Dieter Mehnert, Ulrich Kordon,
Matthias Wolff (Hrsg.)

Systemtheorie
Signalverarbeitung
Sprachtechnologie

TUDpress

Studientexte zur Sprachkommunikation
ISSN 0940-6832
Bd. 68

Dieter Mehnert, Ulrich Kordon,
Matthias Wolff (Hrsg.)

Systemtheorie
Signalverarbeitung
Sprachtechnologie

Rüdiger Hoffmann
zum 65. Geburtstag

TUDpress
2013

Bibliografische Information der Deutschen Nationalbibliothek
Die Deutsche Nationalbibliothek verzeichnet diese Publikation in der Deutschen Nationalbibliografie; detaillierte bibliografische Daten sind im Internet über http://dnb.d-nb.de abrufbar.

Bibliographic information published by the Deutsche Nationalbibliothek
The Deutsche Nationalbibliothek lists this publication in the Deutsche Nationalbibliografie; detailed bibliographic data are available in the Internet at http://dnb.d-nb.de.

ISBN 978-3-944331-19-5

Verlag der Wissenschaften GmbH
Bergstr. 70 | D-01069 Dresden
Tel.: +49 351 47969720 | Fax: +49 351 47960819
http://www.tudpress.de

Gesetzt vom Autor.
Printed in Germany.

Inhaltsverzeichnis

Wolff, M.:
Systemtheorie und Sprachtechnologie
Prof. Dr.-Ing. habil. Rüdiger Hoffmann zum 65. Geburtstag 11

Signalverarbeitung und Systemtheorie

Vich, R.:
Approximate Complex Cepstrum Computation Based on Discrete Cosine Transform..... 15

Lacroix, A.:
Prony und die Prädiktion – Zu den Wurzeln der linearen Prädiktion 23

Hess, W. J.:
Pitch Determination of Acoustic Signals - An Old Problem and Some Recent Solutions 29

Höge, H.:
Modeling of Statistic Dependencies of Feature Vectors within Phonemes 36

Ascoli, A.; Corinto, F.; Senger, V.; Tetzlaff, R.:
Model Dependency of Memristor Circuit Dynamics 45

Pfeifer, G.; Marschner, U.; Starke, E.:
Anwendung von Reziprozitätsbeziehungen in der Messtechnik 59

Sprachtechnologie

Fujisaki, H.:
From „Speech and Language Processing“ to „Spoken Language Processing and Written Language Processing“ 69

Wagner, P.:
(What is) the Contribution of Phonetics to Contemporary Speech Synthesis Research (?) 75

Rhonzhin, A.; Karpov, A.:
Challenges of Russian Speech Processing in Multimodal Applications 82

Möbius, B.:
Exemplarmodelle der Sprachproduktion und ihre Relevanz für die Sprachsynthese 88

Duckhorn, F.; Strecha, G.:
Stille Post mit UASR 96

Kačič, Z.:
Pitch Marking Algorithm Using Short-Time Autocorrelation Function and Zero-Phase Filter Bank 103

Unoki, M.:
Speech Enhancement Based on the Concept of Modulation Transfer Function 109

Möller, S.; Hinterleitner, F.:
Auditive und Instrumentelle Beurteilung der Qualität synthetischer Sprache
in unterschiedlichen Anwendungszusammenhängen 117

Werner, S.:
Sprachdialogsysteme im Automobil - von der Theorie in die Serienproduktion 125

Ding, H.:
Chinese Synthesis in a Multilingual TTS System and a
German CAPT System for Chinese Learners 133

Kraljevski, I.; Gebremedhin, Y. B.:
Development of Speech Technology for Under-resourced Languages 139

Verarbeitung nichtsprachlicher Signale

Paulus, E.:
Die Aussagekraft des Kurzzeit-Frequenzspektrums und der Kurzzeit-
Autokorrelationsfunktion bei der Analyse von Tierstimmen 146

Campbell, N.:
An Acoustic Analysis of 7395 Dog Barks 154

Eichner, M.; Hübler, S.:
Inhaltsbasierte Musikanalyse 171

Altinsoy, E.:
Auditive Wahrnehmung und Beurteilung von instationären Fahrzeuggeräuschen 177

Fehér, T.; Kürbis, S.; Kordon, U.:
Drehzahlmessung aus Auspuffgeräuschen von Kfz 185

Beiträge zur Akustik

Kroschel, K.:
Basics of Saliency Detection in Acoustical Scenes 193

Fuder, G.:
Schallmesspraxis und Anschaulichkeit 201

Klippel, W.:
Nichtlineare Modellierung von Mikrolautsprechern 207

Artikulatorische und multimodale Aspekte

Kröger, B. J.:
Modeling of Speech Production from the Perspective of Neuroscience 218

Braun, A.; Kraft, L.:
Die Erkennbarkeit vertrauter Stimmen bei Verstellung 226

Bissiri, M. P.:
Glottalizations in German-accented English in Relationship to Phrase Boundaries 234

Mixdorff, H.; Hussein, H.:
CALL Mandarin – Results and Conclusions from a Project
for Developing a Computer-Assisted Pronunciation Training Programm 241

Capuano, V.; Riviello, M. T.; Cordasco, G.; Mekyska, J.; Faundez-Zanuy, M.; Esposito, A.:
Assessing Natural Emotional Facial Expressions:
an Evaluation of the I.Vi.T.E. Database 249

Betrachtungen zur Entwicklung des Fachgebiets

Pétursson, M.; Yamaguchi, T.:
Gedanken über die Rolle der Geisteswissenschaften in der Gesellschaft 256

Fellbaum, K.:
Einige Gedanken zum Thema „Kognition“ 261

Ziegenhals, G.:
Akustik, unde venis? 269

Wolff, M.; Tschöpe, C.; Römer, R.
Quo vadis, UASR? 276

Historische Aspekte

Mauersberger, K.:
Die Universitätssammlungen auf dem Weg zu neuen Netzwerken der Wissenskommunikation 286

Költzsch, P.:
August Seebeck – der erste Akustiker der Dresdner "Universität“ 295

Reininger, A.:
Wolfgang von Kempelens Aufenthalt in London:
heißersehnt, jedoch nicht von dem erhofften Erfolg gekrönt. 303

Hirschfeld, U.; Stock, E.:
Wolfgang von Kempelen - ein Wegbereiter modernen phonetischen Denkens 311

Brackhane, F.; Trouvain, J.:
Stationen mechanischer Sprachsynthese vom 18. bis zum 20. Jahrhundert 319

Lobanov, B.:
History and Development of Speech Science and Technology in USSR 327

Mehnert, D.; Dietzel, R.; Kürbis, S.:
Auswertung von Sprachsignalen aus Kymogrammen,
Sonagrammen und digitalen Aufzeichnungen – ein historischer Rückblick 339

Gruber, C.; Koloska, U.; Falk, T.; Wenzel, M.; Schubert, R.;
Hirschfeld, D.; Kurnot, F.:
Sprachkommunikation zwischen Wissenschaft und praktischem Einsatz –
ein Rückblick auf 12 Jahre industrieller Sprachtechnologie-Nutzung.................................. 347

Jokisch, O.:
Technology Transfer for Speech Processing Applications 359

Kortke, M.; Wittenberg, S.:
Eine kurze Geschichte über die Lehre.. 367

Systemtheorie und Sprachtechnologie
Prof. Dr.-Ing. habil. Rüdiger Hoffmann zum 65. Geburtstag

Matthias Wolff

BTU Cottbus
matthias.wolff@tu-cottbus.de

Am 30. August 2013 vollendet Herr Prof. Dr.-Ing. habil. Rüdiger Hoffmann sein 65. Lebensjahr und zum Ende des Wintersemesters 2013/14 seine „offizielle" – wie wir hoffen, jedoch nicht seine aktive – Laufbahn als Hochschullehrer und Wissenschaftler. Aus diesem Anlass dürfen wir eine Zwischenbilanz ziehen und das bisherige Wirken von Professor Hoffmann würdigen.

Rüdiger Hoffmann wurde 1948 in Weltwitz (Thüringen) geboren. Nach dem Abitur und einer Ausbildung zum Chemiefacharbeiter nahm er ein Studium der Hochfrequenztechnik an der Technischen Universität Dresden auf (1966), welches er mit einer Diplomarbeit zum Thema „Zellulare Permutationsstrukturen" abschloss (1971). Begleitend zu einer anschließenden mehr als zehnjährigen Industrietätigkeit promovierte er ebenfalls an der Technischen Universität Dresden mit einer Arbeit über zellulare Systeme (1978). Im Jahr 1982 wechselte er endgültig, zunächst als wissenschaftlicher Mitarbeiter, an die Technische Universität Dresden, an der er nunmehr seit über 30 Jahren wirkt. Er erwarb seine Lehrberechtigung und die Promotion B zum Dr. sc. techn. (1985, entspricht heute der Habilitation), wurde kurz darauf auf eine Dozentur für Mensch-Maschine-Kommunikation (1986) und später auf die Professur für Sprachkommunikation (1992) berufen. Nach der Übernahme des Lehrgebiets Systemtheorie (2002) erfolgte die Umberufung zum Professor für Systemtheorie und Sprachtechnologie (2007). Seit 2010 ist er zusätzlich Gastprofessor an der School of Foreign Languages der Tongji Universität Shanghai. Während seiner Tätigkeit als Hochschullehrer hat Professor Hoffmann bislang über 100 Diplomanden, 25 Doktoranden sowie 4 Habilitanden zum erfolgreichen Abschluss geführt. Fünf seiner Schüler arbeiten heute als Professoren an Universitäten und Hochschulen in Deutschland, China und Mexiko.

Seit seiner Berufung lehrte Professor Hoffmann auf dem Gebiet der Signalverarbeitung, Signalanalyse und -erkennung. In seinen Lehrbüchern „Signalanalyse und -erkennung" (1998) sowie „Grundlagen der Frequenzanalyse" (2001) gibt er eine in ihrer Systematisierung und Klarheit einzigartige Übersicht über diese Themen – jeder seiner Schüler wird sich beispielsweise an den einprägsamen „Transformationswürfel" erinnern. Die Titel sind gleichzeitig auch Fachbücher, die einerseits einen Beitrag zur Weiterentwicklung des Wissensgebiets liefern und andererseits einen Rückbezug auf dessen Ursprünge herstellen. Nach der Übernahme des Lehrgebiets Systemtheorie vertrat Professor Hoffmann mehr als zehn Jahre lang auch dieses für den Ingenieur so grundlegend wichtige Thema in den Vorlesungen Systemtheorie I bis III sowie Einführung in die Systemtheorie. Er verstand es nicht nur, das auf seinen Lehrer Gerhard Wunsch und dessen Nachfolger Helmut Schreiber zurückführende exzellente Niveau dieser Lehrveranstaltungen zu erhalten, sondern auch einen perfekten Anschluss an sein ursprüngliches Lehrgebiet der Signalanalyse und -erkennung herzustellen, was sich – angesichts der Weiterentwicklung des Fachgebiets hin zu intelligenter Signalverarbeitung und zu kognitiven Systemen – inzwischen als richtungsweisend herausgestellt hat. Weitere Lehrveranstaltungen hielt Professor Hoffmann auf seinem besonderen Forschungsgebiet, der elektronischen Sprachsignalverarbeitung.

Professor Hoffmann ist ein international ausgewiesener und anerkannter Experte auf dem Gebiet der Sprachtechnologie, besonders der Sprachsynthese. Neben dem wissenschaftlichen Fortschritt, der sich in neun von ihm betreuten Dissertationen allein auf dem letzteren Gebiet sowie einer Vielzahl von nationalen und internationalen Veröffentlichungen widerspiegelt, standen für ihn auch immer technologische Aspekte im Mittelpunkt. So entstanden unter seiner Leitung der Sprachsyntheseprozessor VOICE 1 (1993), das Dresdner Sprachsynthesesystem „DRESS“ (ab 2000), der erste Hardware-Sprachsynthetisator in Form einer PCMCIA-Karte (1997) sowie die zu ihrer Zeit kompakteste Diphon-Synthese microDRESS (2002), um nur die wichtigsten zu nennen. Die im Rahmen dieser Forschungstätigkeit gewonnenen Erkenntnisse werden derzeit unter seiner Leitung zu einem umfassenden Fachbuch zur Sprachsynthese zusammengetragen, welches sich seiner Fertigstellung nähert.

Mit dem Satz: „Ich würde mir gern *anhören* können, welche Informationen ein Spracherkenner auf den verschiedenen Modellebenen überhaupt noch zur Verfügung hat“ inspirierte Professor Hoffmann das „Vereinheitlichte System zur Sprachsynthese und -erkennung“ (UASR, Unified Approach to Speech Synthesis and Recognition) und mit diesem eine ganze Generation von Doktoranden, darunter auch mich selbst. Er gehörte damit zu den weltweit ersten Forschern, welche das wissenschaftliche und technologische Potenzial eines kombinierten Sprachsynthetisators und -erkenners nicht nur erkannten, sondern auch praktisch nutzbar machten. Der von ihm vorgeschlagenen Architektur liegt die klare Erkenntnis zugrunde, dass wesentliche Fortschritte auf dem Gebiet der Sprachtechnologie nur auf einer soliden systemtheoretischen Grundlage erzielt werden können. UASR wurde in der konsequenten Umsetzung dieses Leitgedankens entwickelt. Im Laufe von nunmehr über 15 Jahren entstanden zu diesem Forschungsthema sieben Dissertationen (weitere zwei sind noch in Bearbeitung), eine Habilitation, eine beachtliche Anzahl von wissenschaftlichen Beiträgen auf nationalen und internationalen Konferenzen, in Fachzeitschriften und in Büchern sowie mehrere Patente. Nicht zuletzt existiert heute eine über 200.000 Programmzeilen umfassende Softwarerealisierung, welche zurzeit zur öffentlichen Freigabe aufbereitet wird. Mit seinen Erweiterungen auf semiotische und kognitive Sprach- und Signalverarbeitung sowie auf die akustische Mustererkennung für technische, Bio- und Musiksignale bildet UASR heute und in Zukunft das konzeptionelle und technologische Fundament für eine wachsende Zahl von Wissenschaftlern an verschiedenen Hochschulen und Forschungseinrichtungen.

Professor Hoffmanns Wirken gibt ein beredtes Zeugnis für seine Überzeugung, dass sich die Ingenieurwissenschaft nicht auf den akademischen „Elfenbeinturm“ beschränken darf. Er hat stets nicht nur die technologische Umsetzung von wissenschaftlichen Erkenntnissen, sondern auch deren Anwendung in der Praxis vehement vorangetrieben. Als Beispiele hierfür seien die von ihm geleiteten Projekte AzAR und EURONOUNCE genannt, in denen Assistenzsysteme zum Sprachlernen entwickelt und in den praktischen Einsatz gebracht wurden. Weiterhin sollen in diesem Zusammenhang seine langjährige und erfolgreiche Kooperation mit Siemens (später Infineon) auf dem Gebiet der Sprachtechnologie sowie seine aktive oder beratende Beteiligung an mehreren Firmenausgründungen (GeSiM mbH, GWT-TUD GmbH, voiceINTERconnect GmbH sowie Linguwerk GmbH) erwähnt werden.

Universitäre Forschungstätigkeit erfordert in zunehmendem Maße Erfolg bei der Einwerbung von Drittmitteln. Professor Hoffmann hat es verstanden, über lange Jahre *kontinuierlich* weit mehr Drittmittelstellen zu finanzieren, als seiner Professur Haushaltsstellen zugeordnet waren. Die von ihm dafür erschlossenen Finanzierungsquellen reichen von Industrieaufträgen über Mittelstandsförderprogramme, DFG- und EU-Förderung von Grundlagenforschung bis hin zur Teilnahme an Großforschungsprojekten wie beispielsweise dem renommierten Verbmobil-Projekt.

Professor Hoffmann ist – das glaube ich so sagen zu dürfen – ein leidenschaftlicher Bücherliebhaber. Abgesehen davon, dass er Autor der schon genannten Lehrbücher, Herausgeber des in

Entstehung befindlichen Fachbuchs zur Sprachsynthese und Mitherausgeber einer Reihe weiterer Bücher ist, hat er die Reihe „Studientexte zur Sprachkommunikation“ ins Leben gerufen. In fast 30 Jahren ist die erstaunliche Zahl von 65 Bänden zusammengekommen, weitere sind in Vorbereitung und ein Ende ist noch lange nicht in Sicht. Die Reihe umfasst Tagungsbände der Konferenz „Elektronische Sprachsignalverarbeitung“ (ESSV) und ihrer Vorläufer, Dissertationen, Habilitationen sowie einige Sonderbände und gibt so einen breit gefächerten Querschnitt der deutschen Forschung auf dem Gebiet der Sprachtechnologie wieder. Professor Hoffmann hat mit dieser Buchreihe schon jetzt ein bleibendes Vermächtnis geschaffen.

Gleiches gilt für die maßgeblich durch ihn ermöglichte Einrichtung der historischen akustisch-phonetischen Sammlung (HAPS) an der TU Dresden. Diese geht ursprünglich auf Exponate der damaligen Professur für Sprachkommunikation zurück, die hauptsächlich die Entwicklung der Sprachsynthese an der TU Dresden und im Kombinat Robotron dokumentieren. In einer gemeinsamen Initiative mit seinem langjährigen Weggefährten Professor Dieter Mehnert sicherte er dann zunächst wertvolle Bestände der inzwischen aufgelösten Fachabteilung für Phonetik der Humboldt-Universität zu Berlin (1999) sowie später des ehemaligen phonetischen Labors der Universität Hamburg (2005). Es ist das große und bleibende Verdienst von Professor Hoffmann, diese Sammlung von inzwischen mindestens europäischem Rang für die Technische Universität Dresden aufgebaut und gemeinsam mit seinen Mitstreitern in jahrelanger akribischer Arbeit konserviert, katalogisiert und dokumentiert zu haben.

Als herausragender Wissenschaftler ist Professor Hoffmann selbstverständlich fester Bestandteil der wissenschaftlichen Gemeinde. Er ist unter anderem Mitglied des IEEE, der ISCA, der ITG und des Deutschen Hochschulverbands, der ISCA Special Interest Groups „Speech Synthesis“ (seit 1999) und „History of Speech Communication Sciences“ (seit 2011), Vorsitzender des ITG-Fachausschusses „Sprachverarbeitung“ sowie Gründungsmitglied des European Center of Excellence in Speech Synthesis (ECESS) und mehrerer COST-Aktionen. Von 2005 bis 2013 war er Vorstandsmitglied des Vogtländischen Fördervereins für Musikinstrumentenbau und Innovation e. V. Das Institut für Musikinstrumentenbau e. V. in Zwota verdankt ihm seinen Status als An-Institut der TU Dresden. Seit 1991 hat Professor Hoffmann regelmäßig die Konferenz „Elektronische Sprachsignalverarbeitung“ (ESSV) ausgerichtet und im Jahr 2009 den Förderverein Elektronische Sprachsignalverarbeitung e. V. gegründet, dessen Vorstandsvorsitzender er seitdem ist. 2006 war er General Chair und lokaler Organisator der „Speech Prosody“, wofür er von der Stadt Dresden mit dem Dresden Congress Award ausgezeichnet wurde. 1994 und 2008 war er Mitorganisator der Jahrestagung für Akustik (DAGA), 2012 wissenschaftlicher Leiter und lokaler Organisator der COST 2012 Final Conference on Cognitive Behavioral Systems. Er war und ist Mitglied der Programmkomitees zahlreicher nationaler und internationaler Konferenzen, Gutachter für die DFG, das BMBF und andere sowie für verschiedene Fachzeitschriften. Die weltweit hohe fachliche Reputation von Professor Hoffmann drückt sich nicht zuletzt in der Vielfalt seiner internationalen Beziehungen, darunter mit so namhaften Wissenschaftlern wie Hiroya Fujisaki, Nick Campbell und Eric Keller, und in einer besonders im letzten Jahrzehnt stetig wachsenden Anzahl internationaler Promotionsstudenten und Gastwissenschaftler, welche den Weg an seine Professur gesucht und gefunden haben, aus.

Während meiner 15-jährigen Tätigkeit als wissenschaftlicher Mitarbeiter an seiner Professur habe ich Herrn Professor Hoffmann als väterlichen Freund, wissenschaftlichen Mentor und wohlwollenden, aber auch kritischen Ratgeber schätzen gelernt. Wir wünschen Herrn Professor Hoffmann alles Gute für seinen weiteren Lebensweg, vor allem Gesundheit und persönliches Wohlergehen. Wir erwarten mit Spannung die Fertigstellung seiner laufenden Buchprojekte und freuen uns auf die weitere Zusammenarbeit mit ihm und auf viele weitere Begegnungen, nicht zuletzt auf der Konferenz „Elektronische Sprachverarbeitung“.

Approximate Complex Cepstrum Computation Based on Discrete Cosine Transform

Robert Vích

Academy of Sciences of the Czech Republic

vich@ufe.cz

Abstract: In the paper a new approximate computation of the complex cepstrum based on Discrete Cosine Transform using the DCT-1 is defined and compared with the classic DFT complex cepstrum. The unwrapping algorithm in the complex cepstrum computation based on DCT is simple and without any approximation. The whole procedure is faster than the complex cepstrum computation based on DFT. For increasing the approximation accuracy of the complex cepstrum the DCT is applied to the delayed signal and a recommendation for the choice of the delay is proposed. For the signal reconstruction by homomorphic deconvolution a proper cepstral window is proposed. The approximate complex cepstrum computation is illustrated on a speech signal.

1 Introduction

In 1984, in a short note [1], the Discrete Cosine Transform (DCT) was for the first time applied to the approximate computation of the complex cepstrum. Up to this time the complex cepstrum had been defined solely using the Discrete Fourier Transform (DFT), see e.g. [2]. For completeness it should be mentioned that the application of the DCT (or symmetrical DFT) for real cepstrum computation was proposed already in 1981 for homomorphic speech modeling in adaptive transform coding [3]. Later in [4], [5] the idea of DCT application for complex cepstrum computation was further developed. In all the mentioned papers the cepstra obtained by DCT were called pseudocepstra. Because the notion pseudocepstrum has been also used by several authors for the cepstrum based e.g. on a rational power instead on the logarithm, we shall not use the attribute pseudo, but the more appropriate feature – approximate cepstrum computation.

The application of the DCT permits in the approximate real cepstrum computation a reduction of the computational load by a factor of two. In the complex cepstrum case the application of the DCT leads to a construction of a simple and accurate phase unwrapping algorithm without iteratively applied numerical integration.

In this paper the approximate computation of the complex cepstrum using the DCT-1 [6], [7] is applied. The approach is compared with the classical DFT complex cepstrum computation and illustrated on a speech signal. For increasing the approximation accuracy of the DCT complex cepstrum a new parameter – the delay of the signal – is introduced prior to the DCT spectrum estimation. The reconstruction of the signal by homomorphic deconvolution and the estimation of the vocal tract frequency response are shortly mentioned.

2 Comparison of the DCT and DFT Spectra

Let $s[n]$ be a real discrete signal defined for $0 \le n \le N_s - 1$, where N_s is the signal length. The DCT-1 is given by the transform pair [6]

$$S_C[k] = 2\sum_{n=0}^{N_C-1}\alpha[n]s[n]\cos(\frac{\pi kn}{N_C-1}),$$
$$0 \le k \le N_C - 1, \quad N_C \ge N_s,$$
$$s[n] = \frac{1}{N_C-1}\sum_{k=0}^{N_C-1}\alpha[k]S_C[k]\cos(\frac{\pi kn}{N_C-1}), \tag{1}$$
$$0 \le n \le N_C - 1,$$

where N_C is the dimension of the DCT, $\alpha[n]=1/2,\ n=0, N_C-1$ and $\alpha[n]=1,\ 1\le n\le N_C-2$.

The DCT spectrum $S_C[k]$ is a real even symmetric sequence and it holds $S_C[k] = S_C[-k]$. The DCT-1 is the most convenient form of the four common forms of the DCTs for the construction of the DCT Complex Cepstrum (DCTCC) for its close relation to the corresponding DFT.

The DFT is defined by the transform pair

$$S[k] = \sum_{n=0}^{N-1} s[n]e^{-i\frac{2\pi}{N}kn},$$
$$0 \le k \le N-1,$$
$$s[n] = \frac{1}{N}\sum_{k=0}^{N-1} S[k]e^{i\frac{2\pi}{N}kn}, \tag{2}$$
$$0 \le n \le N-1,$$

where we choose N=2N_C -2. Using this dimension N of the DFT, the DCT of an N_C -point sequence is identical to the (2N -2)-point DFT of the symmetrically extended sequence $s[n]$. The DFT spectrum $S[k]$ is in general complex even for a real sequence $s[n]$ and the symmetry condition $S[k]=S^*[-k]$ holds. For N even, only the two DFT samples $S[0]$ and $S[N/2]$ are real and distinct.

As an example we use the stationary part of the vowel *a* with the fundamental frequency F_0 = 118 Hz sampled with the sampling frequency F_S = 8 kHz. The signal frame of the length N_s = 200 is weighted using the Hamming window, see Fig. 1.

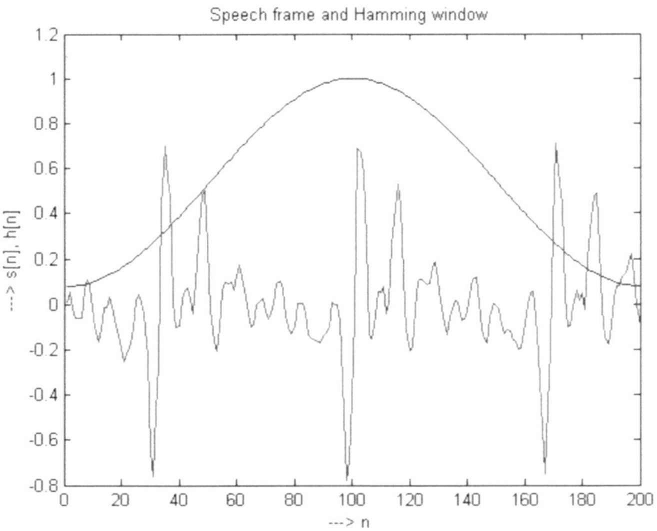

Figure 1 - Frame of the vowel *a* and the Hamming window

For DCT calculation the signal frame is padded with zeros to the length $N_C = 1025$ and for the DFT to the length $N = 2048$. This choice enables the comparison of the DCT spectrum with the DFT magnitude spectrum and it is also convenient for DCTCC computation using the FFT. The DCT-1 spectrum together with the DFT magnitude spectrum is shown in Fig. 2.

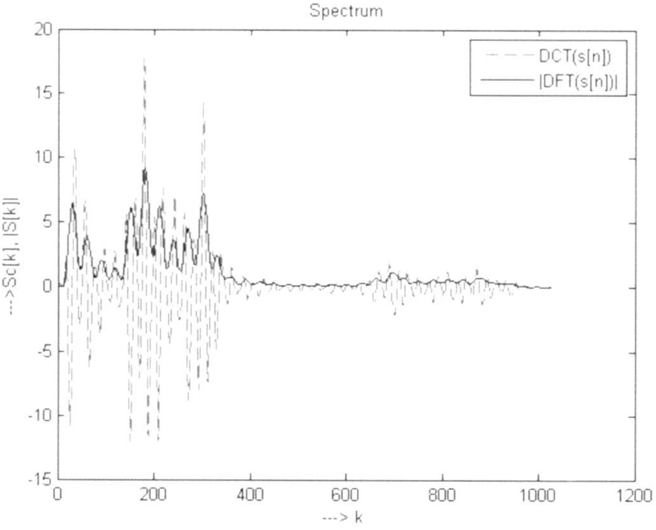

Figure 2 - DCT-1 spectrum and the DFT magnitude spectrum

Even when the DCT spectrum $S_C[k]$ of the sequence $s[n]$ is real, the phase of the DFT spectrum $S[k]$ manifests in the polarity changes of the DCT spectrum $S_C[k]$. It holds

$$S_C[k] = 2|S[k]|\cos(Arg(S[k])),\ k = 0,\ldots,N_C - 1. \tag{3}$$

The sequence $\cos(Arg(S[k]))$ is the "DCT spectrum carrier component" and $2|S[k]|$ corresponds to the DCT magnitude spectrum envelope. The "frequency" of the carrier component is dependent on the period of the even symmetrically extended sequence $s[n]$ in the definition of the DCT, which is for DCT-1 $N_P = 2N_s - 2$. In the DCT spectrum it manifests itself with the period $K_P = F_S / N_P$, see Fig.2.

3 Complex Cepstrum Computation

The traditional complex cepstrum based on DFT (DFTCC) [2], [7] is defined by

$$\begin{aligned} \hat{s}[n] &= \frac{1}{N}\sum_{k=0}^{N-1} \hat{S}[k] e^{i\frac{2\pi}{N}kn}, \\ n &= 0,1,\ldots,N-1, \\ \hat{S}[k] &= \log(S[k]) = \log(|S[k]|) + j\arg(S[k]), \\ k &= 0,1,\ldots,N-1. \end{aligned} \tag{4}$$

The imaginary part of $\hat{S}[k]$ is the unwrapped phase without the linear phase component, obtained usually by the Tribolet algorithm. In order to use the relations (4) also in the case of the DCT, the logarithmic DCT spectrum $\hat{S}_C[k] = \log(S_C[k]) = \log|S_C[k]| + j\arg(S_C[k])$ must be estimated. The phase of the DCT spectrum $S_C[k]$ is given for $k = 0,1,\ldots,N_C - 1$ by

$$Arg(S_C[k]) = 0, \qquad S_C[k] > 0,$$
$$= -\pi, \qquad S_C[k] < 0. \tag{5}$$

The application of the Tribolet algorithm is in this case not possible. In [1] a specific DCT phase unwrapping algorithm is proposed which keeps track of the sign changes of $S_C[k]$. The unwrapped phase can also be obtained alternatively by

$$\arg(S_C[k]) = -\pi\, r[k],$$
$$r[k] = \sum_{i=0}^{k-1} \left|\Delta[\operatorname{sgn}\{S_C[i] < 0\}]\right|, \tag{6}$$
$$k = 0,\ldots,N_C - 1,$$

where $\Delta y[i] = y[i+1] - y[i]$. The sequence $r[k]$ represents the number of zero crossings of the DCT spectrum $S_C[k]$ including the kth spectrum sample. The unwrapped phase $\arg(S_C[k])$ is a monotonically decreasing staircase sequence and its minimum value for $k = N_C$-1 corresponds to the linear phase component, which must be removed from the unwrapped phase. The result is then the corrected unwrapped phase $\arg_C(S_C[k])$, which is an odd sequence

$$\arg_C(S_C[k]) = \arg(S_C[k]) - \arg(S_C[N_C - 1])\frac{k}{N_C - 1},$$
$$k = 0,\ldots,N_C - 1. \tag{7}$$

The complex cepstrum based on DCT can then be defined by a similar expression as in (4), but $N = 2N_C$-2 must be respected. That means that we have to extend the complex logarithmic DCT spectrum so that $\hat{S}_C[k] = \hat{S}_C^*[-k]$ for $k = 0,1,\ldots,N_C - 1,\ldots,N-1$. The DCTCC $\hat{s}_C[n]$ can then be obtained by FFT and is given by

$$\hat{s}_C[n] = \frac{1}{N}\sum_{k=0}^{N-1} \hat{S}_C[k] e^{i\frac{2\pi}{N}kn},$$
$$n = 0,1,\ldots,N-1,$$
$$\hat{S}_C[k] = \log(S_C[k]) =$$
$$= \log\left(\left|S_C[k]\right|\right) + j \arg_C(S_C[k]), \tag{8}$$
$$k = 0,1,\ldots,N-1.$$

The value $r[N_C$-1] in (6) is the delay added to $s[n]$ prior to the computation of the complex cepstrum and must be used for the recover of the signal by the inverse cepstral transform.

The accuracy of the complex cepstrum based on DCT is dependent on the frequency sampling of the DCT spectrum, i.e. on N_C. It can be further enhanced by delaying the time sequence $s[n]$, i.e. using the DCT of the sequence $s[n - M]$, see Fig. 3, where $M = N/4 = 512$. Then the period of the even symmetrically extended sequence $s[n-M]$ increases to $N_{Pd} = 2(N_s+M)$-2 and the period of the carrier component in the DCT spectrum decreases to $K_{Pd} = F_S/(2(N_s+M)$-2), see Fig. 4.

For illustration of the impact of the signal delay M on the DCT spectra, in Fig. 4 are shown for our example the low frequency parts of the logarithmic DCT magnitude spectra of the original and of the delayed signal, together with the logarithmic DFT magnitude spectrum. The logarithmic DFT magnitude spectrum corresponds to the logarithmic speech spectrum envelope and the positions of the maxima of its lobes correspond to multiples of the fundamental frequency F_0. The figure shows that the number of lobes of the logarithmic DCT magnitude spectrum of the delayed signal is greater than that of the logarithmic DCT magnitude spectrum for the not delayed signal. This fact leads to a greater accuracy in cepstrum estimation.

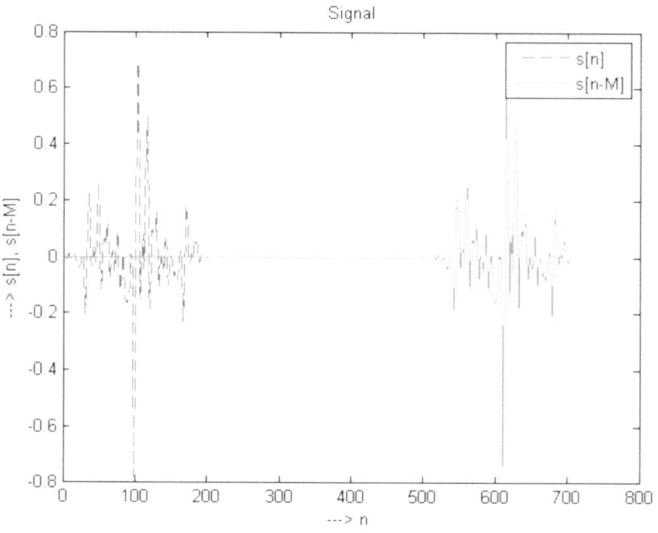

Figure 3 - Windowed speech signal: original and delayed frames

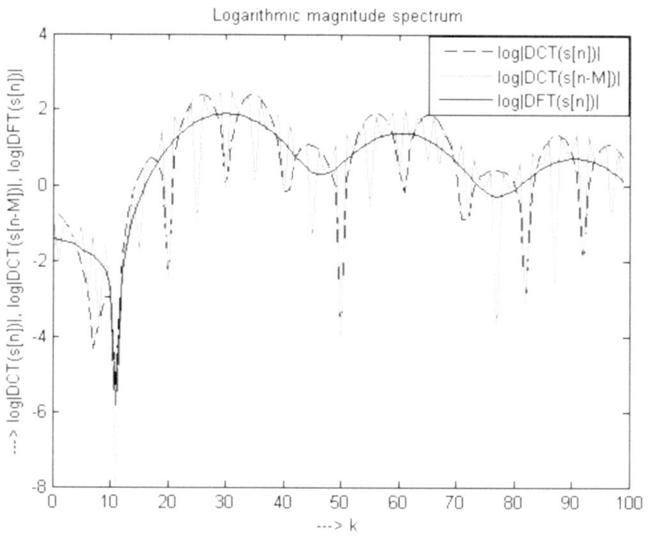

Figure 4 - Low-frequency parts of the DCT and DFT logarithmic magnitude spectra

The main effect of the signal delay M can be seen in the unwrapped phase spectrum without the linear phase component in Fig. 5. The corrected unwrapped DCT phase spectrum of the delayed signal is positioned around the unwrapped DFT phase spectrum, whereas the corrected unwrapped phase spectrum of the not delayed original signal is quite different.

The linear phase component obtained in the phase unwrapping is in our example for the not delayed signal $r[N_C -1]= -100$. In the case of the delayed signal we obtain $r[N_C -1]= -610$. Adding the signal delay $M = 512$ we obtain the linear phase component -98 which is equal to the linear phase component in the DFT complex cepstrum computation.

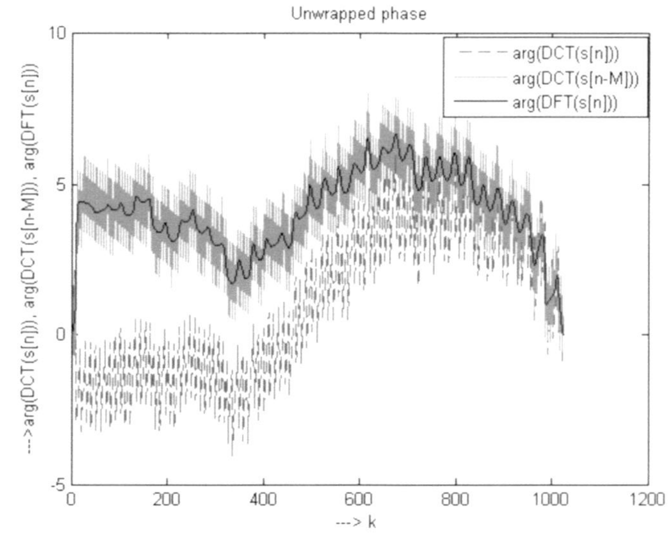

Figure 5 - Unwrapped DCT and DFT phase spectra without the linear phase component

The resulting DFT and DCT complex cepstra are shown in Fig. 6. In the DCTCC of the not delayed signal we can see a dispersed wave group situated approximately at $n = N\text{-}1\text{-}N_s$ and of the length N_s. This is caused by the even signal symmetry in the definition of the DCT with the period N_P. It means that also a minimum-phase signal leads to a non causal DCT complex cepstrum. The delay M of the signal presents itself in the cepstrum by a shift of this wave group to the left by $2M$. The appropriate delay M is signal dependent and for our example approximately holds

$$N/4 = M_{\min} \leq M \leq M_{\max} = \left(N - 5N_s/2\right)/2. \tag{9}$$

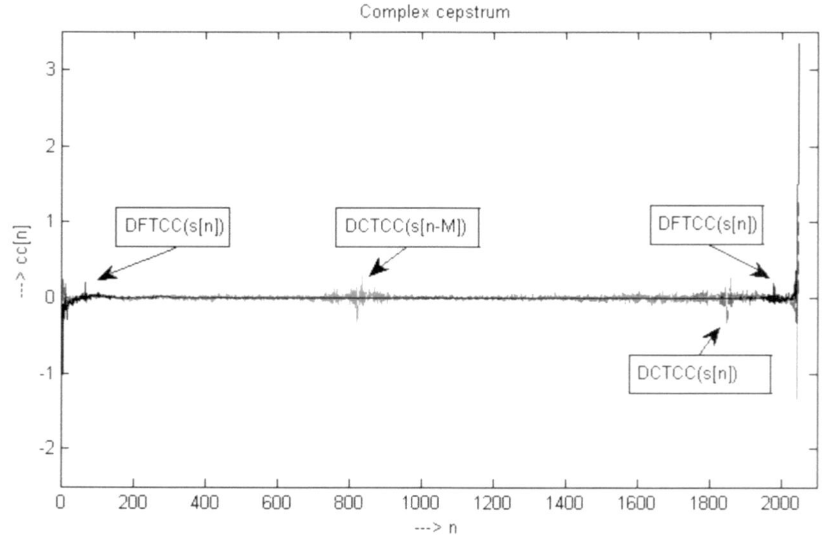

Figure 6 - Complex DFT and DCT cepstra

The increase of the computation accuracy of the DCTCC using the signal delay can be seen in Fig. 7 and Fig. 8. In the figures the initial sections of the causal and anticipative parts of the

DFT and DCT complex cepstra for $0 \leq n$ and for $n < 0$ are shown. The DCTCC for the delayed signal is approximately identical with the DFTCC.

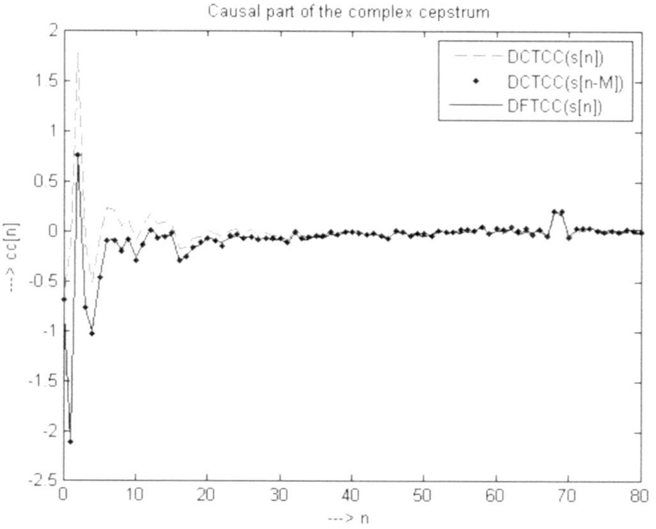

Figure 7 - Causal parts of the complex cepstra

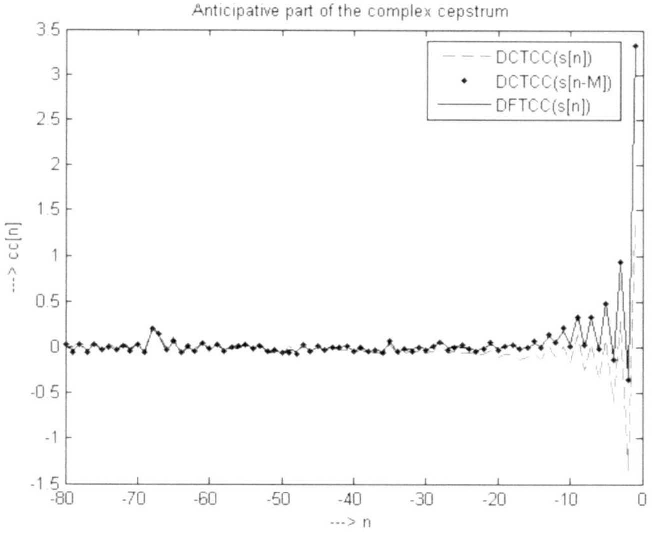

Figure 8 - Anticipative parts of the complex cepstra

4 Reconstruction of Signals

To recover the signal $s[n]$ from the DCTCC a convenient cepstral low-time window must be applied to suppress the wave group in the DCTCC caused by the even symmetry in the DCT definition and also to suppress the associated cepstral noise. Such a window $w[n]$ can be defined as follows

$$
\begin{aligned}
&w[n] = 1, \quad 0 \le n < N_s, \\
&w[n] = 0, \quad N_s \le n \le N - N_s, \\
&w[n] = 1, \quad N - N_s < n \le N - 1.
\end{aligned}
\tag{10}
$$

In case that the frequency response of the vocal tract model or the corresponding impulse response is of interest, a narrower low-time window is needed to suppress the cepstral peaks corresponding to the fundamental frequency period F_0 of the speech signal

$$
\begin{aligned}
&w_0[n] = 1, \quad 0 \le n < N_0, \\
&w_0[n] = 0, \quad N_0 \le n \le N - N_0, \\
&w_0[n] = 1, \quad N - N_0 < n \le N - 1.
\end{aligned}
\tag{11}
$$

The value N_0 is the integer value $N_0 = \lfloor F_S / F_0 \rfloor$. Then the impulse response of the vocal tract model $s_w[n]$ is given by the inverse cepstral transform using FFT

$$
\begin{aligned}
s_w[n] &= \frac{1}{N} \sum_{k=0}^{N-1} S_w[k] e^{i \frac{2\pi}{N} kn}, \\
n &= 0, 1, \ldots, N-1, \\
S_w[k] &= \exp(\hat{S}_w[k]), \\
\hat{S}_w[k] &= \sum_{n=0}^{N-1} w[n] \hat{s}[n] e^{-i \frac{2\pi}{N} kn}, \\
k &= 0, 1, \ldots, N-1
\end{aligned}
\tag{12}
$$

and the frequency response of the vocal tract model is $S_w[k]$.

5 Conclusion

In the paper the approximate computation of the complex cepstrum using the DCT was described and illustrated using a speech signal. The DCTCC is always a two-sided cepstrum also for a minimum-phase signal, which is the consequence of the even symmetrically extended sequence $s[n]$ in the definition of DCT. The approximation accuracy of the DCTCC can be enhanced by a delay of the analyzed signal and using proper cepstral windowing. The unwrapping algorithm in DCTCC computation is straightforward without any approximation and the whole complex cepstrum computation is faster than the classic approach using DFT.

References

[1] Hassainen, H. and Rudko, M.: On the Use of Discrete Cosine Transform in Cepstral Analysis. IEEE Transactions on ASSP, Vol. ASSP-33, no. 4, 1984, pp. 922-925.

[2] Oppenheim, A. and Schafer, R. W.: Discrete-Time Signal Processing. Prentice Hall, New Jersey, 1989.

[3] Cox, R. and Crochiere, R. E.: Real-Time Simulation of Adaptive Transform Coding. IEEE Transactions on ASSP, Vol. ASSP-29, no. 2, 1981, pp. 147-154.

[4] Muralishankar, R. and Ramakrishnan, A. G.: DCT Based Pseudo Complex Cepstrum. ICASSP, Orlando, Florida, USA, Vol. I, 2002, pp. 521-524.

[5] Muralishankar, R. and Ramakrishnan, A. G.: Pseudo Complex Cepstrum using Discrete Cosine Transform. International Journal of Speech Technology, no. 8, 2005, pp. 181-191.

[6] Oppenheim, A. Schafer, R. W. and Buck, J. R.: Discrete-Time Signal Processing, Prentice Hall, 1999.

[7] Vich, R.: *Z* Transform Theory and Applications. D. Reidel Publishing Company, 1987.

PRONY UND DIE PRÄDIKTION – ZU DEN WURZELN DER LINEAREN PRÄDIKTION

Arild Lacroix

Institut für Angewandte Physik, Johann Wolfgang Goethe-Universität, Frankfurt am Main
arild.lacroix@gmail.com

Abstract: Die lineare Prädiktion ist ein Verfahren zur modellbasierten Analyse, das mit dem Beginn der 1970er Jahre zu einem wichtigen Instrument in der Sprachsignalverarbeitung wurde, wohl deshalb, weil die Rechnerentwicklung der damaligen Zeit die Anwendung derartiger Verfahren möglich machte. Die Wurzeln der linearen Prädiktion reichen jedoch weit zurück: PRONY veröffentlichte bereits 1795 ein Verfahren zur Exponentialapproximation, das die lineare Prädiktion vorwegnahm. In dieser Arbeit wird auf die historischen Zusammenhänge näher eingegangen; darüberhinaus wird auch über eine kürzlich gefundene deutsche Übersetzung der französischen Originalarbeit berichtet.

1 Die Lineare Prädiktion

Um 1970 herum wurde unter der Bezeichnung „Linear Prediction" ein Verfahren zur Extrapolation von Sprachsignalen aus äquidistanten Abtastwerten publiziert [1, 2], das sich bald als Standardverfahren zur modellgestützten Analyse von Signalen etablieren sollte. Dabei wird aus einer Linearkombination zurückliegender Abtastwerte ein Schätzwert für den nächsten Abtastwert berechnet; die Minimierung der quadratische Erwartung des Differenzsignals zwischen geschätzten und tatsächlichen Abtastwerten liefert eine Vorschrift zur Berechnung der optimalen Koeffizienten der Linearkombination, den sogenannten Prädiktorkoeffizienten. Das der Analyse zugrunde liegende Modellsystem ist ein rein rekursives zeitdiskretes System, das sogenannte Nur-Pole-System (engl. all-pole-filter), das im Zeitbereich durch eine entsprechende Differenzengleichung (Rekursionsgleichung) beschrieben wird.

Wenngleich die lineare Prädiktion besonders im Kontext von Sprachsignalen bekannt wurde, lassen sich vielfältige Anwendungen in zahlreichen anderen Gebieten, beispielsweise in der Seismik, in der Regelungstechnik und in Biologie und Medizin nachweisen. Eine mathematische Darstellung und Begründung der linearen Prädiktion ist beispielsweise in [3, 4] gegeben; daher wird hier auf weitere Einzelheiten verzichtet.

Bald nachdem die lineare Prädiktion bekannt wurde, ist in [5-7] darauf hingewiesen worden, dass dieses Verfahren schon von PRONY angegeben wurde, um aus äquidistanten Beobachtungen ein Darstellung durch Exponentialsummen zu gewinnen [8]. PRONY erkannte, dass Exponentialsummen einer linearen Differenzengleichung mit konstanten Koeffizienten gehorchen und benutzte diese Tatsache zur Aufstellung eines linearen Gleichungssystems zur Bestimmung der Prädiktorkoeffizienten, die identisch sind mit den Koeffizienten der zur Differenzengleichung gehörigen charakteristischen Gleichung. Bis auf die heute üblichen Verfahren zum Fehlerausgleich (Kovarianzmethode, Autokorrelationsmethode) hat er mit seiner Arbeit die lineare Prädiktion bereits 1795 vorweggenommen.

Das PRONY-Verfahren zur Darstellung von Funktionen durch Exponentialsummen mit i. a. komplexem Argument war zumindest seit den 1920er Jahren in der numerischen und praktische Mathematik wohlbekannt: Stellvertretend seien die Monographien von RUNGE und KÖNIG [9], WILLERS [10], WHITTAKER und ROBINSON [11], und HILDEBRAND [12] genannt. Interessant ist in diesem Zusammenhang der Hinweis bei WILLERS, dass das PRONY-Verfahren sich auch zur Approximation von bestimmten Sprachsignalen, insbesondere denen von Vokalen und Halbvokalen eigen könnte. Beachtenswert ist auch eine Spezialisierung des PRONY-Verfahrens auf den Fall von Eigenwerten ausschließlich auf dem Einheitskreis, die eine bestimmte Symmetrie (gerade oder ungerade) der Koeffizienten des charakteristischen Polynoms erfordert; es ergeben sich dann periodische Eigenfunktionen vom Sinus/Cosinus-Typ allerdings mit i. a. inkommensurablen Argumenten, die im Gegensatz zu FOURIER-Reihen auch nichtharmonische Reihenentwicklungen ermöglichen.

2 Die Originalarbeit von PRONY und die deutsche Übersetzung

Die Arbeit von PRONY wurde in den regelmäßig erscheinenden Berichten der École Polytechnique in Paris veröffentlicht, in denen auch andere bekannte Zeitgenossen wie LAGRANGE oder LAPLACE publizierten. Im Druckvermerk wird das Jahr IV, Nivose (Schneemonat: Dezember/Januar), genannt, wobei dieser Angabe der Revolutionskalender zugrunde liegt, der mit dem 22. Sept. 1792 beginnt; daher gilt als Erscheinungsjahr das Jahr 1795. Der Berichtsband hat Großoktav-Format, das Papier ist handgeschöpftes Büttenpapier, entstanden lange vor Beginn der industriellen Papierproduktion; es bereitet haptisches Vergnügen ein derartiges Büttenpapier in Händen zu halten. Abb. 1 zeigt das Titelblatt des Journals.

Den Titel der Veröffentlichung von Prony zeigt Abb. 2. Die Arbeit beginnt mit dem schon diskutierten mathematischen Teil, gefolgt von dem experimentellen Teil, der sich mit der Ausdehnung von Gasen wie Wasserdampf, Alkoholdampf, Wasserstoff, Sauerstoff, Stickstoff, Luft, Salpetergas, Ammoniakgas und kohlensaures Gas abhängig von der Temperatur befasst. Dabei wird der Versuchsaufbau anhand eines großformatigen Kupfers erläutert. Die Versuchsergebnisse sind in Form von Tabellen und auch in graphischer Weise dargestellt.

Kürzlich konnte der Verfasser dieses Aufsatzes die deutsche Übersetzung der französischen Originalarbeit von PRONY ausfindig machen, die im Jahr 1802 in „Allgemeines Journal der Chemie" erschienen ist [13]; der Übersetzer der Arbeit wird nicht genannt. Im Vergleich zum französischen Original ist der mathematische Teil verkürzt wiedergegeben: Es wird die Reihendarstellung nur für einen Exponentialterm mit einem Konstantanteil behandelt, wie von PRONY für die Approximation der Experiment-Resultate verwendet. Der experimentelle Teil der Arbeit ist so ausführlich wie in der Orignalarbeit dargestellt mit Einschluss des Experiment-Aufbaus und der Experiment-Ergebnisse in Tabellenform und auch als Graphik.

3 Biographische Hinweise zu PRONY

Gaspard Clair Francois Marie Riche de PRONY, geboren am 22. Juli 1755 in Chamelet (Dept. Rhone), gestorben am 29. Juli 1839 in Asnières-sur-Seine bei Paris, war im Hauptberuf Bauingenieur mit profunden Kenntnissen und Fähigkeiten in Mathematik und Naturwissenschaften. Von 1776 bis 79 studierte er an der École Nationale des Ponts-et-Chaussées. Nach einigen Berufsjahren, in denen er sich mit Brücken- und Wasserbau beschäftigte, kehrte er an seine Ausbildungsstätte zurück und wurde dort später Ingenieur-en-chef. 1794 wurde er Professor für Mechanik an der École Polytechnique in Paris. Neben zahlreichen Aufsätzen überwiegend zum Bauwesen und zur Mechanik hat er Lehrbücher verfasst über analytische Mechanik und über Wasserbau. Seit 1795 gehört er der Akademie der Wissenschaften, seit 1817 dem Bureau des Longitudes an. 1828 wird er zum Baron ernannt, 1835 zum Pair erhoben. Er gehört zu den 72 bedeutenden Persönlichkeiten, die auf dem Eiffelturm in Paris verewigt sind. Abb. 3 zeigt ein Bildnis von Prony.

4 Literatur

[1] ATAL, B. S., SCHROEDER, M. R.: Adaptive Predictive Coding od Speech Signals, BSTJ **49** (1970), S. 1973 – 1986.

[2] ATAL, B. S., HANAUER, S. L.:Speech Analysis and Synthesis by Linear Prediction oft he Speech Wave, JASA **50** (1971), S. 637 – 655.

[3] MAKHOUL, J.: Linear Prediction: A Tutorial Review, Proc IEEE **63** (1975), S. 561 – 580.

[4] MARKEL, J. D., GRAY, A. H.: Linear Prediction of Speech, Springer, Berlin-Heidelberg-New York 1976.

[5] MARKEL, J. D.: The Prony Method and its Application to Speech Analysis, 80. Meeting JASA U12, Vol. **49** (1971), S. 105 – 106.

[6] KREMER, H., LACROIX, A.: Praktische Berechnung von Exponentialapproximationen mit dem Prony-Verfahren, Angewandte Informatik **14** (1972), S. 121 – 126.

[7] AUTH, W.: System Identification of Vocaltract and Excitation, Proc. Adv. In Cybernetics and Systems Res., Wien 1973, S. 143 – 150.

[8] PRONY, R.: Essai Expérimental st Analytique Sur les lois de la Dilatabilité des Fluides elastique et sur celles de la Force expansive de la vapeur de l´eau et de la vapeur de l´alkool, à differentes temperatures, Journal de L´École Polytechnique ou Bulletin due Travail fait a cette École, Deuxième Cahier, Paris an IV (1795), S. 24 – 76.

[9] RUNGE, C., KÖNIG, H.: Vorlesungen über numerisches Rechnen, Springer, Berlin 1924, S. 231- 235.

[10] WILLERS, F. A.: Methoden der praktischen Analysis, de Gruyter, Berlin-Leipzig 1928, S. 289 – 295.

[11] WHITTAKER, E., ROBINSON, G.: The Calculus of Observations, Blackie & Son, London-Glasgow, 4th Ed. 1944 (1st Ed. 1924), S. 369 - 371.

[12] HILDEBRAND, F. B.: Introduction to Numerical Analysis, McGraw-Hill, New York-Toronto-London 1956, S. 378 – 382.

[13] PRONY, R.: Versuche zur Bestimmung der Gesetze der Ausdehnung elastischer Flüssigkeiten, Allgemeines Journal der Chemie, 4. Jahrgg., 8. Band, Heft 45, Berlin 1802, S. 245 - 259

JOURNAL

DE L'ÉCOLE POLYTECHNIQUE,

OU

BULLETIN DU TRAVAIL

FAIT

A CETTE ÉCOLE,

PUBLIÉ

PAR LE CONSEIL D'INSTRUCTION ET ADMINISTRATION DE CET ÉTABLISSEMENT.

DEUXIÈME CAHIER.

MOIS DE FLORÉAL ET DE PRAIRIAL.

A PARIS,

DE L'IMPRIMERIE DE LA RÉPUBLIQUE.

NIVÔSE, AN IV.

Et se trouve chez les C.ens REGENT et BERNARD, libraires, quai des Augustins, n.° 37.

Abbildung 1 – Titelblatt des Journal de L´École Polytechnique

24 ESSAI

ESSAI EXPÉRIMENTAL

ET ANALYTIQUE

Sur les lois de la Dilatabilité des fluides élastiques et sur celles de la Force expansive de la vapeur de l'eau et de la vapeur de l'alkool, à différentes températures.

Par R. PRONY.

CONSIDÉRATIONS GÉNÉRALES.

LA physique s'est enrichie depuis environ quarante ans d'un grand nombre d'observations faites avec beaucoup de soin par des hommes savans et exercés. Ce dépôt s'augmente chaque jour, et la collection qu'il renferme devient de plus en plus précieuse, à mesure que la perfection des instrumens nouveaux donne plus de précision aux expériences : déjà l'esprit philosophique s'est emparé des faits multipliés, fournis par les observateurs ; les phénomènes ont été rapprochés, comparés, classés ; la langue d'une partie importante de la science est devenue analytique ; des théories raisonnables ont fait disparaître les systèmes futiles et souvent absurdes, dont on a occupé les écoles jusqu'au milieu de ce siècle.

L'étude de la nature ainsi ramenée à l'examen et à la connaissance effective de ses opérations, me paraît offrir deux objets de recherches qu'il ne faut pas confondre ; l'*explication des effets* et leur *mesure*.

L'explication des effets consiste à trouver, dans une classe de phénomènes composés, les phénomènes simples ou primitifs, dont tous les autres ne sont que les modifications ou les combinaisons diverses, et à faire voir comment on peut, à travers les apparences les plus variées, démêler l'action et la manière d'être des élémens pris pour base du système. Ainsi en partant

Abbildung 2 – Titel der Veröffentlichnung von Prony

Abbildung 3 – Bildnis von Prony

Pitch Determination of Acoustic Signals – An Old Problem and Some Recent Solutions

Wolfgang J. Hess

Communication, Language and Speech, University of Bonn, Germany
wgh@sk.uni-bonn.de

Abstract: This paper briefly reviews three aspects of pitch determination of speech and music signals, (1) methods of short-term analysis pitch determination, (2) detection of the instants of glottal closure, and (3) the question of latency of the pitch estimates.

1 Introduction. Pitch in Time-Variant Acoustic Signals

Pitch, i.e., fundamental frequency F_0 and fundamental period T_0 of a (quasi-)periodic signal, can be measured in many ways. If the signal is completely stationary and periodic, all these strategies - provided they operate correctly - lead to identical results. Since both speech and music signals, however, are nonstationary and time variant, aspects of strategy such as the starting point of the measurement, the length of the measuring interval, the way of averaging (if any), or the operating domain (time, frequency, lag etc.) start influencing the results and may lead to estimates that differ from algorithm to algorithm even if all these results are "correct" and "accurate."

There are three points of view for looking at such a problem of acoustic signal processing [42]: the production, the signal-processing, and the perception points of view, respectively. For speech the production point of view is clearly oriented toward phonation in the larynx; we will thus have to start from a time-domain representation of the waveform as the response of the vocal tract to a train of laryngeal pulses. If a pitch determination algorithm (henceforth called PDA) works in a speech-production oriented way, it measures individual laryngeal excitation cycles or, if some averaging is performed, the rate of vocal-fold vibration. The signal-processing point of view – which can be applied to any acoustic signal – means that (quasi-)periodicity or at least cyclic behavior is observed, and that the task is to concentrate on those features that best represent this periodicity. The perception point of view (again for any acoustic signal) leads to a frequency-domain representation since pitch sensation primarily corresponds to a frequency (cf. e.g. Terhardt [38]). This point of view is associated with the original meaning of the term *pitch.* Yet this term has consistently been used as some kind of "common denominator"and a general name, at least in the technical literature on speech [25]. In the following, we will use the term pitch in this wider sense.

For reasons of space, we cannot present a general overview here; this was done elsewhere (Hess, 1983, 2004, 2008 [15, 16, 18]; Christensen and Jakobsson, 2009 [9]). Instead, we will briefly discuss three aspects: (1) determination of T_0 or F_0 by short-term analysis, both for speech and for music signals, (2) determination of glottal closure instants (henceforth called GCI), which is a subproblem of glottal inverse filtering (see [1] for a review), and (3) the latency question.

2 Some Applications in Speech and Music

Investigating prosodic events like intonation, particularly in spontaneous speech, has become an important issue in speech understanding systems (cf., for instance, [33, 4]), and many of these systems now contain a prosody module. As it is a long-term goal in speech technology to make such devices operable from almost any place, a PDA may even have to cope with signals from mobile phones which can be extremely bad and inconsistent.

Another new application area is data-driven speech synthesis. Algorithms for time-domain pitch modification, such as the well-known PSOLA algorithm, require precise pitch period determination in order to work properly, and in nonuniform unit-selection synthesis systems large speech corpora have to be analyzed, yet usually with good-quality signals free from phase distortions. For this application, GCI determination is the appropriate method.

Automatic notation of melodies and musical tunes is a long-standing problem. As early as 1979 Askenfelt [3] reported about a project how to automatically transcribe folk melodies that had been collected in a large corpus. In this case most of the melodies were one-voiced so that PDAs developed for speech signals could be used. This is not always the case for music, however, and therefore we must count as a particular problem in music that more than one note can be played at the same time, and that PDAs for this application may have to cope with multiple pitches and have to determine them all simultaneously, if ever possible. These applications emerged much later.

Information retrieval from audio data (audio mining) also involves pitch determination of musical signals and speech. This application area is closely related to the preceding ones. Since one has to take into account environmental "noises" such as background music or competing speakers, it also involves the problem of multiple pitches.

3 Short-Term Analysis Pitch Determination

In any short-term analysis PDA a short-term (or short-time) transformation is performed as a first step. The speech signal is split up into a series of frames; an individual frame is obtained by taking a limited number of consecutive samples of the input signal $s(n)$ from a starting point, $n=q-K+1$, to the ending point, $n=q$. The frame length K is chosen short enough so that the parameter(s) to be measured can be assumed approximately constant within the frame. On the other hand, K must be large enough to guarantee that the parameter remains measurable. For most short-term analysis PDAs a frame thus requires two or three complete periods at least. In extreme cases, when F_0 changes abruptly, or when the signal is irregular, these two conditions are in conflict with each other and may become a source of error [13]. The frame interval Q, i.e., the distance between consecutive frames (or its reciprocal, the frame rate), is determined in such a way that any significant parameter change is documented in the measurements.

The short-term transform, so to speak, is intended to behave like a concave mirror which focuses all the information on pitch scattered across the frame into one single peak in the spectral domain from which pitch is extracted. This peak is then determined by a maximum (or, in some methods, minimum) detector. Hence this algorithm yields a sequence of average pitch estimates. The short-term transform causes the phase relations between the spectral domain and the original signal to be lost. At the same time, however, the algorithm gets more robust since it loses much of its sensitivity to phase distortions and signal degradation.

Not all the known spectral transforms show the desired focusing effect. The "conventional" ones which do are in some way related to the power spectrum: correlation techniques, frequency-domain analysis, active modeling (Atal [32]), and a least-squares approach. Among the correlation techniques we find the well-known autocorrelation function (ACF) [31]. Its counterpart is given by applying a distance function, for instance the well-known average magnitude difference function (AMDF) [36, 28]. If the signal were strictly periodic, a distance function would vanish at the lag (delay time) $d=T_0$. For quasi-periodic signals there will be a strong minimum at this value of d. In contrast to other short-term PDAs where the estimate of T_0 or F_0 is indicated by a maximum whose position and value have to be determined, the minimum has an ideal target value of zero so that we only need to determine its position [11]. For this reason, distance functions do not require (quasi-)stationarity within the measuring interval; they can even cope with very short frames of one pitch period or less.

The frequency-domain methods are also split up into two groups. Direct determination of F_0 as the location of the lowest peak in the power spectrum is unreliable and inaccurate. We investigate the harmonic structure of the signal instead. One way to do this is spectral compression, which computes the fundamental frequency as the greatest common divider of all harmonics. The power spectrum is compressed along the frequency axis by a factor of two, three etc., and then added to the original power spectrum. This operation gives a peak at F_0 resulting from the coherent additive contribution of the higher harmonics (Schroeder [34]; Martin [26, 27]). Some of these PDAs stem from theories and functional models of pitch perception in the human ear (e.g., Terhardt et al. [39]; Hermes [14]). Similar to Martin's [26] PDA for speech, Brown [5] developed a frequency-domain PDA for music which uses a logarithmic frequency scale. In this scale that also corresponds to musical intervals, a harmonic structure always takes on the same pattern regardless of the value of its fundamental frequency. Consequently, Brown applied a pattern recognition algorithm to detect such patterns in the spectrum and to locate their starting point corresponding to F_0. The patterns themselves depend on the kind of instrument analyzed and can be adjusted according to the respective instruments.

The second frequency-domain technique leads into the lag domain. An inverse DFT is applied, for instance, to the logarithmic power spectrum. This results in the well-known cepstrum PDA (Noll [29]). Instead of the logarithm, one can also compute the amplitude spectrum or its square root and transform it back (Weiss et al. [39]; Indefrey et al. [20]). Inverse transform of the power spectrum itself leads to the autocorrelation function. All these so-called generalized autocorrelation [11] or double-transform techniques [39] lead to a lag-domain representation which exhibits a strong maximum at the lag $d=T_0$. The independent variable, lag (or "quefrency", as Noll [29] called it), has the physical dimension of time, but as the phase relations have been discarded by the nonlinear processing in the frequency domain, all values of d refer to a virtual point $d=0$ where we will always find a pitch pulse, and then the next one will necessarily show up at $d=T_0$.

Harmonic structure detection and distance functions are also closely related to comb filtering [26] and notch filtering [9], respectively. Note that the principle of generalized autocorrelation can also be applied to distance functions [11].

Although these principles are long standing, they still count among the most successful methods in pitch determination [7]. They have found many refinements and variations which cannot be discussed here for reasons of space. For instance, Talkin's PDA [37] applies a nonstationary approach of the autocorrelation function which proved to work with short frames and performs better for rapidly time-varying signals. Such algorithms are also known to have a short overall latency, see further below (Sect. 6).

The least-squares approach is originally a mathematical procedure to separate a periodic signal of unknown period T_0 (Noll, 1970 [30]) from Gaussian noise within a finite signal segment. This technique paved the way for statistical methods to enter pitch determination. Flexibility and modularity are their main advantages. Such PDAs model the statistical properties of harmonic structures in noisy environments and use standard algorithms such as maximum likelihood (ML) and expectation maximization (EM) to obtain F_0. As they are able to deal with multi-pitch information, they are particularly attractive for analyzing music signals. The monograph by Christensen and Jakobsson (2009 [9]) gives a good overview.

4 Detecting the Instant of Glottal Closure (GCI)

If a PDA in speech is required to be very accurate, it is optimal to synchronize it with the instants of glottal closure. A cascaded PDA for this purpose was developed by Hess [17] based on a former algorithm by Cheng and O'Shaughnessy [6]. It is intended for work in time-domain speech synthesis and determines GCIs from undistorted signals. The first part of the cascade is a short-term PDA applying a double spectral transform [20]. The second part uses its estimate to restrict its momentary F_0 range to an octave around this value.

In the source-filter model, the speech signal is the response of the supraglottal system to the pulse train generated by the source, and a pitch period can be regarded as the (first part of) the impulse response of the vocal tract. If we now compute the correlation function $c(n)$ between the speech signal $s(n)$ and the beginning of the pertinent impulse response $h(n)$ of the vocal tract, there will be maxima at those instants n which correspond to an GCI. The impulse response $h(n)$ is estimated via linear prediction. The main peaks of $c(n)$ synchronize well with the individual GCIs. As strong formants also show up in $c(n)$, further processing is required, in this case by calculating the envelope of $c(n)$ via a Hilbert filter and send it through a high-pass filter and a halfway rectifier to enhance the leading amplitudes at the beginning of each pitch period. This approach, however, has one drawback known from all PDAs that apply some sort of inverse filtering [16]. When the formant $F1$ coincides with F_0, the signal will be almost sinusoidal since most of its energy is concentrated in the F_0- $F1$ region. In this case the envelope becomes a constant which no longer allows detecting GCIs. A possible workaround is to additionally derive the GCIs from $c(n)$ and combine both estimates.

Other approaches involve neural networks [19], wavelet transform [21, 10], group delay function [35], dynamic programming [12] or epoch detection from the linear-prediction residual [2]. Drugman et al. (2012 [12]) carried out a comparative evaluation of five such algorithms and showed that they also work well in the presence of additive noise. They also showed that all these algorithms need some restriction or preset of their range of F_0.

5 Multiple Pitch Determination

Simultaneous tones with different frequencies require some frequency-domain processing since in that domain peaks resulting from different tones show up separately at their respective frequencies. The same holds for the lag domain of a double spectral-transform PDA when the nonlinear processing in the frequency domain is of local nature, such as in computing a cepstrum or an autocorrelation function. Hence PDAs that explicitly or implicitly involve a Fourier transform will have this property which was first shown in [39] using simultaneous speech from two talkers as well as musical signals. This has also been demonstrated in various other places in the literature, e.g. by Karjalainen and Tolonen [23] who used a perception-oriented double-transform PDA. The signal is split into two subbands; the two lag-domain representations for each subband are then added up, and significant maxima are searched. The algorithm works well when the simultaneous tones in the input signal do not differ too much in amplitude. The algorithm by Klapuri (2008 [24]) applies an auditory model which consists of a critical-band filterbank followed by some nonlinear processing in each channel to model neural activity in the auditory nerve fibers. From these signals information on periodicity is derived and combined over the channels using a comb filter approach in the frequency domain. The algorithm then takes the pitch estimate with the highest salience and subtracts the pertinent harmonic structure from the spectrum. This procedure is then repeated until all relevant pitch estimates have been determined.

Statistical methods are particularly advantageous when the number of pitches present in a signal is unknown and/or variable, such as in automatic transcription of polyphonic music [9]. As an example, Kameoka's PDA [22] applies Gaussian mixture modelling. Each possible pitch is represented by a harmonic structure, and each harmonic structure is modeled by a tied Gaussian mixture model (GMM) with one degree of freedom, i.e., its fundamental frequency. The initial number k of pitch estimates is set to a value which will exceed the true number of different tones in the signal and thus overfit the model. The F_0 estimates and their respective weights are then iteratively optimized using an EM algorithm. Then the harmonic structure with the lowest contribution to the overall likelihood is removed, thus decreasing k by one, and the optimization is repeated. To determine the optimum value of k the Akaike information criterion is applied which provides a tradeoff between the maximum log likelihood of the model and the number of free parameters.

6 The Question of Latency

Response time of a PDA depends on two factors, 1) computational complexity and speed of the device running it, and 2) latency, i.e., the amount of signal required to get a reliable estimate plus computing time. A PDA runs in real time if the processing time required is less than the elapsed time, say, between two successive frames. As today's computers are able to run even complex PDAs in real time [9, 12, 24], we can put aside the first issue. With the amount of signal required, however, there may be a hidden problem. An ordinary short-term PDA needs (at least) two complete pitch periods to orderly detect periodicity. If the spectral transform is done in one step for the whole range of F_0, latency will exceed two times the longest possible period in the window. For speech, with F_0 ranging from 50 Hz for a deep male voice up to, say, 1000 Hz for a child in spontaneous speech, this means a latency of at least 40 ms from the beginning of the window (plus the frame interval Q) until we get an estimate. In vocoder telephony (as long as this was an area of research) this might just have been tolerable; online capturing of music in a MIDI application, however, may run into problems. Of course latency will go down when the lower end of the frequency range gets higher. One period of the lowest tone of an ordinary guitar lasts about 12 ms, of a violin about 5 ms. If the PDA, however, applies postprocessing, for instance pitch contour tracking by dynamic programming [37], latencies will go up significantly. It goes without saying that such methods cannot be applied in an online application with tough time constraints. Yoo and Fujinaga [41] tested several hardware and software PDAs for MIDI capture on a violin and found latencies between 15 and 90 ms. For a MIDI application this may already be too much.

So, what to do? If, for reasons of robustness, a short-term PDA has to be used, we have to apply one (without postprocessing) that can deal with short frames, such as nonstationary ACF [37], distance functions [28], or perception-oriented PDAs that apply a short-term Fourier transform with frequency-dependent frame length [24]; where F_0 information can be quickly obtained from higher-frequency channels. In addition, it is preferable to make the frame interval Q as short as possible, in the ideal case equal to the sampling interval of the signal. Here, computational load is significantly reduced if spectra etc. and/or pitch estimates can be updated recursively, as e.g. proposed by Fujisaki et al. [13] already in 1986.

Statistical methods also allow instantaneous and recursive tracking. The recent PDA by Christensen [8] applies a maximum-likelihood approach and an exponential forgetting factor for the pitch estimates, after an initialization, it can thus update the estimates sample by sample without look-ahead. The pitch contour is then processed by a fast Kalman filter which splits it up into a slowly changing part and fast deviations allowing it to track fast pitch variations with low delay.

7 Concluding Remarks

The problem of pitch determination and fundamental frequency tracking is long standing, yet there is no algorithm that yields a general solution. However, for almost any application algorithms have been developed that yield good solutions, so looking for the PDA which covers „everything“ may even no longer be desirable. Applications in speech and music have moved away from the vocoder toward prosody recognition, automatic melody detection, acoustic data retrieval, music transcription, computational auditory scene analysis, and high-precision analysis of speech synthesis corpora. New challenges for the development of PDAs, among others, comprise high-precision pitch period determination, processing of signals with multiple pitches, and PDAs with very short latencies.

References

[1] Alku, Paavo (2011): “Glottal inverse filtering analysis of human voice production – a review of estimation and parameterization methods of the glottal excitation and their applications.” Sādhanā *36*, 623-650 (Indian Academy of Sciences)

[2] Ananthapadmanabha T. V. / Yegnanarayana, B. (1979): “Epoch extraction from LP residual for identification of closed glottis interval.” IEEE Trans. ASSP-27, 309-318

[3] Askenfelt, Anders (1979): ”Automatic notation of played music: The Visa project.” Fontes Artis Musicae *26*, 109-120

[4] Batliner, Anton / Buckow, Jan / Niemann, Heinrich / Nöth, Elmar / Warnke, Volker (2000): “The prosody module.” In Verbmobil: Foundations of speech-to-speech translation, ed. by W. Wahlster, 106-121 (Speinger, Berlin)

[5] Brown, Judith C. (1992); “Musical fundamental frequency tracking using a pattern recognition method.” J. Acoust. Soc. Am. *92*, 1394-1402

[6] Cheng, Y. M. / O’Shaughnessy, Douglas (1989): ”Automatic and reliable estimation of glottal closure instant and period.” IEEE Trans. ASSP-*37*, 1805-1815

[7] Christensen, Mads Græsbøll (2011): “Pitch Estimation: Advances and Speech Applications”, tutorial M2 given at INTERSPEECH 2011 (cf. http://imi.aau.dk/~mgc)

[8] Christensen, Mads Græsbøll (2012): “A method for low-delay pitch tracking and smoothing.” Proc. IEEE ICASSP 2012, 345-348

[9] Christensen, Mads Græsbøll / Jakobsson, Andreas (2009): *Multi-Pitch Estimation* (Morgan & Claypool, http://www.morganclaypool.com)

[10] d'Alessandro, Christophe / Sturmel, Nicolas (2011): “Glottal closure instant and voice source analysis using time-scale lines of maximum amplitude.” Sādhanā *36*, 601-622

[11] de Cheveigné, Alain / Kawahara, Hideki (2002): “YIN, a fundamental frequency estimator for speech and music.” J. Acoust. Soc. Am *111*, 1917-1930

[12] Drugman, Thomas / Gudnason, Jon / Naylor, Patrick / Dutoit, Thierry (2012): “Detection of glottal closure instants from speech signals: a quantitative review.” IEEE Trans. Audio Speech Lang. Proc. *20*, 1994-2006

[13] Fujisaki, Hiroya / Hirose, Keikichi / Shimizu, K. (1986): ”A new system for reliable pitch extraction of speech.” Proc. IEEE ICASSP-86, paper 34.16

[14] Hermes, Dik J. (1988): ”Measurement of pitch by subharmonic summation.” J. Acoust. Soc. Am. *83*, 257-264

[15] Hess, Wolfgang J. (1983): *Pitch determination of speech signals - algorithms and devices* (Springer, Berlin)

[16] Hess, Wolfgang J. (1992): ”Pitch and voicing determination.” In *Advances in speech signal processing*; ed. by M. M. Sondhi and S. Furui (M. Dekker, New York), 3-48

[17] Hess, Wolfgang J. (1995): ”Determination of glottal excitation cycles in running speech.” Phonetica *52*, 196-204

[18] Hess, Wolfgang J. (2008): ”Pitch and voicing determination with an extension toward music signals.” In *Springer Handbook of Speech Processing*; ed. by J. Benesty, M. M. Sondhi, and Y. Huang (Springer, Berlin), 181-212

[19] Howard, Ian S. / Walliker, J. R. (1989): ”The implementation of a portable real-time multilayer-perceptron speech fundamental period estimator.” Proc. EUROSPEECH-89,

206-209 (http://www.isca-speech.org/archive/eurospeech_1989)
[20] Indefrey, Helge / Hess,Wolfgang J. / Seeser, Günter (1985): "Design and evaluation of double-transform pitch determination algorithms with nonlinear distortion in the frequency domain." Proc. IEEE ICASSP-85, vol. 2, paper 11.12
[21] Kadambe, S. / Boudreaux-Bartels, Gloria F. (1992): "Application of the wavelet transform for pitch detection of speech signals. IEEE Trans. IT-*38*, 917-924
[22] Kameoka, Hirokazu / Nishimoto, Takuya / Sagayama, Shigeki (2004): "Multi-pitch detection algorithm using constrained Gaussian mixture model and information criterion for simultaneous speech," In Proc. Speech Prosody (SP2004), 533-536 (http://www.isca-speech.org/archive/sp2004)
[23] Karjalainen, Martti / Tolonen, Tero (1999): "Multi-pitch and priodicity analysis for sound separation and auditory scene analysis." Proc. IEEE ICASSP-99, 929-932
[24] Klapuri, Anssi (2008): "Multipitch analysis of polyphonic music and speech signals using an auditory model." IEEE Trans. Audio Speech Lang. Proc. *16*, 255-266
[25] Kohler, Klaus J. (1982): "25 Years of Phonetica." Preface to the special issue on pitch analysis. Phonetica *39*, 185-187
[26] Martin, Philippe (1987): "A logarithmic spectral comb method for fundamental frequency analysis". Proc. 11th Intern. Congr. on Phonetic Sciences, Tallinn, paper 59.2
[27] Martin, Philippe (2004): "WinPitchPro - a tool for text to speech alignment and prosodic analysis," Proc. Speech Prosody (SP2004), 545-548
[28] Moorer, James A. (1974): "The optimum comb method of pitch period analysis of continuous digitized speech." IEEE Trans. ASSP-*22*, 330-338
[29] Noll, A. Michael (1967): "Cepstrum pitch determination." J. Acoust. Soc. Am. *41*, 293-309
[30] Noll, A. Michael (1970): "Pitch determination of human speech by the harmonic product spectrum, the harmonic sum spectrum, and a maximum likelihood estimate." In *Symp. on Computer Processing in Commun.*, ed. by the Microwave Inst.; vol.*19*, 779-797
[31] Rabiner, Lawrence R. (1977): "On the use of autocorrelation analysis for pitch detection." IEEE Trans. ASSP-*25*, 24-33
[32] Rabiner, Lawrence R. / Cheng, M. J. / Rosenberg, Aaron E. /McGonegal, Carol A. (1976): "A comparative study of several pitch detection algorithms." IEEE Trans. ASSP-*24*, 399-423
[33] Sagisaka, Yoshinori / Campbell, Nick / Higuchi, Norio (eds.) (1996): *Computing prosody. Computational models for processing spontaneous speech* (Springer, New York)
[34] Schroeder, Manfred R. (1968): "Period histogram and product spectrum: new methods for fundamental-frequency measurement." J. Acoust. Soc. Am. *43*, 819-834
[35] Smits, R. / Yegnanarayana, B. (1995): "Determination of instants of significant excitation in speech using group delay function." IEEE Trans. Speech Audio Process *3,* 325-333
[36] Sobolev, V. N. / Baronin, S. P. (1968): "Investigation of the shift method for pitch determination." Elektrosvyaz 12, 30-36 (in Russian)
[37] Talkin, David (1995): "A robust algorithm for pitch tracking (RAPT)", in *Speech Coding and Synthesis*, ed. by B. Kleijn and K. Paliwal (Elsevier, Amsterdam), 495-518
[38] Terhardt, Ernst (1979): "Calculating virtual pitch." Hearing Research *1*, 155-182
[39] Terhardt, Ernst / Stoll, Günther / Seewann, Michael (1982): "Algorithm for extraction of pitch and pitch salience from complex tonal signals." J. Acoust. Soc. Am. *71*, 679-688
[39] Weiss, Mark R. / Vogel, Reinhold P. / Harris, Cyril M. (1966): "Implementation of a pitch-extractor of the double spectrum analysis type." J. Acoust. Soc. Am. *40*, 657-662
[41] Yoo, Lilit / Fujinaga, Ichiro (1999): "A comparative latency study of hardware and software pitch trackers," Proc. 1999 Intern. Computer Music Conf., 36–40
[42] Zwicker, Eberhard / Hess, Wolfgang / Terhardt, Ernst (1967): "Erkennung gesprochener Zahlworte mit Funktionsmodell und Rechenanlage." Kybernetik *3*, 267-272

Modeling of Statistic Dependencies of Feature Vectors within Phonemes

Harald Höge

Universität der Bundeswehr München
harald.hoege@t-online.de

Abstract: We investigate two sets of MFCC based feature vectors with different degree of correlation. Analyzing two databases recorded for Spanish and French, high correlation of those features across phonemes is observed. We model the statistic dependencies of feature vectors within segments, which are defined as sub-phonetic units derived from clustered tri-phones. The acoustic model for the segments are Hidden Chunk Models (HCMs). The acoustic model for phonemes is constructed by concatenating three segments building a phoneme. The model assumes, that the feature vectors taken from different segments are statistic independent. The impact of correlation is investigated by classification of segments and phonemes using Bayes decision rule. Evaluation of error rates, Shannon's conditional entropy and model generated chunks demonstrate, that the HCMs come quite close to the distribution of the feature vectors within segments, approaching minimal classification error for segments. The evaluation of the acoustic model for phonemes shows, that we are far away from the true distribution of all feature vectors realizing a phoneme. For the features investigated phoneme error rates (*PER*) of 32% - 38% are achieved. Analyzing Shannon's conditional entropy and model based chunks leads we derive an upper bound of *PER.* Taking French data the upper bound is 5% - 10%. Further it can be speculated that minimal achievable *PER* is in the range of 10% - 20%.

1 Introduction

The acoustic model for any phonetic unit *PU* is an approximation of the distribution $p_t(\vec{X}_t|PU)$, where $\vec{X}_t = [X_1, \dots, X_t]$ denotes the sequence of feature vectors realizing *PU*. The acoustic model used in HMM technology assumes statistic independence of the feature vectors leading to:

$$p_t(\vec{X}_t|PU) \approx \prod_{n=1}^{t} \tilde{p}(X_n|S(PU)_{w(n)}); \qquad PU = [S(PU)_1, \dots, S(PU)_K] \qquad (1)$$

where *PU* is described symbolically as a sequence of *K* states, which are aligned to the frames n=1,...,t by the warping function *w*(*n*). Given the set S_i $i = 1, \dots, N_j$ of states, which describe any PU, the acoustic model (1) is determined by the 'emission probabilities' $p(X|S_i)\,; i = 1, \dots, N_j$, These conditioned density functions (cdf's) are estimated leading to approximations $\tilde{p}(X|S_i)$.

Segment models [1] are more advanced acoustic models, as they model the statistic dependencies of the feature vectors within a segment. The segments $Q_i, i = 1, \dots, N_Q$ are arbitrary large phonetic or data driven units. We use the segment model in the form

$$\left.\begin{aligned} p_t(\vec{X}_t|PU) &\approx \prod_{m=1}^{K} \tilde{p}_{l(m)}(\vec{X}_{l(m)}|Q(PU)_m); PU = [Q(PU)_1 \dots Q(PU)_K] \\ \vec{X}_t &= [\vec{X}_{l(1)}, \dots, \vec{X}_{l(K)}]; \vec{X}_{l(m)} = [X_n, \dots, X_{n-l+1}]^T \; ; \sum_{m=1}^{K} l(m) = t \end{aligned}\right\} \qquad (2)$$

The cdf $\tilde{p}_l(\vec{X}_l|Q_i)$ is a model of $p_l(\vec{X}_l|Q_i)$, which describes the statistical bindings of all feature vectors of the sequence $\vec{X}_l = [X_1, \dots, X_l]^T$ aligned to a segment Q_i. We call such aligned sequences '**chunks**' of length *l*. It is specific for segment models [1], that the cdf's $p_l(\vec{X}_l|Q_i); l = 1,2,\dots$ depend explicitly on the length *l*. The length of a segment is given by the warping function *l*(*m*), which partitions a sequence $\vec{X}_t$ into a sequence of chunks

$[\vec{X}_{l(1)}, \ldots, \vec{X}_{l(K)}]$. According to (2) we assume, that the feature vectors belonging to different chunks are statistic independent. In this paper we regard as phonetic units *PU* phonemes, which allow to study statistic dependencies of long sequences of feature vectors (see table 2). To model the segment distribution $p_l(\vec{X}_l|Q_i)$ of segments, we use GMMs:

$$\tilde{p}_l(\vec{X}_l|Q_i) = \sum_{k=1}^{K_i} c_{ikl} N(\vec{X}_l; \vec{\mu}_{ikl}, \vec{V}_l) \; ; \mathrm{i} = 1, \ldots, N_Q \quad (3)$$

Under mild restrictions the GMMs have the property, that $\tilde{p}_l(\vec{X}_l|Q_i)$ can approximate with increasing number of modes K_i the distribution $p_l(\vec{X}_l|Q_i)$ with respect to the Kullback-Leibler distance [12,11]. We use the EM algorithm applied for chunks in its unified form [2,3] to estimate $\tilde{p}_l(\vec{X}_l|Q_i)$ i.e. the tied covariance matrices $\vec{V}_l$ of chunks of length *l* and the mean vector sequences $\vec{\mu}_{i,k,l} = [\mu_{i,k,l,1}, \ldots, \mu_{i,k,l,l}]$. Reliable estimates are achieved, if enough chunks for a given *l* are available. Thus an important issue is the choice of the segments fulfilling two conditions. On the one hand side the segments should be as large as possible to capture the statistic dependencies of feature vectors of large portions of a phoneme. On the other hand side the cdf's $\tilde{p}_l(\vec{X}_l|Q_i)$ have to be estimated reliably for those chunks with length *l* covering most chunks observed in the speech databases. Taking a complete phoneme as segment we find a distribution $P(l|Q)$, where many sets of chunks with given length have very low probability (see table 2). To achieve reliable estimation we use as segments Q_i sub-phonetic units derived from clustered tri-phones Ph_c. Each Ph_c is constructed by a sequence of three segments. In the following we call the cdf's $\tilde{p}_l(\vec{X}_l|Q_i)$ - modeled by GMMs (3) and based on segments as defined above - **H**idden **C**hunk **M**odels (HCMs) [10]. Analyzing two speech databases for French and Spanish (see chapter 2) we found, that for $l \leq 3$ (Spanish data) and for $l \leq 5$ (French data) enough chunks are available to estimate the HCMs. Those HCMs cover 92% of the chunks. The handling of chunks for $l > 5$ is treated in chapter 4.

The classification of segments and phonemes - described in chapter 3 - demonstrate, that the correlation of feature vectors has great impact on error rates. Provided $p_t(\vec{X}_t|Ph_j)$ and the a-priori distribution $P(Ph_j|t)$ is known, Bayes decision rule

$$\widehat{Ph} = argmax_j(p_t(\vec{X}_t|Ph_j)P(Ph_j|t)) \quad (4)$$

delivers the minimal classification error (MCE), i.e. the minimal phoneme error rate (*PER*) achievable for given features. Assuming the chunks are statistic independent and $p_l(\vec{X}_l|Q_i)$ is given, the lowest *PER* is already achieved with the acoustic model (2). In chapter 3 we discuss, how far away is (2) from an optimal acoustic model achieving MCE.

2 The Feature Sets

2.1 Experimental Set Up

For deriving features we use speech databases as described [9]. Speech is recorded in Spanish (ES) and French (FR) with a sampling rate of 16kHz. Every 10ms a vector containing 16 MFFCs is calculated. Given the MFCC vectors we construct two sets of feature vectors. The 16 dimensional feature vectors of **set1** are given by transforming each MFCC vector by an LDA. The feature vectors of **set2** are constructed by concatenating 4 right and 4 left MFCC vectors inclusive the central MFCC vector to an 144 dimensional super vector. The super vector is LDA transformed to dimension 24. Both sets are globally normalized to zero mean and variance of 1 for each dimension. The databases are labeled into CART generated segments Q_i. The labels deliver the information to segment the sequence of feature vectors into chunks with their length *l*. In table 1 and table 2 the size of the databases and the length distribution of chunks and phonemes are shown. It is evident, that the length distribution of the 2 languages is quite different. Given the distribution of the chunks and the phonemes we can calculated the entropy $H_l(Q)$ and *H*(*Ph*) (see table 3). Their values is the number of bits needed to recognize the segments for given length and the phonemes without errors. Further we estimated HCMs for different length l=1,...,m_0 depending on the data available.

DB	# chunks for training	# chunks for test	length l of chunks & $P_Q(l)$ in %					
			1	2	3	4	5	≥ 6
ES	7 721 815	570 492	26.3	62.5	6.4	1.9	0.8	2.2
FR	27 164 564	4 095 502	26.8	31.6	20.6	9.4	4.1	7.6

Table 1 - amount of data available for the databases DB and length distribution $P_Q(l)$ of the segments

l	1	2	3	4	5	6	7	8	9	10	11	12	13	14	15	16	17
ES	0.1	0.2	10.5	13.1	18.5	34.1	9.0	4.5	2.4	1.4	0.9	0.6	0.4	0.3	0.2	0.2	0.2
FR	1.5	3.8	4.8	9.0	13.3	14.9	13.0	9.7	6.9	4.8	3.4	2.5	1.9	1.5	1.3	1.1	0.8

Table 2 - length distribution $P_{Ph}(l)$ of the phonemes in % ; $P_{Ph}(l \geq 18|ES) = 3.1\%$; $P_{Ph}(l \geq 18|FR) = 5.9\%$

Speech database	m_0	# of segments \ l	$H_l(Q)[bit]$						# of phonemes	$H(Ph)$
			1	2	3	4	5	≥ 6		
Spanish	3	604	8.8	8.92	8.82	8.53	8.06	3.21	32	4.11
French	5	598	8.77	8.75	8.72	8.62	8.54	7.63	40	4.71

Table 3 - $H_l(Q), H(Ph)$ for segments for l=1-5 and for phonemes; HCMs are trained for l=1,...,m_0

2.2 Statistical Properties of the Features

To analyze the statistic dependencies of feature vectors we use the covariance matrices $\vec{V}_l$ of the HCMs (3). The matrix $\vec{V}_l$ is composed by covariance elements $V_l^{X_v X_{v'}} \equiv \langle X_v X_{v'}{}^T \rangle$, which denotes the covariance matrix of the feature vectors $X_v, X_{v'}$ describing the correlation between two feature vectors within a chunk. Given D-dimensional feature vectors $X_v = [x_v^1, \dots, x_v^D]^T$ from the speech databases used to estimate the matrices $\vec{V}_l$ we see, that the relation $\langle x_l^d x_v^{d'} \rangle = \delta(d, d') \langle x_l^d x_v^d \rangle$ (δ denotes the Kronecker delta) holds roughly, leading to

$$\vec{V}_l = \begin{pmatrix} V_l^{X_l X_l} & \cdots & V_l^{X_l X_1} \\ \vdots & \ddots & \vdots \\ V_l^{X_1 X_l} & \cdots & V_l^{X_1 X_1} \end{pmatrix} ; \; V_l^{X_v X_{v'}} \equiv \langle X_v X_{v'}{}^T \rangle \approx \begin{pmatrix} \langle x_l^1 x_v^1 \rangle & \cdots & 0 \\ \vdots & \ddots & \vdots \\ 0 & \cdots & \langle x_l^D x_v^D \rangle \end{pmatrix} \tag{5}$$

Table 4 and table 5 show the first (d=1) and last value (d=D) of $\langle x_l^d x_v^d \rangle$ for the two feature sets and for Spanish and French. The values are normalized by $\langle x_l^1 x_l^1 \rangle$.

Language	Correlation	Set 1		Set 2	
	v	1	2	1	2
Spanish	$\langle x_l^1 x_v^1 \rangle$	0.873	0.762	0.899	0.809
	$\langle x_l^D x_v^D \rangle$	0.745	0.555	0.589	0.347
French	$\langle x_l^1 x_v^1 \rangle$	0.817	0.667	0.966	0.933
	$\langle x_l^D x_v^D \rangle$	0.739	0.546	0.746	0.557

Table 4 - normalized correlation values for chunks of length l=3

Language	Correlation	Set 1				Set 2			
	v	1	2	3	4	1	2	3	4
French	$\langle x_l^1 x_v^1 \rangle$	0.848	0.683	0.545	0.435	0.930	0.808	0.657	0.534
	$\langle x_l^D x_v^D \rangle$	0.791	0.627	0.501	0.400	0.761	0.382	0.101	0.027

Table 5 - normalized diagonal for chunks of length l=5

The tables demonstrates the long ranging strong correlation between the features within segments. The value of $\langle x_l^d x_v^d \rangle$ is maximal for d=1. The correlation drops with increasing d and is lowest for d=D. There are differences in the *set1* and *set2*. For d=1 the correlation of *set1* drops faster with increasing ν than for *set2*. For d=D the two sets behave just opposite. We further conclude, that the high correlation values shown in table 5 for ν =4 holds also for feature vectors within different chunks. Thus the assumption of statistic independency of feature vectors across chunks made in (2), is a very crude approximation.

3 Evaluation of Acoustical Models

The evaluation of acoustic models is done with the quality measures: segment error rates (*SER*), phoneme error rates (*PER*), Shannon's conditional entropies and the method of 'Model generated Chunks (MgCs)'. The methodology of these quality measures and the generation of MgCs is given shortly in section 3.1 and described in detail in [2]. The error rates are of primary interest for research in ASR. The question, what minimal error rate is achievable and how far a given acoustic model deviates from the optimal model is handled by the entropies and MgCs. In section 3.2. experimental results for the quality measures are given.

3.1 The Quality Measures

The labeled speech databases described in chapter 2 provide boundaries of segments, i.e. the chunks with their length are given. The acoustic model (2) is adapted to classify as *PU* context independent phonemes

$$\tilde{p}_t(\vec{X}_t|Ph_j) = \sum_{c=1}^{N_j}\left[P(Ph_c|Ph_j,t)\prod_{p=1}^{3}\tilde{p}_{l_p}\left(\vec{X}_{l_p}\middle|Q_{i(j,c,p)}\right)\right] \;;\; t = \sum_{p=1}^{3} l_p \qquad (6)$$

In (6) we sum up the probabilities of all tri-phone clusters Ph_c composed by 3 segments $Ph_c \equiv \left[Q_{i(j,c,1)}, Q_{i(j,c,2)}, Q_{i(j,c,3)}\right]$, which have as central phone the phoneme Ph_j. For each context c of a clustered tri-phone with central phoneme Ph_j the function $i(j,c,p)$ maps Ph_c to the indices i of the 3 segments $Q_{i(j,c,p)}$; $p = 1,2,3$ building Ph_c. The segments and the phonemes are classified with the Bayes decision rule using acoustic models:

$$\left.\begin{aligned}\hat{Q} &= argmax_i\left(\tilde{p}_l(\vec{X}_l|Q_i)P(Q_i|l)\right)\\ \widehat{Ph} &= argmax_j\left(\tilde{p}_t(\vec{X}_t|Ph_j)P(Ph_j|t)\right)\end{aligned}\right\} \qquad (7)$$

We assume, that the a-priori distributions $P(Q_i|l)$ and $P(Ph_j|t)$ can be estimated reliably from the databases. Appling (7) to the test databases the segment error rate (*SER*) and the phoneme error rate (*PER*) is determined. The case of long chunks, where no HCM is available to evaluate (7), is handled in chapter 4. Bounds for the error rates are evaluated using Shannon's conditional entropy $H_t(U|\vec{X}_t)$ [4,8], where $U \in \{Q, Ph\}$. These entropies are defined in appendix 7. We use as upper bound the Fano bound [5] and as lower bound the Golic bound [6]. These bounds are functions of the entropy $H_t(U|\vec{X}_t)$. To evaluate $H_t(U|\vec{X}_t)$ the distribution $p_t(\vec{X}_t|U_i)$ must be known. As described in [2] we approximate $H_t(U|\vec{X}_t)$ by

$$\tilde{H}_t(U|\vec{X}_t) \equiv -\sum_{i=1}^{N_{PU}} P(U_i|t)\int p_t(U_i|\vec{X}_t)\log\tilde{p}_t(U_i|\vec{X}_t)\,d\vec{X}_t;\; \tilde{p}_t\left(U_i|\vec{X}_t\right) \equiv \frac{\tilde{p}_t(\vec{X}_t|U_i)P(U_i|t)}{\sum_{i=1}^{N_U} P(U_i|t)\tilde{p}_t(\vec{X}_t|U_i)} \qquad (8)$$

To evaluate (8) we use the cross entropy $E_{p_l}(\log\tilde{p}_l(\vec{X}_t|U_i))$, which is approximated by the Monte Carlo Method [7]:

$$H(\vec{X}_t|U_i) \equiv E_{p_l}(\log p_l(\vec{X}_t|U_i)) \approx -\int p_t(\vec{X}_t|U)\,log(\tilde{p}_t(\vec{X}_l|U_i)\,d\vec{X}_t \approx -\frac{1}{N_{S(i,t)}}\sum_{n=1}^{N_{S(i,t)}} log\,\tilde{p}_l(\vec{X}_t^n|U_i) \qquad (9)$$

$N_{S(i,l)}$ is the number of sequences $\vec{X}_t^n$ $n = 1, \dots, N_{S(i,t)}$ of length t assigned to a U_i. Taking into account the Jensen inequality [13] we can relate $H_t(U|\vec{X}_l)$ to its approximation $\tilde{H}_t(PU|\vec{X}_l)$ by

$$H_t(U|\vec{X}_t) \le \tilde{H}_t(U|\vec{X}_t) \qquad (10)$$

The bounds for the error rates are evaluated by using $\tilde{H}_t(U|\vec{X}_t)$ instead of the unknown entropies $H_t(U|\vec{X}_t)$. Thus the bounds are approximations. The deviation of $\tilde{p}_t(\vec{X}_t^n|U_i)$ from $p_t(\vec{X}_t^n|U_i)$ is evaluated by MgC's, which have exact the distribution chunks of the acoustic model (6) and the GMMs $\tilde{p}_l(\vec{X}_l|Q_i)$ in (3). We evaluate error rates *ER(U)* and the entropies $\tilde{H}_t(U|\vec{X}_t)$ for the given speech databases and for the corresponding MgC generated databases. From the differences of the error rates and entropies evaluated from the 2 databases the deviation of $\tilde{p}_t(\vec{X}_t|U_i)$ of the acoustic model to the real distribution $p_t(\vec{X}_t|U_i)$ is judged.

3.2 Experimental Results

In table 6 and 7 the values of error rates and entropies are depicted for the Spanish and French databases. The tables show the values for the two feature sets *set1* and *set2* for the databases described in chapter 2 with their MgCs generated counterpart. The experiments were performed with different number of modes (NoM). The MgCs are modeled with the same NoM as used for the HCMs i.e. the MgCs have exactly the distribution as the acoustical models (3) and (6). With increasing NoMs the HCMs should converge to the distribution $p_l(\vec{X}_l|Q_i)$ of the chunks. Regarding tables 6,7 the values for the *SER* and $\widetilde{H}_l(Q|\vec{X}_l)$ drop in general with increasing NoMs for the speech database. The corresponding values for the MgC-database converge to the values of those of the speech database. The gap between the corresponding values is bigger for *set2* than for *set1*. Yet *set2* is more relevant, as it delivers lower *SERs*. The acoustic model (6) delivers large MgC-distances for the values of *PER* and $\widetilde{H}_t(Ph|\vec{X}_t)$, especially for the higher correlated features of *set2*.

Set1/2 - MgC	**NoM**	***SER**$_l$*					$\widetilde{H}_l(Q\|\vec{X}_l)$					***PER***	$\widetilde{H}_t(Ph\|\vec{X}_t)$
		1	2	3	4	5	1	2	3	4	5		
1-no	1.812	94.6	87.6	79.1	80.3	83.1	7.53	6.69	6.18	7.66	9.78	50.0	12.65
1-no	21.744	93.2	84.8	75.4	77.9	80.7	7.36	6.23	5.81	7.18	9.27	43.7	5.94
1-yes	1.812	94.3	86.1	74.3	63.8	51.0	7.18	5.82	4.50	3.46	2.60	27.3	1.22
1-yes	21.744	92.2	86.1	76.5	74.2	71.9	6.73	5.96	5.11	5.18	5.14	27.4	1.86
2-no	1.812	82.9	73.1	62.6	64.9	68.5	6.72	6.13	5.91	9.03	12.64	41.8	6.03
2-no	21.744	76.2	70.0	59.4	62.3	68.4	5.99	5.77	5.34	7.98	11.44	37.4	4.58
2-yes	1.812	79.9	61.5	42.9	32.0	12.0	5.38	3.61	2.26	1.09	0.53	10.0	0.42
2-yes	21.744	69.7	59.2	44.2	33.9	25.0	4.31	3.41	2.38	2.14	1.60	6.9	0.31

Table 6 - error rates and the approximated Shannon's conditional entropy $\widetilde{H}_l(Q|\vec{X}_l)$, $\widetilde{H}_t(Ph|\vec{X}_t)$ for the feature sets *set1* and *set2* for **Spanish;** results for model based generated chunks are notated as MgC=yes

set-MgC	**NoM**	***SER**$_l$*					$\widetilde{H}_l(Q\|\vec{X}_l)$					***PER***	$\widetilde{H}_t(Ph\|\vec{X}_t)$
		1	2	3	4	5	1	2	3	4	5		
1-no	2.990	89.4	75.7	70.6	67.4	66.1	6.68	5.28	4.92	4.69	4.72	42.2	8.19
1-no	20.000	87.9	74.1	68.0	64.8	63.5	6.48	4.95	4.63	4.60	4.68	35.7	3.06
1-no	40.000	87.6	73.5	67.5	64.3	63.0	6.37	4.82	4.49	4.49	4.60	34.9	2.92
1-yes	2.990	89.2	71.6	62.4	58.6	55.6	6.02	4.15	3.41	3.11	2.98	21.8	5.21
1-yes	20.000	86.8	72.7	66.8	63.6	61.7	5.71	4.27	3.78	3.55	3.45	15.8	0.73
1-yes	40.000	86.4	73.1	67.7	64.7	62.8	5.68	4.36	3.91	3.70	3.61	16.3	0.77
2-no	2.990	69.6	57.0	53.0	52.1	52.9	5.50	4.38	4.18	4.14	4.25	36.1	5.60
2-no	20.000	63.0	54.3	51.6	51.0	52.1	4.77	4.15	4.12	4.13	4.31	33.6	3.27
2-no	40.000	61.6	54.0	51.6	51.2	52.8	4.51	4.09	4.11	4.17	4.47	33.0	3.37
2-yes	2.990	59.2	36.3	30.1	28.8	29.3	3.32	1.79	1.44	1.37	1.40	8.3	0.39
2-yes	20.000	51.8	37.6	32.8	32.0	31.4	2.81	1.86	1.61	1.61	1.65	9.4	0.45
2-yes	40.000	50.8	37.8	32.8	32.0	31.3	2.75	1.89	1.64	1.67	1.77	9.3	0.46

Table 7 - error rates and Shannon's conditional entropy for the feature set1 and set2 for **French**

3.3 Bounds of Error Rates

The Fano-Golic plots for the bounds of error rates is shown in Figure 1. Selected data points of table 7 with NoM=40.00 and *l*=1,2,3 are depicted. In the case of MgCs, Shannon's entropies fulfill the condition $H(U|\vec{X}_t) = \widetilde{H}(U|\vec{X}_t), U \in \{Q, Ph\}$, as the MgCs are exactly distributed as given by the GMMs (3) and the acoustic model (6). Thus the Fano-Golic bounds are valid for those data points. In the case of chunks derived from speech, $H(U|\vec{X}_t)$ is approximated by $\widetilde{H}_t(U|\vec{X}_t)$ (8). Due to (10) the exact values of $H(U|\vec{X}_t)$ are smaller. This means, that the not filled data points of figure 1 have to be shifted down to an unknown amount. The *PER*-$H(Ph|\vec{X}_t)$ data points measured from chunks of speech is outside of the bounds. A shift down of at least 1 bit is needed to get 'valid' data points. This indicates that the acoustic model (6) is far away from the real distribution of the features. Although we have no proof, it seems that the MgCs deliver lower bounds for Shannon's conditional entropy $H_t(Ph\ \vec{X}_t)$. For MgC we have $H_t(Ph|\vec{X}_t) = 0.45$ for *set2* and $H_t(Ph|\vec{X}_t) = 0.77$ for *set1*. Taking the Fano bound we conclude for French an upper bound of *PER* is 5% for *set2* and 10 % for *set1*. For these sets we could speculate for a MCE for phonemes with an acoustic model taking into account the statistic dependencies of chunks. A minimal of *PER* in the range of 10-20% seems plausible.

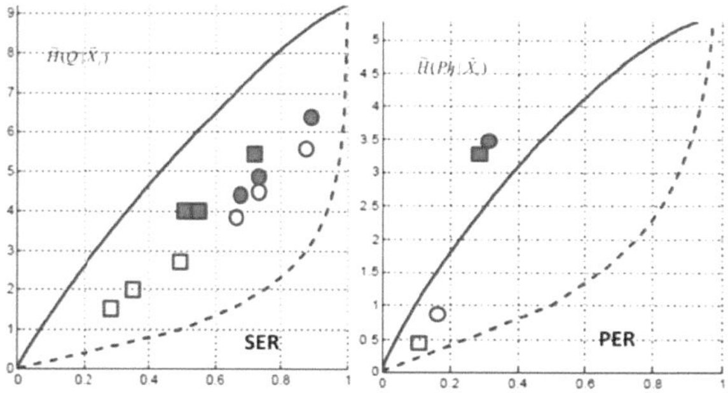

Figure 1 - Bounds of *SER* and *PER* for French with 40.000 modes; not filled data points belong to MgCs; the round points are from *set1* - the quadratic points are from *set2*.

4 Handling of Long Chunks

As shown in table 1 there exist segments realized by long chunks with low probability. In these cases the set of chunks is too small to estimate HCMs reliable. Yet to apply the classifiers (7) we need a value for $\tilde{p}_l(\vec{X}_l|Q_i)$ for any l. In the following we handle this case.
We assume, we can estimate the HCMs for a length till $l=m_0$. Now we have to solve the task to provide for the GMMs (3) the covariance matrix and the means for $l > m_0$. In [9] a 'similarity approach' is presented for handling long chunks. In the next sections we evaluate the similarity approach and extend it by an autoregressive approach. In [2] a specific method for very long chunks is described. The results shown in table 6,7 are achieved using the similarity approach.

4.1 Similarity Approach

The similarity approach is based on two assumption

I. the correlation between feature vectors for $l > m_0$ is the same as for $l=m_0$ and the correlation vanishes between feature vectors with distance $l - v > m_0$
II. the means for $l > m_0$ are the same as for $l=m_0$ for $v \le m_0$. For $v > m_0$ the means are extended with the same value as for $v=m_0$

Assumption I. leads to the approximation:

$$\tilde{V}_l^{X_v X_{v'}} \equiv \begin{cases} V_l^{X_v X_{v'}} \ for\ v, v' \le m_0 \\ \left. \begin{array}{ll} f_0 V_m^{X_{m_0} X_{m_0 - |v-v'|}} & for\ |v-v'| < m_0 \\ 0 & for\ |v-v'| \ge m_0 \end{array} \right\} v, v' > m_0 \end{cases} \quad (11)$$

The scalar f_0 is introduced, because it turned out in the experiences that the extended matrix V_l for $l > m_0$ with the elements $\tilde{V}_l^{X_v X_{v'}}$ using $f_0 = 1$ lead to non positive definite matrices $\vec{V}_l$ especially for larger l. For this reason we set $f_0 \equiv \delta(v, v')$ in the experiments described in chapter 3. For extending the means for $l > m_0$ the assumption II leads to

$$\mu_{i,k,v,l} = \begin{pmatrix} \mu_{i,k,v,m_0} \ for\ v \le m_0 \\ \mu_{i,k,m_0,m_0} \ for\ v > m_0 \end{pmatrix} l > m_0 \quad (12)$$

4.2 Autoregressive Approach

Now we extend chunks $\vec{X} = [X_1, \dots, X_{m_0}]^T$, where each D-dimensional feature vector $X_\nu, \nu = 1, \dots, m_0$ has the components x_ν^d, $d = 1, \dots, D$ to chunks of length $l = m_0 + 1$. We assume, that the components $x_{m_0+1}^d$ are generated by an autoregressive process of order m_0 driven by the transfer functions

$$H^d(z) = \frac{1}{1 + a_2^d z^{-1} + \dots + a_{m_0+1}^d z^{-m_0}} \; ; d = 1, \dots, D$$

Thus the elements $x_{m_0+1}^d$ of the feature vector X_{m_0+1} are generated by

$$x_{m_0+1}^d = -\sum_{\nu=2}^{m_0+1} a_\nu^d \, x_{m_0-\nu+2}^d \; + \; \varepsilon^d \tag{13}$$

from the elements x_ν^d, $\nu = 1, \dots, m_0; d = 1, \dots, D$ of the feature vectors $[X_1, \dots, X_{m_0}]^T$. The autoregressive process (13) is defined by residuals ε^d with zero mean and the prediction coefficients a_ν^d. We assume that the prediction coefficient a_ν^d are the same for all segments Q_i. To apply (13) the prediction coefficients have to be estimated. For this approach we make some assumptions concerning statistic dependencies of the generated elements $x_{m_0+1}^d$. The elements $x_{m_0+1}^d$ are correlated as assumed in the relation (5) leading to

$$V_{m_0+1}^{X_{m_0+1}X_\nu} = \begin{pmatrix} \langle x_{m_0+1}^1 x_\nu^1 \rangle & \cdots & 0 \\ & \ddots & \vdots \\ 0 & \cdots & \langle x_{m_0+1}^D x_\nu^D \rangle \end{pmatrix} \quad \nu = 1, \dots, m_0 + 1 \tag{14}$$

Inspecting reliable estimated covariance matrices $\vec{V}_l$ available for $l \leq m_0$, we see that (14) is an approximation. For low values of d the elements x_ν^d are correlated with elements x_ν^{d-1} and x_ν^{d+1}. To construct the components $\langle x_{m_0+1}^d x_{\nu'}^d \rangle, \nu' = 1, .., m_0 + 1$, we use the similarity approach (11) by setting $f_0=1$. From these components we make a diagonal matrix $V_{m_0+1}^{X_{m_0+1}X_{\nu'}}$ where the diagonal has the values

$$[\langle x_{m_0+1}^1 x_{\nu'}^1 \rangle, \dots, \langle x_{m_0+1}^D x_{\nu'}^D \rangle]^T \equiv diag\,(V_{m_0+1}^{X_{m_0+1}X_{\nu'}})$$

Taking the diagonal elements $V_{m_0+1}^{X_{m_0+1}X_{\nu'}}$ we can extend the covariance matrix $\vec{V}_{m_0+1}$ to the covariance matrix $\vec{V}_{m_0+1}$, which differs from the similarity approach by using only diagonal elements. Given $\vec{V}_{m_0+1}$ we can apply the Levinson algorithm [13, eq. (13-108)] to determine the prediction coefficients a_ν^d and the power of the residual ε^d via the relation

$$\langle x_{m_0+1}^d x_{\nu'}^d \rangle = \begin{Bmatrix} -\sum_{\nu=2}^{m_0+1} a_\nu^d \langle x_{m_0-\nu+2}^d x_{\nu'}^d \rangle + \langle \varepsilon^d \varepsilon^d \rangle \; for \; \nu' = m_0 + 1 \\ -\sum_{\nu=2}^{m_0+1} a_\nu^d \langle x_{m_0-\nu+2}^d x_{\nu'}^d \rangle \qquad else \end{Bmatrix} \tag{15}$$

From the prediction coefficients the related reflection coefficients r can be calculated. For stable filters the condition $|r|<1$ must hold. If this condition is not given, the components $\langle x_{m_0+1}^d x_{\nu'}^d \rangle$ can be corrected by manipulation of the reflection coefficients.

For extending the means $\vec{\mu}_{ikl} = [\mu_{ikl1}, \dots, \mu_{ikll}]$ we use (13) by averaging the feature vectors for all chunks $X_{m_0,m_0-\nu+2}$ aligned to Q_i. The subsets are all features vectors assigned to a mode k. Now we average (13) with respect to these subsets ω_{ikl} resulting in the relation

$$\langle x_{m_0+1}^d \rangle_{\omega_{ikl}} = -\sum_{\nu=2}^{m_0+1} a_\nu^d \langle x_{m_0-\nu+2}^d \rangle_{\omega_{ikl}} + \langle \varepsilon^d \rangle_{\omega_{ikl}}$$

$$\mu_{ik,m_0+1,m_0+1}^d = -\sum_{\nu=2}^{m_0+1} a_\nu^d \, \mu_{ik,m_0,m_0-\nu+2}^d \tag{16}$$

The average $\langle x_{m_0+1}^d \rangle_{\omega_{ikl}}$ has to be interpreted as the average of all $x_{m_0+1}^d$ generated by the feature elements $x_{m_0-\nu+2}^d$ from the set ω_{ikl}. The mean elements $\mu_{ik,m_0,\nu}^d$, $\nu = 1, \dots, m_0$ are those of the HCM for $l = m_0$.

Given the extension from $l = m_0$ to $l = m_0 + 1$ we can iterate the whole process as described above to extent the covariance matrices and means to $l > m_0 + 1$.

4.3 Evaluation

For evaluating the two approaches, we compare covariance matrices and means for the same length l by constructing these items by 2 ways. The first items are estimated with chunks given from the databases, the second items are estimated with one of the two approaches. Covariance matrices $\vec{V}_l$ are compared by the entropy $H_l(\vec{X}_l|Q_i)$ of segments with mono-modal Gaussian distribution $N(\vec{X}_l; \vec{\mu}_{ikl}, \vec{V}_l)$. This entropy depends only on the covariance matrix $\vec{V}_l$:

$$R_{\vec{V}_l} = \frac{a_{\vec{V}}^2}{a_{\vec{V}}^1};\ a_{\vec{V}_l} = \frac{H_l(\vec{X}_l|Q_i)}{l \cdot D} = \frac{ln(2\pi e)}{2ln2} + \frac{ln(|\vec{V}_l|)}{2ln2 \cdot l \cdot D} \qquad (17)$$

In (17) the entropy $H_l(\vec{X}_l|Q_i)$ is normalized by $l \cdot D$. $a_{\vec{V}_l}$ can be interpreted by the mean entropy of single component of a feature vector. The ratio $R_{\vec{V}_l}$ shows the deviation of $a_{\vec{V}}^1$ of the chunk estimated covariance matrix compared to $a_{\vec{V}}^2$ of the matrices of one of the two approaches. The means $\vec{\mu}_{ikl}^1$ and $\vec{\mu}_{ikl}^2$ of two HCMs for chunks of length l are compared by the relative difference

$$R_{\vec{\mu}_l} = \frac{\sum_{i=1}^{N_Q} \sum_{k=1}^{K_i} |\vec{\mu}_{ikl}^1 - \vec{\mu}_{ikl}^2|}{\sum_{i=1}^{N_Q} \sum_{k=1}^{K_i} |\vec{\mu}_{ikl}^1|} \cdot 100\ [\%] \qquad (18)$$

where the means $\vec{\mu}_{ikl}^1$ are estimated from the chunks and $\vec{\mu}_{ikl}^2$ are those estimated by one of the two approaches. Table 8 shows the values of $R_{\vec{V}_l}$ and $R_{\vec{\mu}_l}$ for mono-modal HCMs of *set2*. It can be concluded that the similarity approach leads to better results.

l	3	4	5
$S - R_{\vec{V}_l}$	1.39	1.76	5.70
$AR - R_{\vec{V}_l}$	1.44	2.04	8.72
$S - R_{\vec{\mu}_l}$	29.6	28.7	28.0
$AR - R_{\vec{\mu}_l}$	25.1	28.2	43.1

Table 8 - $R_{\vec{V}_l}$ and $R_{\vec{\mu}_l}$ for the similarity approach *S* and the autoregressive approach *AR* for French

5 Conclusion

In the databases investigated we found that MFCC based feature vectors are strongly correlated within phonemes. The correlation is modeled on segment level using HCMs. Due to the experiments performed in chapter 3 we found that the gap of the HCMs to the true distribution of features of segments gets smaller with increasing number of modes. For the *set1* the gap is quite small. For the highly correlated set *set2* the gap is still high even when using 40.000 modes. It seems that for better approximation unrealistic high number of modes are needed. The GMM approach with tied covariance matrices used as basic distributions has to be reconsidered. Analyzing Shannon's Entropy and MgCs we derived an upper bound for phoneme error rates. For French this bound is 5% for set2 and 10% for set1. We speculate, that the minimal achievable *PER* is about 10-20%. With the current acoustic model an *PER* of 33% (Spanish) and 37% (French) is achieved. In order to achieve minimal *PER* we have to optimize the acoustic models (2, 6). Either we extend (2) to an approach modeling statistical dependencies of chunks, or we use longer segments covering larger portions of a phoneme. Ladder approach runs into the problem of sparse data. As shown in chapter 4, the approaches investigated for long segments with sparse data show low performance yet.

6 Acknowledgements

We would like to thank Christan Pflahl and Hermann Ney from the RWTH, Aachen, Germany for kindly providing the labeled Quaero databases.

7 Appendix

Given phonetic units PU_i, $i=1,\ldots,N_{PU}$ realized by feature vector sequences $\vec{X}_t$ of length t Shannon' conditional entropy $H_t(PU|\vec{X}_t)$ is defined by

$$H_t(PU|\vec{X}_t) \equiv H_t(PU) - I_t(\vec{X}_l; PU);\ I_t(\vec{X}_t; PU) \equiv H_t(\vec{X}_t) - H_t(\vec{X}_t|PU)$$

$$H_t(PU) \equiv -\sum_{i=1}^{N_{PU}} P(PU_i|t)\log(P(PU_i|t));\ H_t(\vec{X}_t) \equiv -\int p(\vec{X}_t) log\, p(\vec{X}_t)\, d\vec{X}_t$$

$$p(\vec{X}_l) = \sum_{i=1}^{N_Q} P(Q_i|l) p_l(\vec{X}_l|Q_i);\ H_l(\vec{X}_l|Q) \equiv -\sum_{i=1}^{N_Q} P(Q_i|l)\int p_l(\vec{X}_l|Q_i)\, log\, p_l(\vec{X}_l|Q_i)\, d\vec{X}_l$$

Now we derive Shannon's conditional entropy of phonemes with given segment boundaries. Setting $PU=Ph$ and considering the segmentation $l^{\vec{S}}$ of phonemes into segments, we get:

$$H\left(Ph\middle|\vec{X}_t, l^{\vec{S}}\right) = H\left(Ph\middle|l^{\vec{S}}\right) - I\left(\vec{X}_t; Ph\middle|l^{\vec{S}}\right);\ I\left(\vec{X}_t; Ph|l^{\vec{S}}\right) = H\left(\vec{X}_t\middle|l^{\vec{S}}\right) - H\left(\vec{X}_t\middle|Ph, l^{\vec{S}}\right)$$

A sequence $\vec{X}_t$ building a phoneme Ph_j has a segmentation $l^{\vec{S}_j}$ of 3 chunks with length $l_{j,}^p, p = 1,2,3$. With this notation we get for the terms for evaluating $H\left(Ph\middle|\vec{X}_t, l^{\vec{S}}\right)$:

$$H\left(Ph\middle|l^{\vec{S}}\right) = -\sum_j \sum_{\vec{S}_j} P(Ph_j, l^{\vec{S}_j}) \log P\left(Ph_j\middle|l^{\vec{S}_j}\right) = -\sum_j \sum_{l_j} P(l_j) P(Ph_j|l_j) \log P(Ph_j|l_j)\ ;\ l_j = \sum_{p=1}^{S_j} l_j^p$$

$$H\left(\vec{X}_t\middle|Ph, l^{\vec{S}}\right) = -\sum_j \sum_{\vec{S}_j} P(l^{\vec{S}_j}) P\left(Ph_j\middle|l^{\vec{S}_j}\right) \int p(\vec{X}_t|Ph_j, l^{\vec{S}_j}) \log p(\vec{X}_t|Ph_j, l^{\vec{S}_j})\, d\vec{X}_t$$

$$p\left(\vec{X}_{l^{\vec{S}_j}}\middle|Ph_j, \vec{S}_j\right) = \sum_c P(Phc_{jc}|Ph_j, l^{\vec{S}_j})\, p\left(\vec{X}_{l_j^1}, \ldots, \vec{X}_{l_j^3}\middle|Phc_{jc}, \vec{S}_j\right);\ p\left(\vec{X}_{l_j^1}, \ldots, \vec{X}_{l_j^3}\middle|Phc_{jc}, \vec{S}_j\right) = \prod_{p=1}^{3} p(\vec{X}_{l_i^p}|Q_{i(c,p)})$$

$$H\left(\vec{X}_n\middle|l^{\vec{S}}\right) = -\int \sum_{\vec{S}_j} P(l^{\vec{S}_j})\, p\left(\vec{X}_n\middle|l^{\vec{S}_j}\right) \log\, p\left(\vec{X}_n\middle|l^{\vec{S}_j}\right) d\vec{X}_n$$

$$p\left(\vec{X}_t\middle|l^{\vec{S}_j}\right) = \sum_j p\left(\vec{X}_t, Ph_j\middle|l^{\vec{S}_j}\right) = \sum_j P\left(Ph_j\middle|l^{\vec{S}_j}\right) p\left(\vec{X}_t\middle|Ph_j, l^{\vec{S}_j}\right) = \sum_j P(Ph_j|l_j) \left\{\prod_{p=1}^{3}\left(\sum_{i\in C_j^p} \frac{P(Q_i|l^p)}{\sum_{i'\in C_j^p} P\left(Q_{i'}\middle|l_j^p\right)} p_{l_p}(\vec{X}_{l_p}|Q_i)\right)\right\}$$

Literature

[1] Ostendorf, M., Digalakis, V., and Kimball, O., “From HMMs to segment models: a unified view of stochastic modeling for speech recognition”, IEEE Trans. on Speech and Audio Proc., 4(5): 360-378, 1996.

[2] Höge, H., “Comparison of HMMs and HCMs”, Proc. ESSV Bielefeld , 2013

[3] Huang, X. D., Ariki, Y. and Jack, M. A., “Hidden Markov Models for Speech Recognition”, Information Technology Series, Edinburg University Press, 1990

[4] Shannon, C.E.: A Mathematical Theory of Communication. Bell System Technical Journal, Vol. 27: July and October 1948, pp. 379-423 and 623-656.

[5] Fano, R.M.: Transmission of Information: A Statistical Theory of Communications. MIT Press and John Wiley & Sons, Inc., New York, third edition: 1991

[6] Golic, J.: On the Relationship between the Information Measures and the Bayes Probability of Error. IEEE Transactions on Information Theory, Vol. IT-33(5): 1987, pp. 681-693.

[7] Robert, C. and Casella, G.: Monte Carlo Statistical Methods. Second edition Springer Verlag: New York 2004

[8] Höge, H., Setiawan, P.: Improvements of Hidden Chunk Models. In Proc. ESSV: Berlin 2010

[9] Höge,H.: The Use of Conditional Gaussians for Hidden Chunk Models. In Proc. ESSV: Cottbus 2012

[10] Rybach, D., Gollan, C., Heigold, G., Hoffmeister, B., Lööf, J., Schlüter, R., and Ney, H., “The RWTH Aachen University open source speech recognition system”, in Proc. Interspeech, Brighton, U.K.:2111–2114, 2009.

[11] Mclachlan, G. and Peel, D., "Finite Mixture Models". Wiley, New York. MR1789474, 2000.

[12] Norets, A., "Approximation of conditional densities by smooth mixtures of regression". The Annals of Statistics, Vol. 38, No. 3, 1733–1766, 2010

[13] Papoulis, A.: Probability, Random Variables, and Stochastic Processes. Third Edition, McGraw-Hill, Inc.: 1991.

Model dependency of memristor circuit dynamics

on the special occasion of the 65th birthday of Prof. Rüdiger Hoffmann

A. Ascoli[1], *F. Corinto*[2], *V. Senger*[1], *R. Tetzlaff*[1]

[1] *Faculty of Electrical and Computer Engineering, Technische Universität Dresden, Germany*
{alon.ascoli, vanessa.senger, ronald.tetzlaff}@tu-dresden.de
[2] *Department of Electronics and Telecommunications, Politecnico di Torino, Italy*
fernando.corinto@polito.it

Kurzfassung: Pickett's model is one of the few memristor models based upon experimental observations. Despite its high degree of accuracy, it is fairly complex and its use in large circuits is problematic. A number of simpler memristor models, specifically Biolek's model, the generalized Boundary Condition Memristor model and the ThrEshold Adaptive Memristor model are capable to track the dynamics of Pickett's model after undergoing a proper optimization process. However, since the parameter values of Pickett's model need to be tuned on the basis of the way the memristor is coupled to other circuit components including the input source, the optimization procedure is not unique but must be repeated on a case by case basis. This is non ideal since the parameters of Pickett's model were only given for a few circuit/input scenarios. Further, employing these models in simple memristor-based circuits without a preliminary necessary optimization step, simulations results reveal the occurrence of distinct nonlinear behaviors under a common setting for the circuit components coupled to the memristor. These issues demonstrate that the current lack of a finalized model for the physical memristor prevents memristor-based electronics to flourish. Preliminary investigations on a novel polynomial model show that Prof. Chua's idea of "unfolding the memristor" by suitably expanding the morphing function in series of polynomials involving state and input could represent the key towards the ultimate model.

1 Introduction

One of Prof. Chua's memorable research breakthrough was the 1971 introduction of the memristor [1], a two-terminal electrical component with nonlinear charge-flux linkage relationship and non-volatile state-dependent memory-resistance which, under the condition of the Passivity Criterion [2] is non negative. In the following 37 years the concept of memristor and memristive systems [2] was of some interest to theoretically inclined researchers only. Then in 2008 Hewlett Packard announced the discovery of memristor behavior at the nano-scale in a TiO_2-based thin film [3] and since then researchers and industry have been investing a large amount of resources on various topics, including the development of models for the physical memristors [4, 5, 6, 7].

This topic is of particular interest nowadays. Considerable progress in memristor circuit design may not be attained without the availability of a faithful model for the physical memristor. In 2009 Pickett introduced a model based upon experimental observations on the TiO_2-based memristor [5]. This model explains the dynamics of this memristor with Simmon's tunnel barrier effect [8] and is taken as reference throughout this manuscript. In 2011 Abdalla presented a PSpice circuit implementation of Pickett's model [9], which shall be used in this paper for the numerical simulations of the reference model.

In a first study this work demonstrates that simple models proposed in literature [4, 6, 7] may be tuned to the reference model through an optimization procedure so as to capture its dynamics in a basic memristor circuit for which the parameters of Pickett's model are publicly available. Parameter sets of Pickett's model for more complicated circuits were not documented. As a result, the second part of our investigation may not benefit from the optimization step. In such investigation the models were used in simulations of a couple of single-memristor oscillators to study the variance in the observed dynamics under a common choice for the values of the circuit components coupled to the memristor. In general the dynamics of the oscillators were found to be sensitive to the memristor model under use [10].

The results of this research further point out the necessity to develop a finalized model for the physical memristor to drive progress in memristor circuit design. Taking inspiration from Prof. Chua's idea [11] of "unfolding the memristor" by expanding the state evolution function (which he named as morphing function) in series of polynomials involving state and input, the final part of the manuscript introduces a novel Polynomial Memristor (PM) model [12], in which the memristance function within the state-dependent Ohm's law may also be described as a polynomial series depending on state and input. The most remarkable feature of the model is its high degree of freedom associated to the large number of polynomial series coefficients which may be independently tuned so as to massage the morphing function in multiple forms. As a Proof-of-Concept here a fitting procedure allows the determination of polynomial series coefficients for a close approximation of the state evolution function in Pickett's model.

2 Review of memristor models

This section briefly reviews the reference model together with some of the most remarkable memristor models from the literature.

2.1 Pickett's model

Pickett's model [5] is assumed as reference since it is one of the few models based on laboratory measurements on the TiO_2-based memristor. Pickett used the Simmons' tunnel barrier model to characterize the nano-device: an insulating TiO_2-based tunnel barrier of width w is interposed between the Platinum contacts and the conductive TiO_{2-x}-based layer.

The time evolution of state w is governed by

$$\frac{dw}{dt} = f_{off}\sinh\left(\frac{|i|}{i_{off}}\right)\exp\left(-\exp\left(\frac{w-a_{off}}{w_c}-\frac{|i|}{b}\right)-\frac{w}{w_c}\right) \tag{1}$$

$$\frac{dw}{dt} = -f_{on}\sinh\left(\frac{|i|}{i_{on}}\right)\exp\left(-\exp\left(\frac{a_{on}-w}{w_c}-\frac{|i|}{b}\right)-\frac{w}{w_c}\right) \tag{2}$$

for $i>0$ and $i<0$ respectively, where i is the tunneling junction current (i.e. the memristor current). The voltage across the barrier is expressed as $v_g = v - R_s i$, where v is the voltage falling across the whole film (i.e. the memristor voltage), while R_S is the resistance of the conductive layer. The following implicit relation between i and v holds:

$$i = \frac{j_o A}{(\Delta w)^2}\left\{\phi_I e^{-B\sqrt{\phi_I}} - (\phi_I + e|v_g|)e^{-B\sqrt{\phi_I+e|v_g|}}\right\}. \tag{3}$$

In section 3 various models described in 2.2 shall be fitted to the reference model in the case of a circuit (see Fig. 1) in which a voltage source generating a periodic non-zero average triangular signal (see Fig. 2), a resistor of value $R_i = 2.4k\Omega$ and a memristor are placed in series and where the negative terminals of voltage source and memristor are connected to ground.

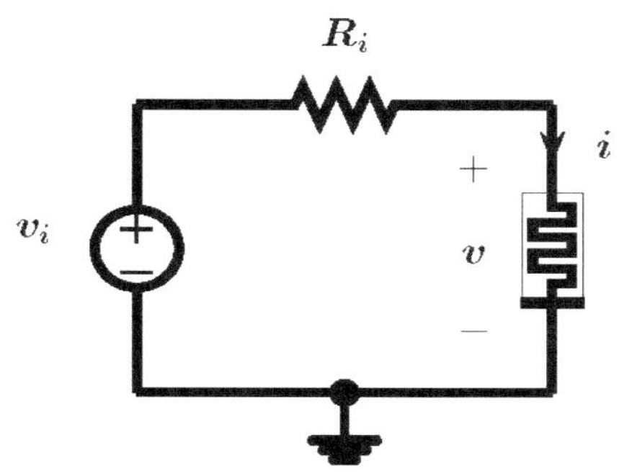

Figure 1 - Memristor circuit used in the fitting procedure of section 3.

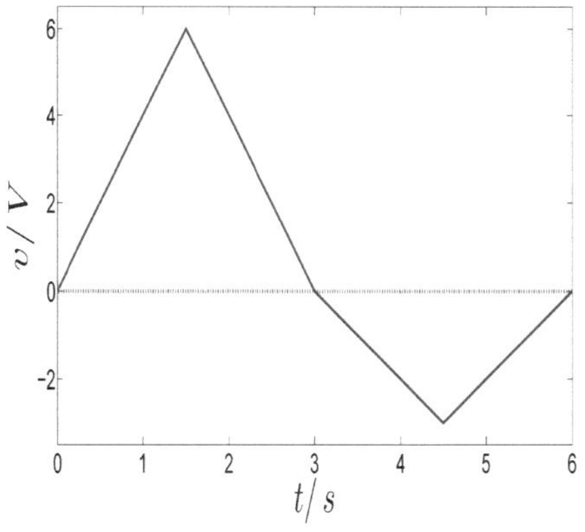

Figure 2 - One period of the triangular waveform generated by the voltage source in the circuit of Fig. 1.

In the fitting procedure R_S was chosen as $215\,\Omega$, while the values of the other parameters in 1-2 are tabulated in Table 1 (see [9] for details).

2.2 Simpler models

This section revisits some of the most notable models available in the literature, i.e. Biolek's model [4], the generalized BCM model [6] and the TEAM model [7]. In the first two models the input u-output y algebraic relation is expressed as $y = g\left(wD^{-1}\right) u$, where state w and constant D respectively denote the length of the conductive layer and the film longitudinal extension. Function $g(wD^{-1})$ stands for the memristance $M\left(wD^{-1}\right) = R_{off} - \Delta R wD^{-1}$ for current control (i.e. $u = i$ and $y = v$, as in Biolek's model) and for the memductance $W\left(wD^{-1}\right) = G_{on}G_{off}\left(G_{on} - \Delta G wD^{-1}\right)^{-1}$ for voltage control (i.e. $u = v$ and $y = i$, as in the generalized

Table 1 - Values of the parameters of the reference model for the input and circuit specified in the text.

f_{off}	f_{on}	i_{off}	i_{on}
$3.5\mu m s^{-1}$	$40\mu m s^{-1}$	$115\mu A$	$8.9\mu A$
a_{off}	a_{on}	b	w_c
$1.2nm$	$1.8nm$	$500\mu A$	$107pm$

BCM model). In both cases the equation defining how the state changes with time is given by $\frac{dw}{dt} = \mu R_{on} D^{-1} i f(w,u)$, where $f(w,u)$ represents the window function. In the fitting procedure of section 3 the common parameters of these models are taken as $R_{on} = 1\,k\Omega$, $R_{off} = 10\,k\Omega$, $\mu = 10^{-16} m^2 V^{-1} s^{-1}$ and $D = 10\,nm$, while the initial state is chosen as $w(0) = 2.2\,nm$. Biolek's window function [4] is defined as $f(w,i) = 1 - \left[\frac{w}{D} - stp(-i)\right]^{2p}$, where $stp(i)$ is 1 if $i \geq 0$ and 0 otherwise. The generalized BCM [6] window function $f(w,v)$ assumes a value of $b \in \mathbb{R}_+$ if either condition C_1 or condition C_2, respectively defined as

$$C_1 = \{ (w \in (0,D) \text{ and } ((v > v_{t0}) \text{ or } (v < -v_{t1})))\}, \quad (4)$$
$$C_2 = \{ (w = 0 \text{ and } v > v_{th0}) \quad \text{or} \quad (w = D \text{ and } v < -v_{th1})\} \quad (5)$$

holds, of 0 if either condition C_3 or condition C_4, respectively defined as

$$C_3 = \{ w = 0 \text{ and } v \leq v_{th0}\}, \quad (6)$$
$$C_4 = \{ w = D \text{ and } v \geq -v_{th1}\} \quad (7)$$

holds, and of $a \in \mathbb{R}_{0,+}$ $(0 \leq a < b)$ if condition C_5, i.e.

$$C_5 = \{ (w = \bar{w} \in (0,D) \text{ and } ((v \leq v_{t0}) \text{ and } (v \geq -v_{t1}))) \quad (8)$$

holds. Parameters $v_{th0} \in \mathbb{R}_{0,+}$ and $v_{th1} \in \mathbb{R}_{0,+}$ represent the *boundary threshold voltages*, while $v_{t0} \in \mathbb{R}_{0,+}$ and $v_{t1} \in \mathbb{R}_{0,+}$ denote the *programmability threshold voltages*, identifying three regions of the memristor voltage v-axis with distinct dynamics. In one of such regions, defined as $v \in [-v_{t1}, v_{t0}]$, the window function assumes a low a value, yielding a small rate of change of memristor state under excitation (i.e. a nano-structure responding slowly to the external perturbation). When the nano-device is operated in this region, it is said to be in read mode. This scenario occurs when there is a need to read the memristor state without affecting it (the reading is carried out by applying a voltage pulse with adequately small amplitude lying within $[-v_{t1}, v_{t0}]$, then registering the resulting current response and finally applying Ohm's Law to derive the memristance value). In each of the other two regions, respectively defined as $v < -v_{t1}$ and $v > v_{t0}$, the window function assumes a large b value, yielding a high rate of change of memristor state under excitation (i.e. a nano-structure responding quickly to the external perturbation). A nano-device operated in this region is said to be in programmable mode. This situation takes place when the memristor state needs to be modified. This may be accomplished by application of a voltage pulse with amplitude $v < -v_{t1}$ or $v > v_{t0}$ depending on the desired outcome of the programming phase, i.e. an increase or a decrease in memristance respectively.
The TEAM model [7], inspired by the reference [5], describes the state equations as

$$\frac{dw}{dt} = \begin{cases} k_{off}\left(\frac{i}{i_{off}}-1\right)^{\alpha_{off}} f_{off}(w) & \text{if } i > i_{off} > 0, \\ 0 & \text{if } i_{on} < i < i_{off}, \\ k_{on}\left(\frac{i}{i_{on}}-1\right)^{\alpha_{on}} f_{on}(w) & \text{if } i < i_{on} < 0, \end{cases}$$

where state w denotes the length of the TiO_2-based tunnel barrier, $k_{off} \in \mathbb{R}_+$ and $k_{on} \in \mathbb{R}_-$ are factors with dimensions ms^{-1}, $\alpha_{off} \in \mathbb{R}_+$ and $\alpha_{on} \in \mathbb{R}_+$ are constants, while thresholds $i_{off} \in \mathbb{R}_+$ and $i_{on} \in \mathbb{R}_-$ are in current form. The functions $f_{off}(w)$ and $f_{on}(w)$ are respectively defined as $f_{off}(w) = \exp\left(-\exp\left(\frac{w-a_{off}}{w_c}\right)\right)$ and $f_{on}(w) = \exp\left(-\exp\left(\frac{a_{on}-w}{w_c}\right)\right)$, where $a_{off} \in \mathbb{R}_+$ and $a_{on} \in \mathbb{R}_+$ are coefficients with dimensions m. The range of variation of state w is limited to closed interval $[w_{on}, w_{off}]$, where the bounds are $w_{on} = a_{off}$ and $w_{off} = a_{on}$. The i-v relation is expressed as $v = R_{on}\exp\left(\lambda\,(w-w_{on})(w_{off}-w_{on})^{-1}\right) i$, where $\lambda = R_{off}R_{on}^{-1}$ and R_{on} and R_{off} are given in Ω. In 9 the initial state $w(0)$ is taken as $1.75\,nm$, while the values of thresholds i_{off} and i_{on} are respectively set to $1\,\mu A$ and $-1\,\mu A$. In the input-output equation $R_{on} = 100\,\Omega$ and $R_{off} = 200k\Omega$.

Note that the state variable in Biolek's and the generalized BCM models is the complement with respect to the length of the memristor of the state variable in Pickett's and the TEAM models. In the next section the symbol used for the normalized state is x.

3 Fitting procedure

The fitting procedure aims at optimizing some parameters of a model so as to tune its dynamics to the behavior of the reference model. It consists of a multiple run of a combination of Simulated Annealing and Gradient Descent algorithms. The optimization process is based upon minimization of a cost function $e(\cdot,\cdot)$, defined as a combination of the root mean squared error of two memristor variables θ and ζ, i.e. as

$$e_{\theta,\zeta} = \sqrt{\frac{\Sigma(\theta_m-\theta_r)^2}{\bar{\theta}_r^2}} + \sqrt{\frac{\Sigma(\zeta_m-\zeta_r)^2}{\bar{\zeta}_r^2}}. \tag{9}$$

where index r denotes the reference time series, index m the time series of the model under study, while a barred variable the time average of the time series of the model itself. In accordance with Chua's theory, appropriate choices for pair of memristor variables θ and ζ are either state and flux-linkage or charge and flux-linkage. The first choice is adopted in the case of Biolek's and the TEAM models, while the latter choice is adopted in the case of the generalized BCM model.

In the case of Biolek's model, the parameter under optimization is coefficient p in the window function. Setting its initial value to 1, the fitting procedure yields an optimized value of 6. Fig. 3 shows dynamics of Biolek's model before and after optimization together with the behavior of the reference model.

In the window function of the generalized BCM model a large number of parameters may be tuned so as to closely track the dynamics of the reference model. In particular it is possible to adjust boundary threshold voltages v_{th0} and v_{th1} and programming threshold voltages v_{t0} and v_{t1}, together with parameters a and b specifying the variation in the speed of the width w of the conductive layer from read-only mode, when $v \in [-v_{t1}, v_{t0}]$ to programmable mode, when $v < -v_{t1}$ or $v > v_{t0}$.

Table 2 reports initial and optimized values for these parameters. Fig. 4 shows the dynamics of the pre- and post-fitting model together with the behavior of the Pickett's model.

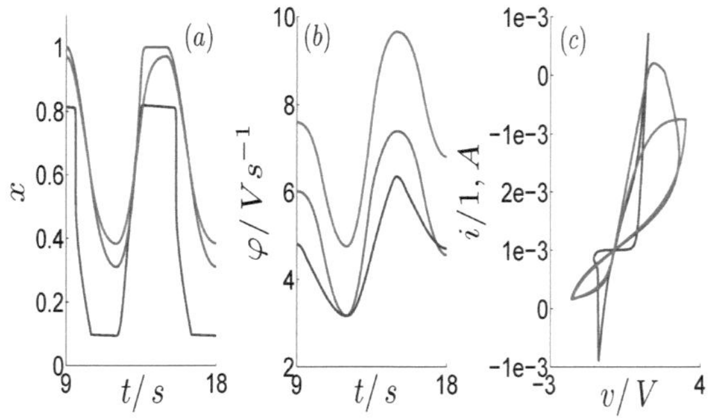

Figure 3 - State (a) and flux-linkage (b) versus time and current-voltage characteristic (c) according to Biolek's model pre- (red) and post- (green) fitting to the reference model (blue).

Table 2 - Steps (1): initial parameter values of the generalized BCM model. Step (2): optimized parameter values of the generalized BCM model. The dimensions of the threshold voltages are V.

step	v_{th0}	v_{th1}	v_{t0}	v_{t1}	a	b
(1)	0.2	0.35	0.15	0.15	$1 \cdot 10^{-5}$	1
(2)	4.7401	2.4629	0.9150	1.3048	0.1494	1.6182

Similarly to the generalized BCM model, the TEAM model also offers a number of tunable parameters for the fitting procedure, particularly α_{off}, k_{off}, α_{on} and k_{on} in the state equation and a_{off}, a_{on} and w_c in functions $f_{off}(w)$ and $f_{on}(w)$. The initial and optimized values of these parameters are tabulated in Table 3. Fig. 5 shows the dynamics of the model before and after fitting it to the reference model.

Table 3 - Step (1): pre-fitting parameter values of the TEAM model. Step (2): post-fitting parameter values of the TEAM model. Parameters k_{off} and k_{on} are expressed in ms^{-1}, while the dimensional units of a_{on}, a_{off} and w_c are m.

parameter	step (1)	step (2)
α_{off}	3	1.7747
α_{on}	3	3.3849
k_{off}	$8 \cdot 10^{-13}$	$7.2794 \cdot 10^{-13}$
k_{on}	$-8 \cdot 10^{-13}$	$-8.1661 \cdot 10^{-13}$
a_{off}	$1.2 \cdot 10^{-9}$	$8.0720 \cdot 10^{-10}$
a_{on}	$2.3 \cdot 10^{-9}$	$2.2579 \cdot 10^{-9}$
w_c	$1.07 \cdot 10^{-9}$	$3.5618 \cdot 10^{-10}$

3.1 Quantitative estimate of the effect of the optimization

This section gives a quantitative estimate of the effect of parameter optimization on the models. The estimate is based upon the calculation of an error function, consisting of a combination of

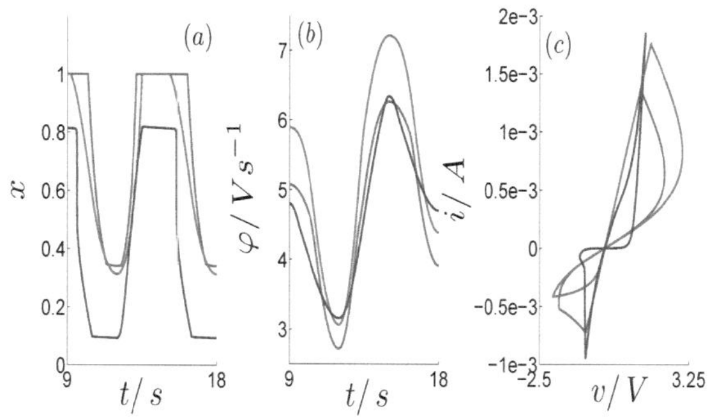

Figure 4 - Pre- (red) and post- (green) optimization dynamics of the generalized BCM model and behavior of the reference model (blue): time evolution of state (a) and flux-linkage (b), and *i*-*v* characteristic (c).

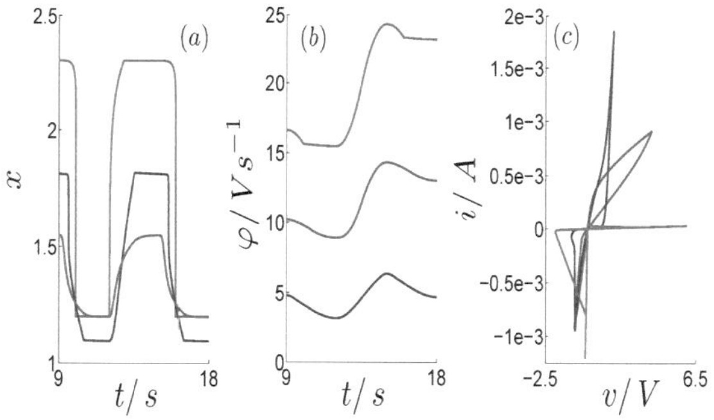

Figure 5 - Time behavior of state (a) and flux-linkage (b), and *i*-*v* characteristic (c) as predicted by the TEAM model previous to (red) and following (green) the fitting to the Pickett's model (blue).

the root mean squared error of voltage and current, previous to and following the fitting procedure. We chose $\theta = i$ and $\zeta = v$ in 9, since current and voltage are the most important physical quantities in circuit design. All the models fitted to the reference model for a certain circuit topology and excitation type in section 3 show some improvement in tracking the dynamics of the Pickett's model after fitting. However, the variation in dynamical behavior from the pre- to the post-fitting scenario is more consistent in the TEAM model than in both Biolek's and the generalized BCM models, as evident from Figs. 3, 4 and 5. This is confirmed in Table 4, reporting for each model the pre- and post-fitting the root mean squared error with respect to the time series of voltage and current.

Table 4 shows that the TEAM model is the one which most benefits from the fitting procedure, since the final value of $e_{v,i}$ is more than halved with respect to its initial value. Nonetheless, the lowest post-fitting root mean squared error pertains to the generalized BCM.

Table 4 - Values of cost function 9 for $\theta = i$ and $\zeta = v$ previous to and following optimization for each of the models under study.

model	pre-optimization $e_{v,i}$	post-optimization $e_{v,i}$
Biolek's	0.4521	0.4256
BCM	0.4201	0.3358
TEAM	0.8342	0.3808

4 Model-dependency of the dynamics of memristor circuits

The dependency of the behavior of a couple of basic memristor circuits upon the memristor model is discussed in this section. Since the reference model parameter values were not reported for the circuit topologies under study in this section, a preliminary optimization step of the parameters of the models under comparison (Biolek's, the generalized BCM and the TEAM) is not possible in these case studies. Due to lack of space the values of the parameters adopted for each memristor model in each of the case studies are omitted in this manuscript. The interested reader may find details in [10].

4.1 Second-order oscillator

Fig. 6 shows the first circuit under test, a second-order oscillator where $R_1 = -50\,\Omega$, $L = 10\,mH$, $C = 1\,\mu F$ and $R_2 = 250\,\Omega$. Perturbing from equilibrium the autonomous system by specifying non-zero initial conditions, it was found to experience oscillatory behavior under each memristor model, as demonstrated in Fig. 7. Table 5 gives the oscillation frequency for each memristor model.

Table 5 - Frequency of the first harmonic of the oscillation for each memristor model.

model	oscillation frequency $/kHz$
Pickett	1.3605
Biolek	1.4085
BCM	1.4286
TEAM	1.3793

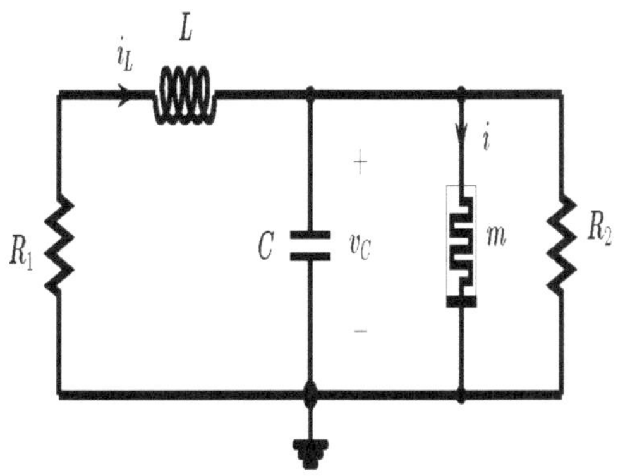

Figure 6 - Second-order memristor oscillator.

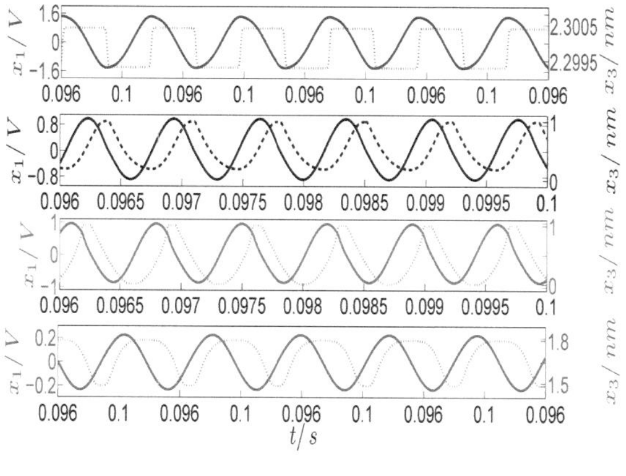

Figure 7 - Time evolution of states $x_1(t) = v_C(t)$ (solid) and $x_3(t) = -R_1 i_L(t)$ (dotted): reference model (blue), Biolek's model (black), generalized BCM model (red) and TEAM model (green).

The TEAM model is the most accurate in reproducing the higher-order harmonic components in the capacitor voltage observed in the case of the reference model. This is clear from Fig. 8, showing the Fast Fourier Transform (FFT) of $x_1(t) = v_C(t)$ for each of the models.

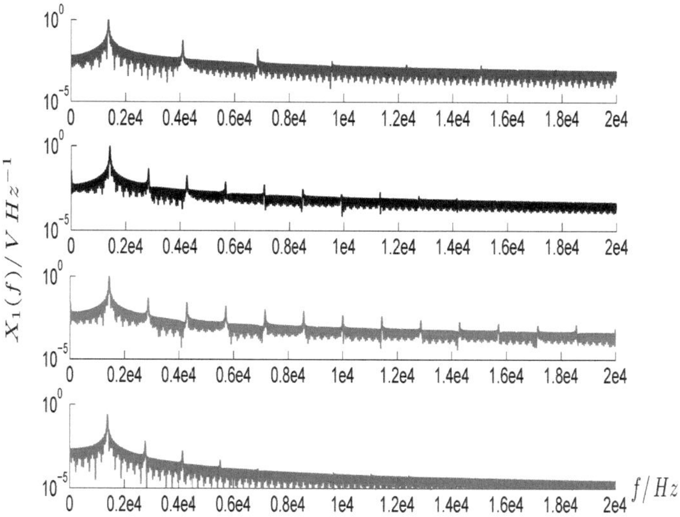

Figure 8 - Spectrum of capacitor voltage ($x_1(t) = v_C(t)$) for the reference model (blue), the Biolek's model (black), the generalized BCM model (red) and the TEAM model (green). A log scale is adopted for the y-axis.

A further test analyzed the response of the circuit of Fig. 6 to a current pulse source inserted in parallel to capacitor C and injecting current into its upper node. Amplitude i_0, time delay t_d, rise time t_r, fall time t_f and width Δt of the current pulse were respectively set to $1\,\mu A$, $1\,ms$, $1\,ms$, $1\,ms$ and $10\,ms$. As shown in Fig. 9, Biolek's and the generalized BCM models most accurately capture the dynamic behavior of the response observed in the case of the reference model. However, the TEAM model better detects the time instant of the on-set of the response pertaining to Pickett's model.

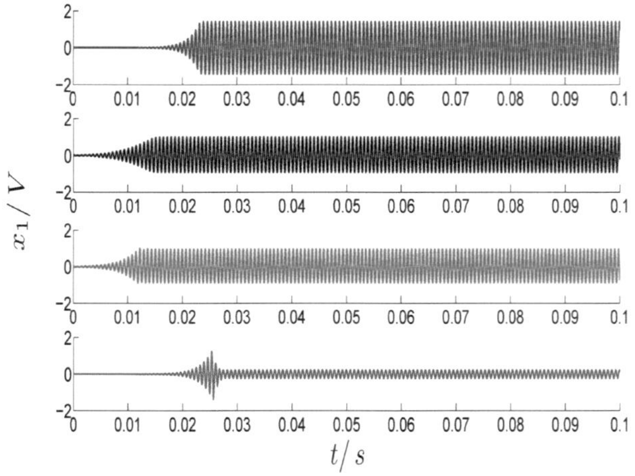

Figure 9 - Response to a current pulse: time evolution of $x_1(t) = v_C(t)$ for the reference model (blue), the Biolek's model (black), the generalized BCM model (red) and the TEAM model (green).

4.2 Third-order oscillator

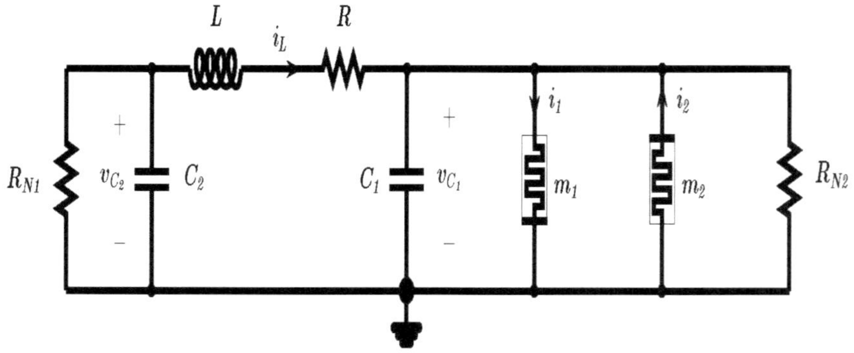

Figure 10 - Memristor version of Chua's canonical oscillator where Chua's diode is replaced by the anti-parallel combination of two memristors.

In another case study we investigated the dependency upon the memristor model of the chaotic dynamics observed in a memristor version of Chua's canonical oscillator after suitable perturbation from equilibrium (see Fig. 10, where $R = 300\Omega$, $R_{N2} = -952.38k\Omega$, $C_2 = 60nF$, $L = 100mH$, $R_{N1} = -2k\Omega$ and C_1 was taken as bifurcation parameter). The result from this analysis revealed that Biolek's and the generalized BCM models are in agreement with each other and undergo chaotic oscillations for nearly the same value of the bifurcation parameter (see Figs. 11 and 12, where $C_1 = 56nF$) as in the case of Pickett's model (see Fig. 13, where

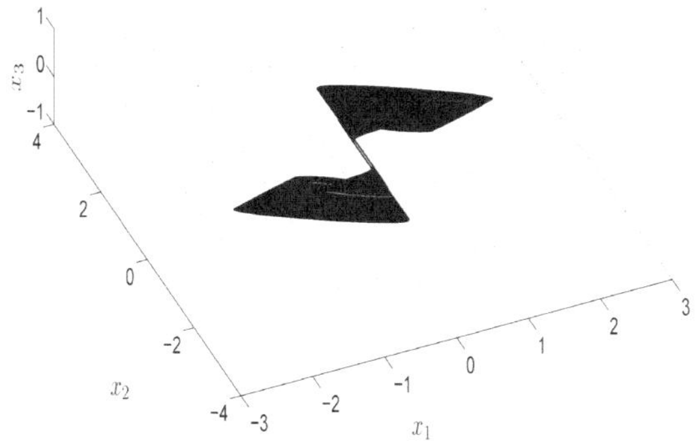

Figure 11 - Chaotic attractor on state space $x_1 - x_2 - x_3$ ($x_1 = v_{C1}$, $x_2 = v_{C2}$, $x_3 = -Ri_L$) according to Biolek's model. Here $C_1 = 56nF$.

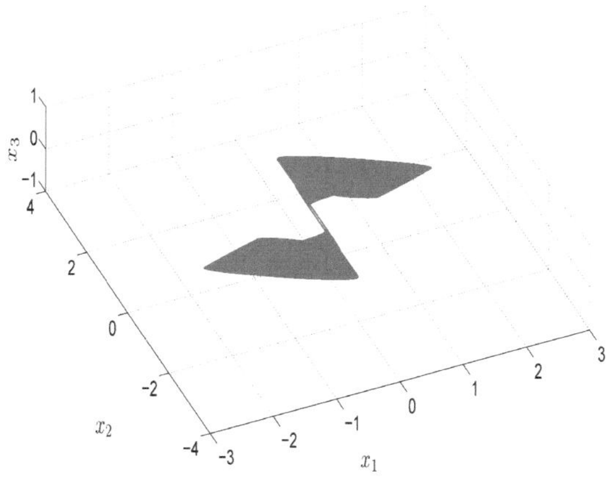

Figure 12 - Chaotic attractor on the space spanned by x_1, x_2 and x_3 in the case of the generalized BCM model. Capacitance C_1 is equal to $56nF$.

, where $C_1 = 55nF$). On the other hand the bifurcation parameter for which the TEAM model manifests chaotic behavior is smaller than in the case of the reference model (see Fig. 14, where $C_1 = 52nF$). Despite each model gives origin to chaotic dynamics, it is clear that in this case none of them is able to track the behavior observed with the reference model.

The strong dependence of the dynamical behaviors of the memristor circuits of Figs. 6 and 10 upon the memristor model under use should serve as a warning to the circuit designer against a blind trust in the simulation results pertaining to any of the memristor models introduced in the literature. This points out the urgent necessity to develop an ultimate memristor model to foster considerable progress in the design of novel memristor circuits and systems.

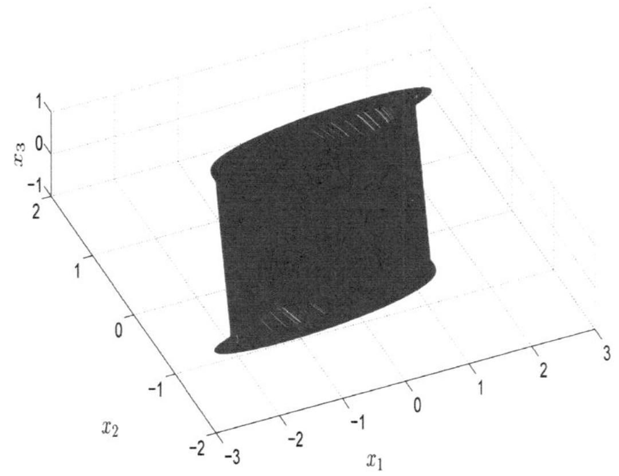

Figure 13 - Chaotic attractor on state space x_1-x_2-x_3 for the Pickett's model. The value of capacitor C_1 is $55\,nF$.

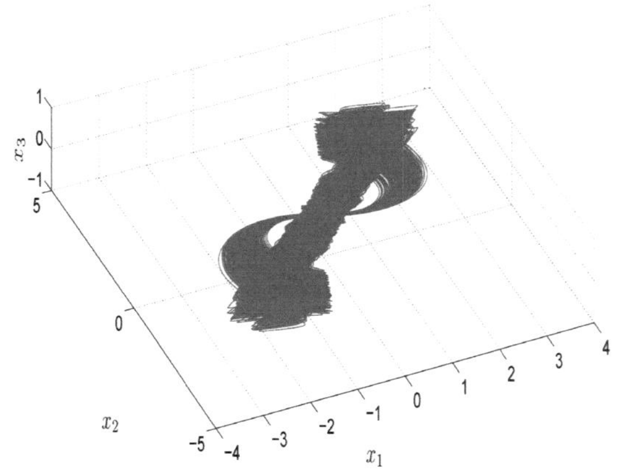

Figure 14 - Chaotic attractor on space x_1-x_2-x_3 as predicted by the TEAM model. Here $C_1 = 52\,nF$.

5 A novel polynomial model

This section introduces a novel current-controlled memristor model based upon a polynomial series representation of the state evolution function $g(w,i)$, hence the name Polynomial Memristor (PM) model coined to identify it. The time evolution of state w is governed by $\dot{w} = g(i,w) = \sum_{n=0}^{N} a_n\, i^n + \sum_{m=0}^{M} b_m\, w^m + \sum_{p=1}^{P} (c_p\, i + d_p)^p (e_p\, w + f_p)^p$, for $|i| > i_{min}$ and 0 for $-i_{min} \leq i \leq i_{min}$. The input-output algebraic equation is $v = R(w,i)i$, where the memristance $R(w,i)$ may be expanded into another series of polynomials involving input and state. Optimizing the series coefficients in $g(w,i)$ and $R(w,i)$, it is possible to reproduce a large number of i-v characteristics observed in experiments on physical memristors. As Proof-of-Concept, we fitted $g(w,i)$ to Pickett's state evolution function in 1-2.

The first investigations focused on the case $i < -i_{min}$ (i_{min} was set to $0.05\,mA$). Fig. 15 shows the switching characteristics of the Pickett's model, of the fitted TEAM and PM models. The variation interval for w and the choices for i were chosen so as to match experimental results from Hewlett Packard Labs. The values of the parameters for the reference model and for the fitted TEAM and PM models are reported in [10].

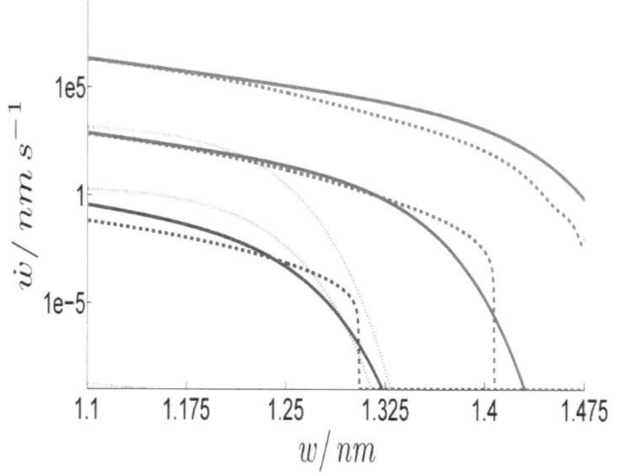

Figure 15 - A comparison among the $\dot{w} - w$ characteristics of Pickett's model (solid), of the TEAM model (dotted) and of the PM model (dashed) for $|i| = 0.06\,mA$ (blue), $|i| = 1\,mA$ (green) and $|i| = 2\,mA$ (red). In the fitted PM model $N = 11$, $M = 13$ and $P = 4$.

Fig. 15 reveals the added value a polynomial series expansion of the state evolution function may bring to the current search for a simplified yet accurate representation of the Pickett's model. In both pictures the PM results clearly outperform the TEAM model predictions.

6 Conclusions

Fitting some of the most remarkable memristor models, namely Biolek's model [4], the generalized BCM model [6] and the TEAM model [7], to Pickett's complex model [5], the dynamics of the latter may be reproduced using simpler mathematical description. However the fitting algorithm may be carried out only for those circuit topologies where Pickett's model parameters were determined by means of experimental measurements. Without a preliminary fit, simulations on basic memristor circuits reveal the high sensitivity of the dynamics to the memristor model [10]. The results of this study pose a serious problem to circuit designers aiming at the investigation of the full potential of the memristor in modern electronics and points out the necessity to develop an ultimate memristor model. A novel memristor model, inspired from Prof. Chua's idea of "unfolding the memristor" by expanding the state evolution function into series of polynomials involving state and input [11], could pave the way towards a finalized mathematical description for the memristor [12].

References

[1] L. O. Chua, "Memristor: the missing circuit element," *IEEE Trans. on Circuit Theory*, vol. 18, no. 5, pp. 507-519, 1971

[2] L. O. Chua, and S. M. Kang, "Memristive devices and systems," *Proc. IEEE*, vol. 64, no. 2, pp. 209-223, 1976

[3] D. B. Strukov, G. S. Snider, D. R. Stewart, and R. S. Williams, "The missing memristor found," *Nature*, vol. 453, pp. 80-83, 2008

[4] Z. Biolek, D. Biolek, and B. Biolková, "Spice model of memristor with nonlinear dopant drift," *Radio Eng.*, vol. 18, no. 2, pp. 210-214, 2009.

[5] M. D. Pickett, D. B. Strukov, J. L. Borghetti, J. J. Yang, G. S. Snider, D. R. Stewart and R. S. Williams, "Switching Dynamics in Titanium Dioxide Memristive Devices," *J. Appl. Phys.*, vol. 106, pp. 074508, 2009.

[6] A. Ascoli, R. Tetzlaff, F. Corinto: "Generalized Memristor Boundary Condition Model and its PSpice circuit," *IEEE Transactions on Circuits and Systems – I*, under revision, 2013

[7] S. Kvatinsky, E. G. Friedman, A. Kolodny, and U. C. Weiser, "TEAM - ThrEshold Adaptive Memristor Model," *IEEE Transactions on Circuits and Systems – I*, vol. 60, no. 1, pp. 211-221, 2013

[8] J. Simmons, "Electric tunnel effect between dissimilar electrodes separated by a thin insulating film," *Journal of Applied Physics*, vol. 34, no. 9, pp. 2581-2590, 1963

[9] H. Abdalla, Pickett, M. D.: "SPICE modeling of Memristors," *IEEE International Symposium on Circuits and Systems*, pp. 1832-1835, May 2011

[10] A. Ascoli, F. Corinto, V. Senger and R. Tetzlaff: "Memristor model comparison," *IEEE Circuits and Systems Magazine*, under press, 2013

[11] L. O. Chua, "Resistance switching memories are memristors," *Applied Physics A*, vol. 102, no. 4, pp. 765-783, 2011

[12] A. Ascoli, F. Corinto, V. Senger and R. Tetzlaff: "A Novel Polynomial Memristor Model," *IEEE Workshop on Nonlinear Dynamics of Electronic Systems*, under press, 2013

Anwendung von Reziprozitätsbeziehungen in der Messtechnik

Günther Pfeifer[*], *Uwe Marschner*[*] *und Eric Starke*[+]

[*]*Institut für Halbleiter- und Mikrosystemtechnik, TU Dresden*
[+]*Institut für Leichtbau und Kunststofftechnik, TU Dresden*
mikrosystemtechnik@tu-dresden.de

Abstract: In der elektromechanischen Messtechnik treten oft passive Wandler und passive elektrische Netzwerke gemeinsam in Wechselwirkung. Bei einigen Anwendungen sind Kontinua, in denen sich Felder ausbilden und Wellen ausbreiten, Bestandteil des Systems. Wenn die Netzwerke, Kontinua und die elektromechanischen Wandler in ihrer jeweiligen Arbeitsumgebung (z. B. bei Aussteuerung um einen Arbeitspunkt) ausreichend amplitudenlineares Verhalten aufweisen und alle Elemente des Systems über die Messzeit konstante Parameter besitzen, kann die geschickte Anwendung der diesen Systemen innewohnenden Reziprozität zu erstaunlich nützlichen Vorteilen führen. Im Beitrag wird das an aktuellen Beispielen aus der Messtechnik gezeigt. Obwohl der Sachstand an sich gut bekannt ist, wird sein Potential in der Messtechnik häufig übersehen oder außer Acht gelassen.

1 Einleitung

Die Beschreibung zeitinvarianter Systeme mit vernachlässigbarer Nichtlinearität durch lineare Netzwerke ist nicht auf eine einzelne physikalische Domäne beschränkt. Gerade elektromechanische und elektroakustische Systeme verschiedenster aktorischer und sensorischer Anwendungen können mit linearen Netzwerken in Form einer Schaltungsdarstellung grafisch beschrieben werden. Das Herzstück der Sensoren und Aktoren sind umkehrbare Wandler, die die physikalischen Größen transformieren oder gyrieren [1-3]. Eine solche übersichtliche Systemdarstellung fördert nicht nur das Verständnis für die physikalische Wirkungsweise des Systems beim Entwurf und bei der Analyse. So gestattet die Anwendung der linearen Netzwerktheorie beispielsweise signifikante Schaltungsvereinfachungen zum Herausarbeiten des Systemkerns. Die Schaltungsdarstellung ist außerdem die Voraussetzung für eine effiziente Simulation des dynamischen Systemverhaltens mit leistungsfähigen Schaltungssimulatoren.

Lineare zeitinvariante Netzwerke besitzen darüber hinaus Eigenschaften, die die Grundlage für präzise Messverfahren bilden. Eine solche Eigenschaft ist die Reziprozität oder Umkehrbarkeit. So lassen sich akustische Felder elegant mit Hilfe von Reziprozitätsbeziehungen analytisch behandeln. In diesem Beitrag wird zunächst die Reziprozität in linearen Netzwerken am Beispiel elektromechanischer Wandler allgemein begründet. Daran schließen sich zwei Beispiele für aktuelle elektroakustische Anwendungen der Reziprozität an. Eine Anwendung ist die Primärkalibrierung von Labor-Normalmikrofonen. Mit keinem anderen Verfahren können geringere Messunsicherheiten erzielt werden. Die andere vorgestellte Anwendung der Reziprozitätsbeziehungen behandelt die Verbesserung messtechnischer Eigenschaften sowie die Linearitätskontrolle eines Netzwerkes.

2 Reziprozität in linearen Netzwerken

Auf die Reziprozitätseigenschaft eines beliebigen passiven linearen elektrischen Systems stößt man bei der Auswertung von zwei Beispielexperimenten. Bezogen auf das System E in Bild 1 mit sechs Toren werden zunächst zwei Tore ausgewählt. In Bild 1 sind das die Tore 3 und 6. Die verbleibenden Tore können offen oder kurzgeschlossen sein. Diese Randbedingungen müssen dann bei beiden Experimenten beibehalten werden. Im ersten Experiment

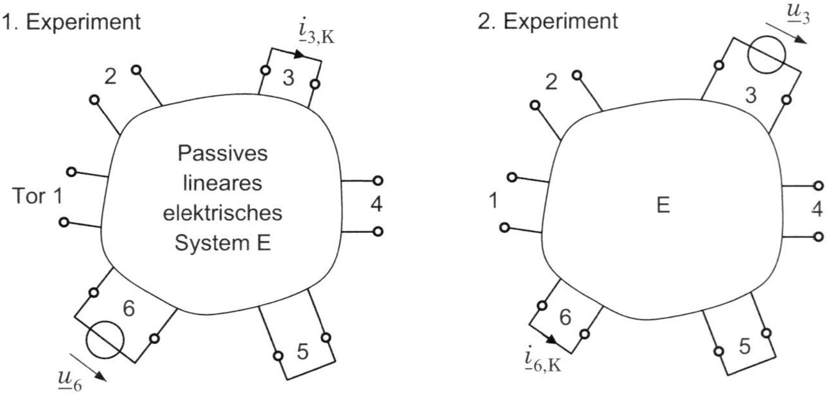

Bild 1: Reziproke Experimente an einem elektrischen System

wird an Tor 6 eine Spannung $\underline{u}_6$ angelegt und an Tor 3 der Kurzschlussstrom $\underline{i}_{3,\mathrm{K}}$ gemessen. Im zweiten Experiment werden Anregungstor und Messtor vertauscht, d.h. $\underline{i}_{6,\mathrm{K}}$ gemessen nachdem $\underline{u}_3$ angelegt wurde. Es stellt sich heraus, dass für die Verknüpfung der zwei Koordinatenpaare

$$\frac{\underline{i}_{3,\mathrm{K}}}{\underline{u}_6} = \frac{\underline{i}_{6,\mathrm{K}}}{\underline{u}_3}$$

gilt. Diese Gesetzmäßigkeit kennzeichnet die Umkehrbarkeit oder Reziprozität eines passiven linearen Netzwerkes.

Die Reziprozität folgt aus der Gültigkeit des Superpositionsgesetzes. Sie ist nicht nur auf elektrische Systeme beschränkt sondern gilt auch für Systeme, die verschiedene physikalische Strukturen enthalten. Analog zu den am elektrischen System E durchgeführten Experimenten können Reziprozitätsbeziehungen an einem passiven elektromechanischen System experimentell nachgewiesen werden. Zur Verdeutlichung sei das passive lineare elektromechanische System S in Bild 2 experimentell untersucht. Das System enthält zwei elektrische Tore und zwei mechanische Tore, von denen je eines für die Untersuchung bestimmt wird. Nacheinander werden einmal die Kurzschlusskraft $\underline{F}_{i,\mathrm{K}}$ bei anregender Spannung $\underline{u}_n$ gemessen und dann die Stromstärke $\underline{i}'_{n,\mathrm{K}}$ bei Anregung mit der Geschwindigkeit $\underline{v}'_i$.

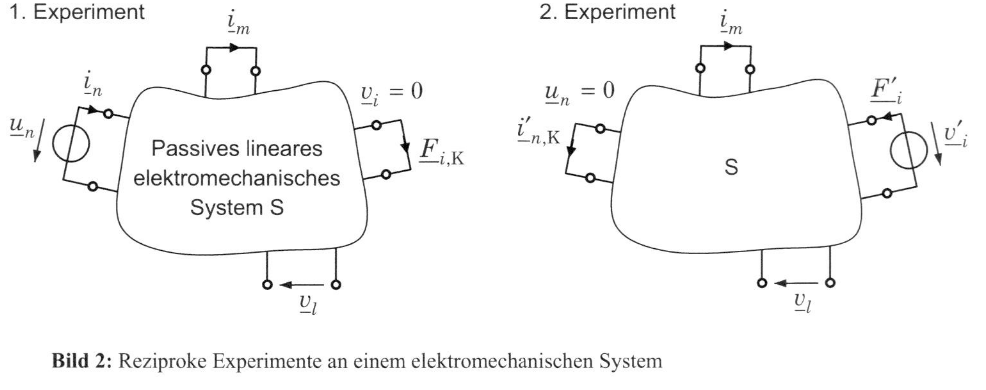

Bild 2: Reziproke Experimente an einem elektromechanischen System

Im Ergebnis der zwei Experimente zeigt sich die Gleichheit der Quotienten

$$\left|\frac{\underline{F}_{i,\mathrm{K}}}{\underline{u}_n}\right| = \left|\frac{\underline{i}'_{n,\mathrm{K}}}{\underline{v}'_i}\right| .$$

Für elektromechanische Wandler können weitere Reziprozitätsbeziehungen als Teilmenge aller Übertragungsfunktionen abgeleitet werden:

$$\frac{\underline{v}_\mathrm{L}}{\underline{i}} = \pm\frac{\underline{u}'_\mathrm{L}}{\underline{F}'} \qquad \frac{\underline{v}_\mathrm{L}}{\underline{u}} = \pm\frac{\underline{i}'_\mathrm{K}}{\underline{F}'} \qquad \frac{\underline{F}'_\mathrm{K}}{\underline{i}'} = \pm\frac{\underline{u}_\mathrm{L}}{\underline{v}} .$$

+ magnetische Wandler, − elektrische Wandler

Die verknüpften Leistungskoordinatenpaare sind die in Bild 3 gekennzeichneten Fluss- und Differenzgrößen. Die Indizes K und L bedeuten Kurzschluss und Leerlauf. Im Wandler sind nur umkehrbare Vorgänge im Sinne der Thermodynamik gestattet. Bei derartigen Wandlern gelingt die Abtrennung der Verluste in das umgebende Netzwerk aus dem Wandler heraus. Bei elektrischen und magnetischen Wandlern ist diese Bedingung erfüllt.

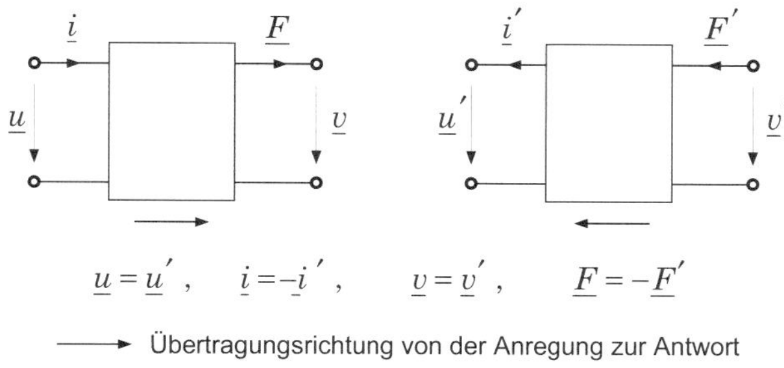

Bild 3: Reziprozitätsbeziehungen zwischen Koordinatenpaaren elektromechanischer Wandler

In der Messtechnik ist die Kalibrierung von Beschleunigungssensoren eine klassische Anwendung der Reziprozitätsbeziehungen. Eine Kalibrierquelle für mechanische Größen ist dabei nicht erforderlich, sondern nur ein beliebiger zusätzlicher elektromagnetischer Wandler. Das System wird so dimensioniert, dass seine Nachgiebigkeit vernachlässigt werden kann.

Die Kalibrierung erfordert zwei Experimente, wie in Bild 4 schematisch gezeigt. Zuerst wird ein elektrischer Strom $\underline{i}$ in den Zusatzwandler eingespeist und die Leerlaufspannung $\underline{u}_{2,1}$ gemessen. Anschließend regt eine äußere Kraft $\underline{F}$ das System an, dass mit den Leerlaufspannungen $\underline{u}_{1\mathrm{L}}$ und $\underline{u}_{2,2}$ reagiert, die gemessen werden.

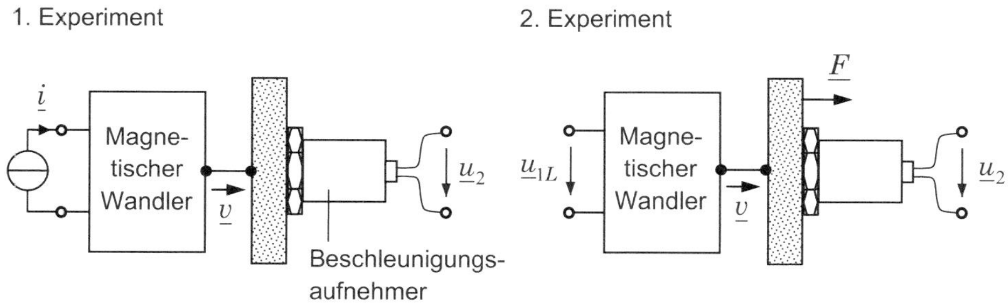

Bild 4: Experimente zur Reziprozitätskalibrierung eines Beschleunigungsaufnehmers

Der Übertragungsfaktor des Beschleunigungsaufnehmers $\underline{B}_\mathrm{a}$ lässt sich durch die Anwendung der Reziprozitätsbeziehungen auf Verhältnisse der gemessenen Spannungen, die Masse m und Kreisfrequenz ω zurückführen:

$$\left|\underline{B}_\mathrm{a}\right| = \sqrt{\frac{m}{\omega}\cdot\left(\frac{\underline{u}_{2,1}}{\underline{i}}\right)_{1.\mathrm{Exp.}}\cdot\left(\frac{\underline{u}_{2,2}}{\underline{u}_{1\mathrm{L}}}\right)_{2.\mathrm{Exp.}}}\;.$$

Da sich diese Größen einfach, schnell und hochgenau messen lassen, ergibt sich ein effizientes Kalibrierverfahren [2,3].

Die Anwendung von Reziprozitätsbeziehungen erweist sich darüber hinaus als vorteilhaft, wenn Kontinua im System berücksichtigt werden müssen. Bereits 1926 hat Schottky die Reziprozitätssätze der klassischen Schwingungslehre für die Bestimmung von Empfangs- und Sendeeigenschaften elektroakustischer Wandler angewendet [4]. Damit konnte die Wirkung einer auf ein Oberflächenelement auftreffenden Quasikugelwelle aus ihrer Emissionswirkung berechnet werden. Schottky illustriert die Methodik am Beispiel eines elektrodynamischen Trichterlautsprechers, der tiefe Frequenzen beim Empfang bevorzugt. Das Gesetz führte auf die mathematische Theorie des Empfangstrichters. Nachfolgend wird die Aktualität der Methodik anhand von zwei Beispielen aus der Elektroakustik demonstriert.

3 Anwendung der Reziprozitätsbeziehung zur Kalibrierung von Messmikrofonen

Eine derzeit unverzichtbare Anwendung der Reziprozität ist die Primärkalibrierung von Labor-Normalmikrofonen. Diese wird in den metrologischen Staatsinstituten (z. B. der Physikalisch Technischen Bundesanstalt) durchgeführt, um die Einheit des Schalldrucks Pascal (Pa) darzustellen. Von diesen primärkalibrierten Normalmikrofonen erfolgt wiederum die Weitergabe der Einheit an alle zu kalibrierenden Mikrofone des Landes mittels Vergleichsverfahren.

Die in ihren Grundsätzen bereits 1940 von MacLean [5] beschriebene Mikrofonkalibrierung nach dem Reziprozitätsverfahren ist heute das Verfahren mit dem die geringsten Messunsicherheiten erzielt werden können. Dafür gibt es zwei maßgebliche Gründe.

1. Die Schalldruckmessung wird auf die Messung von mechanischen und elektrischen Größen zurückgeführt, welche mit sehr hoher Genauigkeit möglich sind.
2. Die Übertragungsfunktion von Messmikrofonen ist abhängig von den akustischen Randbedingen unter denen das Mikrofon genutzt wird.

Nur mit Hilfe des Reziprozitätsverfahrens ist momentan die direkte Kalibrierung für die messtechnisch relevanten Fälle Druckkammer (DIN EN 61094-2 [7]), Freifeld (DIN EN 61094-3 [8]) und diffuses Schallfeld (Vorländer [10]) möglich.

Grundlage für die Reziprozitätskalibrierung ist die Umkehrbarkeit elektrostatischer Messmikrofone, solange diese in ihrem ausreichend linearen Bereich betrieben werden. Bild 5 zeigt die Definition der elektrischen und akustischen Größen für das elektroakustische Zweitor „Mikrofon“. Am elektrischen Tor sind dies die Spannung $\underline{u}$ und der Strom $\underline{i}$ sowie am akustischen Tor der über die Membranfläche gemittelte Schalldruck $\underline{p}$ und der durch die gesamte Membran erzeugte Schallfluss (Volumenstrom) $\underline{q}$. Für den linearen Bereich lässt sich damit die elektroakustische Schaltung des Mikrofons in Bild 6 angeben. Als Impedanzmatrix des Zweitors folgt

$$\begin{pmatrix}\underline{u}\\ \underline{p}\end{pmatrix}=\begin{pmatrix}\underline{Z}_{\mathrm{eB}} & -\underline{M}\cdot\underline{Z}_{\mathrm{aL}}\\ \underline{M}\cdot\underline{Z}_{\mathrm{aL}} & -\underline{Z}_{\mathrm{aL}}\end{pmatrix}\cdot\begin{pmatrix}\underline{i}\\ \underline{q}\end{pmatrix}.$$

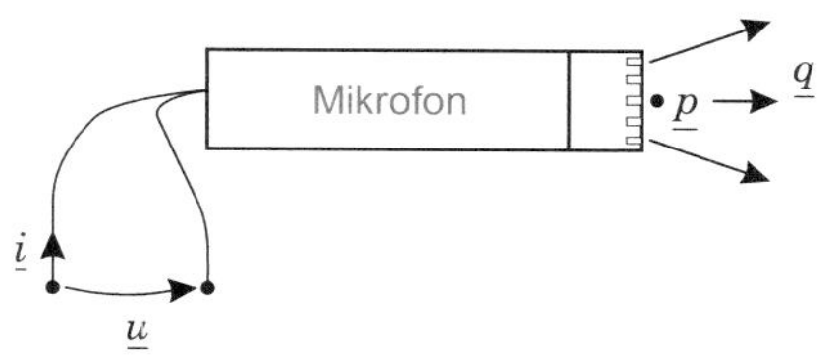

Bild 5 Elektrische und akustische Größen am elektrostatischen Messmikrofon

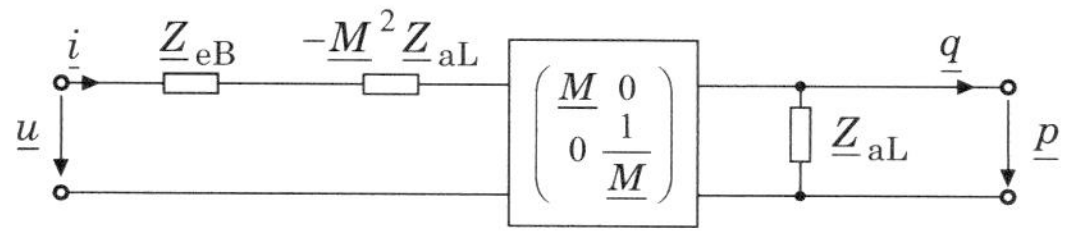

Bild 6 Elektroakustische Schaltung des Mikrofons

Hierbei ist $\underline{Z}_{eB}$ die elektrische Impedanz wenn der gesamte erzeugte oder einwirkende Schallfluss $\underline{q}$ gleich null ist. $\underline{Z}_{aL}$ ist die akustische Impedanz bei elektrischem Leerlauf, d. h. Strom $\underline{i}$ gleich null. Der Übertragungskoeffizient $\underline{M}$ gibt sowohl das Verhältnis der Leerlauf-Spannung (Strom $\underline{i} = 0$) zum anregenden Druck im Empfangsfall als auch das Verhältnis des Kurzschluss-Volumenstroms (Schalldruck $\underline{p} = 0$) zum eingespeisten Strom im Sendefall an:

$$\underline{M} = \underbrace{\left.\frac{\underline{u}}{\underline{p}}\right|_{\underline{i}=0}}_{\text{Empfang}} = \underbrace{\left.\frac{\underline{q}}{\underline{i}}\right|_{\underline{p}=0}}_{\text{Senden}} .$$

Zur Kalibrierung wird wie in Bild 7 dargestellt ein Mikrofon als Sender und ein Mikrofon als Empfänger verwendet (nachfolgend durch die Indizes 1 und 2 unterschieden). Die akustische Übertragungsstrecke zwischen dem durch das Sendemikrofon M1 erzeugten Schallfluss $\underline{q}_1$ und dem Schalldruck $\underline{p}_2$ am Empfangsmikrofon M2 wird durch die die Impedanzmatrix

$$\begin{pmatrix} \underline{p}_1 \\ \underline{p}_2 \end{pmatrix} = \begin{pmatrix} \underline{Z}_{aS1} & -\underline{Z}_{aT} \\ \underline{Z}_{aT} & -\underline{Z}_{aS2} \end{pmatrix} \cdot \begin{pmatrix} \underline{q}_1 \\ \underline{q}_2 \end{pmatrix}$$

abgebildet. Bild 8 zeigt die resultierende Schaltung der gesamten Kalibrieranordnung.

Je nachdem ob die Kalibrierung in der Druckkammer, im Freifeld oder im diffusen Schallfeld stattfindet, ergeben sich unterschiedliche akustische Impedanzmatrizen. Nachfolgend soll das weitere Vorgehen anhand der Freifeldkalibrierung verdeutlicht werden. Für die Freifeldkalibrierung wird nach DIN EN 61094-3 [7] die Freifeldübertragungsfunktion

$$\underline{M}_f = \left.\frac{\underline{u}}{\underline{p}'}\right|_{\underline{i}=0} = \left.\frac{\underline{q}}{\underline{i}}\right|_{\underline{p}'=0}$$

bezüglich des Schalldrucks $\underline{p}$' eingeführt, welcher bei einem einfallenden Schall an einer unbeweglichen Mikrofonmembran ($\underline{q} = 0$) wirken würde. Damit ist die Wirkung der akustischen Strahlungsimpedanzen $\underline{Z}_{aS1}$ und $\underline{Z}_{aS2}$ bereits in den Übertragungsfunktionen $\underline{M}_{f1}$ und $\underline{M}_{f2}$ mit berücksichtigt. Die Übertragungsstrecke zwischen den Mikrofonen vereinfacht sich zu

$$\begin{pmatrix} \underline{p}'_1 \\ \underline{p}'_2 \end{pmatrix} = \begin{pmatrix} 0 & -\underline{Z}_{aT} \\ \underline{Z}_{aT} & 0 \end{pmatrix} \cdot \begin{pmatrix} \underline{q}_1 \\ \underline{q}_2 \end{pmatrix}$$

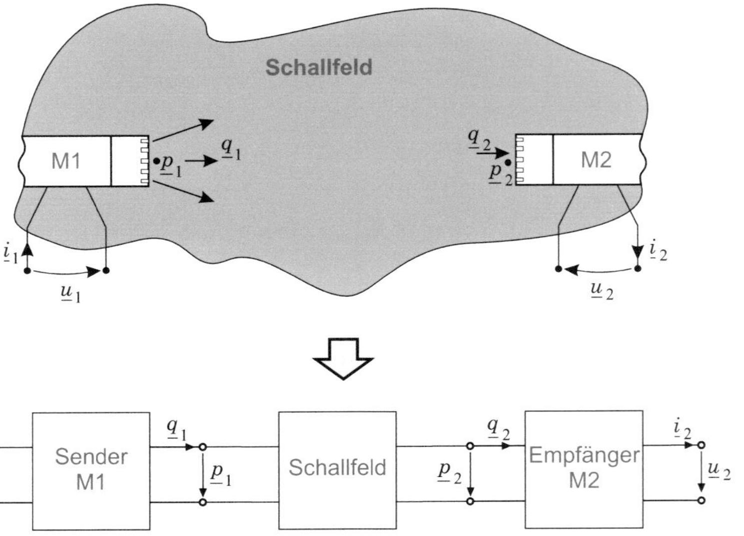

Bild 7 Mikrofonanordnung für die Reziprozitätskalibrierung (oben) und Zweitordarstellung (unten)

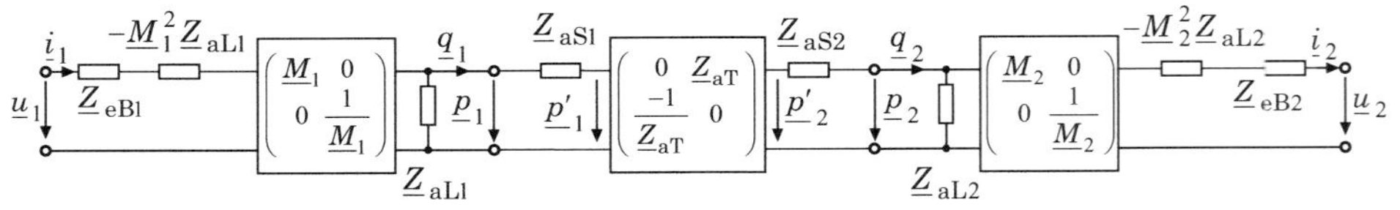

Bild 8 Schaltungsabbildung der Kalibrieranordnung

mit der akustischen Transferimpedanz

$$\underline{Z}_{\mathrm{aT}} = \frac{\mathrm{j}\omega\rho}{4\pi d_{12}} \cdot \mathrm{e}^{-\underline{\gamma} d_{12}},$$

die die Ausbreitung des Schalls im Freifeld beschreibt. Hierbei ist ρ die Dichte der Luft, c die Schallgeschwindigkeit, $\underline{\gamma}$ der komplexe Ausbreitungskoeffizient und d_{12} der Abstand der akustischen Zentren der Mikrofone. Als elektrische Transferimpedanz für die Freifeldkalibrierung folgt

$$\underline{Z}_{\mathrm{e}12} = \frac{\underline{u}_2}{\underline{i}_1} = \underline{M}_{\mathrm{f}1} \cdot \underline{Z}_{\mathrm{aT}} \cdot \underline{M}_{\mathrm{f}2}.$$

Mit der bekannten akustischen Transferimpedanz $\underline{Z}_{\mathrm{aT}}$ erhält man durch die Messung von $\underline{i}_1$ und $\underline{u}_2$ somit das Produkt zweier Übertragungskoeffizienten. Durch die Reziprozität $\underline{Z}_{\mathrm{e}12} = \underline{Z}_{\mathrm{e}21}$ liefert das Vertauschen von Sender und Empfänger keine zusätzliche Information. Da jedoch nicht die Übertragungsfunktion einer Übertragungsstrecke aus zwei Mikrofonen gesucht ist, sondern die Übertragungsfunktion des einzelnen Mikrofons, ist es erforderlich ein drittes Mikrofon hinzuzunehmen und die Mikrofone jeweils paarweise zu vermessen. Damit erhält man drei Gleichungen, aus denen die drei gesuchten Übertragungskoeffizienten

$$\underline{M}_{f1} = \sqrt{\frac{1}{\underline{Z}_{aT}} \frac{\underline{Z}_{e12} \cdot \underline{Z}_{e13}}{\underline{Z}_{e23}}} \qquad \underline{M}_{f2} = \sqrt{\frac{1}{\underline{Z}_{aT}} \frac{\underline{Z}_{e23} \cdot \underline{Z}_{e12}}{\underline{Z}_{e13}}} \qquad \underline{M}_{f3} = \sqrt{\frac{1}{\underline{Z}_{aT}} \frac{\underline{Z}_{e13} \cdot \underline{Z}_{e23}}{\underline{Z}_{e12}}}$$

der Mikrofone berechnet werden können.

Zusammenfassend waren also für die Ermittlung der Mikrofonübertragungsfunktionen nur Messungen von Spannung, Strom und wirksamen Abstand sowie Kenntnisse von Frequenz, Luftdichte und Schallgeschwindigkeit erforderlich. Mit Hilfe der Reziprozitätskalibrierung werden damit im Frequenzbereich von 31,5 Hz bis 8 kHz für die Akustik äußerst geringe Messunsicherheiten von $\leq$0,05 dB erreicht (Freifeld- und Druckkammerkalibrierung, Bork et al. [9]). Selbst im unteren Ultraschallbereich von 20 kHz bis 160 kHz werden für die Freifeldkalibrierung von ¼“ Mikrofonen Messunsicherheiten von weniger als 0,2 dB erreicht (Bouaoua [6]). Derzeit gibt es kein Alternativverfahren, welches ähnlich geringe Messunsicherheiten erzielt und die Kalibrierung in der Druckkammer, im Freifeld und im diffusen Schallfeld erlaubt.

Als künftige Ergänzung zur Reziprozitätskalibrierung, ist die Nutzung optischer Messverfahren für die Kalibrierung von Mikrofonen Gegenstand aktueller Forschung (siehe z. B. Theobald et al. [11] und Koukoulas et al. [12]). Diese Verfahren erzielen zurzeit jedoch noch nicht die geringen Messunsicherheiten der Reziprozitätskalibrierung.

4 Anwendung der Reziprozitätsbeziehungen zur Verbesserung messtechnischer Eigenschaften

Ein weiteres Anwendungsfeld für die Nutzung von Reziprozitätsbeziehungen ist die Verringerung der Messunsicherheit von Messgeräten.

Das wird nachfolgend am Beispiel eines Gasdurchfluss-Messgerätes auf Ultraschallbasis gezeigt. Bild 9 zeigt eines der Wirkprinzipe einer solchen Messanordnung.

Um die mittlere Geschwindigkeit eines in einem Rohr strömenden Gases zu erfassen, könnte z. B. an die elektrischen Anschlussklemmen eines Ultraschallwandler A ein zeitbegrenztes Spannungssignal (z. B. ein Ausschnitt von einigen Wellenzügen aus einer sinusförmigen Zeitfunktion) angelegt werden. Das vom Wandler abgestrahlte Ultraschallsignal breitet sich im Rohr mit der Richtcharakteristik des Wandlers aus und trifft nach der Laufzeit im Gas auf den Wandler B. In diesem Wandler wird eine elektrische Spannung erzeugt, die an den elektrischen Klemmen des Wandlers gemessen werden kann. Um die Zeit zwischen dem Beginn des gesendeten elektrischen Signals und dem Eintreffen am Wandler B zu bestimmen, wird durch eine geeignete mathematische Operation dem elektrischen Empfangssignal ein definierter Empfangszeitpunkt Zeitpunkt zugeordnet.

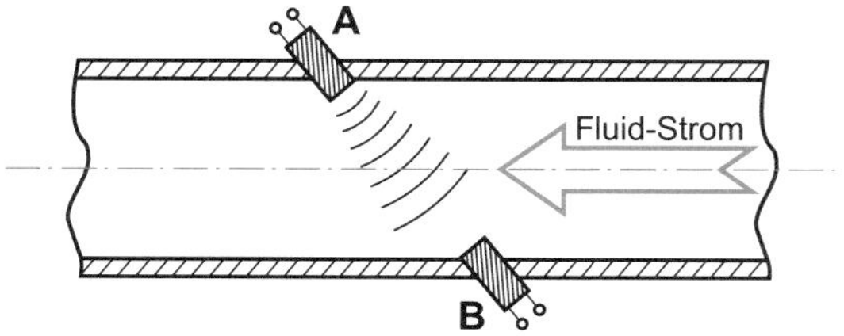

Bild 9 Wirkprinzip der Durchflussmessung mit zwei in ein Rohr hineinragenden Ultraschallwandlern A und B (Ultraschall-Laufzeitverfahren)

Durch die schräge Einbaulage beider Wandler ist die Laufzeit des Ultraschallsignals neben der Laufzeit im Gesamtsystem zwischen den beiden elektrischen Signalen auch von der Geschwindigkeit des Gasstromes abhängig. Für messtechnische Zwecke ist diese Anordnung aber noch nicht zu verwenden, da die Laufzeit auch von der Ausbreitungsgeschwindigkeit von Schallwellen im Gas (und damit von Temperatur und Dichte des Gases) sowie von der Temperaturabhängigkeit der Übertragungsfunktion der Ultraschallwandler abhängt. Um diese Abhängigkeiten zu verringern wird das Differenzverfahren angewendet. Unmittelbar nach dem Ablauf einer Zeitmessung wird die Senderichtung getauscht. Der Wandler B sendet nun das Signal und der Wandler A empfängt. Bei stehendem Gas erwartet man nun, dass beide Zeiten gleich groß sind. Die Differenz der Kehrwerte der beiden Zeiten wird nunmehr vorrangig die Strömungsgeschwindigkeit des Gases widerspiegeln. (Bild 10).

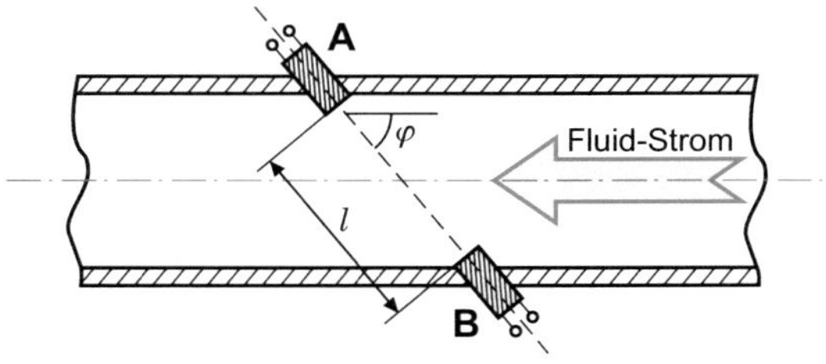

t_1 Laufzeit des Wellenpakets im Fluid von **A** gesendet und von **B** empfangen

t_2 Laufzeit des Wellenpakets im Fluid von **B** gesendet und von **A** empfangen

$\bar{v}$ mittlere Geschwindigkeit des Fluid

$$\bar{v} = \frac{l}{2\cos\varphi} \cdot \frac{t_1 - t_2}{t_1 \cdot t_2}$$

Bild 10 Messprinzip mit Differenzmessung

Die Annahme, dass die beiden Zeiten bei fehlender Gasgeschwindigkeit gleich groß sind, setzt identische Ultraschallwandler voraus. Der Ultraschallwandler besteht meist aus einem piezoelektrischen Wandler in Verbindung mit anderen mitschwingenden mechanischen Bauteilen. So entstehen mechanische Resonanzsysteme, die zum Ausschwingen etwa Zeit benötigen. Um die Zeitbestimmung ausreichend genau ausführen zu können und den Impuls in der Gegenrichtung möglichst zeitnah zum ersten Impuls senden zu können, dürfen die Ultraschallwandler aber nicht lange nachschwingen. Zur Verkürzung des mechanischen Ausschwingens nach Abschluss der elektrischen oder akustischen Anregung sind bei manchen Konstruktionen weitere Bauelemente nötig. Auf der elektrischen Seite werden passive lineare elektrische Bauelemente ergänzt. Außerdem werden mechanisch wirkende Dämpfungselemente in den Ultraschallwandler eingebaut.

Die komplexe Struktur der Wandler ist der Grund dafür, dass es sehr schwer ist, ausreichend gleich wirkende Ultraschallwandler herzustellen. Die verbleibende Ungleichheit zwischen den Ultraschallwandlern erzeugt selbst bei fehlender Gasströmung eine Laufzeitdifferenz. Diese Differenz ist aber nicht konstant sondern von der Temperatur und der Alterung der Wandler in komplizierter Weise abhängig. Sie stellt somit einen nur schwer zu korrigierenden Anteil des Messfehlers bei der Gasgeschwindigkeitsmessung dar.

An dieser Stelle bietet sich die Anwendung von Reziprozitätsbeziehungen helfend an. Um die individuellen Eigenschaften der Ultraschallwandler und ihrer Ergänzungsbauteile aus der Differenzzeit vollständig herauszuhalten, ist es unter der Voraussetzung eines zeitinvarianten und linearen Systems ausreichend, statt der Ausgangsspannung des Empfangswandlers den Kurzschlussstrom zu messen (Bild 11).

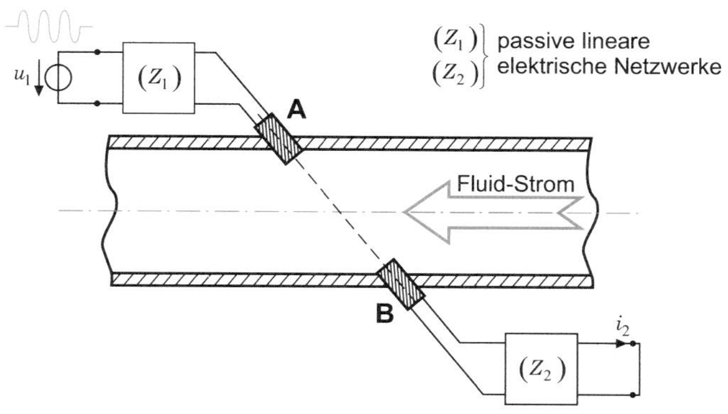

Bild 11 Anordnung für Spannungsspeisung und Strommessung

Bei strenger Anwendung der Messvorschrift (vernachlässigbar kleine Innenwiderstände der Sendespannungsquelle und der Strommessschaltung auf der Empfangsseite) wird die Differenzzeit zwischen den beiden Richtungen genügend klein bleiben, auch wenn die individuellen Eigenschaften der Ultraschallwandler unterschiedlich sind. Nur während der Zeit der zwei Messungen, die für die Differenzzeitbildung verwendet werden, müssen die Eigenschaften konstant bleiben.

Das Verfahren wird sich aber weniger oder gar nicht hilfreich auswirken, wenn die Wandler oder die Ergänzungsbauteile soweit ausgesteuert werden, dass die Forderung nach Linearität verletzt wird. Es ist deshalb von großer Bedeutung die nichtlinearen Eigenschaften zu kennen, um Aussteuerungsgrenzen festzulegen.

5 Anwendung der Reziprozitätsbeziehungen zur Linearitätskontrolle komplexer Systeme

Aus dem bisher dargestellten ergibt sich die naheliegende Möglichkeit Reziprozitätsbeziehungen zu verwenden, um eine Kontrolle auf Linearität eines Systems vorzunehmen. Eine Struktur wird messtechnisch so untersucht, dass die Anordnung die Reziprozitätsbeziehung benutzt. Bei ausreichend kleinen Signalen erwartet man deshalb die Einhaltung der Beziehungen. Bei größeren Signalamplituden wird sich eine zunehmend größer werdende Abweichung ergeben, die letztendlich auf Nichtlinearitäten im System zurückzuführen ist. Über die Quelle der Nichtlinearität und deren Größe lässt sich zunächst keine Aussage treffen. Verwendet man aber eine Anordnung, bei der nur ein Zweig bezüglich seiner Linearität fraglich ist, so kann mit diesem Verfahren durch Austausch der Zweigelemente eine Prüfung auf ausreichende Linearität durchgeführt werden.

Im Beispiel der o. g. Durchflussmessung wird die Differenz zwischen den beiden Messzeiten bei nichtbewegtem Fluidvolumen und bei ausreichend kleiner Anregungsamplitude zu Null erwartet. Bei zunehmender Anregungsamplitude ist eine mit der Anregungsamplitude zunächst zunehmende Zeitdifferenz ein Maß für das Wirksamwerden von Nichtlinearitäten. Dieses Verfahren ermöglicht es somit, zulässige Aussteuergrenzen festzulegen oder Bauteile mit zu großen nichtlinearen Kennwerten zu erfassen.

6 Zusammenfassung

Der Beitrag hat mit einigen Beispielen zur Kalibrierung, zur Verringerung der Messunsicherheit und als Kontrollverfahren zur Erfassung von Nichtlinearitäten gezeigt, wie auf unterschiedliche Weise die Reziprozitätsbeziehungen zeitinvarianter linearer Netzwerke helfend im Fachgebiet der elektromechanischen Messtechnik angewendet werden können. Dies gilt auch und insbesondere für komplexe lineare Netzwerke mit Anteilen kontinuierlich verteilter Medien.

Literatur

[1] Gerlach, G.: Umkehrbare Wandler als Herzstück von Sensoren, in: G. Gerlach, R. Hoffmann (Hg.): Neue Entwicklungen in der Elektroakustik und elektromechanischen Messtechnik – Prof. Dr.-Ing. habil. Günther Pfeifer zum 65. Geburtstag. Dresdner Beiträge zur Sensorik, Band 40. Dresden: TUDpress, 2010, pp. 25-35.

[2] Lenk, A., Pfeifer, G.:, Werthschützky, R.: Elektromechanische Systeme, Springer, New York, 2001.

[3] Lenk, A., Ballas, R.G., Werthschützky, R., Pfeifer, G.: Electromechanical Systems in Microtechnology and Mechatronics, Springer Heidelberg, 2011.

[4] Schottky, W.: Das Gesetz des Tiefenempfangs in der Akustik und Elektroakustik, Zeitschrift für Physik 36, 1926, pp. 689-736.

[5] MacLean, W. R.: Absolute Measurement of Sound without a Primary Standard, J. Acoust. Soc. Am. Volume 12, Issue 1, 1940, pp. 140-146.

[6] Bouaoua, N.: Free-field reciprocity calibration of condenser microphones in the low ultrasonic frequency range, Dissertation, Universität Oldenburg, 2008.

[7] DIN EN 61094-2, Meßmikrofone Teil 2: Primärverfahren zur Druckkammer-Kalibrierung von Laboratoriums-Normalmikrofonen nach der Reziprozitätsmethode (IEC 61094-2:2009), Deutsche Fassung EN 61094-2:2009, 2009.

[8] DIN EN 61094-3, Meßmikrofone Teil 3: Primärverfahren zur Freifeld-Kalibrierung von Laboratoriums-Normalmikrofonen nach der Reziprozitätsmethode (IEC 1094-3:1995), Deutsche Fassung EN 61094-3:1995, 1995.

[9] Bork, I, Fedtke, T, Ratschko, D.: Kalibrierung von Messmikrofonen – die Basis der Bestimmung akustischer Größen, PTB Mitteilungen, 117 Jg., Heft 1, pp. 7-13, 2007.

[10] Vorländer, M.: Maximalfolgen-Reziprozitätskalibrierung von Mikrofonen im Hallraum, Habilitationsschrift TU Dresden, Dresden, 1996.

[11] Theobald, P, Preston, R, Robinson, S, Barham, R, Tyrer, J, Greated, C, et al.: Fundamental standards for acoustics based on optical methods-first stage report., National Physical Laboratory, 2002.

[12] Koukoulas, T., Theobald, P., Schlicke, T., Barham, R.: Towards a future primary method for microphone calibration: Optical measurement of acoustic velocity in low seeding conditions, Optics and Lasers in Engineering, Volume 46, Issue 11, November 2008, Pages 791-796, ISSN 0143-8166, 2008.

From "Speech and Language Processing" to "Spoken Language Processing and Written Language Processing"

Hiroya Fujisaki

The University of Tokyo
fujisaki@alum.mit.edu

Abstract: Instead of the concept of a language as an encoding system common to speech and text, this paper emphasizes the need for introducing the concepts of spoken language and written language as two separate encoding systems. This is illustrated in the case of the well-known schema of statistical speech recognition, indicating its shortcomings as well as directions for future research.

1 Introduction

In the early days of speech communication research, say up to the beginning of 1970s, tasks such as text-to-speech synthesis (TTS) and automatic speech recognition (ASR) were believed to be solvable without utilizing higher-level linguistic knowledge. For instance, researchers on TTS systems were mainly concerned with grapheme-to-phoneme conversion, and did not pay attention to the fact that one needs deep understanding of the text in order to produce natural prosody. Likewise, ASR was believed to be solvable by doing the opposite: phoneme-to-grapheme conversion, followed by dictionary look-up. Since around 1970, the need for more linguistic knowledge was realized, but the efforts did not produce much progress. In fact, at the IBM Research Center, word recognition rate of the ASR system was said to go up by a few percent each time a linguist in the group was fired (F. Jelinek, personal communication). Overt but fragmentary linguistic knowledge was then replaced by the so-called "statistical method" which brought about a remarkable progress in ASR, at least at the beginning [1]. However, we are still far from solving the problem [2].

In the author's opinion, this is mainly due to the lack of insight into the true nature of what people vaguely call "language." In this paper I will explain my concept of "spoken language" [3] as distinct from what is commonly called "language," point out some of the problems that arise from the confusion, especially in the so-called statistical method of ASR, and indicate directions for future research.

2 Language and Speech — Three Alternative Views

2.1 Elementary View

For daily mutual communication humans primarily use speech, which is a physically observable (if not visible) phenomenon. But most of us also believe that speech is an overt signal of a certain underlying message generated by an encoding system for expressing information, and we call the encoding system (henceforth "code" for short) LANGUAGE. Although it is NOT physically observable, from the ancient days scholars have made attempts to assume, analyze, and describe the units, structures and rules, *etc.* of a language. In this sense, all the linguistic concepts are refined artifacts conceived in order to explain what we observe in its physical manifestation, *viz.*, speech. Figure 1 shows the relationship between language and speech in this most elementary view: language as a code and speech as its physically observable signal. This is also the concept that underlies the statistical method of speech recognition with a "language" model.

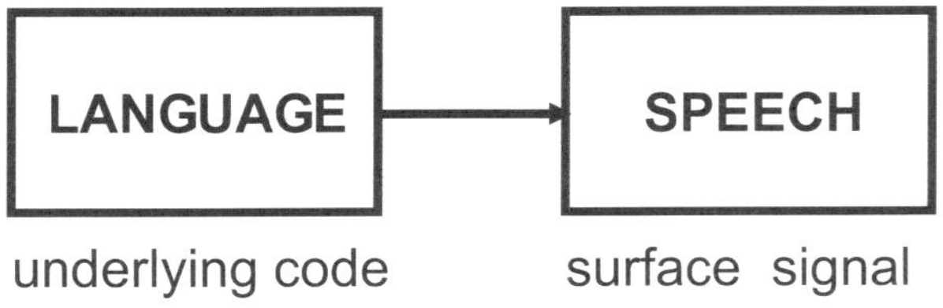

Figure 1: Language as the Underlying Code for Speech

2.2 Conventional View

In the case of text, which is apparently a secondary medium for communication invented by humans much later than speech, the signal is also observable, and is much more durable than speech in most cases. Therefore, it is quite natural that many of the concepts concerning language have been derived by studying text, *viz*., the written manifestation of a language. In doing so, almost everyone believes that the language which has been studied and described is one and the same for both speech and text within a community that uses both of them. This notion is described in Figure 2. Furthermore, it is often believed that the study of written language is the study of natural human language itself (hence the name "natural language processing" which actually deals only with the written language). Also, the concepts, units and rules derived from studies of text are often assumed to apply to speech, and whatever that does not follow the rules is called "ill-formed."

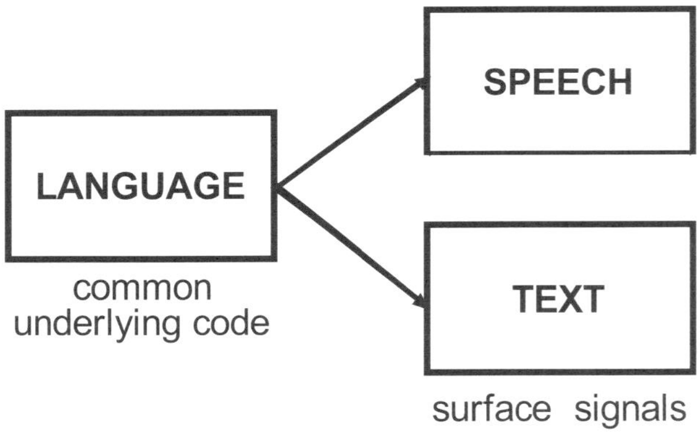

Figure 2: Language as the Common Underlying Code for both Speech and Text

2.3 The Author's View

However, from a careful study of differences between speech and text, it became more and more clear, at least to the present author, that the basic assumptions underlying Figure 2 are not correct. In other words, the underlying codes for speech and text, whenever a human community uses both, cannot be regarded as one and the same, but should be regarded as two distinctly different codes, as shown in Figure 3. Here the term "**spoken language**" is used to cover its aspects as an encoding system and those as the signal, and the same applies to "**written language**". This becomes evident if one notices the difference in the information carried by them.

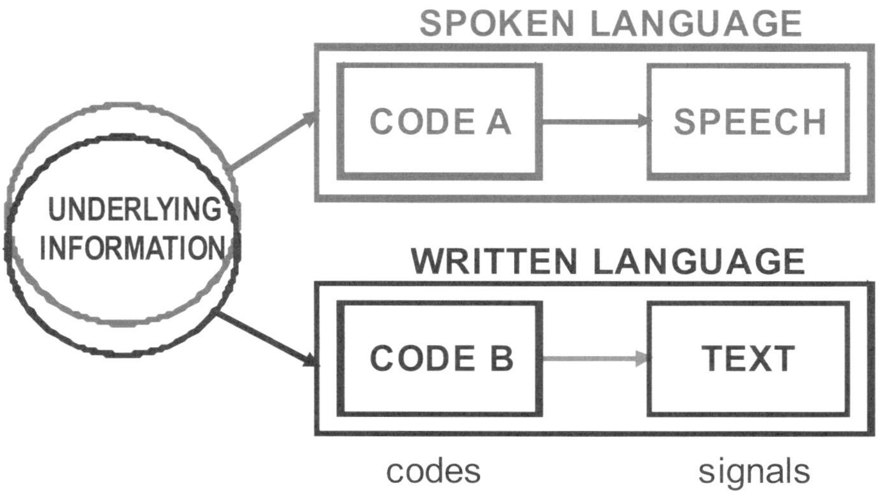

Figure 3: Spoken Language and Written Language as Two Different Languages, Each with Aspects of Code and Signal

3 Examples of Differences Between Spoken Language (SL) and Written Language (WL) as Codes

The following sections show some (but not all) of the differences between SL and WL. The examples are all from English. It should be noted, however, that certain differences are language-specific.

3.1 Difference in Ambiguity

Many expressions exist that are ambiguous in WL but are unambiguous in SL, and *vice versa*; *e.g.*, homographism and homophony at the lexical level.

- Examples of homographism (ambiguous in WL but not in SL):
  close, content, interest, increase, present, record, recreation, wind, *etc.*
- Examples of homophony (ambiguous in SL but not in WL):
  bare/bear, dear/deer, die/dye, flower/flour, knight/night, made/maid, meat/meet, pray/prey, right/write, sea/see, steal/steel, tail/tale, *etc.*

3.2 Presence of Prosody Only in SL

Prosody in SL allows disambiguation of some of the ambiguities (*e.g.*, lexical and syntactic) in WL.

- Examples of syntactic ambiguity in WL that can be disambiguated by prosody in SL:
  (a) All young men went to the war, leaving only old men and women at home.
  (b) Old men and women are called senior citizens.

3.3 Presence of Word Boundary Marking Only in WL

In many (but not all) WLs, word boundaries are explicitly shown, but not in SL, causing ambiguity in SL.

- Examples: I scream/ icecream, an ice cream/a nice cream, night rate/nitrate.

4 Re-examination of Basic Assumptions for Statistical Speech Recognition

4.1 Basic Assumptions for the Statistical Speech Recognition

With the distinction between SL and WL in mind, let us now re-examine the basic assumptions for the statistical speech recognition, which was proposed in the middle of 1970s and has since been widely accepted. Figure 4 shows the formulation of the combined generation/recognition process underlying the statistical speech recognition [2]. It is claimed that the entire operation can be regarded as transmission through a noisy channel, which is the basic problem of information theory.

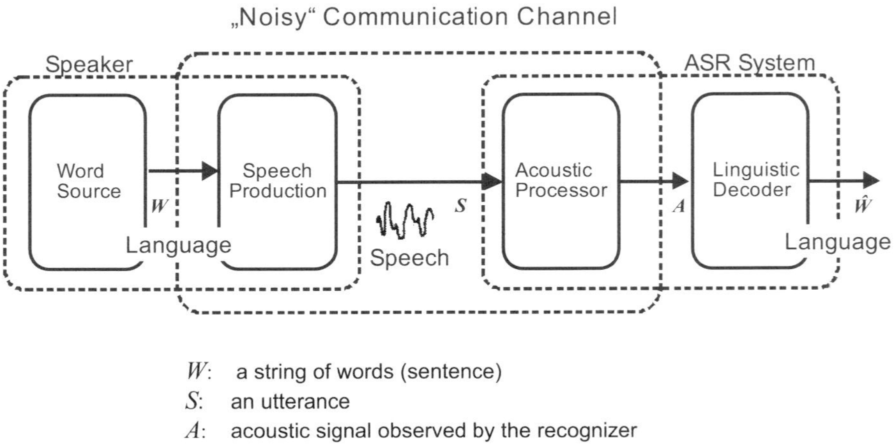

Figure 4: Schematic Diagram of Statistical Speech Recognition (from [2], modified by Fujisaki)

It should be noted that the formulation here was proposed originally for recognition of **strings of isolated words generated by an artificial grammar**, and was quite successful, but the model was subsequently used, without modification, for ASR of utterances produced with less constrained, more natural grammar, *i.e.*, **fluent speech**. Also note that both the input and the output are marked simply as "word strings," without making distinctions between SL and WL. Namely, it is based on the simplest model shown in Figure 1.

In order to examine whether the schematic diagram is valid for ASR of meaningful, fluent speech or not, let us now ask the following three questions:

(a) Is the speaker model true?

(b) Is the noisy communication channel model valid?

(c) Is the language model sufficiently accurate for natural, fluent speech?

4.2 Is the speaker model true?

Since $\hat{W}$ is the estimated output of an ASR system (i.e., a string of words in WL), the input W must also be a string of words in WL. A speaker does not start by constructing W first by himself and then produces speech. Therefore, this diagram is valid only in a situation where the speaker is presented a text written by someone else, and reads it aloud (*i.e.*, dictation).

Therefore, the schematic diagram of Figure 4 must be changed into Figure 5 to describe the real situation: dictation of a given text. In this case, "the word source" is not a part of the speaker. The speaker's actual roles are:

(1) Understanding the input sentence ***W*** of a WL (since reading a sentence aloud is possible only after understanding the sentence), and then

(2) Generating an utterance ***S*** in the corresponding SL.

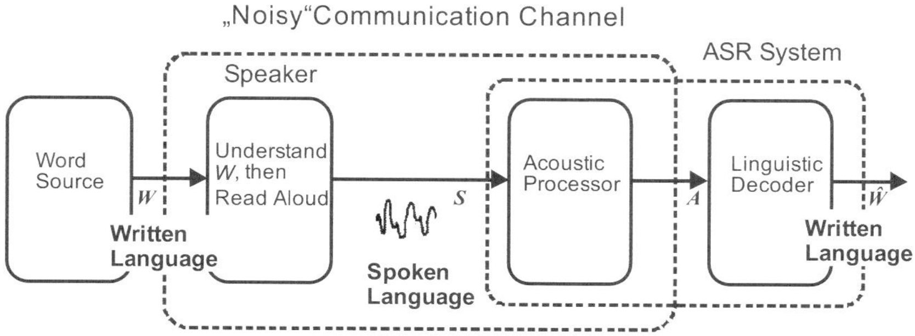

Figure 5: Actual roles of the speaker in Dictation of a Given Text

4.3 Is the noisy communication channel model valid?

Since the conversion of a sentence ***W*** in WL into an utterance ***S*** in SL entails ambiguity of various origin (lexical, syntactic, *etc.*) that cannot be resolved by statistical inference, the channel cannot be regarded as a simple noisy channel, but as a channel with degeneration.

4.4 Is the language model sufficiently accurate for natural, fluent speech?

Since the bigram (*i.e.*, simple Markov) model is known to be quite insufficient for representing syntactic relationships between words within a sentence, it has become a common practice to use the trigram (*i.e.*, second-order Markov) model as the language model. For a thousand word vocabulary, it is necessary to count the number of occurrences of each of one billion trigrams. Since the amount of available data is not enough, smoothing is introduced, but its validity is not guaranteed. Still, trigram is a very poor model for syntactic relationship. Theoretically it should be possible to achieve higher degree of approximation to actual syntactic constraints if we increase N indefinitely for N-grams [4]. However, it is practically impossible to go beyond trigrams even for a modest vocabulary size of one thousand.

5 ASR of Spontanous Speech (*i. e.*, NOT Dictation)

The foregoing section has shown that the original schema of statistical speech recognition is valid only for dictation, where the input to the speaker is a message in WL, and yet the schema has serious limitations. Although dictation may be useful for certain applications, the ultimate goal of ASR is of course recognition of fluent and spontaneous speech. In this case, the communication channel model is no more valid because the speaker is NOT a part of the channel, but is the source of information which directly generates utterances of SL. Thus the real task of an ASR system is to convert an utterance (or a sequence of utterances) ***S*** of SL into a sentence (or a sequence of sentences) ***W*** of WL. In other words, it is Speech-to-Text conversion (STT). This is exactly opposite to a TTS system which converts ***W*** of WL into ***S*** of SL.

Although it is not done in current TTS systems, it will be easily understood that the ultimate TTS system must start from understanding $\boldsymbol{W}$ in order to dissolve lexical and syntactic ambiguities, and then generate $\boldsymbol{S}$ correctly (namely with correct segmental and prosodic features). Conversely, the ultimate ASR system must start from understanding $\boldsymbol{S}$, and then generate $\boldsymbol{W}$ correctly (namely with correct spelling, word boundaries and punctuations). In other words, automatic speech understanding (ASU) is the prerequisite to the ultimate ASR To the present author this is quite evident, but unfortunately this view is not shared by most experts in the field of ASR.

6 Conclusion and Dedication

This short article was meant to explain the rationale that led the author to introduce the concept of Spoken Language Processing, and also to point out some problems in the formulation of statistical speech recognition which is widely accepted. It is dedicated to Professor Rüdiger Hoffmann to commemorate his 65th birthday as a token of thanks for his friendship over the years, as well as of best wishes for many more years of healthy and productive life.

References

[1] Jelinek, F.: Continuous Speech Recognition by Statistical Methods. Proceedings of IEEE, Vol. 64(4), pp. 532-556, 1976.

[2] Jelinek, F.: The Dawn of Statistical ASR and MT. Communications of ACM, Vol. 35(4), pp.483-494, 2009.

[3] Fujisaki, H.: Spoken Language Processing. Opening Keynote Lecture given at the First International Conference on Spoken Language Processing (ICSLP), Kobe, 1990.

[4] Shannon, C.: A Mathematical Theory of Communication. Bell System Technical Journal, Vol. 27(3), pp.379-423, 1948.

(WHAT IS) THE CONTRIBUTION OF PHONETICS TO CONTEMPORARY SPEECH SYNTHESIS RESEARCH (?)

Petra Wagner

Universität Bielefeld
petra.wagner@uni-bielefeld.de

Kurzfassung: Recent advances in speech technology have significantly reduced the necessity for traditional phonetic system components or phonetic expertise, e.g. rule-based prosody models. We therefore need to ask the question, whether and how phonetics ought to play a role in ongoing and future speech synthesis development. The answer can be derived directly from a global analysis of the weaknesses in state-of-the-art systems. Their quality limitations unveil those areas where phonetics can still provide important impulses for system improvement. In this paper, it is argued that even if phoneticians "traditional" tasks have become less influential, with the advent of more dynamically flexible and interactive systems new challenges have arisen and need solutions within the humanities.

1 Phonetics in State-of-Art Speech Synthesis

Traditionally, phoneticians and engineers worked hand-in-hand on developing speech synthesis applications[1]: A lot of explicit phonetic knowledge was needed to hand-craft or statistically motivate rules in order to predict formant trajectories, phone durations, intonation contours and lots of other phonetic detail (e.g. [11] or the collection of many phonetically inspired approaches to synthesis in [27]). With data storage becoming less of a problem, and with data driven methods showing their superior ability to detect regularities and interdependencies in masses of data, phonetic knowledge was still needed when doing symbolic annotations or developing cost functions. In unit selection approaches, phoneticians determined the optimal levels of granularity for segmentation, prediction, unit selection or concatenation. In some sense, the phonetician's task has moved from *building* models him- or herself towards supervising the training of model building algorithms. But even the necessity for this type of expertise has been called into question:

> Fine grained phonetic data/topological rules are not necessarily required for generating plausible intelligible speech – as long as the carriers of those information are present in the text data (and corresponding speech recordings) used for training the system.' [25]

Thus, one could argue that whenever the need of building working applications rather than doing linguistic research is in the foreground, the phonetician's role has become minuscule at best, while the linguist remains somewhat needed for tagging the database. Roux's diagnosis seems to be correct when inspecting at the decreasing percentages of genuinely phonetic or linguistic publications at the latest international Speech Synthesis Workshops (cf. Table 1). It

[1]Many of the thoughts in this paper were presented as an invited talk at the ESSV 2011 meeting in Aachen and published as an abstract in [12]

needs to be stressed that the vast number of papers counted as "phonetic" are by no means non-technological. Rather, they were counted as "phonetic" because they all apply some phonetic insight in order to model the synthetic speech signal.

Table 1 - Relative and total numbers (in brackets) of phonetic or linguistic vs. purely technolgy-related contributions at international conferences focusing on aspects of TTS between 2004 and 2010.

Topic	SSW 5 (2004)	SSW 6 (2007)	SSW 7 (2010)
technology	30% (12)	38% (26)	64% (36)
phonetics/linguistics	70% (28)	62% (43)	36% (21)

The main reasons for this development lie (i) in state-of-the-art architecture specific challenges and chances, (ii) in scientific progress, and (iii) in a shift of interests within those parts of phonetics community sharing an interest in technical systems:

1. Naturally, the main scientific visions and goals of unit selection approaches lie in their data-orientation lending to the idea of using easily available resources such as audio books [4, 24], building on the natural phonetic variety available in large speech corpora (e.g. [6]), or using available resources for building applications for minority languages ([26, 18]). A main problem within statistical-parametric (HMM-based) approaches to speech synthesis [3] is the need to improve the voice quality. The architecture specific chances lie in the possibility to exploit the parametric approach by working on voice conversion algorithms and on modeling the expressive, emotional and gender specific characteristics of speech (e.g. [21, 20]). Despite the clear phonetic relevance of such topics, the solutions are at best marginally touching on phonetic aspects.

2. Progress in automatic labeling has made much of the former manual annotation work superfluous, especially with the advent of semi- or unsupervised machine learning techniques that need only few amounts of training data (e.g. [33]). Furthermore, much progress has been made within objective evaluation procedures, making speech synthesis research more independent of time consuming (phonetic) evaluation work (e.g. [19]). Also, synthesis systems have reached a very good quality, in some applications even outperforming humans, e.g. when being used for announcements in noisy environments such as train stations, where a somewhat machine-like hyperarticulation can be advantageous.

3. Probably linked to the good quality of many TTS systems, the research focus within the speech technologically interested phonetics community has shifted towards other applied research questions, such as using phonetic knowledge in CALL applications (e.g. [10]), modeling human speech processing using embodied, articulatory and neuronal approaches (e.g. [13, 28]), modeling the prosody of discourse and dialogue (e.g. [30, 7]), classifying phenomena of turn organization, overlap and pausing (e.g. [9, 34]), investigating communicative functions of non-verbal expressions such as laughter (e.g. [31]), modeling processes of communicative adaptation such as interactional convergence or entrainment (e.g. [14, 32, 15]) or multimodality (e.g. [29, 2]). Thus, building on a high-quality basic systems, researchers are currently aiming at making the technological applications more communicative, interactive, adaptive, expressive and multimodal.

In sum, it can be said that while it is true that the current fundamental research in speech synthesis are being made largely without phonetic and linguistic competence, the unsolved problems such as building adaptive and interactive systems are still in need of a certain amount of insight probably gained from the humanities. The good news is that it has been the technological progress that has given phoneticians the freedom to tackle these issues. In the following section, I will discuss the current state of the art of speech synthesis applications and make a suggestion on how a reintegration of the technologically inspired communicative trend in phonetics can help improving current synthesis applications.

2 A Qualitative Assessment of State-of-the-Art Synthesis Systems

Speech synthesis has reached a plateau of quality, perhaps now being in a situation similar to speech recognition. In certain fields, synthesis has reached a high degree of acceptance, e.g. in announcement systems at train stations, in car navigation systems, computer games or mobile phone applications. Thus, we have empirical proof that users are able to adapt to synthetic speech even if it is still not perfect in the sense of "human". Interestingly, we do not really know why this is the case and how the systems could be further improved. Despite some success stories of working applications, many of our ongoing research concentrates on the boundaries of the technologically possible without knowing where this, e.g. highly emotional, authentic speech, would be useful in an application. Clearly, research should not be entirely application driven. Still, in a research field focusing on an application, it comes as a surprise that the question of applicability is often ignored. To this day, we have little or no knowledge about the individual user's needs and expectations:

> Even if a model can predict user judgements of "overall quality" with high validity and reliability, this is not necessarily a good indicator of the acceptability of a service. [...] Different users may focus on different quality dimensions in different contexts and weight them according to the task, context of use, price etc. [17]

Indeed, we need to get a understanding of our "typology of users", instead of tuning our applications and evaluations to the "average user" – as it is done by MOS approaches to system evaluation. In some sense or other, most users will belong to a "special user group", e.g. by being young or senior citizens, by being male or female, by being upset, bored, distracted or attentive. In fact, any potential user is likely to approach a system with "peculiar" or somewhat "special" personality or context dependent preferences or dislikes. Just as different people use different sets of options in their operating systems or mobile phones, they might want to use a different set of options in their speech synthesis systems. It is the task of researchers to find out what a good set of options and settings might be.

Some first attempts are being made to better grasp the user needs and expectations, e.g. by investigating preferences within or across special user groups such as blind users or senior citizens (e.g. [16, 35]). Besides the individual differences, typical contexts influencing our system demands need to be better understood. Such contexts could be situations where the user is distracted, e.g. while driving, or highly attentive, e.g. while interacting with a computer game, but there are only few studies of human-human listening behaviour in distracted vs attentive situations (cf. [5] and references therein). A very promising and rather active line of research lies in the better understanding of felicitous system feedback, e.g. using non-verbal expressions such as laughter, verbal or visual backchannels signalling a degree of system attention, similar to a human listener (e.g. [23, 8]). A better understanding of feedback may enable a more efficient communication between human and machine [1]. A better understanding about the adaptations between interlocutors, but also a better understanding of how recipient design, i.e. the way we adapt ourselves to the needs of our interlocutors, may be very helpful to improve these dynamical aspects in human-machine interaction in the future.

3 Discussion

A key problem in improving our current synthetic speech is our lack of understanding our user's needs. Certainly, many insights can be gained from studying human-human interaction but possibly, that approach leads us to wrong conclusions as humans probably do not expect human-like behavior from a machine. While WOZ-scenarios may tell us something about the potential interaction patterns we need to integrate into our systems, these share a problem with many of the recordings made to study human-human interaction (cf. Figure 1): They are carried out in laboratory contexts that are likely to elicit behaviors differing strongly from those in everyday situations. It would be advantageous if users could be studied using their synthetic speech devices in everyday applications. The most problematic aspect of less experimental control is a lack of finding systematic variables influencing the users' behavior. Therefore, just as we need to find better ways of studying authentic human-human-behaviour, we need to find better, systematic ways of evaluating our applications embedded in authentic situations thus making our findings ecologically more valid. Besides investigating better techniques of systematically capturing authentic user-system interactions in a minimally invasive manner, we need to better exploit existing technologies to deal with noisy data – as are typical for authentic situations. Progress in channel separation, audio signal enhancement need to be taken into account if we want to move our system evaluations "out of the lab and into the wild". Besides the technical issues, more work needs to be done to build annotation tools and standards for "noisy speech" occurring out of the lab. Based on these data, a kind of "user typology" may be developed which helps us to determine the system parameters that need to be taken into account when building working applications for "special user groups". The MOS as the still most widely used tool to investigate the quality of synthetic speech, does not appear to be the optimal method for system evaluations, unless we are paying close attention to the "outliers". The expertise of phoneticians should be very helpful in developing alternative methods for system architecture evaluation and in detecting the potential keys to a system's success or failure.

Figure 1 - The Figure on left shows a corpus recording environment where it has been tried to capture video, audio and motion data in a maximally authentic, minimally invasive manner [22]. The picture on the right shows a typical corpus recording under laboratory conditions [5].

4 Conclusion

This article built on the observation that phonetics has become less influential in building synthetic speech synthesis applications, as the state-of-the-art technologies used are less in need of phonetic models predicting the detailed sound structure of the synthesized units. However,

I have argued that with the increased quality of available system's, other, new aspects of system quality need to be addressed in speech synthesis development, which lie more in the area of adequateness in the human-system interaction. While engineers can build and provide the platforms on which appropriate technical systems are built, the way they are of use in human-machine interaction needs insight gained from the humanities. Those can concentrate on the following questions:

- What contexts (speaker or situation specific) exist that need an adjustment of the synthetic voice and style?
- What are the phonetic system parameters that should be subject to a context specific adjustment?
- What kind of phonetic adjustments are needed and useful?

References

[1] BAUMANN, T. and D. SCHLANGEN: *INPROiSS – A component for just-in-time incremental speech synthesis.* In *ACL*, pp. 103–108, 2012.

[2] BERGMANN, K., V. AKSU and S. KOPP: *The relation of speech and gestures: temporal synchrony follows semantic synchrony.* In MALISZ, Z., C. KIRCHHOFF and P. WAGNER (eds.): *Proceedings of GESPIN*, http://gespin.uni-bielefeld.de/?q=node/66, 2011.

[3] BLACK, A. W., H. ZEN and K. TOKUDA: *Statistical parametric speech synthesis.* In *Proceedings of ICASSP*, pp. 1229–1232, 2007.

[4] BREUER, S., S. BERGMANN, R. DRAGON and S. MÖLLER: *Set-up of a Unit Selection Synthesis with a Prominent Voice.* In *Proceedings of LREC 2006*, http://www.lrec-conf.org/proceedings/lrec2006/, 2006.

[5] BUSCHMEIER, H., Z. MALISZ, M. WŁODARCZAK, S. KOPP and P. WAGNER: *'Are you sure you're paying attention?' – 'Uh-huh'. Communicating understanding as a marker of attentiveness.* In *Proceedings of Interspeech*, pp. 2057–2060, Florence, Italy, 2011.

[6] CAMPBELL, N.: *Developments in Corpus-Based Speech Synthesis: Approaching Natural Conversational Speech.* IEICE Trans. Inf. Syst., E88-D(3):376–383, 2005.

[7] CHARFUELAN, M., M. SCHRÖDER and I. STEINER: *Prosody and voice quality of vocal social signals: the case of dominance in scenario meetings.* In *Proceedings of Interspeech*, pp. 2558–2561, 2010.

[8] GRANSTRÖM, B. and D. HOUSE: *Inside out – Acoustic and visual aspects of verbal and non-verbal communication.* In *Proceedings of the 16th Congress of the Phonetic Sciences*, pp. 11–28, 2007.

[9] HELDNER, M. and J. EDLUND: *Pauses, gaps and overlaps in conversations.* Journal of Phonetics, 38:555–568, 2010.

[10] JOKISCH, O., A. WAGNER, R. SABO, R. JAECKEL, N. CYLWIK, M. RUSKO and R. HOFFMANN: *Multilingual Speech Data Collection for the Assessment of Pronunciation and Prosody Training in a Language Learning System.* In *Proceedings of Speech and Computer (SPECOM)*, pp. 515–520, 2009.

[11] KLATT, D.: *Synthesis by rule of Segmental Durations in English Sencences.* In LINDBLOM, B. and S. ÖHMANN (eds.): *Frontiers of Speech Communication Research*, pp. 287–299. London: Academic Press, 1979.

[12] KRÖGER, B. and P. BIRKHOLZ (eds.): *Elektronische Sprachsignalverarbeitung 2011 – Tagungsband der 22. Konferenz*, vol. 61, Studientexte zur Sprachkommunikation, Aachen, September 2011. Dresden, TUD Press.

[13] KRÖGER, B., J. KANNAMPUZHA and C. NEUSCHAEFER-RUBE: *Towards a neurocomputational model of speech production and perception.* Speech Communication, 51:793–809, 2009.

[14] LEVITAN, R. and J. HIRSCHBERG: *Measuring Acoustic-Prosodic Entrainment with Respect to Multiple Dimensions.* In *Proceedings of Interspeech*, pp. 3081–3084, Florence, Italy, 2011.

[15] LEWANDOWSKI, N.: *Talent in nonnative phonetic convergence.* PhD thesis, Universität Stuttgart, URN: urn:nbn:de:bsz:93-opus-74023, 2012.

[16] MOERS, D. and P. WAGNER: *Assessing the adequate treatment of fast speech in unit selection systems for the visually impaired.* In *Proceedings of SSW6*, pp. 282–287, 2007.

[17] MÖLLER, S., K.-P. ENGELBRECHT and R. SCHLEICHER: *Predicting the Quality and Usability of Spoken Dialogue Systems.* Speech Communication, 50:730–744, 2008.

[18] NIEKERK, D. R. VAN and E. BARNARD: *Phonetic alignment for speech synthesis in under-resourced languages.* In *Proceedings of Interspeech*, pp. 880–883, 2009.

[19] NORRENBROCK, C., F. HINTERLEITNER, U. HEUTE and S. MÖLLER: *Instrumental Assessment of Prosodic Quality for Text-to-Speech Signals.* IEEE Signal Proc. Letters, 19(5):255–258, 2012.

[20] NOSE, T. and T. KOBAYASHI: *Recent development of HMM-based expressive speech synthesis and its applications.* In *Proceedings of APSIPA ASC*, p. 189, 2011.

[21] NOSE, T. and T. KOBAYASHI: *Speaker-independent HMM-based voice conversion using adaptive quantization of the fundamental frequency.* Speech Communication, 53(7):973–985, 2011.

[22] OERTEL, C., F. CUMMINS, J. EDLUND, P. WAGNER and N. CAMPBELL: *D64 – A corpus of richly recorded conversational interaction.* Journal of Multimodal User Interfaces, pp. 1–10, 2012.

[23] POPPE, R., K. TRUONG, D. REIDSMA and D. HEYLEN: *Backchannel Strategies for Artificial Listeners.* Intelligent Virtual Agents, pp. 146–158, 2010.

[24] PRAHALLAD, K. and A. W. BLACK: *Segmentations of monologues in audio books for building synthetic voices.* IEEE Trans. Audio, Speeech and Language Processing, 19(5):1444–1449, 2011.

[25] ROUX, J. C.: *Do we need linguistic knowledge for speech technology applications in African languages?.* In PAUW, G. DE, H. GROENEWALD and G.-M. DE SCHRYVER (eds.): *AFLAT 2010 – Proceedings of the Second Workshop on African Language Technology*, p. 1, http://aflat.org/aflat2010, 2010. European Language Resources Association (ELRA).

[26] ROUX, J. C. and A. S. VISAGIE: *Data-driven approach to rapid prototyping Xhosa speech synthesis*. In *Proceedings of SSW6*, pp. 143–147, 2007.

[27] SANTEN, J. P. VAN, R. W. SPROAT, J. P. OLIVE and J. HIRSCHBERG (eds.): *Progress in Speech Synthesis*. Springer: New York, 1997.

[28] ŠIMKO, J. and F. CUMMINS: *Sequencing and Optimization within an Embodied Task Dynamic Model*. Cognitive Science, 35(3):527–562, 2011.

[29] SWERTS, M. and E. KRAHMER: *Facial expressions and prosodic prominence: Comparing modalities and facial areas*. Journal of Phonetics, 36(2):219–238, 2008.

[30] SYRDAL, A., A. CONKIE, Y.-J. KIM and M. BEUTNAGEL: *Speech acts and dialogue TTS*. In *Proceedings of SSW7*, Kyoto, Japan, 2011.

[31] TROUVAIN, J. and N. CAMPBELL (eds.): *Proceedings of the Interdisciplinary Workshop on The Phonetics of Laughter*, http://www.coli.uni-saarland.de/conf/laughter-07/proceedings.html, 2007. Saarland University, Germany.

[32] WAGNER, P., B. INDEN, Z. MALISZ and I. WACHSMUTH: *Interaction Phonology*. In WACHSMUTH, I., P. JAECKS and J. DE RUITER (eds.): *Towards a New Theory of Communication*. Benjamins, to appear.

[33] WATTS, O.: *Unsupervised Learning for Text-to-Speech Synthesis*. PhD thesis, University of Edinburgh, http://www.cstr.ed.ac.uk/publications/, 2012.

[34] WŁODARCZAK, M., J. ŠIMKO and P. WAGNER: *Temporal entrainment in overlapped speech: A cross-linguistic study*. In *Proceedings of Interspeech*, 2012.

[35] WOLTERS, M., P. CAMPBELL, C. DEPLACIDO, A. LIDDELL and D. OWENS: *Making Synthetic Speech Accessible to Older People*. In *Proceedings of SSW6*, 2011.

Challenges of Russian Speech Processing in Multimodal Applications

Andrey Ronzhin and Alexey Karpov

ronzhin@iias.spb.su

Abstract: Some achievements in Russian speech processing research obtained during the collaborative projects headed by Prof. Dr.-Ing. habil. Rüdiger Hoffmann are considered in the paper. The models of audio-visual speech synthesis and speech recognition were used for development of multimodal applications based on natural interaction. An information kiosk and services of a smart meeting room are the main cases, where speech processing technologies were applied.

1 Introduction

Fundamental research of speech synthesis and recognition taking into account peculiarities of Russian was one of the purposes of the three international projects headed by Prof. Dr.-Ing. habil. Rüdiger Hoffmann. As a result of the fruitful cooperation between Dresden University of Technology, Institute of Computer Science University of Bialystok, United Institute of Information Problems of the National Academy of Sciences of Belarus and Saint-Petersburg Institute for Informatics and Automation of the Russian Academy of Sciences the speech based products were developed [1-4]. Short survey of Russian speech recognition peculiarities and features of the developed models for audio visual speech processing are described below.

Russian, Belarusian and Ukrainian are the East Slavic languages of the Balto-Slavic subgroup of the Indo-European family of languages. There are certain common features for all East Slavic languages, such as stress and word-formation. Stress is moveable and can occur on any syllable, there are no strict rules to identify stressed syllable in a word-form (people keep it in mind and use analogies; proper stressing is a big problem for learners of the East Slavic languages). These languages are synthetic and highly inflected with lots of roots and affixes including prefixes, interfixes, suffixes, postfixes and endings; moreover, these sets of affixes are overlapping, in particular one-letter grammatical morphemes set ('a', 'o', 'y'). Nouns and pronouns are identified with certain gender classes (masculine, feminine, common, neuter), which are distinguished by different inflections and trigger in syntactically associated words. Nouns, pronouns, their modifiers, and verbs have different forms for each number class and must be inflected to match the number of the nouns/pronouns to which they refer. Another grammatical category that is characteristic for these languages is case: Russian and Belorussian have 6 cases and Ukrainian has 7 (Ukrainian is the only modern East Slavic language, which preserves the vocative case). Conjugation of verbs is affected by person, number, gender, tense, aspect, mood, and voice. One of the Slavic language features is a high redundancy, e.g. the same gender and number information can be repeated several times in one sentence. Russian is characterized by a high degree of grammatical freedom (but not completely free grammar; random permutation of words in sentences is not allowable); however, the inflectional system takes care of keeping the syntax clear; semantic and pragmatic information is crucial for determining word order.

Word order in Russian sentences is not restricted by hard grammatical constructions, like in modern English or German. While English sentence has a strict structure: subject-verb-object, in Russian, words can change their place without significantly influencing the sentence meaning. This complicates the creation of statistical language model and substantially decreases their predictive power.

Thus, many word-forms of the same words differ only by endings which are usually pronounced not so clearly as the beginnings of words and errors of inflections' recognition lead to errors of phrase recognition because of word discordance. In Russian the subject and object of sentence can only be determined by a word inflection and a verb congruence rather then order of words. Even the interchanging of words does not lead to the loss of the meaning. Also a punctuation play an important role in Russian. Accents and pauses should be used for a correct recognition of the inflective part of speech and sentence as a whole.

2 Speech recognition for Russian

Any modern ASR system requires at least three types of models in order to recognize speech: acoustic, lexical and language model. These models for our very large vocabulary Russian speech recognition system are presented below. The first step, we are faced with in developing any speech recognition system, is choosing appropriate units for acoustic modeling. Phoneme set size determines the number of context-independent models and also influences the number of context-dependent models and the amount of data needed for training. Information from phonological knowledge includes pronunciation rules and phonological alternation information. This allows us to determine acoustically close phonemes. Another important challenge in the development of spoken Russian ASR is the grapheme-to-phoneme conversion (or orthographic-to-phonemic transcription) of all the words in the recognition vocabulary. The aim of grapheme-to-phoneme conversion is to automatically generate pronunciation vocabulary from the lexicon represented in the orthographic form. For the grapheme-to-phoneme conversion, we apply an extended morphological database, consisting of more than 2.3M word-forms with the symbol '!' indicating stressed vowels. This database is a fusion of two different morphological databases: AOT (www.aot.ru) and Starling (http://starling.rinet.ru/morpho.php). The former one is larger and has more than 2M entries, but the latter one contains information about secondary stress for many compound words, as well as words with grapheme 'ë', which is always stressed, but usually replaced with 'e' in official texts which leads to loosing required information on the stress position.

We implemented an integral syntactico-statistical language model that takes advantage of both the statistic and syntactic text analysis. The main aim of the syntactical analysis is to extract syntactical groups in a sentence [6, 7]. The syntactic parsing of sentence produces long-distance word pairs additionally to the statistic processing. N-gram likelihoods in the integral stochastic LM are calculated after merging the results of both analyzers based on their frequency in the training text data. Table 2 summarizes the speech recognition results in terms of WER and letter (includes all the letters and the white-space between words) error rate (LER) as well as perplexity (PPL) and n-gram hit ratios (for bi-grams and tri-grams).

Language model	**PPL**	**n-gram hit, %**	**WER, %**	**LER, %**
Statistical bi-gram model	750	82.7	30.5	9.5
Syntactico-statistical bi-gram model	758	83.2	30.0	9.4
Statistical tri-gram model	569	39.2 (43.5 bi-grams)	27.5	8.6
Statistical tri-gram model interpolated with syntactico-statistical bi-gram model	549	39.2 (44.0 bi-grams)	26.9	8.5
Statistical bi-gram model	750	82.7	30.5	9.5

Table 1 - Large vocabulary Russian speech recognition results using various language models

All LMs were built using the same vocabulary of 204K words. The OOV rate for the combined test set is 2.5%. The best WER and LER results were obtained with the statistical tri-gram model linearly interpolated with the proposed syntactico-statistical bi-gram LM with interpolation coefficient of 0.27. RTF was less than 2.0 for the speech decoder installed on a desktop PC with multi-core Intel Core i7-3770K 3.5 GHz processor. Relatively high word error rates can be explained by the inflective nature of the given Slavic language, where each stem corresponds to tens/hundreds of endings, which are usually pronounced in continuous speech not so clearly as the beginning parts of the words and often different orthographic word-forms have identical phonemic representations. Some other reasons for the recognition errors are out-of-vocabulary words, a few transcription mistakes in tokens of the pronunciation vocabulary, rather high language model perplexity and low n-gram hit values, which are caused by high freedom of the Russian grammar.

3 Audio visual sythesis for Russian

General architecture of the developed audio-visual speech synthesizer for Russian is depicted in Figure 1. A way for implementation of an additional module in the standard architecture of audio-visual speech synthesizer was proposed. This is the module for modeling of asynchrony phenomena between corresponding auditory and visual units. The proposed talking head is an audio-driven model so the visual processing part is controlled by the results of text-to-speech system with the help of modalities asynchrony model. High-quality auditory speech synthesizer was designed for Russian especially [8], while visual part was initially created for Czech and later adopted to Russian, because of the fact that both of the languages belong to Slavic group of languages.

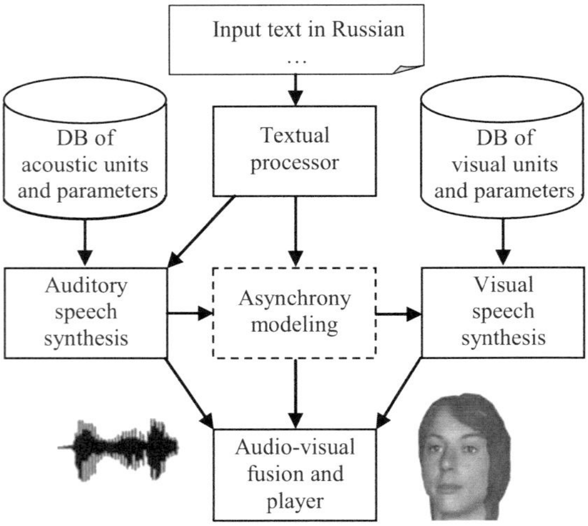

Figure 1 - General architecture of the bimodal synthesizer

The TTS-synthesis model based on allophones and multi-allophones natural waves (ANWs and MANWs) concatenation was applied [8]. The speech prosody synthesis uses an original Accentual Units Portrait (AUP) model for a stylization of tonal, rhythmical and dynamic contours of a phrase. Fusion of these modules allows synthesizing speech with a high degree of intelligibility and naturalness.

Synchronization of virtual face and lip movements with synthesized acoustical signal is realized on the basis of information known about positions of beginning and end boundaries of each context-dependent phoneme (allophone) in the speech flow. Duration of every allophone is set by the auditory TTS system based on allophone average length and required speech tempo. To model bimodal asynchrony in the developed audio-driven talking head and take into account different speech rates the following 16 context-dependent timing rules for transitions between visemes were defined.

Figure 2 shows the results of the experiments on speech intelligibility. Rather low intelligibility values for synthetic speech could be explained by the inflective nature of Russian. Only grammatical rules and experience can help us to choose proper word-forms in a phrase. Phrases proposed to informants are grammatically correct but meaningless, so it was an additional difficulty for them to recognize proper word-forms from acoustic/visual information only.

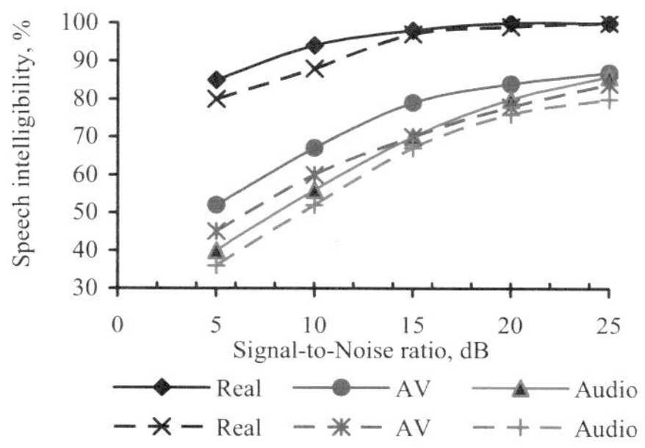

Figure 2 - The speech intelligibility with additive babble noise (solid lines) and white noise (dashed lines)

Figure 2 proves that visual speech cue assists to recognize uttered speech better especially in noisy conditions. One can see that the distance between intelligibility functions grows while decreasing SNR value. In our experiments the AVSS system has outperformed the unimodal TTS by 6% on average. McGurk effect was repeatedly observed, for instance, in pairs of Russian words /oda/ (ode)- /oba/ (both), which were correctly recognized when adding visual speech only.

The intelligibility results are different for additive babble and white noises. In white noise conditions the speech intelligibility is slightly lower than for babble noise. This could be explained: white noise is more disturbing at listening whereas babble noise is a more "pleasant" sound for ears. In babble noise-added speech it is more difficult to detect speech boundaries, but speech is intelligible. However, white noise-added speech is problematic in general which influences intelligibility negatively. Statistically significant differences in user evaluation marks of asynchrony models were not observed in the experiments with babble and white noises.

4 Developed Multimodal Applications

The proposed models of audiovisual speech processing were introduced in two applications: multimodal information kiosk and smart meeting room. The intelligent information kiosk called MIDAS (Multimodal Interactive-Dialogue Automaton for Self-service), is able to detect clients and supports both the standard means for information input/output (touchscreen and loudspeaker) and the devices for contactless HCI (video-cameras and microphones) [9]. The infokiosk offers information about the structure and staff of laboratories, the location and phones of departments and employees of the institution. The infokiosk is able to detect a human being inside the working zone with the Haar-based object detector [10], to track his/her movements and demonstrate awareness by a 3D avatar, which tracks clients by rotation of her talking head [8]. The infokiosk realizes a mixed initiative dialogue strategy, starting from the system's initiative and giving initiative for the query to a user after a verbal welcome. Usability results and the analysis of real exploitation have demonstrated that people prefer to communicate in a multimodal way; more than 60% of the user requests were made by natural speech and the rest by touch.

The developed smart meeting room is intended for holding small and medium events with up to forty participants [11]. The developed technologies of audio-visual data processing were successfully implemented in the room to provide natural and intuitively understandable way of interaction with the room equipment. Figure 3 shows a technological framework of the intelligent meeting room. Most important technologies are automatic speech recognition, speaker identification, sound source localization, detection of position and tracking moving objects and user faces, detection of user pose. Collaborative work of the referred technologies supplies a room control system with data about current situation, participant's behavior and provides robust recognition of voice command due to the analysis of spatial-temporal, situational information and user preferences.

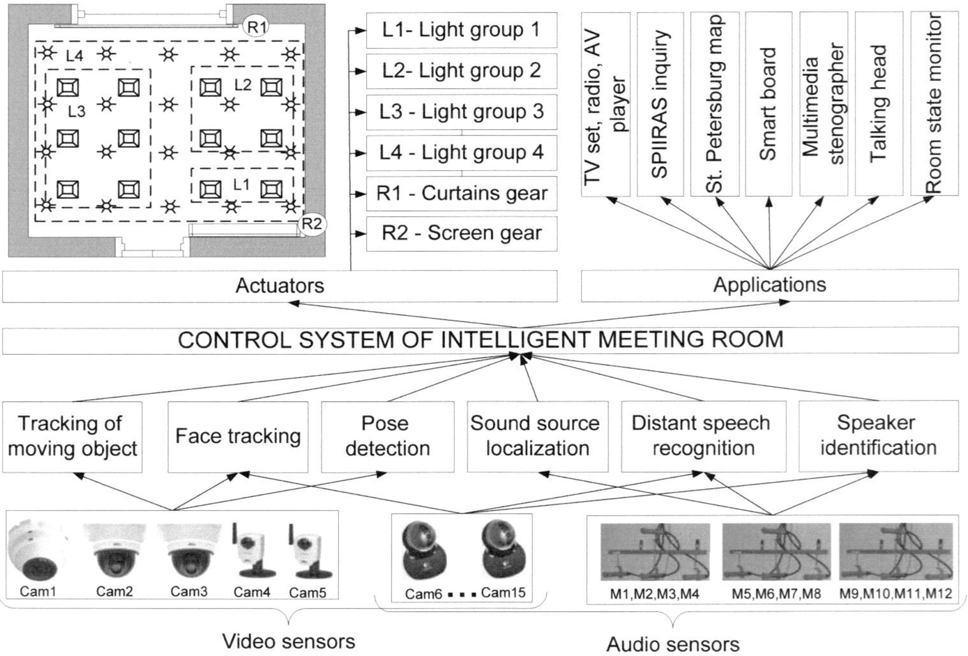

Figure 3 - Technological framework of the intelligent meeting room

A bimodal audio-visual Russian speech synthesis technology (talking head) is used for developed interactive applications. The multimodal applications "SPIIRAS inquiry" and "St. Petersburg map" were adopted based on similar systems realized in a multimodal kiosk [12]. Voice control system for TV set and radio implements commands to select a channel by its number or title, to change the settings of sound and picture. In the application "Smart board" voice commands intended for selecting color, width of pen, brush or other instruments for handwrited sketches on the touchscreen. Moreover, most of the commands could be activated by gestures on the touchscreen. In particular, in map-based applications a direct pointing to a graphical object is more needed, but speech commands are used for operation with objects.

5 Conclusion

Implementation of multimodal user interface capable to perceive speech, movements, poses and gestures of participants in order to determine their needs provides the natural and intuitively understandable way of interaction with intelligent services and solves the main task of ambient intelligent: assignment of easy-to-use and well-timed services in invasive manner. Combination of speech processing models, audio source localization, voice activity detection, face tracking technologies was realized in the developed multimodal infokiosk and smart meeting room services. Using the various combinations of multimodal interfaces and the equipment of the intelligent meeting room the fundamental issues of human-machine interaction are studied and various application in security medicine, robotics, logistics and other scientific areas are investigated now.

References

[1] R. Hoffmann, O. Jokisch, B. Lobanov, L. Tsirulnik, E. Shpilewsky, B. Piurkowska, A. Ronzhin, A. Karpov. Slavonic TTS and SST Conversion for Let's Fly Dialogue System, In Proc. of 12-th International Conference on Speech and Computer SPECOM, Moscow, Russia, 2007, pp. 729 – 733.

[2] Andrey Ronzhin, Alexey Karpov, Milos Zelezny, Roman Mesheryakov, Ruediger Hoffmann. Development of Multimodal Applications for Disabled People. Proc. of the Eighth All-Ukrainian International Conference, Kyjiv, Ukraine, 2006, pp. 163 – 166.

[3] Jokisch O., Jäckel R., Rusko M., Demenko G., Cylwik N., Ronzhin A., Hirschfeld D., Koloska U., Hanisch L., Hoffmann R. The EURONOUNCE Project – an intelligent language tutoring system with multimodal feedback functions, roadmap and specification. Proc. ESSV 2008, Frankfurt/M., 2008, pp. 116 – 123.

[4] O. Jokisch, A. Wagner, R. Sabo, R. Jaeckel, N. Cylwik, M. Rusko, A. Ronzhin, R. Hoffmann. Multilingual Speech Data Collection for the Assessment of Pronunciation and Prosody in a Language Learning System. In Proc. 13-th International Conference SPECOM'2009, St. Petersburg, 2009, pp. 515 – 520.

[5] A. Zaliznjak. Grammatical dictionary of the Russian language. Moscow: Russian dictionaries, 2003, 796 p. (in Rus.).

[6] A. Sokirko. Morphological modules on the website www.aot.ru, In Proc. "Dialogue-2004", Protvino, Russia, 2004, pp. 559 – 564 (in Rus.).

[7] I.M. Nozhov. Realization of automatic syntactic segmentation of a Russian sentence. PhD thesis, 2003, 140 p. (in Rus.).

[8] A. Karpov, L. Tsirulnik, Z. Krnoul, A. Ronzhin, B. Lobanov, M. Zelezny. Audio-Visual Speech Asynchrony Modeling in a Talking Head. In Proc. 10-th International Conference Interspeech-2009, Brighton, UK, 2009, pp. 2911 – 2914.

[9] A.A. Karpov, A.L. Ronzhin, Information Enquiry Kiosk with Multimodal User Interface // Pattern Recognition and Image Analysis, Moscow: MAIK Nauka/Interperiodica, Vol. 19, № 3, 2009, pp. 546 – 558.

[10] R. Lienhart, J. Maydt. An Extended Set of Haar-like Features for Rapid Object Detection, In Proc. IEEE International Conference on Image Processing ICIP-2002, 2002, pp. 900 – 903.

[11] Yusupov R.M., Ronzhin An.L., Prischepa M., Ronzhin Al.L. Models and hardware-software solutions of automated control of intelligent meeting room facilities // Automation and Remote Control, Vol. 72, No. 7, 2011, pp. 39 – 49.

[12] A.L. Ronzhin, V.Yu. Budkov, A. Karpov. Multichannel System of Audio-Visual Support of Remote Mobile Participant at E-Meeting // Springer-Verlag Berlin Heidelberg, S. Balandin et al. (Eds.): NEW2AN/ruSMART 2010, LNCS 6294, 2010, pp. 62 – 71.

Exemplarmodelle der Sprachproduktion und ihre Relevanz für die Sprachsynthese

Bernd Möbius

FR 4.7, Phonetik, Universität des Saarlandes
moebius@coli.uni-saarland.de

Kurzfassung: Sprachsynthese nach der Methode der *Unit Selection* wählt aus einem Korpus akustische Einheiten aus, die nach Verkettung eine gegebene Zieläußerung optimal repräsentieren. Bei der Auswahl werden die akustischen Einheiten danach bewertet, ob sie gute Repräsentanten der jeweiligen Zieleinheit sind und sich zugleich gut mit den benachbarten Einheiten verketten lassen. Wissenschaftshistorisch gesehen ist die *Unit Selection*–Methode nicht durch Modelle der menschlichen Sprachproduktion inspiriert. Exemplarbasierte Modelle der Sprachproduktion, die in den letzten Jahren zunehmend Beachtung gefunden haben, legen jedoch eine Analogie zwischen Modellen der Sprachproduktion und Verfahren der Sprachsynthese nahe. Dieser Beitrag widmet sich der Frage, ob diese Analogie oberflächlicher Art ist oder ob die komputationelle Modellierung von Prozessen der menschlichen Sprachverarbeitung die Implementierung sprachtechnologischer Verfahren informieren kann.

1 Einleitung

Korpusbasierte Sprachsyntheseverfahren orientieren sich nicht primär an den Prozessen der menschlichen Sprachproduktion in dem Sinn, dass sie eine Modellierung der Sprachproduktion anstreben. Sie arbeiten im Gegenteil mit dem Endprodukt dieser Prozesse, dem natürlichen Sprachsignal, dessen Bausteine – üblicherweise beschrieben durch traditionelle strukturelle Einheiten (Laute, Diphone, Silben usw.) – zu neuen, synthetischen Zieläußerungen rekombiniert und resequenziert werden.

Die Exemplartheorie wurde ursprünglich in der Psychologie als ein allgemeines Modell für Wahrnehmung und Kategorisierung eingeführt [11, 18] und ist erst in jüngerer Zeit zur Erforschung von Sprachperzeption [8, 9] und -produktion [19, 28, 30] aufgegriffen worden. Die zentrale Annahme ist hier, dass sprachliche Stimuli als vollspezifizierte Exemplare im Langzeitgedächtnis abgelegt werden, die als Referenzen für die Kategorisierung neuer Stimuli bei der Sprachwahrnehmung und als Ziele bei der Sprachproduktion dienen können. Die Repräsentation der Exemplare enthält phonetische Details, Informationen über den sprachlichen Kontext und den Sprecher und über die kommunikative Situation. Die Exemplarrepräsentation sprachlicher Kategorien wird ständig aktualisiert und ist sensitiv gegenüber Effekten der Auftretenshäufigkeit, die für diverse linguistische Domänen und phonetische Parameter dokumentiert worden sind [3, 4, 5, 10, 16]. Die Varianz der Realisierungen sprachlicher Kategorien drückt sich in der statistischen Verteilung ihrer Exemplare entlang zahlreicher Dimensionen aus.

Eine Herausforderung für Exemplarmodelle ist es zu erklären, wie Exemplare sprachlicher Kategorien auf unterschiedlichen strukturellen Beschreibungsebenen (z.B. Laute, Silben, Wörter) miteinander interagieren und wie sich Exemplare kleinerer Einheiten zu solchen größerer Ein-

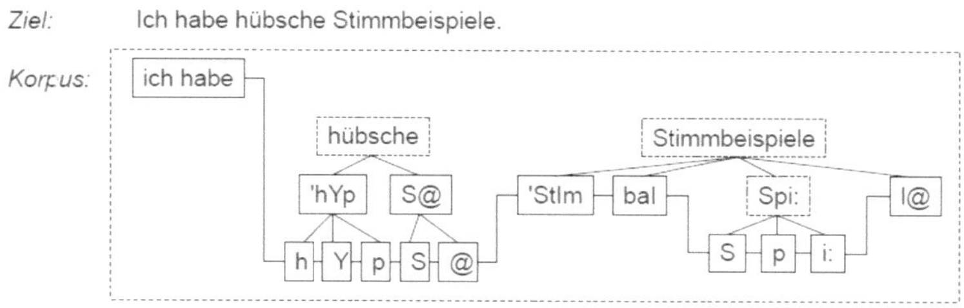

Abbildung 1 - Non-Uniform Unit Selection: Zur Abdeckung der Zieläußerung werden Einheiten im Korpus entlang einer linguistischen Hierarchie gesucht. Wenn auf einer höheren Ebene (z.B. Wort) keine Kandidaten gefunden werden, wird die Suche auf einer niedrigeren Ebene (z.B. Silbe) fortgesetzt.

heiten verbinden. Die Interaktion solcher Einheiten auf unterschiedlichen Ebenen ist eine wichtige Charakteristik der Sprache. Sie ist auch Kern der Strategie der *Non-Uniform Unit Selection* in der Sprachsynthese [20, 22, 24, 26].

2 Sprachproduktion und Sprachsynthese

In den folgenden Abschnitten wird zunächst die als *Unit Selection* bekannte Synthesemethode mit ihren für die Zwecke dieses Artikels relevanten Eigenschaften charakterisiert. Anschließend werden zwei komputationelle Modelle der Sprachproduktion vorgestellt, die im theoretischen und konzeptionellen Rahmen der Exemplartheorie entwickelt wurden und für die Weiterentwicklung der Sprachsynthese potenziell interessante Konzepte und Ergebnisse bieten.

2.1 *Unit Selection*–Synthese

Sprachsynthese nach der Methode der *Unit Selection* [6, 25] wählt aus einem Korpus akustische Einheiten aus, die nach erfolgter Verkettung eine gegebene Zieläußerung optimal repräsentieren. Bei der Auswahl werden die akustischen Einheiten danach bewertet, ob sie gute Repräsentanten der jeweiligen Zieleinheit sind und sich zugleich gut mit den benachbarten Einheiten verketten lassen. Bei der Berechnung der Zielkosten werden akustische, phonetische und linguistische Eigenschaften des Kandidaten selbst sowie die des Kontextes einbezogen. Die Verkettungskosten basieren auf der akustischen Diskontinuität, die bei der Verkettung von je zwei Einheiten entsteht.

Viele *Unit Selection*–Systeme verwenden (sub)segmentale Einheiten (Demiphone, Phone, Diphone) als Basiseinheit. Längere Sequenzen, z.B. Silben, Wörter oder ganze Phrasen, werden bei der Auswahl insofern indirekt begünstigt, als im Korpus bereits adjazente Laute keine Verkettungskosten verursachen. Einige Ansätze zielen auf eine unmittelbarere Auswahl größerer Bausteine ab, indem sie das Korpus entlang einer hierarchischen linguistischen Repräsentation von oben nach unten durchsuchen. Wenn auf einer höheren Ebene (z.B. Wort) keine Kandidaten gefunden werden, wird die Suche auf einer niedrigeren Ebene (z.B. Silbe) fortgesetzt. Die Zielspezifikationen werden ebenenspezifisch formuliert, und die Verkettungskosten zwischen zwei längeren Einheiten entsprechen den Kosten der Verkettung der beiden Lautsegmente an der Verkettungsstelle. Solche Verfahren werden häufig als *Non-Uniform Unit Selection* bezeichnet [20, 22, 24, 26] (Abb. 1). Sie sind am besten für eingeschränkte Anwendungsdomänen geeignet, in denen viele längere Einheiten bereits im Korpus enthalten sind, und sind weniger effizient

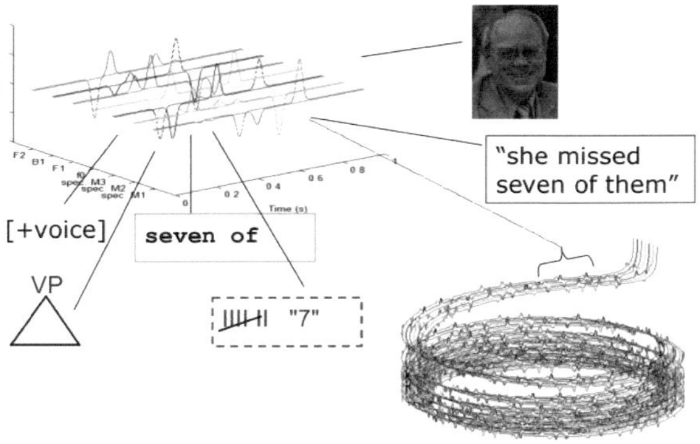

Abbildung 2 - Context Sequence Model: Exemplare sind entlang vieler akustischer, linguistischer und außersprachlicher Dimensionen spezifiziert und bilden ein episodisches Gedächtnis in Form einer langen Sequenz analysierter sprachlicher Ereignisse [28].

in unbeschränkten Domänen, in denen häufig auf die kleinsten, (sub)segmentalen Einheiten zurückgegriffen werden muss.

Die Algorithmen der Einheitenauswahl in *Unit Selection*–Systemen sind nicht an Modellen der Sprachproduktion und nur bedingt, nämlich durch auditorische Skalierung akustischer Parameter, an Erfordernissen der Sprachwahrnehmung orientiert.

2.2 Exemplarbasierte Sprachproduktion

In einem Exemplarmodell der Sprachproduktion dienen Akkumulationen von Exemplaren, die die Zielkategorie repräsentieren, als Produktionsziele [19, 23]. Zur Konstruktion der Produktionsziele werden diejenigen Exemplare herangezogen, die der Zieleinheit im gegebenen Kontext optimal entsprechen. Bei Kategorien mit hoher Auftretenshäufigkeit ist es wahrscheinlich, dass zahlreiche passende Exemplare zur Verfügung stehen. Das daraus gebildete Produktionsziel und das auf dieser Grundlage neu produzierte Exemplar ist somit früheren Realisierungen ähnlich. Die empirisch beobachtete höhere Variabilität hochfrequenter Kategorien im Vergleich zu seltenen Kategorien [23] ist darauf zurückzuführen, dass Exemplare von Kategorien mit hoher Auftretenshäufigkeit in sehr vielen unterschiedlichen Kontexten vorkommen, was die Entstehung von Kategorien mit großer, aber systematischer Variabilität begünstigt.

Im folgenden sollen zwei implementierte Exemplarmodelle vorgestellt werden, die eine komputationelle Simulation von Aspekten der Sprachproduktion erlauben.

Im **Context Sequence Model** (CSM) [28, 29] werden akustische Ziele der Sprachproduktion durch die Auswahl von Einheiten aus einem Gedächtnisspeicher bestimmt. Der Speicher enthält eine große Anzahl früher wahrgenommener (oder produzierter) sprachlicher Einheiten, die sowohl abstrakt (phonologisch) indiziert als auch entlang vieler akustischer Dimensionen spezifiziert sind (Abb. 2). Die Signale im Gedächtnisspeicher entsprechen langen Sequenzen kontinuierlicher Sprache, so dass individuelle Sprachlaute immer in einem größeren Kontext auftreten. Eine zentrale Eigenschaft des Modells besteht darin, dass die Auswahl von Exemplaren für die Produktion auf einer Bewertung der Ähnlichkeit zwischen dem Kontext, in dem sie ursprünglich aufgetreten waren, und dem aktuellen Produktionskontext beruht.

Simulationen der Sprachproduktion mit realistischen akustischen Daten zeigen, dass die opti-

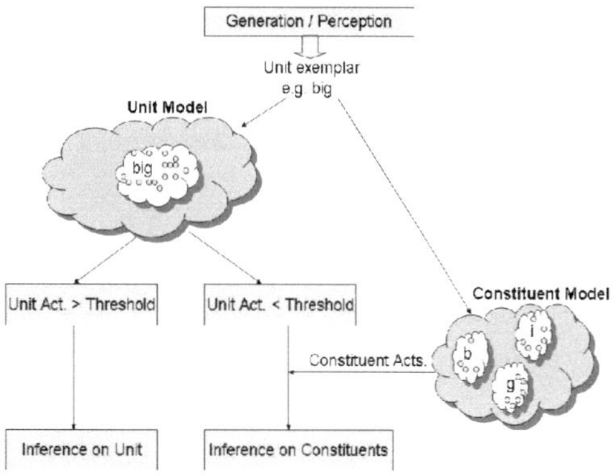

Abbildung 3 - Multilevel Exemplar Model: Interaktion zwischen Einheiten auf unterschiedlichen linguistischen Ebenen; hier: Verarbeitung von Silben als Einheit bzw. als Sequenz der sie konstituierenden Einzellaute, in Abhängigkeit von der Aktivierungsstärke oder Auftretenshäufigkeit [30].

male Auswahl von kontextadäquaten Einheiten auf Lautebene die Berücksichtigung eines linken und rechten Kontextes von etwa 1 Sekunde, zentriert um den Ziellaut, erfordert. Die Ergebnisse legen außerdem die Interpretation nahe, dass die kontextabhängige Produktion auf der Lautebene einige Effekte der Auftretenshäufigkeit bedingt, die bislang als Effekte auf Silben-, Wort- und anderen höheren Ebenen der sprachlichen Organisation betrachtet wurden [28]. Das CSM sieht keine separaten Ebenen für Exemplare von Lauten, Silben, Wörtern oder Phrasen vor. Das episodische Exemplargedächtnis ist einfach eine lange Sequenz analysierter sprachlicher Ereignisse.

Das CSM zeigt, wie die Sprachproduktion unmittelbar durch phonetisches Wissen beeinflusst wird. Das Modell ist jedoch unvollständig, da die Simulationen nur die Akustik des lautlichen Kontextes berücksichtigen, ohne die zugrunde liegenden Artikulationsprozesse einzubeziehen. Damit ist keineswegs impliziert, dass phonetisches Wissen vorrangig akustisch oder auditorisch ist. Im Gegenteil, das Modell sollte dahingehend erweitert werden, dass die Simulationen auch artikulatorische Prozesse und Beschränkungen bei der Sprachproduktion integrieren [7].

Das **Multilevel Exemplar Model** (MLM) [30, 31] wurde entwickelt, um die Interaktion zwischen Einheiten auf unterschiedlichen hierarchischen Ebenen linguistischer Domänen zu untersuchen. Es erlaubt eine Simulation experimenteller Daten, die bislang für zwei Phänomene durchgeführt wurde: die Variabilität von Silbendauern in der gesprochenen Sprache sowie eine exemplarbasierte Fundierung von Grammatikalitätsurteilen in der Syntax [21]. In der phonetischen Domäne wurde das MLM zur Modellierung von Effekten der Auftretenshäufigkeit auf Laut- und Silbenenebene verwendet. Produktionsstudien zeigen, dass häufige Silben variabler sind als seltene Silben [23]. Dieser Effekt der Auftretenshäufigkeit wird von exemplarbasierten Simulationen im Rahmen des MLM bestätigt [30].

Experimentelle Ergebnisse anhand großer lautsprachlicher Korpora legen die Interpretation nahe, dass die Variabilität von Silbendauern eine Funktion der Variabilität der involvierten Lautdauern ist – allerdings nur in Silben mit geringer Auftretenshäufigkeit. Hingegen konnte die Variabilität der Dauern häufiger Silben nicht direkt aus den Dauern der Einzellaute vorhergesagt werden [23]. Die Ergebnisse der MLM-basierten Simulationen untermauern die Hypothese, dass häufige Silben in der Sprachproduktion als eigenständige Einheiten verarbeitet werden, während seltene Silben durch sequenzielle Verarbeitung der sie konstituierenden Laute produziert werden [30, 31] (Abb. 3). Diese Ergebnisse sind mit den Konzepten des *Mental Syllabary* [15], einer Komponente des psycholinguistischen Sprachproduktionsmodells von Levelt und Kollegen [12, 13, 14], und des *Dual Pathway* mit Wettbewerb zwischen Einheitensequenzen auf mehreren Ebenen [32] kompatibel.

Das MLM kann außerdem mit einer Version des CSM in Einklang gebracht werden, in der Intervalle der Exemplargedächtnis-Sequenz bezüglich sprachlicher Kategorien annotiert sind, wobei die Intervalle überlappen und ineinander eingebettet sein können.

3 Synergien und ihre Grenzen

Die Exemplartheorie ist teilweise durch die Beobachtung motiviert, dass nicht alle Elemente der Sprache originell und produktiv sind. Zahlreiche sprachliche Bausteine, die wir produzieren und wahrnehmen, sind vorfabrizierte und wiederverwertbare Versatzstücke [2]. Die Herausforderung liegt in der kontextuell adäquaten Auswahl und Resequenzierung der verfügbaren Bausteine. Ein wichtiger Unterschied zwischen einer Konzeptualisierung der Sprachproduktion etwa im Sinn des *Context Sequence Model* und der korpusbasierten konkatenative Synthese liegt darin, dass die Exemplarbasis kontinuierlich durch Verarbeitung neuer Exemplare aktualisiert wird, während das Sprachkorpus des *Unit Selection*–Systems statisch ist. Bei der Sprachsynthese kommt es also darauf an, schon beim Design des Sprachkorpus eine optimale Abdeckung der Zieldomäne – in der Regel der gesamten Zielsprache – anzustreben. Aber auch die Einheitenauswahl zur Laufzeit kann anhand erfolgreicher Simulationen durch Exemplarmodelle modifiziert werden.

Sprachkorpora von *Unit Selection*–Systemen, einmal aufgezeichnet und annotiert, sind statisch. Im Unterschied dazu wird die Exemplarbasis in der menschlichen Sprachverarbeitung kontinuierlich durch Wahrnehmung und Produktion neuer Exemplare aktualisiert. Exemplarmodelle arbeiten außerdem häufig mit einem Konzept von dynamischer Aktivierung: Die Stärke der Aktivierung gespeicherter Exemplare, die ansonsten mit fortschreitender Zeit sinkt, wird durch Verwendung hinreichend ähnlicher Exemplare wieder angehoben. Dies führt dazu, das Exemplare häufiger Kategorien, die in häufigen Kontexten auftreten, als Referenz für wahrgenommene Exemplare und als Ziele für aktuelle Produktionen in großer Zahl zur Verfügung stehen. Seltene Exemplare hingegen sinken allmählich auf ein Niveau, das sie – ohne weitere Modellannahmen – nicht wieder aktivierbar macht. Auf diese Weise werden in der Exemplartheorie Phänomene wie individueller Lautwandel oder gar Kategorienverfall modelliert [19]. Exemplarbasierte Sprachproduktion beruht also auf der Ähnlichkeit, Häufigkeit und Neuigkeit von Exemplaren.

Grundsätzlich ließe sich in der Sprachsynthese ein Mechanismus der dynamischen Aktivierung von Korpusbausteinen auf der Basis der Häufigkeit ihrer Verwendung durchaus implementieren. Zwei Probleme müssten dabei gelöst werden. Zum einen kann die Verwendung immer wieder derselben Bausteine in häufig auftretenden Konstellationen zu einem Grad an Invarianz führen, der in der menschlichen Sprachproduktion aufgrund inhärenter Ungenauigkeiten des Artikulationsprozesses nicht entstehen kann. In exemplarbasierten Produktionsmodellen werden zumeist Zufallsvariationen der Realisierung ausgewählter Einheiten als triviale Implementierung der artikulatorischen Variabilität eingesetzt. In der Synthese würde ein solcher Mechanismus zusätzliche Signalverarbeitungsschritte erfordern, um häufig ausgewählte Bausteine künstlich zu variieren. Damit würde jedoch eine der grundlegenden Motivationen für *Unit Selection*–Synthese, die weitgehende Vermeidung von Signalverarbeitung, konterkariert. Zum anderen müsste sicher gestellt werden, dass selten verwendete Bausteine dennoch weiterhin für seltene Konstellationen zur Verfügung stehen. Bekanntlich ist die kumulative Wahrscheinlichkeitsmasse sprachlicher Ereignisse, die jedes für sich extrem unwahrscheinlich sind, so hoch, dass seltene Ereignisse nicht generell vernachlässigt werden dürfen [17, 27]. Dies wäre durch die Vermeidung einer Mindestaktivierungsschwelle vermutlich einfach zu erreichen.

Exemplarmodelle nehmen an, dass verarbeitete und gespeicherte Exemplare entlang vieler Dimensionen spezifiziert sind (Abb. 2). Zu diesen Dimensionen gehören akustische Eigenschaften, phonologische Kategorien, linguistische Strukturen (morphologische Struktur, Wortklasse, syntaktische und semantische Information), indexikalische Sprecherinformation bis hin zu Informationen über die kommunikative Situation. Bei weitem nicht alle diese Informationen lassen sich im Sprachsynthesekorpus annotieren, sei es aus praktischen oder theoretischen Gründen. Schwerer wiegt der Umstand, dass – zumindest im klassischen *Text-to-Speech*–Szenario – aus dem Text allein keine Zielspezifikation erstellt werden kann, die indexikalische und außersprachliche Information enthält. Dies gilt zum Teil auch für semantische und pragmatische Informationen.

Dass selbst eine partielle Berücksichtigung einer um kontextuelle Information erweiterten Zielspezifikation die Synthese verbessern kann, zeigt eine Implementierung des *Multilevel Exemplar Model* zum Zweck der exemplarbasierten Lautdauermodellierung in expressiver Sprachsynthese. Die so generierten Stimuli wurden in Perzeptionstests besser beurteilt als die herkömmlich synthetisierten Stimuli: Die exemplarbasierte Synthese klang eher wie ein echter Sprecher, gab die Sprecherintentionen besser wieder, klang flüssiger und erweckte eher den Eindruck einer konversationellen Sprache [1].

4 Ausblick

Dieser Artikel befasste sich mit Analogien und parallelen Konzepten zwischen Exemplarmodellen der Sprachproduktion und korpusbasierter Synthese und diskutierte mögliche Synergien, aber auch die Grenzen der Synergien. Diese Grenzen liegen zum ersten in der Statik von Sprachsynthesekorpora, zum zweiten in der Dimensionalität der Eigenschaften sprachlicher Einheiten und zum dritten in der Repräsentation des außersprachlichen Kontextes. Simulationen und erste Experimente stützen jedoch die Erwartung, dass exemplarbasierte Modelle von Prozessen der menschlichen Sprachverarbeitung interessante Konzepte für die Weiterentwicklung der Sprachsynthese und generell für die Implementierung sprachtechnologischer Verfahren bieten können.

Literatur

[1] ABOU-ZLEIKHA, M., É. SZÉKELY, P. CAHILL und J. CARSON-BERNDSEN: *Multi-level exemplar-based duration generation for expressive speech synthesis.* In: *Proceedings of Speech Prosody 2012 (Shanghai)*, 2012.

[2] BYBEE, J.: *From usage to grammar: The mind's response to repetition.* Language, 84:529–551, 2006.

[3] BYBEE, J. und J. SCHEIBMAN: *The effect of usage on degrees of constituency: the reduction of don't in English.* Linguistics, 37(4):575–596, 1999.

[4] CARREIRAS, M. A. und M. B. PEREA: *Naming pseudowords in Spanish: Effects of syllable frequency.* Brain and Language, 90:393–400, 2004.

[5] CHOLIN, J., W. J. M. LEVELT und N. O. SCHILLER: *Effects of syllable frequency in speech production.* Cognition, 99(2):205–235, 2006.

[6] CLARK, R. A. J., K. RICHMOND und S. KING: *Multisyn: Open-domain unit selection for the Festival speech synthesis system.* Speech Communication, 49(4):317–330, 2007.

[7] DURAN, D., J. BRUNI, H. SCHÜTZE und G. DOGIL: *Context Sequence Model of speech production enriched with articulatory features.* In: *Proceedings of the 17th International Congress of Phonetic Sciences (Hong Kong)*, S. 615–618, 2011.

[8] GOLDINGER, S. D.: *Words and voices—Perception and production in an episodic lexicon.* In: JOHNSON, K. und J. W. MULLENNIX (Hrsg.): *Talker Variability in Speech Processing*, S. 33–66. Academic Press, San Diego, 1997.

[9] JOHNSON, K.: *Speech perception without speaker normalization: An exemplar model.* In: JOHNSON, K. und J. W. MULLENNIX (Hrsg.): *Talker Variability in Speech Processing*, S. 145–165. Academic Press, San Diego, 1997.

[10] JURAFSKY, D., A. BELL, M. GREGORY und W. D. RAYMOND: *Probabilistic relations between words: Evidence from reduction in lexical production.* In: BYBEE, J. und P. HOPPER (Hrsg.): *Frequency and the Emergence of Linguistic Structure*, S. 229–254. Benjamins, Amsterdam, 2001.

[11] KRUSCHKE, J. K.: *ALCOVE: An exemplar-based connectionist model of category learning.* Psychological Review, 99(1):22–44, 1992.

[12] LEVELT, W. J. M.: *Speaking: From Intention to Articulation.* MIT Press, Cambridge, MA, 1989.

[13] LEVELT, W. J. M.: *Producing spoken language: a blueprint of the speaker.* In: BROWN, C. M. und P. HAGOORT (Hrsg.): *The Neurocognition of Language*, S. 83–122. Oxford University Press, Oxford, UK, 1999.

[14] LEVELT, W. J. M., A. ROELOFS und A. S. MEYER: *A theory of lexical access in speech production.* Behavioral and Brain Sciences, 22:1–75, 1999.

[15] LEVELT, W. J. M. und L. WHEELDON: *Do speakers have access to a mental syllabary?.* Cognition, 50:239–269, 1994.

[16] LOSIEWICZ, B. L.: *The Effect of Frequency on Linguistic Morphology.* Doktorarbeit, University of Texas, Austin, TX, 1992.

[17] MÖBIUS, B.: *Rare events and closed domains: Two delicate concepts in speech synthesis.* International Journal of Speech Technology, 6(1):57–71, 2003.

[18] NOSOFSKY, R. M.: *Attention, similarity, and the identification-categorization relationship.* Journal of Experimental Psychology: General, 115(1):39–57, 1986.

[19] PIERREHUMBERT, J.: *Exemplar dynamics: Word frequency, lenition and contrast.* In: BYBEE, J. und P. HOPPER (Hrsg.): *Frequency and the Emergence of Linguistic Structure*, S. 137–157. Benjamins, Amsterdam, 2001.

[20] SAGISAKA, Y.: *Speech synthesis by rule using an optimal selection of non-uniform synthesis units.* In: *Proceedings of the IEEE International Conference on Acoustics and Speech Signal Processing (New York, NY)*, S. 679–682, 1988.

[21] SCHÜTZE, H., M. WALSH, B. MÖBIUS und T. WADE: *Towards a unified exemplar-theoretic model of phonetic and syntactic phenomena.* In: *Proceedings of the 29th Meeting of the Cognitive Science Society (CogSci 2007, Nashville, TN)*, S. 1461–1466, 2007.

[22] SCHWEITZER, A., N. BRAUNSCHWEILER, T. KLANKERT, B. MÖBIUS und B. SÄUBERLICH: *Restricted unlimited domain synthesis.* In: *Proceedings of Eurospeech-2003 (Geneva)*, S. 1321–1324, 2003.

[23] SCHWEITZER, A. und B. MÖBIUS: *Exemplar-based production of prosody: Evidence from segment and syllable durations.* In: *Speech Prosody 2004 (Nara, Japan)*, S. 459–462, 2004.

[24] STÖBER, K., P. WAGNER, J. HELBIG, S. KÖSTER, D. STALL, M. THOMAE, J. BLAUERT, W. HESS, R. HOFFMANN und H. MANGOLD: *Speech synthesis using multilevel selection and concatenation of units from large speech corpora.* In: WAHLSTER, W. (Hrsg.): *Verbmobil: Foundations of Speech-to-Speech Translation*, S. 519–534. Springer, Berlin, 2000.

[25] TAYLOR, P.: *Text-to-Speech Synthesis.* Cambridge University Press, 2009.

[26] TAYLOR, P. und A. W. BLACK: *Speech synthesis by phonological structure matching.* In: *Proceedings of the European Conference on Speech Communication and Technology (Budapest, Hungary)*, Bd. 2, S. 623–626, 1999.

[27] VAN SANTEN, J. P. H.: *Combinatorial issues in text-to-speech synthesis.* In: *Proceedings of the European Conference on Speech Communication and Technology (Rhodos, Greece)*, Bd. 5, S. 2511–2514, 1997.

[28] WADE, T., G. DOGIL, H. SCHÜTZE, M. WALSH und B. MÖBIUS: *Syllable frequency effects in a context-sensitive segment production model.* Journal of Phonetics, 38(2):905–945, 2010.

[29] WADE, T. und B. MÖBIUS: *Speaking rate effects in a landmark-based phonetic exemplar model.* In: *Proceedings of Interspeech 2007 (Antwerpen)*, S. 402–405, 2007.

[30] WALSH, M., B. MÖBIUS, T. WADE und H. SCHÜTZE: *Multilevel Exemplar Theory.* Cognitive Science, 34:537–582, 2010.

[31] WALSH, M., H. SCHÜTZE, B. MÖBIUS und T. WADE: *Accounting for phonetic and syntactic phenomena in a multi-level competitive interaction model.* In: *ESSLLI Workshop on Exemplar Based Models of Language Acquisition and Use (Dublin)*, S. 22–31, 2007.

[32] WHITESIDE, S. P. und R. A. VARLEY: *Dual-Route Phonetic Encoding: Some Acoustic Evidence.* In: *Proceedings of the 5th International Conference on Spoken Language Processing (Sydney)*, Bd. 7, S. 3155–3158, 1998.

Stille Post mit UASR

Frank Duckhorn, Guntram Strecha

Institut für Akustik und Sprachkommunikation
Technische Universität Dresden

Kurzfassung: Spracherkennung wie auch Sprachsynthese sind Gebiete intensiver Forschung. In beiden Gebieten werden Sprachsignale auf verschiedenen Ebenen modelliert und zwischen diesen transformiert. Mittlerweile gibt es für beide Aufgaben Lösungen, welche unter bestimmten Voraussetzungen zufriedenstellend funktionieren. Was liegt nun näher, als einen Spracherkenner und einen Sprachsynthetisator auf der Ebene des akustischen Signals und der Ebene der textuellen Repräsentation zu koppeln. Damit entsteht ein autonomes System, welches nach einer Initialisierung mit einem Sprachabschnitt, diesen iterativ synthetisiert und erkennt. Praktisch wird dadurch das berühmte Gesellschaftsspiel „Stille Post" simuliert. Dieser Beitrag stellt ein System vor mit dem eine solche Simulation möglich ist. Außerdem werden Experimente mit verschiedenen Störungen präsentiert.

1 Motivation

Am Institut für Akustik und Sprachkommunikation der Technischen Universität Dresden wurde in den letzten Jahrzehnten ein System entwickelt welches Sprachsynthese und -erkennung vereinigen soll. Ziel war möglichst die gleichen Datenbanken und Modelle für beide Verfahren zu verwendet. Das System wurde Unified Approach to Speech Synthesis and Recognition (UASR) genannt [4]. Dieser Beitrag benutzt die Verfahren zur Synthese und Erkennung von Sprache, um das Gesellschaftsspiel „Stille Post" mit einem PC zu simulieren.

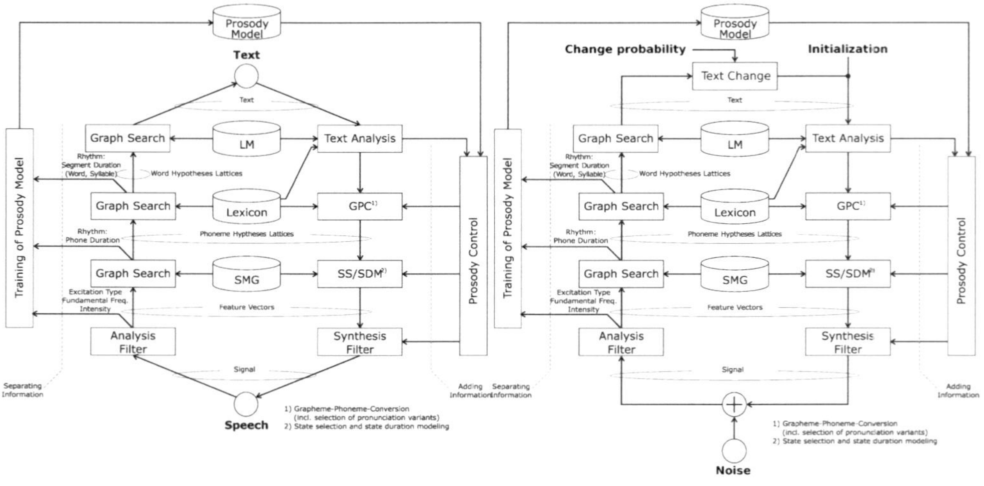

(a) Original UASR (b) Stille Post Ansatz

Abbildung 1 - Änderungen am UASR System für Realisierung der Stillen Post

Die Ablauf des Spiels ist folgender:

- Ein Spieler denkt sich einen Satz aus
- Dieser wird reihum dem Nachbar zugeflüstert, so dass kein anderer mithören kann.
- Anschließend wird der letzte Satz mit dem ursprünglichen verglichen.

Dabei treten im wesentlichen zwei Störfaktoren auf. Zum Ersten ist durch das Flüstern die Verständlichkeit der Sprache stark beeinflusst. Zum Anderen verändert sich der Satz, weil sich die Spieler unter Umständen das Gerhörte nicht exakt einprägen.
Die Simulation soll den Ablauf sowie die Störfaktoren möglichst genau nachbilden. Anstatt der Sätze haben wir gesprochene 9-stellige Zahlen mit drei Nachkommenstellen verwendet. Weiterhin haben wir das UASR System ergänzt. In der Abbildung 1 ist das ursprüngliche und das geänderte System gegenübergestellt. Das System wurde um einen Kurzschluss auf der Ebene des akustischen Signals und auf textueller Ebene erweitert. Nach der Initialisierung mit einer zufällig erzeugten Zahl, wird diese durch die Synthese in ein Sprachsignal gewandelt. Dieses wird anschließend mit weißem Rauschen überlagert. Das Rauschen simuliert die schlechte Verständlichkeit. Das Verhältnis von Signalpegel und Rauschpegel (SNR) ist einstellbar. Anschließend wird das verrauschte Signal erkannt. Bei der erkannten Zahl werden nun einzelne Ziffern der Zahl mit einer Wahrscheinlichkeit P_{chg} geändert. Diese Wahrscheinlichkeit gibt an, wie wahrscheinlich es ist, dass sich die Ziffer ändert. Falls eine Ziffer geändert wird sind alle anderen Ziffern gleich wahrscheinlich. Formel 1 gibt die Wahrscheinlichkeit der Ziffer Z'_k an der k-ten Stelle in Abhängigkeit der ursprünglichen Ziffer Z_k an. Die Wahrscheinlichkeit P_{chg} simuliert somit das Vergessen der Spieler. Abschließend wird die geänderte Zahl mit der ursprünglichen Zahl verglichen und eine Erkennungsrate bestimmt. Die Prozedur wird über mehrere Iterationen wiederholt.

$$p(Z'_k) = \begin{cases} 1 - P_{chg} & : Z'_k = Z_k \\ \frac{P_{chg}}{9} & : Z'_k \neq Z_k \end{cases} \qquad (1)$$

In den folgenden beiden Abschnitten werden die eingesetzten Verfahren zur Sprachsynthese und -erkennung näher beleuchtet. Anschließend folgt eine Auswertung der erzielten Ergebnisse.

2 Sprachsynthese

Die Sprachsignale wurden mit einer konkatenativen akustischen Synthese erzeugt. Das verwendete Inventar besteht aus HMM-kodierten Diphonen [6]. Die zur Erstellung des Inventars und zur Synthese verwendeten HM-Modelle stammen vom Erkenner. Das Schema der Erzeugung des Inventars aus den Trägerwörtern der Diphone sowie der akustischen Synthese ist in Abbildung 2 dargestellt.

2.1 Inventarerzeugung

Unter der Voraussetzung, dass die HM-Modelle bereits trainiert worden, sind zur Erzeugung eines HMM-kodierten Inventars folgende Schritte notwendig:

1. Bestimmen der optimalen Zustandsfolge der Trägerwörter durch eine erzwungene Erkennung und Ausschneiden der Diphonkandidaten,
2. Auswahl jeweils eines Diphons aus den Kandidaten anhand des Log-Likelihood der Erkennung,

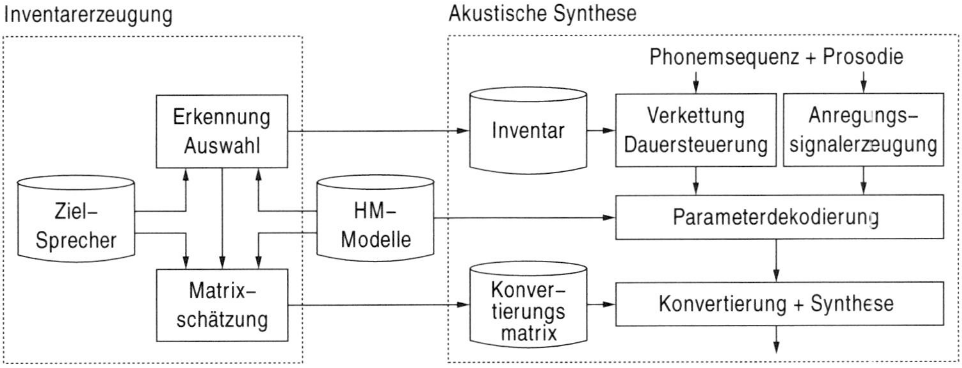

Abbildung 2 - Darstellung der Arbeisweise der akustischen Synthese mit HMM-kodierten Inventaren einschließlich der Inventarerzeugung.

3. Schätzung der Konvertierungsmatrix,
4. Kodieren der ausgewählten Diphone und der Konvertierungsmatrix.

Für jedes ausgewählte Diphone wird die Folge der Indizes, welche den Zuständen und damit den Verteilungsdichten zugeordnet sind, im Inventar gespeichert. Da die Modelle des Erkenners im Allgemeinen von Sprachsignalen einer großen Anzahl an Sprechern trainiert werden, repräsentieren die Modelle einen gemittelten Sprecher. Außerdem bilden die Mittelwerte der Verteilungsdichten der HM-Modelle nicht notwendigerweise zur Sprachsynthese geeignete Parameter. Eine Möglichkeit zur Konvertierung einer gemittelten in eine bestimmte Stimme ist die Adaption der HM-Modelle [9]. Wir verwenden eine einfacheres, aber effektives Verfahren zur Stimmenkonvertierung, welches auch zur Konvertierung der HMM-Parameter in geeignete Syntheseparameter verwendet werden kann [7]. Diese Konvertierung ist eine lineare Transformation der Mittelwerte der Verteilungsdichten, d. h. eine Multiplikation der Mittelwerte mit einer sprecherabhängigen Konvertierungsmatrix.

2.2 Akustische Synthese

Den Eingang der akustischen Synthese bildet die erwünschte Phonemfolge annotiert mit den Zielwerten der Phonemdauern und der Sprechergrundfrequenz. Die Synthese bildet Diphone aus der Phonemfolge, sucht die entsprechenden Indexfolgen der Diphone aus dem Inventar und verkettet diese. Anschließend wird die Parametervektorfolge anhand der Indizes gebildet. Diese wird mit der Konvertierungsmatrix des Zielsprechers multipliziert, um die Folge der Syntheseparameter zu erhalten. In diesem Fall sind die Syntheseparameter das Mel-Cepstrum. Mit dem Mel-Log-Spectrum-Approximation- (MLSA-) Filter nach [3] und nach einer perzeptiven Wichtungs des Cepstrums nach [5] wird daraus das Synthesesignal generiert.

3 Spracherkennung

Der eingesetzte Spracherkenner basiert auf allen Ebenen auf endlichen gewichteten Automaten ([8, 2]). Die Grammatik für 9-stellige deutsche Zahlwörter mit Nachkommastellen wurde in Form eines Automaten implementiert. Dieser Automat verfügt ergänzend über Kellersymbole [1]. Dadurch ist es möglich kontextfreie Grammatiken abzubilden. Für die verwendete

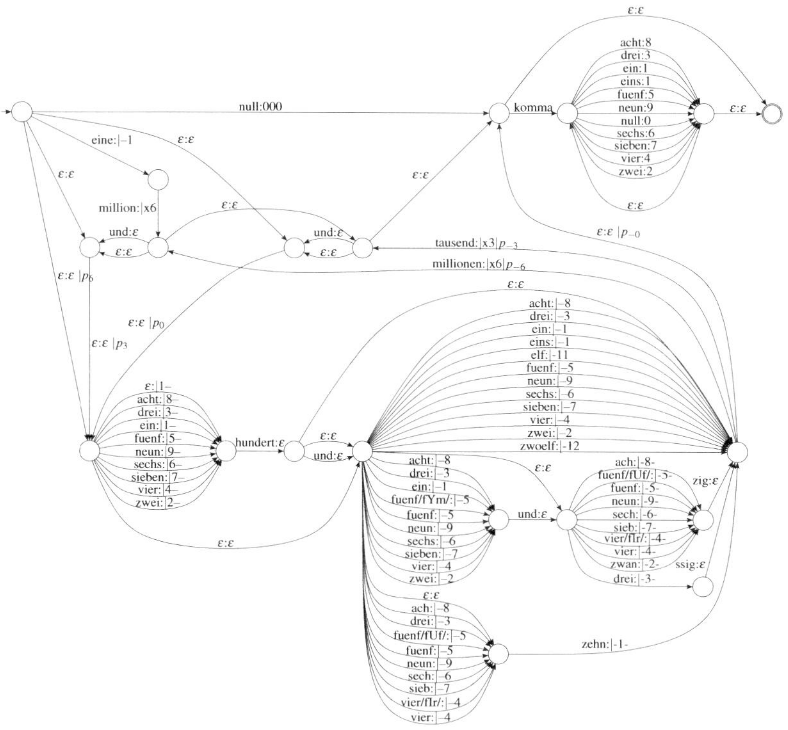

Abbildung 3 - Zahlwortgrammatik für 9-stellige deutsche Zahlen mit Nachkommastellen

Zahlwortgrammatik ergibt sich eine starke Reduktion der Automatengröße. Der Teil des Automaten, welcher 3-stellige Zahlen abbilden kann, wird mehrfach durchlaufen. Vor Beginn dieses Abschnitts markiert ein Kellersymbol, ob es sich um die Millionen, Tausender oder Einer Stelle handelt (p_6,p_3,p_0). Anschließend sind durch die negierten Kellersymbole nur bestimmte Übergänge benutzbar. Die Abbildung 3 zeigt die Grammatik. Anstelle der Übergangsgewichte sind die Kellersymbole dargestellt.

Das Lexikon besteht aus insgesamt 30 Zahlwörtern sowie einer Pause und ist ebenfalls als Automat implementiert. Es basiert auf 43 Phonem Hidden-Markov-Modellen, welche jeweils über 3 Zustände mit einer Mischverteilung aus 8 Normalverteilungen verfügen. Die Normalverteilungen werden mit vollen Kovarianzmatrizen eingesetzt. Sie modellieren die sekundären Merkmale. Diese entstehen durch Erweiterung um dynamische Merkmale sowie durch Reduktion mittels Hauptkomponentenanalyse aus den primären Merkmale. Letzter sind die logarithmierten Werte einer MEL-Filterbank.

4 Experimente

Mit dem beschriebenen Synthetisator und Erkenner wurden verschiedene Experimente durchgeführt. Dabei wurde jeweils das Signal-Rausch-Verhältnis (SNR) des eingebrachten weißen Rauschens sowie die Wahrscheinlichkeit mit der sich einzelne Ziffern ändern (P_{chg}) variiert. Insgesamt wurden jeweils zehn Iterationen durchlaufen und die Zahl jeder Iteration mit der ursprünglichen Zahl verglichen. Die Tabelle 1 zeigt vier Beispiele für Zahlen bei unterschiedlicher Konfiguration. Bei starker akustischer Störung (SNR=10dB) ergibt sich eine stark geänderte Zahl. Es werden hauptsächlich Ziffern erkannt deren Aussprache dem Rauschen ähnelt (vier, fünf).

SNR / P_{chg}		10dB 0%	20dB 0%	30dB 0%	30dB 5%
	Ori	161416076,664	835585884,206	585395118,027	665126427,851
Iteration	1	411500,454	135585444,204	585395118,027	665126627,841
	2	405500,454	135585444,204	585395118,027	665126627,841
	3	405500,454	135545444,204	585195118,027	665126627,841
	4	405500,454	135545444,204	585195118,027	665126627,841
	5	405500,454	135545444,204	585195118,027	665126627,241
	6	405500,454	135545444,204	585195118,027	665126627,241
	7	405500,454	135545444,204	585195118,027	665129627,241
	8	405500,454	135545444,204	585195118,027	635129627,241
	9	405500,454	135545444,204	585195118,027	635129627,241
	10	405500,454	135545444,204	585195118,027	635129627,241

Tabelle 1 - Beispiele für Änderung der Zahlen bei verschiedenen Parametern

Für jede Konfiguration wurde diese Prozedur für 500 Zahlen wiederholt. Anschließend wurde für die einzelnen Iterationen die Rate falscher Zahlen bestimmt. Diese gibt an, wieviele der 500 Zahlen nicht mehr der ursprünglichen Zahl entsprechen. In der Abbildung 4 sind die Ergebnisse für verschiedene akustische Störungen dargestellt. Es fällt auf, das bei starker Störung (SNR=20…30dB) die Fehlerrate sich nach der ersten Iteration nur noch gering ändert. Der Hauptteil der neuer Zahlenfehler geschieht in der ersten Iteration. Das Verhalten ist das gleiche wie im ersten Beispiel in der Tabelle 1. Nach den ersten Iterationen ist eine Zahl gefunden worden, die trotz Störung robust wiedererkannt wird. Daher gibt es deutlich weniger Änderungen in den folgenden Iterationen. Ohne Störung treten keine Fehler auf. Weil Erkenner und Synthetisator auf die gleichen Modelle zurückgreifen, funktioniert die Wiedererkennung perfekt.

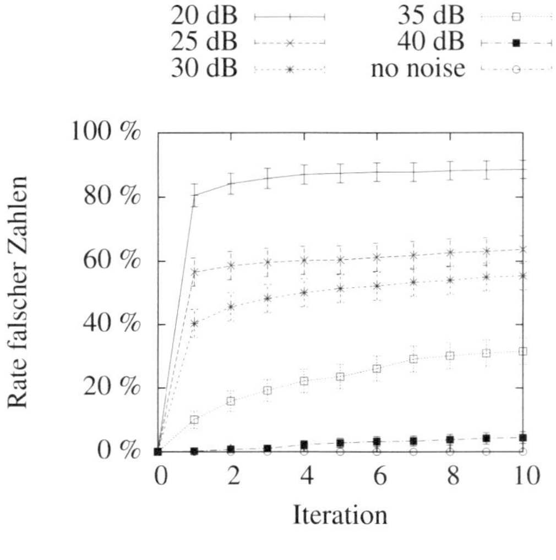

Abbildung 4 - Rate falscher Zahlen für verschiedene akustische Störungen, ohne Ziffernänderung

Wenn man nun beide Störquellen (akustische und textuelle) berücksichtigt erhält man ein anderes Bild. Die Abbildung 5 zeigt die Rate falscher Zahlen für eine akustische Störung mit

SNR=30dB und 50dB sowie mit variierter Wahrscheinlichkeit der Ziffernänderung (P_{chg}). Das Bild gleicht nun eher dem, was wir von der Stillen Post erwartet hätten. Nämlich, dass die Rate falscher Zahlen mit steigender Anzahl von Iterationen weiter ansteigt. Falls man dieses Verhalten auch bei einem realem Spiel „Stille Post“ beobachten könnte, würde es zeigen, dass der Einfluss des Gedächtnisses der Spieler leicht über dem der Sprachverständlichkeit liegt.

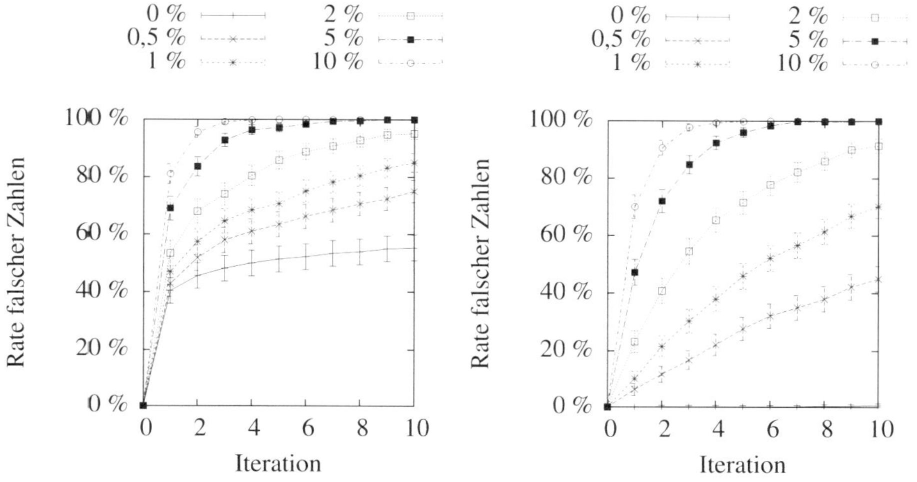

(a) SNR=30dB (b) SNR=50dB

Abbildung 5 - Rate falscher Zahlen mit Ziffernänderung und akustischer Störung

Abschließend ist in der Abbildung 6 die Verwechslungsmatrix für einzelne Ziffern dargestellt. Dabei wurde eine akustische Störung mit SNR=20dB ohne Ziffernänderung verwendet. Die Matrix wurde mit den Werten der 10. Iteration erzeugt. Man sieht, dass sehr häufig anstatt einer acht ein vier und anstatt einer 3 eine 1 erkannt wird. Außerdem fällt auf, dass alle Zahlen häufig als null erkannt werden. Das ist darin begründet, dass die Zahl im Lauf der Iterationen gelegentlich kürzer wird und somit die höhsten Stellen null werden. Dass eine Zahl umgekehrt wieder länger wird, ist hingegen kaum zu erwarten.

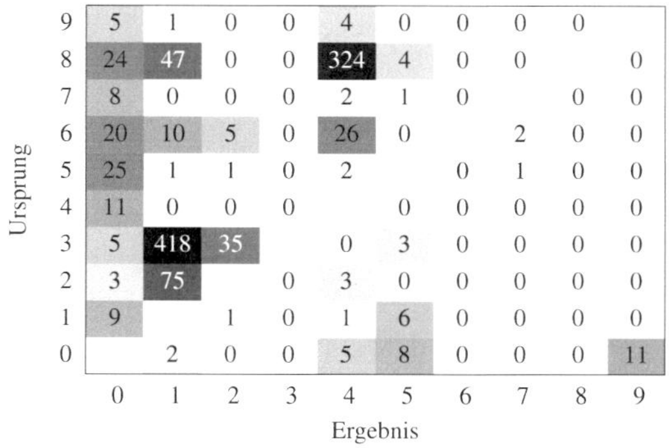

Abbildung 6 - Verwechslungsmatrix einzelner Ziffern SNR=20dB, keine Ziffernänderung, Iteration 10

5 Zusammenfassung

Wir haben gezeigt, dass es möglich ist mit dem UASR das Spiel „Stille Post“ zu simulieren. Interessanterweise hat die akustischen Störung einen anderen Einfluss, wie man von Spiel erwartet. Der Zahl ändert sich nach den ersten Iterationen nur noch wenig. Die Simulation des Vergessens bildet den erwarteten Verlauf deutlicher ab.

Literatur

[1] DUCKHORN, F., M. WOLFF und R. HOFFMANN: *A new epsilon filter for efficient composition of weighted finite-state transducers.* In: *Proceedings of the 12th Annual Conference of the International Speech Communication Association (Interspeech 2011)*, S. 897–900, Florence, Italy, Sep. 2011.

[2] EICHNER, M., M. WOLFF und R. HOFFMANN: *A unified approach for speech synthesis and speech recognition using stochastic Markov graphs.* In: *Proceedings of the 6th Internation Conference on Spoken Language Processing (ICSLP 2000)*, Bd. 1, S. 701–704, Beijing, China, Okt. 2000.

[3] FUKADA, T., K. TOKUDA, T. KOBAYASHI und S. IMAI: *An adaptive algorithm for mel-cepstral analysis of speech.* In: *Proceedings of IEEE International Conference on Acoustics, Speech, and Signal Processing 1992 (ICASSP '92)*, Bd. 1, S. 137–140, San Francisco, California, USA, März 1992.

[4] HOFFMANN, R., M. EICHNER, S. WERNER und M. WOLFF: *The project UASR (unified approach for speech synthesis and recogition) - a progess report.* In: *Proceedings of 25th DAGM Symposium*, Bd. 2781 d. Reihe *Lecture Notes in Computer Science*, S. 17–24, Magdeburg, Germany, 2003. Springer. ISBN 3-540-40861-4.

[5] KOISHIDA, K., K. TOKUDA, T. KOBAYASHI und S. IMAI: *Efficient encoding of mel-generalized cepstrum for CELP coders.* In: *Proceedings of IEEE International Conference on Acoustics, Speech, and Signal Processing 1997 (ICASSP '97)*, Bd. 2, S. 1355–1358, München, Germany, Apr. 1997.

[6] STRECHA, G. und M. WOLFF: *Speech synthesis using HMM based diphone inventory encoding for low-resource devices.* In: *Proceedings of IEEE International Conference on Acoustics, Speech, and Signal Processing 2011 (ICASSP '11)*, S. 5380–5383, Prague, Czech, Mai 2011.

[7] STRECHA, G., M. WOLFF, F. DUCKHORN, S. WITTENBERG und C. TSCHÖPE: *The HMM Synthesis Algorithm of an Embedded Unified Speech Recognizer and Synthesizer.* In: *Proceedings of the 10th Annual Conference of the International Speech Communication Association (Interspeech 2009)*, S. 1763–1766, Brigthon, United Kingdom, Sep. 2009.

[8] WOLFERTSTETTER, F. und G. RUSK: *Structured Markov Models for Speech Recognition.* In: *Proceedings of IEEE International Conference on Acoustics, Speech, and Signal Processing 1995 (ICASSP '95)*, Bd. 1, S. 544–547, Detroit, Michigan, USA, Mai 1995.

[9] YAMAGISHI, J., K. OGATA, Y. NAKANO, J. ISOGAI und T. KOBAYASHI: *HSMM-Based Model Adaptation Algorithms for Average-Voice-Based Speech Synthesis.* In: *Proceedings of IEEE International Conference on Acoustics, Speech, and Signal Processing 2006 (ICASSP '06)*, Bd. 1, S. 77–80, Toulouse, France, Mai 2006.

Pitch Marking Algorithm using Short-Time Autocorrelation Function and Zero-Phase Filter Bank

Zdravko Kačič

University of Maribor, Faculty of Electrical Engineering and Computer Science, Slovenia
kacic@uni-mb.si

Abstract: A novel pitch marking algorithm using a short-time autocorrelation function and zero-phase band-pass filter bank is proposed. The short-time autocorrelation is used to select the filter bank channel, which contains pitch waveform. By analysing the pitch waveform, the pitch periods are defined, which denote the pitch segments. The mapping of the pitch segment to the speech signal is performed to define the region of pitch mark, where the pitch mark is defined as a negative peak within the pitch segment. The evaluation of the proposed method was performed using the ECESS evaluation framework. The experimental results showed good success rate and robustness of the proposed method, especially for moderate signal/noise ratios. Further analysis showed the inconsistencies of the reference pitch marks used in evaluation, especially in the speech segments with less expressed periodicity, what influenced the evaluation results of the proposed method.

1 Introduction

Pitch is a fundamental feature of speech signal. In time domain it is denoted by a pitch period within the voiced segment of speech. Pitch marking means marking of time instants of glottal closure, also referred as glottal closure instants (GCIs) or epochs. Usually, the pitch mark is set at time instant of speech signal amplitude extreme within a pitch period - most often negative peak, which corresponds to the time instant of glottal closure. The instants of glottal closing can be defined also by electroglottograph, which enables non-invasive measurement of the time variation of the contact between vocal cords (measuring the electroglottograph (EGG) signal). However, use of electroglottograph is rather limited and many times EGG signal is not available. Therefore, accurate and robust definition of pitch marks from speech signal only is still an interesting research issue.

The accurate marking of epochs is important in number of speech processing areas including speech analysis and processing [1], automatic phonetic segmentation [2], pitch-synchronous speech enhancement [3], clinical diagnosis, speech coding [4], voice conversion [5], speaker characterization [6], speech synthesis [7], and speech recognition [8].

Many pitch marking algorithms have been proposed that are based on different speech processing techniques, like autocorrelation function [9], cepstral analysis [10], average magnitude difference function [11], group delay based methods [12], linear prediction [13], Cohen's class time-frequency representations (TFR) [14], ensemble empirical mode decomposition [15], multiphase algorithm [16], threshold based and peak picking methods [17], group delay methods [18]. Many of these techniques face problems like averaging, windowing effect, low time or frequency resolution, epoch insertion or deletion etc. By using the EGG signal it is possible to accurately define a glottal closure instant in speech. By time alignment of EGG and speech signals the glottal closure instants can be mapped to the speech signal. The analyses of the aligned EGG and speech signals showed that the GCI usually corresponds to the instants of peaks in speech signal, being positive or negative (depending on the polarity of speech). When no EGG signal is available, it should be decided whether the pitch marks will be placed at positive or negative peaks of a speech waveform. In many cases the time instant of negative peak is selected as pitch mark position, like in [19].

To achieve an accurate and robust pitch marking with high success and accuracy rates, with no windowing problem, and good time resolution a novel pitch marking method is proposed in this article based on the use of autocorrelation function, bandpass zero phase filter bank, mapping of pitch waveform to speech signal and performing peak- picking within the pitch segment.

2 Pitch marking algorithm using an autocorrelation function and zero-phase filter bank (AFB)

The basic idea of the proposed method is based on the source-filter model of speech production in which voiced sounds have a source due to periodic glottal excitation. This can be approximated by an impulse train in the time domain and by harmonics in the frequency domain. The shape filter, which is the second part of the source-filter model, defines the position and the form of formants. Its shape depends on tongue position, lip protrusion etc.

The proposed method extracts the pitch signal from the periodic excitation (first component of the harmonic excitation, i.e. the fundamental frequency) using the narrow band band-pass filter. The pitch signal is further used to define the pitch segments within which the pitch marks are defined. Figure 1 shows the block diagram of the proposed method. To achieve time alignment of pitch signal with speech waveform a zero phase filters should be used.

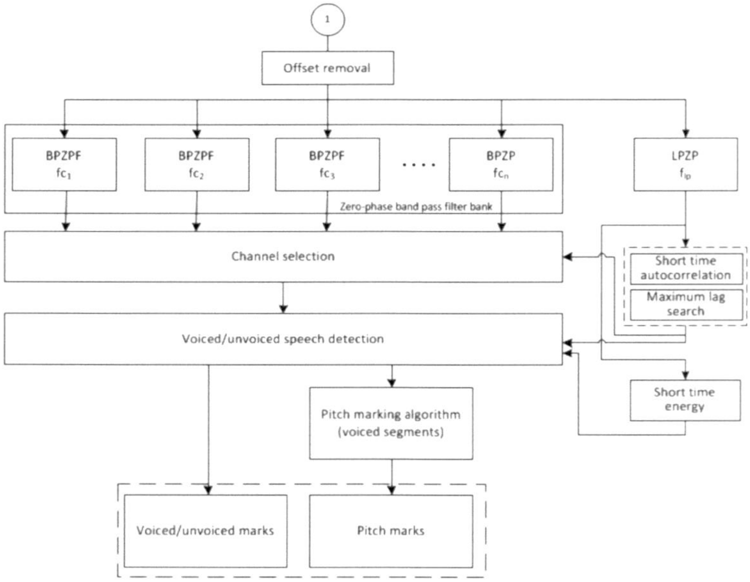

Figure 1 - Block diagram of the pitch marking algorithm using zero-phase filter bank and short-time autocorrelation function (BPZPF – band-pass zero-phase filter, LPZP – lowpass zero-phase filter).

As pitch of the speech signal is changing over time, a time varying filter should be applied to extract the changing pitch signal. To achieve similar results the proposed method uses a zero phase filter bank instead, with the narrow band pass-band filters. To define the appropriate filter channel, which defines the pitch signal corresponding to the temporal pitch, the short term normalized autocorrelation function of the lowpass filtered speech signal is used. The value of the maximum lag of the short-time autocorrelation function indicates the filter channel to be used in further analysis. In the next step a simple pitch period extraction algorithm is performed on the pitch waveform by extracting half periods of the pitch signal to define pitch segments. Next, mapping of the pitch segments to the speech waveform is performed. Using the peak picking algorithm within the pitch segment the GCI is defined as a negative peak value of the pitch period. Fig. 2a shows the speech waveform and the output signal of the filter bank. Fig. 2b shows the pitch signal of the selected filter bank channel aligned with the speech waveform, the defined pitch period marks (dashed lines) and the defined pitch marks (solid lines) as the negative peaks of the speech periods.

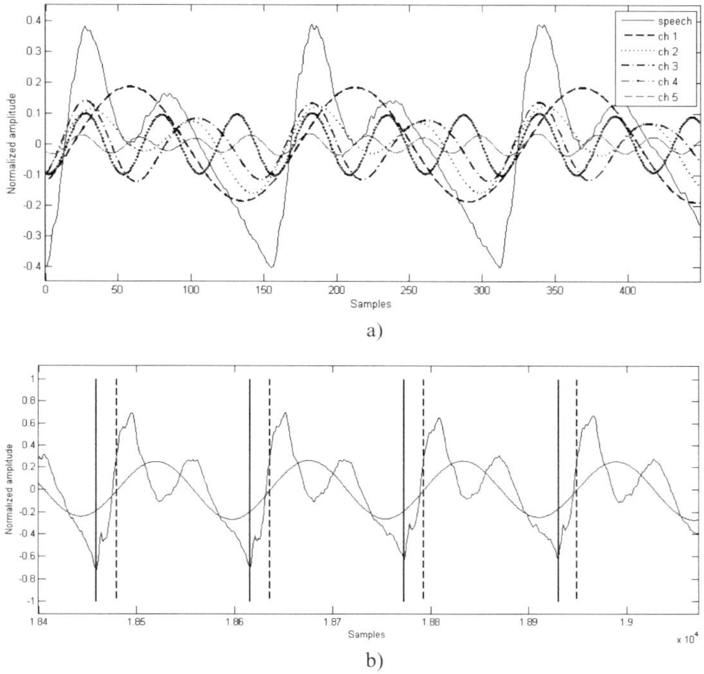

Figure 2 - Speech waveform and the output signals of the filter bank aligned with the speech signal a), speech signal, selected filter channel - pitch signal, pitch period marks (dashed lines) and the pitch marks (solid lines) defined as negative peaks of the speech periods b).

Voiced/unvoiced speech detection is based on the short term autocorrelation function and short term energy of low pass filtered signal using the thresholding technique. The voiced segments of speech signal are defined when the normalized autocorrelation function exhibits at least two peaks, which are greater than the predefined threshold value (or one peak in which case the threshold value is higher) and at the same time if the short-time energy value is greater than the predefined threshold. The unvoiced segment is defined when short-term energy falls below the predefined threshold and the peak of autocorrelation function does not reach the threshold.

3 Evaluation setup

3.1 The implementation of the AFB algorithm

The proposed AFB algorithm was implemented in the following way. The filter bank was implemented as a set of zero-phase band pass FIR filters with the bandwidth of 80Hz. The Constrained Least Squares (CLS) FIR filter design function was used in filter design. The filter bank consisted of five filters with the central frequencies from 80 Hz to 400 Hz. For short-time energy and autocorrelation calculation the filtering with the zero-phase low pass filter with the cut-off frequency of 400 Hz was performed. The length of all FIR filter impulse responses was 320 samples. The length of the window for short-time energy calculation was 64 samples and the window step was 10 samples. The autocorrelation window length was 640 samples, and the window step was 10 samples. If at least two autocorrelation peaks were detected in the autocorrelation function, the thresholds applied for the two maximum peaks were 0.25 and 0.2 for the first and the second peak, respectively. If only one peak was detected, the threshold of 0.4 was applied.

1.1 The experimental setup

The proposed method was evaluated using the ECESS evaluation framework [19]. According to the evaluation framework the most negative peak of the voiced speech signal was defined as the position of the epoch. In the PMA evaluation the Speecon speech database was used [20]. The acoustical environments in which the database was recorded were car interior, office and living rooms. The database was recorded at 16 kHz sampling rate and quantized using the 16-bit linear coding. In the PMA evaluation database a subset of 60 speakers was selected (30 male and 30 female speakers, speaker age from 19 to 79 years). The signal was recorded simultaneously with four microphones, where each microphone was placed at a different distance from the speaker: a head mounted close-talk microphone (channel C0), a Lavalier microphone (placed below the chin of the speaker, channel C1), a directional microphone placed at 1 meter from the speaker (channel C2), and an omni-directional microphone placed at 2-3 meters from the speaker (channel C3). In order to define a reference pitch marks, the close-talk microphone recordings in the amount of 1 minute per speaker were selected. The reference database consists of 60 minutes of manually verified pitch-marked speech signal.

In counting the correct epochs, a maximal tolerance deviation of 20% of the period time T at maximal presumable pitch frequency was allowed, what is consistent with the definition of the gross error in the case of pitch detection – in case of assumed maximal pitch frequency of 600 Hz at the 16kHz sampling rate, the tolerance interval for epoch detection is +/- 6 samples [19]. This value was used in the evaluation of the proposed algorithm. The success rate ($SR_{\%}$) of the PMA was computed as follows:

$$SR_{\%} = \frac{|\{x(x \in T) \wedge (x \in R)\}|}{|R|} \cdot 100\% \qquad (1)$$

where R represents the set of all reference epochs, and T represents the set of epochs generated by the AFB method. The number of the correct epochs is the sum of the epochs generated by the AFB method, which are on the same positions as the reference pitch-marks (encountering the allowed tolerance). Duplicated pitch-marks are not considered as correct pitch-marks. The accuracy of the PMA was computed by the equation:

$$ACC_{\%} = \frac{|Corr| - |Ins|}{|Ref|} \cdot 100\% \qquad (2)$$

|Ins| is the number of all inserted pitch marks and |Corr| is the number of correct pitch marks. The latter can be calculated as follows:

$$|Corr| = |Ref| - |Del| \qquad (3)$$

where |Ref| is the number of reference pitch marks and |Del| is the number of deleted pitch marks.

accuracy (AR%) of the proposed method on the SPEECON pitch marking task. In comparison with the success rate reported in [19] worse results were obtained for channel C0, however, better results were obtained for channels C1 and C2. In general more gradual decrease of success rate can be observed in Table 1 regarding the channel quality than reported in [19].

Condition	**|Ref|**	**|Test|**	**|Corr|**	**|Ins|**	**|Del|**	**SR%**	**ACC%**
Channel C0	314066	304139	278062	26077	36004	88.53	80.23
Channel C1	314066	260893	196500	64393	117566	62.56	42.06
Channel C2	314066	292137	147705	144432	166361	47.03	1.04
Channel C3	314066	271210	85071	186139	228995	27.08	-32.18

Table 1 – Overall evaluation results of PMA for SPEECON speech database.

Detailed analysis of the pitch marks generated by the AFB method and the reference pitch marks of the SPEECON database showed that errors were mostly encountered in regions of low energy speech, where the periodicity of speech signal was very weak or not present at all, however the speech segments were still marked as voiced. It was further revealed that in the low energy segments of speech signal a significant inconsistency of reference pitch marks appears. In most such cases pitch marks are not denoting the most negative peak or if there is no periodicity present in the signal, the pitch marks are inconsistent. Therefore additional evaluation was performed in which small energy speech segments with inconsistent pitch marks or signal segments with no periodicity were excluded from the analysis. Table 2 shows the evaluation results. It can be seen that the results improved especially for channels C0 and C1. The proposed method shows good success rate and robustness to noise, what can be seen in gradual decrease of success rate with decrease of speech quality, compared to the results reported in [19].

Condition	**|Ref|**	**|Test|**	**|Corr|**	**|Ins|**	**|Del|**	**SR%**	**ACC%**
Channel C0	291735	288073	268468	19605	23267	92.02	85.30
Channel C1	293959	250110	191268	102691	58842	65.06	45.04
Channel C2	290014	272596	141916	130680	148098	48.93	3.87
Channel C3	284647	229585	79351	150234	205296	27.87	-24.90

Table 2 - Overall evaluation results of PMA for SPEECON speech database, where small energy speech segments with inconsistent pitch marks were excluded from evaluation.

5 Conclusion

A pitch marking algorithm using a short-time autocorrelation function and zero-phase band-pass filter bank was proposed. The short-time autocorrelation was used to select the filter bank channel, which contains pitch waveform. The mapping of the pitch segment to the speech signal is performed to define the region of pitch mark, which was then defined as a negative peak within the pitch segment. For evaluation the ECESS evaluation framework was used with the SPEECON database. The algorithm achieved good success rate and accuracy for channel C0 and demonstrated good noise robustness for channels C1 and C2. It was further revealed that the evaluation database contains inconsistent reference pitch marks in small energy speech segments or segments with no periodicity. By excluding these regions further performance improvements of the proposed method were achieved.

References

[1] Schoentgen, J.: Decomposition of vocal cycle length perturbations into vocal jitter and vocal microtremor, and comparison of their size in normophonic speakers. In: Journal of Voice, Vol. 17, No. 2, 2003, pp. 114-125.

[2] Matoušek, J., Romportl, J.: Automatic pitch-synchronous phonetic segmentation. In: Proc. Interspeech, Brisbane, Australia, 2008, pp. 1626-1629.

[3] Kleijn, W. B.: Enhancement of coded speech by constrained optimization. In: Proc. IEEE Workshop on Speech Coding, Tsukuba, Ibaraki, Japan, 2002, pp. 163-165.

[4] Ertan, A. E., Barnwell, T. P.: Improving the 2,4 KB/s Military Standard MELP (MS-MELP) Coder using pitch-synchronous analysis and synthesis techniques. In: Proc. IEEE ICASSP 2005, pp. 761 - 764.

[5] Sündermann, D., Ney, H., Höge, H.: VTLN-based cross-language voice conversion. In: Proc. ASRU. Virgin Islands, USA, 2003, pp. 676- 681.

[6] Kim, S., Eriksson, T., Kang, H. G., Young, D. H.: A pitch synchronous feature extraction method for speaker recognition. In: Proc. IEEE ICASSP, 2004, pp. II-405 II-408.

[7] Drugman, T. Wilfart, G., Moinet, A., Dutoit, T.: Using a pitch-synchronous residual codebook for hybrid HMM/frame selection speech synthesis. In: Proc. IEEE ICASSP, 2009, pp. 3793-3796-

[8] Li, M., Yu, T.: Robust and efficient pitch tracking method for tonal feature extraction. In: Proc. IEEE ICASSP, 2001.

[9] Rabiner, L. R.: On the use of autocorrelation analysis for pitch detection. In: IEEE Trans. on acoustics, speech, and signal processing, Vol. Assp-25, No. 1, 1977, pp: 24- 33.

[10] Noll, A. M.: Cepstrum pitch determination. In: J. Acoust. Soc. Amer. Vol. 41, No. 2, 1967, pp. 293-309.

[11] Ross, M.J., Shaffer, H.L., Cohen, A., Freudberg, R., Manley, H. J.: Average magnitude difference function pitch extractor. In: IEEE Trans. acoust., speech, signal processing. Vol. ASSP-22, 1974, pp. 353-362.

[12] Rao, K., Prasanna, S., Yagnanarayana, B.: Determination of instants of significant excitation in speech using Hilbert envelope and group delay function. In: IEEE Signal process. letters. Vol. 14, No. 10, 2007, pp. 762-765.

[13] Plante, F., Meyer, G., Ainsworth, W.: Pitch detection: auditory versus inverse filtering. In: Proc. Inst. Acoust., Vol. 16, 1996, pp. 81-88.

[14] Navaro-Mesa, J. L., Lleida-Solano, E., Moreno-Bilbao, A.: A new method for epoch detection based on the cohen's class of time frequency representations. In: IEEE Signal processing letters, Vol. 8, No. 8, 2001, pp. 225-227.

[15] Galhotra, P., Kumar Patil, M.: Determine the pitch markers in speech signal using ensemble empirical mode decomposition. In: Int. journal of advanced research in computer science and software engineering. Vol. 2, Issue 7, 2012, pp. 90-96.

[16] Legat, M., Matoušek, J., Tihelka, D.: On the detection of pitch marks using robust multi-phase algorithm. In: Speech communication, Vol. 53, Issue 4, 2011, pp.552-566.

[17] Rothenberg, M., Mahshie, J. J.: Monitoring vocal fold abduction through vocal fold contract area. In: Journal of speech and hearing research. Vol. 31, 1998, pp. 338-351.

[18] Brooks, M., Naylor, P. A., Gudnason, J.: A quantitative assessment of group delay methods for identifying closures in voiced speech. In: IEEE Trans. audio, speech and language process. Vol. 14, No. 2, 2006, pp. 456-466.

[19] Höge, H., Kotnik, B., Kačič, Z., Pfitzinger, H. R.: Evaluation of pitch marking algorithms. In: ITG-report 192: voice communication . VDE Verlag, Berlin, Offenbach, 2006.

[20] Iskra, D., J., Grosskopf, B., Marasek, K., van den Heuvel, H., Diehl, F., Kiessling, A.: Speecon speech database for consumer devices: Database specification and validation. In: Proc. LREC, 2002, pp. 329–333.

SPEECH ENHANCEMENT BASED ON THE CONCEPT OF MODULATION TRANSFER FUNCTION

Masashi Unoki

School of Information Science, Japan Advanced Institute of Science and Technology
unoki@jaist.ac.jp

Abstract: This paper proposes a speech enhancement framework based on the concept of the modulation transfer function (MTF) in reverberant environments. This framework can be used to enhance reverberant speech without having to measure the room impulse response. The temporal power envelopes (TPEs) and temporal fine structures (TFSs) in this framework are decomposed from a reverberant speech signal using an N-channel band-pass filterbank. Then, the TPEs are restored by using the inverse MTF and the TFSs are quasi-generated by using carrier regeneration. Finally, each channel signal is reproduced by multiplying the restored TPEs with the quasi-generated TFSs, and then the channel signals are reconstructed into the dereverberated speech signal by using the same filterbank. We carried out 15,000 simulations of dereverberation for reverberant speech signals to evaluate the proposed method. We also subjectively evaluated the method with listening tests (word intelligibility tests). The results from both evaluations indicated that in addition to reducing the averaged log-spectrum distortion by about one decibel the new method reduced the loss of speech intelligibility caused by reverberation by 30%.

1 Introduction

Reverberation generally smears significant features in speech and lowers speech intelligibility. Speech dereverberation is therefore needed in various forms of speech signal processing, such as that in hearing aid systems and the front-ends of ASR systems. The ultimate goal of our work was to construct a method of blind speech dereverberation that could restore the speech signal from reverberant speech without using useful prior information such as the room impulse response (RIR), which caused less loss of speech intelligibility due to reverberation.

Several well-known inverse filtering methods can be used to dereverberate the original signal from the reverberant signal in room acoustics. There are, for example, the methods used by Neely and Allen [1] and Miyoshi and Kaneda [2], which use a single microphone or microphone array to dereverberate signals. Miyoshi and Kaneda's method can be applied to room acoustics with non-minimum phase characteristics, but that of Neely and Allen can only be applied to minimum phase characteristics in room acoustics. However, the RIR for these methods must be measured before dereverberation to determine inverse filtering. Moreover, RIR is generally time variant. These methods would therefore require remeasurements of RIR for each dereverberation to be processed. This is a significant drawback with regard to the use of these methods for various speech applications.

Nakatani and Miyoshi recently proposed a blind method of dereverberation for a single-channel speech signal based on the harmonic structure without having to measure RIR [3]. This method, however, required the fundamental frequency to be accurately estimated from reverberant speech, and they pointed out that it was difficult to meet this requirement. It also seems that this method does not precisely dereverberate parts corresponding to consonants.

Methods of temporal envelope inverse filtering, on the other hand, have been proposed that not only restore the temporal envelope from reverberant speech, but also improve speech intelligibility that has been degraded by reverberation. There are the methods of Avendano and Hermansky [4] and Hirobayashi *et al.* [5], for example, which are based on the concept of the modulation transfer function (MTF) [6] and can restore the temporal power envelope (TPE) (temporal fluctuation or modulation index) from reverberant speech without having to measure the RIR. They should therefore be useful for preprocessing in such applications. However, they do not effectively improve the speech intelligibility of the restored speech signal. We think this shortcoming is due to artifacts in the temporal fine structure (TFS) of the restored speech since these methods disregard the carrier of the speech signal in their dereverberation processing.

We improved Hirobayashi *et al.*'s method [5] to solve the problems they encountered [7] in the first step of our previous work and then extended the improved basic approach to one based on a filterbank by taking into consideration issues regarding speech applications [8]. We refined our method in the second step to enable a reverberant speech signal to be restored and a speech waveform to be reconstructed after dereverberation [9]. We propose a speech enhancement framework to improve TPE restoration by inverse MTF and TFS quasi-generation by using carrier regeneration in this paper to develop a method of MTF-based speech dereverberation that will enable the loss of speech intelligibility to be recovered.

2 Concept of modulation transfer function

The MTF concept was proposed by Houtgast and Steeneken [6] to account for the relationship between the transfer function in an enclosure in terms of the envelopes of input and output signals and the characteristics of the enclosure such as reverberation, as shown in Fig. 1(b). This is defined as the characteristics between the TPE of input and output signals $\overline{I_i^2}(1+\cos(2\pi f_m t))$ and $\overline{I_o^2}\{1+m(f_m)\cos(2\pi f_m(t-\tau))\}$, where $\overline{I_i^2}$ and $\overline{I_o^2}$ represent the magnitude of the input and output signals. Here, f_m represents the modulation frequency and τ represents the initial phase. The $m(f_m)$ represents the modulation index, i.e., MTF. This concept was introduced as a measure in room acoustics for assessing the effect of the enclosure on speech intelligibility [6].

The observed reverberant signal, the original signal, and the stochastic idealized RIR are assumed to correspond to $\mathbf{y}(t)$, $\mathbf{x}(t)$, and $\mathbf{h}(t)$, as shown in Fig. 1. The signal is also assumed to be composed of the temporal envelope, $e(t)$, and the carrier, $\mathbf{c}(t)$, as random variables. By assuming linear systems and the mutual independence between carriers, the TPE, $e_y^2(t)$, can be represented as $e_y^2(t) = e_x^2(t) * e_h^2(t)$, where "$*$" indicates convolution [7, 8], and they are also represented as

$$e_x^2(t) = \overline{e_x^2}(1+\cos(2\pi f_m t)), \tag{1}$$

$$e_y^2(t) = \frac{\overline{e_x^2}}{\alpha}\{1+m(f_m)\cos(2\pi f_m t)\}, \tag{2}$$

where $\alpha = \int_0^\infty \mathbf{h}^2(t)dt$. Here, the stochastic RIR (Schroeder's RIR [12]), $\mathbf{h}(t)$, is represented as $\mathbf{h}(t) = e_h(t)\mathbf{c}_h(t) = a\exp(-6.9t/T_R)\mathbf{c}_h(t)$, where $\mathbf{c}_h(t)$ is a white noise carrier acting as a random variable and a is a gain factor of RIR. From these, the MTF is represented as

$$m(f_m) = \left|\frac{\beta}{\alpha}\right| = \left[1+\left(2\pi f_m \frac{T_R}{13.8}\right)^2\right]^{(-1/2)}, \tag{3}$$

where $\beta = \int_0^\infty \mathbf{h}^2(t)\exp(-j\omega_m t)dt$ and a has been normalized to be one. Here, T_R is a parameter of RT. The MTF, $m(f_m)$, has characteristics of low-pass filtering as a function of f_m and T_R.

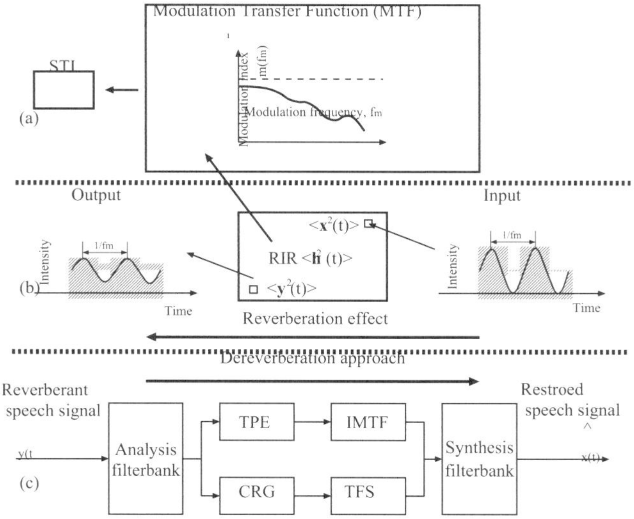

Figure 1 - Schematic of reverberation and dereverberation for speech intelligibility based on MTF concept and STI prediction.

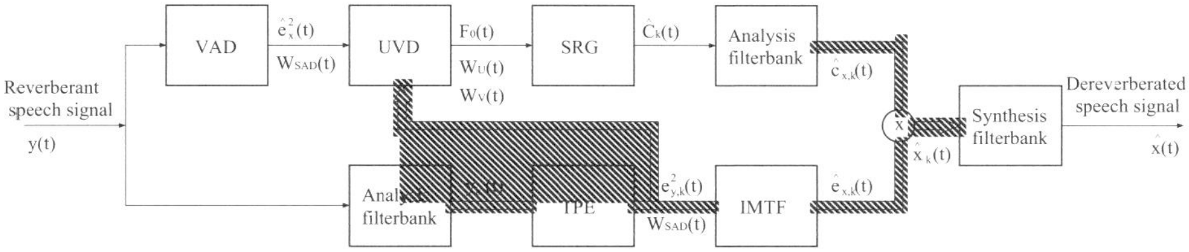

Figure 2 - Framework for speech enhancement based on MTF concept.

Figure 1(a) shows a general scheme for MTF, $m(\omega)$, as a function of modulation frequency f_m (i.e., the dominant frequency in the temporal envelope) and the speech transfer index (STI) for predicting speech intelligibility derived from MTF. The MTF is only of interest for the range of f_m relevant for the speech signal; thus, this is for the range of fluctuation rhythms, which is determined by the spectrum of the temporal envelope of speech, that is encountered in speech. Based on the MTF concept, we can know how much reverberation affects reduction in the modulation index, and we can then predict reduced speech intelligibility using STI derived from MTF. The approach of temporal dereverberation is aimed at restoring reduced MTF and then enhancing speech intelligibility using the restored MTF, as outlined in Fig. 1(c).

3 Method of speech dereverberation

The proposed framework for speech dereverberation is outlined in Fig. 1(c). This framework consists of two parts: TPE restoration by Inverse MTF (IMTF) and the quasi-regenerated TFS by the carrier regeneration (CRG). This is also implemented as outlined in Fig. 2. First, reverberant speech signal $y(t)$ is decomposed into the TPEs, $e_{y,n}(t)$, and the TFSs, $c_{y,n}(t)$, in N-channels ($1 \leq n \leq N$, bandpass filtering using a filterbank (analysis processing).

$$x(t) \quad = \quad \sum_{n=1}^{N} x_n(t) = \sum_{n=1}^{N} e_{x,n}(t) \cdot c_{x,n}(t), \tag{4}$$

$$y(t) = \sum_{n=1}^{N} y_n(t) = \sum_{n=1}^{N} e_{y,n}(t) \cdot c_{y,n}(t), \quad (5)$$

where $x_n(t)$ and $y_n(t)$ are the band-limited signals, $e_{x,n}(t)$ and $e_{y,n}(t)$ are the temporal envelopes, and $c_{x,n}(t)$ and $c_{y,n}(t)$ are the carriers in the channels. Then, the IMTF is used in the TPE restoration process to recover the TPE of speech, $\hat{e}^2_{x,n}(t)$, from the reverberant envelope, $e^2_{y,n}(t)$ as described in Section 4. The CRG in the TFS regeneration process based on the pulse source interpolated frequency modulation (PIFM) method [10] is used to reconstruct the source information of the dereverberated speech from voiced/unvoiced information based on the estimated fundamental frequency (F0). This information was detected by using the voice activity detection (VAD) and unvoiced/voiced detection (UVD). The TFS with regard to source information is decomposed into the carriers in the channels, $\hat{c}_{x,n}(t)$, described in Section 5. Finally, each channel signal is reproduced by multiplying the restored TPE with the quasi-regenerated TFS (i.e., $\hat{x}_n(t) = \hat{e}_{x,n}(t) \cdot \hat{c}_{x,n}(t)$) and then the channel signals are reconstructed into the dereverberated speech signal, $\hat{x}(t)$, using the same filterbank (resynthesis processing).

4 Restoration process for temporal power envelope

The observed reverberant signal, the original signal, and the stochastic-idealized RIR [6] correspond to $y(t)$, $x(t)$, and $h(t)$ in the basic model to inverse-filter the power envelope proposed by Hirobayashi *et al.* [5], and these are modeled as follows:

$$y(t) = x(t) * h(t), \quad (6)$$
$$x(t) = e_x(t)c_1(t), \quad (7)$$
$$h(t) = e_h(t)c_2(t) = a\exp(-6.9t/T_R)n_2(t), \quad (8)$$

where "*" denotes the convolution operation, $e_x(t)$ and $e_h(t)$ are the envelopes of $x(t)$ and $h(t)$, and $c_1(t)$ and $c_2(t)$ are mutually independent respective white noise functions, i.e., $< c_k(t), c_k(t-\tau) >= \delta(\tau)$, $k = 1$ and 2.

The power envelope of the reverberant signal, $e^2_y(t)$, in this model can be determined as

$$\langle y^2(t) \rangle = e^2_x(t) * e^2_h(t) = e^2_y(t), \quad (9)$$

where $< \cdot >$ is a set-averaging operation [5]. This equation shows that there is a significant relationship between the envelopes; i.e., the MTF concept. Based on this result, $e^2_x(t)$ can be recovered by deconvoluting $e^2_y(t)$ with $e^2_h(t)$. Here, the transmission functions of power envelopes $E_x(z)$, $E_h(z)$, and $E_y(z)$ are assumed to be the respective z-transforms of $e^2_x(t)$, $e^2_h(t)$, and $e^2_y(t)$. Thus, the transmission function of the power envelope of the original signal, $E_x(z)$, can be determined from

$$E_x(z) = \frac{E_y(z)}{a^2} \left\{ 1 - \exp\left(-\frac{13.8}{T_R \cdot f_s} \right) z^{-1} \right\}, \quad (10)$$

where f_s is a sampling frequency. Finally, power envelope $e^2_x(t)$ can be obtained from the inverse z-transform of $E_x(z)$ [5]. This model concept, therefore, enables the TPE of an original signal to be recovered from an observed signal.

We have extended this model to the filterbank model for speech applications [8] in this paper because most envelopes are not co-modulated envelopes throughout the entire range. Here, a constant bandwidth filterbank is used to decompose speech into channel components that are then dereverberated using the same method in each channel. However, two problems are associated with the basic model: (1) how to precisely extract the power envelope from the observed signal, and (2) how to determine the parameters of the reverberant time and the amplitude terms (T_R and a) of the RIR. We resolved these problems, as we previously reported [8].

(a) Extraction of power envelope:

$$\hat{e}^2_{y,n}(t) = \mathrm{LPF}\left[|y_n(t) + j\mathrm{Hilbert}(y_n(t))|^2\right]. \tag{11}$$

(b) Estimation of reverberation time:

$$\hat{T}_R = \max\left(\underset{0\le T_R\le T_{R,\max}}{\arg\min}\left\{\int_0^T \left|\min\left(\hat{e}^2_{x,n,T_R}(t),0\right)\right| dt\right\}\right). \tag{12}$$

(c) Determination of amplitude term:

$$\hat{a} = \sqrt{1/\int_0^T \exp(-13.8t/T_R)dt}. \tag{13}$$

where Hilbert$(\cdot)$ is the Hilbert transform, LPF$[\cdot]$ is low-pass filtering, and $\hat{e}^2_{x,n,T_R}(t)$ is the restored TPE using any T_R. We used LPF$[\cdot]$ with a cut-off frequency of 20 Hz to remove the high-pass envelope [8]. Here, T is the signal duration of $y(t)$, $\hat{e}^2_{x,T_R}(t)$ is the set of candidates of the TPE restoration as a function of T_R, and $T_{R,\max}$ is the upper limited region of T_R.

5 Carrier regeneration process

Since the previous method in our studies [7, 8], did not deal with carrier signal ($c_{x,n}(t)$ from $c_{y,n}(t)$) in each channel, this model cannot resynthesize the restored signal in the waveform using only $\hat{e}^2_{x,n}(t)$. As was described in Section 1, all other MTF-based methods [5] used $c_{y,k}(t)$ instead of $\hat{c}_{x,n}(t)$ to resynthesize dereverberated signal $\hat{x}(t)$ from the set of channel signals $\hat{e}_{x,n}(t)\cdot c_{y,n}(t)$. This processing is based on Drullman's study [13] where the temporal envelope appeared to be most important for speech intelligibility rather than carrier differences. However, there was no improvement in speech intelligibility in the restored signal. Hence, we have to consider how to restore carrier signal $c_{x,n}(t)$ from $c_{y,n}(t)$ or $y(t)$ using any useful information.

The top block in Fig. 2 has the signal flow for the carrier regeneration process. This block separately processes in voiced and unvoiced durations based on the estimated F0. These durations are extracted by using a robust VAD that the author proposed [14]. We used our proposed methods of estimating F0 from reverberant speech [15].

First, the carrier regeneration block in the voiced duration is based on the facts: source information of voiced speech consisting of harmonicity and/or periodicity with F0 and this harmonicity can smoothly vary with F0 fluctuations; the harmonicity is frequency-modulated together with F0. Thus, this block generates harmonicity with the estimated F0 based on the PIFM model [10]. The generated carrier, $\hat{c}_v(t)$, in this block is represented as

$$\hat{c}_v(t) = \frac{1}{K(t)}\sum_{k=1}^{K(t)} \sin\left(k\int_0^t 2\pi F_0(\tau)d\tau + \phi_k(t)\right) \tag{14}$$

where $F_0(t)$ is the fundamental frequency, $\phi_k(t)$ is the initial phase, k is the index of harmonics ($1 \le k \le K(t)$), and $K(t)$ is the maximum number of harmonics. Next, the carrier regeneration block in the unvoiced duration generates a white noise carrier, $\hat{c}_u(t)$. All carriers corresponding to a speech signal are then added together; i.e., $c_x(t) = c_v(t) + c_u(t)$. Finally, this carrier is decomposed into carriers in each channel of the same filterbank to multiply carriers with the dereverberated envelopes. Carriers are then reconstructed into dereverberated speech using the same filterbank as is used for speech resynthesis.

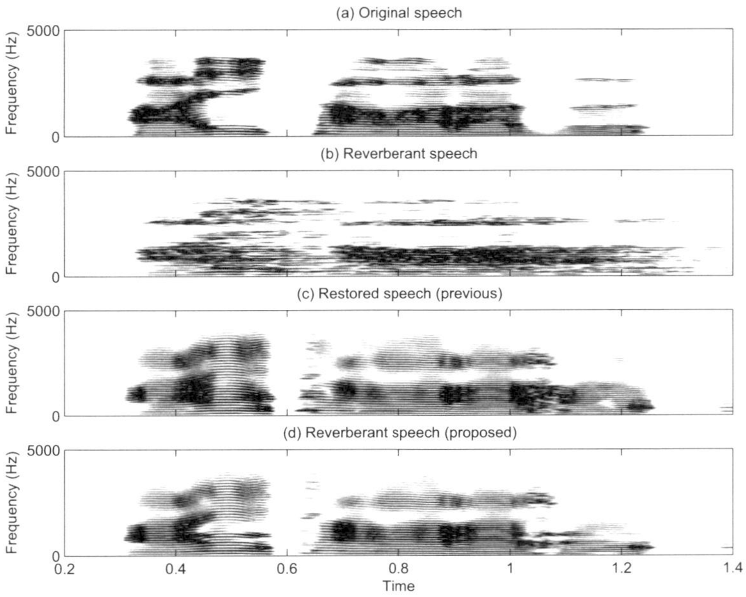

Figure 3 - Sound spectrograms: (a) original speech$x(t)$, (b) reverberant speech $y(t)$, (c) $\hat{x}(t)$ restored with previous method, and (d) $\hat{x}(t)$ restored with proposed method. Reverberation time, $T_R = 1.0$ s.

6 Evaluations

We carried out simulations to evaluate the proposed method. The speech signals were three Japanese words (/aikawarazu/, /shinbun/, and /joudan/) uttered by ten speakers (five males: Mau, Mht, Mnm, Mtm, and Mtt and five females: Faf, Ffs, Fkn, Fsu, and Fyn) from the ATR-database [11]; 100 types of RIR $h(t)$ were used, and five reverberation times of $T_R = 0.1, 0.3, 0.5, 1.0$, and 2.0 were used. All stimuli, $y(t)$s, were composed through 15,000 (=$3 \times 10 \times 5 \times 100$) convolutions of $x(t)$s with $h(t)$s.

We evaluated the distortion in the restored speech using Log-spectrum distortion (LSD) as

$$\mathrm{LSD} = \sqrt{\frac{1}{W}\sum_{\omega}^{W}\left(20\log_{10}\frac{|S(\omega)|}{|\hat{S}(\omega)|}\right)} \qquad \text{(dB)} \tag{15}$$

where W is the upper frequency (here, it is 10 kHz), and $|S(\omega)|$ and $|\hat{S}(\omega)|$ are the amplitude spectrum of $\tilde{x}(t)$ and $\tilde{y}(t)$ or $\hat{x}(t)$, respectively. Here, $\tilde{x}(t)$ is the original speech resynthesized using carrier generation, and $\tilde{y}(t)$ is the reverberant $\tilde{x}(t)$ (i.e., $\tilde{x}(t) * h(t)$). Figure 3 shows the amplitude spectrograms for (a) $\tilde{x}(t)$ and (b) $\tilde{y}(t)$ where $T_R = 1.0$ s. (c) is $\hat{x}(t)$ with the previous method, and (d) is $\hat{x}(t)$ with the proposed method. Comparing Figs. 3 (a)-(d), we can see that the proposed model recovered more of a silence interval from reverberant speech.

We then compared the proposed method with the previous method to determine improvements that could be attained through the use of CRG. Figure 4 shows that while both methods reduced LSD, restoration was better when using time division and/or frequency division with the previous model. The improved method provided the greatest improvement in restoration accuracy under all conditions: LSD was one decibel lower than that with the previous model.

We evaluated our previous and proposed models through listening tests. We conducted the listening tests in a soundproof room with five subjects who had normal hearing. The speech

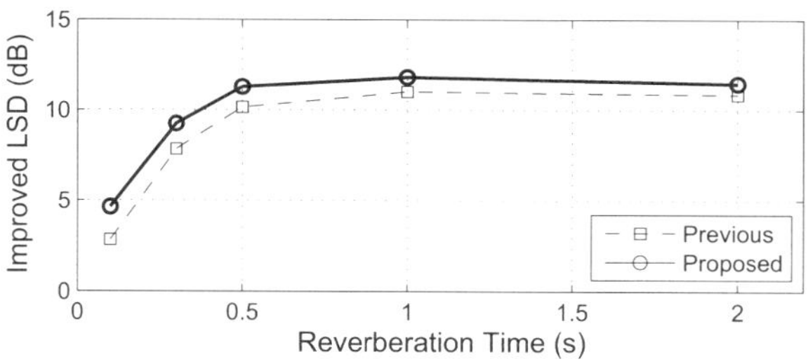

Figure 4 - Improvements in restoration accuracy (LSD).

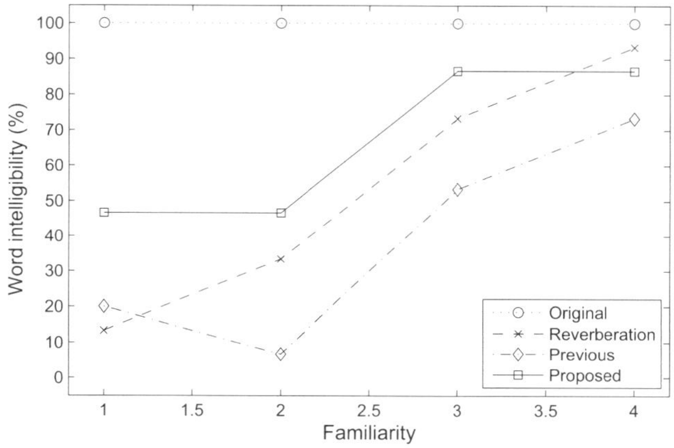

Figure 5 - Results for word intelligibility tests.

signals in these experiments were eight words from Japanese sentences from an NTT database for speech intelligibility testing [16], and the stimuli were manipulated under four conditions (original, reverberant, and dereverberated by the previous and proposed models).

We measured the speech intelligibility of dereverberated speech with the same subjects. The speech signals were 12 words (4 familiarity levels $\times 3$ words) from the database. Subjects in this test were asked to compare the intelligibility of the four versions (reverberant, dereverberated by the previous model, dereverberated by the improved model, and the original) of each word. Word intelligibility improved as the familiarity level increased, and was higher with the improved model than with the previous model or with the reverberant version (Fig. 5). The improved model particular recovered about 30% of the reduction in speech intelligibility caused by the reverberation. We thus believe that the improved speech quality greatly contributed to improving speech intelligibility.

7 Conclusions

We proposed a speech enhancement framework based on the MFT concept, which did not require RIR to be measured. The TPEs and TFSs in this model were decomposed from the reverberant speech signal using an N-channel band-pass filterbank and were then dereverberated in each respective channel. We used the IMTF in TPE restoration to restore the TPE of a reverberant speech signal. The CRG method in TFS regeneration was based on voiced/unvoiced intervals from the estimated fundamental frequency based on the PIFM method. We found that the proposed model could accurately dereverberate both reverberant speech and power envelopes through 15,000 simulations of the dereverberation of reverberant speech. LSD was improved by about one decibel compared with that of the previous method. TPE restoration based on the MTF concept and CRG related to the control of group delay for speech synthesis contributed to the recovery of reverberant speech with regard to the signal and speech intelligibility.

References

[1] Neely S. T. and Allen J. B., "Invertibility of a room impulse response," *J. Acoust. Soc. Am.*, **66**(1), 166-169, 1979.

[2] Miyoshi, M. and Kaneda, Y., "Inverse filtering of room acoustics," *IEEE Trans. ASSP*, **36**(2), 145–152, 1988.

[3] Nakatani, T. and Miyoshi, M., "Blind dereverberation of single channel speech signal based on harmonic structure," *Proc. ICASSP2003*, **I**, 92–95, Hong Kong, 2003.

[4] Avendano, C. and Hermansky, H. "Study on the dereverberation of speech based on temporal envelope filtering," *Proc. ICSLP96*, 889–892, Philadelphia, USA, 1996.

[5] Hirobayashi, S., Nomura, H., Koike, T., and Tohyama, M., "Speech waveform recovery from a reverberant speech signal using inverse filtering of the power envelope transfer function," *IEICE Trans. A*, **81-A**(10), 1323–1330, 1998 (in Japanese).

[6] Houtgast, T. and Steenken, H. J. M., "A review of the MTF concept in room acoustics and its use for estimating speech intelligibility in audioria," *J. Acoust. Soc. Am.*, **77**(3), 1069–1077, 1985.

[7] Unoki, M., Furukawa, M., Sakata, K., and Akagi, M., "An improvemed method based on the MTF concept for restoring the power envelope from a reverberant signal," *Acoust. Sci. & Tech*, **25**(4), 232–242, 2004.

[8] Unoki, M., Sakata, K., Furukawa, M., and Akagi, M., "A speech dereverberation method based on the MTF concept in power envelope restoration," *Acoust. Sci. &Tech.*, **25**(4), 243–254, 2004.

[9] Unoki, M., Sakata, K., and Akagi, M., "A speech dereverberation method based on the MTF concept," *Proc. Interspeech2003*, 1417–1420, Geneva, Switzerland, Sept. 2003.

[10] Hamagami, T., "Speech synthesis using source wave shape modification technique by harmonic phase control," *J. Acoust. Soc. Jpn.*, **54**(9), 623–632, 1998

[11] Takeda, T. et al., Speech Database User's Manual, ATR Technical Report, TR-I-0028, 1988.

[12] Schroeder, M. R., "Modulation transfer functions: definition and measurement," *Acustica*, **49**, 179–182, 1981.

[13] Drullman, R., "Temporal envelope and fine structure cues for speech intelligibility," *J. Acoust. Soc. Am.*, **97**(1), 585–592, 1995.

[14] Unoki, M., Lu, X., Petrick, R., Morita, Sh., Akagi, M., and Hoffmann, R., "Voice activity detection in MTF-based power envelope restoration," *Proc. Interspeech2011*, 2609–2612, Florence, Italy, 2011.

[15] Unoki, M., Hosorogiya, T., and Ishimoto, Y., "Comparative evaluations of robust and accurate F0 estimates in reverberant environments," *Proc. ICASSP2008*, 4569–4572, Las Vegas, March 2008.

[16] Database for speech intelligibility testing using Japanese word lists. NTT-AT, 2003.

AUDITIVE UND INSTRUMENTELLE BEURTEILUNG DER QUALITÄT SYNTHETISCHER SPRACHE IN UNTERSCHIEDLICHEN ANWENDUNGSZUSAMMENHÄNGEN

Sebastian Möller und Florian Hinterleitner

Quality and Usability Lab, Telekom Innovation Labs, TU Berlin
sebastian.moeller@telekom.de

Abstract: In diesem Aufsatz beleuchten wir Methoden zur Beurteilung der Qualität synthetischer Sprache. Zunächst werden psychophysikalische Merkmale analysiert, welche der menschlichen Wahrnehmung und Qualitätsbeurteilung zugrunde liegen. Darauf aufbauend werden Testmethoden und –ergebnisse beschrieben, die diese Merkmale in unterschiedlichen Anwendungsszenarien auditiv quantifizieren. Abschließend wird ein Überblick auf laufende Arbeiten gegeben, welche versuchen, auditive Testergebnisse zu einem gewissen Maße instrumentell zu schätzen. Die Nutzbarmachung solcher instrumenteller Verfahren für die Syntheseentwicklung und –optimierung wird diskutiert.

1 Motivation

“If you cannot measure it, you cannot improve it.” Dieses Zitat, welches Lord Kelvin zugeschrieben wird, bezog sich eigentlich auf physikalische Sachverhalte, wie aus folgenden Erläuterungen in seinem Werk „Popular Lectures and Addresses“ (1891-1894) hervorgeht:

> „In physical science the first essential step in the direction of learning any subject is to find principles of numerical reckoning and practicable methods for measuring some quality connected with it. I often say that when you can measure what you are speaking about, and express it in numbers, you know something about it; but when you cannot measure it, when you cannot express it in numbers, your knowledge is of a meagre and unsatisfactory kind; it may be the beginning of knowledge, but you have scarcely in your thoughts advanced to the state of Science, whatever the matter may be.”[1]

Wenn man den Begriff der Messung auch auf psychophysikalische Sachverhalte erweitert, so weist das Zitat auf die zentrale wissenschaftliche Bedeutung der Messung für die wissenschaftliche Forschung wie auch die praktische Nutzbarmachung der Forschungsergebnisse hin. Dies gilt in besonderem Maße für die maschinelle Sprachsynthese, bei der weiterhin grundlegende Mechanismen unbekannt und – teilweise als Folge davon – Anwendungen von nicht ausreichender Qualität sind, um den Massenmarkt zu bedienen. Rüdiger Hoffmann trug nicht unwesentlich dazu bei, diesem Umstand Abhilfe zu verschaffen.

Eine moderne Definition sieht Qualität als einen Abgleich von wahrgenommenen und erwarteten oder erwünschten Eigenschaften einer Einheit [2]. Das Wahrgenommene wird häufig durch ein physikalisches Ereignis (z.B. die Schallwelle, die von einer Sprachsynthese über einen Lautsprecher ausgegeben wird) getriggert; es „geschieht“ also gewissermaßen, und ist daher durch den Ort, die Zeit und die Eigenschaften des Ereignisses gekennzeichnet. Wird ein solches Ereignis mit dem Erwarteten oder Erwünschten verglichen, entsteht daraus wiederum ein Ereignis – hier ein Qualitätsereignis, welches bislang nur durch Introspektion der Versuchsperson erfasst werden kann (zu zukünftigen alternativen Methoden vgl. den Ausblick dieses Abschnitts).

Zur qualitativen und quantitativen Erfassung der Qualität synthetisierter Sprache bedient man sich normalerweise psychoakustischer Experimente mit menschlichen Versuchspersonen. Dabei werden vorher synthetisierte Sprachproben bezüglich ihrer relevanten Qualitätsmerkmale „vermessen“ oder vorher bekannte Qualitätsmerkmale „gemessen“, d.h. quantifiziert. Die Messung geschieht durch menschliche Versuchspersonen, welche ihre Wahrnehmungsereignisse nach vorher definierten Regeln mit Erwartungen und Wünschen abgleichen.

Wichtig ist in diesem Zusammenhang der Begriff der Relevanz: Wenn man davon ausgeht dass die Wahrnehmungsmerkmale konstant sind, so sollten sie sich eigentlich vom Anwendungszusammenhang unabhängig für alle Wahrnehmungsereignisse eines bestimmten Typs (z.B. die Wahrnehmungen synthetischer Sprache) gleichermaßen quantifizieren lassen. Ergebnisse psychophysikalischer Untersuchungen, wie sie in Abschnitt 2 vorgestellt werden, zeigen jedoch, dass je nach Anwendung unterschiedliche Merkmale von den Versuchspersonen genannt und beurteilt werden. Diesem Umstand trägt die Referenz (d.h. das Erwartete oder Erwünschte) Rechnung, die einzelne Wahrnehmungsmerkmale verstärkt oder abschwächt – ähnlich einem Filter für Wahrnehmungsmerkmale.

Im folgenden Abschnitt 2 stellen wir Ergebnisse psychoakustischer Studien vor, die die wahrgenommenen Merkmale synthetischer Sprache zu ergründen suchen. Abschnitt 3 beschreibt experimentelle Untersuchungen, in denen diese Merkmale in unterschiedlichen Anwendungszusammenhängen quantitativ erfasst wurden. Abschnitt 4 erläutert das Prinzip der Qualitätsschätzung und zeigt, dass auch mittels instrumenteller Messungen Aussagen zu einzelnen Qualitätsmerkmalen getroffen werden können. Abschnitt 5 beschließt den Aufsatz mit einem kritischen Rückblick und Ausblick auf offene Fragen.

2 Wahrnehmungsdimensionen synthetischer Sprache

Obwohl moderne Text-To-Speech (TTS) Systeme inzwischen ein Qualitätsniveau erreicht haben, das sie geeignet für eine Vielzahl unterschiedlicher Anwendungen macht, so z.B. Email-Vorlesedienste und Telefoninformationssysteme, werden einzelne Qualitätsaspekte synthetischer Sprache immer noch durch unterschiedliche systemabhängige Störungen beeinflusst: Diphone-Synthesizer hören sich wegen der zahlreichen Verkettungen von Spracheinheiten meistens sehr künstlich an, HMM-Synthesizer können zwar zu sehr natürlich klingender, aber gleichzeitig auch stark verrauschter Sprache führen, und die Qualität von Unit-Selection-Systemen hängt nicht nur davon ab, wie gut die einzelnen Einheiten zueinander passen, sondern auch davon, wie gut sie zu dem zu synthetisierenden Text passen.

Diese Störungen klingen allesamt unterschiedlich, d.h. sie stören die wahrgenommene Qualität somit entlang unterschiedlicher Wahrnehmungsdimensionen. Die Qualität synthetischer Sprache muss also als multidimensional angesehen werden.

Im Folgenden stellen wir die Ergebnisse mehrerer Studien vor, in denen die synthetischer Sprache zugrundeliegenden perzeptiven Qualitätsdimensionen untersucht wurden.

In einer ersten Versuchsreihe [4] wurden die Qualitätseindrücke der Versuchspersonen mittels eines semantischen Differentials (SD) erfasst. Dabei bewerten die Probanden vorgespielte Stimuli, wie sie für Telekommunikationsdienste typisch sind, auf vorgefertigten Attributskalen. Um zu garantieren, dass in diesem Versuch auch alle perzeptiven Qualitätseindrücke erfasst werden, müssen die Attributskalen durch aufwendige Vorversuche entwickelt werden. In einem ersten Schritt wurde eine Testdatenbank erstellt. Um eine möglichst große Anzahl unterschiedlicher Störungen zu erfassen wurden synthetische Sprachdaten von 14/15 unterschiedlichen weiblichen/männlichen TTS-Systemen erstellt. Einige von ihnen lagen mit bis zu 6 unterschiedlichen Stimmen vor.

In einem ersten Vorversuch wurden 296 unterschiedliche qualitätsbeschreibende Attribute gesammelt, die in 44 Attributskalen komprimiert wurden. Ein zweiter Vorversuch diente dazu, aus diesem Satz an Skalen die relevantesten herauszufiltern. Diese dienten im eigentlichen Hauptversuch dazu, die Qualität der präsentierten Stimuli zu erfassen.

Mittels einer Hauptachsen-Faktorenanalyse und einer daran anschließenden Promax-Rotation ließen sich 4 Faktoren extrahieren. Diese repräsentieren die *Natürlichkeit*, *Störungen*, *zeitliche Verzerrungen* sowie die *Geschwindigkeit*.

In einer zweiten Studie [5] sollten diese Ergebnisse durch einen Versuch mit multidimensionaler Skalierung (MDS) bestätigt werden. Während die Bewertungen der Probanden in einem semantischen Differential immer auf die vorgegebenen Skalen beschränkt sind, umgeht die multidimensionale Skalierung diese Einschränkung, indem die Versuchspersonen nicht die einzelnen Stimuli bewerten, sondern die Ähnlichkeit je zweier paarweise präsentierter Stimuli. Da die Anzahl solcher Paarvergleiche selbst bei wenig umfangreichen Datenbanken schnell Werte größer 100 annimmt und jeder Proband somit mehrere Stunden beschäftigt wäre, wurde in diesem Versuch statt auf Paarvergleiche auf eine Sortierungsaufgabe zurückgegriffen. Dabei sollten die Versuchspersonen die präsentierten Stimuli in mehrere Gruppen einteilen mit der Vorgabe, dass sich Stimuli einer Gruppe auditiv ähnlich sind während sie sich von Stimuli in anderen Gruppen unterscheiden. Aus den Ergebnissen aller Probanden wurde eine Unähnlichkeitsmatrix erstellt, die mittels eines MDS-Algorithmus ausgewertet wurde. Bei diesem Versuch ergaben sich drei Dimensionen, die sich der *Natürlichkeit der Stimme*, *zeitlichen Verzerrungen* und der *Gelassenheit des Sprechers* zuordnen lassen.

Damit ergeben sich in den Ergebnissen der beiden Versuche einige Übereinstimmungen, aber auch Unterschiede:

- Die sehr breit angelegte Dimension Natürlichkeit aus dem SD-Experiment findet sich in der Dimension Natürlichkeit der Stimme sowie in prosodischen Teil der Dimension zeitliche Verzerrungen des MDS-Versuchs wieder.
- Die Dimensionen zeitliche Störungen repräsentieren zeitliche Ansätze, wie sie beim Verknüpfen von Sprachbausteinen in einer Unit-Selection-Synthese vorkommen. Der Hörer hat dann, sofern die Spracheinheiten nicht genau zueinander passen, den Eindruck, als würden zwei Sprecher gleichzeitig reden.
- Die Dimension Geschwindigkeit und Gelassenheit des Sprechers repräsentieren beide Ruhe/Trägheit bzw. Unruhe/Hektik des Sprechers.
- Die Dimension Störungen aus dem ersten Versuch, die z.B. Rauschen, Zischen, Kratzen usw. wiedergibt, konnte im zweiten Versuch nicht bestätigt werden.

Die in den vorangegangenen Abschnitten untersuchten Stimuli wiesen alle eine Dauer von ca. 5-10s auf und bezogen sich somit auf Use-Cases wie z.B. Smart-Home-Umgebungen oder Telefon-Informationssysteme. Im nun folgenden Abschnitt werden die Ergebnisse zweier Studien zu Qualitätsdimensionen synthetisch erzeugter Hörbüchern vorgestellt. In [6] wurde ein Evaluationsverfahren zu Bestimmung der Qualität synthetisch erzeugter Hörbücher entwickelt. Neben bereits standardisierten Skalen [7] wurden einige Bewertungsskalen speziell für diese Aufgabe entwickelt. Um ein möglichst großes Spektrum unterschiedlicher Text abzudecken wurden Bücher aus mehreren Bereichen (Science Fiction, Komödie, Thriller, Kinderbuch usw.) und mit verschiedenen Schreibstilen (direkte/indirekte Sprache, gehobenes Vokabular, kurze/lange Sätze, komplexer Satzbau, poetische Sprache usw.) ausgewählt. Die von zwei Sprachsynthesen mit jeweils weiblicher und männlicher Stimme erstellten Stimuli hatten eine durchschnittliche Länge von ca. 50s. Die Stimuli wurden in einem Hörversuch auf den vorliegenden 8 Skalen bewertet und die Ergebnisse im Anschluss mittels einer Hauptachsen-Faktorenanalyse ausgewertet. Dabei ergaben sich zwei Qualitätsdimensionen, die sich dem *Hörgenuss* und der *Prosodie* zuordnen lassen.

Nach einer abschließenden Verbesserung am Messprotokoll kam das entwickelte Verfahren in der Blizzard Challenge [8] zum Einsatz. Diese ist ein jährlich stattfindender Wettbewerb für Entwickler von Sprachsynthesesystemen, in dem im Jahr 2012 zum ersten Mal auch synthetisch erzeugte Hörbücher evaluiert wurden. In dieser groß angelegten Studie wurden unter Anderem 230 TTS-Hörbuchstimuli auf 7 der im vorgehenden Abschnitt präsentierten Skalen bewertet. Aus einer Faktorenanalyse gingen auch hier zwei Faktoren hervor, die sich ebenfalls dem *Hörgenuss* und der *Prosodie* zuordnen lassen.

Im Vergleich zu den Dimensionen der anfangs beschriebenen Use-Cases zeigt sich, dass die Dimension Hörgenuss der Dimension Natürlichkeit der Stimme zugeordnet werden kann, während die Dimension Prosodie die Rhythmik aus den Dimensionen Natürlichkeit (SD) und zeitliche Störungen (MDS) wiedergibt.

3 Auditive Beurteilung bei unterschiedlichen Anwendungen

Exemplarisch sollen in diesem Abschnitt experimentelle Untersuchungen zur Quantifizierung der Qualität synthetischer Sprache in einem prototypischen System vorgestellt werden. Hierbei handelt es sich um das Infotainment-System INSPIRE, welches im Rahmen des gleichnamigen EU-geförderten IST-Projektes erstellt wurde und die Bedienung verschiedener Geräte in einem intelligenten Haus ermöglicht, wie den Fernseher, den Videorekorder, den Anrufbeantworter, die Leuchten und die Rollos. Einige Funktionen (elektronische Programminformationen, Videorekorder-Programmierung und Anrufbeantworter) sind auch über einen Telefonzugang erreichbar, und insbesondere in diesem Fall kommt der synthetischen Sprache besondere Bedeutung zu.

Ziel der Evaluierung war es deshalb, verschiedene Versionen des Systems mit verschiedenen Synthesesystemen auf ihre Gebrauchstauglichkeit für die geplante Anwendung zu untersuchen. Hierzu wurden 3 Experimente in unterschiedlichen Anwendungsszenarien durchgeführt:

- *Hausumgebung*: Der Fokus der Evaluation lag dabei auf dem Erscheinungsbild, welches der Nutzer vom System bekommt (sog. Metaphor), sowie auf dem Einfluss der Raumakustik bei der Sprachwiedergabe. Dabei konnte INSPIRE entweder als eine Ansammlung von „intelligenten Geräten“ agieren, die unabhängig voneinander eine sprachliche Interaktion mit dem Nutzer führen konnten, oder als „Assistent“, der auf einem Bildschirm in Form eines Avatars sichtbar war, oder als unsichtbarer Assistent (sog. „Geist“).
- *Telefonbedienung aus dem Büro*: Hier wurde der Effekt unterschiedlicher Übertragungskanäle, Endgeräte sowie möglicher Hintergrundgeräusche getestet.
- *Telefonbedienung aus dem fahrenden Auto*: Hier wurde die Robustheit der Sprachausgabe gegen Hintergrundgeräusche sowie bei kognitiver Belastung (Ablenkung durch die Fahraufgabe) des Nutzers gemessen.

Für das erste Szenario wurde das System in einer simulierten Wohnumgebung am IKA der Ruhr-Universität Bochum aufgebaut. Dabei hörten Testnutzer zum einen die Sprachausgabe des Systems vom Sofa aus und realisierten zum anderen die Reaktion der adressierten Hausgeräte. Nach jeder Sprachausgabe wurde zunächst der Inhalt des Gesagten abgefragt; hierdurch sollte erreicht werden, dass sich die Probanden auf den sprachlichen Inhalt konzentrierten (wie dies in einer realen Situation auch der Fall wäre), und nicht allein auf die Oberflächenform. Danach beurteilten sie 4 Merkmale der Sprachausgabe (Gesamtqualität,

Höranstrengung, Annehmlichkeit der Stimme, Passgenauigkeit der Stimme zum System) auf kontinuierlichen Skalen, welche durch Attribute beschriftet waren.

Im zweiten Szenario fehlte das direkte Feedback der Hausgeräte, dafür wurden Telefonverbindungen mit unterschiedlichen Übertragungseigenschaften (Leitungsrauschen, Kodierer mit und ohne Paketverluste) simuliert sowie Endgeräte mit unterschiedlichen akustischen Eigenschaften (Handapparat, realer und idealer Freisprecher), z.T. bei Hintergrundgeräusch verwendet. Im dritten Szenario wurden in einem Fahrsimulator ebenfalls unterschiedliche Übertragungseigenschaften simuliert, allerdings wurde hier nur der Freisprecher als realistisches Endgerät betrachtet; außerdem hatten die Probanden dort eine Fahraufgabe, und es wurde nur die (wahrgenommene) Verständlichkeit sowie die Gesamtqualität abgefragt, welche im Fahrsimulator auf einem Bildschirm bewertet werden sollten. Die Sprachprompts bestanden in allen Fällen aus Sätzen oder Doppelsätzen, welche sowohl statischen als auch dynamisch generierten Inhalte enthielten. Für die statischen Inhalte stand entweder ein natürlicher Sprecher oder verschiedene Sprachsynthesen zur Verfügung, für die dynamischen Inhalte nur die Sprachsynthesen; somit enthielten die Sprachprompts entweder nur synthetische oder auch gemischt natürlich-synthetische Stimmen.

Detaillierte Informationen zum Versuchsaufbau, den Sprachstimuli, den Bewertungsverfahren sowie den Ergebnissen finden sich in [3]. Im Folgenden sollen nur einige Kern-Ergebnisse aufgelistet werden, die veranschaulichen, dass die Qualitätsmesswerte – selbst bei einem einzigen getesteten System und einer einzigen synthetischen Stimme – in starkem Maße vom Anwendungsszenario bestimmt werden:

- In der *Hausumgebung* zeigten sich deutliche Unterschiede zwischen den Qualitätsurteilen für unterschiedliche natürliche und synthetische Stimmen. Allerdings kam die beste synthetische Stimme manchmal einer natürlichen bezüglich der Gesamtqualität gleich. Bei den Metaphoren „Assistent“ und „Geist“ war die Kombination von natürlicher und synthetischer Stimme am vorteilhaftesten. Je nach Metaphor schnitten die Stimmen unterschiedlich ab: Die natürlichen Stimme wurde beim „Assistenten“ besser beurteilt als bei den „intelligenten Geräte“, bei der synthetischen Stimme war es umgekehrt.
- In der *Büroumgebung* zeigte sich ein starker Einfluss des Übertragungskanals auf die Qualitätsurteile. Quantitativ war der Einfluss bei synthetischer Sprache ungefähr mit dem bei natürlicher Sprache vergleichbar, allerdings schien die synthetische Stimme robuster bei Leitungsrauschen. Hintergrundgeräusche am Empfangsort beeinträchtigten insbesondere die Höranstrengung.
- Im *Auto* wurde ebenfalls die natürliche bzw. die Kombination von natürlicher und synthetischer Stimme bevorzugt. Die Übertragungskanäle zeigten wiederum einen deutlichen Einfluss, allerdings war dieser für synthetische Sprache bei Sprachkodierern etwas geringer und bei Paketverlusten etwas stärker ausgeprägt als bei natürlicher Sprache.

Insgesamt kann das Testprotokoll als ein gutes Beispiel für die anwendungsorientierte Evaluierung synthetischer Sprache dienen. Es zeigt, dass das Anwendungsszenario einen signifikanten Einfluss auf die wahrgenommene Qualität hat, und dass vielfach einzelne Einflussfaktoren nur mit einem speziell gestalteten Testprotokoll adäquat berücksichtigt werden können. Dies ist für die Validität der Messergebnisse von großer Bedeutung.

4 Instrumentelle Schätzung

Auditive Bewertungen, wie sie in dem vorangegangenen Abschnitt vorgestellt wurden, stellen immer noch die einzige verlässliche Methode zur Qualitätsbestimmung von Sprachsynthesen dar. Da TTS-Entwickler ihre Systeme innerhalb eines Entwicklungszyklus jedoch des Öfteren evaluieren müssen, um sowohl Algorithmus als auch Korpus zu optimieren, sind zeit- und kostenintensive Nutzerstudien ein ineffizientes Mittel. Um den Aufwand für Hörversuche auf ein Minimum zu reduzieren ist ein rein instrumentelles Verfahren zur Vorhersage der Qualität wünschenswert.

In den vergangenen Jahren wurden einige Verfahren vorgestellt, mit denen sich erste Ergebnisse im Bereich der Qualitätsvorhersage für synthetische Sprache erzielen ließen. Im Folgenden wird ein einführender Überblick über mögliche Ansätze gegeben.

Bereits in [9] wurden unterschiedliche Verfahren miteinander verglichen.

- *HMM-basierter Merkmalsvergleich*

  Im Vergleich zu natürlicher Sprache können in synthetischer Sprache durch die Verknüpfung einzelner Sprachbausteine zu einem Sprachsignal spontane spektrale Veränderungen auftreten, die durch die Trägheit des Vokaltrakts bei Menschen sonst nicht gegeben sind. Diese Störungen dienen als Hinweis auf die Qualität des erzeugten Sprachsignals. Im vorliegenden Ansatz werden deshalb Hidden-Markov-Modelle (HMM) auf natürlich erzeugte Sprache trainiert. Die spektralen vom HMM erfassten Informationen dienen dann dazu, Unterschiede z.B. zwischen natürlichen Wortendungen und durch Sprachsynthese erzeugten Signalunterbrechungen zu quantifizieren.

  Als Basis dienen melskalierte cepstrale Koeffizienten (MFCC) 12. Ordnung. Diese wurden zunächst aus einer Trainingsdatenbank mit natürlichen Sprechern extrahiert und anschließend zum Training des HMMs verwendet. In einem zweiten Schritt lassen sich dieselben Sprachmerkmale aus den zu evaluierenden TTS-Daten extrahieren.

  Über den Forward-Backward-Algorithmus kann nun ein Log-Likelihood-Wert bestimmt werden, der die perzeptive Ähnlichkeit zwischen einem TTS-Signal und dem auf natürliche Sprache trainierten HMM ausdrückt.

- *Linearkombination extrahierter Merkmale*

  Im zweiten Ansatz werden Parameter aus dem TTS-Signal extrahiert, die mit den durch den Syntheseprozess induzierten Störungen in Zusammenhang stehen können. Als Basis dienten zum einen die 44 internen Parameter des in der ITU-T-Empfehlung P.563 [10] beschriebenen Algorithmus. Dieser erlaubt eine zuverlässige Qualitätsschätzung von über einen Telefonkanal übertragener Sprache. Da diese Parameter unter Anderem Signalcharakteristiken wie z.B. Rauschen, zeitliches Clipping und Robotereffekte (metallisch klingende Stimmen) ausdrücken, erschienen sie auch für die durch Sprachsynthese erzeugten Artefakte von Bedeutung. Des Weiteren stand ein Set an Sprachmerkmalen zur Verfügung, das umfangreiche Informationen über den Vokaltrakt liefert und zur Klassifikation von menschlichen Emotionen eingesetzt wird. Enthalten sind unter anderem Informationen zu: Grundfrequenzverlauf, Lautheit, MFCCs, spektralen Komponenten, Formanten und der Intensität. Dadurch ergaben sich insgesamt 1495 Sprachmerkmale pro TTS-Signal.

  Um insbesondere aus dem zweiten sehr umfangreichen Satz an Merkmalen die für die Qualitätsschätzung bedeutsamsten Informationen zu ermitteln wurde eine korrelationsbasierte sequentielle Merkmalsauswahl durchgeführt. Aus der Untermenge an Merkmalen ließ sich mittels einer Hauptkomponentenanalyse ein kleiner Satz relevanter Faktoren ermitteln, die über eine lineare Regressionsanalyse zu einem Qualitätsschätzwert kombiniert wurden.

Neben diesen drei ermittelten Schätzwerten wurden alle Schätzer durch eine weitere lineare Regression miteinander kombiniert. Für die meisten der vorhandenen evaluierten TTS-Datenbanken konnten dadurch sehr gute Vorhersagegenauigkeiten erzielt werden, während die Ergebnisse auf einigen Datenbanken weiter optimiert werden müssen. Dies trifft insbesondere für die weiblichen TTS-Stimuli zu. Die Kombination mehrerer Schätzer führte durchweg zu deutlich stabileren Vorhersagen.

5 Ausblick

Wir haben in den vorangegangenen Abschnitten Methoden zur auditiven Messung und zur instrumentellen Schätzung der Qualität synthetisierter Sprache vorgestellt. Dabei diente die auditive Messung stets als Mittel der Wahl, lassen sich doch nur damit valide und zuverlässige Qualitätsmesswerte erzielen. Allerdings zeigte sich, dass die von Versuchspersonen gelieferten Urteile stark von der Anwendung abhängig sind; Merkmale – oder perzeptive Dimensionen – welche in einem Anwendungszusammenhang als relevant erachtet werden, sind dies nicht unbedingt in einem anderen Zusammenhang.

Die Abhängigkeit der auditiven Qualitätsmessung vom Anwendungszusammenhang erschwert auch eine instrumentelle Schätzung, denn hierbei müsste der Anwendungszusammenhang ja ebenfalls berücksichtigt werden. So lassen sich derzeit zwar für einzelne Datenbanken mit den o.a. Verfahren zufriedenstellende Korrelationen zwischen auditiven Urteilen und instrumentellen Schätzungen herstellen; es bleibt aber noch zu zeigen, in wie weit sich solche Schätzungen auch auf andere Datenbanken, die womöglich andere Anwendungszusammenhänge widerspiegeln, übertragen lassen.

Wir gehen davon aus, dass eine solche instrumentelle Schätzung sich einfacher für einzelne Qualitätsdimensionen als für die Gesamtqualität bewerkstelligen lässt. Dies gilt unter der Annahme, dass der perzeptive (Qualitäts-)Raum von synthetischer Sprache grundsätzlich feststeht, und dass einzelne Dimensionen dieses Raumes je nach Anwendungsszenario unterschiedlich gewichtet werden müssen. Dieser Annahme entspricht die Idee der in Abschnitt 1 genannten „Filterung“ der Wahrnehmungsmerkmale durch die Referenz. Im Ergebnis könnte eine Qualitätsschätzung also in Form eines multidimensionalen Profils erfolgen. Dieser Ansatz wird derzeit in einem gemeinsam mit der Christian-Albrechts-Universität zu Kiel bearbeiteten DFG-Projekt verfolgt (DFG MO 1038/11-2).

Ein Profil von Qualitätsschätzern wäre für die Entwickler von TTS-Systemen von großer Bedeutung. So könnten Entwickler einzelne Parameter ihres Systems (oder den verwendeten Korpus) verändern und direkt (ohne Zeitverlust für die Durchführung eines auditiven Tests) Feedback zur erzielten Qualitätsverbesserung oder –verschlechterung erhalten. Mehr noch, das Profil von Qualitätsschätzern, welche je eine perzeptive Dimension vorhersagen, würde Aufschluss über verbleibende Probleme – und somit Hinweise auf mögliche Lösungen – liefern. Dadurch könnte die Entwicklung besserer Sprachsynthesesysteme stark beschleunigt werden.

Wie oben beschrieben beruhen Messungen von Qualität auf bewussten Urteilen von Probanden eines auditiven Tests. Dies ist notwendig, da das Qualitätsereignis (vgl. Abschnitt 1) innerhalb des Probanden liegt und damit unzugänglich erscheint. Neuere Untersuchungen belegen aber, dass sich durch physiologische Messungen Rückschlüsse auf die Wahrnehmung von Qualität ziehen lassen [11]. So wurde bspw. in [12] gezeigt, dass sich mittels Elektroenzephalographie (EEG) auch nicht bewusst wahrgenommene Störungen von Sprachsignalen messen lassen. Bei der Analyse ereigniskorrelierter Potenziale im EEG zeigte sich, dass vor allem die Amplitude der Reaktion des Gehirns ca. 300 ms nach dem Einsetzen eines Triggers bei gestörten Stimuli größer ist, und dass die Reaktion bei starken Störungen etwas früher eintritt. Die verringerte Latenz kann als geringerer „neuronaler Effort“ bei der

Störungsentdeckung verstanden werden. Am Quality and Usability Lab der TU Berlin wird derzeit in Zusammenarbeit mit dem INRS in Montreal untersucht, ob sich diese Methode auch für synthetisierte Sprache einsetzen lässt [13].

Danksagung

Dieser Beitrag wurde im Rahmen des Projektes „Instrumentelle Schätzung der Qualität synthetisierter Sprachsignale“ (MO 1038/11-2) von der DFG gefördert.

Literatur

[1] Thomson, W. Lecture on “Electrical Units of Measurement” (3 May 1883). Published in Popular Lectures Vol. I, p. 73. Quoted in Encyclopaedia of Occupational Health and Safety (1998) by Jeanne Mager Stellman, p. 1992.

[2] Jekosch, U. Voice and Speech Quality Perception — Assessment and Evaluation. Signals and Communication Technology Series, Springer, Berlin, 2005.

[3] Möller, S., Krebber, J., Smeele, P. Evaluating the Speech Output Component of a Smart-Home System, Speech Communication 48, 1-27, 2005.

[4] Hinterleitner, F., Möller, S., Norrenbrock, C., Heute, U. Perceptual Quality Dimensions of Text-To-Speech Systems, Proceedings Interspeech 2011, Florenz, S. 2177-2180, 2011.

[5] Hinterleitner, F., Norrenbrock, C., Möller, S., Heute, U. What makes this voice sound so bad? A multidimensional analysis of state of the art text-to-speech systems, Proceedings of the Spoken Language Technology Workshop (SLT) 2012, Miami, S. 240-245, 2012.

[6] Hinterleitner, F., Neitzel, G., Möller, S., Norrenbrock, C. An Evaluation Protocol for the Subjective Assessment of Text-To-Speech in Audiobook Reading Tasks, Proceedings of the Blizzard Challenge Workshop, Florenz, 2011.

[7] ITU-T Rec. P.85, A Method for Subjective Performance Assessment of the Quality of Speech Voice Output Devices, International Telecommunication Union, Genf, 1994.

[8] Hinterleitner, F., Norrenbrock, C., Möller, S. Perceptual Quality Dimensions of Text-To-Speech Systems in Audiobook Reading Tasks, Proceedings of the ESSV 2012, Bielefeld, 2013.

[9] Möller, S., Hinterleitner, F., Falk, T., Polzehl, T. Comparison of Approaches for Instrumentally Predicting the Quality of Text-To-Speech Systems, Proceedings Interspeech 2010, Kyoto, S. 1325-1328, 2010.

[10] ITU-T Rec. P.563, Single-Ended Method for Objective Speech Quality Assessment in Narrow-Band Telephony Applications, International Telecommunication Union, Genf, 2004.

[11] Möller, S., Antons, J.-N., Arndt, S., Porbadnigk, A., Schleicher, R. Zum Einsatz von Elektroenzephalographie bei der Messung der Wahrnehmung gestörter Sprache, in: Elektronische Sprachsignalverarbeitung 2012. Tagungsband der 23. Konferenz, Cottbus, 29.-31. Aug., M. Wolff (Hrsg.), TUDpress, Dresden, S. 81-88, 2012.

[12] Antons, J.N., Blankertz, B., Curio, G., Möller, S., Porbadnigk, A.K., Schleicher, R. Subjective listening tests and neural correlates of speech degradation in case of signal-correlated noise, in: Audio Engineering Society (AES) 129th Convention, 2010.

[13] Laghari, K.u.R., Gupta, R., Arndt, S., Antons, J.-N., Schleicher, R., Möller, S., Falk, T.H. Auditory BCIs for Visually Impaired Users: Should Developers Worry About the Quality of Text-to-Speech Readers?, angenommen zur Veröffentlichung: International BCI Meeting (Brain-Computer Interface 2013), Asilomar, Pacific Grove CA, 3-7 June 2013.

Sprachdialogsysteme im Automobil – Von der Theorie in die Serienproduktion

Steffen Werner

steffen.s.werner@daimler.com

Kurzfassung: Die Fahrzeugentwicklung erfordert leistungsfähige Prozesse, um das Gesamtfahrzeug zu einem definierten Termin produzieren und dann dem Kunden übergeben zu können. Ein Prozess davon ist die Entwicklung eines integrierten und modernen Infotainmentsystems, welches mittlerweile einen marken- und einen wertbestimmenden Faktor eingenommen hat. Ein Bestandteil dieses Systems ist ein Sprachdialogsystem welches die Sicherheit und den Komfort bei der Bedienung implementierter Funktionen erhöht und die Fahrablenkung reduziert.

Die einzelnen Stufen bei der Entwicklung eines Sprachdialogsystems für das Infotainmentsystem müssen sich dabei den Prozessschritten der Fahrzeugentwicklung selbst unterwefen. Dieses Paper versucht die einzelnen Stufen den Prozessschritten der Gesamtfahrzeugentwicklung zu zu ordnen. Das Ergebnis sind 7 Entwicklungsstufen, die hier im Einzelnen beschrieben werden.

1 Einleitung

Die Entwicklung von Sprachdialogsystemen (SDS) und dem damit notwendigerweise verbundenen Sprachdialogdesign hat in den letzten Jahren stetig zugenommen (z. B. [McT04, Mei06, Wah06, Hem08, Lew10, Mei10, MLNM11, Sün11]). Viele Sprachdialogsysteme wurden und werden entwickelt bzw. eingesetzt, um bestimmte Geschäftsprozesse zu automatisieren und dementsprechend Kosten zu senken (vor allem in Call Centern). Diese Dialogsysteme und deren zugrunde liegenden Strukturen sind auch die am häufigsten beschriebenen in der Literatur.
Unter einem Sprachdialogsystem ist ein sprachverstehendes Sytem gemeint, welches „dem Erreichen von Zielen im gegenseitigen kooperativen Dialog" ([Ham09]) dient. Hierfür muss das System „Benutzeräußerungen adäquat verarbeiten und darauf sinnvoll reagieren können" [Ham09]. Der kürzeste Dialog ist ein einfacher Turn und entspricht der Äußerung eines Dialogpartners und der Reaktion des anderen (Command&Control). Damit können Systeme entworfen werden, die es dem Nutzer gestatten, mit einer gezielten Spracheingabe eine gewünschte Systemreaktionen hervorzurufen (z. B. DragonTV in [Nua]). Allerdings echte Dialoge, im Sinne eines wechselnden Kommunikationsprozesses beider Dialogpartner, werden hierbei eher selten durchlaufen. Dies findet vor allem in sogenannten Besprechungsszenarien statt [SM10].
Sprachdialogsysteme, wie sie in heutigen Infotainmentsystemen im Fahrzeug eingesetzt werden [Web, Ham09] und Drageon Drive in [Nua], verbinden Command&Control (z. B. Radiosenderwechsel) als auch Interaktionsdialoge (z. B. Sonderzielsuche und anschließender Start der Zielführung) je nach zu erfüllender Aufgabe miteinander.
In diesem Paper stelle ich meine persönliche (idealisierte und stark vereinfachte) Sicht auf die Enwicklung und Umsetzung des Sprachdialogsystems im Automobil dar. In der Realität ist eine solche Entwicklung weit komplexer und unterliegt wesentlich mehr Einflussfaktoren, als hier dargestellt werden (können). Auch die zeitliche Dauer der einzelnen Zuordnungen sind nicht identisch und wurden hier der Einfachheit halber außer acht gelassen.

Die im Rahmen des Papers genannten Beispiele basieren auf dem bereits im Markt befindlichen Sprachdialogsystem LINGUATRONIC der Mercedes-Benz Fahrzeuge. Dieses SDS wurde 1996 eingeführt und vorerst als Sonderausstattung angeboten. Der Funktionsumfang war damals sehr bescheiden und begrenzt auf Nummernwahl, Namenwahl mittels Voice Enrollments und wenige Radio-Steuerungsbefehle. 1998 kam dann die erste Zieleingabe dazu, allerdings musste man noch buchstabieren. Mit der Einführung der Ganzworteingabe für die 800 größten Städte in 2001 und die ersten Sonderzielauswahlmöglichkeiten wie Tankstelle, Parkplatz oder Restaurant stieg auch die Akzeptanz des Sprachdialogsystems.

2006 wurde die LINGUATONIC Sprachbedienung fest an das Infotainmentsystem mit Navigation gekoppelt und erfuhr somit ein weite Verbreitung. Dieses System hatte breits robuste Sprachdialoge für die Ganzwortzieleingabe in mehreren Sprachen, die Auswahlmöglichkeit von Sonderzielen, eine komplette Radio-, Telefon- und Adressbuchbedienung, sowie erste Dialoge zur Multimedia-Steuerung.

Mittlerweile ist eine sog. *OneShot*-Zieleingabe (Ort, Straße, Hausnummerin einer Äußerung), eine Sonderzielsuche und eine Musiksuche ebenfalls selbstverständlich. Kontakten aus dem Telefonbuch können Adressdaten zugeordnet und so direkt zur Navigation ausgewählt werden. Die Eingabe von Telefonnummern erfolgt in einem natürlichen, ununterbrochenem Sprachfluss. Kontakte werden direkt aufgerufen. Namen mit abweichender Schreibweise und Aussprache können mit Sprachtags hinterlegt werden. Der Aufruf und Bedienung der Audioquellen Radio, CD, MP3 kann ebenfalls über Spracheingabe erfolgen.

Nachfolgend sind die persönlich angepassten Entwicklungsstufen kurz beschrieben.

2 Neue Technologien – Träume bewerten

Sprachtechnologie wird zwar nicht jedes Jahr neu erfunden und es passieren auch keine Quantensprünge (mehr), allerdings entwickelt sie sich dennoch stetig weiter.

Allein die Weiterentwicklung der automatischen Spracherkennung (von einzelen Wörtern hin zu *Natural Language Understanding* (NLU)) ermöglichte in den letzten Jahren einen Wandel in der Bedienphilosophie der Dialogsysteme. Anfänglich konnten die Systeme nur Einzel-Wort-Kommandos erkennen und direkt ausführen. Mittels Command&Control war es dann möglich kurze Eingabephrasen zu erkennen und auszuführen, aber auch komplexere (allerdings geführte) Frage&Antwort Dialoge zu gestalten. Heutzutage sind bereits kleinere (oft Domaineingeschänkte) freie natürlich-sprachliche Eingaben möglich.

Auch die Sprachsynthese erfährt Weiterentwicklungen. Vor allem die Qualität der Sprachausgaben nimmt stetig zu. War man vor einigen Jahren noch froh, wenn man in den doch sehr gekünstelten Ausgaben zumindest die Ankunftszeit und/oder die Fahrtrichtungsempfehlung richtig verstanden hat, so lauscht man heutzutage ganzen Textpassagen in Emails und/oder Tages-Nachrichten.

Allerdings ist nicht alles, was auf dem PC und/oder in Simulationen heute bereits darstellbar ist, auch ohne weiteres ins Fahrzeug portierbar. Oft benötigt es von der ersten PC Simulation bis ins Fahrzeug noch einige Jahre Entwicklung. Um eine realistische Einschätzung treffen und hinter den sogenannten „Sales Talk“ blicken zu können, helfen nur eigene praxisnahe Tests und Benchmarks.

3 Design – Wünsche festlegen

Jede Fahrzeugmarke soll als diese auch erkennbar sein, d. h. ein Mercedes-Benz muss immer als Mercedes-Benz erkennbar sein, und das nicht nur über das Fahrzeugdesign sondern auch die Art und Weise der Bedienung. Damit die Sprachbedienung auch den gewünschten Bedienkomfort und die Sicherheit bietet, neben der eigentlichen Fahraufgabe auch noch sicher bedienen zu können, müssen die Konzepte entsprechend ausgearbeitet werden. Das Sprachdialogsysteme den Bedienkomfort und auch die Bediensicherheit während der Fahrt erhöhen, wurde bereits in [Boe01] nachgewiesen. Auch neuere Studien belegen dies.

Es ist deshalb nicht verwunderlich, wenn die Anzahl der möglichen Sprachbefehle und damit der Umfang der mittels Sprache bedienbaren Funktionen immer weiter wächst. Abb. 1 zeigt die Entwicklung über die letzten Jahre am Beispiel des im Mercedes-Benz C-Klasse verbauten Infotainmentsystems. Dabei ist es heutzutage selbstverständlich, dass Adressen über einen

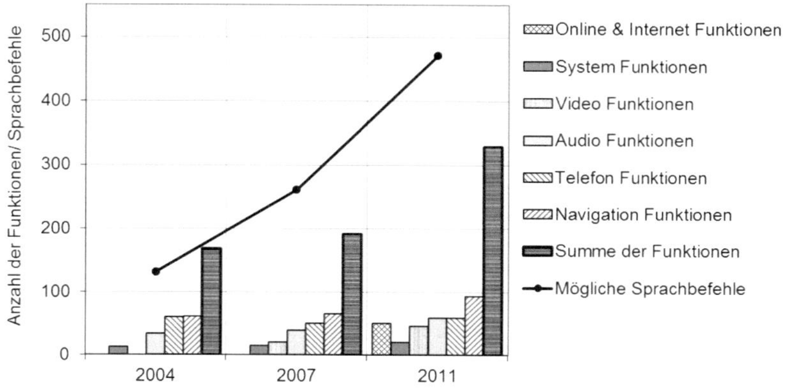

Abbildung 1 - Entwicklung verfügbarer Funktionen/Sprachbefehle am Beispiel des Infotainmentsystems der Mercedes-Benz C-Klasse (aus [Lue13])

sogenannten „OneShot“ (Ort, Strasse und Hausnummer in einer Sprachäußerung) direkt ins Navigationssystem diktiert werden können. Aber auch die Verwendung von Adressen aus den Telefonkontakten eines gepairten Telefons oder einer Restaurantsuche im Internet muss hierbei bedacht werden. Die Architekur des Dialogsystems ist festzulegen, vor allem welcher Erkenner kann welche Erkenneraufgabe am besten meistern und wo befindet sich dieser (On- oder Offboard). Bei Offboard Erkenneraufgaben wie dem Diktieren von SMS und/oder Email kann ein cleveres Dialogdesign auch Konnektivitätsprobleme und/oder längere Antwortzeiten kaschieren.

Die designten Bedienkonzepte und Sprachdialoge verknüpfen das „Look&Feel“ mit den technischen Funktionen und sollen die Gebrauchstauglichkeit (engl. usabilty) maximieren. Diese wird entsprechend der internationalen Norm EN ISO 9241 als „das Ausmaß, indem ein Produkt durch bestimmte Benutzer in einem bestimmten Nutzungskonzept genutzt werden kann, um bestimmte Ziele effektiv, effizient und mit Zufriedenheit zu erreichen“, definiert [DIN11]. In besagter Norm sind ebenfalls Grundsätze für die Gestaltung interaktiver Systeme (wie die Sprachdialogsysteme (SDS)) wie folgt formuliert (frei nach [DIN11] und [Lue13]):

Aufgabenangemessenheit: SDS unterstützt den Benutzer seine Aufgabe effektiv und effizient zu erledigen (z. B. minimale Anzahl an Dialogschritten).

Selbstbeschreibungsfähigkeit: Jeder einzelne Dialogschritt ist unmittelbar verständlich bzw. wird dem Benutzer erklärt (z. B. aussagekräftige Systemprompts).

Steuerbarkeit: Der Benutzer ist in der Lage, den Start, die Richtung, die Geschwindigkeit und den Dialogfortschritt selber zu wählen (z. B. stetige Abbruchmöglichkeit).

Erwartungskonformität: Das SDS soll konsistent sein, d. h. es soll den allgemein anerkannten Konventionen entsprechen und so dem Kenntnisstand des Benutzers widerspiegeln (z. B. durch Vergleich mit anderen Systemen).

Fehlertoleranz: Eine fehlerhafte Eingabe und/oder Systemsetzung muss mit minimalem Aufwand korrigiert werden können (z. B. durch Integration von Korrekturkommandos).

Individualisierbarkeit: Das Einstellen von individuellen Vorlieben des Benutzers ist möglich (z. B. Einstellen der Kartenausrichtung).

Lernförderlichkeit: Der Benutzer soll beim Erlernen des SDS unterstützt werden (z. B. Hilfefunktion).

Aber nicht nur die definierten Konzepte und Dialoge entscheiden über einen positiven Kundeneindruck, sondern auch die verwendeten Sprachaus- und -eingaben.
Letztere sollten ein großes Spektrum der verwendeten Bezeichnungen und Kommandos abdecken und nicht nur die im Infotainment System zur optischen Anzeige verwendeten. So sollte es dem System egal sein, ob ein Nutzer beispielsweise *CD* oder *DISK* sagt und dies Englisch oder Deutsch ausspricht. Aber auch die Eingabe fremder Städtenamen wie *Nizza* oder *Nice* sollte dem System keine Schwierigkeiten machen.
Ein wesentlicher Teil des Markenimage kann über eine geschickte Auswahl der Sprachausgaben und der dazu verwendeten Stimme erreicht werden (vgl. auch die Werbekampagne auf der IFA 2009, z. B. [Wel09]). Damit das Stimmbranding erfolgreich ist, müssen semantische, syntaktische, kontextuelle und prosodische Aspekte beachtet werden und wie diese von einer Stimme transportiert werden. Dieser Möglichkeit wird heutzutage bei Sprachdialogsystemen immer noch viel zu wenig Aufmerksamkeit geschenkt.

4 Virtuelle Erprobung – Möglichkeiten evaluieren

Das Festlegen der Wünsche ist das eine, ob diese aber auch im Fahrzeug umsetzbar sind das andere. Lütze fasst es wie folgt zusammen: „Revolutionäre Bedienkonzepte sind wertlos, wenn die Umsetzung scheitert und eine mangelhafte Qualität den Bedienkomfort und die Bediensicherheit einschränkt. Mehr noch, qulitative Mängel der MMS sind für den Kunden mit hoher Wahrscheinlichkeit wahrnehmbar und haben einen unmittelbaren Einfluss auf die Wertigkeit und den Qualitätseindruck des gesamten Produkts“ [Lue13].
Deshalb ist es um so wichtiger, so zeitig wie möglich aufzuzeigen, ob bestimmte Sprachdialoge im Fahrzeug überhaupt realisiert werden können. Neben den üblichen Randbedingungen wie beschränkter Speicherplatz (Kosten) und beschränkte Rechenleistung (Verbrauch) gibt es ebenfalls technische Herausforderungen wie beispielsweise sehr unterschiedliche Geräusche: Fahrbahn, Wind, Scheibenwischer, Blinker, usw. Aber auch der Kunde selbst möchte in endlicher Zeit eine Reaktion auf seine Eingabe. Das Zusammenspiel dieser Faktoren wird häufig in prototypischen Umsetzungen evaluiert. Mit diesen Demosystemen kann auch das Zusammenspiel verschiedener Bedienmodalitäten untersucht und die mögliche Fahrablenkung gemessen werden.

5 Digitale Entwicklung – Soll-Zustandes spezifizieren

Nach dem Wünsche formuliert und auf Machbarkeit untersucht wurden, muss das Zielsystem noch so niedergeschrieben werden, das es auch implementiert werden kann.
Die Beschreibung eines Sprachdialogsystems erfolgt durch die Darstellung der verschiedenen Dialogaktivitäten durch definierte Elemente, die sich wie folgt einteilen lassen (aus [LW12]):

Benutzeraktionen:

- Haptische Aktivierung des Sprachdialogsystems
- Spracheingaben

Systemreaktionen:

- Akustische Rückmeldung durch Sprachausgaben
- Optische Rückmeldung durch Textausgabe
- Systemaktivität im Hintergrund, ohne optische oder akustische Rückmeldung

Formale Modellelemente zur Beschreibung des Dialogablaufs:

- Startpunkt und Endpunkt
- Variablen mit Zuweisung von Werten
- Dialogverzweigungen mit Abfrage von Zuweisungen oder Systemzuständen
- Vorbedingungen (Preconditions)

Neben (Pseudo-)Progammiersprachen (z. B. VoiceXML) können sowohl *Ablaufdiagramme* als auch *Zustandsdiagramme* zur Modellierung des Dialogablaufs mit den beschriebenen Elementen verwendet werden.

Ablaufdiagramme beschreiben das Systemverhalten als eine Folge von voneinander klar abgegrenzten Aktivitäten. Sie eignen sich gut zur Beschreibung von statischen Systemen, deren Verhalten kaum durch Ereignisse und Bedingungen beeinflusst wird. Zustandsdiagramme beschreiben das Systemverhalten, welches von verschiedenen auf das System einwirkenden Ereignissen und Bedingungen abhängt. Befindet sich das System in einem Zustand, ist es in diesem stabil und verlässt diesen erst durch externe Stimuli. [LW12]

Sprachdialogsysteme zur Bedienung von Infotainmentsystemen im Kraftfahrzeug sind bedienfreundlich gestaltet und die Dialogführung einfach, um den Fahrer nicht von der eigentlichen Fahraufgabe abzulenken. Die Dialoge sind sequenziell und bevorzugt von geringer Tiefe. Im Rahmen dieser Voraussetzungen kann ein Ablaufdiagramm den Sprachdialog sehr gut beschreiben. Abb. 2 zeigt ein Beispiel für einen kleinen Navigationsdialog, wobei sich die Darstellung im wesentlichen an das in [Ham09] vorgestellte Spezifikationsformat hält.

Bei der Definition des Soll-Zustandes muss ebenfalls das statische Vokabular und/oder das statische natürlichsprachliche Sprachmodell festgelegt werden, mit dem das Dialogsystem später arbeiten soll. Statisch deshalb, weil es bereits im Vorfeld ermittelt werden kann und nicht erst zur Laufzeit des Systems bekannt wird. Letzteres entspricht dem dynamischen Vokabular wie beispielsweise die Namen im Telefonbuch des Kundentelefons. Das heißt es muss festgelegt

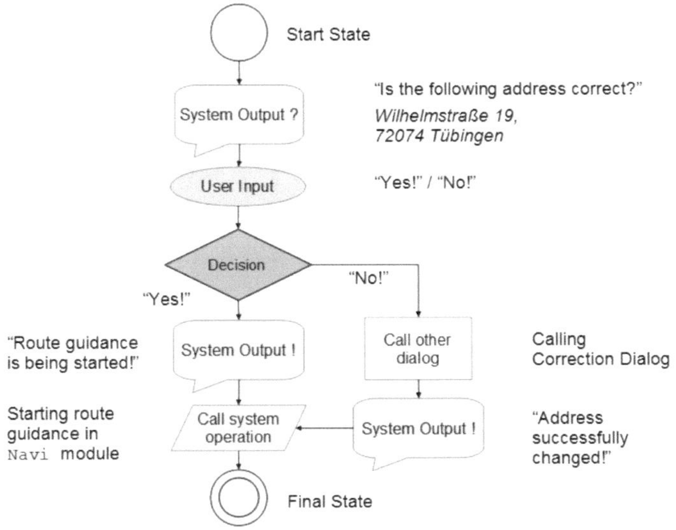

Abbildung 2 - Flowchartbeschreibung eins Navigationsdialoges. (aus [SWH13]

werden, welche Teile mittels Command&Control, welche mit einer erweiterten Frage/Antwort-Modellierung und welche mittels freier natürlichsprachlicher Eingabe umgesetzt werden sollen. Hierbei sind durchaus auch Kombinationen möglich, beispielsweise kann nach einer freien initialen Eingabe noch fehlende Information direkt nachgefragt werden.

Aber auch die Sprachausgaben müssen definiert werden oder es müssen Concept-to-Speech Modelle angelernt werden (welche bisher im Fahrzeug kaum Verwendung finden). Dabei können ebenfalls statische Ausgaben (z. B. Navi-Ansagen, Prompts für Sprachdialoge) und dynamische Ausgaben (z. B. Richtungsangaben, TMC, SMS, Fernsehsender) unterschieden werden. Für eine bessere Sprachqualität ist das Aufnehmen oder Tunen der statischen Prompts zu überlegen.

6 Aufbau von Versuchsfahrzeugen – Können implementieren

Die im Vorfeld spezifizierten Sprachdialoge, müssen nun in den Gesamtkontext des Infotainmentsystems integriert werden. Da Sprachtechnologie heutzutage meist „nur" ein Softwarebaustein innerhalb des Infotainmentsystems ist, unterliegt sie natürlich auch den Softwareentwicklungsregeln die häufig als Entwicklung in the Loop-Modell oder als *V-Modell* [Spi08] dargestellt werden.

Viele Fahrzeughersteller (häufig auch *Original Equipment Manufacturer*, kurz OEM genannt) lassen die Infotainmentkomponente nach ihrer im Vorfeld erstellten Spezifikation fertigen und zuliefern. Beim Zulieferer läuft damit ein Softwareentwicklungsprozess, entsprechend dem V-Modell. Da die Softwareentwicklung in den meisten Fällen über mehrere Releases verteilt wird, um nicht erst am Entwicklungsende Kentniss über die Integrationsqualität zu haben, wird das V-Modell häufig zum sogenannten W-Modell [Spi03] erweitert. Berücksichtigt man ferner die Schnittstelle zwischen Auftragnehmer und Systemlieferant entsteht das in Abb. 3 dargestellte *erweiterte W-Modell*. „Der funktionale Systementwurf und die Anforderungsdefinition bilden den Ausgangspunkt im Entwicklungsprojekt und die zentrale Schnittstelle" [Lue13] zwischen OEM und Zulieferer. Auf dieser Basis kann auf Seiten des Systemlieferanten „das klassische V-Modell gelebt werden und nach technischem Systementwurf und Komponentenspezifikation die Implementierung stattfinden" [Lue13].

7 Fahrzeugtests – Ist-Zustande testen

Nachdem ein Sprachdialogsystem integriert wurde, findet die Qualitätssicherung über separate Testprozesse statt. Allerdings findet nicht ein großer Test „gebündelt am Ende des Entwicklungsprozesses statt, sondern vielmehr iterativ während des gesamten Produktentstehungsprozesses und müssen entsprechend geplant werden" [Lue13].

Wie in Abb. 3 dargestellt, kann der OEM parallel zum Zulieferprozess Testaktivitäten durchführen, wenn auf Basis der Anforderungsdefinition die Tests geplant und das Systemmodell erstellt werden. „Durch die Erstellung des Modells können konzeptionelle, inhaltliche oder formale Fehler in den Spezifikationsdokumenten bereits äußerst frühzeitig identifiziert und korrigiert werden. Gleiches gilt nach Generierung der Testfälle. Ein Review der generierten Testfälle ermöglicht nicht nur die Identifikation von Modellierungsfehlern, sondern offenbart auch konzeptionelle Schwächen des Systems. Ein Großteil der Testaktivitäten kann bereits zu einem Zeitpunkt stattfinden, an welchem die Implementierung des Systems noch nicht begonnen wurde oder noch am Anfang steht. Eine fehlerhafte Implementierung aufgrund fehlerhafter Anforderungsdokumente kann deutlich besser verhindert werden als im bisherigen, klassischen V-Modell." [Lue13]

Durch die Erstellung eines Systemmodells kann der OEM also aktiv die Softwareentwicklung mitgestalten und gleichzeitig die Vorteile des modellbasierten Testens nutzen. Im Rah-

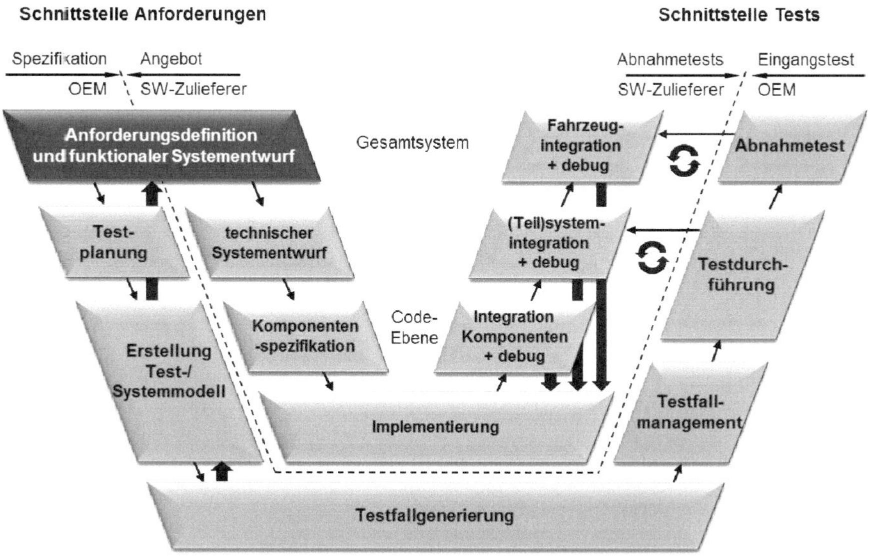

Abbildung 3 - Erweiter W-Modell des automatisierten Testens (aus [Lue13]

men des modellbasierten Testprozesses wird aus der Systemspezifikation ein formales Modell des Sprachdialogsystems erstellt. Durch die Modellierung kann eine automatische Testfallgenerierung ermöglicht werden. Dieser Prozessschritt unterscheidet den modellbasierten Test von automatischen und manuellen Testprozessen (vgl. Abb. 4). [LW12]

Der Vorteil liegt unter anderem darin, dass Testfälle gezielt, in kurzer Zeit und mit einem definierbaren Abdeckungsgrad generiert werden können. Zwar werden Ressourcen investiert, um das Modell zu erstellen, die ressourcenintensive und fehleranfällige manuelle Testfallerstellung entfällt jedoch. [LW12]

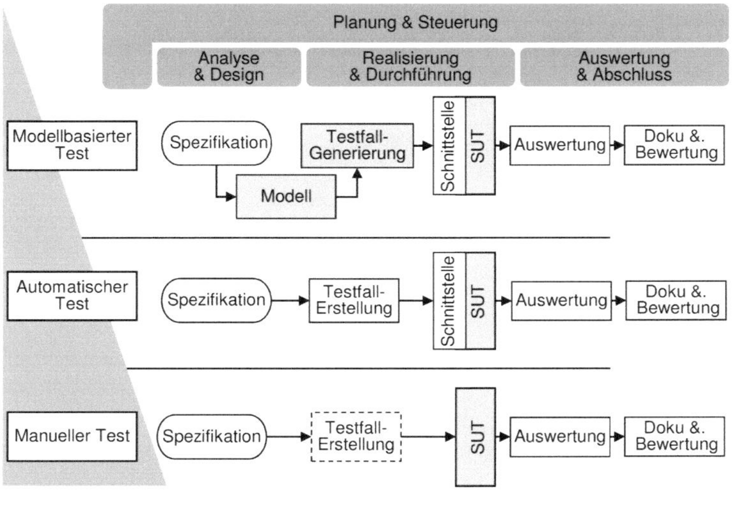

Abbildung 4 - Die verschiedenen Testprozesse des SDS (aus [LW12].
SUT = System Under Test

8 Kundenerlebnis – Kundenzufriedenheit evaluieren

Hat man in den vorherigen Schritten alles richtig gemacht so ist hoffentlich das Produkt auch beim Kunden beliebt und die Absatzzahlen stimmen.

Moderne Infotainmentsysteme haben mittlerweile einen wertbestimmenden und markenspezifischen Rang im Automobil erobert. Deshalb werden auch häufig unabhängige Vergleichtest von verschiedenen Automobilherstellern durchgeführt. Auch wenn man die wirkliche Unahbängigkeit anzweifeln kann, so bieten diese Tests den Kunden auch eine Vergleichsmöglichkeit. In den letzten Jahren werden immer häufiger auch der Bedienkomfort und die Bediensicherheit untersucht und bewertet.

9 Zusammenfassung

In diesem Paper wurde die persönliche Sicht auf die Abbildung der Entwicklung von Infotainment-Sprachdialogsystemen auf den Fahrzeugentwicklungsprozess dargestellt. In der nächsten Ausbaustufe müssen noch die zeitliche Dauer und auch agile Prozesse der Softwareentwicklung betrachtet werden.

Literatur

[Boe01] Erwin R. Boer. Behavioral entropy as a measure of driving performance. In *International Driving symposium on Human Factors in Driver Assessment, Training and Vehicle Design*, USA, 2001.

[DIN11] DIN. EN ISO 9241: Ergonomie der Mensch-System-Interaktion, 2011.

[Ham09] Stefan W. Hamerich. *Sprachbedienung im Automobil: Teilautomatisierte Entwicklung benutzerfreundlicher Dialogsysteme*. Springer Berlin Heidelberg, 2009.

[Hem08] Thomas Hempel. *Usability of Speech Dialog Systems – Listening to the Target Audience*. Springer Verlag, 2008.

[Lew10] James R. Lewis. *Practical Speech User Interface Design (Human Factors and Ergonomics)*. Crc Pr Inc, 2010.

[Lue13] Lars Luetze. *Modellbasierter Test der akustischen Mensch-Maschine-Schnittstelle eines Infotainmentsystems im Kraftfahrzeug*. PhD thesis, Universität Stuttgart, 2013.

[LW12] Lars Luetze and Steffen Werner. Qualitätssicherung im LINGUATRONIC Entwicklungsprozess – Modellbasiertes Testen auf Basis formaler Beschreibung von Sprachdialogsystemen. In *Elektronische Sprachsignalverarbeitung (ESSV), Tagungsband*, 2012.

[McT04] Michael F. McTear. *Spoken Dialogue Technology: Towards the Conversational User Interface*. Springer London, 2004.

[Mei06] Bill Meisel. *VUI Visions – Expert views on Effective Voice User Interface Design*. Trafford Publishing, 2006.

[Mei10] Bill Meisel. *Speech in the User Interface: Lessons from Experience*. Trafford Publishing, 2010.

[MLNM11] Wolfgang Minker, Gary Geunbae Lee, Satoshi Nakamura, and Joseph Mariani. *Spoken Dialogue Systems Technology and Design*. Springer Verlag, 2011.

[Nua] Nuance. http://www.nuance.com/products/.

[SM10] Petra-Maria Strauß and Wolfgang Minker. *Proactive Spoken Dialogue Interaction in Multi-Party Environments*. Springer Verlag, 2010. ISBN 13: 978-1441959911.

[Sün11] David Sündermann. *Advances in Commercial Deployment of Spoken Dialog Systems*. SpringerBriefs in Speech Technology. Springer Verlag, amy neustein edition, 2011.

[Spi03] A. Spillner. Das W-Modell, Vorteile der agilen Prozesse in einem konservativen Umfled nutzen. Technical report, Hochschule Bremen/Oldenburg, 2003.

[Spi08] A. Spillner. *Praxiswissen Softwaretest – Testmanagement*. dPunkt.verlag, 2008.

[SWH13] Maria Schmidt, Steffen Werner, and Tobias Heinroth. Herausforderungen der kombinierten Verwendung von On-Board- und Off-Board-Sprachdialogsystemen in Telematikeinheiten im Automobil. In *Elektronische Sprachsignalverarbeitung (ESSV), Tagungsband*, 2013.

[Wah06] Wolfgang Wahlster. *SmartKom: Foundations of Multimodal Dialogue Systems*. Cognitive Technologies. Springer Verlag, 2006.

[Web] http://www.mercedes-fans.de/inside/inside_artikel/id=1059.

[Wel09] http://www.welt.de/motor/article4459936/Dies-sind-die-Stimmen-in-der-sprechenden-S-Klasse.html, 04.Sept.2009.

Chinese Synthesis in a Multilingual TTS System and a German CAPT System for Chinese Learners

Hongwei Ding

School of Foreign Languages, Tongji University, China
hongwei.ding@tongji.edu.cn

Abstract: One characteristic of IAS TU Dresden is the research of the tone language Mandarin Chinese, in addition to other European intonation languages. There are two important developments related to Mandarin Chinese in the laboratory: 1) The first development is to integrate a Mandarin Chinese synthesis into the multilingual text-to-speech system; 2) Another important event is the extension of the German CAPT system for Chinese learners. In this paper, the researches we have carried out in both fields will be briefly summarized.

1 Introduction

State-of-the-art speech synthesis systems sound no longer mechanical and robotic, especially Chinese speech synthesis has progressed remarkably in recent years. Since 2008, not only synthesizers of English, but also synthesizers of Mandarin Chinese will be evaluated in the annual open, international event – Blizzard Challenge. Both English and Chinese are regarded as important languages for the international research institutions of speech synthesis. The importance of Chinese speech synthesis was foreseen in the laboratory, since 1995 a lot of efforts have been devoted to Chinese TTS to enlarge the multilingual Dresden Speech Synthesizer (DreSS) [8]. Besides the DreSS synthesis system, a German CAPT system is another important product of speech technology. Based on the accomplishment of a CAPT system for European learners [9], IAS has been cooperated with Tongji University to extend the system for Chinese learners [6]. Because there are so many Chinese students studying in Germany, a German CAPT system meets great requirements both in China and in Germany.

2 Mandarin Synthesis

A TTS system normally begins with the orthographic text input, then generates the prosodic parameters, and finally outputs the synthesized speech. However, the development of our Mandarin Chinese synthesis system started from the bottom up: 1) We began with the task to build an acoustic inventory; 2) After we concatenated the syllables and synthesized the Chinese speech, we made efforts to modify the prosody; 3) After acceptable synthesis was generated, we managed to convert the orthographic Chinese characters to phonetic pinyin transcriptions. In the following sections, these three steps will be introduced with the emphasis on the new approaches applied in our Mandarin Chinese synthesis [1]: 1) The first was the construction of a syllable-based inventory to model the coarticulatory effects that cross syllable boundaries; 2) The second was the superposition of a rule-based sentence intonation with the inherent tone structure to maintain the natural tone contours of Chinese syllables.

2.1 Acoustic inventory

The original contribution of our Mandarin synthesis was the acoustic inventory construction. In the early 1990s diphones were the most favorite units for acoustic inventory to model the coarticulation in speech. Syllables are actually the best unit choice in Chinese synthesis for several reasons: 1) a limited number of about 420 syllables can cover almost all pronunciations in Chinese; 2) the lexical tone can be stored together with the syllable; 3) a syllable is longer than a diphone, syllable-based synthesis can reduce concatenation points and provide better synthesis quality. Due to the difficulty in modeling coarticulation across syllables, diphones were widely used in Chinese synthesis. We were among the first to use syllable as the phonetic unit and were successful in modelling the coarticulation across syllables, which proves to be the right decision. With the rapid development of computer processing power and storage capacity, syllable has long become the most favorite acoustic unit for most Chinese speech synthesis systems.
The challenge in inventory design is to capture key coarticulation phenomena while at the same time to keep the number of units in practical limit. This was achieved by the following two approaches:

1. To introduce typical allophonic variations of vowel-ending syllables into the synthesis inventory, so that the coarticulation effects across syllables could be modelled in time domain without the need of spectral manipulation; and

2. To store all the possible tonal variations for the syllables, so that least prosodic manipulations was required in the process of synthesis.

To illustrate the adequacy of the coarticulation-oriented inventory, one example is shown in Figure 1, in which the formant transitions are smoother with the availability of such an inventory:

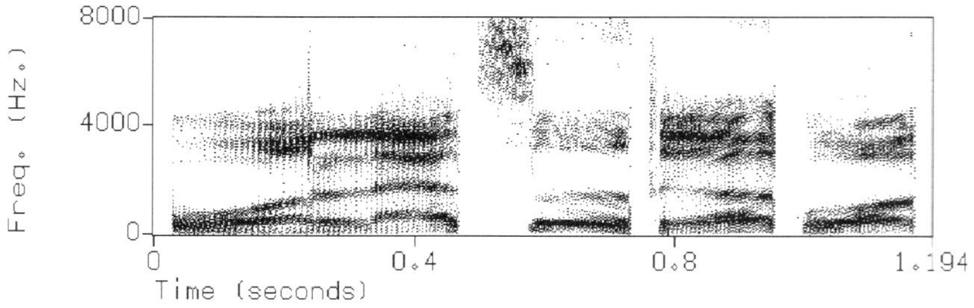

Figure 1: The spectrogram of a synthesized sentence "wo3 lai2 zi4 de2guo2 (I come from Germany.)"

From the above spectrographic patterns, it is obvious that the formant transitions across syllables are not abrupt. And listening tests also confirmed that concatenation of syllables with correct coarticulation patterns out of the inventory did sound more natural than the simple concatenation without any consideration in the aspect of coarticulation.

2.2 Prosody modelling

In the intonation model, both rule-based and data-driven approaches have been attempted. In the rule- and parameter-based model in Chinese [2, 3, 1], the intonation model was resulted from the superposition of suprasegmental sentence intonation and segmental tonal components.

One synchronization point in the middle of the syllable was chosen for each tonal change due to sentence intonation effect, which can be illustrated in Figure 2.

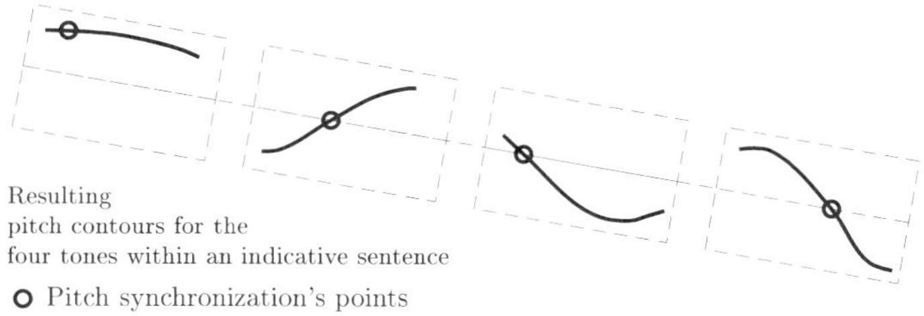

Figure 2: Superposition of syllable inherent tone contours and sentence intonation pattern

This theory was also reflected in a rule-based data-driven model for Chinese [7], which employed the linguistic and prosodic information to treat these in combined effects, and predicted parameters for both duration and intonation. In order to catch the peaks and lows in the syllable contours, f0 was calculated at three points in the syllable final (at the onset and offset, and in the middle). An additional point at the beginning of the syllable initial was also introduced, thus we had four points in the syllable to capture the maximum and minimum of the tonal contours and tonal coarticulation effects. Listening tests proved that both rule-based and data-driven models improved the naturalness substantially.

2.3 Text analysis

Word segmentation proves to be the most difficult task in Mandarin text analysis. It is well known that Chinese is an ideographic language and there is no word delimiter between words in written text. No meaningful spaces are used to separate larger units of words (or phrases) in the sequence. Native speakers typically agree on which characters form a semantic unit. In automatic processing, it is particularly difficult to segment words correctly.

The lexicon-based matching approach was adopted in our system. The basic strategy was to match the input characters string with a large set of entries stored in a pre-compiled lexicon to find all (or part of) possible segmentations. In this method, the lexicon played the critical role in the result of word segmentation. A list of about 100,000 Mandarin Chinese words with pronunciations in pinyin was used as the lexicon in our system. In order to resolve the ambiguities, a set of heuristic rules, time and numeral expressions, and name identifiers were also applied in the analysis [4]. This lexicon-based method was very simple, but could achieve a relatively satisfactory performance. The accuracy amounted to 96% with a test of the database which consisted of 63 sentences.

However the lexicon-based algorithm could not identify some unknown words in texts. In order to achieve further improvements in the future, a statistical model should be integrated into the system, and part of speech tagging is also necessary for an accurate word segmentation.

3 German CAPT for Chinese Learners

With the progress of speech technology, language educators become more interested in CAPT (Computer Assisted Pronunciation Training) systems. All these systems intend to capture segmental and suprasegmental error patterns of the learners and provide the learners with targeted training to improve their pronunciation. With the same approach, a German learning tutoring system EURONOUNCE has been developed [9] at TU Dresden. It is a corpus-based learning system, which integrates large speech corpora and multilingual speech databases. Special speech corpora are needed for each pair of languages. With the aim to extend the system to German-Chinese language pair, we have been making efforts to collect speech data [6] and analyze the segmental and suprasegmental deviations of Chinese learners from German native speakers, some of the researches will be introduced in the following.

3.1 Segmental investigation

Tense-lax vowel contrast, consonant clusters and consonant codas of Chinese learners are the main focus of segmental investigation.
Since Chinese vowels do not have tense-lax contrast as those in German, our investigations have found that Chinese learners have greater difficulty in pronouncing German lax vowels than tense vowels [5]. The differences can be observed by comparing the F1-F2 vowel chart produced by Chinese subjects in Figure 3 (a) with that by a German native speaker presented in Figure 3 (b). These Chinese speakers exhibited a similar pattern of vowel charts as those of the native speaker, F1 of most lax vowels (/I/, /E/, /a/, /O/, /U/, /Y/, /9/) are higher than their corresponding tense vowels (/i/, /e:/, /a:/, /o:/, /u:/, /y:/, /2:/); and all the short vowels connected with dotted lines are located inside the triangle of the long vowels connected with solid lines. The difference is that lax vowels produced by Chinese speakers (Figure 3 (a)) are not centralized as those by the German native speaker in Figure 3 (b).

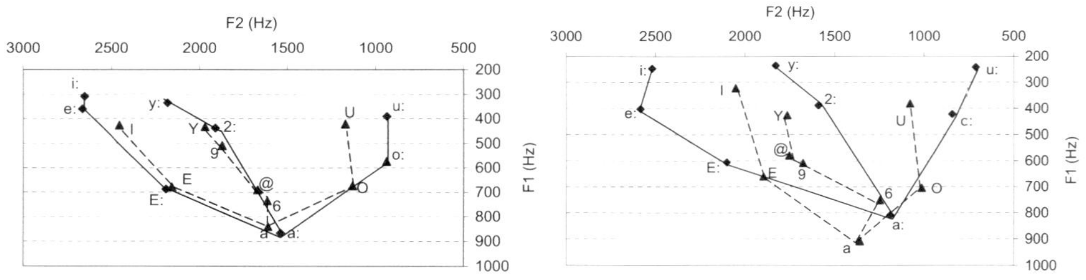

(a) produced by Chinese learners (b) produced by a native female speaker

Figure 3: Chart of German vowels produced by Chinese and German speakers

In addition to vowel investigation, consonant clusters and post-vocalic German /l/ of Chinese learners were also investigated. It has been found that:

1. Chinese students employed all kinds of modification strategies: epenthesis, feature change and absence, with epenthesis as the major strategy. There were certain relationship between coda length and accuracy of pronunciation, the longer the codas were, the more inaccurate were the pronunciation.

2. Beginners had some preference for a CV syllable structure on German word-final coda acquisition. But advanced learner were getting used to CVC pronunciation.

3. Different categories of consonants demonstrated different degrades and different types of modification, a clear /l/ was usually replaced by a dark /l/ after vowels, which was classified as feature change. All kinds of consonants could be modified by epenthesis, but /t/ was by far the most favorite phone for epenthesis.

3.2 Prosodic investigation

Deviation of pitch movements and duration in German speech by Chinese learners have been studied in the aspect of suprasegmentals.
Chinese language is a tonal language, pitch can be changed greatly on the syllable level. Trying to attach a lexical tone to each syllable final, Chinese speakers speak vividly. German language is, however, an intonation language, pitch changes are spread across a stretch of speech such as sentences. Moreover, German intonation is more monotonous and less lively compared with the other European languages, such as English, Swiss German, etc. The intonational differences pose a great difficult for Chinese learners.
Based on the investigations we conducted, findings can be summarized as follows:

- Chinese learners were reluctant to use the rising boundary tone to express yes/no questions, while Chinese question particles can take the role of pitch movement in this case.
- Chinese learners tended to use falling pitch accent (H*+L) to stress syllables, which is not popular in German at non-final positions.
- Major intonational deviations were: inappropriate insertion of pauses and non-reduced syllables; incorrect placement of pitch accent and boundary tones; different phonetic strategies to realize accentuation; more frequent pitch changes and enlarged pitch ranges; higher beginning pitch levels of intonation phrase.

Besides intonational differences, Chinese speakers also deviate from the native German rhythmic patterns. As reported in the previous literature that stress-timed languages like German have a relatively lower $\%V$ and a high ΔC, while syllable-stressed languages like Chinese have a relatively high $\%V$ and a lower ΔC. When Chinese learners read German sentences, because of the organization of German text, they showed a lowerer $\%V$ than that when they read Chinese, but they still produced a high percentage of the vocalic intervals. The values of $\%V$ and ΔC are the averages of 10 sentences of each speaker, which is illustrated in Figure 4.

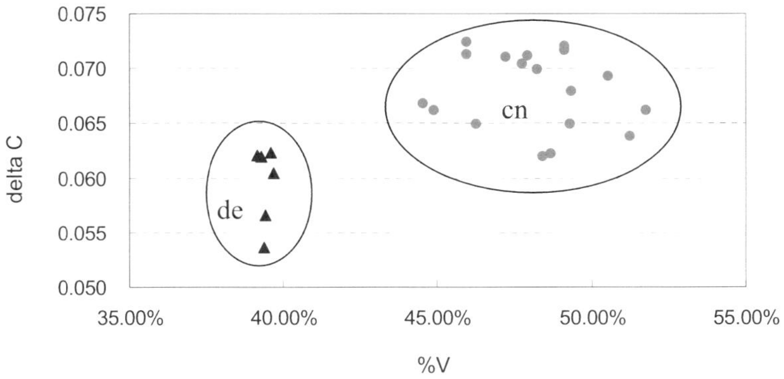

Figure 4: Vocalic proportion (%V) and standard deviation of consonantal intervals (delta C) for all Chinese speakers (cn) and the German native speakers (de)

One reason is that Chinese learners did not reduce vowels as the natives do, another reason is that they added an extra schwa to get a CV syllable structure out of German. And because of the nature of German text, Chinese learners produced a much higher ΔC than that in their Chinese speech, and even higher than those of German speakers. The explanation for that might be due to their slower rate of speech than that of the German natives.

Because of the deviations in vowels and consonants, in intonation and rhythm, foreign accents are perceptible in German speech of Chinese learners. With the help of visualization and feedback of the CAPT system, all these segmental and suprasegmental aspects can be improved.

4 Discussions and Conclusions

Under the leadership of Prof. Hoffmann, holder of the Chair of System Theory and Speech Technology, the research on Chinese has been continuously carried out since I joined the group in the early 1990s. Speech technology products and numerous publications have been produced, and cooperation relationship with China (esp. Tongji University) has been established. All these achievements are best indications of the internationalization of the chair.

5 Acknowledgements

Some of the cooperative research work with China is supported by the Shanghai Social Science project (Project No. 2011BYY002).

References

[1] DING, H.: *A Syllable-based Chinese Synthesis System*, vol. 19 of *Studientexte zur Sprachkommunikation*. w.e.b. Universitätsverlag, 2001.

[2] DING, H. and J. HELBIG: *Natural Tone Contours in a Mandarin Chinese Speech Synthesizer*. ESCA Workshop on Intonation, pp. 95–98, 9 1997.

[3] DING, H. and J. HELBIG: *Modeling Duration and Tonal Coarticulation in a Mandarin Chinese Synthesis*. In *Proc. ISCSLP*, pp. 243–248, Singapore, 1998.

[4] DING, H. and O. JOKISCH: *Grapheme-to-Phoneme Conversion in Mandarin Chinese Text-to-Speech*. In *Joint Congress of 7th Congres Francais d'Acoustique CFA and 30. Deutsche Jahrestagung für Akustik DAGA*, pp. 1151–1152, France, 2004.

[5] DING, H., O. JOKISCH and R. HOFFMANN: *Perception and Analysis of Chinese-accented German Vowels*. Archives of Acoustics, 32(1):89–100, 2007.

[6] DING, H., O. JOKISCH and R. HOFFMANN: *An Audiovisual Feedback System for Pronunciation Tutoring – Mandarin Chinese Learners of German*. In *Cognitive Behavioural Systems*, vol. 7403 of *Lecture Notes in Computer Science*, pp. 191–197. Springer, 2012.

[7] DING, H., O. JOKISCH and H. KRUSCHKE: *Duration and intonation in Mandarin Chinese synthesis with a neural network*. In *Proc. 3rd Intern. Symposium on Chinese Spoken Language Processing (ISCSLP)*, pp. 265–268, Taiwan, 2002.

[8] HOFFMANN, R., D. HIRSCHFELD, O. JOKISCH, U. KORDON et al.: *Evaluation of A Multilingual TTS System with Respect to the Prosodic Quality*. In *Proc. ICPhS*, pp. 2307–2310, San Francisco, 1999.

[9] JOKISCH, O., R. JÄCKEL, M. RUSKO, G. DEMENKO, N. CYLWIK, A. RONZHIN, D. HIRSCHFELD, U. KOLOSKA, L. HANISCH and R. HOFFMANN: *The EURONOUNCE Project - An Intelligent Language Tutoring System with Multimodal Feedback Functions: Roadmap and Specification*. In *Proc. Konferenz Elektronische Sprachsignalverarbeitung (ESSV)*, pp. 116–123, Frankfurt, 2008.

Development of Speech Technology for Under-resourced Languages

Ivan Kraljevski and Yitagessu Birhanu Gebremedhin

TU Dresden, Chair for System Theory and Speech Technology, Dresden, Germany
{ivan.kraljevski, yitagessu_birhanu.gebremedhin}@tu-dresden.de

Abstract: This paper presents two case studies about development of speech recognition and synthesis for under-resourced languages. One case is for Macedonian, which is small population language with unavailable electronic speech resources. The other case is for Amharic, which is language with larger population but with sparse and inappropriate speech databases. Both cases cover the development of speech recognition and synthesis, but use different approaches to create the speech resources. In the first case, cross-language transfer was employed from existing German acoustic model, at first, to transcribe recorded speech sequences, to adapt the source acoustic model for speech recognition and to create completely new model for synthesis. In the second case, smaller amount of the collected Amharic speech data was manually transcribed and used to bootstrap initial acoustic model and create automatic labeler for the rest of the corpus. In both cases, it was shown that the created recognition and synthesis systems provide good recognition performance and acceptable quality, respectively.

1 Introduction

With recent advances in the speech technology and the usage of faster and more available hardware, the state-of-the-art Automatic Speech Recognition (ASR) and synthesis technology becomes more accessible for numerous speech enabled human-computer interaction (HCI) applications. However, in order to develop speech enabled applications with high level of performance and usability, acquisition of large quantity of carefully prepared and transcribed acoustic data is required.

This requirement is especially emphasized for under-resourced languages, where little or no electronic speech and language resources exist. This is the case with the languages used by smaller (Macedonian), as well as large speaker population languages (Amharic) but with sparse language resources. The acquisition and transcription of speech data is very time consuming and costly process and presents one of the major limiting factors in development of speech enabled applications. Transcription process of newly recorded speech material requires manual labeling by human language experts, usually 20-40 times the real-time where the labeling accuracy is inconsistent and error prone.

Therefore, availability of sophisticated speech recognition and synthesis technology is limited to the most widespread world languages. Many different approaches exists which support rapid creation and development of speech enabled systems for under-resourced languages.

The most common approach is the exploitation of acoustical similarities between the sounds in different languages. Some methods as cross-language transfer uses generalized set of acoustic models capable to perform speech recognition on multiple languages without the need of any target language training data.

In [1] the authors examined the performance in the scenario of cross-language transfer of LVCSR systems to other languages when no training data is available at all. The authors in [2] used ASR systems on six source languages to build a system on Vietnamese with cross-language transfer, unsupervised training and bootstrapping.

With bootstrapping approach, the target language acoustic models are initialized with models developed for another language. Usually, this method is limited to context independent monophonic models initialized for the target language by source language seed models. Then, these initial acoustic models could be recreated or re-adapted using training data of the target language [3-4].

Cross-language adaptation method is based on adapting of existing acoustic models of one language in order to improve discriminatory ability on another language using very small amount of available transcribed data [5-6].

In this paper, two different approaches for development of speech technologies for under-resourced languages are presented. In the first case, cross-language adaptation was used after bootstrapping for creation of acoustic-model for ASR and synthesis on Macedonian language. In the second case, innovative approach was used to build a syllable based, speaker independent, continuous, Amharic ASR using smaller number of acoustic models for the 196 distinctly pronounced Consonant-Vowel (CV) syllable. Because there were no available commercial nor appropriate speech databases on Amharic, the textual and speech corpus was prepared and transcribed by human expert.

2 UASR experimental setup

The UASR (Unified Automatic Speech Recognition and Synthesis) [7] system was used for speech recognition and synthesis. UASR is a speech dialogue system where the speech recognition and synthesis components uses common databases at each processing level. During the recognition process, prosodic information is separated from the data flow and later this information can to be added again for the synthesis. This process is crucial for the naturalness of the synthesized speech. The modular software structure of the framework enables flexible application of different algorithms. Also, this framework allows an inverse function of the recognizer system thus offering the potential for applying analysis-by-synthesis methods for improving the performance of speech recognition systems.

The UASR system uses arc-emission HMMs with one single Gaussian density per arc and an arbitrary topology. The Gaussians are assigned to arcs and create one incoming and one loop arc for every Gaussian at the state for that distribution. The mixture weights are represented through different transition probabilities for each Gaussian distribution.

The structure is built iteratively during the training process by state splitting from an initial HMM model. Applying these topologies as acoustic models in a speech synthesis process requires finding of optimal state sequence within a phoneme model in a given context. In these experiments the synthesis algorithm uses specific textual data, diphone inventory, intonation and phoneme duration modeling as an input for the following processing steps:

- Selecting a path through the HMMs according to a demanded length and modeling the duration of each state in the path [8];
- Assembling the feature sequence for the chosen path;
- Generating the speech signal using a synthesis filter [9].

In order to create the diphone inventory, as a first step, pitch mark analysis must be performed over the data set and the intonation statistics for each speech sequences will be estimated. The diphone inventory will be produced using these statistics and the speaker dependent acoustic model with the highest quality. This acoustic model will be used in speech recognition process on each unique diphone found in the data set and the recognition path throughout the feature space described by the phoneme models will be stored. If more than one example of the same diphone unit occurred, the path of the recognized diphone with the highest accuracy will be preserved [8].

3 Small population language case (Macedonian)

Macedonian is official language of the Republic of Macedonia and an official minority language in parts of Albania, Romania and Serbia. It is a South Slavic language, spoken as a first language by some two million people, principally in the Republic of Macedonia and the Macedonian diaspora; variants are also spoken in some neighboring states. Standard Macedonian was implemented as the official language in 1945 and most of the codification was formalized during the same period.

3.1 Acoustic modeling

In this case, a fast and inexpensive cross-language adaptation method is presented where the source model used as a bootstrapping platform was trained on large German speech corpus. Based on the assumption that the articulatory production of phonemes is very similar across different languages, it is supposed that most phonemes can be considered independent of specific language. However, there is no reliable way to predict and match one language to other. There is a relation of the size of the phoneme set and the cross-language performance. Languages with larger phoneme set (like German, English) enable better possibilities for phoneme mapping compared to languages with more compact phoneme sets (like Japanese).

Firstly, the German acoustic model with phoneme mapping table was used to transcribe and align the only available small amount of speaker dependent recordings. German vowels are represented with more distinct symbols like checked vowels (SAMPA): I, E, a, O, U, Y, 9, the free vowels, i:, e:, E:, a:, o:, u:, y:, 2:, and three free diphthongs aI, aU, OY, while in Macedonian language there are only 6 vowels: i, e, a, @, o, u. This leads to unacceptable phoneme error rate as observed in the speech recognition experiments. Twenty of thirty three units found in Macedonian phonetic inventory can be directly mapped with exact SAMPA German counterpart. The remaining 13 phonemes were replaced with the nearest possible match or replaced by phoneme combinations.

The former is applied for the Macedonian phonemes "ѓ" (IPA: /ɟ/, SAMPA: J\), "s" (IPA: /dz/, SAMPA: dz), "љ" (IPA: /ʎ/, SAMPA: L), "ќ" (IPA: /c/, SAMPA: c). Because there are no similar phonemes in German language, it is assumed that these phonemes could be successfully modeled by combining two other existing phonemes from the source language.

Post-alveolar phoneme "ж" (IPA: /ʒ/, SAMPA: Z) is also present in the German phonetic inventory, but it is rarely found in available training data, thus, this phoneme is not contained in existing acoustic model and it is matched with the alveolar "z" (IPA: /z/, SAMPA: z). The phonemes "s" (IPA: /dz/, SAMPA: dz) and "џ" (IPA: /dʒ/, SAMPA: dZ) were modeled as a combination of the existing model for /d/ and /z/.

In this case, acoustic models were tied and the resulting phoneme inventory for the target language is reduced from 33 to 24. For the recognition problem, this suboptimal modeling can be successfully compensated using proper language modeling, either by constrained formal grammar or statistical language modeling. Opposite, for the speech synthesis these compromises will introduce false pronunciation for those particular phoneme units.

Small speaker-dependent speech recordings on Macedonian were used in the experiments, the corpus was created for the diphone concatenation based TTS system [10]. It consists of 758 short word sequences recorded in less controlled (office) conditions (with present background noise) under following restrictions: constant volume, without intonation, average pronouncing speed, clear articulation and single recording session.

For training and evaluation, the subset of Verbmobil German Database was used (32337 of total 41512 (1022 speakers, 96 hours) turns [11]. The acoustic model structure consists of 42 monophonic HMMs plus one pause and one garbage model. During the training phase on clean speech, the phoneme states were split in 3 iterations thus giving 24 Gaussian different distributions per phoneme or total of 48 for incoming and loop arcs.

In order to examine whether even small amount of available speech data can be successfully used for seed acoustic model adaptation, a development set was created by randomly choosing ~10% of the available data set. The remained sequences (682 sentences, 1004 seconds) forms the training set for the new speaker dependent HMM synthesis acoustic model.

3.2 Speech recognition experiments

In the recognition experiments, the test set of VM2 database with total duration of 9133 seconds was used to evaluate phoneme recognition for the German (47.7%). The recognition performance for the transcribed Macedonian speech was only 17.3%. After confusion analysis it was obvious which phonemes introduces biggest recognition errors and the phoneme mapping was adjusted, which consequently improved the recognition rate (29.4%).

Keeping in mind that small target language data set was produced from only one speaker, the adapted model achieved recognition rate of 66.50%. This gives an indication that the source language acoustic model adapted on the target language with appropriate phoneme mapping can be successfully used in speaker-dependent speech recognition with small to medium vocabulary and constrained language model.

3.3 HMM synthesis experiments

In the HMM speech synthesis experiments, the same UASR configuration was used to create new acoustic model with 25 phoneme models and 3 states per model. The used phonetic units represent a subset with total phoneme count smaller than can be found in Macedonian language. However, this was not a critical issue for the speech recognition task where the language model and the given context could inhibit the effects of monophonic state tying and contribute to better recognition rate. This issue can be compensated during the acoustic model training by using larger number of Gaussian distributions per model.

The training process was performed with 5 splits, producing total number of 2400 distributions, 96 different per phoneme model. The resulting speech is intelligible, but still lacks the naturalness of the original recorded speech. The naturalness can be improved with better intonation and duration modeling by statistical analysis of the Macedonian language.

4 Large population language case (Amharic)

Amharic is the official language of the Federal Democratic Republic of Ethiopia and the second widely spoken Semitic language in the world, after Arabic. The name Amharic comes from the Amhara region in northern Ethiopia, which is thought to be the historic center of the language. Outside Ethiopia, Amharic is the language of some 2.7 million emigrants mainly in Israel, the USA, Canada, and Sweden.

Amharic is written from left to right using a scripting system known as Ge'ez, which has 33 consonants and 7 vowels. This scripting system is unique in that the consonants and vowels in its orthography do not exist independent of each other. Previous attempts to build ASR on Amharic were conducted with variable success [12-15].

4.1 The Amharic speech recognizer

The Amharic speech recognizer is built using CV-syllables as the fundamental sub-word units as their number is very small in Amharic. A number of experiments are conducted to determine the best HMM structure for representing the syllables. The experiments revealed that a left-right structure with 5 states per HMM for longer syllables and 3 states per HMM for relatively shorter syllables are the best HMM structures to use. In both cases, there are 32 Gaussians per state.

Unfortunately, speech corpora are not commercially available for under-resourced languages such as Amharic. Therefore, a large speech corpus of more than 35 hours duration is collected from 133 different speakers. The corpus has a total of 16,292 speech files. A large percentage of the speakers read 120 sentences (some speaker read more than 130 sentences, while others read 100 sentences). The speakers in the database were selected from all geographic regions of Ethiopia where Amharic is spoken predominantly. The ratio between male and female speakers is nearly fifty-fifty and the utterances contain all syllables in as many contexts as possible. In order to generate well-trained acoustic models, the utterances were recorded in three different environments. The first part is recorded in a very quiet office environment (in the middle of the night) so that it does not contain any background noise or background speech. The second part is recorded in a different office under similar circumstances. The last part is recorded in a standard acoustic studio. In spite of our best effort to avoid background noises, a portion of the corpus still has mouth noises, such as smacking, sniffing or loud breaths.

In order to build the initial syllable recognizer using UASR, it is required that part of the speech corpus must be manually labeled. Therefore, some speech files are manually labeled and used to train the initial syllable recognizer. The manual labeling is done until the automatic labeler shows an acceptable accuracy, which happened after it is trained using a manually labeled speech set of 4 hours and 36 minutes duration. The speech recognizer is finally retrained using both the manually and automatically labeled files.

The syllable level recognition accuracy of the ASR is tested using a set of utterances from a single male speaker. The initial syllable level recognition correctness was 58.3 % whereas the accuracy was 50%. In order to improve the accuracy, the confusion matrix has been studied very carefully; and it is observed that the recognizer confuses some syllables with other similarly pronounced ones in a consistent manner. This confusion pattern can best be explained with the help of the following example: Syllables ሰ (sa), ሱ (su), ሲ (si), ሳ (sA), ሴ (sE), ስ (se), and ሶ (so) are derived from the consonant ሰ by combining it with the 7 vowels. Three wrong recognition patterns are observed in the confusion matrix. The first pattern shows that the recognizer confuses syllables ሰ (sa), ሳ (sA), and ስ (se) with each other. Similarly, syllables ሱ (su) and ሲ (si) are confused with ሶ (so) and ሴ (sE), in the second and third patterns respectively. A similar observation can be made for each set of 7 CV-syllables derived from the same consonant.

4.2 Speech recognition experiments

A special mapping file is prepared to combine the syllables that have similar pronunciation. This has brought the number of acoustic models down to 93 from 196. The recognizer is then retrained for the new set of syllables. The original syllables are regenerated through context information in the lexical model. This is possible because there are no words in the dictionary whose pronunciations differ based on only the syllables combined.

The final syllable based, speaker independent, continuous, Amharic ASR is built for weather forecast and business report applications. The training speech corpus, which is of more than 35 hours duration, is a collection of corpora recorded in three different environments. This is purposefully done in order to make the recognizer less sensitive to recording environment and microphone changes. The grammar is finite state transducer based and the lexical model consists of thousands of words. Though acoustic models for only 93 syllables are trained, a recognition accuracy of 93.26% is achieved on a test set that has 4,000 words collected from 10 speakers.

4.3 HMM synthesis experiments

An HMM based Amharic synthesis system is built using phonemes as the fundamental acoustic unit. A speech corpus uttered by a single speaker, and consisting of all diphones of the Amharic language is used for training. The corpus consists of more than 640 phonetically balanced sentences. It is carefully prepared so that all of the 1156 diphones of Amharic are covered in a fairly equal proportion. The speech signals are recorded in a standard studio at a rate of 16 kHz and quantified to 16 bit. The speech signals are windowed by a 25.6ms Hamming window with a 5ms shift, and then cepstral coefficients were obtained using cepstral-coefficient analysis. The feature vectors consist of 24 cepstral coefficients including the 0th coefficient, and their delta and delta-delta features.

The complete system consists of a training part with the inventory generation and the synthesis part. The parameters of the statistical models used in the system are estimated in the training part. Initially, the speech parameters related to the spectrum are extracted. The spectral parameters consist of the mel-cepstral coefficients and the delta and delta-delta coefficients. These parameters are then used to train the acoustic models that represent the phonemes. The HMM models are used to generate the diphone inventory. The inventory consists of the optimal state sequences of the diphones measured by a forced Viterbi alignment of the training database. This inventory is used by the synthesis part to build a Gaussian sequence according to the desired input phoneme sequence by concatenating the diphone state sequences of the inventory. We use the MLSA filter to synthesize the mel-cepstrum sequence taken from the means of the probability density functions (codebook) of the generated Gaussian sequence. Initial results show that the phoneme HMM based Amharic speech synthesizer has acceptable intelligibility and naturalness.

5 Conclusion

In this paper, two different approaches for development of speech technologies for under-resourced languages are presented. In the first case, cross-language adaptation was used after bootstrapping for creation of acoustic-model for ASR and synthesis on Macedonian language.

Using very limited amount of speech data in the target language (hundreds of seconds for adaptation and tens of minutes for model training), acceptable recognition performance can be achieved for speaker dependent speech recognition. Also, the resulting synthesized speech is intelligible, but still lacks the naturalness of the original speech. The naturalness can be improved with better intonation and duration modeling by statistical analysis of the Macedonian language.

In the second case, innovative approach was used to build a syllable based, speaker independent, continuous, Amharic ASR using smaller number of acoustic models for the 196 distinctly pronounced Consonant-Vowel (CV) syllable. Because of the unavailability of neither commercial nor appropriate Amharic speech databases, the textual and speech corpora were prepared and transcribed by human expert.

The final syllable based, speaker independent, continuous, Amharic ASR is built for weather forecast and business report applications. Initial results show that the phoneme HMM based Amharic speech synthesizer has acceptable intelligibility and naturalness.

References

[1] Tanja Schultz, Alex Waibel, "Experiments on Cross-language Acoustic Modeling", Proceedings of the 7th European Conference on Speech Communication and Technology, Eurospeech 2001, pp. 2721, Aalborg, Denmark.

[2] Ngoc Thang Vu, Franziska Kraus, Tanja Schultz, "Rapid building of an ASR system for Under-Resourced Languages based on Multilingual Unsupervised training", Interspeech 2011, Florence, Italy.

[3] V. B. Le, L. Besacier, "First steps in fast acoustic modeling for a new target language: application to Vietnamese", ICASSP'05, Vol. 1, pp. 821-824, Philadelphia, USA, 19-23 March 2005.

[4] T. Martin and S. Sridharan, "Cross-language acoustic model refinement for the Indonesian language", Int. Conference on Acoustics, Speech, and Signal Processing, 1:865–868, Mar. 2005.

[5] Jonas Lööf, Christian Gollan, Hermann Ney, "Cross-language Bootstrapping for Unsupervised Acoustic Model Training: Rapid Development of a Polish Speech Recognition System", In Interspeech (September 2009), pp. 88-91.

[6] Viet Bac Le, Laurent Besacier, Tanja Schultz, "Acoustic-Phonetic Unit Similarities for Context Dependent Acoustic Model Portability", In IEEE International Conference on Acoustics, Speech and Signal Processing (ICASSP 2006) (2006).

[7] R. Hoffmann, M. Eichner, and M. Wolff: "Analysis of verbal and nonverbal acoustic signals with the Dresden UASR system". In: A. Esposito et al. (eds.), Verbal and Nonverbal Communication Behaviours. Berlin etc.: Springer 2007, Lecture Notes in Artificial Intelligence, vol. 4775, pp. 200-218.

[8] Strecha, G.; Wolff, M., "Speech synthesis using HMM based diphone inventory encoding for low-resource devices", 2011 IEEE International Conference on Acoustics, Speech and Signal Processing (ICASSP), pp. 5380-5383, 22-27 May 2011.

[9] Imai, S., Sumita, K., and Furuichi, C., "Mel log spectrum approximation (MLSA) filter for speech synthesis", Trans. IECE, vol. J66-A, 122-129, 1983.

[10] S. Chungurski, I. Kraljevski, D. Mihajlov, S. Arsenovski, "Concatenative speech synthesizers and speech corpus for Macedonian language", ITI 2008, 30th International Conference on Information Technology Interfaces, 2008. 23-26 June, Pages: 669-674, Dubrovnik, Croatia.

[11] T. Bub, J. Schwinn, "VERBMOBIL: The Evolution of a Complex Large Speech-to-Speech Translation System", Int. Conf. on Spoken Language Processing, 1996, Philadelphia, PA, USA, October 1996, vol. 4, pp. 2371-2374.

[12] Solomon Berhanu, "Isolated Amharic consonant-vowel syllable recognition: An experiment using the Hidden Markov Model", Msc Thesis, School of Information Studies for Africa, Addis Ababa University, Ethiopia, 2001.

[13] Kinfe Tadesse, "Sub-word based Amharic speech recognizer: An experiment using Hidden Markov Model (HMM)", MSc Thesis, School of Information Studies for Africa, Addis Ababa University, Ethiopia, June 2002.

[14] Martha Yifiru, "Automatic Amharic speech recognition system to command and control computers", MSc Thesis, School of Information Studies for Africa, Addis Ababa University, Ethiopia, 2003.

[15] Zegaye Seifu, "HMM based large vocabulary, speaker independent, continuous Amharic speech recognizer", MSc Thesis, School of Information Studies for Africa, Addis Ababa University, Ethiopia, 2003.

Die Aussagekraft des Kurzzeit-Frequenzspektrums und der Kurzzeit-Autokorrelationsfunktion bei der Analyse von Tierstimmen

Erwin Paulus

Institut für Nachrichtentechnik, Technische Universität Braunschweig
e.paulus@tu-braunschweig.de

Abstract: Unter der Annahme des Quelle-Filter-Modells für die Lauterzeugung bei Wirbeltieren wird die Frage untersucht, welche Aufschlüsse die Kurzzeit-Spektralanalyse und die Kurzzeit-Autokorrelationsanalyse über etwaige subharmonische Signalkomponenten während quasi-stationärer stimmhafter Signalabschnitte liefern kann und wie die Analyseergebnisse für die visuelle Beurteilung anschaulich dargestellt werden können.

1 Einleitung

Für die Analyse von Tierstimmen werden sehr oft Verfahren eingesetzt, die sich bei der Analyse von menschlichen Sprachsignalen bewährt haben. Mehr und mehr richtet sich die Aufmerksamkeit auch auf die automatische Unterscheidung bzw. Erkennung von Tierlauten. Und auch dafür werden hochentwickelte Verfahren der Mustererkennung und insbesondere der automatischen Spracherkennung übernommen [1] [2], wobei zuvor aber die Frage geklärt werden muss, welche Merkmale aus den akustischen Signalen extrahiert werden sollen. Auch dieses im Vorfeld der automatischen Erkennung auftretende Problem erfordert meist umfangreiche Studien, bei denen Verfahren der Signalanalyse auf Tierlaute anzuwenden sind und bei denen auch die visuelle Beurteilbarkeit der Analyseergebnisse eine bedeutsame Rolle spielen kann. Signalanalyse in Verbindung mit der visuellen Beurteilung ist aber nicht unbedingt nur im Hinblick auf die Vorstudien zur automatischen Erkennung zu sehen, und im Folgenden wird sie als eigenständiges Aufgabengebiet aufgefasst, bei dem es gilt, Kenntnisse über Tierlaute zu gewinnen. Natürlich kann dieses Aufgabengebiet hier nicht umfassend behandelt werden. Einschränkungen betreffen die Methoden der Signalanalyse, die Art der Kenntnisse die gewonnen werden sollen und nicht zuletzt auch die Tierstimmen, die betrachtet werden.

Was die Methoden angeht, wird nur die Kurzzeit-Spektralanalyse in Verbindung mit der Kurzzeit-Autokorrelationsanalyse behandelt. Als Gegenstand der Analyse werden nur Tierstimmen von Wirbeltieren angesehen, und zwar nur unter der zusätzlichen Voraussetzung, dass die Annahme des Quelle-Filter-Modells für die Lauterzeugung berechtigt ist. Und als Ziel der Analyse werden Kenntnisse über etwaige subharmonische Signalkomponenten in quasi-stationären stimmhaften Abschnitten des akustischen Signals angestrebt. Um die Zweckmäßigkeit der behandelten Methoden zu demonstrieren, können aus Platzgründen nur zwei kleine Beispiele angeführt werden. Zur Vorbereitung folgen zunächst noch einige allgemeine Bemerkungen über die Kurzzeit-Spektralanalyse, die Kurzzeit-Autokorrelationsanalyse, und über eine aus der Literatur bekannte Methode zur Feststellung von subharmonischen Komponenten in menschlichen Sprachsignalen.

Die Kurzzeit-Spektralanalyse ist eine ‚klassische', weithin geläufige Methode bei der Untersuchung akustischer Signale. Wichtige Anwendungsgebiete sind z. B. die Sprachsignalanalyse und die damit verwandte Analyse von Lauten aus dem Repertoire von Wirbeltieren. Die Verwandtschaft ergibt sich aus dem Quelle-Filter-Modell der Lautproduktion, das zwar eine weitgehende Idealisierung bedeutet, bekanntlich aber bei der Sprachsignalanalyse vielfach und mit großem Erfolg angewendet wird und das in vielen Fällen auch bei der Analyse von Tierlauten angenommen werden kann [3].

Bei der Kurzzeit-Frequenzanalyse wird die Kurzzeit-Fouriertransformierte des Signals – ein Kurzzeit-Amplituden- oder Kurzzeit-Leistungsspektrum - bestimmt und als Sonagramm dargestellt. Dadurch werden wesentliche Eigenschaften sowohl der Quelle als auch des Filters einer visuellen Beurteilung zugänglich gemacht. Was die Quelle angeht, kann z. B. Ausschau nach stimmhaften und nach stimmlosen Signalabschnitten gehalten werden, und für stimmhafte Abschnitte ergibt sich für den Betrachter zumindest auch ein erster Eindruck von etwaigen zeitlichen Veränderungen der Frequenz der Grundschwingung. Für das Filter lässt sich der Frequenzgang und dessen zeitliche Veränderung grob abschätzen, indem im Sonagramm z. B. die Anzahl, die Frequenzlage und die zeitlichen Verläufe von ‚Formanten' festgestellt werden.

Im Vergleich zur Kurzzeit-Frequenzanalyse wird die Kurzzeit-Autokorrelationsanalyse wesentlich seltener bei der Untersuchung von Sprachsignalen oder Tierlauten eingesetzt. Insbesondere gibt es keine allgemein gebräuchliche Form der Veranschaulichung der Kurzzeit-Autokorrelationsfunktion. Diese ist bekanntlich zu jedem Zeitpunkt als inverse Fouriertransformierte des augenblicklichen Kurzzeit-Leistungsspektrums aufzufassen und kann daher keine grundsätzlich anderen Aufschlüsse über Signaleigenschaften liefern als das Sonagramm. Allerdings kann die Kurzzeit-Autokorrelationsanalyse Vorteile bieten, wenn es nicht um die visuelle Beurteilung der Signale, sondern um die ‚Messung' von Signalparametern geht. Ein bekanntes Beispiel ist die Bestimmung der Grundfrequenz in ihrem zeitlichen Verlauf. Dafür gibt es aber auch zahlreiche alternative Methoden, durch die die Bedeutung der Kurzzeit-Autokorrelationsanalyse wieder eingeschränkt wird.

Im Folgenden wird aber trotzdem versucht, die Kurzzeit-Autokorrelationsfunktion zusätzlich zum Sonagramm einzusetzen, selbst wenn es dabei vorwiegend nur um die visuelle Beurteilung geht. Allerdings sollen dabei nur stimmhafte, quasi-stationäre Signalabschnitte berücksichtigt werden, die sich bei der Betrachtung des Sonagramms gut feststellen lassen. Es wird erwartet, dass für diese Abschnitte dann durch geeignete Darstellung, Betrachtung und Auswertung der Kurzzeit-Autokorrelationsfunktion eine Eigenschaft der Quelle offenbar wird, durch welche die Stimmhaftigkeit genauer beschrieben werden kann. Im einfachsten Fall werden dabei Oberwellen danach unterschieden, ob sie bei geraden oder bei ungeraden Vielfachen einer bestimmten Frequenz auftreten. In [4] wird diese Frequenz der ‚Subharmonischen' zugeordnet, während das Doppelte davon als ‚Grundfrequenz' f_0 angesehen wird. Die dort beschriebenen Arbeiten betreffen Sprachsignale und zeigen, dass sich die beim Anhören ausgelöste Tonhöhenempfindung sowohl nach der Subharmonischen als auch nach der Grundfrequenz richten kann, je nach dem, wie sich die Energie des Signals auf die geraden und ungeraden Oberwellen der Subharmonischen verteilt. Diese Erkenntnisse werden für die automatische Bestimmung der Tonhöhe (*Pitch*) durch eine aufwendige Verarbeitung des Kurzzeit-Frequenzspektrums verwendet. Es ist aber nicht leicht, allein durch das Betrachten des Sonagramms die maßgebliche Energieaufteilung auf die verschiedenen Oberwellen zu beurteilen. Hier soll nun versucht werden, diese ‚Stimmqualität' einer visuellen Beurteilung zugänglich zu machen, indem zusätzlich zum Sonagramm auch eine Kurzzeit-Autokorrelationsfunktion und die Ergebnisse von einigen weiteren einfachen Verarbeitungsschritten zur Betrachtung angeboten werden. Dabei geht es also nicht um die automatische Bestimmung von Tonhöhen oder Tonhöhenverläufen, und anstelle von Sprachsignalen (d. h. anstelle der menschlichen Stimme) werden zu Demonstrationszwecken zwei Beispiel für die Analyse von Tierstimmen berücksichtigt.

In den folgenden Abschnitten wird die Kurzzeit-Autokorrelationsfunktion ideal periodischer und quasi-periodischer Funktionen behandelt (Abschnitt 2), der Bezug zwischen dem Quelle-Filter-Modell und etwaigen Subharmonischen beleuchtet (Abschnitt 3) und die Zweckmäßigkeit der Unterscheidung zwischen Oberwellen bei ungeraden und bei geraden Vielfachen von $f_0/2$ erläutert (Abschnitt 4). In Abschnitt 5 werden die Ergebnisse der vorangegangenen Abschnitte zu einer Methode für die visuelle Verdeutlichung von Subharmonischen verwertet, die an zwei Beispielen demonstriert wird. Abschnitt 6 bringt eine Zusammenfassung und eine abschließende Diskussion.

2 Normierte Kurzzeit-Autokorrelationsfunktion ideal periodischer und quasi-periodischer Funktionen

Bekanntlich ist die normierte Autokorrelationsfunktion $r(\tau)$ einer ideal periodischen Funktion ebenfalls ideal periodisch, und sowohl für das Signal als auch für $r(\tau)$ gilt dieselbe Periodenlänge. Außerdem gibt es in Abständen der Periodendauer gleich große Maxima der Größe $r(0) = 1$, und zwischen diesen Maxima gibt es allenfalls lokale Maxima, die aber allesamt < 1 sind. Für die Kurzzeit-Autokorrelationsfunktion einer ideal periodischen Funktion gibt es einen ähnlichen – wenn auch nicht mehr ganz so einfachen – Zusammenhang.

Im Folgenden wird das für die normierte Kurzzeit-Autokorrelationsfunktion $r(\tau, t)$ maßgebliche Fenster im Zeitbereich immer als Rechteckfenster der Dauer 2T vorausgesetzt. Damit ist $r(\tau, t)$ die normierte Autokorrelationsfunktion eines von $t - T$ bis $t + T$ reichenden Signalausschnitts der Dauer $2T$. Für eine ideal periodische Funktion hat $r(\tau, t)$ als Funktion von $|\tau| < 2T$ betrachtet (d. h. für jedes konstant gehaltene t) in Abständen der Periodendauer besondere Maxima. Die Besonderheit besteht darin, dass die dort erreichten maximalen Werte sehr nahe an die normierte Autokorrelationsfunktion des Rechteckfensters herankommen. (Diese hat bekanntlich die Form eines Dreiecks; sie steigt im Bereich von $\tau = -2T$ bis $\tau = 0$ linear von 0 auf 1 und sinkt danach linear bis zum Verschwinden bei $\tau = 2T$) In jedem Intervall von der Länge der Periodendauer, das von zweien dieser Maxima begrenzt wird, gibt es allenfalls lokale Maxima, die aber allesamt größere Abstände zur normierten Autokorrelationsfunktion des Rechteckfensters aufweisen. Das größte unter den besonderen Maxima ist $r(0, t) = 1$. Mit wachsendem τ (bei konstant gehaltenem t) folgt dann das nächste im Abstand von einer Periodendauer.

3 Stimmqualität

Bekanntlich steht im Quelle-Filter-Modell bei stimmhaften Signalabschnitten die Quelle für die ‚Phonation' durch die Glottis und das Filter für die ‚Artikulation' durch den Vokaltrakt. Während quasi-stationärer stimmhafter Signalabschnitte bleibt der Vokaltrakt praktisch konstant und die Quelle liefert – grob gesprochen – eine quasi-periodisches, sehr obertonreiches ‚Anregungssignal'. Im Allgemeinen wird unter einem quasi-stationären Signal ein Signal verstanden, das sich abschnittsweise als Ausschnitt aus einem periodischen Signal der augenblicklichen Grundfrequenz f_0 auffassen lässt. Die Dauer des Ausschnitts muss dabei einerseits möglichst groß im Vergleich zur Periodendauer sein, andererseits aber auch so klein sein, dass die Periodendauer innerhalb des Ausschnitts als praktisch konstant gelten kann. Damit verbunden ist die Vorstellung, dass sich jede Periode in ihrer Dauer oder Signalform von der nächsten Periode weniger unterscheidet als von der übernächsten. Sowohl bei der menschlichen Stimme als auch bei Tierstimmen trifft diese Vorstellung auf manche stimmhafte Signalabschnitte aber nicht zu. Im Folgenden wird der häufigste – bzw. der einfachste – Fall betrachtet, bei dem die Übereinstimmung jeder Periode mit der jeweils übernächsten besser als mit der nächsten Periode ist. Dadurch ergibt sich die Summe der Dauern zweier aufeinanderfolgenden Perioden als Periodendauer einer ‚Subharmonischen'. Unter der Voraussetzung, dass im Quelle-Filter-Modell ein lineares Filter wirksam ist, prägt sich diese Subharmonische des Anregungssignals auch im Ausgangssignal des Filters aus.

Auch wenn die Subharmonische als ein Merkmal der Quelle anzusehen ist, kann dieses Merkmal also auch ohne die direkte Beobachtung des Anregungssignals festgestellt werden.

Was die menschliche Stimme angeht, gibt es für die mit der Ausprägung von Subharmonischen verbundene Stimmqualität mehrere Bezeichnungen, wie z. B. *creaky voice*, *vocal fry*, *laryngealisation* und Strohbass. Für Tierstimmen soll hier aber keine dieser Bezeichnungen verwendet werden. Es wird aber auch kein anderer Fachausdruck vorgeschlagen, sondern einfach nur von der Ausprägung einer Subharmonischen gesprochen, wobei immer nur der einfachste Fall einer Subharmonischen im Oktavabstand bzw. der Fall von Oberwellen einer solchen Subharmonischen gemeint ist.

4 Subharmonisches Signal mit zugeordneten Oberwellen

Im Folgenden wird die Sinnfälligkeit der Unterscheidung zwischen ‚ungeraden' und ‚geraden' Oberwellen erläutert, je nach dem ob sie bei ungeraden und bei geraden Vielfachen von $f_0/2$ auftreten. Betrachtet wird ein ideal periodisches Signal $h(t)$ mit der Frequenz f_0, dem ein ideal periodisches ‚subharmonisches' Signal $g(t)$ mit der Frequenz $f_0/2$ überlagert ist. Die Überlagerung ergibt ein ideal periodisches Signal $s(t) = h(t) + g(t)$ mit der Frequenz $f_0/2$. Unter diesen Voraussetzungen gibt es für $h(t)$ allfällige Oberwellen nur bei ganzzahligen Vielfachen von f_0, d. h. bei geraden Vielfachen von $f_0/2$. Demnach werden alle zu $s(t)$ gehörigen Oberwellen bei ungeraden Vielfachen von $f_0/2$ allein vom subharmonischen Signal $g(t)$ verursacht.

Für die normierte Autokorrelationsfunktion (AKF) von $s(t)$ gilt:
Der Maximalwert 1 wird im Allgemeinen in Abständen von $P = 2/f_0$ erreicht. Für die Verschiebung P trifft nämlich maximale Autokorrelation sowohl für $h(t)$ als auch für $g(t)$ zu. Bei der Verschiebung $p = 1/f_0$ trifft maximale Autokorrelation nur für $h(t)$ zu. Das führt nicht zwangsläufig zu einem lokalen Maximum der AKF, und selbst wenn, muss es < 1 sein. Nur im Sonderfall $g(t) \equiv 0$ wird der Maximalwert 1 in Abständen von p erreicht. Diese Aussagen treffen sinngemäß zu jedem Zeitpunkt t auch auf die normierte Kurzzeit-AKF $r(\tau, t)$ quasi-periodischer Funktionen zu. Allerdings wird der Wert 1 nur bei $\tau = 0$ erreicht, die anderen Maximalwerte kommen nur möglichst nahe an die AKF des Rechteckfensters heran.

In den weiter unten angeführten Beispielen wurde als Periodendauer P der Subharmonischen die Lage des globalen Maximums der Funktion $r(\tau, t) - r_w(\tau)$ im Intervall $\tau_{min} < \tau < T$ herangezogen. Dabei ist $r_w(\tau)$ die AKF des Rechteckfensters und $\tau_{min} > 0$ ist ein willkürlich anzunehmender Parameter, der dazu dient, zu kleine Werte für die gesuchte Periodendauer auszuschließen. Das Verfahren ist einfach zu automatisieren, ist aber etwas fehleranfällig, weniger wegen des frei wählbaren Parameters τ_{min}, sondern wegen der mit der Automatisierung verbundenen Diskretisierung und Rechenungenauigkeit.

Die Beschränkung der Suche auf $\tau < T$ ist sinnvoll. Ein Ergebnis $> T$ bedeutet nämlich, dass der im Rechteckfenster der Dauer $2T$ erfasste Signalabschnitt nicht einmal zwei Perioden vollständig erfasst. In diesem Fall müsste also ein größeres Fenster gewählt werden. Bei der Wahl der Fenstergröße ist ein Kompromiss zwischen zwei gegensätzlichen Anforderungen notwendig: einerseits sollten möglichst viele Perioden erfasst werden, andererseits wächst aber mit der Fenstergröße die Gefahr, dass die Annahme einer konstanten Periodendauer innerhalb des erfassten Signalabschnitts nicht mehr hinreichend gut zutrifft.

5 Beispiele

Das erste hier zu Demonstrationszwecken behandelten Beispiel betrifft einen Warnschrei von einem Totenkopfaffen Für die mit 40 kHz abgetastete und digitalisierte Tonaufzeichnung wurde jeweils das Kurzzeit-Amplitudenspektrum in Abständen von 2ms unter Verwendung eines 8ms breiten Hamming-Fensters für 117 Zeitpunkte und 512 äquidistante Frequenzen zwischen 0 und 20 kHz berechnet. Das Ergebnis ist in Abbildung 1 links als Sonagramm dargestellt, wobei nur der Frequenzbereich 0 bis 12500 Hz berücksichtigt ist.

Die Tonaufzeichnung stammt aus einer verschiedene Säugetierarten betreffenden Sammlung, die dem Institut für Nachrichtentechnik der TU Braunschweig von Prof. Jahns von der Bundesanstalt für Landwirtschaft (FAL, jetzt Johann Heinrich von Thünen Institut) in Braunschweig im Rahmen einer Studienarbeit überlassen worden ist. Was Totenkopfaffen angeht, stammen die Tonaufzeichnungen ursprünglich aus dem Primatenzentrum (DPZ) in Göttingen.

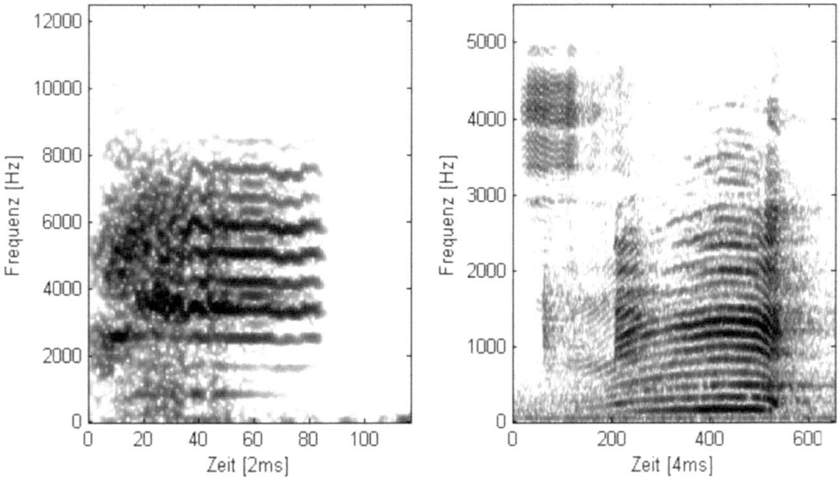

Abbildung 1 – Sonagramme von Tierrufen (links Totenkopfaffe , rechts Kuh)

Im Sonagramm lassen sich mehrere quasi-stationäre stimmhafte Abschnitte erkennen; und bei zumindest einem davon, nämlich bei dem mit Zentrum beim 60. der 117 Zeitpunkte, scheint es eine ausgeprägte Subharmonische zu geben.

Abbildung 2 zeigt oben die augenblickliche normierte Kurzzeit-AKF zum 60. Zeitpunkt. Aus Symmetriegründen kann sich die Darstellung auf positive Verschiebungen beschränken. Ebenfalls eingezeichnet ist die AKF des zutreffenden 8ms breiten Rechteckfensters (als gestrichelte Gerade). Durch Rauten markiert sind das Maximum bei der Verschiebung 0 und insbesondere dasjenige Maximum der normierten Kurzzeit-AKF das zwischen den Verschiebungen 0 und der halben Fensterdauer (hier 4ms) liegt und dabei am wenigsten von der AKF des Rechteckfensters abweicht. Dieses markierte Maximum liegt hier bei 2,38 ms (bei der geltenden Abtastfrequenz von 40kHz sind das 96 Abtastintervalle) und bedeutet die augenblickliche Periode P der Subharmonischen. Abbildung 2 zeigt unten auch das augenblickliche Kurzzeit-Amplitudenspektrum zum 60. Zeitpunkt (als punktierte Linie) Besonders hervorgehoben sind die Amplituden bei den Vielfachen von $1/P$ = 421,05 Hz: ungerade Vielfache durch Punkte und gerade Vielfache durch kleine Kreise. Die meist sehr deutlichen Unterschiede in der Amplitude bei einem ungeraden Vielfachen und den benachbarten geraden Vielfachen lassen im Hinblick auf das Quelle-Filter-Modell zwei gegensätzliche Erklärungen zu: Entweder der Frequenzgang des Filters ist wellig nach Art eines Kammfilters oder die genannten Unterschiede charakterisieren eine augenblickliche Stimmqualität der Quelle. Eine Kammfiltercharakteristik des Frequenzgangs des Filters mag in Ausnahmefällen tatsächlich vorkommen - in der Regel sollten die genannten Unterschiede aber als Stimmqualität zu werten sein.

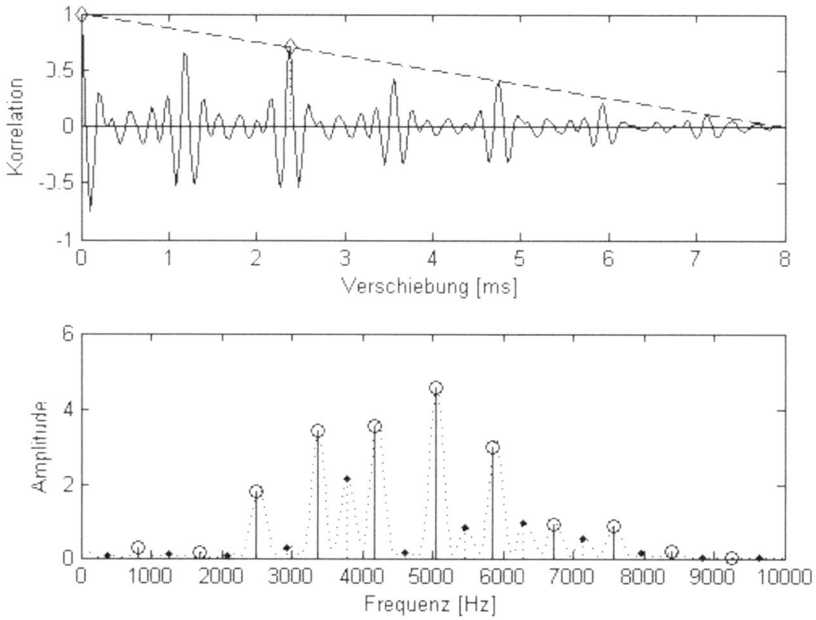

Abbildung 2 - Augenblickliche Kurzzeit-AKF (oben) und augenblickliches Kurzzeit-Amplitudenspektrum für den Ruf des Totenkopfaffen (s. Abb. 1 links) zum Zeitpunkt 60 (120ms)

Abbildung 3 betrifft den Fall einer nur schwach ausgeprägten oder gar fehlenden Subharmonischen. Es zeigt in der linken Hälfte die normierte Kurzzeit-AKF zu den Zeitpunkten 75 (oben) und 71 (unten). Die beiden Funktionen unterscheiden sich nur wenig, die Unterschiede führen aber dazu, dass jeweils ein anderes Maxima durch eine Raute automatisch markiert worden ist. In der rechten Bildhälfte sind die zu den Zeitpunkten 75 (oben) und 71 (unten) gehörigen Kurzzeit-Amplitudenspektren dargestellt. Die beiden Spektren sind ebenfalls nahezu gleich. Aber oben gibt es eine sehr schwach ausgeprägte und unten gar keine Subharmonische. Im zuletzt genannten Fall ist die Unterscheidung zwischen geraden und ungeraden Oberwellen zwar automatisch getroffen worden – ist aber nicht sinnvoll und sollte bei der visuellen Kontrolle ignoriert werde. Entscheidungshilfen dafür ergeben sich einerseits aus der Betrachtung der augenblicklichen Kurzzeit-AKF und andererseits aus der Betrachtung des augenblicklichen Kurzzeit-Amplitudenspektrums: Wenn in der Kurzzeit-AKF links vom markierten Maximum nur vergleichsweise kleine lokale Maxima vorkommen, sollte die Annahme einer Subharmonischen in Zweifel gezogen werden. Gleiches gilt, wenn sich alle im Kurzzeit-Amplitudenspektrum ausgeprägten Oberwellen durch eine gedachte Einhüllende verbinden lassen, die keine tief eingeschnittenen Minima oder einzeln herausragende Maxima aufweist und die demnach auf den Frequenzgang des im Quelle-Filter-Modell enthaltenen Filters hinweist. Sobald beide Kriterien Zweifel an der Existenz der Subharmonischen aufkommen lassen, sollte die Annahme einer Subharmonischen verworfen werden.

Wie schon in der Einleitung festgestellt, kann die Kurzzeit-AKF grundsätzlich keine Aufschlüsse über das Signal liefern, die nicht auch allein aus dem Kurzzeit-Amplituden- bzw. dem Kurzzeit-Leistungsspektrum gefolgert werden können. Was das erste Beispiel betrifft, wäre es für den 60. Zeitpunkt tatsächlich ziemlich einfach, allein aus dem augenblicklichen Kurzzeit-Amplitudenspektrum und ohne die in Bild 2 unten bereits eingetragenen Ergebnisse aus der automatschen Analyse der augenblicklichen Kurzzeit-AKF die Unterscheidung zwischen geraden und ungeraden Oberwellen zu treffen. Bei den in der Abbildung 3 behandelten Grenzfällen schwach ausgeprägter oder fehlender Subharmonischer kann die automatisierte Analyse der augenblicklichen Kurzzeit-AKF aber zumindest hilfreich erscheinen

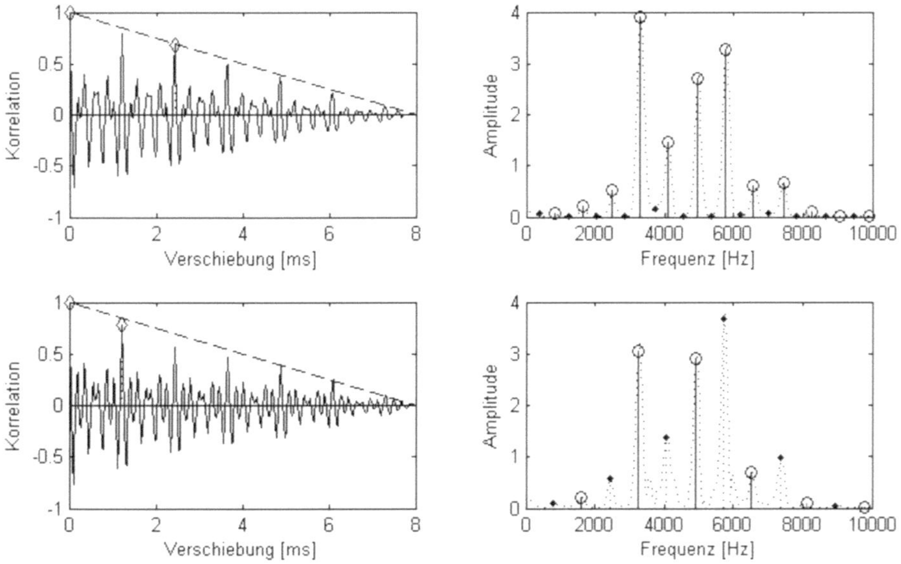

Abbildung 3 – Augenblickliche Kurzzeit-AKF (links) und augenblickliches Kurzzeit-Amplituden-Spektrum (rechts) für den Ruf des Totenkopfaffen zu den Zeitpunkten 75 (oben) und 71 (unten)

Um den potenziellen Nutzwert der Analyse der Kurzzeit-AKF zusätzlich zur Analyse des Kurz-zeit-Amplitudenspektrum weiter zu unterstreichen, wird hier ein zweites Beispiel behandelt, bei dem die alleinige Auswertung des Kurzzeit-Amplitudenspektrums wegen der Vielzahl und der unterschiedlich Ausprägung von Oberwellen kompliziert erscheint. Es betrifft den Schrei einer kalbenden Kuh. Für die mit 11025 Hz abgetastete und digitalisierte Tonaufzeichnung wurde jeweils das Kurzzeit-Amplitudenspektrum in Abständen von 4ms unter Verwendung eines 24ms breiten Hamming-Fensters für 624 Zeitpunkte und 512 äquidistante Frequenzen zwischen 0 und rund 5,5 kHz berechnet. Das Ergebnis ist in Abbildung 1 rechts als Sonagramm dargestellt. Die Tonaufzeichnung stammt aus der schon erwähnten, dem Institut für Nachrichtentechnik der TU Braunschweig von Prof. Jahns überlassenen Sammlung.

Hier sei zu Demonstrationszwecken nur der 225. Zeitpunkt herausgegriffen. Abbildung 4 zeigt oben die augenblickliche normierte Kurzzeit-AKF zu diesem Zeitpunkt zusammen mit der AKF des zutreffenden 24ms breiten Rechteckfensters. Das der Periode *P* der Sub-harmonischen entsprechende Maximum ist durch eine Raute markiert; es liegt bei 7,9ms. (Bei der geltenden Abtastfrequenz sind das 88 Abtastintervalle.)

Abbildung 4 zeigt unten auch das augenblickliche Kurzzeit-Amplitudenspektrum zum 225. Zeitpunkt. Besonders hervorgehoben sind die Amplituden bei den Vielfachen von $1/P$ (d, h. hier 126,7 Hz) - ungerade Vielfache durch Punkte und gerade Vielfache durch kleine Kreise. Da einerseits die ungerade Oberwelle bei $3/P$ deutlich kleinere Amplitude als die benach-barten geraden Oberwellen bei $2/P$ und $4/P$ besitzt und andererseits die gerade Oberwelle bei $10/P$ deutlich kleinere Amplitude als die benachbarten ungeraden Oberwellen bei $9/P$ und $11/P$ besitzt, ist keine Einhüllende vorstellbar, die alle Oberwellen ohne tief eingeschnittene Minima oder einzeln herausragende Maxima verbindet. Demgemäß erscheint die Annahme einer Subharmonischen gerechtfertigt.

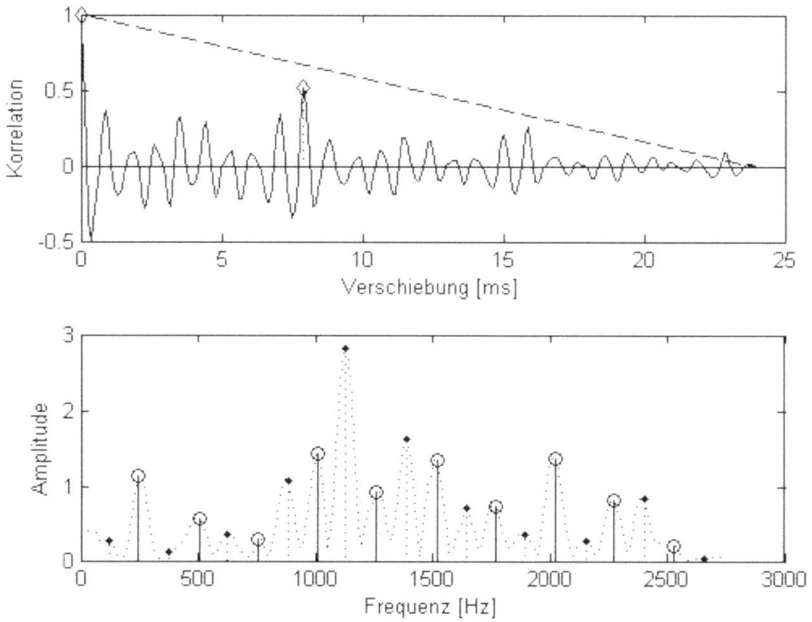

Abbildung 4 - Augenblickliche Kurzzeit-AKF (oben) und augenblickliches Kurzzeit-Amplituden-spektrum für den Ruf der Kuh (s. Abb. 1 rechts) zum Zeitpunkt 225 (900ms).

6 Zusammenfassung und Diskussion

Unter der Annahme des Quelle-Filter-Modells für die Lauterzeugung bei Wirbeltieren wurde gezeigt, dass in stimmhaften quasi-stationären Abschnitten des akustischen Signals etwaige subharmonische Signalkomponenten einer visuellen Beurteilung besser zugänglich gemacht werden können, wenn nicht nur das Sonagramm (d. h. das Ergebnis einer Kurzzeit-Frequenzanalyse), sondern zu ausgewählten Zeitpunkten neben dem jeweiligen augenblicklichen Kurzzeit-Amplitudenspektrum auch die augenblickliche Kurzzeit-Autokorrelationsfunktion betrachtet wird, wobei die Anschaulichkeit und Interpretierbarkeit der Funktionsverläufe durch einfache und leicht automatisch bestimmbare Zusatzinformationen noch gesteigert werden kann. Vorerst wurden zwar nur Subharmonische im Oktavabstand (und ihre Oberwellen) berücksichtigt, eine Erweiterung auf Subharmonische in anderen Abständen ist aber möglich, wenn auch mit etwas höherem Aufwand für die Bestimmung der Zusatzinformationen.

Literatur

[1] Mitrovic, D., M. Zeppelzauer, and Ch. Breiteneder: Discrimination and Retrieval of Animal Sounds. Proc. IEEE Multimedia Modeling Conference, Beijing 2006, pp. 339 – 343.

[2] Jahns,G.: Automatischer Ruferkenner für landwirtschaftliche Nutztiere – Tierstimmerkennung. Landbauforschung Völkenrode, Band 56 (2006), Heft 1-2, Seiten 31-37.

[3] Paulsen, K.: Prinzipien der Stimmbildung in der Wirbeltierreihe und beim Menschen. Akademische Verlagsgesellschaft, Frankfurt a. M. 1967.

[4] Sun, X.: Pitch determination and voice quality analysis using subharmonic-to-harmonic ratio. Proc. ICASSP 2002, Vol. I, Orlando Florida 2002, pp. 333 – 336.

AN ACOUSTIC ANALYSIS OF 7395 DOG BARKS

Nick Campbell
Speech Communication Lab
Trinity College Dublin, Ireland

Kurzfassung: This paper presents the results of a preliminary analysis of the sounds of dog barks in various everyday situations. Seven types of bark were recorded from twenty-seven dogs of the Hungarian breed Mudi. Barks were recorded in the following situations: alone,playing with a ball, fighting with a human, food time, at play with a human, warning of a stranger, and taking a walk. Not all dogs were recorded in every situation, but a few were, and the analysis of these barks forms the core of this technical report. Statistical analysis of the acoustic parameters of each bark was performed, and a principal components analysis determined which were the main contributing factors in each case. A statistical model was then trained (we used both classification trees and state-vector machines) to predict the most likely category for each bark by training either with barks from other dogs opr from barks of the same dog with a subset held back for testing. N-fold cross-validation was tested at n=5, n=10, and n=15. Good categorisation was possible for each dog when trained on similar material from the same dog, but models trained on one or more different dogs were very poor at categorising the barks of another. The paper provides many example using the free software statistical processing package R and serves as a guide for similar acoustical processing for classification.

1 Introduction

This paper is presented as an example of statistical analysis and aims to provide a student with examples of the types of processing that can be carried out in order to classify acoustic samples. It shows how the barks of dogs differ according to activity and attempts to classify the barks from their acoustic features to predict activity type. Recordings were made available by Professor Ádám Miklósi and the analysis was carried out by the author while working with Géza Németh as a guest of the BME during the summer of 2010. Table 1 shows counts of the barks recorded in each of the seven categories. Table 2 shows the total number of barks recorded for each of the twenty-seven dogs for each category.of bark. It is clear from Table 2 that not all dogs were recorded in all conditions, and that some dogs only produced a small number of barks. Those dogs that were not prolific were clustered into a single category (shown by an 'x' in Table 3) which was used for non-specific training and testing. The most prolific dogs were d12, d23, and d24. Only d24 barked in all categories. These three dogs formed the core of our training and testing material, and numbers of data-points are given in Table 3.

Tabelle 1 - Showing the number of barks recordes for 7 categories of bark: a=alone, b=ball, f=fight, fo=food, p=play, s=stranger, and w=walk

a	b	f	fo	p	s	w
853	1105	1236	877	880	1593	851

Tabelle 2 - Showing the total number of barks (in all categories) recorded for each dog. Dogs are numbered from d01 to d27 to preserve their privacy, though identities are noted in a separate file kept in a locked drawer.

d01	d02	d03	d04	d05	d06	d07
22	40	15	10	303	20	40
d08	d09	d10	d11	d12	d13	d14
95	728	108	20	1045	8	480
d15	d16	d17	d18	d19	d20	d21
33	354	38	277	20	720	9
d22	d23	d24	d25	d26	d27	-
9	970	1701	91	111	128	-

Tabelle 3 - Showing the number of barks in each category for the dogs with most recordings. A separate category 'x' has been made to contain the data of dogs with fewer barks. See Table 1 for explanation of category labels.

	a	b	f	fo	p	s	w
d05	10	-	-	-	158	135	-
d09	-	50	-	163	-	487	28
d12	152	193	345	99	-	194	62
d14	168	158	34	101	-	9	10
d16	-	20	100	3	44	118	69
d18	48	63	-	-	147	10	9
d20	-	177	161	137	146	9	90
d23	140	201	139	187	0	150	153
d24	277	165	235	168	313	208	335
d27	-	23	64	-	-	26	15
x	58	55	158	19	72	247	80

2 Principal Components Analysis

The acoustic features for each bark were calculated using the Snack speech processing library [?], part of the Tcl/Tk programming language. The features we tested were measures of fundamental frequency, speech amplitude, and spectral tilt. For fundamental frequency and power, we calculated the mean, maximum, and minimum values measured across each bark, as well as the position of the maximum in relative percentage values within the waveform. We measured spectral tilt by the difference between the first harmonic and the amplitude of the third formant, after Hansen '90 [?], and included duration of the bark as well as the amount of voicing it contained. The following values were obtained for the set of barks as a whole:

```
    fmean            fmax             fmin             fpct
 Min.   :118.5   Min.   :121.5   Min.   :113.8   Min.   :0.0000
 1st Qu.:403.5   1st Qu.:510.3   1st Qu.:278.9   1st Qu.:0.3300
 Median :529.3   Median :634.5   Median :394.6   Median :0.4600
 Mean   :503.6   Mean   :585.8   Mean   :392.0   Mean   :0.4822
 3rd Qu.:618.5   3rd Qu.:698.2   3rd Qu.:504.0   3rd Qu.:0.6100
 Max.   :774.1   Max.   :824.6   Max.   :767.5   Max.   :0.9800

     pmean            pmax             pmin             ppct
 Min.   :26.43   Min.   :43.86   Min.   : 0.04   Min.   :0.110
 1st Qu.:43.11   1st Qu.:67.09   1st Qu.:15.31   1st Qu.:0.290
 Median :50.01   Median :71.41   Median :24.24   Median :0.340
 Mean   :50.31   Mean   :71.81   Mean   :25.18   Mean   :0.351
 3rd Qu.:57.14   3rd Qu.:77.90   3rd Qu.:33.10   3rd Qu.:0.410
 Max.   :76.32   Max.   :83.82   Max.   :74.21   Max.   :0.790

      h1h2              h1a3              h1                a3
 Min.   :-23.710   Min.   :-17.25   Min.   :-61.69   Min.   :-70.82
 1st Qu.:  3.558   1st Qu.: 15.14   1st Qu.:-45.35   1st Qu.:-63.35
 Median :  8.080   Median : 20.84   Median :-39.87   Median :-61.32
 Mean   :  8.278   Mean   : 21.62   Mean   :-39.00   Mean   :-60.62
 3rd Qu.: 12.550   3rd Qu.: 27.16   3rd Qu.:-33.80   3rd Qu.:-58.60
 Max.   : 35.520   Max.   : 70.95   Max.   :  7.98   Max.   :-38.17

      fvcd              dn
 Min.   :0.0300   Min.   :0.1100
 1st Qu.:0.3400   1st Qu.:0.2600
 Median :0.5600   Median :0.3000
 Mean   :0.5523   Mean   :0.3183
 3rd Qu.:0.7600   3rd Qu.:0.3700
 Max.   :1.0000   Max.   :0.9200
```

A principal components analysis showed these parameters to be largely independent, and a combination of the first seven components cumulatively accounted for 83% of the variance in the data:

Importance of components:

	Cmp.1	Cmp.2	Cmp.3	Cmp.4	Cmp.5	Cmp.6
Standard deviation	1.7597	1.5894	1.3210	1.12837	1.0773	1.00134
Proportion of Variance	0.2211	0.1804	0.1246	0.09094	0.0829	0.07162
Cumulative Proportion	0.2211	0.4016	0.5262	0.61724	0.7001	0.77177

	Cmp.7	Cmp.8	Cmp.9	Cmp.10	Cmp.11	Cmp.12
Standard deviation	0.94532	0.89067	0.71722	0.69154	0.62758	0.253054
Proportion of Variance	0.06383	0.05666	0.03674	0.03415	0.02813	0.004574
Cumulative Proportion	0.83560	0.89226	0.92900	0.96316	0.99130	0.995876

	Cmp.13	Cmp.14
Standard deviation	0.240279	3.220e-04
Proportion of Variance	0.004123	7.4104e-09
Cumulative Proportion	0.999999	1.000e+00

Loadings: (shown here only for the first 9 components):

	Comp.1	Comp.2	Comp.3	Comp.4	Comp.5	Comp.6	Comp.7	Comp.8	Comp.9
fmean	-0.429		0.224	-0.406			-0.194	0.189	
fmax	-0.447	0.120	0.147	-0.375			-0.192	0.252	
fmin	0.149	-0.194	0.442	-0.183	0.318	-0.363		-0.157	-0.209
fpct	-0.178	0.247	-0.407		-0.319	-0.117	0.115	0.209	-0.622
fvcd	-0.248	0.314	-0.315	0.151	0.184	0.121		0.102	0.476
pmean	0.164	0.540	0.271						
pmax		0.319	0.351		-0.490	0.104		-0.111	-0.195
pmin	0.192	0.484	0.207						0.250
ppct		0.134	-0.282	-0.124		-0.769	0.252	-0.325	0.176
h1h2	-0.163	0.201	-0.189	-0.139	0.222	0.279	-0.346	-0.764	-0.215
h1a3	0.443		-0.234	-0.427			-0.104	0.152	
h1	0.452		-0.240	-0.290	0.119		-0.283	0.200	
a3		0.110		0.544	0.121	-0.366	-0.672	0.172	-0.133
dn		-0.265		-0.167	-0.651		-0.409	-0.166	0.364

As can be seen from the loadings, the first principal component is largely related to a combination of (mean & max) fundamental frequency and spectral slope, the second to power of the bark (mean & min), and the third to minimum fundamental frequency and position of the peak. These three axes alone account for little over half of the variance observed in the sound of the barks. Blanks in the table above indicate non-significant relations, held out for ease of viewing.

Figures 1 and 2 plot the acoustic data for two dogs (d12 and d24) to illustrate the difference in the distribution of barks in the two most relevant dimensions. Figures 3 and 4 show the equivalent data for dog D12 plotted according to the PCA, Figure 3 showing the first and second components (rotated features) with vectors representing the similarity of the various features. Figure 4 is an amalgam showing the same data plotted according to combinations of the first four dimensions.

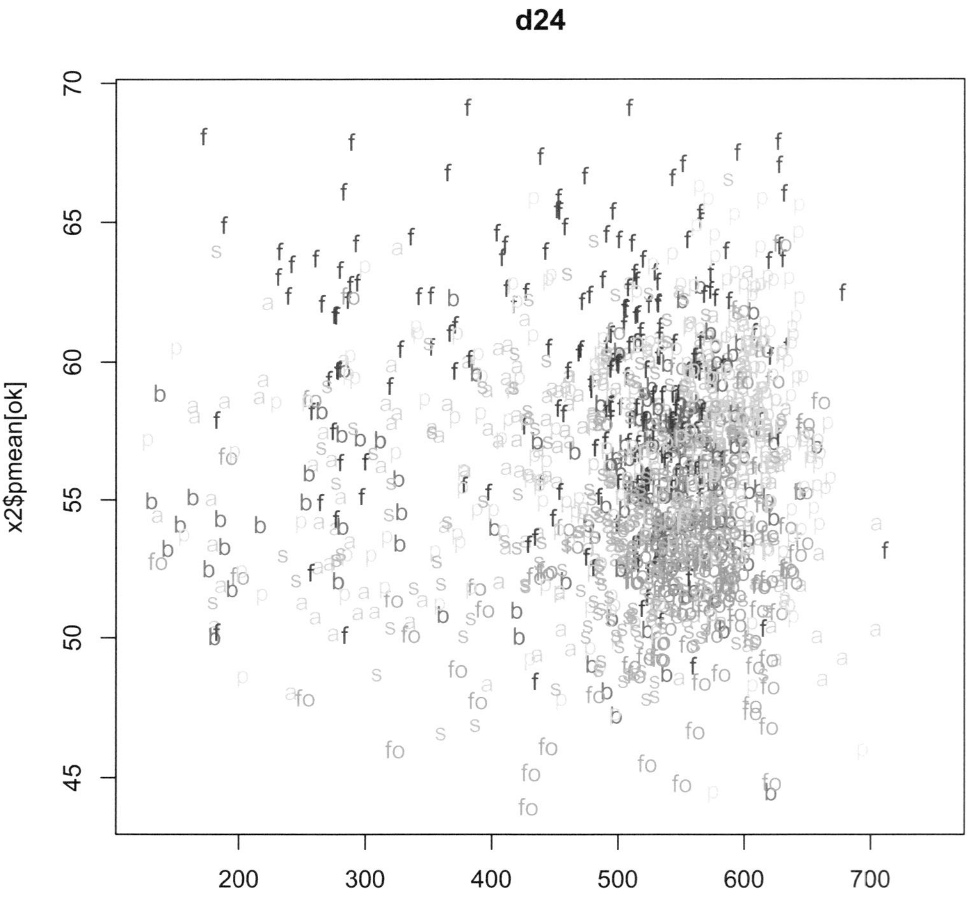

Abbildung 1 - Plotting the seven types of bark (see Table 1 for explanation) in terms of pitch and power of the acoustics. Note for example that 'f' (fighting) is characterised by relatively high mean power, and that 'b' (playing with a ball) is characterised by relatively low mean power. Most barks are in the region of high pitch (fundamental frequency) and there is considerable spread of bark categories across the whole of this two-dimensional feature space.

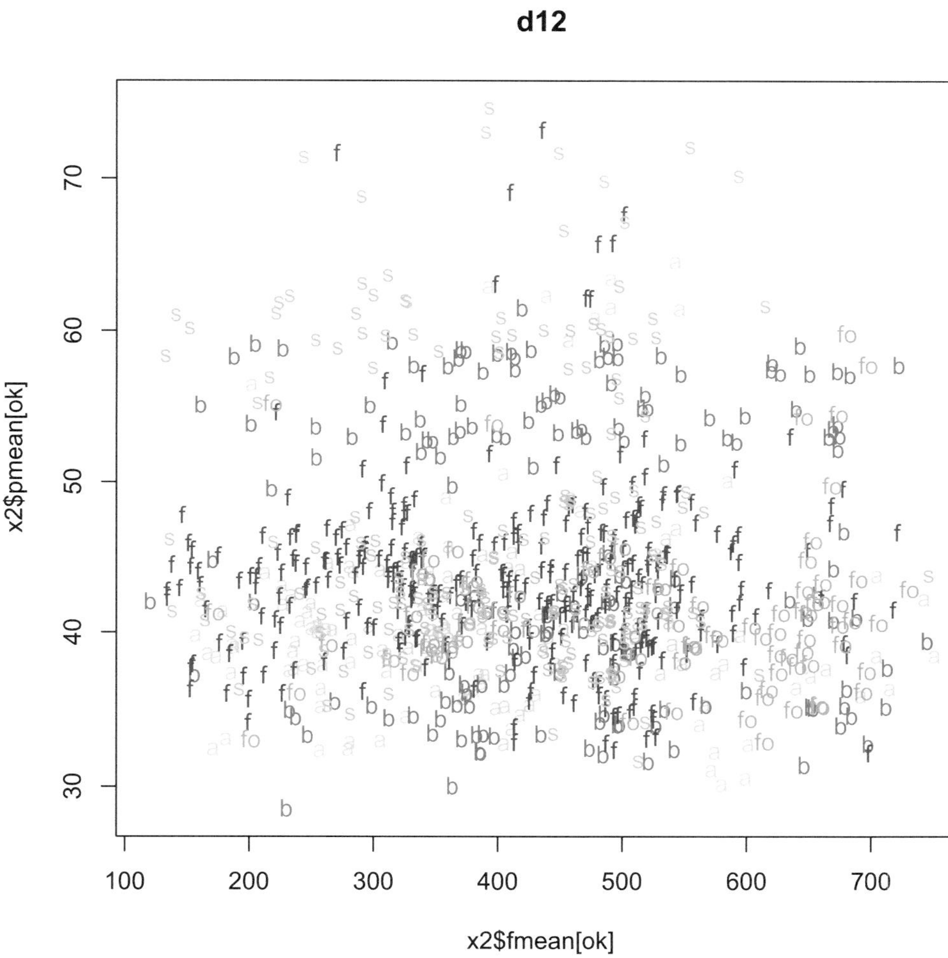

Abbildung 2 - Dog 12 shows a very different distribution of categories across the same feature space, making better use of the range of fundamental frequency (fmean) Note especially that the 'b' category appears to exhibit two clear variants or subsets; one with high mean power, overlapping with 's' (stranger), and the other with relatively low mean power, overlapping with 'fo' (food). One is tempted to speculate here that the dog is playing two types of game with the same ball perhaps?

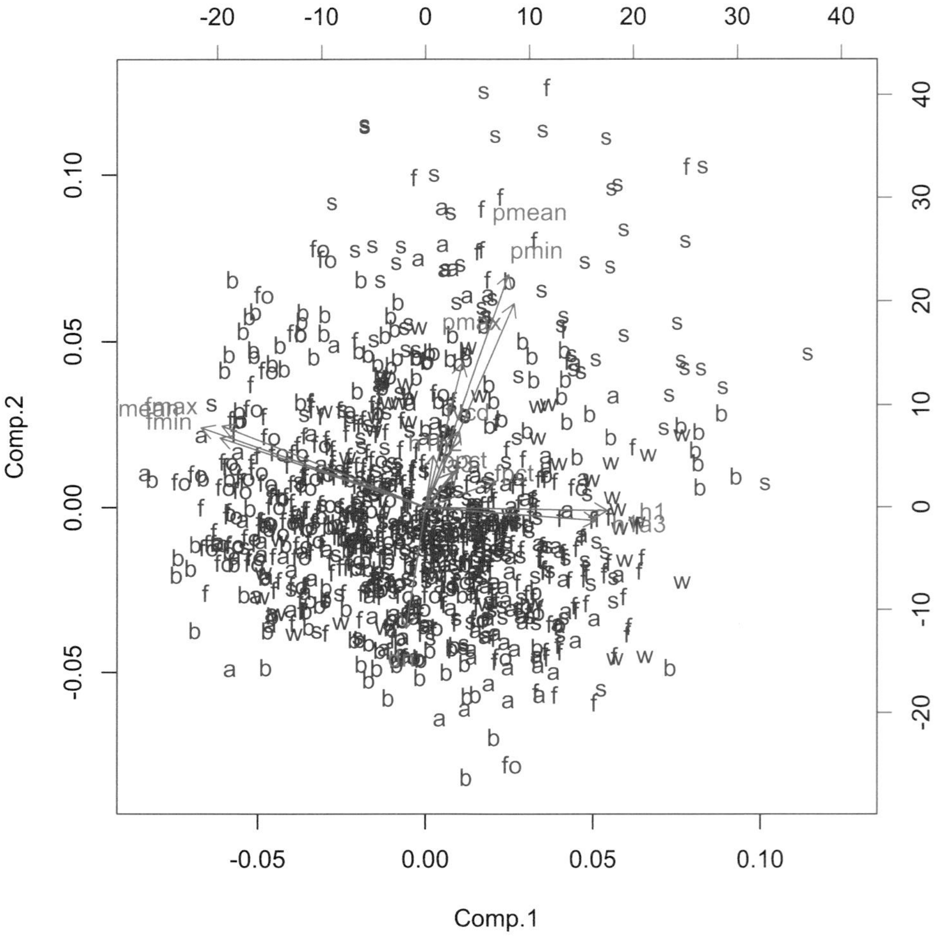

Abbildung 3 - Biplots of the first two principal components of dog D12's acoustic features and associated categories.

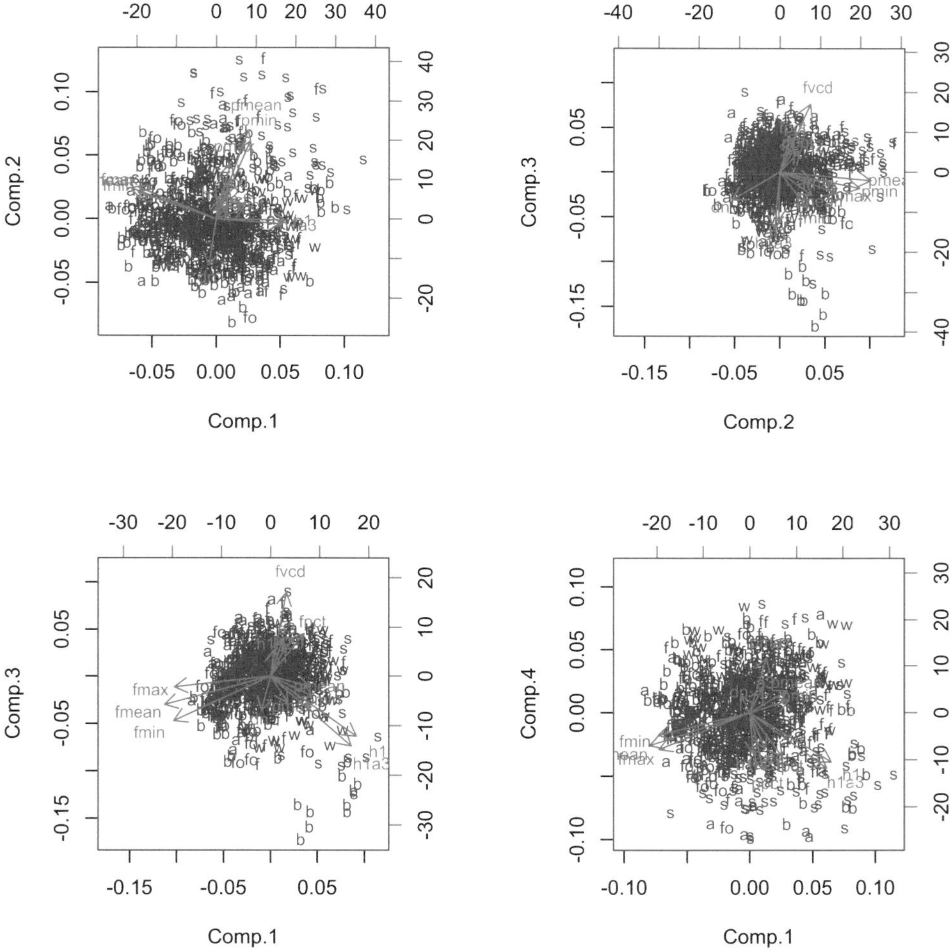

Abbildung 4 - Biplots of the first 4 principal components of dog D12's acoustic features and their categories, showing the overall shape of the data space.

3 Prediction using Classification Trees

We used the 'R' statistical package [?] to perform a statistical modelling and prediction of the above acoustic material, learning the correlation of each acoustic category to the category of barks and predicting from the characteristics of unseen samples to classify each sound into one of the seven types of bark.

Both Classification Trees and SVMs were tested; the former being relatively weak at prediction but very useful for examining the contribution of the factors, and the latter being perhaps the strongest classifier available for general use.

The classification tree was trained with the 'R' command 'Tree', taking d2$ctxt (the object containing the contexts or categories of the barks, and learning the factors of x2 (the object containing the acoustic variables) that best predict those categories. Here we examine the subset containing the barks of dog D24 first. The '>' symbol indicates an 'R' command line:

```
> ttt=tree(d2$ctxt ~ ., x2,subset=d2$id=="d24")
> summary(ttt)
Classification tree:
tree(formula = d2$ctxt ~ ., data = x2, subset = d2$id == "d24")
Variables actually used in tree construction:
[1] "dn"    "pmax"  "a3"    "ppct"  "pmean" "fvcd"
Number of terminal nodes:  10
Residual mean deviance:  2.889 = 4886 / 1691
Misclassification error rate: 0.575 = 978 / 1701
```

Next we use the tree to predict a classification for the same data. Since the tree has been pruned so strongly, it only predicts less than half of the tokens correctly, but the confusion matrix allows us to see the typical confusability in the data (see also Figure 5):

```
> ttp=predict(ttt,type="class")
> table(ttp,ctxt[d2$id=="d24"])

ttp    a   b   f  fo   p   s   w
  a   43  13  36   2   0   1  17
  b   22  77  14  59   4  13  19
  f   23  42 140  19   5  46  25
  fo  29   6   0  40  39   0  18
  p   70   0   1  16 128  14  56
  s   48   5   4  19  11 117  22
  w   42  22  40  13 126  17 178
```

Play (p) and Stranger (s) appear to be well predicted, and we can assume that they have characteristic or distinctive acoustical features that distinguish them, but Ball (b) and Fight (f) show some confusion, indicating that their acoustic features are not so clearly distinguished at this simple level of statistical decision making. Not surprisingly perhaps, Walk (w) and Play (p) appear to be highly confused (similar?). Stranger (s) is similarly confused with Fight (f). For completeness, we look next at the performance through detailed counts (note the use of '==' here):

```
> table(ttp==d2$ctxt[d2$id=="d24"])

FALSE  TRUE
  978   723
```

We turn next to dog D12.

```
> ttt=tree(d2$ctxt ~ ., x2,subset=d2$id=="d12")
> summary(ttt)

Classification tree:
tree(formula = d2$ctxt ~ ., data = x2, subset = d2$id == "d12")
Variables actually used in tree construction:
[1] "pmin"  "pmax"  "dn"    "pmean" "fmean" "fvcd"  "fmin"
```

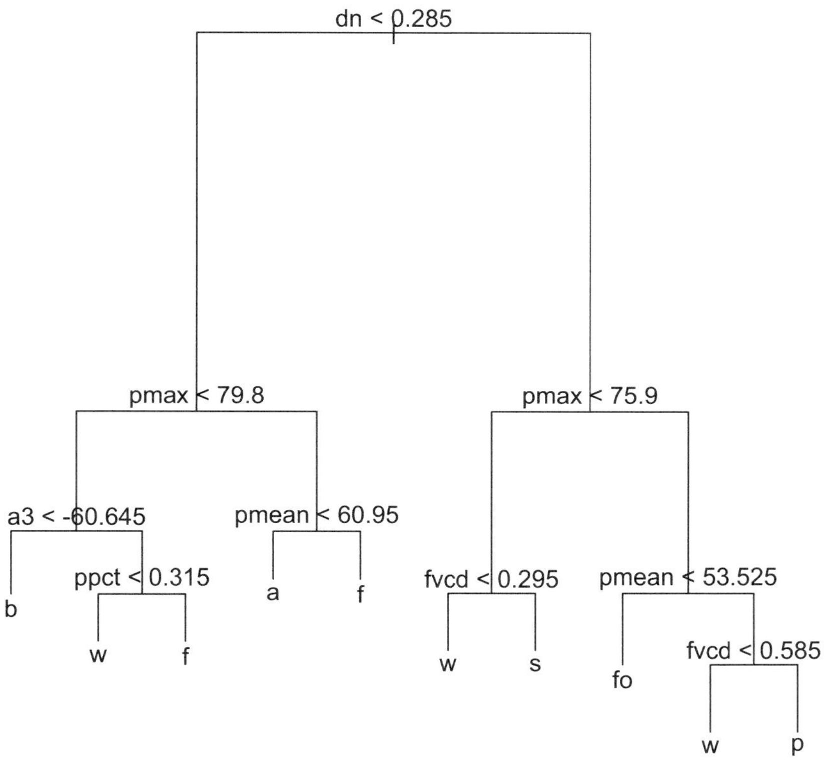

Abbildung 5 - The Classification Tree for predicting barks from D24 - with 10 leaves, showing duration to be the first determining factor, followed by pmax, a3, and f0-voicing respectively. This simple tree predicts less than half of the barks correctly, but confirms that most of the features are being used in making the classification.

```
Number of terminal nodes:  15
Residual mean deviance:  2.087 = 2150 / 1030
Misclassification error rate: 0.4134 = 432 / 1045
> table(ttp,d2$ctxt[d2$id=="d24"])

ttp    a   b   f  fo   p   s   w
  a   43  13  36   2   0   1  17
  b   22  77  14  59   4  13  19
  f   23  42 140  19   5  46  25
  fo  29   6   0  40  39   0  18
  p   70   0   1  16 128  14  56
  s   48   5   4  19  11 117  22
  w   42  22  40  13 126  17 178

> table(ttp==d2$ctxt[d2$id=="d24"])

FALSE  TRUE
  978   723
```

This time the tree predicts almost 60% of the tokens correctly, but as the plot (Figure 6) shows, a completely different set of features is used. Finally we test the entire dataset. The tree only develops 5 terminal nodes, and fails to predict more than 69% of the tokens, with no predictions of Walk, Food, or Alone barks Interestingly, Fight and Stranger appear to be well predicted but internally confusable. However, it is clear that there is considerably individuality in the remaining categories of barks for these dogs.

```
Classification tree:
tree(formula = d2$ctxt ~ ., data = x2)
Variables actually used in tree construction:
[1] "pmin" "dn"   "a3"   "pmax"
Number of terminal nodes:  5
Residual mean deviance:  3.581 = 26470 / 7390
Misclassification error rate: 0.6944 = 5135 / 7395
>  ttp=predict(ttt,type="class")
> table(ttp,d2$ctxt)

ttp     a    b    f   fo    p    s    w
  a     0    0    0    0    0    0    0
  b    72  398  134  370   67  182  134
  f   215  117  549   76  167  308  234
  fo    0    0    0    0    0    0    0
  p    66   93   24   38  259   49   93
  s   500  497  529  393  387 1054  390
  w     0    0    0    0    0    0    0
```

4 Prediction by SVM

Support Vector Machines are included in the library **e1071** in 'R'. Training an SVM on the same data gives a much more successful result, since it employs a total of 6744 Support Vectors to predict the data, rather than the 10 to 15 terminal nodes determined by the Classification Tree. Since it is not feasible to examine those vectors individually (as it was with the branches of the tree) we use n-fold cross validation to hold out n% of the data, train with the rest and then test with the held-out samples. Here we set n=15 (it is usually about 10, so this is a stricter test perhaps) and find that on average the SVM can successfully predict less than half of the samples.

```
> sss=svm(d2$ctxt ~ ., x2,cross=15)
> summary(sss)

Call:
```

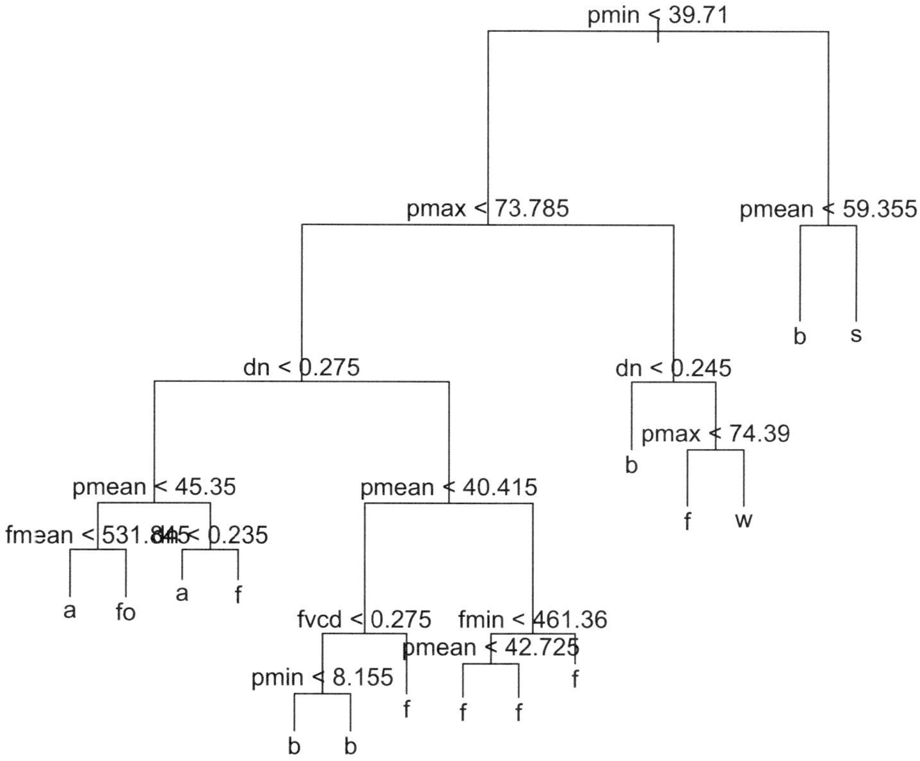

Abbildung 6 - The Classification Tree for predicting barks from D12 - with 15 leaves, using a different set of parameters and parameter ordering from that determined for D24, starting from min-pitch, then looking at mean and max of the same. This tree predicts about 60% of the barks correctly,

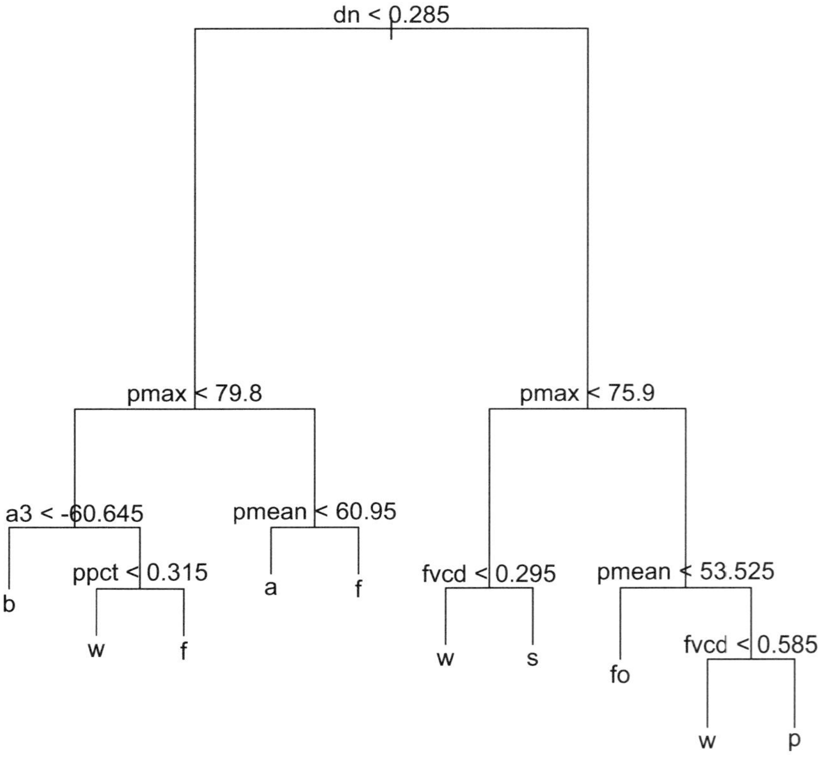

Abbildung 7 - The Classification Tree for predicting barks from D24 - with 10 leaves, showing duration to be the first determining factor, followed by pmax, a3, and f0-voicing respectively. This simple tree predicts less than half of the barks correctly, but confirms that most of the features are being used in making the classification.

```
svm(formula = d2$ctxt ~ ., data = x2, cross = 15)

Parameters:
   SVM-Type:  C-classification
 SVM-Kernel:  radial
       cost:  1
      gamma:  0.07142857

Number of Support Vectors:  6744

 ( 1070 845 1339 1019 839 828 804 )

Number of Classes:  7

Levels:
 a b f fo p s w

15-fold cross-validation on training data:

Total Accuracy: 45.94997
Single Accuracies:
 38.94523 50.91278 46.65314 48.27586 44.62475 47.66734  43.20487
 46.4503 48.88438 47.66734 47.87018 46.04462 45.23327 46.24746 40.56795
```

However, when we limit the prediction to a subset of the barks, predicting in this case those of dog D12, we achieve an accuracy of greater than 60% in the general case:

```
Call:
svm(formula = d2$ctxt ~ ., data = x2, cross = 15, subset = d2$id == "d12")

Parameters:
   SVM-Type:  C-classification
 SVM-Kernel:  radial
       cost:  1
      gamma:  0.07142857

Number of Support Vectors:  923

 ( 149 157 280 89 188 60 )

Number of Classes:  6

Levels:
 a b f fo p s w

15-fold cross-validation on training data:

Total Accuracy: 60.86124
Single Accuracies:
 31.88406 54.28571 62.85714 62.31884 75.71429 77.14286  75.36232
 64.28571 65.71429 69.56522 65.71429 62.85714 57.97101 51.42857 35.71429
```

When we then examine the individual prediction accuracy for each category by running the SVM in 'predict' mode and comparing with the original categories, we obtain the following confusion matrix:

```
> ssp=predict(sss)
> table(ssp,ctxt[d2$id=="d12"])
```

```
ssp    a   b   f  fo   p   s   w
  a   93   2   2  11   0  15   1
  b   11 142   8   4   0   6   1
  f   33  35 320   9   0  68   7
  fo  11  11   7  72   0   6   1
  p    0   0   0   0   0   0   0
  s    3   3   7   1   0  99   1
  w    1   0   1   2   0   0  51
```

This can be compared with a similar exercise for dog D24, achieving similar accuracy (given the larger number of classes) and clear discrimination, as confirmed by the two clear confusion matrices.

```
> sss=svm(d2$ctxt ~ ., x2,subset=d2$id=="d24",cross=15)
 . . . . .
Total Accuracy: 56.61376
Single Accuracies:
 46.90265 56.63717 55.26316 57.52212 64.91228 50.44248 58.40708
 50.87719 66.37168 52.63158 63.71681 67.25664 56.14035 61.9469 40.35088

> ssp=predict(sss)
> table(ssp,ctxt[d2$id=="d24"])

ssp    a   b   f  fo   p   s   w
  a  187   9   6  12  16  18  29
  b   10 109   5  28   1   7  15
  f   12  13 188   1   1  11  17
  fo  15  20   4 103   2   3   8
  p   21   1   7  19 237   2  47
  s   21   8   8   0   5 154  10
  w   11   5  17   5  51  13 209
> ==================================
```

5 Cross Prediction (across dogs)

The final exercise in this report concerns the training of a SVM on one dog and then testing the results on another. To do this, we first make a subset of the data containing the material related to each dog. Here we use for example dogs D12, D23, and D24:

```
> d12=subset(d2,id=="d12")
> d23=subset(d2,id=="d23")
> d24=subset(d2,id=="d24")
```

then make a training subset of each, separating the predictor variables from the independent categories:

```
> x12=subset(d12, select=c(-ctxt,-n,-id,-wav))
> y12=d12$ctxt
> x23=subset(d23, select=c(-ctxt,-n,-id,-wav))
> y23=d23$ctxt
> x24=subset(d24, select=c(-ctxt,-n,-id,-wav))
> y24=d24$ctxt
```

and then perform the model training to build the SVM:

```
> m12=svm(x12,y12)
> m23=svm(x23,y23)
> m24=svm(x24,y24)
```

and test the results on the closed data, where perfect prediction can be expected (but considerable confusion remains in certain categories of bark):

```
> table(y12,predict(m12))

y12    a   b   f  fo   p   s   w
  a   93  11  33  11   0   3   1
  b    2 142  35  11   0   3   0
  f    2   8 320   7   0   7   1
  fo  11   4   9  72   0   1   2
  p    0   0   0   0   0   0   0
  s   15   6  68   6   0  99   0
  w    1   1   7   1   0   1  51

> table(y23,predict(m23))

y23    a   b   f  fo   p   s   w
  a  124   0  11   2   0   1   2
  b    3 155   2  33   0   1   7
  f   16   0 123   0   0   0   0
  fo   3  40   0 133   0   1  10
  p    0   0   0   0   0   0   0
  s    4  27   0   9   0  96  14
  w    0   8   0  20   0  10 115
```

and then between dogs, in the open data case, training first on one and then testing on the other:

```
> table(y12,predict(m23,x12))

y12    a   b   f  fo   p   s   w
  a   20  11  59  29   0   8  25
  b    3  32  58  17   0  41  42
  f   30  71 149  26   0  20  49
  fo  12  20  24  12   0   8  23
  p    0   0   0   0   0   0   0
  s   24  24 109  10   0  18   9
  w    3   5  23   0   0  25   6

> table(y23,predict(m12,x23))

y23    a   b   f  fo   p   s   w
  a   20   0  59  10   0  51   0
  b    0   2 190   0   0   5   4
  f   19   0  55   1   0  64   0
  fo  10   5 161   0   0  10   1
  p    0   0   0   0   0   0   0
  s    6   0  91   0   0  40  13
  w    5   5 128   0   0   9   6
```

or expressing the above in simpler numerical terms:

```
> table(y23==predict(m12,x23))

FALSE  TRUE
  847   123

> table(y12==predict(m23,x12))

FALSE  TRUE
  808   237
```

we see from these very poor cross-prediction results that the previously effective SVM cannot be trained on one dog to predict the bark categories of another. Results are similar for tests with dog D24, but for reasons of space have not been included here.

6 Discussion

From the above results, we conclude that barks are generally consistent in their acoustic realisation and that simple statistical models can be trained to predict the category of bark from the acoustics of that bark type for several different dogs. Within dog, we can obtain good prediction accuracies, of around 60% for a seven-category task, but *across* dogs the prediction accuracy drops considerably. It might be concluded from this that dogs learn to bark in a given situation individually, rather as a species, and that they bark to communicate with their owner, rather than with each other. This is speculation by the first author, a non-expert, but such an interpretation would be supported by the above data.

Within dogs, barks appear to be clearly distinguished and can be recognised to a large extent from their acoustics, but there is also considerable variety that prevents a more successful classification. This remains as work in progress. We will look next at the sequence of barks, to see if there is an effect for position in the bark sequence that might explain the apparent confusion in the data.

7 Acknowledgement

This work reported was carried out at BME in Budapest while the author was a summer guest of the BME (Budapest University of Technology and Economics) and the Hungarian Academy of Sciences as part of the ETOCOM project (TÁMOP-4.2.2-08/1/KMR-2008-0007) through the Hungarian National Development Agency in the framework of Social Renewal Operative Programme supported by the EU and co-financed by the European Social Fund. The author also wishes to acknowledge the Science Foundation Ireland SFI Stokes Professorship Award 07/SK/I1218).

Inhaltsbasierte Musikanalyse

Matthias Eichner und Stephan Hübler

Kurzfassung: Das Interesse an Systemen zur automatischen Musikanalyse und Annotation hat in den letzten Jahren stark zugenommen. Eine Hauptursache dafür liegt in der stetig wachsenden Menge digital gespeicherter und über das Internet abrufbarer Musik. Lag einst die Herausforderung in der Beschaffung einer bestimmten Aufnahme eines Musikstücks oder Werkes, liegt sie heute im Navigieren und dem Einschränken der Suche innerhalb der riesigen Menge an verfügbarer Musik. Das Forschungsgebiet des Music Information Retrieval beschäftigt sich mit Methoden zum Auffinden gewünschter Informationen innerhalb von Musikstücken oder Musikdatenbanken, sowie der Manipulation von Musik und der automatischen Erzeugung neuer Musik. Es ist so vielschichtig wie das Medium Musik selbst. Dieser Betrag soll einen Überblick über das Forschungsgebiet und typische Anwendungsfälle geben.

1 Einleitung

Sowohl die Art und Weise wie wir Musik konsumieren, als auch die Musikindustrie haben sich im letzten Jahrzehnt drastisch verändert. Klassische Tonträger wie Schallplatten, Kassetten und Compact Disks wurden durch MP3 Downloads und Streaming-Angebote verdrängt. Traditionsunternehmen, wie zum Beispiel HMV, das fast ein Jahrhundert existierte, können sich nicht mehr gegen die großen Online-Shops behaupten und melden Insolvenz an [8]. Hat man früher neue Musik durch Stöbern im Plattenladen entdeckt, wird man heute eher im Internet auf Musikportalen nach den Neuerscheinungen seiner Lieblingsinterpreten suchen. Dabei möchte man möglichst nicht nur Alben angezeigt bekommen die man schon kennt, sondern vor allem Musik, die den persönlichen Geschmack trifft und neu ist. Betreiber solcher Portale benötigen eine entsprechende Infrastruktur, um diese personalisierten Empfehlungen anbieten zu können.
Diese Entwicklung hat zu einer starken Nachfrage nach Methoden und Systemen geführt, die in der Lage sind Musikdatenbanken automatisch zu annotieren und durchsuchbar zu machen. Das Forschungsgebiet, was sich mit dieser Aufgabe beschäftigt, wird als *Music Information Retrieval* (MIR) bezeichnet. Die Anfänge des MIR reichen bis in die 60er Jahre zurück [9], größere Beachtung hat es aber erst mit der Gründung des *International Symposium on Music Information Retrieval* (ISMIR)[1] im Jahre 2000 erfahren. Seit dem ist die jährlich stattfindende ISMIR die wichtigste Konferenz auf diesem Gebiet.

2 Anwendungsgebiete der inhaltsbasierten Musikanalyse

Drei unterschiedliche Gruppen sind an MIR-Technologien interessiert: a) die Musikindustrie, welche Musik produziert und verwertet, b) Konsumenten, die Musik nach ihrem Geschmack finden möchten und c) Fachleute, die sich beruflich mit Musik beschäftigen, sei es als Musiker, Lehrer oder Musikwissenschaftler. Aus den speziellen Anforderungen dieser Gruppen an die MIR-Technologie ergeben sich eine Vielzahl von Arbeits- und Anwendungsgebieten.

[1] http://www.ismir.net

Die meisten vorgestellten Anwendungsgebiete aus Tabelle sind aktive Forschungsgebiete, für die es im Rahmen des *Music Information Retrieval Evaluation eXchange* (MIREX) [2] jährliche Evaluierungen der besten Systeme auf dem jeweiligen Gebiet gibt. Im Folgenden gehen wir auf die möglichen Repräsentationen eines Musikstückes ein. Anschließend stellen wir Anwendungen vor, welche auf einer Suche innerhalb einer Musikdatenbank basieren.

2.1 Repräsentationen eines Musikstückes

Ein Musikstück kann unterschiedlich repräsentiert werden. Abbildung 1 zeigt die drei möglichen Repräsentationen als Signal (wav, mp3,...), symbolisch (Noten, Midi,...) und textuell (Metadaten).

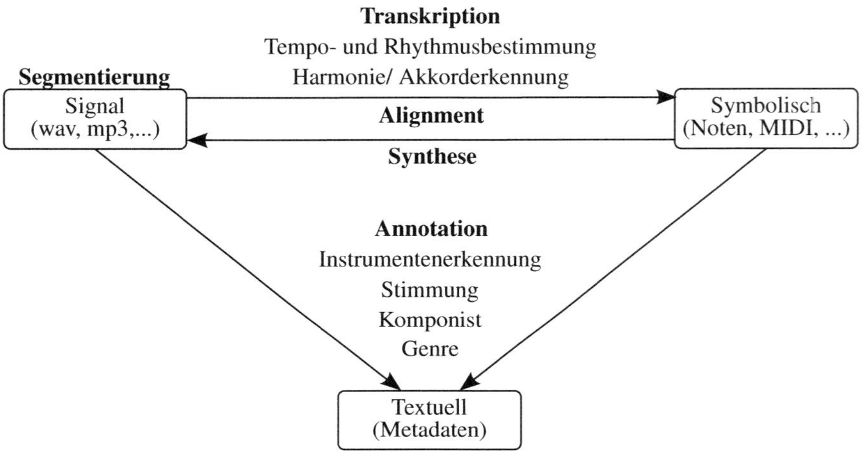

Abbildung 1 - Verschiedene Repräsentation eines Musikstückes und die damit verbundenen MIR-Anwendungsgebiete

Vielfältige aktuelle Forschungsgebiete innerhalb des Music Information Retrieval beschäftigen sich mit der automatischen Überführung der Repräsentationen. Zwischen dem Signal und der symbolischen Darstellung wird eine vollständige Übersetzung angestrebt. Metadaten als textuelle Repräsentation werden lediglich aus dem Signal oder der symbolischen Darstellung gewonnen und können nicht als Grundlage dienen für eine Rücküberführung dienen. Tabelle 1 erläutert die verwendeten Anwendungsgebiete. Jede Anwendung auf der Grundlage des Signals, ist der inhaltsbasierte Musikanalyse zuzuordnen.

2.2 Anwendungen basierend auf einer Musikdatenbank

Vielfältige Anwendungen in dem Bereich des Music Information Retrieval benötigen eine Musikdatenbank. Die Systeme unterscheiden sich in der Herkunft der Information über ein Musikstück. Es existieren Systeme, welche auf der Grundlage von Metadaten von Plattenfirmen, Experten und Nutzern arbeiten und inhaltsbasierten Systeme, welche auf der Grundlage des Audiosignals arbeiten. Sie haben gegenüber den Metadaten-basierten Ansätzen den Vorteil, dass sie keine manuelle Interaktion erfordern und große Musikdatenbanken vollautomatisch verarbeiten können. Sie sind damit in der Lage Musikbestände zu erschließen, über die es keine

[2] http://www.music-ir.org/mirex

Anwendungsgebiet	Beschreibung
Segmentierung	Finden von Segmentgrenzen, z.B. Sprache / Musikunterscheidung, Strophe / Refrain
Transkription	Erstellen eines Notenbildes aus Audiomaterial
Harmonie- / Akkord-Erkennung	Identifizieren der Harmonien innerhalb eines Musikstücks
Tempo- und Rhythmus-Bestimmung	Bestimmung des Tempo, Beat und rhythmischer Pattern
Alignment	Zeitliche Synchronisation von unterschiedlichen Aufführungen des selben Stücks
Synthese	Erzeugung von Audiomaterial aus Mididaten, Erzeugung neuer Musik
Komponist	Identifizieren des Komponisten ohne auf Metadaten zurückzugreifen
Stimmung	Gruppieren von Musik nach bestimmten emotionaler Stimmung
Genre	Identifikation des musikalischem Genres oder Stils
Instrumentenerkennung	Identifizieren der Instrumente, die in einem Musikstück vorkommen

Tabelle 1 - Auswahl typischer MIR-Anwendungsgebiete in Bezug auf verschiedene Repräsentationen eines Musikstückes

oder wenige Informationen gibt, bzw. die auf Grund ihrer geringen Popularität keine Beachtung finden. Die dritte Kategorie stellen hybride Systeme dar, die sowohl Metadaten als auch inhaltsbasierte Verarbeitung miteinander kombinieren.

Abbildung 2 zeigt schematisch die verschiedenen Anwendungen von Systemen, welche eine Musikdatenbank benutzen. Eingabe eines solchen Systems kann ein Musikstück (als Signal oder Symbolisch) sein, aber auch der Mensch, welcher eine Melodie summt, ein Lied singt oder einen Rhythmus klopft. Die zwei Hauptanwendungsgebiete sind die Bereiche der Musikidentifikation und der Musikempfehlung. In Tabelle 2 werden die Anwendungsgebiete erläutert.

Als praktisch gelöst gilt die Musikidentifikation. Auf sie wollen wir etwas genauer eingehen, da sie die in der Öffentlichkeit bekannteste MIR-Anwendung darstellt. Insbesondere das durch die Firma *Shazam* entwickelte und patentierte Verfahren hat der Musikidentifikation zum Durchbruch verholfen [14]. Mit diesem Verfahren ist es möglich, ein Musikstück aus einem Datenbestand von mehreren Millionen Titeln anhand einer nur wenige Sekunden langen, mit einem Mobiltelefon unter stark gestörten Umgebungsbedingungen erstellten Aufnahme, eindeutig zu identifizieren, vorausgesetzt der Titel befindet sich in der Datenbank. Diese erstaunliche Leistung ist aber weniger dem tiefen Verständnis von menschlicher Musikwahrnehmung und ausgeklügelter Signalverarbeitung zu verdanken, als vielmehr der konsequenten Anwendung existierender Such- und Indexierungsstrategien aus dem Gebiet des Data-Mining und Information Retrieval. So lässt sich das Verfahren auch auf andere Arten von Audiosignalen anwenden und wird zum Beispiel zur Synchronisation von Smartphones und Tablet-Computern mit dem Fernseher eingesetzt. Diese als *Second Screen* [7] bezeichnete Anwendung zielt darauf ab, das klassische Fernseherlebnis durch zusätzliche, zum Programm passende und auf den Nutzer zugeschnittene interaktive Inhalte zu bereichern.

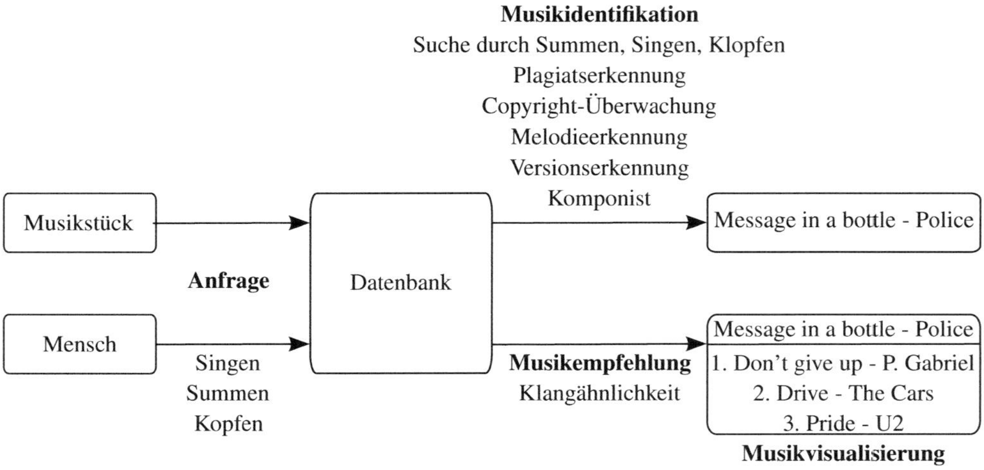

Abbildung 2 - MIR-Anwendungsgebiete unter Verwendung einer Musikdatenbank

3 Typische Analyseverfahren

In Musik existieren meistens mehrere Informationsströme oder Ebenen, die parallel zur selben Zeit ablaufen. Wir nehmen sie als verschiedene Dimensionen der Musik wahr: Tonhöhe, Rhythmus, Tempo, Melodieverlauf, Klangfarbe / Timbre und Dynamik [10]. Entsprechend vielfältig sind die Analyse- und Modellierungsmethoden, die im Music Information Retrieval angewendet werden. Einige Techniken wurden aus verwandten Gebieten übernommen. Dazu zählen Merkmalextraktionsverfahren wie Mel Frequency Cepstrum Coefficients (MFCC) oder Klassifikationsverfahren wie Support Vector Machines und Hidden Markov Modelle (HMM).
Viele Verfahren sind aber musikspezifisch und angepasst an die jeweilige Aufgabe. Ein typischer Vertreter ist das Chroma-Merkmal, bei dem das gesamte Spektrum auf 12 Frequenzbänder abgebildet wird. Diese Abbildung entspricht der in westlicher Musik üblichen Unterteilung einer Oktave in 12 Halbtöne. Töne, welche genau eine Oktave voneinander entfernt sind, werden als besonders ähnlich empfunden und fallen bei der Chroma-Analyse in das selbe Band. Die Energieverteilung zwischen den 12 Halbtönen innerhalb eines Musikstückes ohne die absolute Frequenz bzw. Oktave zu berücksichtigen, liefert wertvolle Informationen über ein Stück und wird zum Beispiel zur Synchronisation unterschiedlicher Aufführungen des selben Musikstücks eingesetzt [3].
Ein weiteres Beispiel für ein typisches Signalanalyse-Verfahren im MIR-Umfeld ist die Constant-Q Transformation (CQT). Sie ist mit der Wavelet Transformation eng verwandt und transformiert ein Zeitsignal in den Frequenzbereich mit einer geometrischen Einteilung der Frequenzachse. Diese Einteilung resultiert in einer Abnahme der Frequenzauflösung von niedrigen zu hohen Frequenzen und einer Zunahme der Zeitauflösung mit steigender Frequenz. Die Anzahl der Frequenzbänder je Oktave liegt typischerweise bei $12-96$ [13]. Die QCT eignet sich besonders deshalb gut für die Analyse von Musiksignalen, weil auch die Grundfrequenzen der Töne in westlicher Musik eine geometrische Anordnung besitzen. Zum Beispiel lassen sich die Grundfrequenzen für die gleichstufige Standardstimmung mit zwölf Tönen nach folgender Formel berechnen: $F_k = 440\text{Hz} \times 2^{k/12}$, mit $k \in [-50, 40]$.

Anwendungsgebiet	Beschreibung
Musikidentifikation	Erkennen einen Musikstücks anhand des Audiosignals oder eines Ausschnitts dessen
Komponist	Identifizieren des Komponisten ohne auf Metadaten zurückzugreifen
Plagiatserkennung	Schutz des geistigen Eigentumsrecht
Copyright-Überwachung	Aufdecken von Urheberrechtsverletzungen, automatische Tantiemenermittlung
Versionserkennung	Identifizieren von Remixes, Live bzw. Studioaufnahmen des selben Titels oder von Coverversionen
Melodieerkennung	Finden der Titel in einer Datenbasis, in der eine bestimmte Melodie vorkommt
Suche durch Summen, Singen oder Klopfen	Finden eines Titels anhand der gesummten oder gesungenen Melodie bzw. geklopften Rhythmus
Klangähnlichkeit	Finden aller Titel, die so ähnlich wie eine vorgegebene Aufnahme klingen
Musikempfehlung	Finden von Musik, die dem persönlichen Geschmack eines Nutzers entspricht
Musikvisualisierung	Grafische Darstellung von Musiktiteln, die eine intuitive Navigation innerhalb der Sammlung ermöglicht

Tabelle 2 - Auswahl typischer MIR-Anwendungsgebiete mit einer Musikdatenbank

4 Herausforderungen und aktuelle Forschungsschwerpunkte

Die automatische Transkription von komplexen polyphonen Musikaufnahmen gilt als der Heilige Gral im Music Information Retrieval. In den letzten Jahren wurden bemerkenswerte Fortschritte auf diesem Gebiet gemacht und es sind mittlerweile kommerzielle Lösungen verfügbar, mit denen sich die einzelnen Töne eines Instrumentes oder einer Stimme innerhalb einer Aufnahme separieren und editieren lassen [11]. Nichtsdestotrotz erreichen diese Systeme bei weitem nicht die Leistungsfähigkeit der menschlichen Wahrnehmung.
Bisher wurden die meisten Verfahren für die Analyse von westlicher Musik entwickelt und optimiert. Es ist nicht davon auszugehen, dass sie für Musik aus anderen Regionen mit komplett verschiedenen Musiksystemen gleich gut funktionieren. Es wird also eine weitere Herausforderung sein, die bestehenden Techniken an die Verarbeitung von Musik aus anderen Teilen der Welt anzupassen. Dieser Aspekt gewinnt besonders im Hinblick auf die fortschreitende Globalisierung an Bedeutung [4].
Für eine zuverlässige automatische Analyse und Annotation von Musik sind noch eine Reihe weiterer Herausforderungen zu meistern [2]. Viele dieser Herausforderungen liegen weniger in der technischen Umsetzung geeigneter Analyseverfahren, als vielmehr im Verständnis der komplexen Zusammenhänge der Musikwahrnehmung und des Mediums Musik selbst. Musikwissenschaftler, Kognitionswissenschaftler und Ingenieure arbeiten zunehmend interdisziplinär zusammen, um diesem Ziel näher zu kommen [5, 1].

5 Zusammenfassung

Erkenntnisse und Forschungsergebnisse aus dem Music Information Retrieval begegnen uns zunehmend im Alltag. Produkte wie die Musikidentifikation, Web-Applikationen zum Erlernen oder Üben eines Musikinstruments [12] oder die automatische Akkordtranskription von Musiksignalen [6] demonstrieren, dass die Algorithmen zur inhaltsbasierten Musikanalyse nicht nur unter Laborbedingungen beeindruckende Resultate liefern.

Es gibt aber noch viele Herausforderungen. Dazu zählen vor allem Anwendungen bei denen die subjektive Wahrnehmung von Musik im Mittelpunkt steht, wie z.B. die Bestimmung der empfundenen Ähnlichkeit zwischen Musikstücken, die Zuordnung von emotionalen Beschreibungen zu einem Musikstück oder die Dekomposition des Musiksignals in Teilsignale, die mit der menschliche Wahrnehmung korreliert. Diese Herausforderungen werden nicht ohne ein besseres Verständnis der Prozesse der Musikperzeption gemeistert werden können.

Literatur

[1] AUCOUTURIER, J.-J. und E. BIGAND: *Mel Cepstrum and Ann Ova: The Difficult Dialog Between MIR and Music Cognition.* In: *Proceedings of the 13th International Society for Music Information Retrieval Conference*, Porto, Portugal, October 8-12 2012.

[2] BYRD, D. und T. CRAWFORD: *Problems of music information retrieval in the real world.* In: *Information Processing and Management*, Bd. 38, S. 249–272. Pergamon Press, Inc., März 2002.

[3] EWERT, S., M. MÜLLER und R. B. DANNENBERG: *Towards Reliable Partial Music Alignments Using Multiple Synchronization Strategies.* In: *Proceedings of the International Workshop on Adaptive Multimedia Retrieval (AMR)*, Madrid, Spain, Sep. 2009.

[4] GRAEFF, N.: *Towards a Transcultural Approach to Automatic Music Classification.* In: *Joint Annual Meeting of the British Forum for Ethnomusicology and ICTM-Ireland*, 2013.

[5] GRAEFF, N., P. KÜPPERS, F. PFEIFER und T. D. O. PINTO: *Automatic Retrieval of Rhythmic Patterns for the Global Music Database, a Joint-Project Between Musicologists and Audio Engineers.* In: *Musikwirtschaft 2.0: Perspektiven für die Musik*, 2012.

[6] HAAS, B. DE: *Chordify.* `http://www.chordify.net/`, 2013. [Online; accessed 12-March-2013].

[7] HEISE ONLINE: *Microsoft-Studie: 68 Prozent der Verbraucher nutzen Second Screen.* `http://heise.de/-1824092`, 2013. [Online; accessed 16-March-2013].

[8] HEISE ONLINE: *Traditionsreiche Musikladen-Kette HMV in Insolvenz.* `http://heise.de/-1784447`, 2013. [Online; accessed 12-March-2013].

[9] KASSLER, M.: *Toward musical information retrieval.* In: *Perspectives of New Music*, Bd. 4, S. 59–67, 1966.

[10] LEVITIN, D.: *This Is Your Brain on Music: The Science of a Human Obsession.* Penguin Group, 2006.

[11] NEUBÄCKER, P.: *Celemony Software GmbH.* `http://www.celemony.com`, 2013. [Online; accessed 12-March-2013].

[12] RYYNÄNEN, M.: *GuitarBots.* `http://guitarbots.com`, 2013. [Online; accessed 12-March-2013].

[13] SCHOERKHUBER, C. und A. KLAPURI: *Constant-Q transform toolbox for music processing.* In: *7th Sound and Music Computing Conference*, 2010.

[14] WANG, A. L.: *An industrial-strength audio search algorithm.* In: *Proceedings of the 4 th International Conference on Music Information Retrieval*, 2003.

AUDITIVE WAHRNEHMUNG UND BEURTEILUNG VON INSTATIONÄREN FAHRZEUGGERÄUSCHEN

Ercan Altinsoy

Lehrstuhl für Kommunikationsakustik, Technische Universität Dresden
ercan.altinsoy@tu-dresden.de

Abstract: Die Qualität von Fahrzeuggeräuschen ist eine mehrdimensionale Größe. Das Ziel dieser Studie ist die Erfassung des auditiven Wahrnehmungsraums von instationären Fahrzeugaußengeräuschen mit Blick auf deren Qualität. In dieser Studie, wurden als Betriebszustände „Motorstart-Leerlauf" und „Beschleunigte Vorbeifahrt" ausgewählt. Um das oben genannte Ziel zu erreichen, wurden zuerst Ähnlichkeitsuntersuchungen durchgeführt. Das Ergebnis dieser Ähnlichkeitsuntersuchungen sind Distanzen der Fahrzeuggeräusche zueinander. Diese Distanz basiert auf komplexen Zusammenhängen von Wahrnehmungsmerkmalen und ermöglicht einen übergeordneten Blick auf die Welt der Fahrzeuggeräusche. Anschließend wurden Hörversuche mit dem Ziel durchgeführt, die Ausprägung von 36 Eigenschaften der einzelnen Fahrzeuggeräusche zu ermitteln. So entstand quasi ein „footprint" von jedem Fahrzeuggeräusch für die zwei untersuchten Betriebszustände. Um die Zusammenhänge der Merkmale und ihre Rolle für die Gesamtqualität, die Sportlichkeit und den Komfort einordnen zu können, wurde eine Faktorenanalyse durchgeführt.

1 Einleitung

Jedes Fahrzeug weist bestimmte technische Merkmale auf, die maßgeblich sind für unterschiedliche Qualitäten von Fahrzeugmodellen und –typen. Zu ihnen gehören technisch-mechanische Vorgänge unterschiedlicher Betriebszustände. Viele von ihnen verursachen Geräusche. Diese Geräusche werden von den Insassen hörend, also auditiv wahrgenommen. Benutzer von Fahrzeugen lernen im Allgemeinen sehr schnell, wie sich bestimmte Fahrzeuge in unterschiedlichen Betriebszuständen anhören. Das wahrgenommene Geräusch hat somit Verweischarakter: es weist nicht nur auf den jeweiligen Betriebszustand des Fahrzeugs hin, sondern es steht auch stellvertretend für die Gesamtqualität des jeweiligen Fahrzeugtyps bzw. Fahrzeugmodells.

Die auditive Wahrnehmung von Fahrzeugen ist ein sehr komplexer Vorgang. Die Abbildung eines Schallereignisses durch rein physikalische Messgrößen kann jedoch nur einen kleinen Einblick geben. Auch die psychoakustische Beschreibung vermag nicht alles zu erfassen, was zur Qualitätsbeurteilung des Produkts Automobil notwendig ist. Die Qualitätsbeurteilung instationärer Signale ist ein Themenschwerpunkt für Produktentwickler, da viele Produkte instationäre Betriebszustände besitzen. Bisherige Untersuchungen konzentrieren sich hauptsächlich auf die Lautheitsbeurteilung von instationären Signalen [1,2,3,4,5].

Das Ziel dieser Studie ist die Erfassung des auditiven Wahrnehmungsraumes von instationären Fahrzeugaußengeräuschen mit Blick auf deren Qualität, Sportlichkeit und Komfort. Um dieses Ziel zu erreichen, wird zuerst eine Ähnlichkeitsuntersuchung durchgeführt. Sie ist die einzige Möglichkeit einer Untersuchung ohne Merkmal- und Wertvorgabe. Anschließend werden 38 Fahrzeuggeräusche mit einem Semantischen Differenzial beurteilt. Die Begriffswelt von Experten spiegelt zu einem Themenkomplex nicht zwangsläufig auch die von Laien benutzten Begriffe wider. Die Beurteilungsmerkmale, aus denen das Semantische Differenzial gebildet wird, sollen eine repräsentative Stichprobe jener Beurteilungsmerkmale darstellen, die die Befragten selbst gewöhnlich zur Beschreibung der untersuchten Beurteilungsgegenstände verwenden [6]. In unserer vorherigen Studie ist es gelungen, eine umfassende Zusammenstellung von wahrnehmbaren Eigenschaften von Fahrzeuggeräuschen für verschiedene Betriebszustände u.a. „Motorstart-Leerlauf“ und „Beschleunigte Vorbeifahrt“ zu erstellen [7]. Diese Beschreibungen beruhen auf den Wahrnehmungen, die nicht akustisch vorgebildete Versuchspersonen in einem Hörversuch beschrieben.

2 Ähnlichkeit von Fahrzeuggeräuschen

Die Ähnlichkeit von Fahrzeuggeräuschen ist ein multidimensionaler Raum, basierend auf allen wahrgenommenen Merkmalen. Die Befragung der Probanden nach der Ähnlichkeit ist die einzige Möglichkeit einer Untersuchung ohne Merkmal- und Wertvorgabe. Die Ergebnisse der Ähnlichkeitsuntersuchung liefern strukturierte Merkmalzusammenhänge, welche zum Sound und Brand Design verwendet werden können.

2.1 Stimuli

Als Stimuli wurden Außengeräusche von 38 Fahrzeugen in den Betriebszuständen „Motorstart-Leerlauf“ und „Beschleunigte Vorbeifahrt ab 30 km/h im 2. Gang“ binaural aufgenommen. Im ersten Betriebszustand startet der Fahrer des Fahrzeugs das Auto und bleibt für fünf Sekunden im Leerlauf stehen. Der Kunstkopf steht vier Meter neben der Fahrbahn und „schaut“ auf die Beifahrerseite. Im zweiten Betriebszustand fährt der Fahrer am Hörer von links nach rechts mit v = 30km/h im 2. Gang vorbei und beschleunigt, wenn er auf dessen Höhe ist. Der Kunstkopf ist genauso platziert wie im ersten Betriebszustand. Folgende Kriterien waren ausschlaggebend für die Fahrzeugwahl: Motorart (Diesel, Otto), in der Regel gleich verteilt; Fahrzeugklasse (hierbei handelt es sich um die Kleinwagen-, Mittel-, Ober- und Sportwagenklasse), in der Regel gleich verteilt und die Fahrzeug-Marke.

2.2 Versuchspersonen

Vierzig Versuchspersonen (dreißig Männer und zehn Frauen) mit Normalhörfähigkeit nahmen an den Experimenten teil. Sie waren zwischen 25 und 55 Jahren alt (Mittelwert: 41 Jahre). Alle Versuchspersonen fahren täglich Auto.

2.3 Versuchsmethode

Es wurden Hörversuche durchgeführt mit dem Ziel, die wahrgenommene Ähnlichkeit von einzelnen akustischen Fahrzeuginnenraumgeräuschen im Paarvergleich zu ermitteln. Die Versuchspersonen hatten die Frage zu beantworten: „Wie ähnlich sind diese Geräusche?“. Um sicher zu stellen, dass die Stimuli kalibriert wiedergegeben werden, wird das Softwarepaket „Artemis“ verwendet.

Bei der Befragung nach der Ähnlichkeit wurde eine quasi-kontinuierliche Skala benutzt. In dieser Skala wurden die in der Psychometrik üblichen äquidistanten Rohrmann-Begriffe verwendet. Als Unterstützung der Bewertung sind unterhalb der Skala die Ähnlichkeitsprozentwerte aufgetragen. Die Bewertungsoberfläche wurde mit Matlab-GUI implementiert. Diese graphische Benutzeroberfläche ist in Abbildung 1 dargestellt. Sie belegt eine Bildschirmseite der Versuchsoberfläche. Die andere Bildschirmhälfte wurde für die Tasten der Stimuliauswahl verwendet. Die Versuchsperson konnte sich die beiden Stimuli beliebig oft anhören bevor sie die Bewertung durch Verschieben des Sliders auf der Skala abgibt. Um den Probanden ein Gefühl für die Breite der Palette der dargebotenen Geräusche zu vermitteln, wurde dem Versuch ein Training vorangestellt. In diesem Training wurden zehn Vergleichsbeispiele zur Bewertung dargeboten. Diese zehn Beispiele umfassten eine repräsentative Auswahl. In dem Versuch wurden die Stimuli randomisiert dargeboten.

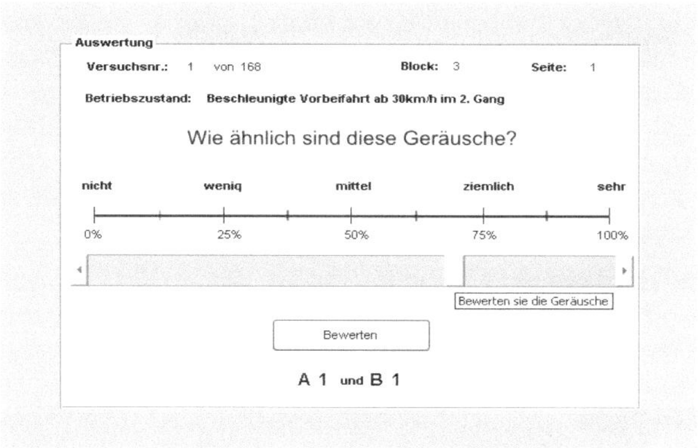

Abbildung 1 - Bewertungsoberfläche für den „Ähnlichkeits-Versuch"

2.4 Ergebnisse

Da bei psychoakustischen Untersuchungen eine Probandengruppenbildung auftreten kann, wurden die Ergebnisse der vierzig Versuchspersonen daraufhin geprüft. Im Ergebnis dieser Prüfung konnte keine Gruppenbildung nachgewiesen werden. Bis auf die Ausnahme der Extremwerte der Ähnlichkeit lag die Standardabweichung bei etwa 22 %. Die weiteren Auswertungen beziehen sich auf Mittelwerte über alle Probanden.

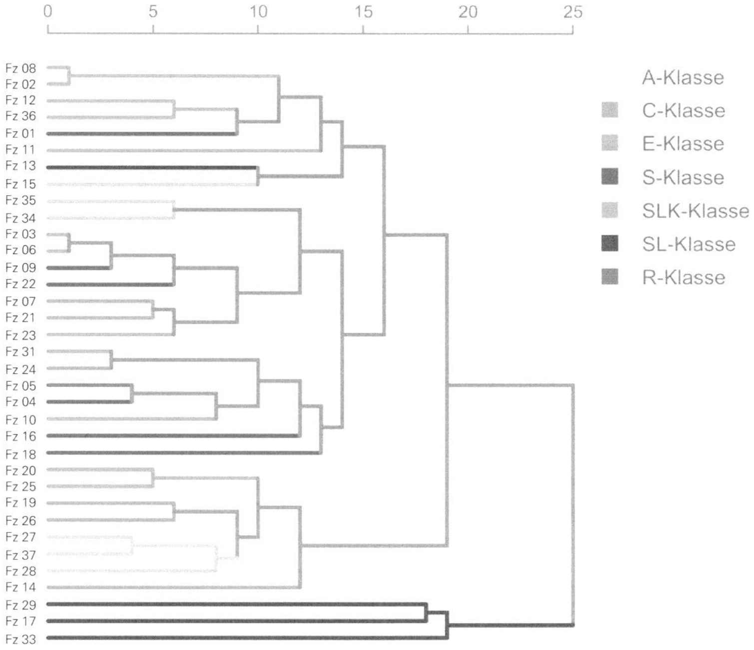

Abbildung 2 - Dendrogramm für den Betriebszustand „Motorstart-Leerlauf"

Die Auswertung aller Probandenbefragungen ergibt Ähnlichkeitsdistanzen zwischen den angebotenen Fahrzeuggeräuschen. Die mathematische Auswertung der Ähnlichkeitsdistanzen nach der Methode der hierarchischen Clusteranalyse ergibt eine Baumstruktur, welche in der Regel mit einem Dendrogramm visualisiert wird. In Abbildung 2 ist das Ergebnis der Clusteranalyse in Form des Dendrogrammes für den Betriebszustand „Motorstart-Leerlauf" dargestellt.

Je weiter links die „Fahrzeugäste“ in einem Knoten münden, desto ähnlicher sind sie sich. Die Fahrzeugäste und Knoten verschiedener Klassen sind mit unterschiedlichen Farben gekennzeichnet. Es ist klar erkennbar, dass Fahrzeuge gleicher Klassen häufiger Gruppen bilden. Allerdings besitzen auch einige Fahrzeuge aus ganz unterschiedlichen Klassen große Ähnlichkeiten. Das auffälligste Beispiel sind die Fahrzeuge 3 (E-Klasse) und 6 (SLK-Klasse). Die beiden Geräusche wurden mit 86 % Ähnlichkeit bewertet, obwohl Fahrzeug 3 Limousinencharakter und Fahrzeug 6 Sportwagencharakter besitzt.

In Abbildung 3 ist das Ergebnis der Clusteranalyse für den Betriebszustand „Beschleunigte Vorbeifahrt ab 30 km/h im 2. Gang“ dargestellt. Ein Ergebniss ist z. B., dass die Sportfahrzeuge 8 und 17 (SL-Klasse) eine Gruppe bilden, auch wenn sie sich erst relativ spät verknüpfen. Grundsätzlich kann man sagen, je später die Knoten (größere Distanz) mit anderen Fahrzeugen gebildet werden, desto größer ist das Alleinstellungsmerkmal eines Fahrzeuggeräusches. In einigen Fällen, bilden die Fahrzeuge gleicher Marke (19, 26, 27) eine Gruppe, obwohl die Fahrzeuge unterschiedlicher Klassen gehören.

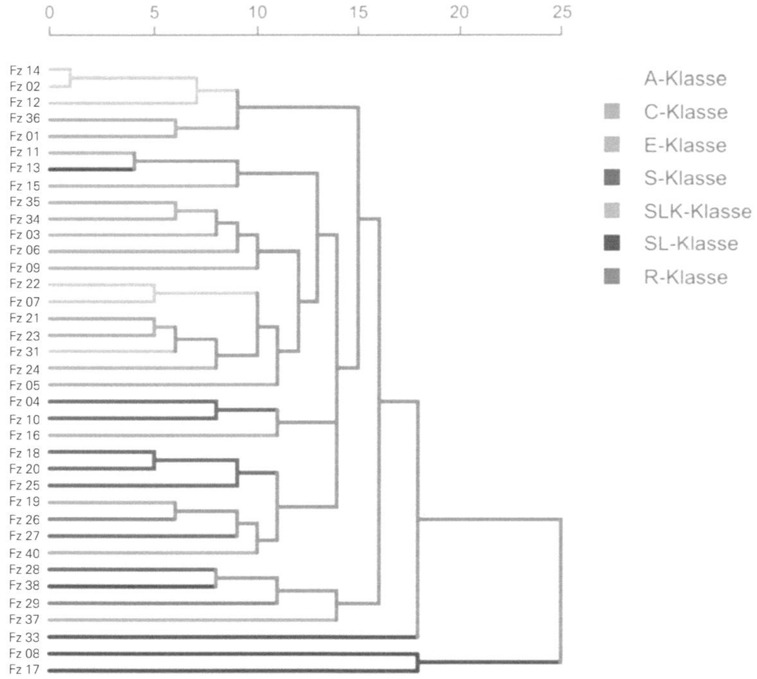

Abbildung 3 - Dendrogramm für den Betriebszustand „Beschleunigte Vorbeifahrt 30 km/h“

3 Eigenschaftsprofil von Fahrzeuggeräuschen über ein Semantisches Differenzial (Faktorenanalyse)

3.1 Stimuli und Versuchspersonen

Für die Erstellung der Fahrzeugprofile nach dem Semantischen Differenzial wurden die gleichen Geräuschsequenzen wie bei den Ähnlichkeitsuntersuchungen verwendet. Auch die Auswahl der Betriebszustände blieb unverändert. Vierzig Versuchspersonen (28 Männer und 12 Frauen) mit Normalhörfähigkeit nahmen an den Experimenten teil. Bis auf wenige Ausnahmen stimmte die Probandengruppe mit der aus den Ähnlichkeitsuntersuchungen überein.

3.2 Versuchsmethode

Es wurden Hörversuche mit dem Ziel durchgeführt, die Ausprägung verschiedener Eigenschaften von einzelnen akustischen Fahrzeuggeräuschen zu ermitteln. Die Versuchspersonen hatten die Frage zu beantworten: „Wie intensiv ist die Ausprägung folgender Eigenschaften?". Da die Wahrnehmungsuntersuchung das durchschnittliche Konsumentenverhalten widerspiegeln soll, mussten Attribute gefunden werden, welche für alle Fahrzeugnutzer verständlich sind. Die befragten Eigenschaften basieren auf unserer vorherigen Studie [7] (siehe Tabelle 1). Die Bewertungsoberflächen wurden mit Matlab-GUI implementiert. Die Versuchsperson konnte sich die Stimuli beliebig oft anhören bevor sie die Bewertung durch Verschieben des Sliders auf der Skala abgibt. Um den Probanden ein Gefühl für die Breite der Palette der dargebotenen Geräusche zu vermitteln, wurde auch diesem Versuch wieder ein Training vorangestellt.

3.3 Ergebnisse

Eine Faktorenanalyse wurde basierend auf den Urteilen der einzelnen Versuchspersonen für beide Betriebszustände durchgeführt. Die Standardabweichung liegt, wie auch schon bei den Bewertungen nach der Ähnlichkeit im Mittel bei etwa 20. Als die Extraktionsmethode wurde die Hauptkomponentenanalyse benutzt und als die Rotationsmethode wurde „Promax" ausgewählt. Das Kaiser-Meyer-Olkin-Kriterium (Maß der Stichprobeneignung) liefert für den Betriebszustand „Motorstart-Leerlauf" einen Wert von 0,86 und für den Betriebszustand „Beschleunigte Vorbeifahrt" einen Wert von 0.92. Beide Betriebszustände besitzen eine sehr gute Eignung für die Faktorenanalyse. Die Ergebnisse der Faktorenanalyse sind in Tabelle 1 dargestellt.

In der Darstellung wurden alle nach Expertenmeinung relevanten Koeffizienten (in der Regel ab ±0,8) farblich markiert. Es wurde versucht, für jeden Faktor (komplexe Hintergrundvariable) eine verbale Beschreibung zu finden. Die Hauptfaktoren für den Betriebszustand „Motorstart-Leerlauf" wurden mit aggressiv (rosafarben markiert), hochwertig (grün) und mit hochfrequent/tonal (türkis) beschrieben. Für den Betriebszustand „Beschleunigte Vorbeifahrt" wurden als Hauptfaktoren aggressiv (rosa), hochwertig (grün), hochfrequent/tonal (türkis) und tieffrequent (gelb) bestimmt.

Tabelle 1 - Hauptfaktoren der Analyse der Betriebszustände Motorstart-Leerlauf und Beschleunigte Vorbeifahrt

	Motorstart-Leerlauf		
promax	1	2	3
angenehm	-,85	,33	-,35
brummen	,80	,15	-,49
dröhnen	,88	,38	-,24
Fahrfreude	,03	,88	-,38
Gesamtqualität	-,21	,85	-,41
hämmern	,38	-,77	-,40
heulen	,44	,54	,64
klappern	,10	-,97	-,12
komfortabel	-,65	,65	-,31
lästig	,83	-,34	,31
pfeifen	-,02	,38	,86
quietschen	,00	-,10	,85
rasseln	,04	-,92	,22
rattern	,25	-,90	-,27
röhren	,87	,42	-,17
scheppern	,38	-,89	-,08
schnurren	-,55	,74	,15
sportlich	,69	,70	-,05
summen	-,11	,79	,44
surren	-,23	,66	,45
turbinenartig	,67	,61	,29
wummern	,85	,13	-,41
neues Modell	-,18	,91	-,12
Diesel	-,03	-,85	-,38
aufgemotzt	,92	,36	-,08
aggressiv	,95	,25	-,02
hallend	,88	-,19	,22
besonders	,64	,71	-,13
robust	,18	,86	-,32
unregelmaessig	,61	-,39	,39
ueberdreht	,89	,04	,42
laut	,97	-,12	-,01
angestrengt	,57	-,26	,58
luxuriös	,59	,75	-,17
stark	,84	,38	-,32
verbraucht viel	,95	,26	,06
hoch	-,44	,03	,83
vibrierend	,59	-,65	-,38

	Acc30g2			
promax	1	2	3	4
angenehm	-,79	,69	-,15	-,43
brummen	,57	-,35	-,57	,98
dröhnen	,84	-,31	-,40	,85
Fahrfreude	,08	,86	,07	-,11
Gesamtqualität	-,29	,87	,16	-,34
hämmern	,73	-,64	-,36	,81
heulen	,46	,02	,60	-,18
klappern	,19	-,97	-,10	,20
komfortabel	-,55	,89	,13	-,49
lästig	,80	-,68	,15	,46
pfeifen	-,27	,17	,94	-,65
quietschen	-,26	-,08	,89	-,58
rasseln	,11	-,90	-,01	,11
rattern	,41	-,92	-,22	,49
röhren	,84	-,33	-,45	,82
scheppern	,51	-,92	-,19	,48
schnurren	-,75	,51	,12	-,56
sportlich	,91	,09	-,01	,47
summen	-,76	,69	,09	-,59
surren	-,31	,30	,31	-,29
turbinenartig	,31	,31	,86	-,29
wummern	,76	-,49	-,40	,91
neues Modell	-,14	,90	,39	-,32
Diesel	-,18	-,63	-,13	,21
aufgemotzt	,98	-,29	-,08	,58
aggressiv	,98	-,33	-,08	,56
hallend	,90	-,57	-,10	,57
besonders	,85	,03	,06	,38
robust	,17	,80	,07	,13
unregelmaessig	,67	-,78	,20	,30
ueberdreht	,90	-,45	,12	,35
laut	,93	-,47	-,13	,68
angestrengt	,37	-,87	-,07	,27
luxuriös	,66	,43	,25	,26
stark	,83	,14	,00	,56
verbraucht viel	,98	-,29	-,03	,58
hoch	-,41	,23	,65	-,96
vibrierend	,62	-,84	-,34	,67

4 Diskussion

Die beiden untersuchten Betriebszustände (Motorstart-Leerlauf und beschleunigte Vorbeifahrt) sind Zustände mit zeitlich stark veränderlichen Ereignissen. Für beide wurde der Hauptfaktor mit „aggressiv“ beschrieben. In unserer vorherigen Studie ist der dominanteste Faktor für den quasistationären Betriebszustand Leerlauf als „Komfort“ festgestellt worden [8]. Diese Ergebnisse zeigen, dass die Aggressivität stark mit zeitlichen Änderungen gekoppelt ist. Aggressivität beinhaltet als Teilfaktoren Sportlichkeit und Lästigkeit. Mit anderen Worten kann die Aggressivität Sportlichkeit oder/und Lästigkeit hervorrufen. Die Bedeutung der Sportlichkeit ist im Alltag eng mit „hoher Leistung“, „überdurchschnittlicher Geschwindigkeit bzw. Beschleunigung“, „Bewegung“ und in bestimmter Weise auch mit „Aggressivität“ verknüpft. Wenn wir die visuelle Modalität betrachten, kann allein das äußere Erscheinungsbild eines Fahrzeugs als „statische“ Information ein Sportlichkeitsgefühl hervorrufen. Zum Beispiel assozieren wir häufig eine lange Motorhaube, ein kurzes steiles Heck oder eine aggressive Fahrzeugfront (Kühlergrill, Scheinwerfer) mit einem sportlichen Fahrzeug. Die Farbe des Lackes kann das sportliche Erscheinungsbild ebenfalls unterstützen, z. B. Farben wie „rot“, „weiß“ oder „dunkelgrün“ [9]. Die auditive und taktile Aggressivität bzw. Sportlichkeitswahrnehmung ist jedoch mit zeitlichen Signalveränderungen verknüpft. In diesen Modalitäten spielen also dynamische statt statische Informationen eine Rolle. Die Aktion/Reaktion-Beziehung stellt einen weiteren wichtigen Aspekt bei der Sportlichkeitsbeurteilung dar. Die Beziehung zwischen dem vom Fahrer betätigten Gaspedal und dem daraus resultierenden Geräusch- und Schwingungssignal wird für die Sportlichkeits- und Leistungsabschätzung benutzt.

Korreliert man die Ergebnisse aus beiden Untersuchungen (Ähnlichkeit und Semantisches Differenzial) mit dem physikalischen Signal (siehe Abbildung 4) für den Betriebszustand „Beschleunigte Vorbeifahrt“, erkennt man, dass die Existenz der dominanten Motorordnungen im tieffrequenten Bereich eine Ähnlichkeitsgruppierung (erste drei Fahrzeuge) verursacht. Diese tieffrequenten Motorordnungen führen zu höherer Sportlichkeits- und Aggressivitätsbeurteilungen (Vergleich zur unteren Gruppe aus drei Fahrzeugen) aber zu keiner bemerkenswerten Komfortverschlechterung oder Komfortverbesserung.

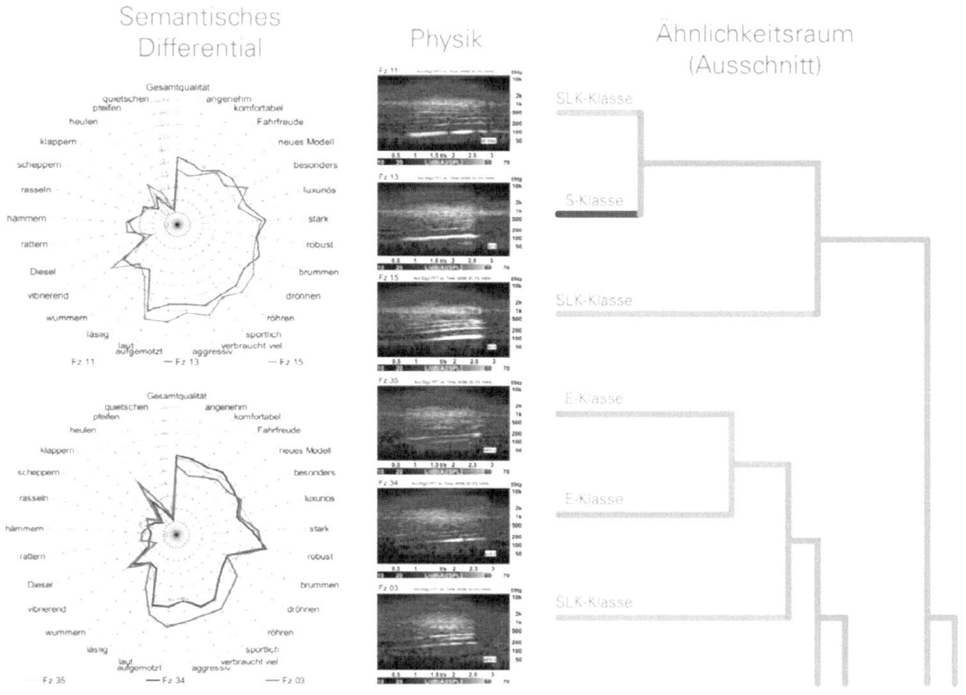

Abbildung 4 - Korrelation der Ergebnisse aus beiden Untersuchungen mit dem physikalischen Signal für den Betriebszustand „Beschleunigte Vorbeifahrt“

Außerdem ist in Abbildung 4 erkennbar, dass die Ergebnisse beider Untersuchungen hohe Übereinstimmung besitzen. Die Geräusche von den ersten drei Fahrzeugen bilden eine Ähnlichkeitsgruppierung und haben auch sehr ähnliche semantische Profile.

Die Beurteilungen in der Semantischen Differenzial-Untersuchung haben ergeben, dass die Geräusche von Fz 8 und Fz 17 jeweils als sehr sportlich wahrgenommen werden, obwohl sie mit nur 33% ähnlich bewertet wurden. Die Signalanalyse in Form einer FFT vs. Zeit (siehe Abbildung 5) verdeutlicht, dass die Motorordnungen von Fz 8 über die gesamte Zeit erkennbar bleiben, wohingegen die Motorordnungen des Fz 17 nur deutlich kürzer dominant sind. Insbesondere beim Fz 17 ist der Pegelanstieg stärker erkennbar. Das Fz 8 besitzt im niedrigen Frequenzbereich (40 Hz bis 200 Hz) mehrere Motorordnungen, die einen raueren Geräuschcharakter vermitteln. Gleichzeitig besitzt der Fz 8 mehr höhere Frequenzanteile als der Fz 17.

Dieses Ergebnis zeigt, dass Fahrzeugakustiker eine breite Variationsmöglichkeit bezüglich des Signals besitzen, wenn Sie eine komplexe Hintergrundvariable wie z. B. „Sportlichkeit“

oder „Qualität“ im Fokus ihres Designs haben. Besonders instationäre Betriebszustände erhöhen diese Parameter-Variationsmöglichkeit über die Zeit. Die Ergebnisse zeigen, dass besonders im Betriebszustand „Beschleunigte Vorbeifahrt“ aber auch im „Motorstart-Leerlauf“ die Fahrzeuge starke individuelle Charaktere haben.

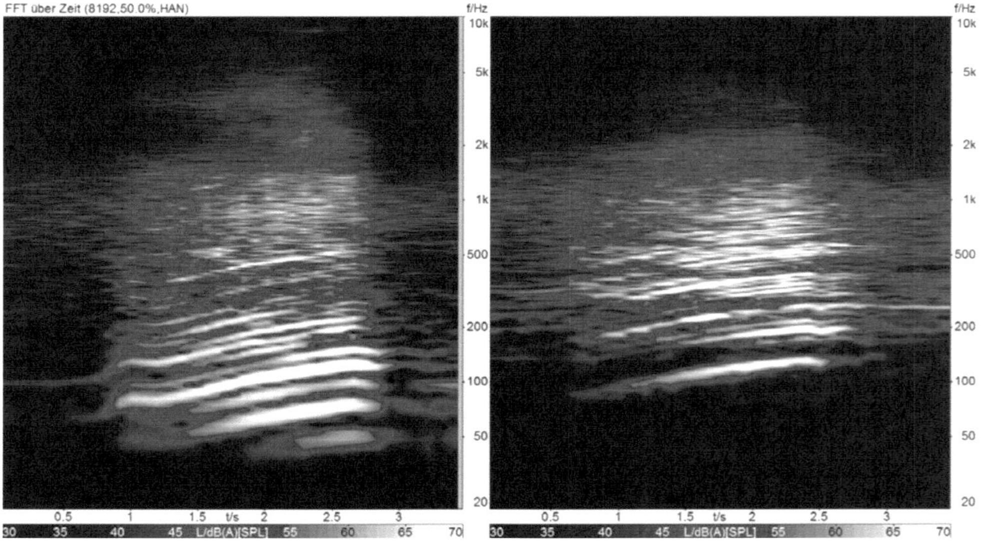

Abbildung 5 - FFT vs. Zeit-Analyse von Geräuschen der Fahrzeuge 8 (links) und 17 (rechts)

Literatur

[1] Meunier S. & Marchioni, A. (2002) “Loudness of sounds with temporal variable intensity”. In Forum Acusticum, Sevilla, France.

[2] Namba, S., Kato, T., Kuwano, S. (1995) “Long-term evaluate on of the loudness of train noise in laboratory situation” 15th International Congress on Acoustics. M. Newman (ed.). Trondheim, Norway, pp. 215–218.

[3] Kuwano, S. & Namba S. (1978) On the loudness of road traffic noise of longer duration (20 min) in relation to instantaneous judgment. J. Acoust. Soc. Am. Vol. 64, pp. 127–128.

[4] Susini P., McAdams S. et al. (2007) “Loudness asymmetry for tones with increasing and decreasing levels using continuous and global ratings” Acta Acoustica/Acustica, Vol. 93, pp. 623-631.

[5] Kuwano, S., Namba, S., Kato T. & Hellbrück, J. (2003) “Memory of the Loudness of Sounds in Relation to Overall Impression” Acoustical Science and Technology, Vol. 24, No. 4, pp. 194-196.

[6] Micko, H.C. (1962) „Die Bestimmung subjektiver Ähnlichkeiten mit dem semantischen Differential“ Zeitschrift für experimentelle und angewandte Psychologie, Vol. 9, pp. 242-280.

[7] Altinsoy, M.E. and Jekosch, U. (2012) „The Semantic Space of Vehicle Sounds: Developing a Semantic Differential with Regard to Customer Perception,“ Journal of the Audio Engineering Society, Vol. 60, No. 1/2, pp. 13-20.

[8] Altinsoy, M.E. (2013) „Identification of Quality Attributes of Automotive Idle Sounds and Whole-Body Vibrations“ International Journal of Vehicle Noise and Vibration, Vol. 9, No. 1/2, pp. 4-27.

[9] Menzel, D., Fastl, H., Graf, R. und Hellbrück, J. (2008) Influence of Vehicle Color on Loudness Judgments. Journal of Acoustical Society of America, Vol. 123, No.5, pp.2477–2479.

Drehzahlmessung aus Auspuffgeräuschen von Kfz

Thomas Fehér, Steffen Kürbis und Ulrich Kordon

Technische Universität Dresden - Institut für Akustik und Sprachkommunikation
Thomas.Feher@tu-dresden.de

Kurzfassung: In diesem Beitrag wird ein Verfahren beschrieben, das die in den Abgasgeräuschen von Kraftfahrzeugen enthaltenen drehzahlabhängigen Anteile zur Bestimmung der Motordrehzahl nutzt. Diese werden am Auspuff des jeweiligen Fahrzeugs aufgezeichnet. Aus diesen Auspuff-Geräuschsignalen können Drehzahl-Zeit-Verläufe bestimmt werden, deren maximale Abweichung von den tatsächlichen Drehzahlen max. 100 U/min betragen soll.

1 Problemstellung

Im Rahmen technischer Überprüfungen von Kraftfahrzeugen sind bei verschiedenen Messungen Drehzahl-Vorgaben des Motors einzuhalten, die vor der Messung entsprechend eingestellt bzw. während der Messung kontrolliert werden müssen. Dazu können einerseits spezielle Testsysteme eingesetzt werden, die dazu bei modernen Fahrzeugen die On-Board-Diagnosis-Daten (OBD) nutzen. Andererseits besteht in der täglichen Praxis Bedarf an einer Messmethode, die zumindest überschlägige Drehzahlwerte liefert, keine spezielle Messtechnik erfordert und ggf. einfach in die eigentliche Messaufgabe integriert werden kann. Eine Möglichkeit dazu ist, die Motordrehzahl von Kraftfahrzeugen (PKW, Krad) auf der Basis entsprechender Fahrzeuggeräusche zu ermitteln. Voruntersuchungen ([4]) haben dabei gezeigt, dass in den Abgasgeräuschen von Fahrzeugen drehzahlabhängige Anteile enthalten sind. Deshalb soll die Drehzahl-Bestimmung auf Basis von Abgasgeräuschen erfolgen, die digital am Auspuff des jeweiligen Fahrzeugs aufgezeichnet werden und als Basis für die Berechnung der Drehzahlinformationen dienen. Dabei wird davon ausgegangen, dass die drehzahlrelevanten Anteile in den Abgasgeräuschen vor allem durch das Zündgeräusch verursacht werden und somit in Abhängigkeit von der Momentandrehzahl in einem bestimmten zeitlichen Abstand periodisch im jeweiligen Geräuschsignal auftreten. Für die Detektion solcher periodischen Signalanteile hat sich bei vergleichbaren Aufgabenstellungen (z. B. Grundfrequenzdetektion in der Sprachsignalverarbeitung, [3]) eine Transformation in den Spektralbereich als vorteilhaft erwiesen. Dort führen diese zu einer mehr oder weniger stark ausgeprägten Linienstruktur des Spektrums, die in der Regel eine stabilere Auswertung als im Zeitbereich erlaubt.

In Abbildung 1 sind typische PKW-Geräuschsignale sowie die entsprechenden Zeit-Frequenzdarstellungen und Ist-Drehzahlverläufe dargestellt.

Ein Vergleich der Zeit-Frequenzdarstellungen mit den Ist-Drehzahlverläufen zeigt, dass die Spektrallinien prinzipiell dem Drehzahlverlauf folgen. Allerdings wird ebenfalls deutlich, dass es sich um relativ breitbandige Spektren handelt, d. h. eine direkte Zuordnung Spektrallinie - Drehzahl (z. B. durch Detektion des energiereichsten Spektralanteils) ist nicht möglich. Offensichtlich sind in den Auspuffgeräuschen neben den Zündgeräuschen weitere drehzahlabhängige periodische Geräuschanteile enthalten, die z. B. durch mitschwingende Karosserie-, Motor- oder Getriebeteile o. a. verursacht werden können. Das Prinzip der Drehzahldetektion aus Auspuffgeräuschen besteht damit vor allem darin, im Spektralbereich die Drehzahlen zuordenbaren Zündgeräuschanteile von den störenden anderen Geräuschanteilen zu trennen.

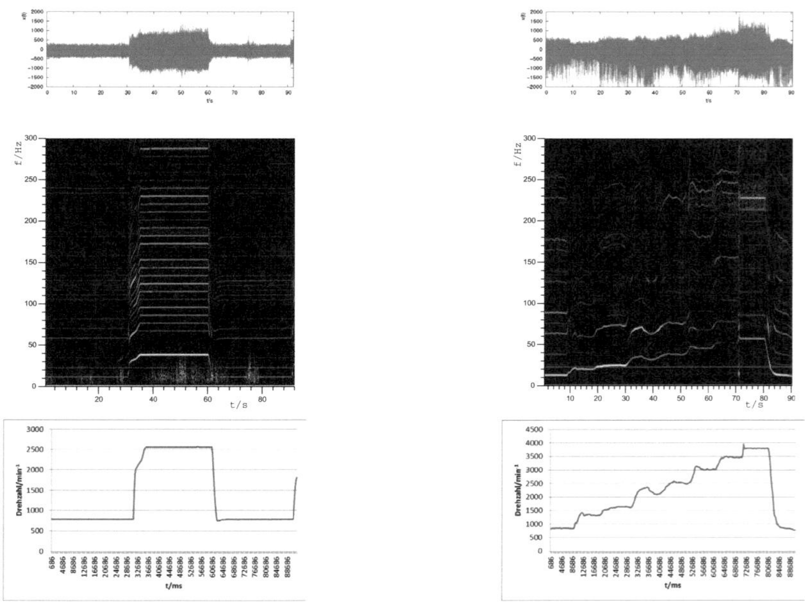

Abbildung 1 - Geräuschsignal (oben), Zeit-Frequenzdarstellung (mitte), Ist-Drehzahl (unten)
links: Geräuschsignal A (Dieselmotor), rechts: Geräuschsignal B (Benzinmotor), vgl. Abschnitt 3

Die maximale Abweichung der aus den Abgasgeräuschen ermittelten Drehzahlen von den tatsächlichen soll max. 100 U/min betragen. Die spätere technische Realisierung ist in Form einer Applikation für ein geeignetes Smart-Phone vorgesehen.

2 Verfahren zur Drehzahlbestimmung

2.1 Prinzip

Abbildung 2 zeigt den prinzipiellen Ablauf des entwickelten Algorithmus zur Drehzahlbestimmung aus dem Auspuffgeräusch.

Die Verarbeitung der Geräuschsignale, die in eine zeitliche Folge von mit einem HANNING-Fenster gewichteten Abschnitten unterteilt wurden, erfolgt sequentiell. Die nachfolgenden Ausführungen beziehen sich auf jeweils einen Abschnitt.

2.2 Bestimmung drehzahlrelevanter Spektralkomponenten

Entsprechend den im Abschnitt 1 getroffenen Annahmen wird jeder Abschnitt zur weiteren Verarbeitung durch eine Fast Fourier Transformation (FFT, z. B. [6]) in den Spektralbereich transformiert. Das Entfernen von nicht relevanten Spektralanteilen oberhalb einer wählbaren Frequenz begrenzt einerseits den rechentechnischen Aufwand in den folgenden Verarbeitungsstufen, andererseits minimiert es den Einfluss evtl. störender Spektralanteile. Vom damit vorliegenden komplexen Spektrum des jeweiligen Abschnitts wird nur die Betragsinformation (Amplitudenspektrum) weiterverarbeitet.

Die folgende Bildung der Autokorrelationsfunktion (AKF, z. B. [5]) vom Amplitudenspektrum verschärft die Linienstruktur des Spektrums als prinzipiellen Träger der Drehzahl-Information

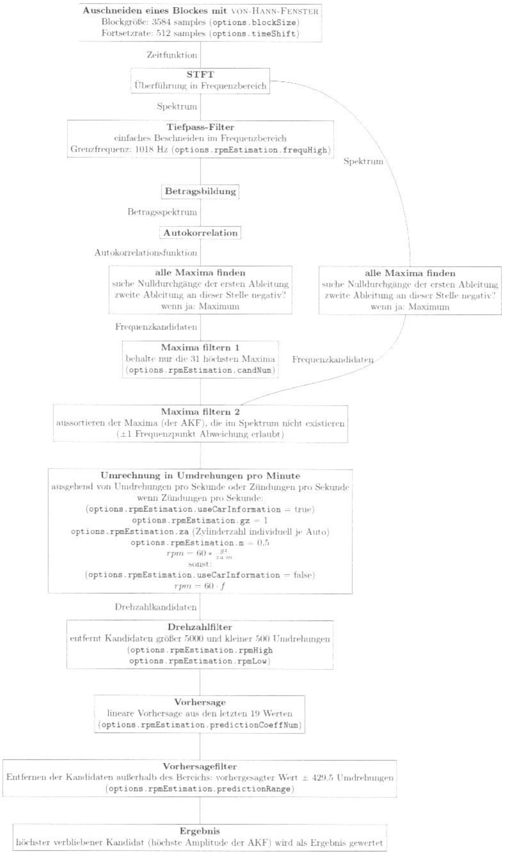

Abbildung 2 - Ablauf der Drehzahlbestimmung aus dem Auspuffgeräusch

und minimiert den Einfluss zufälliger Spektralanteile. Anschliessend werden die Maxima in dieser spektralen Autokorrelationsfunktion bestimmt. Sie sind durch Ermittlung der Nullstellen der ersten Ableitung dieser Funktion bei gleichzeitig positivem Wert der zweiten Ableitung an dieser Stelle detektierbar. Von diesen Maximum-Kandidaten kommt nur eine begrenzte wählbare Anzahl der höchsten zur Weiterverarbeitung, sofern an der Position auch ein lokales Maximum im Spektrum auftritt. Dieser Verarbeitungsschritt dient zur Unterdrückung formal entstandener lokaler Maxima ohne spektraler Entsprechnung. Die zulässige Abweichung der Maxima-Positionen in der spektralen AKF und im Spektrum beträgt $\pm f_A / Signalabschnittslänge$ wobei f_A die Abtastfrequenz ist. In Abbildung 3 ist der zeitliche Verlauf der spektralen AKF für das Geräuschsignal A (links) bzw. B (rechts) dargestellt.

2.3 Drehzahlermittlung

Zur Bestimmung der Drehzahl rpm sind die Frequenzangaben in den spektralen AKF (Abszisse) in Drehzahlen umzurechnen. Mit den Vorgabe- bzw. Fahrzeug-spezifischen Größen Zündungen pro Sekunde gz und Zylinderzahl za wird die Umrechnung nach Gleichung (1) vorgenommen.

$$rpm = 60 \cdot \frac{gz}{za \cdot m} \tag{1}$$

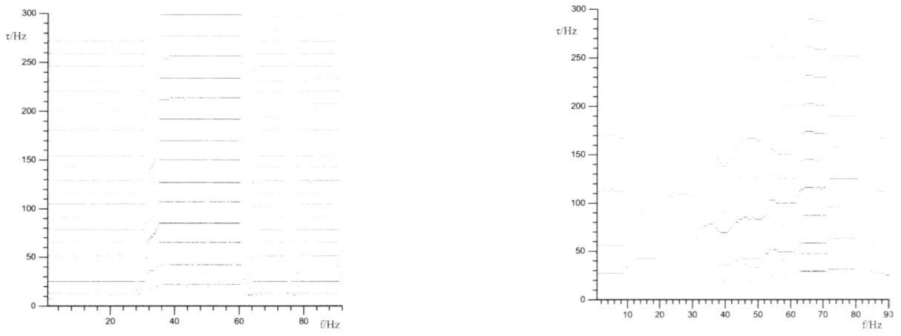

Abbildung 3 - Zeitlicher Verlauf der spektralen Autokorrelationsfunktionen

$1/m$ gibt die Anzahl der Umdrehungen pro Zündung an und hängt von der Motorart ab. Bei Viertakt-Motoren ist $m = 0,5$.

Das nachfolgende Filter eliminiert Komponenten in den Drehzahl-AKF die außerhalb eines vorgebbaren Drehzahlbereichs liegen. Abbildung 4 zeigt den Verlauf der Drehzahl-Kandidaten für das Geräuschsignal A (links) und B (rechts).

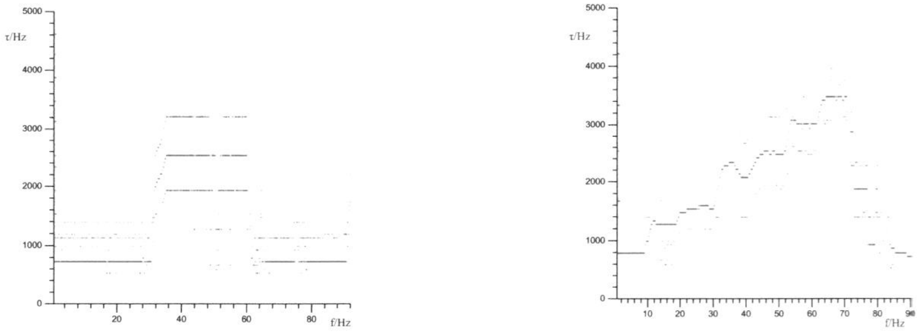

Abbildung 4 - Verlauf der Drehzahl-Kandidaten

Der Drehzahlwert des höchsten Drehzahl-Kandidaten in der umskalierten spektralen AKF wird als ermittelte Drehzahl im aktuellen Signalabschnitt ausgegeben.

2.4 Glättung des Drehzahlverlaufs

Voruntersuchungen haben gezeigt, dass die Drehzahlbestimmung auf Basis dieser Drehzahl-AKF Verläufe liefert, die durch kurzzeitige mehr oder weniger starke Abweichungen (Ausreißer) von den Istwert-Verläufen abweichen können. Zur Minimierung dieser Fehlereinflüsse dient ein Vorhersagefilter, das aus den Drehzahlwerten n vorhergehender Signalabschnitte einen Drehzahlbereich schätzt, innerhalb dessen der Drehzahlwert im aktuellen Signalabschnitt zu erwarten ist. Dabei wird angenommen, dass sich die Ist-Drehzahl über der Zeit ebenfalls nur innerhalb gewisser Grenzen verändert. Diese Einschränkung kann bei dem vorgesehenen Einsatzszenarium des Algorithmus aber berechtigt vorausgesetzt werden. Als Schätzwert wird die Linearkombination der Drehzahlwerte einer bestimmten Anzahl vorhergehender Signalabschnitte verwendet. Mit $r\hat{p}m_i$ als zu schätzenden Drehzahlwert im aktuellen Signalabschnitt i und der Anzahl n in die Schätzung einzubeziehender vorhergehender Drehzahlwerte rpm_{i-k} $(k = 1, ..., n)$ ergibt sich der aktuelle Schätzwert nach Gleichung (2).

$$r\hat{p}m_i = \sum_{k=1}^{n} a_k \cdot rpm_{i-k} \tag{2}$$

Die Gewichtsfaktoren a_l der Linearkombination lassen sich durch Minimierung der Summe der quadratischen Abweichungen zwischen den n vorhergehenden Drehzahlwerten (jeweils Maximum der Drehzahl-AKF-Kandidaten) und ihren Schätzungen bestimmen. Damit ist für jeden Signalabschnitt das lineare Gleichungssystem (3) mit n Gleichungen für die n unbekannten Faktoren a_l zu lösen.

$$\frac{\partial}{\partial a_l}\left[\sum_{j=i-n-1}^{i-1}(rpm_j-\sum_{k=1}^{n}a_k\cdot rpm_{j-k})^2\right]=0 \quad ; \quad 1\le l\le n \tag{3}$$

Die Vorhersage wird erst gestartet, wenn n vorhergehende Werte vorliegen, d. h. n Signalabschnitte verarbeitet worden sind. Dieses Verfahren basiert auf der Theorie der Optimalfilter und stellt in Form des Linear-Predictive-Coding (vgl. z. B. [7]) einen weit verbreiteten Ansatz zur Signal- bzw. Spektrenmodellierung (insbsondere für Anwendungen in der Sprachsignalverarbeitung) dar.

Der Drehzahlwert des aktuellen Zeitfensters ist der größte Drehzahl-Kandidat in der spektralen AKF, der sich innerhalb eines wählbaren Bereichs um diesen Vorhersagewert befindet. In Abbildung 5 ist der ermittelte Drehzahlverlauf für das Geräuschsignal A (links) bzw. B (rechts) und der jeweilige Ist-Drehzahlverlauf (vgl. Abb. 1) gegenübergestellt.

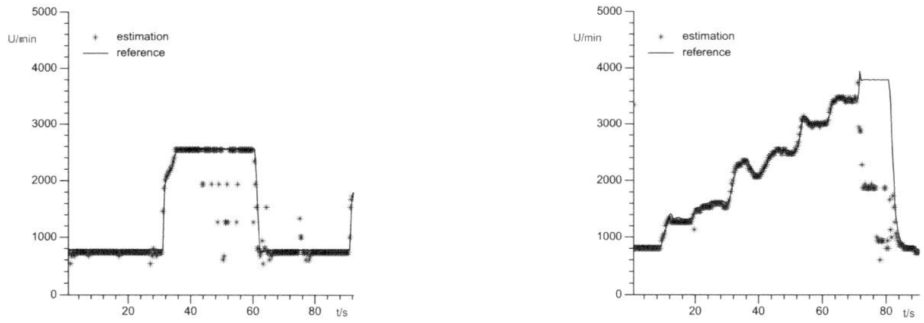

Abbildung 5 - Ermittelter Drehzahlverlauf

3 Geräuschdatenbasis

Die Aufnahmen der Testgeräusche (44 PKW unterschiedlicher Klasse, Motorart, Hubraum und Zylinderzahl und 1 Krad) erfolgten unter Verwendung eines Electret-Kondensator-Mikrofons Philips SBC ME570 und einem Notebook als Aufzeichnungsgerät. Die Mikrofonposition entsprach dabei im Wesentlichen den in [2] vorgegebenen Richtlinien für die Messung von Auspuffgeräuschen (Auspuffhöhe, Abstand 0,5 m, 45° Winkel zur Ausströmrichtung, 3 m Abstand des Fahrzeugs zu evtl. Hauswänden).

Neben den Geräuschsignalen wurden die zugehörigen Ist-Drehzahlverläufe in Form der entsprechenden Ausgangssignale eines parallel betriebenen OBD-Diagnosesystems erfasst, um die Genauigkeit der aus den Geräuschsignalen berechneten Drehzahlinformationen quantitativ bewerten zu können. Zur zeitlichen Synchronisation diente ein in den Ist-Drehzahlverläufen und den zugehörigen Geräuschsignalen gleichermaßen aufgezeichnetes akustisches Klick-Signal. Die Abtastfrequenz von zunächst 44,1 kHz wurde für die weitere Verarbeitung auf 8 kHz reduziert.

Ein Datensatz für jedes Fahrzeug besteht aus je 2 Varianten eines Geräuschsignals vom Typ A (schnelles Gas geben und Erreichen einer Drehzahl von ca. 3000 U/min bzw. Erreichen der U.2 Drehzahl) und eines Geräuschsignals vom Typ B (stufenweises Halten einer Drehzahl in Schritten von etwa 500 U/min aller 10 s bis ca. 4000U/min).

4 Ausgewählte ermittelte Drehzahlverläufe

Durch die Belegung von Konfigurationsvariablen können die Eigenschaften des Verfahrens an verschiedene Verarbeitungsaufgaben angepasst werden. Zur Optimierung dieser Parameter wurde ein unter [1] frei verfügbarer Algorithmus verwendet, dessen drei mögliche Strategien Genetic Algorithm, Differential Evolution und Particle Swarm Optimzation parallel genutzt wurden. Die durch diesen Algorithmus optimierten Werte sind die Signalabschnittslänge (3584 Abtastwerte), die obere Grenzfrequenz (1018 Hz), die Anzahl Drehzahl-Kandidaten (31 Werte), der Bereich für die Drehzahl-Vorhersage (19 Werte) sowie das Vorhersagefenster (700 rpm).

In den Abbildungen 6 bis 9 sind zur Demonstration der Eignung bzw. Grenzen des entwickelten Verfahrens im Sinne der Aufgabenstellung typische Drehzahl-Verläufe von PKW für Geräuschsignale A (links, 4-Zylinder-Dieselmotor) bzw. B (rechts, 4-Zylinder-Benzinmotor) dargestellt. Sie zeigen dabei typische Ergebnisse, die in die vier Kategorien nahezu fehlerfrei, geringe Fehler (z. B. Ausreißer bzw. temporäre Fehler in Phasen starker kurzzeitiger Drehzahländerung), größere systematische Fehler und unbrauchbar unterteilt werden können.

Abbildung 6 zeigt weitgehend fehlerfreie Drehzahlverläufe. Abgesehen von einzelnen geringfügigen Abweichungen entspricht der ermittelte Drehzahlverlauf den Ist-Drehzahlverläufen.

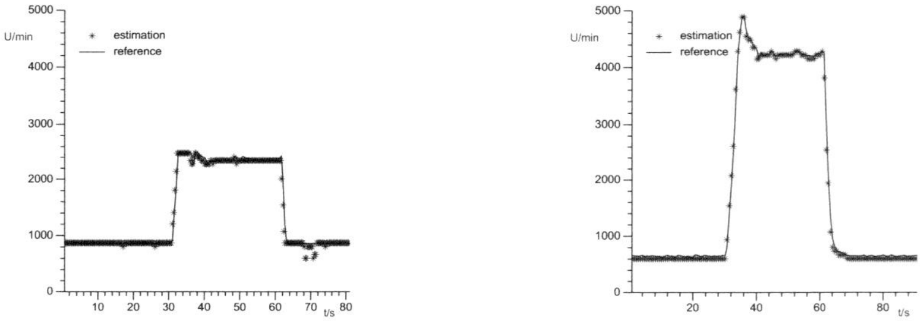

Abbildung 6 - Fehlerfreier Drehzahlverlauf

Die Drehzahl-Verläufe in der Abbildung 7 weisen geringe Differenzen zu den Ist-Drehzahlveräufen auf. Die Abweichungen bestehen entweder in vereinzelten Ausreißern oder in einer kurzzeitigen systematischen Abweichung vom Ist-Verlauf (Abweichung um festen Betrag bei konstanter Drehzahl bzw. prozentuale Abweichung, z. B. in Phasen stärkerer Drehzahländerungen).

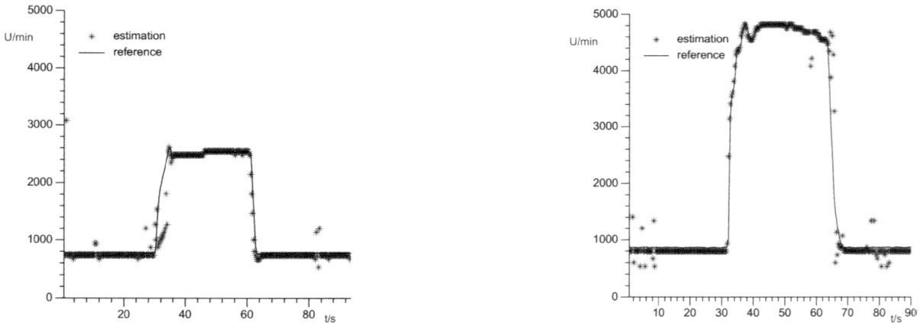

Abbildung 7 - Drehzahlverlauf mit geringen Fehlern

Größere typische Fehler sind in den Verläufen der Abbildung 8 erkennbar. Diese äußern sich vor allem in Form größerer systematischer Abweichungen über einen längeren Zeitbereich bzw. durch eine höhere Anzahl von Ausreißern, die über den gesamten Verlauf verteilt sind oder sich in einem Drehzahlbereich konzentrieren.

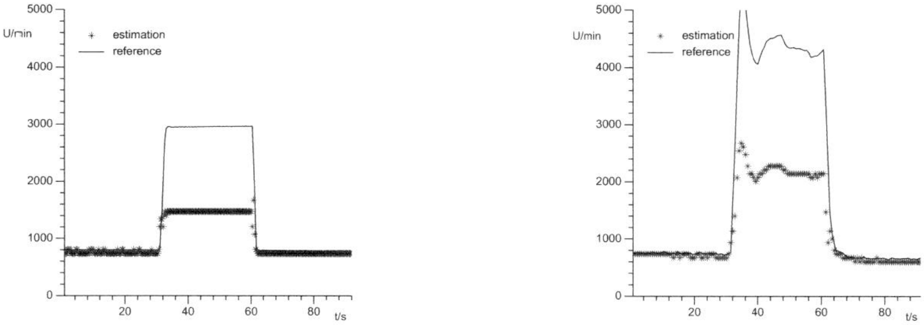

Abbildung 8 - Drehzahlverlauf mit größeren typischen Fehlern

Schließlich zeigt die Abbildung 9 Verläufe, die kein brauchbares Ergebnis darstellen. Hierunter sind einmal Drehzahl-Verläufe zu zählen, die zwar die Phasen des Ist-Drehzahlverlaufs abbilden (z. B. Drehzahl-Änderungen führen auch zu Änderungen im ermittelten Verlauf), allerdings quantitativ nicht interpretierbar sind. Zum anderen sind hierzu Verläufe zu zählen, die ein nahezu regelloses Verhalten aufweisen bzw. eine sehr große Anzahl von Ausreißern enthalten.

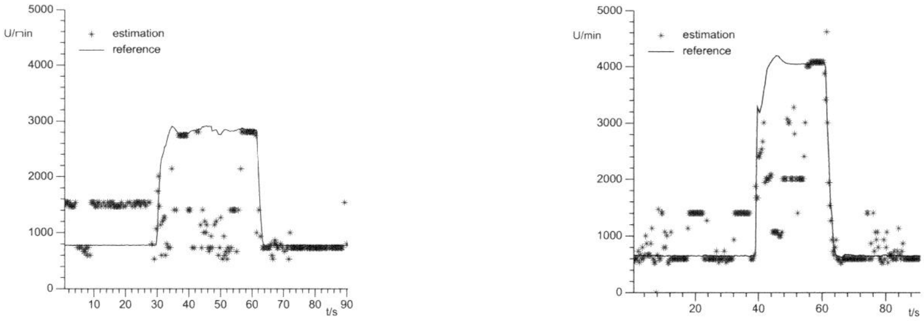

Abbildung 9 - Drehzahlverlauf mit starken, regellosen Fehlern

5 Zusammenfassung

Aus den Ergebnissen kann abgeleitet werden, dass der entwickelte Algorithmus prinzipiell zur Messung der Drehzahl auf der Basis von Auspuffgeräuschen in der geforderten Genauigkeit geeignet ist. Abbildung 10 zeigt die Verteilung der korrekt ermittelten Drehzahlwerte im Signalabschnitt bezogen auf die Gesamtzahl der Signalabschnitte.

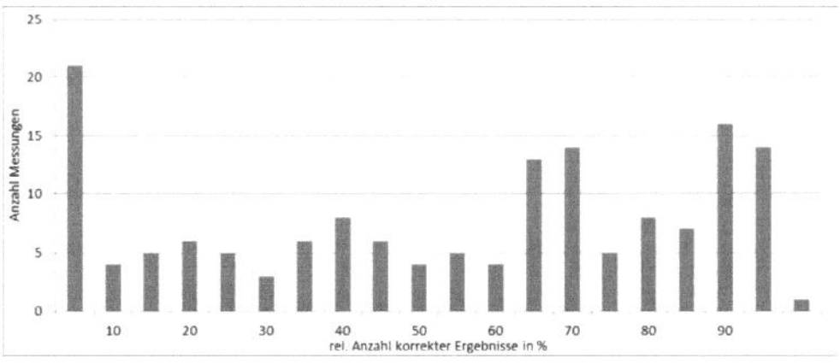

Abbildung 10 - Verteilung der korrekt ermittelten Drehzahlwerte im Signalabschnitt bezogen auf die Gesamtzahl der Signalabschnitte

Die Detektionsraten liegen dabei je nach Fahrzeugtyp zwischen ca. 1,5 % und ca. 92 %. Diese Ergebnisse hängen stark von den eingestellten Parametern des Algorithmus ab. Um eine stabile praktische Nutzung zu gewährleisten, ist deshalb insbesondere eine Optimierung der Parameter notwendig.

Die auftretenden Fehler in den ermittelten Drehzahl-Verläufen sind vor allem in der noch nicht optimalen Selektion des besten Drehzahl-Kandidaten in der Drehzahl-AKF begründet. Das führt meist zu relativ oder absolut konstanten Abweichungen von den Ist-Drehzahlen (ganzzahlige Vielfache einer scheinbaren „Grund-“ Frequenz bzw. -drehzahl). Weitere Ursachen liegen im Einfluss von Störsignalen in den Geräuschsignalen, die insbesondere zu starken Ausreißern in den ermittelten Drehzahlverläufen oder zum „Springen“ der Drehzahl auf ein anderes Vielfaches der oben erwähnten Grundfrequenz bzw. -drehzahl führen. Mögliche Störsignale tragen dabei nicht nur inkohärenten Charakter (externe unabhängige Störquelle) sondern werden vor allem auch durch kohärent mitschwingende Fahrzeugteile oder andere drehzahlproportionale Geräusche des Fahrzeugs selbst verursacht. Die gewählten Testsignale stellen von ihrem Verlauf allerdings relativ harte Anforderungen an den Algorithmus (schnelle starke Drehzahländerungen und kurze Drehzahl-“treppen“ mit geringer Änderung der Drehzahl), die für den vorgesehenen praktischen Einsatzfall nicht unbedingt relevant sind.

Für einen stabilen praktischen Einsatz sind zusammenfassend insbesondere die weitere Optimierung der wählbaren Parameter (evtl. Ermittlung mehrerer optimaler Fahrzeugklassen-spezifischer Parametersätze, die entsprechend zu untersuchendem Fahrzeug ggf. automatisch nach Erkennung der Fahrzeugklasse aktiviert werden) sowie die Ermittlung geeigneter Testsignale bzw. Testszenarien, die z. B. durch Einbeziehung zusätzlicher Informationen (spezielle zeitliche Signalstruktur u. a.) zu einer Stabilisierung der Ergebnisse beitragen, erforderlich.

Die Idee zur Anwendung von Smartphones zur Messung der Geräuschemission von Kraftfahrzeugen in Abhängigkeit der Motordrehzahl stammt von der fsd Fahrzeugsystemdaten GmbH Dresden, die als zentrale Stelle der Bundesrepublik Deutschland Vorgaben für die periodische Fahrzeugüberwachung entwickelt.

Literatur

[1] *www.mathworks.com/matlabcentral/fileexchange/24838-godlike-a-robust-single-multi-objective-optimizer*. Website.

[2] *Auszug aus der Richtlinie des Rates zur Angleichung der Rechtsvorschriften der Mitgliedstaaten über den zuläassigen Geräuschpegel und die Auspuffvorrichtung von Kraftfahrzeugen (70/157/EWG). ABl. L 42*, 23.2.1970. S. 16.

[3] BERDAHL, E. und J. J. BURRED: *Abschlussbericht Moderne Methoden der Signalanalyse: Grundfrequenzanalyse musikalischer Signale.* Techn. Ber., TU Berlin - FG Kommunikationswissenschaft, SoSe 2002.

[4] FEHÉR, T., S. KÜRBIS und U. KORDON: *Studie über Drehzahlmessung aus Auspuffgeräuschen von Kfz.* Techn. Ber., TU Dresden - Institut für Akustik und Sprachkommunikation, 2013.

[5] HOFFMANN, R.: *Signalanalyse und -erkennung.* Springer, Berlin, Heidelberg, New York, ..., 1. Aufl., 1998.

[6] HOFFMANN, R.: *Grundlagen der Frequenzanalyse.* Expert-Verlag, Renningen, 2. Aufl., 2005.

[7] MARKEL, J. D. und A. H. GRAY: *Linear prediction of speech.* Communication and cybernetics 12. New York, ..., 1. Aufl., 1976.

Basics of Saliency Detection in Acoustical Scenes

Kristian Kroschel

Karlsruher Institut für Technologie (KIT)
Fraunhofer Institut für Optronik, Systemtechnik und Bildauswertung (IOSB)
kristian.kroschel@kit.edu

Dedicated to Prof. Dr.-Ing. habil. Rüdiger Hoffmann

Abstract: Saliency is a property of an item which makes it different from its neighbouring environment and thus evokes attention or surprise. Humans are able to detect salient acoustic events in a scene with background signals carrying no information due to their stationarity, e.g. A lot of research results are available covering saliency detection in the video domain. The most reliable detection results are based on the Kullback-Leibler divergence which is based on prior and posterior information carried by the appropriate probability densities. This approach known from video analysis is transferred to audio scenes. It is shown that an utterance and a falling object can be detected reliably in a background composed of coloured noise or a sinusoid. It is planned to install this method of saliency detection on a humanoid robot observing an acoustic environment.

1 Introduction

Assume that your eyes are closed and you listen to the acoustic events in your environment. If there is a vacuum cleaner running you might realize this event when it is switched on or off, but if it is running continuously you will not pay attention to it. This is different if a human starts to speak: you will listen to the utterance to find out whether it carries information adressed to you. If not, you might not be interested to listen and the utterance is not salient any more.

The question is how can we extract saliency from the sensed data? In the case of images, saliency might be based on a change of colour or texture - a red rose in a green environment of leaves - or in video streams the speed of the movement of objects - a police car is driven at high speed - might be salient. A similar event in an acoustic scene is the sound of the siren of a police car with the background of traffic noise.

But how to detect salient events and how to measure saliency? No doubt: the change of a feature in a given environment is the key to detect salient events. But which are the appropriate features? On the field of visual saliency many features have been proposed [1][2][3].

An acoustic signal can be described in the time and frequency domain, respectively. If a signal carries information it will be the sample function $s(t)$ of a random process [4] which is only short-time stationary. Thus we need a description of the process along the time and the frequency axis. An appropriate tool for this description is the spectrogram $S(t, f)$. Using this tool we are able to discriminate between salient events and those without saliency. Imagine you listen to the sound of a sine wave with no changes in amplitude, frequency and phase: it will carry no information. In the spectrogram such a sinusoid corresponds with a line parallel to the time axis with no change in intensity. Similar to that is a white noise process with a homogenious - ideally a constant - pattern

all over the spectrogram. Both signals are not salient and do not evoke attention for a listening human.
No question: without intensity there is no salient event [5]. But intensity alone and even changes in intensity are not sufficient to detect salient events. Instead, statistical properties of the sensed data are exploited and a measure based on Bayesian Surprise [2] is used.
This measure is the basis for the Kullback-Leibler divergence [6] which compares the probability density of the prior state with the probability density of the posterior state when the sensed data are exploited.

2 A General Measure of Saliency

Assume that prior information about an event is given by the probability density function $f_{S_{pri}}(s_{pri})$ which is calculated from old data. Receiving new data, the posterior probability density $f_{S_{pri}|S_{pos}}(s_{pri}|s_{pos})$ can be calculated. Applying the Bayes rule [4], the prior information given the posterior data yields

$$f_{S_{pri}|S_{pos}}(s_{pri}|s_{pos}) = \frac{f_{S_{pos}|S_{pri}}(s_{pos}|s_{pri})}{f_{S_{pos}}(s_{pos})} \cdot f_{S_{pri}}(s_{pri}). \tag{1}$$

If the new data determining the conditional density $f_{S_{pri}|S_{pos}}(s_{pri}|s_{pos})$ do not carry saliency, the prior density $f_{S_{pri}}(s_{pri})$ is not affected. Only if the conditional density differs significantly from the prior density the data carry saliency. For the comparison of both densities the Kullback-Leibler divergence is used

$$D_{KL}(f_{S_{pri}|S_{pos}}(s_{pri}|s_{pos}), f_{S_{pri}}(s_{pri})) = \int_s f_{S_{pri}|S_{pos}}(s_{pri}|s_{pos}) \cdot \log_2 \left(\frac{f_{S_{pri}|S_{pos}}(s_{pri}|s_{pos})}{f_{S_{pri}}(s_{pri})} \right) ds_{pri} \tag{2}$$

The problem is to allocate the probability densities from the available data: what are the prior data, what the posterior data? To calulate both entities, the data stream of the sound is cut into overlapping blocks. The prior data are given by all available data up to the actual data block and the posterior data include in addition the actual data block.

3 Saliency of Audio Data

Audio signals can be described in the time and the frequency domain. A representation of both domains is given by the spectrogram $S(k, n)$ with k denoting the discrete time parameter and n denoting the discrete spectral or frequency parameter

$$S(k, n) = \left| \sum_{i=k-N+1}^{k} s(i) e^{-j2\pi in/N} \right|^2, \qquad 1 \leq n \leq N \tag{3}$$

with N the length of the observed data $s(k)$ from which the spectrum is calculated.
From the samples $S(k, n)$ of the spectrogram given in Eq. 3 the prior density $f_{S_{pri}}(s_{pri})$ and the posterior density $f_{S_{pri}|S_{pos}}(s_{pri}|s_{pos})$ have to be calculated. For this calculation the vectors

$$\mathbf{S}_{pri} = (S(k-1, n), S(k-2, n), \ldots, S(k-K, n))^T$$

and

$$\mathbf{S}_{pos} = (S(k, n), S(k-1, n), \ldots, S(k-K, n))^T$$

are used with K a free parameter which in principle can approach $K \to \infty$. Thus we have

$$f_{S_{pri}|S_{pos}}(s_{pri}|s_{pos}) = g(s|\mathbf{S}_{pos}), \qquad f_{S_{pri}}(S_{pri}) = g(s|\mathbf{S}_{pri}) \tag{4}$$

in a simplified representation.
For the saliency depending on the frequency paramater n follows

$$\begin{aligned} S_A(k,n) &= D_{KL}(g(s|\mathbf{S}_{pos}), g(s|\mathbf{S}_{pri})) \\ &= \int_{-\infty}^{\infty} g(s|\mathbf{S}_{pos}) \cdot \log_2 \left(\frac{g(s|\mathbf{S}_{pos})}{g(s|\mathbf{S}_{pri})} \right) ds \end{aligned} \tag{5}$$

which is known as the saliency map [5].
To simplify the calculation it is assumed that the densities $g(s|\mathbf{S}_{pri})$ and $g(s|\mathbf{S}_{pos})$ are Gaussian. In this case only the means μ_{pri}, μ_{pos} and variances σ_{pri}, σ_{pos} of the densities are required. From Eq. 4 follows [7]

$$\begin{aligned} S_A(k,n) &= D_{KL}(g(s|\mathbf{S}_{pos}), g(s|\mathbf{S}_{pri})) \\ &= \frac{1}{2} \left[\log_2 \frac{\sigma_{pri}^2}{\sigma_{pos}^2} + \frac{\sigma_{pos}^2}{\sigma_{pri}^2} - 1 + \frac{(\mu_{pos} - \mu_{pri})^2}{\sigma_{pri}^2} \right] \end{aligned} \tag{6}$$

with the means and variances as unbiased estimates [4] given by

$$\begin{aligned} \mu_{pri}(k,n) &= \frac{1}{K} \sum_{i=1}^{K} S(k-i,n) \\ \mu_{pos}(k,n) &= \frac{1}{K+1} \sum_{i=0}^{K} S(k-i,n) \\ \sigma_{pri}^2(k,n) &= \frac{1}{K-1} \sum_{i=1}^{K} (S(k-i,n) - \mu_{pri}(k,n))^2 \\ \sigma_{pos}^2(k,n) &= \frac{1}{K} \sum_{i=0}^{K} (S(k-i,n) - \mu_{pos}(k,n))^2. \end{aligned} \tag{7}$$

The measure in Eq. 6 depends on time and frequency. Since only the dependency on time is of interest, the dependency on frequency is suppressed by averaging:

$$S_A(\ell) = \frac{2}{N} \sum_{n=0}^{N/2-1} S_A(\ell, n). \tag{8}$$

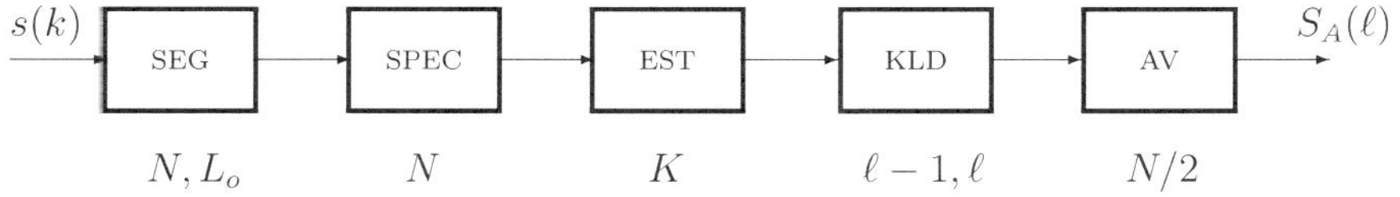

Figure 1 - Signal flow for data processing: SEGmentation, SPECtrum, ESTimation of μ and σ, Kullback-Leibler Divergence, AVeraging.

The calculation of the saliency measure $S_A(\ell)$ is visualized by the block diagram in Fig. 1 with the blocks SEG for segmenation, SPEC for calculation of the spectrum, EST for estimation of the means μ_{pri}, μ_{pos} and variances σ^2_{pri}, σ^2_{pos}, KLD for the calculation of the Kullback-Leibler divergence, and AV for the averaging over the $N/2$ frequency dependent saliency values $S_A(\ell, n)$.
The signal $s(k)$ to be analysed is first cut in block SEG into overlapping data blocks of length N as shown in Fig. 2. This is also the length of the fast Fourier transform (FFT) which is calculated in block SPEC. The consecutive blocks have an offset of L_o samples in order to reduce the computational load on one hand and to increase the difference of the densities compared by the Kullback-Leibler divergence on the other hand. The parameter N controls the spectral resolution and the parameter L_o depends on the correlation of the analysed signal.

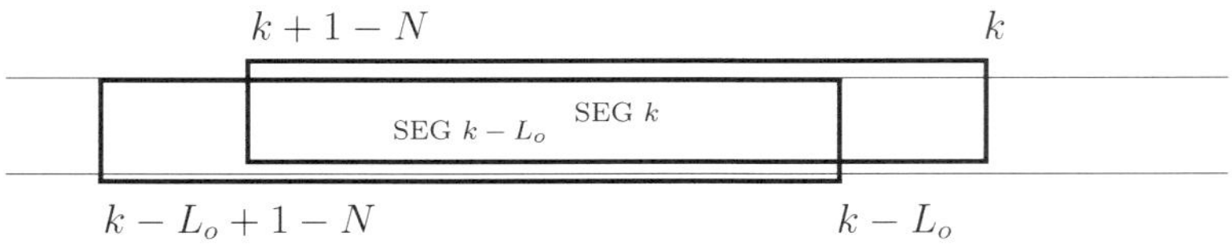

Figure 2 - Segmentation of the analysed signal $s(k)$ into consecutive overlapping data blocks.

By the block SEG the sampling rate is reduced by $1/L_o$ and thus the counter k is replaced by ℓ. In block SPEC the block-dependent spectrogram $S(\ell, n)$ according to Eq. 3 is calculated by FFT. As shown in Fig. 3, the estimates of the means and variances according to Eq. 7 are determined in block EST using $0 \leq \ell \leq K$ values for the prior estimates and $1 \leq \ell \leq K+1$ values for the posterior estimates of the spectrogram $S(\ell, n)$, repectively. The parameter K determines the reliability of the estimate, i.e. the larger K is the lower is the variance of the estimate but the larger is the computational load and the time delay. From estimates of the prior and posterior means and variances the values $S_A(\ell, n)$ of the saliency map according to Eq. 6 are calculated in block KLD. Finally, these values are averaged over the frequency parameter n using $N/2$ values since $S_A(\ell, n)$ is symmetric with respect to $N/2$ and thus averaging over N does not improve the accuracy of the result.

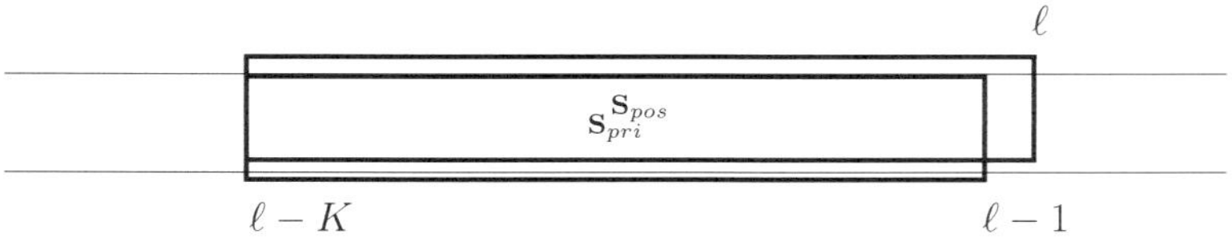

Figure 3 - Data blocks used for estimation of the prior and posterior means and variances.

4 Examples for Saliency Calculation

The investigated signal of interest is the combination of the utterance of the German word *gut* by a female speaker and the sound of a key falling on a table. It is assumed that both, the utterance and the sound of the falling key will be detected as salient events. It is not the task of the saliency detection to identify the salient events as speech and the sound of the falling key or something similar. The representations of the signal $s(k)$ in the time and frequency domain are given in Fig. 4 with the sampling frequency $f_s = 48$ kHz and 80,000 samples. There is some residual noise visible in the time domain caused by the microphone and the amplifier. Finally there is a sinusoid at roughly $f = 18$ kHz which can be seen in the spectrogram.

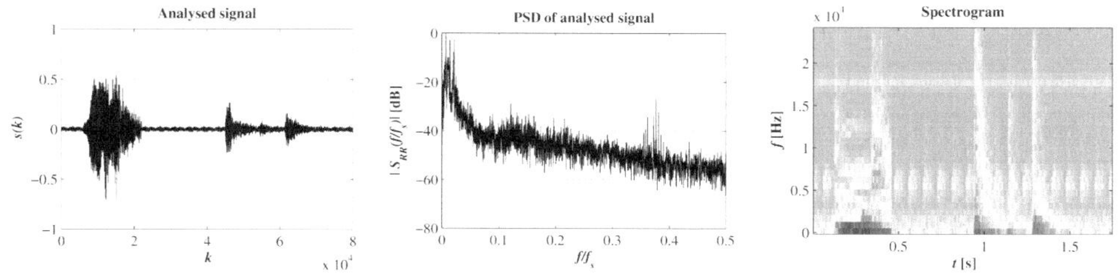

Figure 4 - Two acoustic events, uncorrupted. Time representation (left), spectrum (center), spectrogram (right).

In the time domain the utterance in the first half and the sound of the falling key in the second half of the data record are clearly visible because of the low level of the residual background noise which is almost not audible for the human ear. The spectrum $S_{SS}(f/f_s)$ is plotted in a logarithmic scale and calculated from the whole signal by the Welch method [4]. The utterance covers the lower spectral components whereas the sound of the falling key influences the higher spectral components. Furthermore the spectrogram $S(k, n)$ is given with $n = N \cdot f/f_s$, $N = 256$ or $f = n \cdot N/f_s$ along the frequency axis and $k = t \cdot f_s$ or $t = k/f_s$ along the time axis.

In the sequel the influence of corrupting background sounds will be investigated. For this purpose a coloured noise process and a sinusoid are used. The coloured noise is a white noise process shaped by a Butterworth filter [4] of order $n_0 = 5$, the cutoff frequancy $f_c = 7.2$ kHz or $f_c/f_s = 0.15$ and the amplitude $a_n = 0.125$. This results in a signal to noise ratio $SNR = 6.67$ dB for the speech segment and $SNR = -6.25$ dB for the segment with the falling key. In Fig. 5 the representations in the time and frequency domain and as spectrogram are given.

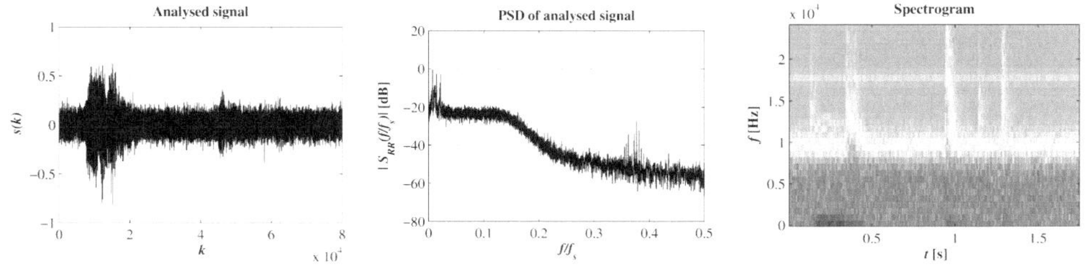

Figure 5 - Two acoustic events, corrupted by coloured noise. Time representation (left), spectrum (center), spectrogram (right).

From the recording the noise is clearly audible and also visible in the time and frequency domain. The cutoff frequency can be read from the spectrum and the spectrogram.

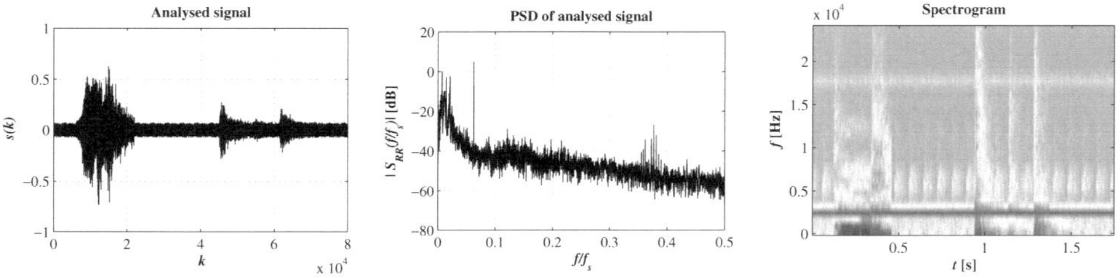

Figure 6 - Two acoustic events, corrupted by a sinusoid. Time representation (left), spectrum (center), spectrogram (right).

As a second interferer a sinusoid of frequency $f_0 = 3$ kHz or $f_0/f_s = 0.0625$ and amplitude $a_s = 0.05$ is investigated which corresponds to $SNR = 13.39$ dB for speech and $SNR = -0.49$ dB for the falling key. Due to resolution the frequency of the sinusoid cannot be read from the time domain representation as Fig. 6 shows. But both, the spectrum and the spectrogram contain a sharp spectral line at $f/f_s = 0.0625$ in the power spectrum $S_{SS}(f/f_s)$ and a horizontal line at $f = 3$ Hz in the spectrogram $S(t, f)$.
The saliency is calculated with the parameters $N = 256$ for the block length and FFT-analysis, $L_o = 100$ for the offset between data blocks and $K = 100$ for the estimation of the means and variances of the density functions. The result of the calculation of the saliency for the three cases is given in Fig. 7.

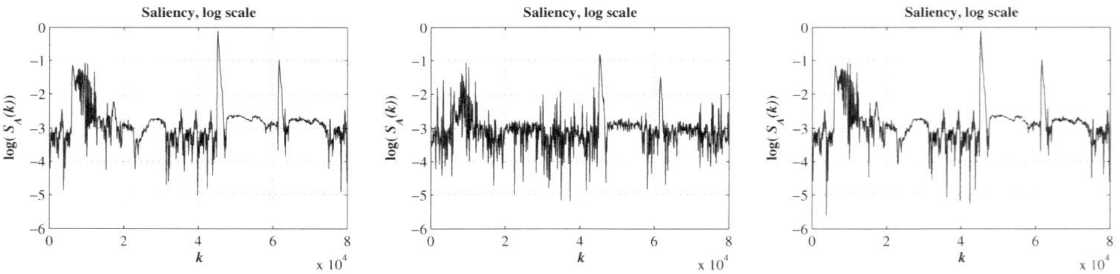

Figure 7 - Saliency of the uncorrupted signal (left), corrupted by coloured noise (center) and by a sinusoid (right).

The saliency $S_A(k)$ for the uncorrupted signal shows a set of maxima for the utterance and two distinct maxima for the sound of the falling key. It is interesting that only the beginning of a salient event is monitored. With the ongoing sounds the saliency decays because the signals then do not carry any novelty. Furthermore, between salient events the saliency measure is not zero but keeps a more or less constant low level. Many reasons can be given for this effect: first, there is some background noise, even if it is low so that it would not be registered by a human listener. Second, the parameters to calculate the saliency measure are based on estimates with a limited accuracy.
A further experiment has been made without the utterance and the sound of the falling key. Instead, the coloured noise, the sinusoid and the mixture of both have been applied to the saliency calculation. The parameters of the corrupting signals have not been changed. The result is given in Fig. 8.
As mentioned above, the saliency is not zero for an event without saliency. But in this case there are random fluctations of approximately the same amplitude. This is true for both corrupting signals, the coloured noise and the sinusoid. In the case of the sinusoid additionally spikes are visible which seem to idicate salient events. The reason for this

pattern is the selection of parameters for the analysis. The spikes are not any more visible if the coloured noise is added as can be seen in the plot on the right. Since in most cases environmental noise will corrupt the signal of interest, the selection of parameters is not a problem for practical applications.

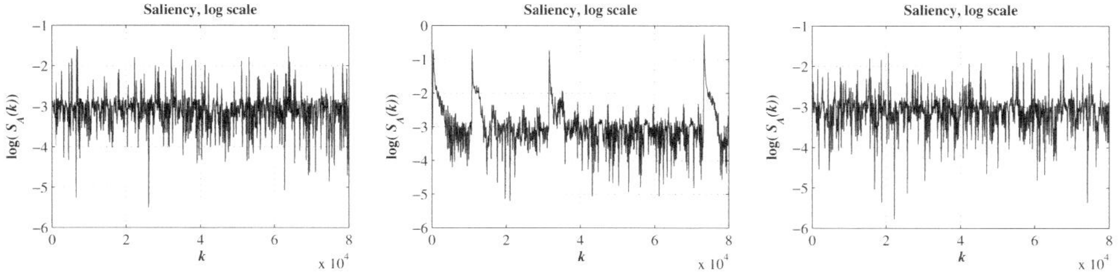

Figure 8 - Saliency for the coloured noise (left), the sinusoid (center), the mixture of both (right).

In the saliency of the sinusoid with $f = 3.0$ kHz is shown. It shows spikes again despite an offset of $L_o = 97$. In the center the frequency has been shifted slightly to $f = 3.1$ kHz or $f = 0.0645833 \cdot f_s$ and $L_o = 97$ has been kept. On the right the parameters $f = 3.0$ kHz and $L_o = 100$ have been chosen. The saliency like spikes are caused by the fact that the sampling frequency f_s is a multiple of the investigated frequency f_0 of the sinusoid. In pratical cases this will apply very rarely.

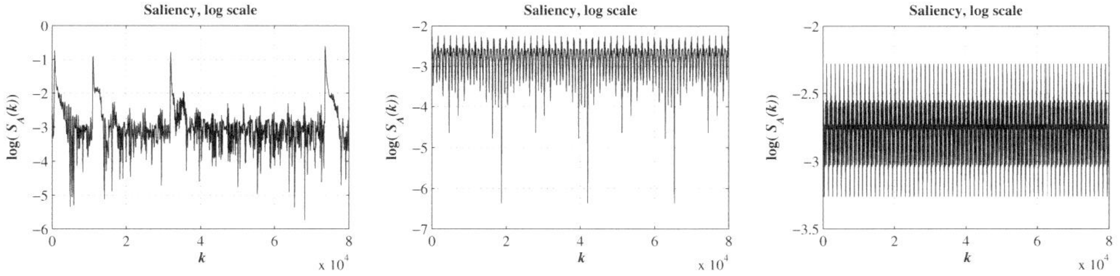

Figure 9 - Saliency of the sinusoid $f_0 = 3.0$ kHz with offset $L_o = 97$ (left), $f_0 = 3.1$ kHz with offset $L_o = 97$ (center), frequency $f_0 = 3.1$ kHz and offset $L_o = 100$ (right).

Another question of interest is how background noise influences the saliency measure. For this purpose the signal of interest has been corrupted by the coloured noise with amplitudes $a_n = 0.125$, $a_n = 0.25$, and $a_n = 0.5$, respectively. The result is given in Fig 10.

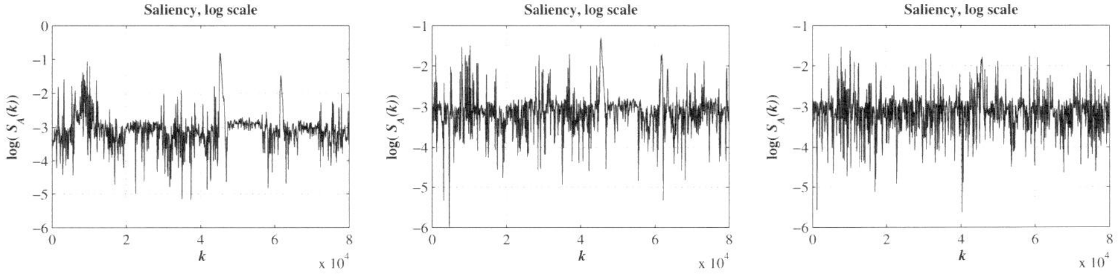

Figure 10 - Saliency of the signal of interest corrupted by coloured noise with amplitudes $a_n = 0.125$ (left), $a_n = 0.25$ (center), and $a_n = 0,5$ (right).

In the first case, i.e. the amplitude $a_n = 0.125$ equivalent to $SNR = 7.67$ dB for speech and $SNR = -6.25$ dB for the falling key the spikes caused by speech and the falling key are clearly separated by their amplitudes from the spikes caused by the background noise. For $a_n = 0.25$ or $SNR = 1.66$ dB for speech and $SNR = -12.31$ dB for the falling key some of the spikes caused by the background noise approach those of the signal of interest. In the third case, for $a_n = 0.5$ or $SNR = -4.37$ dB for speech and $SNR = -18.32$ dB for the falling key, the spikes of the signal of interest and the background noise are more or less of the same hight so that no threshold is given which separates the signal of interest and the background noise reliably.

5 Conclusion

In this paper it has been shown that the saliency measure $S_A(k)$ based on the Kullback-Leibler divergence is a useful tool to extract saliency from an acoustic scene. Background noise and sinusoids can be suppressed significantly which is shown by comparing the spectrogram and the saliency diagram which is calculated from the saliency map $S_A(k, n)$ by averaging over the frequency parameter n. The selection of the parameters of the algorithm to determine the saliency influences the accuracy of the result but deteriorates the result not in such a way that the method is not usefull for practical applications.

6 Acknowledgement

This investigation has been executed in the framework of the SFB 588 Humanoid Robots supported by the German Science Foundation (DFG). Many important and helpful hints have been given by Dipl.-Inf. Benjamin Kühn.

References

[1] Itti, L, Koch, C..: Computational Modelling of Visual Attention. Nature Reviews, Neuroscience, vol. 2, pp. 194-203, March 2001.

[2] Itti, L., Baldi, P.F.: Bayesian Surprise Attracts Human Attention. Advances in Neural Information Processing Systems, 2006.

[3] Schauerte, B. et al.: Multimodal Saliency-based Attention for Object-based Scene Analysis. 2011 IEEE/RSJ, Intl. Conf. on Intelligent Robots and Systems, pp. 1173-1179, 2011.

[4] Kroschel, K. et al.: Statistische Informationstechnik. Springer, Heidelberg, Dordrecht, London, New York, 2011.

[5] Kayser, C. et al.: Mechanisms for Allocating Auditory Attention: An Auditory Saliency Map. Current Biology, vol. 15, pp. 1943-1947, 2005.

[6] Kullback, S.: Information Theory and Statistics. Dover Publications, 1968.

[7] Hershey, J.R. et.al.: Approximating the Kullback-Leibler Divergence between Gaussian Mixture Models. Proc. Interntl. Conf. on Acoustics, Speech and Signal Processing, ICASSP, 2007.

SCHALLMESSPRAXIS UND ANSCHAULICHKEIT

Günther Fuder

TU Dresden, Institut für Akustik und Sprachkommunikation
Guenther.Fuder@mailbox.tu-dresden.de

Abstract: Schall ist vom Prinzip her ein physikalisches Phänomen, das mit Hilfe physikalischer Methoden untersucht und messtechnisch erfasst werden kann. Die Besonderheit ist, dass der Mensch für dieses physikalische Phänomen Sinneswahrnehmungen hat, so dass er Schall hören, fühlen und weiterverarbeiten kann. Damit sind vielfältige und z. T. hochkomplexe Wahrnehmungs- und Verarbeitungsprozeduren verbunden. Deren näherungsweise qualitative und quantitative Beschreibung mit Hilfe eigens dafür entwickelter Kenngrößen und Modellalgorithmen führt in vielen Fällen zu Ergebnissen, die für sich genommen unanschaulich sind. Bei der Bearbeitung akustischer Problemstellungen und der Diskussion der erhaltenen Ergebnisse sollte deshalb in Ergänzung üblicher verbaler und grafischer Darstellungen stärker als bisher von Auralisierungsmöglichkeiten Gebrauch gemacht werden.

1 Problemstellung

Bei der ingenieurtechnischen Erfassung von Schall wird von den physikalischen Phänomenen des Schalls ausgegangen. Dabei werden insbesondere die akustischen Feldgrößen Schalldruck und Schallschnelle mit Hilfe dafür entwickelter Wandler erfasst, in elektrische Signale umgewandelt und datentechnisch verarbeitet. Es lassen sich damit in direkter Weise zunächst nur die physikalischen Aspekte des Schalls untersuchen.

Wirkungen, die der Schall beim Menschen hervorruft, können bei alltagsrelevanten Problemstellungen mit physikalischen Methoden unmittelbar nicht erfasst werden. Aussagen, wie ein Schallereignis gehört wird, wie laut es z. B. wahrgenommen wird, ob es störend wirkt oder nicht, kann man nur unter Einbeziehung des Menschen mit Hilfe von Befragungstechniken erhalten.

Allerdings erfordern Befragungen, die ausreichend statistisch abgesichert sind, einen hohen Aufwand an Personal und Zeit und sind z. B. in der Lärmbekämpfung in den meisten Fällen völlig unpraktikabel. Seit jeher wird deshalb nach Möglichkeiten gesucht, aus der Erfassung der physikalisch vorliegenden Schallsituation auf Wirkungen beim Menschen schließen zu können.

2 Beschreibungsebenen

Physikalische Phänomene des Schalls wie etwa Schallentstehung, Schallausbreitung oder Schallabsorption werden mathematisch beschrieben, d. h. auf der höchstmöglichen Abstraktionsebene. Damit wird von der eindeutigsten und dichtesten Möglichkeit der Beschreibung qualitativer und quantitativer Situationen und Zusammenhänge Gebrauch gemacht.

Wird dagegen Schall vom Menschen aufgenommen und er danach befragt, liegen Beschreibungen und Ergebnisse zunächst auf einer niedrigeren Abstraktionsebene z. B. als verbal formulierte Antworten vor.

Für den Fall, dass Problemstellungen sowohl die physikalische Ebene als auch die Wahrnehmungsebene enthalten, wie es z. B. in der Lärmbekämpfung der Fall ist, muss eine Arbeitsebene eingerichtet werden, auf der beide Beschreibungsformen zusammengeführt werden. Da die mathematische Ebene für die physikalischen Aspekte ohnehin benutzt wird und für

Beschreibungen und die Untersuchung funktioneller Verknüpfungen die meisten Vorteile bietet, ist es naheliegend, sie als Arbeitsebene einzurichten.

Es ergibt sich daraus die Aufgabe, den Abstraktionsgrad der Aussagen auf der Wahrnehmungsebene so zu erhöhen, dass sie mathematisch formuliert und in die Arbeitsebene eingefügt werden können. Erreichen lässt sich diese Erhöhung des Abstraktionsgrades mit Hilfe dafür entwickelter Kenngrößen und Modellalgorithmen.

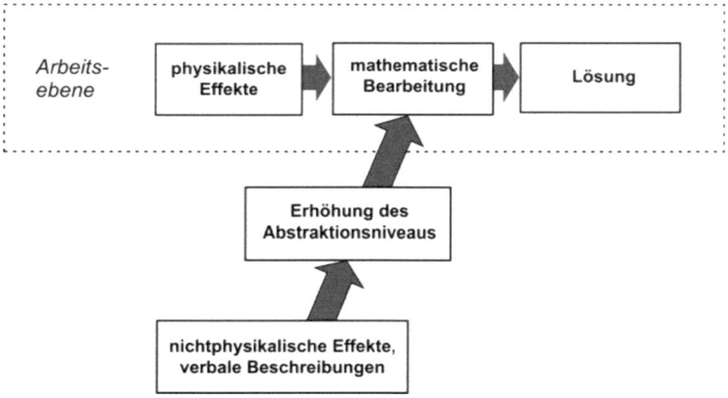

Abbildung 1 – Einrichtung der durchgängigen Arbeitsebene zur mathematischen Bearbeitung

3 Die Kenngröße Schalldruckpegel

3.1 Charakteristik der Kenngröße Schalldruckpegel

Das prominenteste Beispiel der Kenngrößen, die zur Verknüpfung der physikalischen mit der Wahrnehmungsebene dienen, ist der Schalldruckpegel. Das grundlegende Ziel dabei ist, ausgehend von der Schallfeldgröße Schalldruck eine Aussage über die vom Menschen wahrgenommene Schallstärke eines Schallereignisses zu haben ohne den Menschen befragen zu müssen.

Die Basis für die Definition des Schalldruckpegels wird durch das Weber-Fechnersche Gesetz vorgegeben, was besagt, dass zwischen Reizstärke und Sinneswahrnehmung ein logarithmischer Zusammenhang besteht. Weiterhin wird berücksichtigt, dass bei sich ändernder Reizstärke hinsichtlich der Hörwahrnehmung eine minimal unterscheidbare Stufung zu beachten ist und dass eine bestimmte Mindestreizstärke – ein Mindestschalldruck p_0 – vorliegen muss, um eine Hörwahrnehmung auszulösen.

Man erhält dann die Kenngröße Schalldruckpegel L_p in der nach DIN 1320 [1] festgelegten Form zu

$$\boxed{L_\mathrm{p} = 10 \lg \frac{p^2}{p_0^2} \,\mathrm{dB}} \qquad (1)$$

p Schalldruck

p_0 Bezugsschalldruck $(p_0 = 2 \cdot 10^{-5}\ \mathrm{Pa})$

Als Abbildung des Verhältnisses zweier gleichartiger Schalldruckgrößen ist die Kenngröße Schalldruckpegel dimensionslos. Der Zusatz „Dezibel“ (dB) dient lediglich der deutlicheren Erkennbarkeit, dass es sich um Schalldruckpegelwerte handelt.

Zu beachten ist, dass die Zielstellung, den Zusammenhang zwischen Schalldruck und Schallstärkewahrnehmung herzustellen nur in mehr oder weniger guter Näherung erreicht wird. Das liegt u. a. an folgenden Gründen:

- Es gibt Abweichungen vom Weber-Fechnerschen Gesetz insbesondere in der Nähe der Hörschwelle.
- Die Definition des Schalldruckpegels geht zunächst von der Bezugsfrequenz $f = 1000$ Hz aus. Insgesamt liegt eine ausgeprägte Frequenzabhängigkeit vor.
- Es werden zunächst stationäre Dauertöne zugrunde gelegt. Es kann jedoch ein starker Einfluss der Zeitstruktur vorliegen.

3.2 Modifikationen des Schalldruckpegels

3.2.1 Bewertete Schalldruckpegel

Sehr deutlich zeigen die Normalkurven gleichen Lautstärkepegels (DIN ISO 226 [2]), dass es in Abhängigkeit von der Frequenz große Abweichungen zwischen dem Schalldruckpegel nach der Grunddefinition entsprechend Gl.(1) und der wahrgenommenen Schallstärke geben kann.

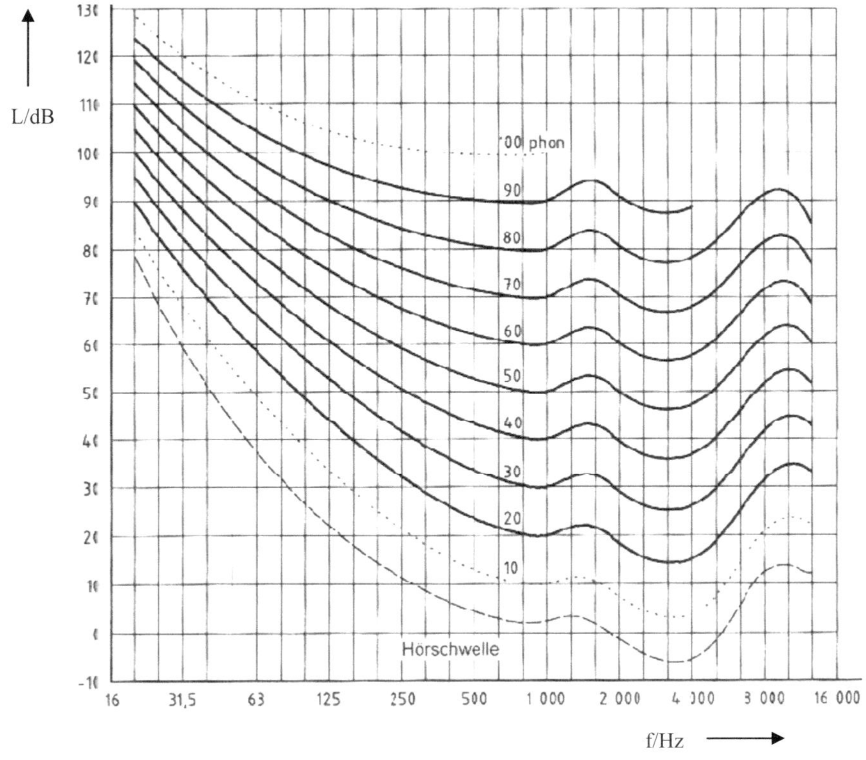

Abbildung 2 – Normalkurven gleicher Lautstärkepegel nach DIN ISO 226 [2]

Um besser zutreffende Aussagen zu erhalten, kann deshalb eine Frequenzbewertung des Schalldruckpegels vorgenommen werden. In der Praxis wird meistens die A-Bewertung nach DIN EN 60651[3] verwendet.

Weiterhin sind auch Zeitbewertungen des Schalldruckpegels möglich, die in Näherung berücksichtigen, dass das Gehör sprunghaften Änderungen der Schalldruck-Zeit-Funktion nicht trägheitslos folgen kann.

Aber auch für die bewerteten Schalldruckpegel gilt, dass dabei Modellierungen verwendet werden, bei denen je nach Konstellation mehr oder weniger große, z. T. sogar drastische Abweichungen zum Verhalten des Gehörs auftreten können.

3.2.2 Pegelmittelwerte

In vielen praktischen Fällen ist es günstig, wenn eine vorliegende Schallsituation durch eine Einzahlangabe gekennzeichnet wird. Damit ist dann ein einfacher Vergleich mit Grenz-, Richt- oder Orientierungswerten möglich.

Schalldruck-Zeit-Funktionen, die in der Praxis auftreten, weisen in der Regel mehr oder weniger ausgeprägte Zeitstrukturen auf. Um sie durch eine einzelne Zahl kennzeichnen zu können, muss die in der Schalldruck-Zeit-Funktion enthaltene Information verdichtet werden. Das wird durch Mittelung erreicht, wobei so vorgegangen werden kann, dass ein Mittelungspegel der Schalldruck-Zeit-Funktion z. B. nach DIN 45641[3] gebildet wird.

Dabei muss in Kauf genommen werden, dass diese Informationsverdichtung mit Verlusten hinsichtlich der gesamten in der Schalldruck-Zeit-Funktion enthaltenen Informationen verbunden ist.

3.3 Bedeutung der Kenngröße Schalldruckpegel für die Praxis

Trotz der Abweichungen, die bei Verwendung des Schalldruckpegels hinsichtlich der tatsächlich wahrgenommenen Schallstärke auftreten können, ist die Bedeutung dieser Kenngröße für die Praxis groß.

Es ist damit möglich, ausgehend von den physikalischen Effekten des Schalls wie Schallentstehung und Schallausbreitung orientierende Aussagen hinsichtlich der Schallwahrnehmung des Menschen zu erhalten. Unter Benutzung der Arbeitsebene nach Abbildung 1 können Schallsituationen für Aufenthaltsorte von Menschen analysiert werden, es kann die Wirksamkeit zu planender Lärmminderungsmaßnahmen abgeschätzt werden und vieles mehr.

Es ist jedoch ausdrücklich festzuhalten:

Die Kenngröße Schalldruckpegel L_p wird vom Prinzip her nicht benötigt, wenn physikalische Aspekte des Schalls wie etwa Schallentstehung oder Schallausbreitung für sich genommen zu untersuchen sind. Das leisten Feldgrößen des Schalls wie Schalldruck und Schallschnelle. Der Schalldruckpegel L_p dient dazu, näherungsweise Aussagen über Schallstärkewahrnehmungen in Abhängigkeit vom Schalldruck zu machen, ohne dass Menschen befragt werden müssen.

4 Anschaulichkeit

4.1 Problem

Obwohl in die Definition des Schalldruckpegels Eigenschaften der Hörwahrnehmung einbezogen sind, besteht das Problem, dass quantitative Angaben von Schalldruckpegelwerten unanschaulich sind.

Bei der Angabe einer Länge - z. B. s = 2 m - entstehen sofort gedankliche Vorstellungen, die mit Alltagserfahrungen verbunden werden können. Diese Möglichkeit des Bezugs zu quantitativen Alltagserfahrungswerten besteht beim Schalldruckpegel nicht.

Das ist in der Praxis von großem Nachteil. Wenn beispielsweise bei einem Lärmminderungsprojekt aufgrund physikalischer Maßnahmen wie etwa der Verminderung der Schallabstrahlung eine Absenkung des Schalldruckpegels am Messpunkt um 4 dB prognostiziert wird, ergibt sich daraus keine alltagsbezogene Vorstellung, welche Verbesserung das tatsächlich bedeutet.

4.2 Herstellung von Anschaulichkeit

Es ergibt sich die Frage, welche Möglichkeiten bestehen, im vorliegenden Fall Anschaulichkeit herzustellen.

Verallgemeinert bedeutet die Herstellung von Anschaulichkeit, dass von der Arbeitsebene ausgehend, auf der das Ergebnis zunächst vorliegt (Abbildung 1), der Abstraktionsgrad der Lösungsbeschreibung herabgesetzt wird, so dass eine anschauliche Lösungsinterpretation erreicht wird (Abbildung 2).

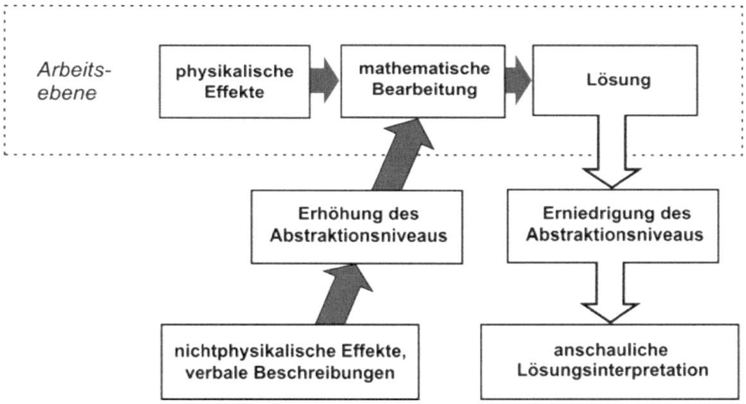

Abbildung 3 – Einbeziehung einer anschaulichen Lösungsinterpretation

Es gibt verschiedene Möglichkeiten der anschaulichen Lösungsinterpretation. Dazu gehören:

- verbale Erläuterungen
- grafische Darstellungen
- pegelkalibrierte Auralisierung (Hörbarmachung)
- pegelkalibrierte Auralisierung und Visualisierung

Verbale Erläuterungen können sehr hilfreich sein, ausgehend von der Aufgabenstellung die erarbeitete Lösung zu kommentieren und zu werten. Davon Gebrauch zu machen wird seine Bedeutung behalten. Das gleiche gilt für grafische Darstellungen. So ist die grafische Darstellung eines Frequenzspektrums immer anschaulicher als eine Liste von Werten.

Eine besonders überzeugende Möglichkeit der Veranschaulichung bietet jedoch die pegelkalibrierte Auralisierung (Hörbarmachung), auch in Erweiterung mit Visualisierung. Es können damit Ausgangssituationen und Ergebnisse in einer Weise realitätsnah akustisch verdeutlicht werden, wie es auf andere Art nicht möglich ist.

Der technische Aufwand, der mit pegelkalibrierten Auralisierungen verbunden ist, hängt von den Aufgabenstellungen ab, die bearbeitet werden sollen. Geht es darum, lediglich Pegelunterschiede zu demonstrieren, die z. B. in der Lärmbekämpfung bei verschiedenen Lösungsansätzen erreicht werden, kann bereits eine kalibrierte Darbietung über Kopfhörer einen sehr guten Eindruck hinsichtlich zu erwartender Ergebnisse vermitteln. Bei darüber hinausgehenden Fragestellungen kommen als hochwertige Möglichkeit auch Darbietungen mittels Wellenfeldsynthese und Videoprojektion in Betracht. Unverzichtbar ist in jedem Falle eine sorgfältige Pegelkalibrierung der Darbietung, erst damit kann der Problemstellung ausreichend entsprochen werden.

Im konkreten Fall wird es immer darum gehen abzuwägen, welche Möglichkeiten ausreichend sind oder am besten geeignet sind, auf der Arbeitsebene ermittelte Ergebnisse zu veranschaulichen. Dabei ist immer zu beachten, dass Veranschaulichung einen Zusatzschritt darstellt, der sich an die auf der Arbeitsebene ermittelten Ergebnisse anschließt.

5 Fazit

Schallmessungen werden in den meisten Fällen nicht mit dem Endziel vorgenommen, physikalische Gesichtspunkte zu klären, sondern weil das Schallereignis von Menschen aufgenommen und in vielfältiger Form verarbeitet wird.

Es wurden deshalb Kenngrößen und Modellalgorithmen entwickelt, die es ermöglichen, von physikalischen Messungen ausgehend, näherungsweise Aussagen zur Schallwahrnehmung zu machen ohne dass Menschen befragt werden müssen Es können damit akustische Projekte effizient bearbeitet werden, die sowohl physikalische Aspekte wie Schallentstehung und Schallausbreitung als auch die Schallwahrnehmung des Menschen betreffen.

Eine in der Praxis häufig benutzte Kenngröße ist der Schalldruckpegel. Damit wird in Näherung eine Beziehung hergestellt zwischen der physikalischen Schallfeldgröße Schalldruck und der Schallstärkewahrnehmung des Menschen.

Nachteilig ist, dass Werte des Schalldruckpegels unanschaulich sind. Mit ihnen lassen sich keine Alltagserfahrungen verbinden, wie es z. B. bei Längenangaben der Fall ist.

Da es aufgrund der technischen Entwicklung immer bessere Möglichkeiten gibt, zu untersuchende Schallsituationen im Labor hörbar zu machen, sollten in stärkerem Maße in die Bearbeitung akustischer Problemstellungen auch pegelkalibrierte Auralisierungen - u. U. erweitert mit Visualisierungen - einbezogen werden.

Beispielsweise lassen sich bei Problemstellungen der Lärmbekämpfung Ausgangssituation und erarbeitete Lösungen durch pegelkalibrierte Auralisierung in eindrucksvoller Weise anschaulich machen. Es kann damit der Verbesserungserwartung, die sich mit vorausberechneten Absenkungen des Schalldruckpegels verbindet, auch Nichtfachleuten eine realitätsnahe Orientierung gegeben werden.

Literatur

[1] DIN 1320, Akustik: Begriffe. 1992
[2] DIN ISO 226, Akustik: Normalkurven gleicher Laustärkepegel. 2006
[3] DIN 45641, Mittelung von Schallpegeln. 1990

NICHTLINEARE MODELLIERUNG VON MIKROLAUTSPRECHERN

Wolfgang Klippel

Klippel GmbH, Dresden, Germany

Das nichtlineare Übertragungsverhalten eines Mikrolautsprechers kann bei großen Signalamplituden mit einem erweiterten Netzwerkmodell beschrieben werden. Das Modell berücksichtigt die Nichtlinearität des mechanischen Widerstandes $R_{ms}(v)$, die bei Mikrolautsprechern erhebliche Signalverzerrungen verursacht. Diese Nichtlinearität und andere freie Parameter des Modelles können mit Methoden der Systemidentifikation aus den gemessenen elektrischen Signalen an den Eingangsklemmen des Wandlers bestimmt werden. Das für den konkreten Wandler identifizierte Modell erlaubt eine Vorhersage der internen Zustandsvariablen und eine Berechnung des Übertragungsverhaltens für ein beliebiges Test- oder Audiosignal. Der Vergleich von Messung und Simulation bestätigte die Gültigkeit des Modelles und eine ausreichende Genauigkeit der Parameteridentifikation.

1 Einleitung

Viele Anwendungen erfordern kleinere und leichtere Lautsprecher, die den erforderlichen Schalldruck am Empfangspunkt mit höherem Wirkungsgrad erzeugen. Mikrolautsprecher, wie sie in portablen Audio- und Telekommunikationsgeräten verwendet werden, sind ein typisches Beispiel dieses Prozesses. Abb. 1 zeigt eine schematische Darstellung dieser Wandler, die eine extrem flache Bauform besitzen und als mechanische Aufhängung der Schwingspule nur eine einfache Sicke der Membran nutzen. Für eine zusätzliche Gewebescheibe wie sie zur Zentrierung und Unterdrückung von Schaukelbewegungen der Schwingspule in Tieftonlautsprechern verwendet wird, fehlt in diesem Wandler der Platz.

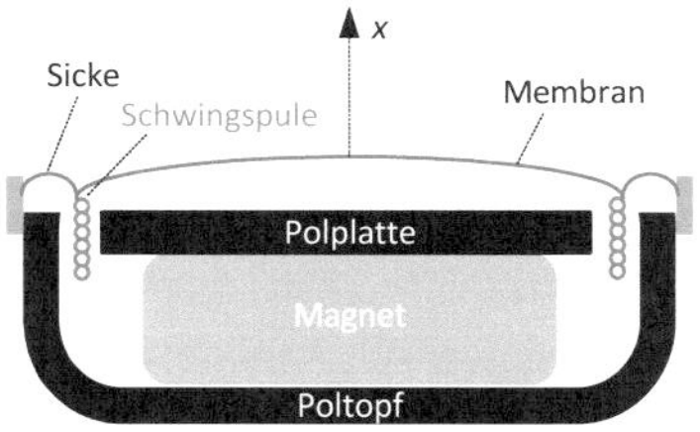

Abb. 1: Schematisches Schnittbild eines Mikrolautsprechers

Freisprechfunktionalität und die Musikwiedergabe in Smartphones, Tablets und Notebooks erfordern Mikrolautsprecher mit begrenzter Membranfläche S_d, die den erforderlichen Volumenfluss q_a für die Schallwiedergabe bei tiefen Frequenzen durch maximale Schwingspulenauslenkung x erzeugen. Die Erzeugung einer hohen Spitzenauslenkung (> 1 mm) erfordert die Ausnutzung aller materiellen Ressourcen und den Betrieb des Wandlers im stark nichtlinearen Arbeitsbereich bis zu den physikalischen Grenzen, die sich zum Beispiel durch das Aufschlagen der Schwingspule auf der Polplatte ergeben.

Der optimale Entwurf der mechanischen Aufhängung (Sicke der Membran) und des elektrodynamischen Antriebes erfordert ein Verständnis der nichtlinearen und thermischen Vorgänge im Wandler. In diesem Beitrag wird ein erweitertes Großsignalmodell vorgestellt, das auch die Nichtlinearität des mechanischen Widerstandes $R_{ms}(v)$ berücksichtigt, die sich im Mikrolautsprecher als eine dominante Verzerrungsursache erweist. Um die Besonderheit dieser Nichtlinearität und die Wechselwirkungen mit anderen Nichtlinearitäten zu beschreiben, werden

in diesem Beitrag verschiedene Methoden der Modellierung vorgestellt und miteinander verglichen. Ausgehend von der klassischen elektroakustischen Modellierung mit Hilfe von elektrischen Analogien wird die nichtlineare Differentialgleichung entwickelt und mit Hilfe von Signalflussplänen interpretiert. Diese Modellierung bildet die Grundlage für die dynamische Bestimmung der freien Parameter des Modelles mit Hilfe der Systemidentifikation unter ausschließlicher Benutzung der elektrischen Signale an den Eingangsklemmen des Wandlers. Die Gültigkeit der Modellierung wird durch Vergleich des simulierten und des gemessenen Übertragungsverhaltens an einem konkreten Mikrolautsprecher untersucht.
Dieser Beitrag in der Festschrift für Prof. Hoffmann zeigt die enge Verbindung zwischen Netzwerkmodellierung und Systemtheorie, die in der Dresdner Schule der Elektroakustik immer eine wesentliche Rolle gespielt hat.

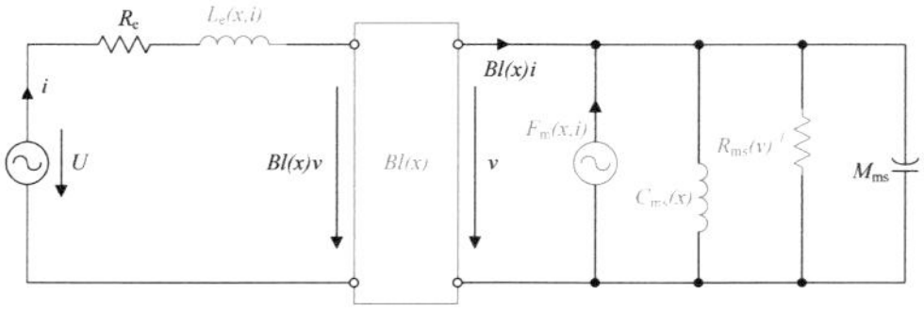

Abb. 2: Ersatzschaltbild des elektromechanischen Wandlers mit konzentrierten linearen und nichtlinearen Elementen

2 Modellierung

2.1 Elektromechanisches Netzwerk

Bei tiefen Frequenzen bewegt sich der innere Teil der Membran als starrer Körper und lediglich die Sicke wird durch die Bewegung der Schwingspule verformt. Die elektro-mechanischen Wechselwirkungen können in diesem Frequenzbereich mit Hilfe konzentrierter Elemente modelliert werden. Abb. 2 zeigt das äquivalente Netzwerk, das neben den bekannten linearen Elementen auch nichtlineare Elemente [1] enthält, die keinen konstanten Parameterwert besitzen, sondern eine Abhängigkeit von den Zuständen des Wandlers aufweisen:

R_e	Elektrischer Widerstand der Schwingspule,
$L_e(x,i)$	Induktivität der Schwingspule als Funktion der Auslenkung x und des Eingangsstromes i,
$Bl(x)$	Kraftfaktor als Funktion der Auslenkung x,
$F_m(x,i)$	Elektromagnetische Anziehungskraft als Funktion der Auslenkung x und des Eingangsstromes i,
$K_{ms}(x)$	Steifigkeit (inverse Nachgiebigkeit $C_{ms}(x)^{-1}$) als Funktion der Auslenkung x,
M_{ms}	Bewegte Masse der mechanischen Elemente und der Luft,
$R_{ms}(v)$	Reibungsstandwert als Funktion der Schwingspulenschnelle v.

Der Kraftfaktor $Bl(x)$ und die Steifigkeit $K_{ms}(x)$ sind die dominanten Nichtlinearitäten in den meisten elektro-dynamischen Wandlern und stehen in einem direkten Zusammenhang mit der Form der Schwingspule, den Abmessungen der Polflächen und der Geometrie der mechanischen Aufhängung. Die Nichtlinearität der Induktivität $L_e(x,i)$ verändert sich durch eine Verschiebung der Schwingspule im Eisenkreis und durch die Veränderung der Permeabilität des Materials. Das

durch den Eingangsstrom i erzeugte magnetische Wechselfeld kann bei großen Tieftonlautsprechern durchaus den Arbeitspunkt in der $B(H)$-Kennlinie verschieben und die Sättigung des Magnetflusses im Eisenkreis verändern. In Mikrolautsprechern ist die Induktivität der Schwingspule im Vergleich zum Gleichstromwiderstand jedoch sehr klein und ihre Nichtlinearität kann in der Praxis vernachlässigt werden.
Dafür besitzen Mikrolautsprecher eine ausgeprägte Nichtlinearität des Widerstandes $R_{ms}(v)$, die durch turbulente Luftströmungen im Luftspalt zwischen Schwingspule und Polplatte und anderen Öffnungen entsteht.

2.2 Differentialgleichung

Die Verkopplung dieser konzentrierten Elemente und der Zustand des Wandlers für eine beliebige Klemmenspannung $u(t)$ kann mit der folgenden nichtlinearen Differentialgleichung beschrieben werden:

$$\begin{aligned} &K_{ms}(x)x + \left(R_{ms}(v) + \frac{Bl(x)^2}{R_e} \right) v + M_{ms}\frac{dv}{dt} \\ &= \frac{Bl(x)}{R_e}\left(u(t) - \frac{d\left(L_e(i,x)i\right)}{dt} \right) + \frac{i^2}{2}\frac{dL_e(i,x)}{dx} \end{aligned} \tag{1}$$

Die Terme auf der linken Seite beschreiben die Rückstellkraft der Feder und andere Kräfte, die durch den mechanischen Widerstand, die elektrische Bedämpfung und die Trägheit der Masse verursacht werden. Auf der rechten Seite erscheinen eine elektrodynamische und eine elektromagnetische Antriebskraft. Die Trägheitskraft ist der einzige lineare Term in dieser Gleichung, da durch die konstante Masse M_{ms} lediglich die Beschleunigung skaliert wird. Alle anderen Terme der Differentialgleichung enthalten veränderliche Parameter, die nichtlineare Funktionen der Zustandsvariablen (Auslenkung x, Schnelle v und Strom i) sind.
In den nichtlinearen Termen entstehen durch die Multiplikation von Zeitsignalen nichtlineare Verzerrungen, die sich im Spektrum der Zustandsvariablen als zusätzliche Signalkomponenten (Gleichanteil, Harmonische, Intermodulationsprodukte) zeigen.
Jedoch besitzen die von jedem nichtlinearem Term erzeugten Verzerrungen sehr unterschiedliche Eigenschaften, die sich aus den spektralen und zeitlichen Eigenschaften der Zustandsvariablen x, v, i und der Klemmenspannung u sowie der Stellung des nichtlinearen Terms in der Differentialgleichung (1) ergeben.
Die Rückstellkraft der mechanischen Aufhängung ist eine nichtlineare Funktion der Auslenkung x und enthält nichtlineare Verzerrungsprodukte, deren Amplitude mit steigender Frequenz f (oberhalb der Resonanzfrequenz f_s) sehr stark abfallen.
Der nichtlineare Kraftfaktor $Bl(x)$ tritt in zwei nichtlinearen Termen auf. Die elektrodynamische Antriebskraft auf der rechten Seite der Gl. (1) führt zu einer Multiplikation des Eingangsstromes $i(t)$ mit einer Funktion der Auslenkung x. Diese nichtlineare Verkopplung von zwei unterschiedlichen Zuständen führt zu Intermodulationsverzerrungen, die nur durch ein Mehrtonsignal messtechnisch erfasst werden können. Für große Auslenkungen x, bei der die Schwingspule den Magnetspalt verlässt, vermindert der abfallende Kraftfaktor $Bl(x)$ die Übertragung aller Signalkomponenten in dem Transformator in Abb. 2. Der elektrische Dämpfungsterm $vBl(x)^2/R_e$ auf der linken Seite der Gl. (1) bedingt eine multiplikative Verknüpfung von Auslenkung x und Schnelle v. Da die Schnelle eine Bandpasscharakteristik besitzt, erzeugt dieser Term maximale Verzerrungen für Anregungssignale nahe der Resonanzfrequenz f_s. Während sich die elektrische Dämpfung mit $Bl(x)^2$ für steigende Auslenkung x vermindert und die effektive Gesamtgüte des Resonators erhöht, steigt die mechanische Dämpfung mit $R_{ms}(v)$ an und verkleinert die Gesamtgüte. Bei Tieftonlautsprechern ist dieser zweite Effekt kaum messbar, da die elektrische Bedämpfung die mechanischen und

akustischen Verluste dominiert. Bei Mikrolautsprechern bestimmen beide nichtlineare Dämpfungsmechanismen das Großsignalverhalten bei der Resonanzfrequenz.
Die nichtlineare Induktivität $L_e(x,i)$ erscheint ebenfalls in zwei Termen in Gl. (1). Die Selbstinduktionsspannung vermindert die Klemmenspannung und ist die zeitliche Ableitung des magnetischen Wechselflusses, der sich mit der Auslenkung und dem Eingangsstrom verändert. Die elektromagnetische Antriebskraft wird in einem elektro-dynamischen Wandler nicht benötigt und ist eine unerwünschte Verzerrungsquelle. Dieser Term verschwindet, wenn die Induktivität $L_e(x,i)$ sich mit der Auslenkung x der Schwingspule nicht ändert. Bei preiswerten Tieftonlautsprechern ohne Kurzschlussring steigt die Induktivität beim Eintauchen der Schwingspule in den Eisenkreis an. In diesem Fall ist die Ableitung nach x nahezu konstant und die Quadrierung des Eingangsstromes ist die entscheidende nichtlineare Verzerrungsquelle.

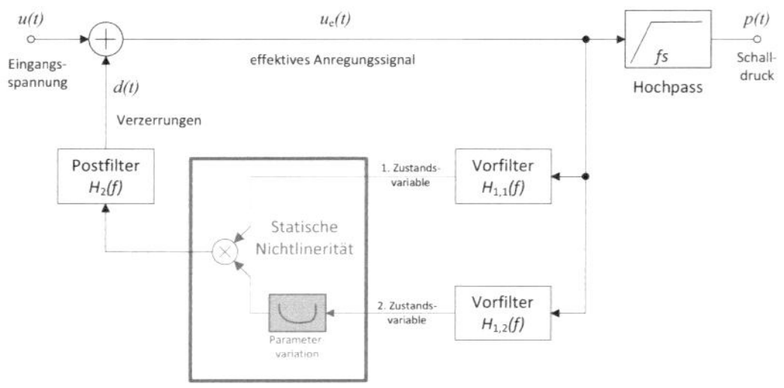

Abb. 3: Signalflussplan zur Modellierung der Wirkung eines nichtlinearen Terms in der Differentialgleichung

2.3 Signalflussplan

Der Entstehungsprozess und die Eigenschaften jeder Verzerrungsursache kann mit Hilfe des allgemeinen Signalflussplanes in Abb. 3 erklärt werden. Diese Modellierung benutzt lineare und nichtlineare Subsysteme, und einen Addierer als Verknüpfungselement. Bei dieser Modellierung wurde die gesamte Dynamik des Gesamtsystems in linearen Subsystemen konzentriert, und mit Hilfe von Impulsantworten oder Übertragungsfunktionen beschrieben. Das Hochpassfilter am Ausgang des Signalflussplans modelliert das lineare Übertragungsverhalten des Wandlers bei kleiner Signalamplitude und entspricht der Lösung der linearen Differentialgleichung, in der die nichtlinearen Parameter durch Konstanten ersetzt wurden (z.B. Kraftfaktor $Bl(0)$ in der Ruheposition $x=0$).
Das nichtlineare Subsystem erfasst die Veränderung des nichtlinearen Parameters (z.B. Kraftfaktor $Bl(x)-Bl(0)$) und ihre multiplikative Verknüpfung mit der Zustandsvariablen (z.B. Strom i). Dieses nichtlineare Subsystem ist ein statisches System ohne Speicherelemente und erzeugt für die momentanen Zustandssignale (z.B. x und i) ein Ausgangssignal, das nicht von der Vorgeschichte der Zustände abhängig ist. Die nichtlinearen Subsysteme sind Bestandteil eines Rückkopplungszweiges, das ein Verzerrungssignal $d(t)$ zum Eingangssignal $u(t)$ addiert.
Tabelle I zeigt für jeden Effekt der nichtlinearen Parameter die Übertragungseigenschaften der Vorfilter $H_{1,1}(f)$, $H_{1,2}(f)$ und des Postfilters $H_2(f)$ und das generierte Zustandssignal am Ausgang des Subfilters.

Tabelle I: Eigenschaften der Vorfilter und des Postfilters im Signalflussplan in Abb. 3 für die isolierten nichtlinearen Verzerrungsursachen.

Nichtlinearer Parameter	**Interpretation**	**Vorfilter $H_{1,1}(f)$** (Ausgangssignal)	**Vorfilter $H_{1,2}(f)$** (Ausgangssignal)	**Postfilter $H_2(f)$**
Steifigkeit $K_{ms}(x)$	Rückstellkraft	Tiefpass (Auslenkung)	Tiefpass (Auslenkung)	1
Kraftfaktor $Bl(x)$	Elektrodynamische Antriebskraft	Bandsperre (Eingangsstrom)	Tiefpass (Auslenkung)	1
	elektrische Dämpfung	Bandpass (Schnelle)	Tiefpass (Auslenkung)	1
Induktivität $L_e(x)$	Positionsabhängige Selbstinduktion	Bandsperre (Eingangsstrom)	Tiefpass (Auslenkung)	Differenzierer
	Elektromagnetische Antriebskraft	Bandsperre (Eingangsstrom)	Tiefpass (Auslenkung)	1
Induktivität $L_e(i)$	Sättigung des Magnetmaterials	Bandsperre (Eingangsstrom)	Bandsperre (Eingangsstrom)	Differenzierer
Widerstand $R_{ms}(v)$	Mechanische, (akustische) Dämpfung	Bandpass (Schnelle)	Bandpass (Schnelle)	1

Die nichtlineare Steifigkeit $K_{ms}(x)$ erfordert zum Beispiel eine Tiefpasscharakteristik beider Vorfilter, um das Auslenkungssignal x den Eingängen der statischen Nichtlinearität zuführen zu können. Das Postfilter $H_2(f)$ besitzt für diesen nichtlinearen Effekt einen frequenzunabhängigen Übertragungsfaktor und kann in diesem Fall entfallen. Da das Verzerrungssignal $d(t)$ Signalkomponenten enthält, die die gleiche Frequenz wie die anregten Signalkomponenten im Eingangssignal $u_e(t)$ besitzen, entsteht durch die Rückkopplung der Grundschwingung eine weiche Begrenzung der mechanischen Auslenkung bei tiefen Frequenzen. Die geradzahligen Potenzen der Auslenkung x in der Reihenentwicklung der statischen Nichtlinearität $K_{ms}(x)x$ können ebenfalls einen Gleichanteil im Verzerrungssignal $d(t)$ erzeugen, der den Arbeitspunkt der Schwingspule im Magnetspalt dynamisch verändert. Dieser Gleichanteil erscheint vor allem in der Auslenkung x aber nicht in der Schnelle v, Schalldruck p und im Strom i, da der Gleichanteil in diesen Zustandsvariablen durch zeitliche Ableitungen beseitigt wird. Der nichtlineare Rückkopplungszweig kann auch ein instabiles Verhalten des Gesamtsystems verursachen. Der nichtlineare Term in der Duffingschen Differentialgleichung entspricht genau diesem nichtlinearen Rückkopplungszweig und verursacht bei einer progressiv ansteigenden Steifigkeitskennlinie und hoher Gesamtgüte Q_{ts} des mechanischen Resonators eine Bifurkation der Zustände oberhalb der Resonanz und Sprungeffekte bei Annäherung von tieferen oder höheren Frequenzen.

Die Modellierung des elektrodynamischen Antriebes mit dem nichtlinearen Kraftfaktor $Bl(x)$ erfordert zwei unterschiedliche Vorfilter. Neben dem Tiefpass zur Generierung der Auslenkung x wird eine Bandsperre benötigt, die den Eingangsstrom i erzeugt.

Die gleichen Vorfilter werden zur Beschreibung der auslenkungsabhängigen Selbstinduktion durch $L_e(x)$ benutzt, allerdings enthält das Postfilter einen Differenzierer, der die Verzerrungsprodukte bei höheren Frequenzen verstärkt.

Die Beschreibung der elektrischen und mechanischen Dämpfung erfordert einen Bandpass als Vorfilter, um die Schnelle v bereitzustellen.

Aufgrund der unterschiedlichen Eigenschaften der linearen Vor- und Postfilter und der nichtlinearen Kurvenform erzeugt jeder nichtlineare Term in der Differentialgleichung (1) sehr unterschiedliche Symptome (Verzerrungen, Gleichanteil, Kompression, Bifurkation) in den inneren Zustandsvariablen *x, v, i* und im Ausgangssignal *p*.

3 Bestimmung der Parameter

Um die Modelle auf reale Wandler anwenden zu können, wird eine einfache Messtechnik für die Bestimmung der freien Parameter dieser Modelle benötigt. Hierfür wurden statische, quasi-statische, inkrementelle und dynamische Methoden entwickelt [5]. Die dynamische Methode regt den Wandler mit einem breitbandigen Stimulus (Testsignal, Musik) ausreichender Amplitude an und erfasst die elektrischen Signale (Strom *i* und Spannung *u*) an den Eingangsklemmen des Wandlers und bildet den Zusammenhang zwischen den elektrischen Signalen mit Hilfe eines adaptiven Modelles nach. Die nichtlineare Systemidentifikation liefert nicht nur die linearen und nichtlinearen Parameter des Wandlers, sondern auch die momentanen Zustandssignale als Funktion der Zeit.

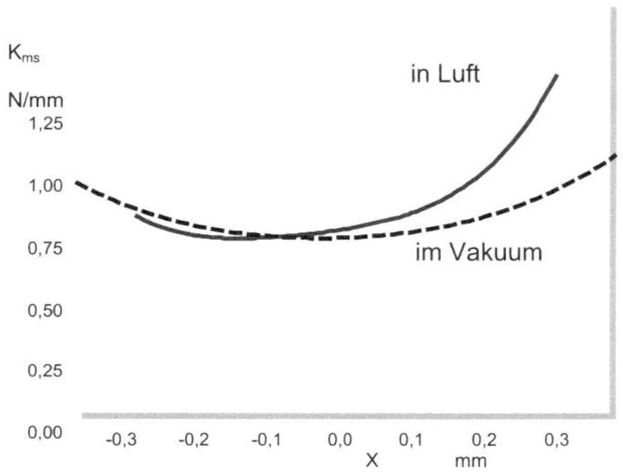

Abb. 4: Nichtlineare Steifigkeit $K_{ms}(x)$ als Funktion der Auslenkung *x* für einen Mikrolautsprecher gemessen in Luft und im Vakuum (gestrichelt)

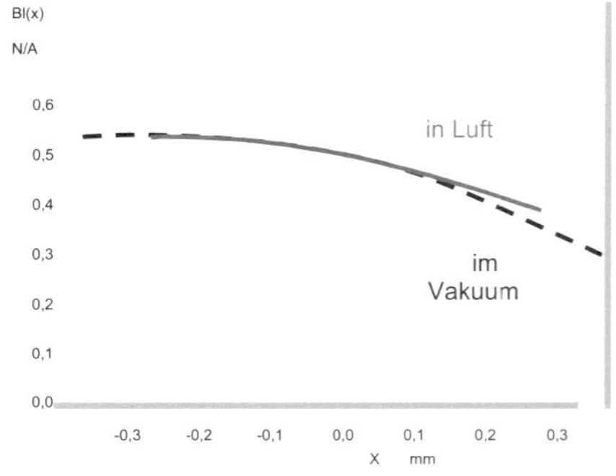

Abb. 5: Nichtlinearer Kraftfaktor *Bl(x)* als Funktion der Auslenkung *x* für einen Mikrolautsprecher gemessen in Luft und im Vakuum (gestrichelt)

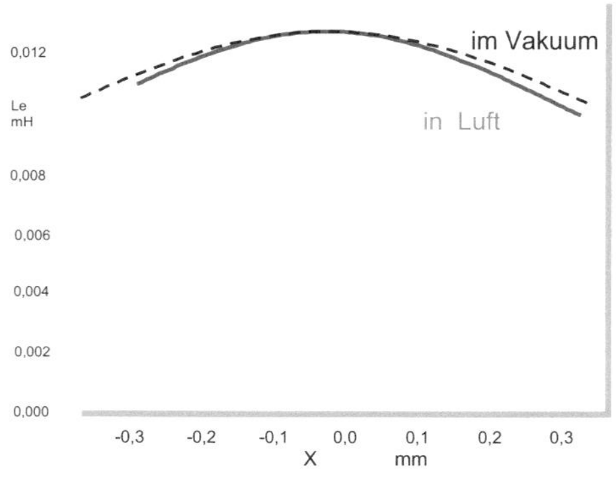

Abb. 6: Nichtlineare Induktivität $L_e(x)$ als Funktion der Auslenkung *x* für einen Mikrolautsprecher gemessen in Luft und im Vakuum (gestrichelt)

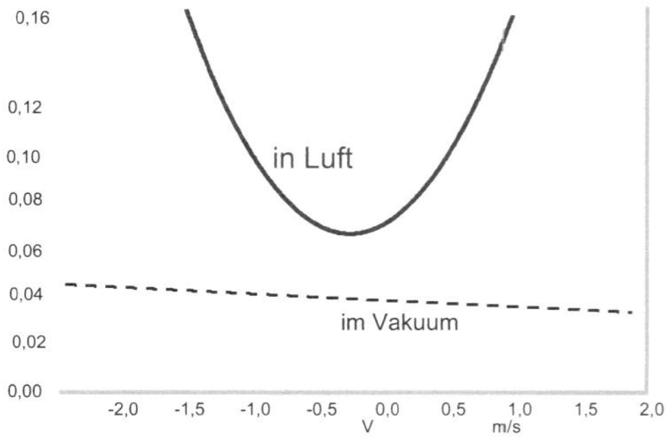

Abb. 7: Nichtlinearer Widerstand $R_{ms}(v)$ als Funktion der Schnelle *v* für einen Mikrolautsprecher gemessen in Luft und im Vakuum (gestrichelt)

Die Abb. 4 – 7 zeigen die nichtlinearen Parameter eines Mikrolautsprechers, der in freier Luft ohne Gehäuse und im Vakuum während der Systemidentifikation betrieben wurde. Signifikante Unterschiede zwischen beiden Messungen treten in den Kennlinien der Steifigkeit $K_{ms}(x)$ und

des Widerstandes $R_{ms}(v)$ auf. Die Vakuummessung zeigt die Eigenschaften des rein mechanischen Systems ohne den Einfluss des eingeschlossenen Luftvolumens auf die Gesamtsteifigkeit. Die starke symmetrische Veränderung des mechanischen Widerstandes $R_{ms}(v)$ für positive und negative Werte der Schnelle der Schwingspule verschwindet vollständig im Vakuum und ist keine Eigenschaft der mechanischen Aufhängung, sondern wird durch Luftströmungen im Spalt und Öffnungen im Gehäuse verursacht.
Der Kennlinien des Kraftfaktors $Bl(x)$ und der Induktivität $L_e(x)$ sind im Vakuum und in der Luft nahezu identisch. Die Ruheposition der Schwingspule befindet sich nicht im Maximum der Kraftfaktors $Bl(x)$. Durch eine Verschiebung der Schwingspule um 0.25 mm in Richtung rückseitiger Polplatte kann die Symmetrie der Kraftfaktorkurve erheblich verbessert werden. Die Nichtlinearität der Induktivität $L(x)$ ist vernachlässigbar, da die Induktivität aufgrund ihres geringen Wertes von maximal 0.013 mH nur einen sehr kleinen Beitrag zur elektrischen Impedanz leistet.

Tabelle 2: Anteil der von jeder Nichtlinearität verursachten Verzerrungen im akustischen Schalldruck eines Mikrolautsprechers, der in Luft und im Vakuum betrieben wurde

VERZERRUNGEN verursacht durch	Luft	Vakuum
$K_{ms}(x)$	28%	36 %
$Bl(x)$	20 %	17 %
$L_e(x)$	2%	2%
$R_{ms}(v)$	45%	6%

Das Wandlermodell mit den identifizierten Parametern erlaubt es, das Verhältnis der Spitzenwerte der Verzerrungen und des abgestrahlten Gesamtschalldruckes während der Wiedergabe eines Test- oder Audiosignals zu berechnen. Tabelle 2 zeigt, dass der nichtlineare Widerstand $R_{ms}(v)$ des Mikrolautsprechers in Luft den höchsten relativen Verzerrungsanteil (45%) erzeugt. Im Vakuum verschwinden diese Verzerrungen nahezu und die Steifigkeit $K_{ms}(x)$ erweist sich als die dominante Verzerrungsursache.

4 Übertragungsverhalten

Das nichtlineare Modell mit den für den realen Wandler identifizierten Parametern erlaubt eine Berechnung der internen Zustandsvariablen und des abgestrahlten Schalldruckes für einen beliebigen elektrischen Stimulus (Testsignal oder Audiosignal). Die simulierten Zustände können mit den an dem gleichem Wandler gemessenen Zuständen verglichen werden. Hierbei ist es zweckmäßig, nichtlineare Symptome aus den Zuständen durch eine geeignete Signalanalyse zu extrahieren, die sich für die Verifikation des Modelles und praktische Bewertung des Großsignalverhaltens eignen. Die bisher dargestellten theoretischen Zusammenhänge erleichtern die Interpretation dieser Symptome. Die Wirkung jedes einzelnen nichtlinearen Parameters kann durch Deaktivierung aller anderen Nichtlinearitäten (Nullsetzen aller höheren Koeffizienten der Potenzreihenentwicklung) sehr einfach in dem Modell simuliert werden. Der Vergleich dieser virtuellen Varianten mit dem realen Lautsprecher zeigt die dominanten Ursachen der Verzerrungen, der Begrenzung der Amplitude und für auftretende Instabilitäten.

4.1 Schwingspulenauslenkung

Da die nichtlinearen Parameter $Bl(x)$, $K_{ms}(x)$ und $L_e(x)$ von der Schwingspulenauslenkung x abhängen, ist die Messung des positiven und negativen Spitzenwertes der Auslenkung als

Funktion der Anregungsfrequenz eines sinusförmigen Stimulus ein wichtiges nichtlineares Symptom.

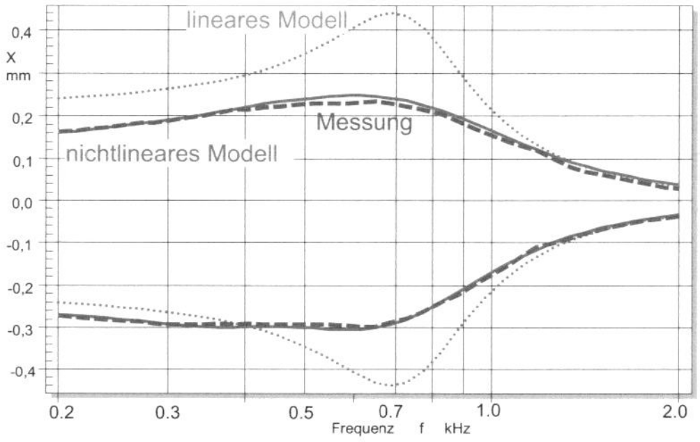

Abb. 8: Positiver und negativer Spitzenwert der gemessenen und berechneten Auslenkung unter Benutzung eines linearen (gepunktete Linie) und eines nichtlinearen (durchgezogene Linie) Modelles

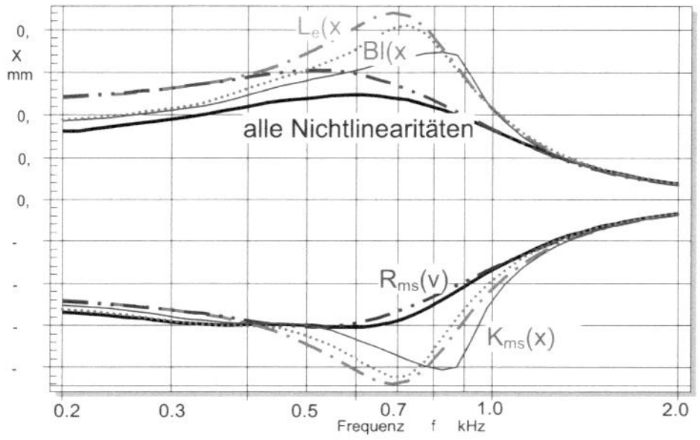

Abb. 9: Positiver und negativer Spitzenwert der berechneten Auslenkung unter Berücksichtigung aller und ausgewählter Nichtlinearitäten

Abb. 8 zeigt eine gute Übereinstimmung zwischen dem gemessenen Ausschlag und dem mit Hilfe des nichtlinearen Modelles berechneten Verhaltens. Das lineare Modell kann die Amplitudenkompression, die gerade bei Resonanzfrequenz f_s=700 Hz sehr stark ausgeprägt ist, nicht nachbilden.

Abb. 9 zeigt den Einfluss jeder isolierten Nichtlinearität auf die Spitzenauslenkung. Die Induktivität $L_e(x)$ ist im Falle des Mikrolautsprechers eine sehr schwache Nichtlinearität und beeinflusst die Auslenkung x kaum. Weder der Kraftfaktor $Bl(x)$ noch die Steifigkeit $K_{ms}(x)$ kann die Amplitudenkompression bei f_s = 700 Hz erklären. Die Bedämpfung der Resonanzspitze wird ausschließlich durch den nichtlinearen Widerstand $R_{ms}(v)$ verursacht, dessen Wirkung bei tiefen und sehr hohen Frequenzen verschwindet.

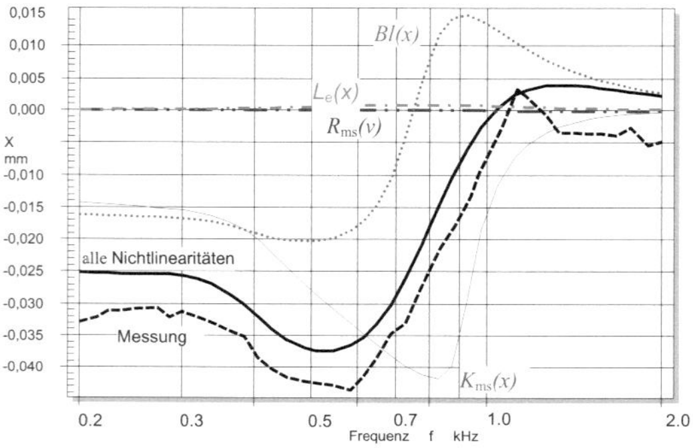

Abb. 10: Gemessener und berechneter Gleichanteil in der Auslenkung bei Berücksichtigung aller und ausgewählter Nichtlinearitäten

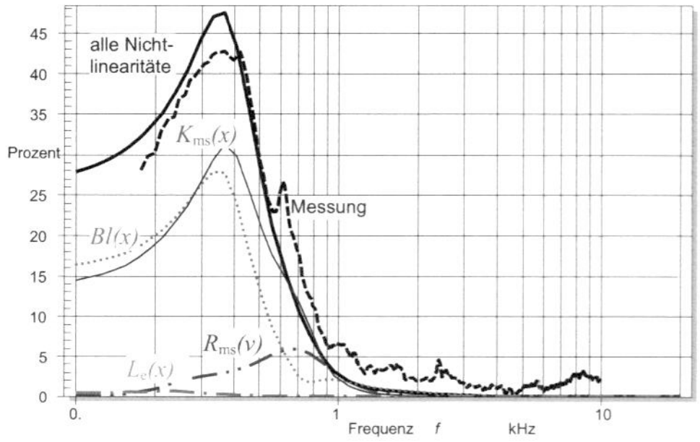

Abb. 11: Harmonische Gesamtverzerrungen bezogen auf den Schalldruck als Funktion der Anregungsfrequenz f als Ergebnis einer Messung (gestrichelt) und modelliert unter Berücksichtigung aller und ausgewählter Nichtlinearitäten

Der genaue Vergleich der positiven und negativen Spitzenwerte in Abb. 9 zeigt bereits eine unsymmetrische Auslenkung der Schwingspule um die Ruheposition, die sich auch im dynamisch generierten Gleichanteil in Abb. 10 ausdrückt. Die gemessene Kurvenform (gestrichelte Linie) konnte durch Berücksichtigung aller Nichtlinearitäten im Modell nachgebildet (dicke Linie) werden. Die kleine negative Verschiebung kann durch visko-elastische Kriecheffekte [6] erklärt werden. Die Asymmetrie der Steifigkeitskurve $K_{ms}(x)$ des in Luft betriebenen Mikrolautsprechers führt zu einem negativen Gleichanteil von -40 µm bei der Resonanzfrequenz f_s= 700 Hz. Bei tiefen Frequenzen liefern Steifigkeit $K_{ms}(x)$ und Kraftfaktor $Bl(x)$ ungefähr den gleichen Beitrag zum Gleichanteil. Bei der Resonanzfrequenz erzeugt der Kraftfaktor $Bl(x)$ keinen Gleichanteil, da die Auslenkung x zum Strom i 90° phasenverschoben ist. Für Frequenzen oberhalb der Resonanzfrequenz bildet sich durch die Asymmetrie der $Bl(x)$-Kennlinie ein positiver Gleichanteil, der den negativen Beitrag der Steifigkeit bei 1 kHz kompensiert. Die Nichtlinearitäten $L_e(x)$ and $R_{ms}(v)$ des hier untersuchten Mikrolautsprechers liefern aufgrund ihrer symmetrischen Form nur einen sehr kleinen Beitrag zum Gleichanteil.

4.2 Harmonische Verzerrungen

Die Messung der gesamten harmonischen Verzerrungen ist ein sehr verbreitetes Messverfahren [7], um das nichtlineare Verhalten des Systems für einen einzelnen Ton bei verschiedenen Anregungsfrequenzen zu untersuchen. Abb. 11 zeigt eine gute Übereinstimmung zwischen den gemessenen harmonischen Verzerrungen des Mikrolautsprechers und den Ergebnissen der Modellierung unter Benutzen aller identifizierten nichtlinearen Parameter. Der Verzerrungsanteil von 40% unterhalb der Resonanzfrequenz f_s entsteht durch das Hochpassfilter am Ausgang des Signalflussplanes in Abb. 3, der die Grundschwingung vermindert. Bei tiefen Anregungsfrequenzen erweisen sich Kraftfaktor $Bl(x)$ und Steifigkeit $K_{ms}(x)$ als die dominanten Verzerrungsursachen. Die von der nichtlinearen Induktivität $L_e(x)$ erzeugten harmonischen Verzerrungen sind bei diesem Mikrolautsprecher vernachlässigbar. Die harmonischen Verzerrungen aller auslenkungsabhängigen Nichtlinearitäten $K_{ms}(x)$, $Bl(x)$ und $L_e(x)$ fallen oberhalb der Resonanzfrequenz f_s stark ab, da hier die Auslenkung x mit 12 dB pro Oktave sinkt. In der Nähe der Resonanzfrequenz gewinnt auch der nichtlineare Widerstand $R_{ms}(v)$ an Bedeutung, da hier die Schnelle v und die Verluste maximal sind.

4.3 Intermodulationen

Die Messung der harmonischen Verzerrungen als Funktion der Anregungsfrequenz liefert keine vollständige Beschreibung des nichtlinearen Übertragungsverhaltens. Die Verwendung eines zweiten Messtones [7] liefert weitere Symptome des nichtlinearen Systems, die hilfreich für die Überprüfung des Modelles und die diagnostische Bewertung des Wandlers sind. Durch die Anregung des Wandlers mit einem Zweitonsignal entstehen neben harmonischen Komponenten auch Intermodulationsprodukte, deren Frequenzabhängigkeit in einem direktem Zusammenhang mit dem Frequenzgang der Vorfilter $H_{1,1}(f)$, $H_{1,2}(f)$ und des Postfilters $H_2(f)$ in dem Signalflussplan in Abb. 3 steht.

Die Wahl der beiden Anregungsfrequenzen in einem Zweitonstimulus ist entscheidend für die Interpretierbarkeit der Ergebnisse. Deshalb wird für den ersten Ton eine feste Frequenz f_1=400 Hz gewählt, die unterhalb der Resonanzfrequenz f_s liegt und eine hohe Schwingspulenauslenkung erzeugt. Die Frequenz f_2 des zweiten Tones wird in einem ausreichenden Frequenzabstand $f_2 >> f_1$ verändert, um die Intermodulationsprodukte von den harmonischen Komponenten eindeutig trennen zu können.

Abb. 12 zeigt, dass die vom Mikrolautsprecher erzeugten Intermodulationen zweiter Ordnung nahezu unabhängig von der Anregungsfrequenz f_2 sind und mit 15 % den Wert der harmonischen Verzerrungen oberhalb der Resonanzfrequenz weit übersteigen. Diese Frequenzunabhängigkeit der Intermodulationen ist ein eindeutiger Hinweis auf die Verzerrungsursache. Nur die Nichtlinearität des Kraftfaktors *Bl(x)* kann dieses Verhalten erzeugen, da der Ton bei der Frequenz f_2 einen nahezu konstanten Strom *i* am Ausgang des Vorfilters $H_{1,1}(f)$ erzeugt, während der Ton bei der Frequenz f_1 eine konstante Auslenkung *x* verursacht. Bei Vernachlässigung der nichtlinearen Steifigkeit $K_{ms}(x)$ bei der nichtlinearen Modellierung, erzeugt die *Bl(x)*-Nichtlinearität etwas höhere Intermodulationsverzerrungen, da die Amplitudenkompression der Schwingspulenauslenkung nicht exakt nachgebildet wird. Die nichtlineare Steifigkeit selbst kann keine signifikanten Intermodulationen bei höheren Frequenzen erzeugen, da beide Vorfilter $H_{1,1}(f)$ und $H_{1,2}(f)$ ein tiefpassgefiltertes Signal erzeugen und die Intermodulation zweiter Ordnung proportional mit der Auslenkung *x* um 12 dB pro Oktave zu höheren Frequenzen $f_2 > f_s$ abfallen. Die durch die Induktivität $L_e(x)$ bedingten Verzerrungen sind im Mikrolautsprecher sehr klein, steigen aber aufgrund des Differenzierers im Postfilter $H_2(f)$ mit ungefähr 6 dB pro Oktave zu höheren Frequenzen f_2 an. Die durch den nichtlinearen Widerstand $R_{ms}(v)$ erzeugten Intermodulationen zweiter Ordnung fallen proportional mit der Schwelle mit 6 dB pro Oktave für Frequenzen $f_2 > f_s$ ab. Aufgrund der geringen Asymmetrie in der Kurvenform von $R_{ms}(v)$ sind die geraden Verzerrungskomponenten gering

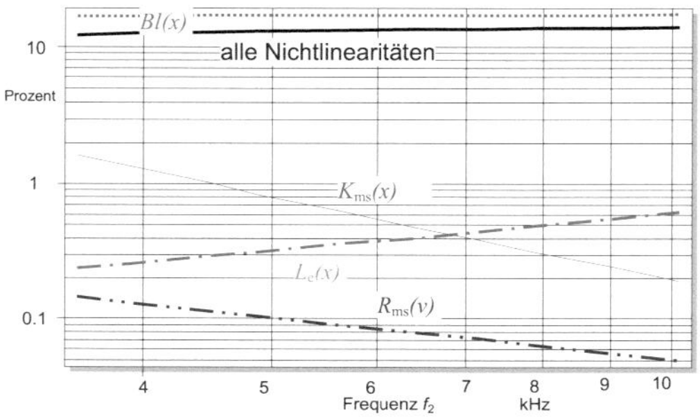

Abb. 12: Quadratische Intermodulationsverzerrungen als Funktion der Frequenz f_2 eines Zweitonstimulus (mit $f_2 >> f_1$=400 Hz) bei Berücksichtigung aller (dicke Linie) und ausgewählter Nichtlinearitäten

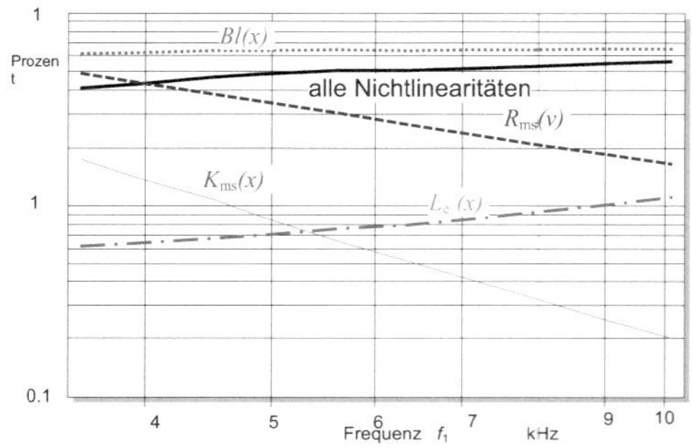

Abb. 13 : Intermodulationsverzerrungen dritter Ordnung als Funktion der Frequenz f_2 eines Zweitonstimulus (mit $f_2 >> f_1$=400 Hz) bei Berücksichtigung aller (dicke Linie) und ausgewählter Nichtlinearitäten

Die Intermodulationen dritter Ordnung werden ebenfalls durch den Kraftfaktor *Bl(x)* dominiert. Der Beitrag des nichtlinearen Widerstandes $R_{ms}(v)$ ist für den Mikrolautsprecher in Luft aufgrund der symmetrischen Kurvenform in Abb. 7 erheblich größer als bei den Verzerrungen zweiter Ordnung. Die Intermodulationsprodukte dritter Ordnung fallen jedoch proportional mit dem Quadrat der Schnelle (12 dB pro Oktave) für Frequenzen $f_2 > f_s$ ab. Bei tiefen Frequenzen interferieren die Beiträge des Kraftfaktors *Bl(x)* und des Widerstandes $R_{ms}(v)$ und vermindern die Gesamtverzerrungen. Die durch die Induktivität $L_e(x)$ erzeugten Intermodulationen dritter Ordnung steigen ebenfalls mit 6dB pro Oktave an, da das Postfilter $H_2(f)$ die Verzerrungskomponenten unabhängig ihrer Ordnung in gleicher Weise filtert.

5 Schlussfolgerungen

Die nichtlinearen Vorgänge begrenzen die Amplitude der internen Zustandsvariablen und des abgestrahlten Schalldrucksignals. Die dominanten Nichtlinearitäten eines Mikrolautsprechers können mit Hilfe konzentrierter Elemente in einem Netzwerkmodell beschrieben werden. Die nichtlinearen Parameter sind leicht interpretierbar, da ein enger Zusammenhang zwischen elektroakustischer Modellierung und konstruktiver Gestaltung des Wandlers besteht. Die nichtlineare Abhängigkeit der Induktivität $L_e(x,i)$ von der Auslenkung *x* und dem Strom *i* spielt

im Mikrolautsprecher im Unterschied zum Tieftonlautsprecher und Druckkammerlautsprecher eine untergeordnete Rolle. Der Kraftfaktor *Bl(x)* des Mikrolautsprechers ist wie bei Tieftonlautsprechern, die eine erhebliche Auslenkung x erzeugen, eine dominante Nichtlinearität und Verzerrungsursache. Eine verbesserte Linearität des Kraftfaktors, d.h. eine Verminderung des symmetrischen Abfalls der *Bl(x)*-Kurve verringert tendenziell den Wirkungsgrad und die Kennempfindlichkeit des Schallsenders oder erfordert ein größeres und kostenintensiveres Magnetsystem. Asymmetrien in der Kraftfaktorkennlinie können durch eine sorgfältige Justierung der Ruheposition der Schwingspule und optimale Gestaltung des magnetischen Feldes vermindert werden. Die nichtlineare Steifigkeit $K_{ms}(x)$ besitzt im Mikrolautsprecher vielfach eine ausgeprägte asymmetrische Kurvenform, die durch die Sickengeometrie bedingt wird. Die Nichtlinearität des Widerstandes $R_{ms}(v)$ ist im Mikrolautsprecher vorrangig ein strömungsakustisches Problem, das im Luftspalt zwischen Schwingspule und Polflächen und durch Undichtheiten im Gehäuse entsteht.
Die numerische Lösung der Differentialgleichung unter Benutzung der identifizierten Parameter erlaubt die Simulation des Übertragungsverhaltens des Wandlers für ein beliebiges Eingangssignal. Neben der Bewertung der einzelnen Verzerrungsursachen, wie in diesem Beitrag gezeigt, können hiermit auch Konstruktionsvarianten virtuell bewertet werden.
Die systemtheoretische Modellierung des Wandlers ist weiterhin die Grundlage für die Entwicklung von aktiven Steuerungssystemen, die die nichtlinearen Verzerrungen aktiv kompensieren und den Wandler gegen mechanische oder thermische Überlastung schützen.

References

[1] W. Klippel, Tutorial: "Loudspeaker Nonlinearities - Causes, Parameters, Symptoms," J. Audio Eng. Society 54, No. 10 pp. 907-939 (2006 Oct.).

[2] "Sound system equipment - Electroacoustical transducers - Measurement of large signal parameters", International Electrotechnical Commission, PAS 62458 IEC:2006(E).

[3] M. Dodd, et. al., "Voice Coil Impedance as a Function of Frequency and Displacement" presented at the 117th Convention of the Audio Eng. Soc. , 2004 October 28–31, San Francisco, CA, USA.

[4] J. M. Kaizer, "Modeling of the Nonlinear Response of an Electrodynamic Loudspeaker by a Volterra Series Expansion," J. Audio Eng. Soc., vol. 35, pp. 421-433 (1987 June).

[5] W. Klippel, "Measurement of Large-Signal Parameters of Electrodynamic Transducer," presented at the 107th Convention of the Audio Engineering Society, New York, September 24-27, 1999, preprint 5008.

[6] M.H. Knudsen et. al., "Low-Frequency Loudspeaker Models that Include Suspension Creep," J. Audio Eng. Soc., vol. 41, pp. 3-18, (Jan./Feb. 1993).

[7] "Sound System Equipment. Part 5: Loudspeakers," IEC Publication 60268-5.

Modeling of Speech Production from the Perspective of Neuroscience

Bernd J. Kröger[1,2]

[1]*Neurophonetics Group, Department of Phoniatrics, Pedaudiology, and Communication Disorders, Medical School, RWTH Aachen University, Germany*

[2]*Cognitive Computation and Applications Laboratory, School of Computer Science and Technology, Tianjin University, P.R.China*

bernd.kroeger@rwth-aachen.de

Abstract: Recent neural models are capable of generating quantitative patterns of speech articulation and speech acoustics. Five models are discussed here: the DIVA model, the task dynamics model, the ACT model, the Warlaumont model and the Hickok model. These models have a more or less strong background in neuroscience. Directions are identified in this paper for a further development of quantitative production models in order to bring models more in line with recent research outcomes from neuroscience.

1 Introduction

The perhaps best-known model of speech production is the Levelt model [1]. This approach describes the whole process of speech production from intention to articulation. The Levelt model includes the whole linguistic processing from utterance planning towards the generation of a phonological representation and subsequently towards the generation of articulatory speech patterns. In contrast to the Levelt model we will focus in this paper on models which particularly describe the *sensorimotor processes of speech production*, starting with a phonological representation of a speech item, and subsequently generating articulatory movement trajectories and an acoustic speech signal [2, 3, 4, 5, and 6]. These models are *quantitative production models* because they generate measurable articulatory movement patterns and subsequently measurable acoustic speech signals (or at least are prepared to generate these signals in future versions: Hickok model [7]). These models already include some knowledge gained from brain imaging as well as from behavioral experiments and thus are at least particularly *neuroscience based models*.

It is the goal of this paper to identify directions how a quantitative model should be organized in order to be in line with neuroscience related knowledge. Furthermore it should be stated here that it is not the goal of this paper to give a complete survey on all existing models of speech production. This paper mainly reflects models which are closely related to our own model [4] and which to our opinion are important for the future development of this type of speech production models.

2 Existing Production Models

2.1 DIVA Model

The structure of the DIVA model (directions into velocities of articulators model [2]) comprises a feedforward and a feedback control subsystem. The starting level of this model is a *speech sound map*, where a set of model neurons represent language specific speech items (i.e. phonemes, syllables, or short sequences of syllables, with the syllable being the most typical unit represented by a single model neuron [8]). Starting with the activation of a specific model neuron at the level of the speech sound map (i.e. activation of a specific speech item), a *feedforward command* (also labeled as motor command) is activated. At the same time neural representations of an auditory and a somatosensory target region (sensory expectation for that speech item) are co-activated. The forward command generates an articulatory movement pattern via a subsequent co-activation of neural patterns at the level of articulator velocity and position maps (level of primary motor map) and subsequently generates an acoustic speech signal by using an articulatory-acoustic model (speech synthesizer). If the auditory and somatosensory feedback signals derived from these articulatory and acoustic signals (generated by the articulatory-acoustic model) are within the expected auditory and somatosensory target regions mentioned above, no additional motor command (i.e. no additional feedback command) is generated. But if one or both sensory feedback signals exceed the limits defined by sensory target regions at least for a short time interval within the time interval representing the whole speech item, *sensory error signals* are generated for that speech item at the level of the auditory and/or somatosensory error map, and a corrective motor command, also called *feedback command* is activated at the level of the feedback control map within the feedback control loop.

In the DIVA model, the activation of feedforward commands, the co-activated associated sensory target regions for each language specific word or syllable, as well as the sensory-to-motor mapping is part of the feedback control map. This map and its mapping towards other neural maps are trained during a *babbling* and during an *imitation learning process*. The synaptic projections between sensory error maps and motor cortex are tuned during babbling (by using prelinguistic proto-speech items) and build up the feedback control map. All other synaptic projections are trained during imitation. Firstly, an auditory target is learned for each word or syllable of a language. If the model then attempts to produce that speech item, corrective motor commands (feedback commands) are activated for updating and storing the current forward command for that speech item. Normally, more than one attempt is needed in order to train the association of speech items and appropriate forward commands. Secondly, during these production (or imitation) attempts in addition somatosensory target regions are learned from the somatosensory states which were activated for each production attempt.

Auditory error signals mainly occur during early phases of speech acquisition and thus are mainly used for the adjustment and storage of feedforward commands during imitation. Auditory error signals in addition occur, if speech production is perturbed externally, e.g. by shifting the frequencies of F1 and/or of F2 for a defined time interval. DIVA produces fast *compensation* via feedback motor commands (added to the already learned feedforward motor commands) starting approximately 75-150 msec after the perturbation onset. In addition, if the auditory perturbation lasts over a longer time period (e.g. for 25-50 epochs, including approximately 30 word productions within each epoch), the auditory error cell activation leads to a further tuning or *adaptation* of feedforward commands (i.e. to an additional learning effect) which subsequently in addition results in a significant after effect, i.e. which results in occurrence of altered feedforward commands, even after removal (switch off) of the auditory feedback perturbation [9].

In a series of experiments, brain regions are identified to host specific maps of the DIVA model. These results are reported in detail in [10]. Interestingly the (language specific) speech sound map here is mainly associated with the left ventral premotor cortex while the feedback control map, which mainly develops during prelinguistic babbling training, and thus merely reflects general sensorimotor than language-specific behavior, is mainly associated with the right ventral premotor cortex. This is in agreement with studies, reporting a more bilateral activation of brain regions for more general (not langue specific) lower-level speech production mechanismus [11]. Also the locations of auditory and somatosensory feedback processing are listed in detail here [10]. In addition, beside the cortex, the role of cerebellum hosting processing routines for motor commands, and the role of basal ganglia and thalamus, hosting processing routines for initiation of articulation is emphasized.

2.2 Task Dynamic Model

From a linguistic perspective, syllables are structured with respect to constituents like syllable onset, nucleus, and coda, where the syllable nucleus in most cases is represented by a vowel and where syllable onset as well as syllable coda (if occurring) are represented by one or more consonants (consonant clusters). Thus, between the level of phonemic representation (abstract symbolic level) and the primary motor level (i.e. level of representation of ongoing articulatory movement patterns) at least one level should exist, reflecting this organization of syllables. Such a *planning level* as well as the calculation of movement patterns on the basis of this planning is introduced in a quantitative form in the task dynamic approach [3, 13]. Here *vocal tract action units (gestures)* are assumed as basic units of speech production and phasing relations are assumed for quantifying the temporal coordination of these basic speech action units within a syllable.

The task dynamics approach separates two levels, i.e. an intergestural coordination level and an interarticulatory coordination level. At the *intergestural coordination level*, gesture activation is specified (gesture activation "…can be interpreted as the strength with which the associated gestures "attempts" to shape vocal tract movements …" [3, p. 335]) and activation intervals as function of time indicate the temporal organization of all gestures within a syllable, called "gestural score" [13]. At the *interarticulatory coordination level*, the movement pattern is calculated for each model articulator on the basis of articulator-related as well as on the basis of vocal-tract-shape-related (i.e. tract variable) coordinates. Tract variables are assumed in this approach to specify the goal of each gesture (i.e. location and aperture of the vocal tract constriction) in a context independent way, while model articulator variables show the resulting context dependent movement pattern for each model articulator during the articulation of a speech item.

Gestures are modeled quantitatively as *time-invariant dynamical systems* (more specifically *point-attractor systems* or critically damped *oscillator systems*) and thus each gesture defines a *class* of goal-directed movements. But the production of a speech item and thus the underlying gestures (i.e. group of dynamical systems) become time dependent with respect to the fact that gesture activation is time-dependent: gesture activation starts and ends at specific points in time. The contextual variation of articulation is simulated in this approach by the interplay of intergestural and interarticulatory coordination. In addition this approach is capable of modeling *compensatory articulation* with respect to mechanical perturbations at the level of the vocal tract (e.g. fixation of the lower jaw by bite-blocks [14, 15]) due to the interplay between the two basic levels introduced in the task dynamic model.

2.3 ACT Model

Our ACTion-based model of speech production, speech perception, and speech acquisition [4] is comparable to the DIVA model but augmented in a way that we not only assume a phonemic map, were one model neuron represents one syllable, but that in addition a *high-level motor representation (motor plan)* is assumed, where the temporal coordination and degree of activation of all vocal tract actions, building up a syllable, is represented in a comparable way as it is represented in a gesture score in the task dynamic approach. Model articulator movements are calculated on the basis of this motor plan for each syllable [16]. Subsequently an articulatory-acoustic model (articulatory synthesizer) generates articulatory movement patterns and an acoustic speech signal [17]. Auditory and somatosensory feedback signals are generated and these signals can be compared with auditory and somatosensory expectations, co-activated with the activation of a specific speech item at the phonemic level (cf. DIVA model).

A main difference to DIVA can be seen in the fact that a supramodal self-organizing map, called *phonetic map* is introduced in ACT, which is associated with the higher-level motor map (containing the motor plan of a syllable), with the high-level auditory and somatosensory map (containing neural activation patterns of the sensory expectations for each syllable), and with the phonemic map (where each phonological representation of a syllable is represented by one model neuron). During imitation training (see below) the model neurons within the phonetic map represent phonetic realizations of syllables. The neural connections between a model neuron of the phonetic map and the neurons of the high-level motor and sensory map store the motor plan and sensory representation for a specific realization of a syllable.

Thus, our model in parallel to Levelt and Wheeldon [18] and to Levelt et al. [1] emphasizes the importance of knowledge and *sensorimotor skill repositories*. A higher level cognitive repository is the *mental lexicon*, comprising concepts, lemmas, and word forms (all symbolic), while a lower level sensorimotor repository, i.e. a *mental syllablary* is assumed, comprising complete gesture scores and sensory expectations of at least high frequent syllables for the spoken language [1, 18]. The existence of this repository reduces the computational load (i.e. the load for generation of the motor plan) during syllable articulation. After a syllabification process [1], the motor program for syllables need not to be assembled (or generated) on the basis of a segment chain, but can be activated as a whole at the level of the mental syllabary.

Babbling training is performed in ACT in order to supply the model with first auditory-to-motor associations. This enables first *language specific imitation* trials since due to babbling the model already has available some auditory-to-motor associative knowledge and thus is capable of producing first motor plans. If the resulting speech item is not awarded by the caretaker, more imitation trials are performed (cf. DIVA, but target "regions" are replaced here by a perceptual "acceptance range" defined by a caretaker). Thus in contrast to DIVA the *communicative interaction process* between model (or toddler) and teacher (or caretaker) is emphasized in our model. Sensorimotor babbling knowledge (sensory-to-motor associations for proto-syllables) as well as language specific knowledge after imitation training (i.e. motor plans and sensory expectations for syllables) is both stored by (i) the organization of the phonetic map and (ii) within the synaptic link weights between phonetic map and motor plan map, between phonetic map and sensory maps, and between phonetic map and phonemic map.

In contrast to the task dynamics approach, *no rules* are predefined in ACT for the relative timing of vocal tract actions within a syllable. This timing of vocal tract actions is (intuitively) learned by the model during imitation training. But due to the resulting self-organized phonetic map, language specific phasing rules can be derived from the occurring motor plans, which are already stored within the neural associations between phonetic map and motor plan map. Typically self-organizing maps allow generalization and thus the extraction of rules, if the number of training items is much larger than the number of model neurons within the self-organizing map.

Last but not least it should be mentioned that ACT includes a model of *speech perception* as well. Since DIVA as well as our approach include auditory feedback, it is obvious to widen the production model in order to become a production-perception model. In the case of ACT we are capable to show, that a stronger *categorical perception* occurs for consonants in comparison to vowels, which is related to the spatial (self-)organization of syllables within the phonetic map [4].

2.4 Warlaumont Model: Emphasizing reinforcement

This model concentrates on prespeech motor learning (mainly babbling) but beside babbling also includes the emergence of phoneme learning by using *reinforcement-gated self-organized learning* [5]. Thus, not imitation of caretakers' productions of speech items is focused on in this approach. But reinforcement by caregivers (i.e. whether a speech items sounds like a phoneme realization in the target language; extrinsic reinforcement) as well as self-reinforcement (intrinsic reinforcement) is introduced. A *self-organizing map* is postulated here at the motor neuron level. Learning results indicate that reinforcement learning leads to an emergence of muscle activation patterns for stable phonations and to an emergence of muscle activation patterns for phoneme realizations.

2.5 Hickok Model: Emphasizing Hierarchy and Neuroanatomy

Hickok [6] argues for a neuroanatomically grounded, hierarchical state feedback control model of speech production. The hierarchy comprises four levels, (i) a *conceptual level*, (ii) a *lemma level*, (iii) an *auditory level* and (iv) a *somatosensory level*. Hickok assumes that "the auditory system (is) driving higher-level control of the (syllabic opening-closing) cycles or half-cycles" [ibid., p. 139], while "the somatosensory system (is) driving lower-level online control that target the end point of a vocalic opening or closing" [ibid., p.139], i.e. consonantal and vocalic target points. This hierarchy is motivated by the fact that especially consonants like plosives show different acoustic (and thus auditory) patterns in different syllable contexts and thus cannot be associated with simple invariant auditory targets (as is the case for vowels and consonants, which can be produced in isolation), while clear articulatory and somatosensory targets or target regions exist.

Neuroanatomical locations are specified explicitly for the higher-level auditory and lower-level somatosensory control loop. The higher-level auditory control loop comprises auditory processing regions (superior temporal gyrus STG and superior temporal sulcus STS), the Spt-region (Sylviain fissure at the pariotemporal boundary) for auditory-motor-association, and the Brodman area 44 for the activation of higher-level (syllable sized) motor programs. The lower-level somatosensory control loop comprises somatosensory processing regions (anterior supramarginal gyrus aSMG and primary somatosensory cortex S1), the cerebellum for somatosensory-motor-association, and the ventral Brodman area 6 as well as primary motor cortex for the activation of lower-level (speech sound sized) motor programs.

Furthermore Hickok [6] emphasizes the importance of *internal forward models* (cf. [19]) because "sensory feedback alone cannot support ... a (high) correction effiency" [6, p. 136] and thus an "internal forward-looking mechanism" [ibid., p. 136], is needed, capable of "mak(ing) predictions regarding the current (articulatory) state" [ibid.; see also 19]. But it is emphasized that this "internal forward-looking mechanism is particularly useful for online movement control" [6, p.136], while feedback is crucial for three purposes: (i) learning sensorimotor relationships, (2) update of the internal model in case of persistent mismatches and (iii) to detect and correct for sudden perturbations [ibid., p. 136]. It is stated that we have to separate *external feedback control* and *internal feedback control* [ibid., p. 136], both occurring within the higher-level as well as within the lower-level feedback control circuits.

3 Directions for Developing Future Quantiative Neural Models

Models of speech production should clearly separate *structure* and *knowledge*. Structure should be hierarchical and should include top-down (e.g. motor commands) as well as with bottom-up interaction (e.g. generation and processing of feedback signals). We argue for a separation of a cognitive phonological level (phonemic map, processing abstract symbolic linguistic units), a multi- or supramodal phonetic level (phonetic map), unimodal high-level motor levels [3, 4] and sensory levels [2], as well as lower-level motor as well as sensory levels. With respect to Hickock [6], a lower-level somatosensory level should directly provide feedback towards motor representations via the cerebellum, while the auditory level provides feedback to at least syllable-sized motor plans. Thus in our model ACT, lower-level sensory representations cover time intervals of 10-50msec, while higher-level sensory representations cover syllable sized time intervals from 50-500msec. Moreover lower-level somatosensory signals are assumed to be tactile and articulator-related proprioceptive information (relative coordinates) while higher-level somatosensory signals are assumed to be tactile as well as vocal-tract-related articulator positions (absolute coordinates), directly defining the vocal tract shape.

A further important concept is the introduction of a *sensorimotor repository*. A mental syllabary [1, 18] allows that 80% of all spoken syllables is based on just 500 (frequent) syllables (in the case of Standard German [20]). Thus the storage of motor plans of just 500 syllables discharged computational effort for motor plans dramatically. Thus in ACT a sensorimotor syllable repository is assumed. Lower frequent syllables can be assembled by co-activating phonetically similar higher frequent syllables and thus by taking motor plan parameters from these already learned syllables [21].

Concerning *learning* it is very interesting to state that the Warlaumont model [5] is capable of learning phoneme realizations without giving reference targets, i.e. without using imitation training [cf. 4]). The targets (phoneme regions) learned here, are derived exclusively from reinforcing specific babbling items. This allows training a speech production model without using imitation and thus the model (learner, toddler) has no to deal with the *vocal tract normalization problem* [22], because the learning only takes into account the speech items produced by the model itself.

The Warlaumont model [5] as well as the ACT model [4] use *self-organizing neural networks* (Kohonen networks [23]) for simulating neural learning and processing processes. Kohonen networks as well as the network approach used in DIVA [2] can be summarized as *rate models* (in contrast to *spiking neuron models*). Rate models integrate neuron activity over specific time intervals (e.g. 20 … 50 msec) and "model neurons" (i.e. groups on real neurons located close together and having similar functions) are defined in order to integrate over space as well. Rate models process neuron spike *rates* in contrast to real (but complex) *spike time patterns* [24]. Currently no comprehensive spiking neuron model is known, capable to describe main aspects of speech production and speech acquisition (e.g. as in ACT [4]), so that currently rate models seem to be the appropriate choice.

A very important feature, which has been highlighted by Hickok [6] is, that two different types of feedback need to be differentiated (see above). *External feedback* allows adaptation (see also DIVA model [2]) while *internal feedback (inner models)* allow online corrections during motor execution of a motor plan (see also the *state feedback control model* of Houde and Nagarajan [19]). In concepts like ACT [4], computational or programming processes are assumed as not thus important. Moreover, neural processes are mainly forwarding neural activation by using already adjusted synaptic link weights (adjusted during learning phases). Correction processes as proposed by state feedback models are mainly motivated from models for arm and hand movement control, where the human with his arms and hands always needs to interact with *different environments* (i.e. different locations, different rooms etc.). But especially in the case of speech the target directed articulator movements always occur in the same "room", i.e. within speakers vocal tract. Thus the importance of state feedback control should remain a matter of debate.

4 Concluding Remark

We are at the very beginning concerning the development of neuroscience based models of speech production. Neuroscience based architectures (i.e. architectures based on imaging experiments) are already suggested and used in some of these models. Also behavior based learning concepts have been used in simulation experiments for speech acquisition by using these models. But there is still a long way in order to model (or imitate) speech production from brain to articulation (including feedback) in a natural way, so that realistic neural function processes like spiking neuron approaches are used and so that a lot of "macroscopic" behavioral data (e.g. learning of articulatory skills, adaptation, compensation etc.) can be explained by realistic "microscopic" neural processes.

Acknowledgements

This work is partially supported by the National Natural Science Foundation of China (Grant No. 61233009)

Literature

[1] Levelt WJM, Roelofs A, Meyer AS (1999) A theory of lexical access in speech production. Behavioral and Brain Sciences 22, 1-75

[2] Guenther FH, Ghosh SS, Tourville JA (2006) Neural modeling and imaging of the cortical interactions underlying syllable production. Brain and Language 96, 280-301

[3] Saltzman EL, Munhall KG (1989) A dynamical approach to gestural patterning in speech production. Ecological Psychology 1, 333-382

[4] Kröger BJ, Kannampuzha J, Neuschaefer-Rube C (2009) Towards a neurocomputational model of speech production and perception. Speech Communication 51: 793-809

[5] Warlaumont AS, Westermann G, Buder EH, Oller DK (2013) Prespeech motor learning in a neural network using reinforcement. Neural Networks 38, 64-75

[6] Hickok G (2012) Computational neuroanatomy of speech production. Nature Reviews Neuroscience 13, 135-145

[7] Walker G, Rong F, Hickok G (2012) An artificial neural network (ANN) model of sensorimotor development for speech. Abstracts of Neurobiology of Language Conference 2012 (San Sebastian, Spain), pp. 58-59

[8] Guenther FH, Vladusich T (2012) A neural theory of speech acquisition and production. Journal of Neurolinguistics 25, 408-422

[9] Guenther FH (2006) Cortical interaction underlying the production of speech sounds. Journal of Communication Disorders 39, 350-365

[10] Golfinopoulos E, Tourville JA, Guenther FH (2010) The integration of large-scale neural network modeling and functional brain imaging in speech motor control. NeuroImage 52, 862-874

[11] Riecker A, Mathiak K, Wildgruber D, Erb M, Hertrich I, Grodd W, Ackermann H (2005) fMRI reveals two distinct cerebral networks subserving speech motor control. Neurology 64, 700-706

[13] Goldstein L, Byrd D, Saltzman E (2006). The role of vocal tract action units in understanding the evolution of phonology. In: Arbib MA (Ed.) Action to Language via the Mirror Neuron System. (Cambridge University Press, Cambridge), pp. 215-249

[14] Fowler CA, Turvey MT (1980) Immediate compensation in bite-block speech. Phonetica 37, 306-326

[15] McFarland DH, Baum SR (1995) Incomplete compensation to articulatory perturbation. Journal of the Acoustical Society of America 97, 1865-1873

[16] Kröger BJ, Birkholz P, Kannampuzha J, Eckers C, Kaufmann E, Neuschaefer-Rube C (2011) Neurobiological interpretation of a quantitative target approximation model for speech actions. In: Kröger BJ, Birkholz P (eds.) Studientexte zur Sprachkommunikation: Elektronische Sprachsignalverarbeitung 2011 (TUDpress, Dresden, Germany), pp. 184-194

[17] Kröger BJ, Birkholz P (2007) A gesture-based concept for speech movement control in articulatory speech synthesis. In: Esposito A, Faundez-Zanuy M, Keller E, Marinaro M (eds.) Verbal and Nonverbal Communication Behaviours, LNAI 4775 (Springer Verlag, Berlin, Heidelberg) pp. 174-189

[18] Levelt WJM, Wheeldon L (1994) Do speakers have access to a mental syllabary? Cognition 50, 239-269

[19] Houde JF, Nagarajan SS (2011) Speech production as state feedback control. Frontiers in Human Neuroscience 5, 82: doi: 10.3389/fnhum.2011.00082

[20] Kröger BJ, Birkholz P, Kannampuzha J, Kaufmann E, Neuschaefer-Rube C (2011) Towards the acquisition of a sensorimotor vocal tract action repository within a neural model of speech processing. In: Esposito A, Vinciarelli A, Vicsi K, Pelachaud C, Nijholt A (eds.) Analysis of Verbal and Nonverbal Communication and Enactment: The Processing Issues. LNCS 6800 (Springer, Berlin), pp. 287-293

[21] Kröger BJ, Miller N, Lowit A, Neuschaefer-Rube C. (2011) Defective neural motor speech mappings as a source for apraxia of speech: Evidence from a quantitative neural model of speech processing. In: Lowit A, Kent R (eds.) Assessment of Motor Speech Disorders. (Plural Publishing, San Diego, CA), pp. 325-346

[22] Johnson K (2008). Speaker normalization in speech perception. In: Pisoni DB, Remez RE (Eds.) The Handbook of Speech Perception. (Oxford, UK: Blackwell), pp. 363-389

[23] Kohonen T (2001) Self-Organizing Maps. (Springer, Berlin, Germany, 3rd edition)

[24] Kasabov N (2010) To spike or not to spike: A probabilistic spiking neuron model. Neural Networks 23, 16-19

DIE ERKENNBARKEIT VERTRAUTER STIMMEN BEI VERSTELLUNG

Angelika Braun und Lydia Kraft

Universität Trier, Fachbereich II, Phonetik

brauna@uni-trier.de

Abstract: Dieser Beitrag befasst sich mit den Auswirkungen zweier Verstellungstypen des stimmlichen Verhaltens (Flüstern und Falsett) auf die Erkennbarkeit eines Sprechers durch vertraute Personen. Zehn Sprecher wurden von 32 Hörern beurteilt, die jeweils einen der Sprecher sehr gut kannten. Während die Erkennungsrate bei Modalstimme fast perfekt ist, sinkt sie im Modus "Flüstern" deutlich ab und fällt im Modul "Falsett" weiter. Gleichzeitig steigt die Rate der Falschidentifizierungen an. Männliche Zielsprecher werden generell besser erkannt als weibliche; signifikant ist diese Differenz jedoch lediglich im Modus "Falsett". Weibliche Hörer weisen allgemein eine bessere Identifizierungsleistung auf als männliche, wobei der Unterschied allerdings nur für den Modus "Flüstern" Signifikanzniveau erreicht.

1 Einleitung

In der forensischen Sprachverarbeitung geht es bei der Durchführung von Stimmenvergleichen normalerweise um eine hochspezialisierte Leistung von einschlägig ausgebildeten Experten (vgl. z.B. Rose 1998, Braun 2011, Jessen 2012). Diese Vergleiche basieren auf dem Abgleich zwischen mindestens einer fraglichen Aufzeichnung und mindestens einer Vergleichsaufzeichnung.

Es sind allerdings auch immer wieder Fälle zu verzeichnen, in denen keine fragliche Aufzeichnung existiert, sondern lediglich Opfer und/oder Zeugen vorhanden sind, die behaupten, den jeweiligen Sprecher identifizieren zu können. Dies geschieht regelmäßig bei Raubüberfällen in Banken oder Tankstellen (sofern die vorhandenen Überwachungssysteme keine Tonaufzeichnung beinhalten) bzw. in Wohnungen oder auch bei Vergewaltigungsdelikten.

In den meisten dieser Fälle findet die Familiarisierung des Opfers/Zeugen mit der Täterstimme in der Tatsituation statt. Im Rahmen einer sog. akustischen Wahlgegenüberstellung (*voice line-up*) wird die Stimme einer verdächtigen Person den Opfern/Zeugen zusammen mit einer Reihe von Distraktoren vorgespielt in der Hoffnung, dass die Betroffenen eine Zuordnung vornehmen können. Die Aufgabe des forensisch-phonetischen Sachverständigen besteht in der Erarbeitung eines für alle Beteiligten fairen Wiedererkennungsexperiments. Hier ist vor allem die Auswahl der Distraktoren wichtig, die der Stimme des Verdächtigen weder zu unähnlich (unfair gegenüber dem Verdächtigen) noch zu ähnlich (unverhältnismäßig schwierig für die Opfer/Zeugen) sein dürfen. Broeders und van Amelsvoort (1999) haben eine hilfreiche Richtlinie erarbeitet, die international auf breite Zustimmung stößt und auch in Deutschland Anwendung findet.

Ein Sonderfall der Wiedererkennung einer Stimme durch Opfer und/oder Zeugen liegt dann vor, wenn nicht die Familiarisierung, sondern die Wiedererkennung in der Tatsituation stattfindet, weil ein Opfer oder Zeuge behauptet, im Täter eine – oft seit Jahren oder gar Jahrzehnten – vertraute Person wiederzuerkennen. In diesen Fällen ist eine "klassische" akustische Wahlgegenüberstellung nicht sinnvoll, da die Erkennungsleistung ja bereits stattgefunden hat (Broeders / Rietveld 1995, 26-27). Sie kann allenfalls dazu dienen, den Nachweis dafür zu erbringen, dass die Betroffenen tatsächlich in der Lage sind, den behaupteten Sprecher zu erkennen, wenn seine Stimme zusammen mit ähnlichen Stimmen dargeboten wird.

Dennoch ist es von Interesse zu untersuchen, wie gut (oder schlecht) vertraute Personen erkannt werden, besonders wenn das stimmlich-sprachliche Verhalten verstellt wird bzw. besonderen situativen Einflüssen unterliegt. Ersteres ist nicht selten bei Drohungen zu beobachten, die beispielsweise im Rahmen von Nachbarschaftskonflikten telefonisch geäußert werden. Letzteres tritt auf, wenn Eltern oder Ehepartner in Entführungsfällen entscheiden sollen, ob es sich bei einer Sprachaufzeichnung als "Lebenszeichen" tatsächlich um die Stimme des Kindes oder Partners handelt. Da solche Aufzeichnungen unter erheblichem Stress entstehen, ist diese Entscheidung nicht immer trivial.

Da die Erkennung vertrauter Stimmen im forensischen Kontext recht selten auftritt und das Interesse an Grundlagenforschung zu einem möglichen Vertrautheitsvorsprung bei der Wiedererkennung eines Sprechers noch in den Anfängen steht, ist die Forschungslage überaus spärlich. Hollien et al. (1982) untersuchten die Erkennungsleistung unterschiedlicher Hörergruppen anhand von zehn männlichen Sprechern, die je eine Probe ihrer Modalstimme, eine Probe unter Stress (induziert durch leichte Elektroschocks) und eine verstellte Probe abgaben. Die Sprecher durften die Art der Verstellung frei wählen; allerdings waren Flüstern und die Vortäuschung eines fremdsprachigen Akzents ausgeschlossen. Drei Gruppen von Hörern absolvierten ein Wiedererkennungsexperiment mit diesen zehn Sprechern: die erste kannte die Sprecher seit Jahren gut, die zweite kannte die Sprecher nicht, wurde jedoch mit deren Modalstimmen familiarisiert, die dritte Gruppe kannte die Sprecher nicht und verstand den Inhalt der Sprachprobe nicht. Die Hörer hatten die Aufgabe, sechs Proben pro Sprecher (je zwei modale, verstellte und unter Stress produzierte) dem richtigen Sprecher zuzuordnen. Ausgewertet wurde der Prozentsatz der korrekten Identifizierungen. Es zeigte sich zum einen ein signifikanter Vertrautheitsvorsprung bei der Identifizierung der jeweiligen Zielsprecher (alle drei Hörergruppen unterschieden sich signifikant), zum anderen war die Performanz bei Verstellung in allen drei Gruppen signifikant schlechter als bei Modalstimme und induziertem Stress. Selbst bei den mit den Sprechern vertrauten Hörern nahm sie von 98% auf 79% ab.

Wagner und Köster (1999) untersuchten den Effekt von Falsett auf die Erkennung eines vertrauten Sprechers. Sie verwendeten fünf männliche Sprecher als Zielsprecher und weitere drei als Distraktoren. Sowohl modale Proben als auch Falsett-Proben wurden nach Telefonübertragung aufgezeichnet. Insgesamt 20 Hörer, die alle jahrelang mit den Sprechern zusammengearbeitet hatten, bekamen die Aufgabe, auf der Basis von insgesamt 48 je 15 Sekunden langen Proben den jeweiligen Sprecher zu benennen (*familiar speaker naming task*), wobei es sich bei der Hälfte der Proben um Falsett-Stimuli handelte. Die Anzahl der korrekten Identifizierungen sank von 97% bei Modalstimme auf 4% bei den Falsett-Stimuli ab. Andererseits war bei modalen Stimuli mit 29% Falschidentifizierungen eine aus forensischer Sicht alarmierende Rate zu verzeichnen. Diese Art von Fehler trat bei Falsett nur in 1% der Fälle auf.

Die der hier vorgelegten am ehesten vergleichbaren Studien stammen von Rose und Duncan (1995) sowie von Daniel Yarmey und Kollegen. Rose und Duncan untersuchten die Erkennung unverstellter vertrauter Stimmen. Insgesamt wurden sechs Sprecher (vier Zielsprecher und zwei *foils* aufgezeichnet. Zehn Hörer führten verschiedene Erkennungsexperimente durch, von denen hier dasjenige referiert wird, bei dem die Stimulusdauer ca. 45 Sekunden betrug. Die Trefferrate betrug 97% bei einer Gesamt-Fehlerrate von 15%. Die Autoren schätzen die Wahrscheinlichkeit einer Falschidentifizierung auf ca. 5% (Rose / Duncan 1995, 15-16).

Orchard und Yarmey familiarisierten unterschiedliche Hörergruppen mit "markanten" oder weniger "markanten" Stimmen in zwei verschiedenen Modi: modal und Flüstern. Die Dauer der Familiarisierung betrug 30 Sekunden oder acht Minuten. Zwei Tage nach der Familiarisierung wurden *voice line-ups* mit insgesamt sechs Sprechern durchgeführt, in denen der fragliche Sprecher entweder enthalten (*suspect present*) oder nicht enthalten (*subject absent*) war. Die Modalitäten der Darbietung in der Familiarisierungs- und Testsituation waren entweder übereinstimmend oder inkongruent. Die Ergebnisse zeigten signifikant bessere Erkennungsleistungen durch Hörer, die eine längere Familiarisierungsphase durchlaufen hatten. Bei den "markanten" Stimmen unterschied sich die Erkennungsleistung zwischen Modalstimme und Flüstern nicht signifikant, solange Familiarisierung und Wiedererkennung im gleichen Modus erfolgten. Wenn der Modus allerdings wechselte (z.B. Familiarisierung mit Modalstimme, Erkennungsexperiment anhand geflüsterter Stimuli), war die Erkennungsleistung signifikant schlechter. Bei den "unmarkierten" Stimmen war die Leistung der Hörer signifikant besser, wenn ausschließlich modale Stimuli involviert waren, als bei geflüsterten oder gemischt-modalen Stimuli.

Aus dieser Studie kann man vorsichtig folgern, dass die Dauer der Exposition offenbar auch unter ungünstigen Umständen einen Unterschied in der Erkennungsleistung mit sich bringt, wobei aufgrund des Untersuchungsdesigns unklar bleibt, welche Auswirkungen ein Wechsel der Modalität für Menschen hat, die über viele Jahre hinweg mit dem Sprecher vertraut sind.

Alle erwähnten Studien weisen unterschiedliche Designs auf, so dass die Ergebnisse nur schwer vergleichbar sind. Übereinstimmend finden sie einen Vertrautheitsvorsprung bei Hörern, die mit dem fraglichen Sprecher gut bekannt sind, sowie eine Abnahme der Erkennungsleistung bei geflüsterten und mit Kopfstimme gesprochenen Stimuli. Die Frage des Sprecher- und Hörergeschlechts wird in keiner der Untersuchungen thematisiert.

Diese Untersuchung beschäftigt sich mit folgenden Fragestellungen, wobei sie sich ausdrücklich um Nähe zu forensisch relevanten Szenarien bemüht:

- Ist die Erkennungsleistung durch vertraute Hörer bei Flüsterstimme geringer als bei Modalstimme?
- Ist die Erkennungsleistung durch vertraute Hörer bei Kopfstimme geringer als bei Modalstimme?
- Unterscheidet sich die Erkennungsleistung durch vertraute Hörer bei Flüsterstimme von der bei Kopfstimme?
- Beeinflusst das Sprechergeschlecht die Erkennungsleistung?
- Beeinflusst das Hörergeschlecht die Erkennungsleistung?

2 Material und Methode

2.1 Sprecher

Insgesamt zehn Sprecher (fünf Frauen und fünf Männer) dienten als Zielsprecher. Sie waren 20 bis 42 Jahre alt, wobei das Durchschnittsalter der Männer 30 und das der Frauen 26 Jahre betrug. Alle sprachen muttersprachliches Deutsch ohne deutliche regionale Prägung oder Sprechfehler. Die Sprecher hatten die Aufgabe, das Bild einer bunten Unterwasserwelt in ganzen Sätzen ohne "Aufzählungsintonation" zu beschreiben, und zwar jeweils 60 Sekunden lang in Modalstimme, Flüsterstimme und Falsett. Die Proben wurden jeweils in drei Abschnitte à 20 Sekunden unterteilt. Auf diese Weise entstanden insgesamt 90 Proben (zehn Sprecher x drei Bedingungen x drei Proben).

2.2 Hörer

Jeder Sprecher benannte mindestens drei Hörer, die als nahe Verwandte oder sehr gute Freunde jahrelangen engen Kontakt zum Zielsprecher in einer großen situativen Variationsbreite besaßen. Auf diese Weise wurden 32 Hörer ausgewählt, von denen 15 männlich und 17 weiblich waren. Ihr Alter betrug im Mittel 38 Jahre bei einer Spannweite von 20 bis 69 Jahren. Die Zuordnung männlicher und weiblicher Hörer zu männlichen und weiblichen "Zielsprechern" war fast ausgewogen: von den 15 männlichen Hörern hatten sieben weibliche und acht männliche Zielsprecher; von den 17 weiblichen Hörern hatten zehn weibliche und sieben männliche Zielsprecher.

2.3 Hörtest und Aufgabe

Die erwähnten 90 Proben wurden randomisiert und zu einem Hörtest von ca. 35 min. Dauer zusammengefasst. Auf eine Differenzierung nach Sprechergeschlecht wurde bewusst verzichtet, weil dieses in beiden Verstellungsmodi – und im übrigen selbst bei Modalstimme – erfahrungsgemäß nicht sicher erkennbar ist. Durch getrennte Darbietung von männlichen und weiblichen Stimuli wäre die Aufgabe der Hörer erheblich erleichtert worden.

Die Hörer bekamen ihre jeweilige Zielperson genannt. Sie hatten die Aufgabe, in einem *forced choice* Design zu entscheiden, ob es sich bei dem jeweiligen Stimulus um die Zielperson handelt oder nicht. Zusätzlich wurde die Urteilssicherheit erfragt. Aus Platzgründen werden hier ausschließlich die kategorialen Entscheidungen berücksichtigt.

3 Ergebnisse

3.1 Erkennungs- und Falschidentifizierungsraten allgemein

Bei Perzeptionsstudien können neben korrekten Identifizierungen (*hits*) zwei Arten von Fehlern vorkommen, die aus forensischer Perspektive sehr unterschiedliche Auswirkungen haben: Falschidentifizierungen (*false alarms*) und Falschzurückweisungen (*missed hits*). In dem hier diskutierten Rahmen sind besonders die ersteren problematisch, weil sie in einem konkreten Fall einen Unschuldigen belasten würden. Sie werden daher in den Abbildungen gesondert ausgewiesen. (So könnte ein Hörer theoretisch eine perfekte Identifizierungsleistung dadurch erreichen, dass er oder sie alle Stimuli als Treffer markiert. Dadurch würden zwar alle Zielstimuli erkannt, aber gleichzeitig alle anderen fälschlich als Treffer gekennzeichnet. Aus diesem Grund ist es unabdingbar, neben den Treffern auch die Falschidentifizierungen in die Auswertung einzubeziehen.)

Die statistischen Analysen wurden – je nachdem, ob die Daten normalverteilt waren oder nicht – als Paarvergleiche mittels t-Test oder Mann-Whitney U-Test durchgeführt. Da angenommen werden durfte, dass zum einen unverstellte Stimuli besser erkannt werden würden als verstellte und zum zweiten Falsett schwieriger zu erkennen ist als Flüstern, kamen hier jeweils einseitige Tests zur Anwendung. Bei der Untersuchung des Sprecher- und Hörergeschlechts wurden zweiseitige Tests verwendet. Das Signifikanzniveau wurde bei 5% angesetzt. – Abbildung 1 zeigt die Treffer und Falschidentifizierungen aller Hörer, aufgeschlüsselt nach Sprechmodi:

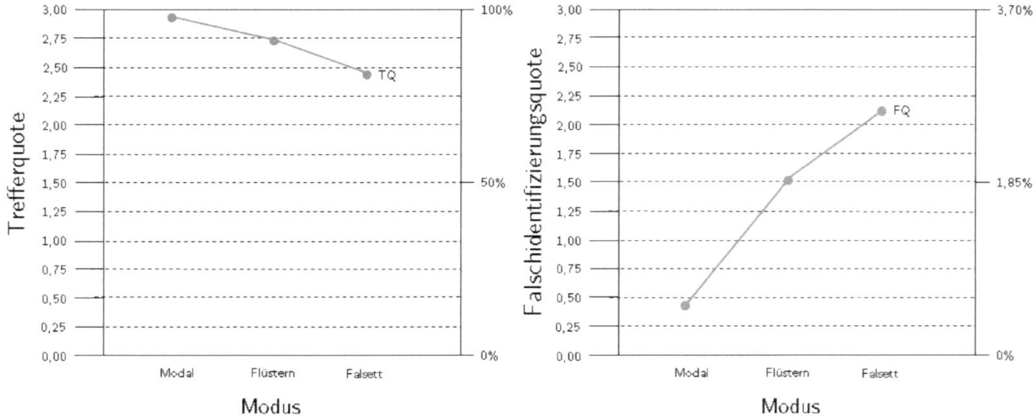

Abbildung 1: Trefferquoten und Falschidentifizierungen nach Sprechmodus, gemittelt über alle Hörer. (Die linke Skala in der Ordinate bezieht sich auf die maximal mögliche Zahl von drei korrekten Identifizierungen pro Sprecher pro Bedingung.)

Tabelle 1 enthält die genauen Prozentsätze für die drei untersuchten Sprechmodi:

Modus	**Geschlecht Zielperson**	**TQ in %**	**FQ in %**
Modal	weiblich und männlich	99,0	0,6
Flüstern	weiblich und männlich	91,0	1,9
Falsett	weiblich und männlich	81,2	2,6

Tabelle 1: Trefferquoten (TQ) und Falschidentifizierungen (FQ) nach Sprechmodus, gemittelt über alle Sprecher und Hörer.

Die Trefferquote bei den Stimuli mit Modalstimme ist nahezu perfekt.[1] Dies spricht für die Validität der Auswahl der Hörer – sie sind unter optimalen Bedingungen in der Lage, ihre Zielperson zuverlässig zu erkennen. Es zeigt sich, dass die Anzahl korrekter Identifizierungen auch unter erschwerten Bedingungen nicht dramatisch absinkt; dennoch unterscheidet sich die Differenz zwischen der Trefferquote bei Modalstimme (99%) und der beim Flüstern (91%) signifikant (p = 0,016). Die Differenz zwischen Modalstimme und Falsett (Trefferquote = 81%) ist noch wesentlich deutlicher: In diesem Fall ist der Unterschied hochsignifikant (p = 0,002). Das bedeutet, dass beide Verstellungstypen selbst bei vertrauten Hörern zu einer deutlichen Verschlechterung der Erkennungsleistung führen. Die Differenz in der Erkennungsleistung zwischen Flüstern und Falsett verfehlt allerdings das Signifikanzniveau knapp (p = 0,063).

Bemerkenswert – und aus forensischer Sicht ermutigend – ist die geringe Zahl an Falschidentifizierungen, die selbst unter erschwerten Bedingungen (Falsett) unter drei Prozent liegt. Die Hörer waren somit nicht nur ausgezeichnet mit den Stimmen ihrer Zielpersonen vertraut, sondern offenbar auch sehr konservativ in ihrem Antwortverhalten, d.h. sie zeigten

[1] Der eine Fall von Falsch-Rückweisung könnte lt. Auskunft des betreffenden Hörers auf ein "Verrutschen" in der Antwortzeile zurückzuführen sein. Da sich dies im nachhinein nicht objektivieren lässt, wird die Antwort gleichwohl als falsch bewertet.

wenig Neigung, Sprecher fälschlicherweise als Zielsprecher zu bezeichnen. Die statistische Analyse (t-Test einseitig) zeigt jeweils höchstsignifikante Unterschiede zwischen Modalstimme und Flüstern sowie zwischen Modalstimme und Falsett (p = 0,000). Flüstern und Falsett unterscheiden sich hochsignifikant (p = 0,003).

3.2 Erkennungs- und Falschidentifizierungsraten nach Geschlecht der Zielperson

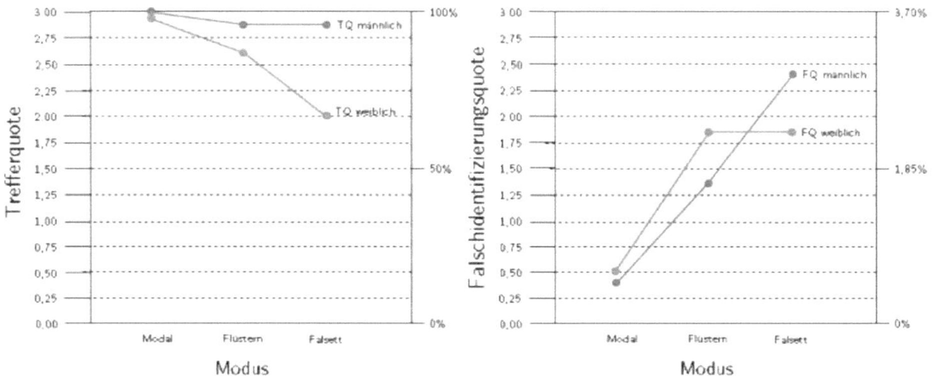

Abbildung 2: Trefferquoten und Falschidentifizierungen nach Sprechergeschlecht und Sprechmodus

Modus	Geschlecht Zielperson	TQ in %	FQ in %
Modal	weiblich	98,0	0,6
	männlich	100,0	0,5
Flüstern	weiblich	86,3	2,3
	männlich	95,7	1,6
Falsett	weiblich	66,7	2,3
	männlich	95,7	3,0

Es fällt auf, dass sich die Identifizierungsquoten für weibliche (98%) und männliche (100%) Zielsprecher bei modaler Sprechlage sehr stark gleichen. Der zweiseitige t-Test ergibt, dass sie sich nicht signifikant unterscheiden (p = 1,0). Gleiches gilt für die Falschidentifizierungen bei diesem Sprechmodus (p = 0,557).

Im Flüstermodus sinkt die Trefferquote bei weiblichen Sprechern stärker als bei männlichen, (86% verglichen mit 96%), die Differenz erweist sich jedoch als nicht signifikant (p = 0,347). Dies trifft auch für die Falschidentifizierungsraten zu, die für weibliche Sprecher geringfügig höher liegen als für männliche Sprecher.

Im Falsett-Modus hingegen zeigt sich ein deutlicher Abfall der Erkennungsraten. Die Trefferquote bei weiblichen Sprechern ist zudem mit 67% hochsignifikant niedriger als bei männlichen (p = 0,007). Der Trend bei den Falschidentifizierungen kehrt sich um insofern, als hier – anders als bei Flüstersprache – männliche Stimmen häufiger einer Fehleinschätzung unterliegen als weibliche. Diese Differenz ist allerdings nicht signifikant (p = 0,64).

3.3 Erkennungs- und Falschidentifizierungsraten nach Geschlecht der Hörer

Modus	Geschlecht Hörer	TQ in %	FQ in %
Modal	weiblich	100,0	0,3
	männlich	97,7	0,9
Flüstern	weiblich	98,0	1,7
	männlich	82,3	2,3
Falsett	weiblich	78,3	1,9
	männlich	82,3	3,4

Tabelle 3: Erkennungsraten (TQ) und Falschidentifizierungsraten (FQ) in Prozent, aufgeschlüsselt nach Geschlecht der Hörer

Es zeigt sich insgesamt eine bessere Performanz der weiblichen Hörer, die sich bei Modalstimme und Flüstern sowohl in höheren Trefferquoten als auch in geringeren Falschidentifizierungsquoten manifestiert. Der Mann-Whitney U-Test ergebt keinen signifikanten Geschlechterunterschied für die modalen Stimuli (p = 0,469), sehr wohl hingegen für die Trefferquote der geflüsterten Stimuli (p = 0,029). Im Modul "Falsett" liegt die Erkennungsleistung der männlichen Hörer geringfügig, aber nicht signifikant höher als die der weiblichen (p = 0,1 bei der Trefferquote und p = 0,442 bei den Falschidentifizierungen).

4 Diskussion

Das hier dargestellte Experiment zeigt, dass Hörer, die mit einer Stimme gut vertraut sind, diese auch unter ungewöhnlichen Umständen (hier: Falsett und Flüstern) sehr gut erkennen können. Die Erkennungsraten liegen nahe 100% und damit im Bereich dessen, was auch in früheren Studien (Hollien et al 1982, Wagner/Köster 1999, Rose/Duncan 1995, Orchard/Yarmey 1995) beobachtet wurde. Allerdings nimmt die Identifizierungsrate von der Modalstimme im Vergleich zum Flüstern signifikant ab; zum Falsett ergibt sich eine erneut signifikante Differenz. Die Erkennungsrate ist auch unter diesen erschwerten Bedingungen mit über 80% immer noch sehr hoch, insbesondere wenn man in Betracht zieht, dass nur in 2,6% der Fälle Falschidentifizierungen auftraten. Die verminderte Erkennbarkeit im Modus "Falsett" gegenüber dem Modus "Flüstern" kann durch den aufgrund der geringeren Obertondichte drastisch verminderten Informationsgehalt im akustischen Signal erklärt werden.

Ein (hoch)signifikanter Effekt des Sprechergeschlechts findet sich nur im Modus "Falsett". Dies überrascht auf den ersten Blick nicht, wenn man berücksichtigt, dass die durchschnittliche Grundfrequenz der weiblichen Sprecherinnen im Modus "Modal" bei 222 Hz und im Modus "Falsett" bei 322 Hz liegt. Diese Differenz von 100 Hz im Mittel bedeutet den Verlust etwa eines Drittels der Harmonischen und damit eine erheblich erschwerte Erkennbarkeit. Die Modalstimme der männlichen Sprecher liegt hingegen bei 123 Hz im Mittel, die Falsettstimme bei 298 Hz. Damit sind deren Falsettstimmen nicht nur den weiblichen in der Grundfrequenz sehr ähnlich, sondern die männlichen Sprecher weisen auch eine wesentlich größere Differenz zwischen Modalstimme und Falsett auf als die weiblichen (15 Halbtöne verglichen mit 6,4). Damit müsste sich eigentlich die Erkennbarkeit der männlichen Stimmen deutlicher verschlechtern als die der weiblichen. Dies ist allerdings nicht der Fall, so dass zu vermuten ist, dass hier auch andere Kriterien als die mittlere Grundfrequenz eine Rolle gespielt haben. Zu denken ist an Merkmale im temporalen Bereich wie Sprechgeschwindigkeit oder Pausenverhalten. Dem wird in Folgeuntersuchungen näher auf den Grund zu gehen sein.

3 Literatur

Braun, A. (2011): Forensische Sprach- und Signalverarbeitung. In: Bockemühl, J. (ed.): Handbuch des Fachanwalts Strafrecht. 5. Auflage. Köln: Wolters Kluwer, pp. 1632-1654.

Broeders, A.P.A. / Rietveld, A.C.M. (1995): Speaker Identification by Earwitnesses. In: Braun, A. / Köster, J.P. (eds): Studies in Forensic Phonetics. Trier: Wiss. Verlag, pp. 24-40.

Broeders, A.P.A. / van Amelsvoort, A.G. (1999): Line-up Construction for Forensic Earwitness Identification: a Practical Approach. In: Proceedings of the XIVth International Congress of Phonetic Sciences, San Francisco, pp. 1373-1376.

Hollien, H. / Majewski, W. / Doherty, E. Th. (1982): Perceptual identification of voices under normal, stress and disguise conditions. In: Journal of Phonetics, 10, pp. 139-148.

Jessen, M. (2012): Phonetische und linguistische Prinzipien des forensischen Stimmenvergleichs. München: LINCOM.

Braun, A. (2006): Stimmverstellung und Stimmenimitation in der forensischen Sprechererkennung. In: Kopfermann, Thomas (ed.): Das Phänomen Stimme: Imitation und Identität. St. Ingbert: Röhrig, pp. 177-181.

Köster, O. / Wagner, I. (1999): Perceptual recognition of familiar voices using falsetto as a type of voice disguise. In: Proceedings of the XIVth International Congress of Phonetic Sciences, San Francisco, pp 1381-1384.

Orchard, T.L. / Yarmey, A.D. (1995): The Effects of Whispers, Voice-Sample Duration, and Voice Distinctiveness on Criminal Speaker Identification. In: Applied Cognitive Psychology 9, pp. 249-260.

Rose, Ph. (1998): Forensic Speaker Identification. London/New York: Taylor & Francis.

Rose, Ph. / Duncan, S. (1995): Naive auditory identification and discrimination of similar voices by familiar listeners. In: Forensic Linguistics 2, pp. 1-17.

Glottalizations in German-accented English in relationship to phrase boundaries

Maria Paola Bissiri

TU Dresden, Chair for System Theory and Speech Technology, Dresden, Germany
maria_paola.bissiri@tu-dresden.de

Abstract: The present study investigates the extent of glottalization before word-initial vowels in German-accented English in relationship to phrase boundaries. In German, as in Czech, glottalizations before word-initial vowels are frequent, while in English they are less frequent and more likely to occur at phrase boundaries. A previous investigation showed that glottalizations in Czech-accented English are pervasive and less influenced by the presence of phrase boundaries [3]. Results of the present study indicate that Germans transfer their word-linking habits from their native language to their English productions. German speakers of English glottalized a great number of tokens (82%), and the most frequent glottalization type they produced was creaky voice. In German-accented English, glottalizations were significantly more frequent at phrase boundaries than at non-phrase boundaries. Specifically, glottal stops were more frequent at phrase-boundaries and absence of glottalization at non-phrase boundaries. These results are in line with previous studies on native German. Other than in German, creaky voice in German-accented English was not more frequent at non-phrase than at phrase boundaries, possibly because of differences in labeling criteria and speech style across studies. The German speakers who had a longer experience in an English speaking environment showed lower glottalization frequencies and higher influence of phrasing. Further research is needed to investigate the impact of glottalization on the perception of foreign accent by English native speakers.

1 Introduction

Second language research traditionally investigates phonemes, i.e. sounds that in a specific language differentiate word meaning. However, non-phonemic information plays an important role in speech communication [7]. Since their communicative function can vary across languages, non-phonemic phenomena should be analyzed in non-native speech production and perception. The present study investigates the glottalization of word-initial vowels, non-phonemic in English and in German, in German-accented English productions in relationship to phrase boundaries.

In this study, glottalization is used as a cover term indicating several glottal phenomena. One is the canonical glottal stop, created by the closing and abrupt opening of the vocal folds. Perceptually equivalent is creaky voice, consisting of irregular and usually low-frequency glottal fold vibrations [14]. A sudden drop in fundamental frequency can also be sufficient for perceiving glottalization [8, 12]. Traditionally, glottalization has been associated with low pitch perception, however Bissiri and Zellers 2013 [4] found that this association is not straightforward.

Glottalizations can have different communicative functions across languages. In some languages (e.g. in Arabic [18]) glottalizations are phonemes, in other languages, such as English, German and Czech, they are related to prosodic structure. Prosodic structure consists a) in the alternation of stressed and unstressed syllables and of accented and unaccented words, and b) in the grouping of higher than segmental units in a hierarchical structure (e.g. syllables into words, words into phrases, smaller phrases into larger phrases) [17]. The relationship between glottalization and prosodic structure can differ across languages.

Glottalizations of word-initial vowels are frequent word-boundary markers in German [10] and in Czech [16]. In English, they are less frequent [5] and are more likely to occur at stressed syllables, pitch accented words and phrase boundaries [13, 5, 6]. In German, glottalization frequency also increases at stressed vowels and accented words [10, 15, 11]. Regarding glottalization and phrasing in German, Rodgers 2000 [15] found a significant main effect of position in the utterance (phrase-initial vs. phrase medial) while Malisz et al. 2013 [11] did not. However, in both studies glottal stops were more frequent phrase-initially than phrase-medially, while creaky voice was more frequent phrase-medially than phrase-initially.

Glottalization is also influenced by speech style. Glottal stops are more frequent in German read speech, while creaky voice as well as absence of glottalization are more frequent in spontaneous speech [15]. The most frequent form of glottalization of word-initial vowels in German is creaky voice [10].

Bissiri and Volín 2010 [3] investigated glottalizations in Czech-accented English compared to British English in relationship to phrase boundaries. The study was carried out on BBC news bulletins read by Czech and English speakers. Czech speakers glottalized nearly 100% of the tokens at phrase boundaries and showed slightly lower glottalization frequencies at non-phrase boundaries. British speakers, instead, seldom glottalized at non-phrase boundaries, while they glottalized 50% of the tokens at phrase boundaries. These results show that glottalizations in Czech English are more pervasive and therefore less influenced by prosodic structure compared to British English.

It is well known that non-native speakers transfer their native language characteristics to their second language productions. Therefore, basing on the above mentioned literature on German and considering that the present investigation on German-accented English is carried out on read speech, the following hypotheses are formulated:

a) Glottalization frequency in German-accented English will be similar to the frequencies reported for German read speech in [10, 15] (respectively 79% and 74%).
b) The most frequent form of glottalization will be creaky voice.

Considering that 1) a main effect of phrasing was found in a German corpus including read speech [15], and that 2) canonical glottal stops are more frequent in read speech and their number increases at phrase boundaries, following hypotheses are formulated:

c) Glottalization will be more frequent at phrase boundaries than at non-phrase boundaries.
d) Glottal stops will be more frequent at phrase boundaries than at non-phrase boundaries.
e) Creaky voice will be more frequent at non-phrase boundaries than at phrase boundaries.

2 Method

In order to facilitate the comparison of German-accented English results with findings previously obtained for Czech-accented English and British English, identical materials as in [3] were employed: two BBC news bulletins of 966 words in total. The speakers were six German natives, three females and three males, employees and students at the Technical University of Dresden, aged 21-55. Five of the speakers were from Saxony, while speaker L6 was from the south of Brandenburg. Speakers L6 and P4 spent respectively one year and six months in the United States, and speaker A7 had daily contact to a native American English speaker since six months. The other three speakers had no longer experience in English-speaking environments and defined their English level as intermediate. The data was recorded in studio at the Institute of Acoustics and Speech Communication of the Technical University of Dresden with a Microtech Gefell M 930 microphone and 44.1 kHz sampling rate.

An automatic labeling of the words starting per vowel with an acoustic model of the glottal stop was carried out by means of the UASR (Unified Approach for Speech Synthesis and Recognition) system [9, 2].

As in [3], glottal phenomena were classified as follows:

- no-glottalization: 0 = absence of glottalization; C = contraction (e.g. "he's" for "he is")
- glottalization: G = canonical glottal stop, if a closure had a duration of at least two third of the whole glottalization; Cr = creaky voice; L = low F0, F0 drop of more than one semitone in 40 ms; H = breathy voice, air escaping from the vibrating vocal folds.

Phrase boundaries were marked according to the Tone and Break Indices (TOBI) system of prosodic labeling [1]. Break Indices (BI) 0 and 1 indicate non-phrase boundaries. BI 3 and 4 indicate intermediate intonational phrase and full intonational phrase boundaries respectively. BI 2 was excluded from the analysis because it can mark both phrase and non-phrase boundaries [1, p.35]. Cutoffs, marked as 1p, and hesitations, marked as 2p and 3p, were also excluded since they are more frequent in non-native speech and can also trigger glottalization, although not necessarily as a transfer from the native language.

3 Results

German speakers of English glottalized 82% of the tokens and creaky voice was the most frequent glottalization category (s. Table 1). Except for the female speaker B5, who produced more canonical glottal stops, for all other speakers creaky voice was the most frequent realization (s. Figure1). Speakers R1 and G3 had an overall tendency of producing breathy phonation, which explains their high percentage of breathy voice tokens.

The three speakers who had at least six months experience in an English speaking environment, A7, L6 and P4, produced 12% less glottalizations than the others, a highly significant difference (χ^2 (1, N = 1304) = 29.5004, p <0.001).

At phrase boundaries 98% of the tokens were glottalized vs. 63% at non-phrase boundaries, a highly significant difference (χ^2 (1, N = 1304) = 257.0569, p <0.001). Each German speaker presented a higher frequency of glottalization at phrase boundaries than at non-phrase boundaries (s. Figure 2). The influence of phrase boundaries on glottalization can be represented as the ratio of the percentage of glottalizations at phrase boundaries to the percentage of glottalizations at non-phrase boundaries (s. Table 2). Except for speaker B5, the ratios of the Germans are higher than the ratios of the Czechs and lower than the ratios of the native English speakers reported in the previous study [3, p.27]. The ratios are higher for the more experienced German speakers of English A7, L6 and P4.

Table 1 - Percentages (and counts) of tokens for the different glottalization categories (s. Section 2).

no-glott.		**glottalization**			
0	C	Cr	G	H	L
15% (200)	3% (38)	48% (627)	25% (328)	8% (105)	0% (6)

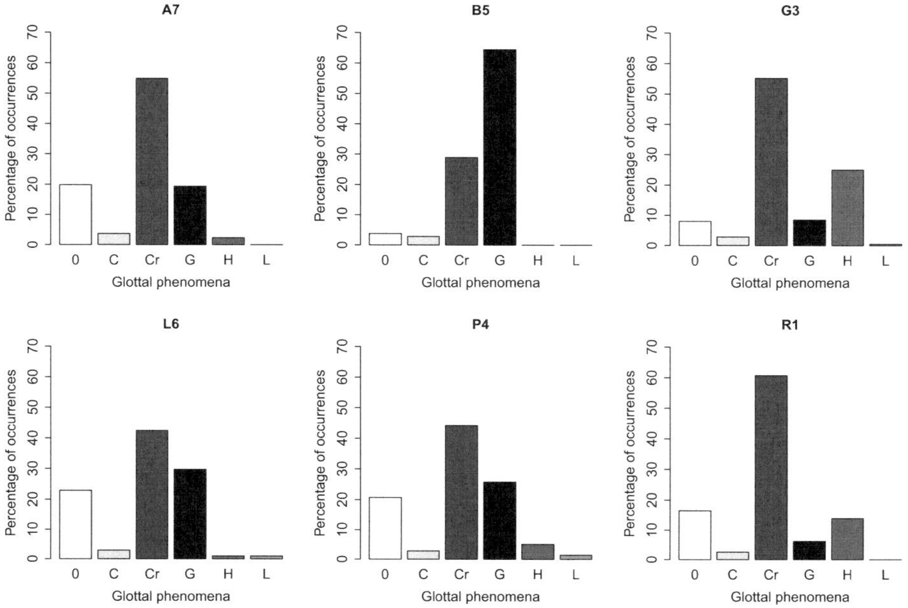

Figure 1 - Percentage of tokens of each glottalization category for the six German speakers.

Figure 3 shows the percentage of glottalization categories at phrase and non-phrase boundaries. Glottal stops (G) were significantly more frequent at phrase-boundaries than at non-phrase boundaries, 38% vs. 11% respectively (χ^2 (1, N = 1304) = 122.8883, p <0.001). Absence of glottalization (0) was significantly more frequent at non-phrase boundaries, 30% vs. 2% at phrase-boundaries (χ^2 (1, N = 1304) = 198.4096, p <0.001). No difference was found between the frequency of creaky voice (Cr) at phrase and non-phrase boundaries, 47% and 50% respectively (χ^2 (1, N = 1304) = 0.9447, n.s.).

4 Discussion

Results support hypothesis a), that in German-accented English the overall glottalization frequency would be approximately as high as in previous studies on native German read speech [10, 15]. Hypothesis b), indicating creaky voice as the most frequent glottalization type in German-accented English as in native German, is also supported. The prevalence of canonical glottal stops for speaker B5 indicates possible individual variations [14]. In the previous study [3], the most frequent glottalization type found for Czech-accented English was the canonical glottal stop.

Table 2 - Ratio of the percentage of glottalized tokens at phrase boundaries to the percentage of glottalized tokens at non-phrase boundaries for each German speaker.

Speakers	A7	B5	G3	L6	P4	R1
Phr. bound./Non-phr. bd.	1.63	1.22	1.36	2.15	1.68	1.41

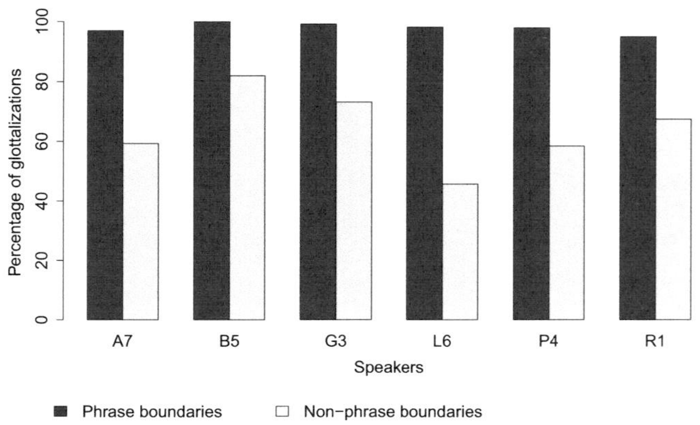

Figure 2 - Percentage of glottalizations at phrase and non-phrase boundaries for each German speaker.

Results also support hypothesis c), that glottalizations would be more frequent at phrase than at non-phrase boundaries, and this was the case for all speakers. In accordance with hypothesis d) and with previous studies on native German [15, 11], glottal stops were more frequent at phrase boundaries than at non-phrase boundaries. A preceding pause possibly facilitates a more precise articulation, necessary to produce a glottal stop [11, p.146]. 35% of the glottal stops produced by the German speakers in the present study were preceded by a pause. However, the frequency of glottal stops can vary from study to study according to the labeling criteria employed. The duration of a glottal stop closure, which is a criterion for distinguishing between glottal stop and creaky voice in the present study (s. Section 2), cannot be determined precisely if the glottalization is preceded by silence. Therefore, glottalizations preceded by pauses were labeled as creaky voice only when the whole vowel was glottalized or the glottalization had a duration comparable to the neighboring segments.

Hypothesis e) is not confirmed since creaky voice was not significantly more frequent at non-phrase boundaries than at phrase boundaries. One reason could be the different labeling criteria across studies. Tokens labeled as creaky voice in the present study could include a closure (s. Section 2). Hence, they could also correspond to the glottal category of "glottal stop and glot-

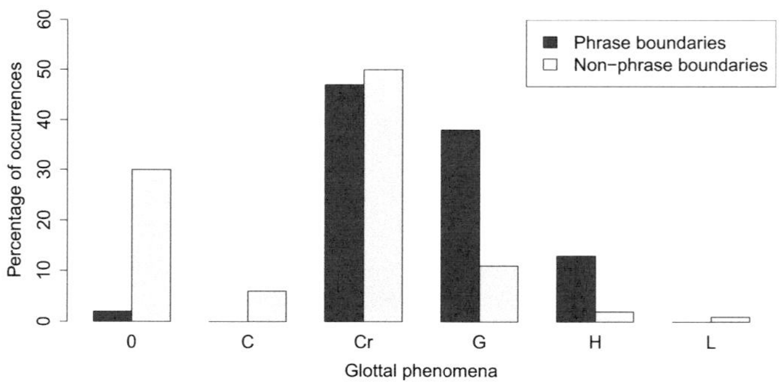

Figure 3 - Percentage of glottalization categories at phrase vs. non-phrase boundaries.

talization" (labeled as Q -q) in [10, 15], which was found more frequently at phrase-boundaries than at non-phrase boundaries [15]. Another reason could be the difference in speech style since creaky voice is less frequent in German read speech [15].

In order to analyze the frequency of glottalization in relationship to proficiency level in English, it would be necessary that expert English listeners perceptually evaluate German speakers' productions. Results of the present study give indications that a lower glottalization frequency can be related to a higher proficiency in English since the German speakers with at least six month experience in an English speaking environment significantly pronounced less glottalizations. Moreover, the ratio of their glottalization frequency at phrase boundaries to their frequency at non-phrase boundaries was higher than the ratio by the other German speakers. Still, the more experienced speakers produced a larger amount of glottalized tokens and showed lower ratios than the English native speakers in the previous study [3]. Therefore, glottalizations might be a persistent characteristic of German-accented English, affecting also advanced speakers. Further investigations are needed to shed light on this and on the influence of glottalizations on the perception of foreign accent by native English speakers.

5 Conclusions

The results presented indicate that Germans, as Czech speakers, transfer their word-linking habits from their native language to their English productions. In German-accented English, a high percentage of the tokens (82%) were glottalized and creaky voice was the most frequently produced glottalization type. These findings are in line with previous studies on native German.

In German-accented English, glottalizations were more frequent at phrase boundaries than at non-phrase boundaries. Glottal stops were significantly more frequent at phrase boundaries, as in native German. Differently than in German, no significant difference was found in the frequency of creaky voice at phrase boundaries compared to non-phrase boundaries. The reason could be different glottalization labeling criteria across studies and different speech style.

More research is needed to find out if glottalization rate is influenced by the level of proficiency in English. German speakers with longer experience in an English speaking environment showed lower glottalization frequencies than the other German speakers, but higher than English natives in the previous study [3]. This could mean that the transfer of word-linking habits from the native language is a persistent characteristic of German-accented English and that it should be explicitly addressed in language teaching and training. Further research is required to test the impact of glottalization on the perception of foreign accent by native English speakers.

6 Acknowledgements

The author is thankful to Ivan Kraljevski for his comments on a previous version of this paper and to all the speakers. This research was supported by a Marie Curie Intra European Fellowship within the 7th European Community Framework Programme. Grateful thanks to Rüdiger Hoffmann for supporting this research project.

References

[1] M. E. Beckman and G. Ayers Elam. *Guidelines for ToBI labelling*. The Ohio State University Research Foundation, 3.0 edition, 1997.

[2] M. P. Bissiri, I. Kraljevski, and R. Hoffmann. Glottal stop detection in German-accented English using ASR. In *Proceedings of AIA-DAGA 2013*, Meran, Italy, 2013.

[3] M. P. Bissiri and J. Volín. Prosodic structure as a predictor of glottal stops before word-initial vowels in Czech English. In R. Vích, editor, *20th Czech-German Workshop, Speech Processing*, pages 23–28. Prague, 2010.

[4] M. P. Bissiri and M. Zellers. Perception of glottalization in varying pitch contexts across languages. In *Proceedings of Interspeech 2013*, Lyon, France, 2013 (accepted).

[5] L. Dilley, S. Shattuck-Hufnagel, and M. Ostendorf. Glottalization of word-initial vowels as a function of prosodic structure. *Journal of Phonetics*, 24(4):423–444, 1996.

[6] M. Garellek. Glottal stops before word-initial vowels in American English: distribution and acoustic characteristics. *UCLA Working Papers in Phonetics*, 110:1–23, 2012.

[7] S. Hawkins. Roles and representations of systematic fine phonetic detail in speech understanding. *Journal of Phonetics*, 31(3-4):373–405, Oct. 2003.

[8] J. Hillenbrand and R. Houde. Role of F0 and amplitude in the perception of intervocalic glottal stops. *Journal of Speech and Hearing Research*, 39(6):1182–1190, 1996.

[9] R. Hoffmann, M. Eichner, and M. Wolff. Analysis of verbal and nonverbal acoustic signals with the Dresden UASR system. In A. Esposito, M. Faundez-Zanuy, E. Keller, and M. Marinaro, editors, *Verbal and nonverbal communication behaviours*, volume 4775 of *Lecture Notes in Artifcial Intelligence*, pages 200–218. Springer, Berlin, Heidelberg, 2007.

[10] K. J. Kohler. Glottal stops and glottalization in German. *Phonetica*, 51:38–51, 1994.

[11] Z. Malisz, M. Żygis, and B. Pompino-Marschall. Rhythmic structure effects on glottalisation: A study of different speech styles in Polish and German. *Laboratory Phonology*, 4(1):119–158, 2013.

[12] J. Pierrehumbert and S. Frisch. Synthesizing allophonic glottalization. In J. van Santen, R. Sproat, J. Olive, and J. Hirschberg, editors, *Progress in speech synthesis*, pages 9–26. Springer, New York, 1997.

[13] J. Pierrehumbert and D. Talkin. Lenition of /h/ and glottal stop. *Papers in laboratory phonology II: Gesture, segment, prosody*, pages 90–117, 1992.

[14] L. Redi and S. Shattuck-Hufnagel. Variation in the realization of glottalization in normal speakers. *Journal of Phonetics*, 29(4):407–429, Oct. 2001.

[15] J. Rodgers. The phonatory correlates of juncture in German. In *Proceedings of the 5th Seminar on Speech Production: Models and Data*, pages 289–292, Kloster Seeon, Bavaria, 2000.

[16] R. Skarnitzl. Acoustic categories of nonmodal phonation in the context of the Czech conjunction “a”. *AUC Philologica, Phonetica Pragensia X*, 1/2004:57–68, 2004.

[17] N. Veilleux, S. Shattuck-Hufnagel, and A. Brugos. *6.911 Transcribing Prosodic Structure of Spoken Utterances with ToBI. January IAP 2006.* Massachusetts Institute of Technology: MIT OpenCourseWare, http://ocw.mit.edu (Accessed 29 May, 2013). License: Creative Commons BY-NC-SA, 2006.

[18] J. Watson. *The Phonology and Morphology of Arabic.* Oxford linguistics. OUP Oxford, 2007.

CALL Mandarin - Results and Conclusions from a Project for Developing a Computer-Assisted Pronunciation Training Program

Hansjörg Mixdorff[1], *Hussein Hussein*[2,3]

[1] *Department of Computer Science and Media, Beuth University, Berlin, Germany*
[2] *Chair for System Theory and Speech Technology, Dresden University of Technology, Dresden, Germany*
[3] *Linguwerk GmbH, Research and Development, Dresden, Germany*
mixdorff@beuth-hochschule.de; hussein.hussein@mailbox.tu-dresden.de

Abstract: This paper presents an overview over the development of a computer-assisted pronunciation training system for German learners of Mandarin. It is based on speech signal analysis using phone and tone recognizers. Speech signal as well as F_0 contour were visualized in real-time, in contrast to many common pronunciation training systems. Visual feedback was assessed to be beneficial for pronunciation improvement. During the course of the project, several perception and production studies were performed in order to determine the most relevant problems for German learners of Mandarin. Tone correctness was assessed on readings and imitations of tokens of varying complexity. Results show that tone 2 is most frequently confused with tone 3. Tone 4 has the highest correctness, which is probably related to the similar F_0 contour of stressed syllables in German. The paper also presents our observations regarding software development problems as well as shortcomings in the the project outcome.

1 Foreword by Hansjörg Mixdorff

Since this article appears in the Festschrift honouring the retirement of Rüdiger Hoffmann, a few personal words are in order. To start with, without his belief in this project none of the research presented in this paper would have been realized. Rüdiger's assistance was essential in my Dr Eng and Dr habil graduation and will certainly help complete Hussein's Dr Eng degree. I remember meeting Rüdiger back in 1995 after I had returned from Japan, unemployed - somehow nobody needed engineers back then - with a half-finished Dr Eng thesis, and without a Doktorvater. A few months later I became a research assistant at TU Dresden and subsequently received my Dr Eng degree from the Department of Electrical Engineering. The relationship between me and Dresden intensified and I cannot count the times I traveled to the Elbe. Many projects developed from this connection, up to now, most commemorable possibly Speech Prosody 2006, but also ESSV 2010 in Berlin, not to mention all the collaborations between Rüdiger's coworkers and myself, also leading to Hussein Hussein's involvement in the project described hereafter. Rüdiger's and my personal relationship took a while to develop, in hindsight maybe partly owing to a prevailing east-west gap, partly to differences in character, mine impatient and insensitive at times, his calm and unpretentious, but sometimes a touch reserved. Eventually I have come to appreciate most that Rüdiger does not make a fuss: Not about being a professor, not about being a great expert in speech science and digital signal processing, not about running one of Germany's most renowned speech labs for many years, not about being internationally recognized. He still has got his feet firmly on the ground. I sincerely wish Rüdiger health and energy for the things he loves, now with much more time on his hands - hopefully one of those things will still be speech.

2 Introduction

A globalized world brings about the need to speak foreign languages and stimulates activities towards Computer-Assisted Language Learning (CALL). CALL facilitates individualized language learning and pronunciation training when a human teacher is not available. However, pronunciation training is probably the most difficult part to be transferred to a computer, because providing useful and robust feedback on learner errors is far from being a solved problem [1]. A useful computer-assisted pronunciation training (CAPT) system must be able to distinguish speaker-individual differences (e.g. voice characteristics) from foreign accent-related ones, provide feedback when actual errors occur and at the same time be robust against minor deviations whose flagging would discourage the learner. A special case arises when the target language belongs to a completely different group and exhibits features alien to the learner's mother tongue - a situation certainly given for Germans acquiring Mandarin.

It is commonly known that Mandarin or standard Chinese is a tone language and hence tonal contours of syllables change the meaning. There are 22 consonant initials (including glottal stop) and 39 vowel finals. Mandarin comprises a relatively small number of syllables. The most important acoustic correlate of tones is F_0. Mandarin has four syllabic tones, that is, high, rising, low, and falling (Tones 1-4) and a neutral tone (Tone 0) in unstressed syllables. In citation forms of monosyllabic words the tonal patterns are very distinct as shown in figure 1, but when several syllables are connected, F_0 contours observed vary considerably due to tonal coarticulation. German is a stress-timed non-tonal language. Mandarin differs from German on the segmental level, but it is the tonal distinctions that pose serious problems to German learners, especially in the context of two or more syllables [1]. Therefore tone display, recognition and correction are paramount features for a pronunciation training system.

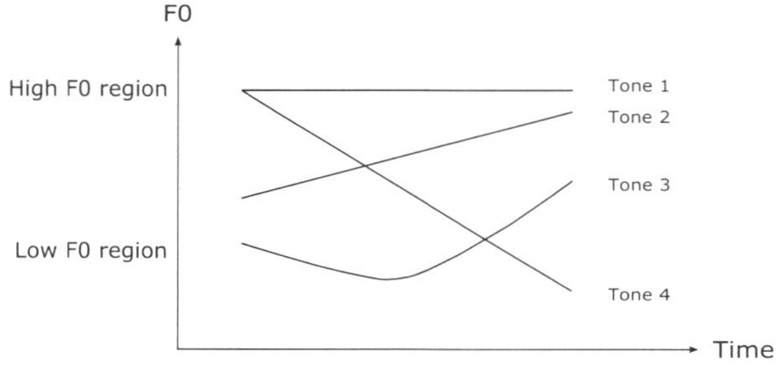

Figure 1 - Typical F_0 patterns of tones 1-4 in mono-syllables.

3 Project Overview - Structure, Partners and Organization

The aim of the project was to develop a CAPT system for teaching Mandarin to German learners (henceforth "*CALL-Mandarin system*"). The development of the *CALL-Mandarin system* was funded by the German Federal Ministry of Education and Research (BMBF) within a three-year project through its program for stimulating applied research at Universities of Applied Sciences

(Fachhochschulen). Two part-time research assistants - Hussein Hussein as a speech technology expert, and a Chinese Studies expert, during the first part Daniel Külls, then Hue San Do - as well as two student helpers worked for the development of the CAPT system. Tasks included, inter alis, speech data collection and annotation, construction of recognizer components and creation of appropriate exercises for typical problems, as well as the technical and pedagogical integration.

The project was based at the Department of Computer Science and Media, Beuth University Berlin, Germany. Due to the wide array of competences required, we gathered a large number of cooperation partners:

- IFLYTEK company, Hefei, China.
- East Asian Institute at the Free University Berlin (FUB), Berlin, Germany.
- Digital Publishing (DP) company, Munich, Germany.
- Institute of Phonetics and Digital Speech Processing, University of Kiel, Kiel, Germany.

Further cooperations developed over the course of the project:

+ Dresden University of Technology (TUD), Dresden, Germany.
+ National Taipei University of Technology (NTUT), Taipei, Taiwan.
+ Tongji University, Shanghai, China.

A prerequisite for BMBF funding to be granted was the collaboration with Digital Publishing, as the ultimate aim of the project was a CAPT prototype which would later turn into a product to be included in DP's portfolio. The formulation of requirements for the future product, technical considerations regarding preexisting DP components and development platforms were therefore critical issues. However, ultimately it was decided to decouple the development of the prototype from such constraints posed by DP's technical framework, mostly due to the lack of innovative functions we planned to implement. The cooperation with FUB was important for accessing students through a pronunciation tutorial and as testbed for the CAPT system to be developed. The company IFLYTEK was planned to provide speech technology for Mandarin (E-Learning Chinese (ECL)) some components of which, however, could not be utilized due to license problems. The final version of CALL Mandarin features syllable and tone recognizers by IFLYTEK. TUD and Tongji University provided annotations of databases which were collected from German students. NTUT supplied databases from Chinese native speakers and components of a Mandarin phone recognizer.

4 Project Considerations - Technical and Pedagogic

A state-of-the-art CAPT system should be able to detect the deviation from the native standard and to provide instructions for improving pronunciation. Therefore, a specialized recognizer is required to detect the kind and place of deviation. *CALL-Mandarin system* was projected to offer the following functionality (+ indicates functions actually implemented):

- (+) Programmed material for training syllables, words and short phrases. In our case based on the vocabulary of the New Practical Chinese Reader, one of the most frequently used text books for Mandarin [2], including recordings of all training items by Chinese native speakers.
- (+) Recording and playback of utterance and audiovisual feedback, that is, visualisation of the speech signal, F_0 contour and intensity contour in real-time.
- (+) A specialized recognizer trained with data from native speakers of Mandarin and optimized using knowledge of probable errors of German learner.

- (+) Indication of probable pronunciation errors by measuring the deviation between learner and native speakers in real-time.
- Generation of instructions (verbal or visual) for improving the pronunciation.
- Auxiliary materials for clarifying the error, for example video films or animated sagittal sections of vocal tract.
- Generation of a corrected, prosodically modified imitation signal using speech resynthesis technology which enable the learner to hear an improved version of his/her utterance.

Pronunciation training is a typical case in which over-learning is aimed at, in other words: The more training, the better. It requires the student to repeatedly rehearse the same tokens, for attaining better fluency while following the feedback of the system for improving errors. In a typical training session of the *CALL-Mandarin system* the student will choose the items s/he wishes to aquire and imitates the native original while monitoring the intonation and intensity contours of the imitation. To this end, the training item is recorded non-stop and displayed aligned with the original. Only after a pause longer than 1.2 sec, recording terminates and the recognizer-based evaluation and subsequent display of results is performed. Reaction time of the system is about 1-3 sec depending on the length of the training item.

5 Implementation - Architecture, Components and Problems

For its core technology, the CAPT system is based on Automatic Speech Recognition (ASR) and tone recognition systems. Initially, the HTK-based phone recognizer [3] of NTUT was employed and run inside the real-time HTK Application Programming Interface (HAPI) [4] provided by Digital Publishing. During later stages of the project, owing to their better performance, phone and tone recognizers by IFLYTEK were used. Hussein redesigned the tone recognizer by combining spectral and prosodic features [5]. The redesigned tone recognizer matched or surpassed the performance of the reference recognizer of IFLYTEK and was therefore deployed in the current CALL system.

Figure 2 shows the Graphical User Interface (GUI) of the *CALL-Mandarin system*. The framework contains a set of reference utterances produced by native speakers of Mandarin. Audiovisual feedback is an important part to detect the the pronunciation errors of users [6]. Therefore, F_0 contours and energy envelope curves of audio signals are shown in real-time as an audiovisual feedback. Once started, the training session can be repeated continuously. The redrawing of the imitation is controlled by an energy threshold.

The alignment of imitation signals to reference signals and the seamless repetition process are intended to help learners exploit instantaneous visual feedback. Especially the real-time display of F_0 contours, which is a distinct function of the *CALL-Mandarin system* in contrast to common CALL systems, was assessed to be beneficial.

However, implementing such seemingly simple funcionality posed many technical problems. Robust F_0 contour detection, problematic still in the off-line case, is even more difficult when on-line visualization is required. In *CALL-Mandarin system*, a raw contour is drawn as the student speaks which is post-processed after recording stopped. Determining when to redraw the training item, especially in the presence of background noise, required dynamic end-point detection.

6 Perception and Production Tests - Main Results

The acquisition of Mandarin tones is the greatest challenge for German learners. Therefore, a tone analysis of the perception and the production of disyllabic words was performed in order

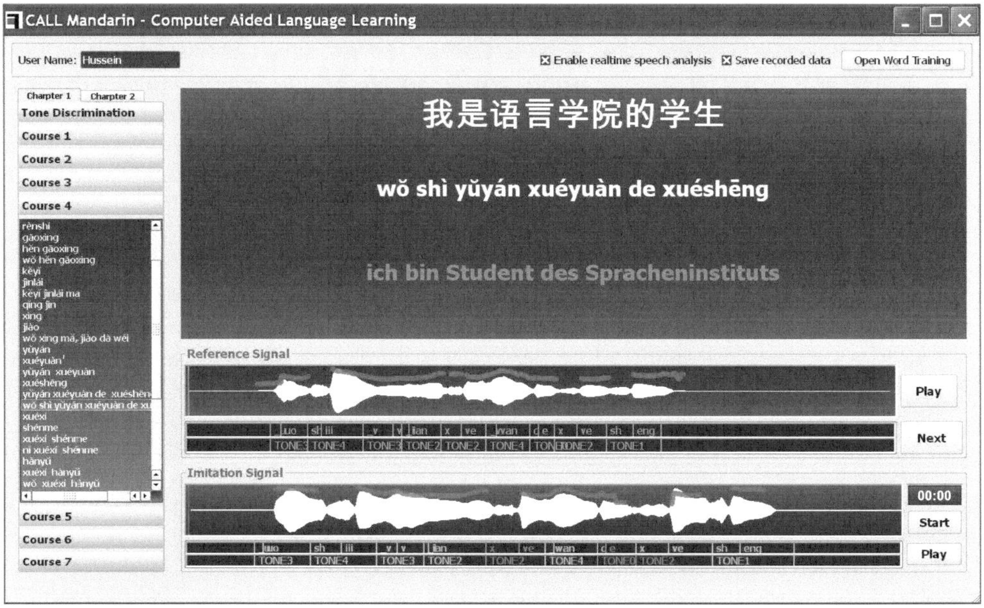

Figure 2 - GUI of the *CALL-Mandarin system.*

to detect the confusion partners of tones. Furthermore, the correctness of syllable tones was determined for readings, as well as imitations of the same sentences after a native speakers [7].

6.1 Speech Material (DE)

The database consists of recordings from German learners of Mandarin. The German data (henceforth "*DE*") consists of recordings from 13 first-year German students (seven seminar students (*WS*) and six non-seminar students (*WOS*)). At the time of recording, students had completed 12 weeks of Mandarin language training. The data consists of the following parts:

1. Identification of disyllables (henceforth "*DE_Perception*"): German students listened to ten Chinese disyllables and identified tone combinations by showing prepared tone cards. These cards had tones marked as tone 1, 2, 3, 4 and 0 for the neutral tone.

2. Production of disyllabic words in reading mode (henceforth "*DE_Production 1*"): The same ten Chinese disyllables as in *DE_Perception* were presented to German students in Pinyin transcription. The students had to read them aloud, yielding a total of 130 speech signals.
   Disyllables chosen for both *DE_Perception* and *DE_Production 1* consisted of real Chinese words with different tonal combinations. The *WS* students had encountered the words in the pronunciation training system before, whereas the *WOS* students had not.

3. Production of sentences in reading mode (henceforth "*DE_Production 2*"): The students were asked seven questions in Chinese and they read seven sentences as answers aloud. Thereafter, students read three questions. Sentences and questions were presented to students both in Chinese characters and in Pinyin transcription.

4. Production of sentences in speaking mode (henceforth "*DE_Production 3*"): Subsequently, the same questions were asked again in Chinese, but this time only a German cue (consisting of two or three German words) was presented. The students had to give the same Chinese answers and ask the same questions as in *DE_Production 2*.
   Both *DE_Production 2* and *DE_Production 3* tests consist of 20 sentences. Each sentence contains both monosyllabic and disyllabic words with a minimum of three and a maximum of nine syllables, yielding a total of 260 utterances. Students had encountered the respective sentences in the *WS*.

The data *DE* was annotated by an expert. The expert listened to the data several times and annotated the perceived tones using numbers 1, 2, 3 and 4 for Mandarin tones and 0 for the neutral tone. Annotations produced by the expert were used as a reference for judging the correctness of tones produced by German learners of Mandarin.

6.2 Results of Perception and Production of Disyllabic Words

Table 1 shows the correctness rate and confusion partners of tones when German students identified disyllables (*DE_Perception*). Tone 2 has the lowest correctness (< 50%) and is most frequently confused with tone 3. Tone 3 also has a relatively low correctness, but is mostly confused with tone 4 and less with tone 2. Tone 4 has the highest correctness, which is probably related to the similar F_0 contour of stressed syllables in German. Tone 1 is mostly confused with tones 2 and 4, but rarely with tone 3. The neutral tone, which is similar to unstressed syllables in German, is mostly confused with tone 4.
The correctness of disyllables produced by German students (*DE_Production 1*) is quite different (see table 1). Tones 1, 2 and 4 have a similar correctness (> 70%) whereas tone 3 is half of the time pronounced as tone 2. This problem is common among German learners of Mandarin who have difficulties with the falling-rising tone. Tone 3 is only realized half-way to the bottom of the tonal range by the combination of tone 3 with other tones. Therefore, tone 3 combined with other tones differs from tone 3 produced in isolation. German learners of Mandarin tend to produce the rising movement of tone 3 as in isolated syllables, which makes tone 3 more likely to be confused with tone 2 [1]. Unlike the identification test, German students confuse both tones 1 and 4 more often with the neutral tone.

Tone	*DE_Perception*					*DE_Production 1*				
	T1	T2	T3	T4	T0	T1	T2	T3	T4	T0
T1	67	15	4	13	0	71	6	4	6	13
T2	12	49	33	6	0	10	71	10	3	6
T3	0	17	56	25	2	4	50	38	4	2
T4	9	8	11	71	2	5	9	5	71	9
T0	8	15	0	23	54	15	0	0	23	62

Table 1 - Correctness and confusion partners of tones for perception and production of disyllabic words (in %).

6.3 Results of Production of Sentences (Reading and Speaking Mode)

Table 2 shows the correctness rate of tones during the production of sentences for reading (*DE_Production 2*) and imitation (*DE_Production 3*) mode. Correctness of the *DE_Production 2* is only slightly better than of the *DE_Production 3*. When Pinyin transcription or Chinese characters is presented (*DE_Production 2*), the neutral tone has the highest correctness, followed by tone 2 which is more often confused with tones 1 and 3. When only a cue spoken in German is presented (*DE_Production 3*), the neutral tone is produced more often in the responses. Consistent with the production of disyllables, tone 1 is often confused with tone 4, whereas tone 3 is commonly pronounced as tone 2. Notably, when reading aloud complete sentences in contrast to mere disyllables, German students more often produce a neutral tone for all four tones, even more so when neither Pinyin transcription nor Chinese characters are available.

Tone	*DE_Production 2*					*DE_Production 3*				
	T1	T2	T3	T4	T0	T1	T2	T3	T4	T0
T1	69	0	0	8	23	63	2	2	13	19
T2	10	70	10	3	7	5	69	8	5	13
T3	6	18	62	3	12	5	20	55	1	18
T4	6	2	1	64	27	7	1	1	60	32
T0	9	0	0	5	86	4	2	0	5	89

Table 2 - Correctness and confusion partners of tones during the reading and speaking of sentences (*DE_Production 2* and *DE_Production 3*) (in %).

7 Discussion and Conclusions

As they say: You learn by experience. In retrospect, developing a running CAPT while performing several scientific studies, teaching students of Mandarin and writing papers was a formidable feat, at times overstretching the means of our small team. First of all, there was the software engineering which started from scratch, but soon turned into a nightmarish web of dependencies ever harder to disentangle. Special credits go to Marijo Mateljan for implementing vital functions, especially for the real-time display. Second, for various reasons the collaboration with DP did not develop as planned and hence the key goal of converting our project outcome into a product was not achieved. Some of the functions projected were not even touched, for instance, providing a corrected resynthesized learner utterance by transplanting the native original's prosody. Third, as a consequence of development delays and other issues, only few students were actually able to use the *CALL-Mandarin system*, and the "great" final study showing the benefits of the system over the traditional method was never performed. In a much smaller study towards the end of the project we showed that users who trained with our system systematically improved their pronunciation, however, a peer reviewer of the associated article rightfully criticized that we lacked a control-group to prove that the gain was owing to our system and not just to the fact they had trained at all [8]. Taking the sobering facts of project management into account we still believe that endowing people with a means of improving their pronunciation is one of the most valuable applications of speech technology. The need for better CAPT systems is stressed by many studies of communicative obstacles that language students encounter (see, for instance, [9]). Pronunciation errors disregarded at an early stage of foreign language acquisition will become bad habits impeding the verbal performance and causing frustration even as fluency and vocabulary grow.

8 Acknowledgements

This work was funded by the German Ministry of Education and Research grant 1746X08 and supported by DAAD-NSC (Germany/Taiwan) and DAAD-CSC (Germany/China) project related travel grants for 2009/2010.

References

[1] H. Mixdorff, D. Külls, H. Hussein, G. Shu, H. Guoping, and W. Si. Towards a computer-aided pronunciation training system for german learners of mandarin. In *Proc. of the Workshop (SLaTE)*, Wroxall Abbey, Warwickshire, England, September 2009.

[2] Xun Liu. *New Practical Chinese Reader Vol. 1.* Beijing Language and Culture University Press, Januar 2009.

[3] S. Young, G. Evermann, M. Gales, T. Hain, D. Kershaw, X. Liu, G. Moore, J. Odell, D. Ollason, D. Povey, V. Valtchev, and P. Woodland. *The HTK Book (Version 3.4).* Cambridge University Press, 2006.

[4] J. Odell, D. Kershaw, D. Ollason, V. Valtchev, D. Whitehouse, and D. Wood. *THE HAPI BOOK: A description of the HTK Application Programming Interface.* Entropic Ltd., September 1998.

[5] H. Hussein, H. Mixdorff, and R. Hoffmann. Real-Time Tone Recognition in A Computer-Assisted Language Learning System for German Learners of Mandarin. In *Proc. of Workshop on Speech and Language Processing Tools in Education, COLING*, pages 37–42, Mumbai, India, December 2012.

[6] G. Demenko, A. Wagner, N. Cylwik, and O. Jokisch. An Audiovisual Feedback System for Acquiring L2 Pronunciation and L2 Prosody. In *Proc. the 2th Workshop on Speech and Language Technology in Education (SLaTE)*, Wroxall Abbey, Warwickshire, England, September 2009.

[7] H. Hussein, H. S. Do, H. Mixdorff, H. Ding, Q. Gao, G. Hu, S. Wei, and Z. Chao. Mandarin Tone Perception and Production by German Learners. In *Proc. of Workshop on Speech and Language Technology in Education (SLaTE)*, Venice, Italy, August 2011.

[8] H. S. Do, H. Hussein, H. Mixdorff, O. Jokisch, H. Ding, Q. Gao, S. Wei, and G. Hu. Evaluation of Benefits from a Computer-Aided Pronunciation Training System for German Learners of Mandarin Chinese. In *Proc. the 6th International Conference on Speech Prosody*, Shanghai, China, May 2012.

[9] U. Hirschfeld, B. Neuber, and E. Stock. Phonetische Sprechwirkungsforschung im Bereich der interkulturellen Kommunikation. In *Hirschfeld, Ursula / Stock, Eberhard (Hg.): Sprechwissenschaftlich-phonetische Untersuchungen zur interkulturellen Kommunikation Russisch - Deutsch. Band 33*, pages 43 – 67, Frankfurt, Germany, 2010. Peter Lang.

Assessing Natural Emotional Facial Expressions: an evaluation of the I.Vi.T.E. Database

Vincenzo Capuano[1], Maria Teresa Riviello[1], Gennaro Cordasco[1], Jiri Mekyska[2], Marcos Faundez-Zanuy[3], Anna Esposito[1]

[1]Second University of Naples, Department of Psychology, Caserta, and IIASS, Italy
[2]Brno University of Technology, Faculty of Electrical Engineering and Communication, Department of Telecommunications, Brno, Czech Republic
[3]EUP Mataró, Avda. Puig i Cadafalch 101, 08303 Mataró (Barcelona), Spain

vincenzo.capuano@unina2.it, m.teresa.riviello@gmail.com, gennaro.cordasco@unina2.it
xmekys01@stud.feec.vutbr.cz, faundez@eupmt.es, iiass.annaesp@tin.it

Abstract: The use of expressions portrayed by actors is a popular method for researching on the perception of emotion however some recent experiments suggest that since actors do not feel the acted emotion, the produced expressions are far from being genuine and realistic. This work presents experimental results on the assessment of 428 selected image frames derived from I.Vi.T.E. (Italian Visible Thermal Emotional database). I.Vi.T.E. is a naturalistic database of visible (e.g., standard) and thermal images developed by video-capturing emotional facial expressions naturally produced by 49 Italian students during induced emotional contexts (happiness, fear, sadness, disgust and neutral). The facial emotional expressions have been evaluated by 100 subjects (balanced by gender) who were asked to tag each of them according to the emotion they considered appropriate. The results will be used to create a database of quasi-spontaneous facial expressions of emotions which will be useful for researchers to develop models describing and/or reproducing human interactions.

1 Introduction

The vital role of emotions in human cognitive processes [4, 18, and 5] represents a challenging topic for recent studies in Human Computer Interaction (HCI), where researches aim at developing advanced user-friendly and emotionally colored automatic system and avatars. Detecting and recognizing emotional cues is crucial to understand and respond to user's need and facilitate human-computer interaction.

At the light of these considerations, facial expressions are considered by several authors as the most informative visible cues to convey and infer information about interactant emotional states [6, 17]. These authors investigated (for a complete review see [1, 10]) the perceptual and automatic recognition of emotional facial signals exploiting static images recorded in an acted situation [3]: an actor is sitting on a chair and play an emotional expression according to the experimenter's requests.

The conceptual debate is on whether an acted expression is able to completely reproduce a genuine emotional signal. Indeed, since the actor tends to reproduce stereotypical expressions of the requested emotion he/she is not feeling, the portrayed expressions may result unnatural.

Batliner [2] illustrated the limitations of the acted simulation technique to get emotional facial expressions, and suggested another approach to get more natural data. The proposed approach is based on the induction of emotional states.

This work aims at defining a database of quasi-spontaneous emotional facial expressions evaluating facial emotional stimuli derived from the Italian Visible and Thermal Emotional Database (I.Vi.T.E.) [11], naturally produced by Italian students in several induced emotional contexts.

1.1 The I.Vi.T.E. Database

I.Vi.T.E. (Italian Visible Thermal Emotional database, [11]) is a database of quasi-spontaneous emotional expressions obtained inducing emotional states in 49 Italian undergraduated students. The participants were asked to watch and listen to a series of pre-defined and assessed emotional video stimuli able to provoke emotional states such as happiness, fear, sadness and disgust, plus a neutral state. The emotional expressions produced by participants were recorded through a system including thermal and visible cameras.

The size of the database is 29.8GB (Thermal: 1.2GB, temperature range 23-38 °C, 160 × 120 pixels; Visible: 28.6GB, 640 × 480 pixels) and consists of video frames (one digital video frame per second for each participant) of emotional expressions of happiness, fear, sadness, disgust and neutral. For each emotion considered the 428 couple of visible/thermal frames, representing the apex of the facial expressions, were selected and classified by an expert judge through a Matlab software. The selected frames were then used to verify possible thermal differences among the corresponding emotional faces in order to define a high rated database of induced facial emotional expressions.

Figure 1 shows a snapshot of the software used to select and tag images. For each set of frames, the application visualizes the current visible (left-side) and the corresponding thermal image (right-side).

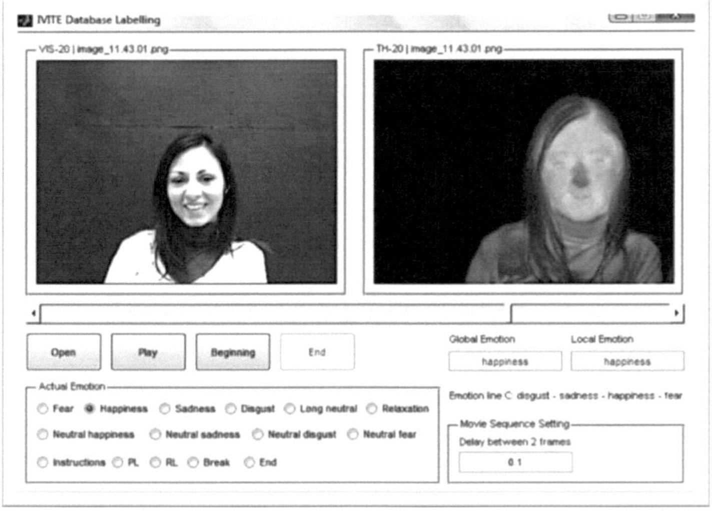

Figure 1 The I.Vi.T.E. Database Labeling software.

1.2 Theoretical background

Fernandez-Dohls et al. [12] highlighted that humans easily recognize a set of prototypical facial expressions of some emotions considered as *basic* [5, 7, 8, 16, 21, and 22]. Moreover, they observed that the recognition ability and the mental categories, through which recognition occurs, are innate and universal. The theoretical assumptions are: (a) basic emotional facial expressions are universal; (b) the universality of the allocation process; (c) the Ekman standard paradigm. The universality of facial expressions theory sustains the existence of six basic (primary) universal emotions: happiness, fear, sadness, disgust, surprise and anger [10, 13] and hypothesizes that members of different cultures reacting to the same emotion-eliciting film, spontaneously generate strongly similar emotional facial expressions.

The universality of the allocation process states that observers from various cultures similarly categorize emotional facial configurations, attributing to them the same emotional meaning [20]. This assumption suggests that "when judges make the expected attribution, they *recognize* a basic emotion (e.g., happiness) in an expression (e.g., through a smile)", thus, facial expression decoding tasks can be exploited as an experimental assessment procedure to validate facial emotional data [12].

The facial expression decoding methodology was first exploited by Ekman that defined what is currently named as the Ekman standard paradigm [19]. This paradigm includes the participation of university students as observers and judges, the use of pre-selected emotional facial expressions for six basic emotions (happiness, fear, sadness, disgust, surprise and anger), a within-subjects experimental design to assess emotional facial expressions, presented in a random order, and a data collecting procedure letting subjects choose an emotional label they consider appropriate for the portrayed facial expression, from a list of definite emotional labels (forced choice).

The present work applies the abovementioned paradigm to assess the 428 facial expressions selected from the I.Vi.T.E. Database, involving 100 Italian students in the emotion decoding task.

2 Experimental set-up

2.1 Participants

The 100 Italian undergraduate students participating to the experiment were divided into five different groups of 20, each made up of ten male and ten female students aged between 18 and 30 years. The participants filled and signed an agreement form declaring their voluntary participation and authorized the researchers to use the collected data for scientific purposes.

2.2 Materials

The 428 selected static frames of facial emotional expressions extracted from I.Vi.T.E. were categorized as: 74 for happiness, 72 for fear, 90 for sadness, 43 for disgust and 147 for neutral state. Five experimental conditions were created in order to keep the length of the emotional decoding task reasonable (each task required around 12 minutes). The set of conditions (a-e), described in Table 1, represents a randomly generated partition of the initial set of frames.

	Happiness	Fear	Sadness	Disgust	Neutral	Tot
Condition a	15	15	18	9	29	86
Condition b	15	15	19	8	30	87
Condition c	15	15	17	9	29	85
Condition d	15	15	18	8	30	86
Condition e	14	14	18	9	29	84
tot.	74	74	90	43	147	428

Table 1 The distribution of the 428 frames over the five conditions (a-e).

2.3 Procedure

The decoding task was presented through the Superlab software [23]. Each group of 20 participants was randomly assigned to one of the five experimental conditions.

The subject seated in front to a computer and the instructions appeared on the monitor. The data collecting procedure was started by pushing the space bar. During the data collection, the screen displayed either a male or female face expressing randomly happiness, fear, sadness, disgust and what can be thought as a neutral state labeled previously by expert judges according to the emotional contents of the watched movie. The naïve subjects were asked to label the face choosing among the six abovementioned labels and the label "other" by pressing on the keyboard the key corresponding to the first letter of the chosen label. The recognition task lasted 12 minutes on average: 3 minutes for the instructions and 9 minutes to complete the decoding task.

3 Results

The data obtained by the participants assessing the emotional expressions was analyzed by computing the percentage of correct decoding computed as the correspondence between the labels assigned to the faces by the naïve participants and those previously assigned to them by the expert judges.

A threshold of 70% of correct decoding was established in order to include a face with a given label in the resulting assessed database. Only 74 out of 428 frames (17%) scored above the threshold: 54 for happiness, 5 for disgust, and 15 for neutral. The remaining set of faces obtained a score below the threshold. Through this selection no stimuli for fear and sadness were identified. Figure 2 illustrates three examples of faces highly rated in accordance with the previously assigned emotional labels.

Figure 2 Examples of highly rated frames in accordance with expert judges. The first row displays the label provided by the expert judges and the percentage of subject's agreements. The second row displays the stimulus code, i.e. a numeric identifier, and the label given to the face as it was defined in I.Vi.T.E, (h= happiness, d=disgust; n=neutral). The last letter indicates the experimental conditions (a-e).

Table 2 shows the confusion matrix describing the percentage of association for each couple of visible/thermal frame. On the columns are the labels chosen by the naïve subjects, on the rows the labels given by the expert judges. The percentage of agreement is displayed on the matrix's diagonal in bold. The percentages were computed summing up the answers the participants provided for all the stimuli and all the proposed labels.

The results show that among the proposed emotions happiness is the one that receive the highest agreement, The naïve subject's answers However, for the remaining facial emotional expressions the agreement was below the chance, and it was particularly poor for sad and fear faces. A sensible number of subjects, indeed, labeled stimuli of sadness as neutral, and stimuli of fear as disgust.

%	Happiness	Fear	Sadness	Disgust	Neutral	Other
Happiness	**75,61**	1,82	4,19	3,78	8,45	6,15
Fear	5,41	**11,99**	12,19	26,51	37,33	20,48
Sadness	5,33	4,89	**22,28**	10,50	21,74	19,67
Disgust	5,35	4,88	17,33	**32,79**	23,42	17,91
Neutral	11,46	17,79	11,87	5,75	**35,54**	17,59

Table 2 – Confusion matrix displaying the percentage of agreement between expert judges and naïve subjects.

It is worth noticing that some stimuli were improperly labeled but in a coherent way (*false recognition*), i.e. a high number of subjects tagged the faces with the same label which was however, different from the one given by the expert judges. In particular, *false recognition* occurred for the 28 facial emotional expressions listed below:

- **Fear**: 8 faces were decoded as disgust (mean: 81,87%, SD: 13,8); 1 face was decoded as neutral (90%).
- **Neutral**: 4 faces were decoded as happiness (mean: 78,75%, SD: 11,1); 4 faces were decoded as disgust (mean: 72,5%, SD: 2,9); 1 face was decoded as sadness (75%).
- **Sadness**: 8 faces were decoded as neutral (mean: 78,12%, SD: 5,9); 1 face was decoded as happiness (80%); 1 face was decoded as disgust (85%).

Figure 3 Examples of *false recognition*. The percentage of improper decoding accuracy is reported on the first row. For instance the left-hand stimulus is the subject's facial expression while watching a fear movies. The naïve subjects tagged the stimulus as a facial expression of disgust.

4 Discussion and Conclusion

The aim of this work was to collect a high rated database of quasi-spontaneous emotional facial expressions through the assessment of the induced facial expressions of happiness, fear, sadness, disgust and neutral state extracted from the I.Vi.T.E. Database, adopting the Ekman standard paradigm.

Unfortunately, only 17%, 74 out of the initial 428 selected frames were in agreement with the contextual induced emotion with a percentage higher than 70%. This selection produced 54 facial expressions of happiness, representing the best decoded expressions among those proposed, 5 facial expressions of disgust and 15 neutral facial expressions. Facial expressions for fear and sadness were often confused with neutral and disgust respectively, producing a highly rated *false recognition accuracy*.

Hence, natural facial expressions, at least for some emotions, seem to be hard to decode when spontaneously produced in an emotion induced paradigm. We can speculate that, several factors such as the contextual, environmental and interactional characteristics, the personal emotional expressive attitude as well as the individual emotional regulation strategies [14] may affect the production of natural facial emotional expressions. Therefore, quasi-spontaneous facial configurations do not follow a stereotypical model and are very peculiar.

On the other hand, inferring emotional states from facial expressions during a decoding task, requires assigning an emotional meaning to a given expression [12]. This semantic inferential process unfolds in the personal experience of the observer.

The results of this pilot study seem to contradict both the universality of the basic emotional facial expressions and the universality of the allocation process. They suggests that, even there exists a universal substrate tying the expression and decoding of emotional faces, this process can be less influential than it was previously hypothesized in regulating social emotional exchanges. To this aim stereotypical emotional models may be more useful for synthesizing emotional faces rather than for their decoding and therefore for identifying features for their automatic recognition. The correct decoding process is more complex and subtle, requiring information on the physical, organizational and social context where it unfold, relying on the degree of sensibility of the observer and on his ability to read emotional signals from a variety of sources (gesture, voices, faces, postures).

More data are needed to explain the above results. New research studies must investigate whether the false recognition occurrence is a phenomenon produced by emotion-induction paradigms, or whether quasi-spontaneous face stimuli alone do no convey enough emotional information to increase its accuracy and therefore, which other subtle emotional cues play a role in allowing humans to succeed in the decoding of emotional facial expressions during social emotional exchanges.

These investigations may support the implementation of socially and emotionally believable Information Communication Technology (ICT) interfaces which will facilitate human-computer interaction and improve the life quality of their users.

Future work will focus on the implementation of a natural setting to elicit emotional facial expressions, as well as the assessment of the personal emotional attitude and emotional regulation strategies both producers and observers exploit during interactions.

References

[1] Anitha, C., Venkatesha, M. K., & Adiga, B. S. (2010). A survey on facial expression databases. International Journal of Engineering Science and Technology, 2(10), 5158-5174.

[2] Batliner A., Fischer K., Huber R., Spilker J., Nöth E. (2003), How to find trouble in communication. Speech communication 40, pp. 117-143.

[3] Cowie, R., Douglas-Cowie, E., Cox, C. (2005). Beyond emotion archetypes: databases for emotion modeling using neural networks. Neural Networks 18

[4] Damasio, A., (1994). Descartes' Error: Emotion, Reason, and the Human Brain. Gosset/Putnam Press,New York, NY.

[5] Ekman P. (1984). Expression and the nature of emotion. In: Scherer, K., Ekman, P.

[6] Ekman P. (1989). The argument and evidence about universals in facial expressions of emotion. In H. Wagner, H., Manstead, A. (1989). (eds.). Handbook of social

psychophysiology, Chichester: Wiley, pp. 143-164.
[7] Ekman P. (1992). An argument for basic emotions. Cognition and Emotion 6, pp. 169–200.
[8] Ekman, P. Friesen, W. V., & Ellsworth, P. (1972). Emotion in the human face: Guidelines for research and an integration of findings.
[9] Ekman P., Friesen W. V., Hager J.C. (2002). The facial action coding system Second edition. Salt Lake City: Research Nexus eBook.London: Weidenfeld & Nicolson.
[10] Ekman, P. (2003). Emotions revealed (2nd ed.). New York: Times Books.
[11] Esposito A., Capuano V., Mekyska J., Faundez-Zanuy M. (2012), A Naturalistic Database of Thermal Emotional Facial Expressions and Effects of Induced Emotions on Memory. Cognitive Behavioural Systems Lecture Notes in Computer Science Volume 7403, pp. 158-173.
[12] Fernandez-Dohls J.M., Carrera P., Barchard K.A., Gacitua M. (2008). False recognition of facial expressions of emotion: Causes and implications. Emotion. 8. pp. 530–539.
[13] Friesen W. V. (1972). Cultural differences in facial expressions in a social situation: An experimental test of the concept of display rules. Doctoral dissertation, University of California, San Francisco. (eds.)Approaches to Emotion, Lawrence Erlbaum, Hillsdale, pp. 319–343.
[14] Gross J. J., & Thompson, R. A. (2007). Emotion regulation: Conceptual foundations. Handbook of emotion regulation, 3, 24.
[15] Isen, A.M., (2000). Positive Affect and Decision Making. In: Lewis, M., Haviland, J. (Eds.), Handbook of Emotions. Guilford, New York.
[16] Izard C.E. (1992). Basic emotions, relations among emotions, and emotion–cognition relations. Psychological Review 99, pp. 561–565.
[17] Izard C. E., Ackerman B.P. (2000). Motivational, organizational, and regulatory functions of discrete emotions. In J.M. Lewis, M. Haviland-Jones (Eds.), Handbook of Emotions, 2nd edition, New York: Guilford Press, pp. 253-264.
[18] LeDoux, J.E., (1996). The Emotional Brain. Simon & Schuster, New York.
[19] Rosenberg, E. L., & Ekman, P. (1995). Conceptual and methodological issues in the judgment of facial expressions of emotion. Motivation and Emotion,19(2), 111-138.
[20] Russell J. A. & Fernandez-Dols J. M. (1997). What does a facial expression mean? In J. A. Russell and J. M. Fernandez-Dols (Eds.) The psychology of facial expression. Cambridge, United Kingdom: Cambridge University Press. pp. 3–30.
[21] Scherer, K.R. (1989). Vocal correlates of emotional arousal and affective disturbance. In: Wagner H., Manstead A. (1989). (eds.) Handbook of Social Psychophysiology, Wiley, New York, pp. 165–197.
[22] Scherer K.R. (1997). The role of culture in emotion-antecedent appraisal. Journal of Personality and Social Psychology 73, pp. 902–922.
[23] www.superlab.com/. Copyright 2012 Cedrus Corporation.

Gedanken über die Rolle der Geisteswissenschaften in der Gesellschaft

Magnús Pétursson und Toshiko Yamaguchi

Institut für Phonetik, Allgemeine Sprachwissenschaft und Indogermanistik der Universität Hamburg, Bogenallee 11, 20144 Hamburg

Department of English, University of Malaya, 50603 Kuala Lumpur, Malaysia

Email-Adressen : magnus.petursson@uni-hamburg.de; tyamag@um.edu.my

Abstract: Es wird auf die große wissenschaftliche Bedeutung der Geisteswissenschaften hingewiesen und nachgewiesen, dass nicht nur der wissenschaftliche Faktor sondern auch der wirtschaftliche Faktor der Geisteswissenschaften völlig unterschätzt wird. Geisteswissenschaftliche Arbeitsplätze sind sehr anspruchsvoll, aber auch sehr nützlich für die Gesellschaft. Wir möchten daher die Rolle und die Besonderheiten der Geisteswissenschaften genauer hervorheben und erläutern, da wir der Meinung sind, dass die gegenwärtige Diskussion zu einseitig ist und den tatsächlichen Gegebenheiten nicht entspricht, denen eine zu geringe Bedeutung beigemessen wird.

1 Einleitung

Die ältesten Universitäten waren ursprünglich in der geisteswissenschaftlichen Tradition gegründet. Die philosophische Fakultät, die noch an vielen Universitäten vorhanden ist, ist in dieser Tradition entstanden. Neben Philosophie gehörte der philosophischen Fakultät auch die Theologie und später gehörten ihr auch sprachliche Fächer, klassische und moderne Sprachen, eventuell auch Pädagogik, Psychologie, Kunstgeschichte und Musikwissenschaft. Die Phonetik ist hier eine typische Grenzwissenschaft, da sie durch die Anwendung experimentalphonetischer Methoden sowohl materielle als auch immaterielle Aspekte besitzt (Pétursson 1979) [4]. Als besonderes selbständiges Fach an den Universitäten entstand die Phonetik ohnehin erst durch die Gründung der experimentellen Phonetik Ende des 19. Jahrhunderts. Die Phonetik wurde dann richtigerweise in die philosophische Fakultät eingegliedert.

2 Besonderheiten der geisteswissenschaftlichen Fächer

2.1 Gemeinsamkeiten der Geisteswissenschaften

Den geisteswissenschaftlichen Disziplinen ist es gemeinsam, dass sie nicht materielle Disziplinen sind. Sie können nicht als materielle Gegenstände gemessen, identifiziert und klassifiziert werden. Sie sind nichtsdestotrotz wirkliche Objekte, d.h. keine Einbildung. Selbstverständlich haben sie auch vielfältige Beziehungen zur realen Welt. In der Realisierung der Sprache werden die Sprechorgane und das Hörorgan benötigt, aber trotzdem kann die Sprache mit diesen Organen nicht identifiziert werden. Sie bleibt nach wie vor immateriell. Die distinktive Funktion der Sprachlaute bzw. der Phoneme und die Semantik sprachlicher Einheiten sind nicht messbar und häufig unsichtbar, obwohl sie interpretierbar und für die Kommunikation unverzichtbar bleiben[1]. Daher bleibt die Sprache immateriell, obwohl die Beziehungen zur materiellen Welt evident, unerlässlich und notwendig sind. Am deutlichsten zeigt uns die Semantik diesen Sachverhalt. Die Bedeutung braucht sicher einen sprachlichen Ausdruck, aber von dem sprachlichen Ausdruck kann trotzdem nicht abgeleitet werden, wie die Bedeutung kodiert ist. Gute Beispiele hierfür liefert die Untersuchung von Yamaguchi (2009, 135)[6], in der Bedeutungselemente isoliert werden, die gar keine lexikalische Darstellung haben. Sie ergeben sich aus den Umständen, unter denen der sprachliche Ausdruck zustande kommt. Langacker (1993)[3] zeigt auf eindrucksvolle Weise wie zahlreiche semantische Elemente ‚unsichtbar' sind, und trotzdem eine wichtige Rolle in der Identifikation der linguistischen Bedeutung spielen. In der Begriffsbildung haben sie eine entscheidende Funktion, die in der Kognitiven Sprachwissenschaft intensiv untersucht wird. Das sind nicht nur Elemente, die der Sprachwissenschaftler identifiziert. Auch der Sprecher erkennt sie unbewusst und verwendet sie in der sprachlichen Kommunikation.

2.2 Bereich der Geisteswissenschaften

Die *European Science Foundation* [1] beschreibt den Bereich der Geisteswissenschaften (*Humanities*) folgendermaßen:

> Humanities research explores the origins and products of the human capacity for creativity and communication ….. Humanities research investigates transcultural and supranational challenges on a global scale, thus lending meaning to the complexity of modern societies, for example through comparative studies of science and societal values, religion and migration.

Geisteswissenschaftliche Forschungsbereiche bauen Brücken zwischen Geisteswissenschaften und Naturwissenschaften. Bereiche, die hier typisch sind, sind Untersuchungen zum Geist und Bewusstsein, zu menschlicher Würde, menschlicher Wesensart und menschlichen Werten, zur Kultur und Nachhaltigkeit, Gesundheit und Kognition, Globalisierung und Integration sowie zum Einfluss von Technik und Innovation auf die Gesellschaft.

Dies ist ein sehr weiter Bereich, der große Teile der Gesellschaft umfasst, weitaus größer als der eingeschränkte klassische Bereich von Philosophie und Theologie, die traditionell den Kern der Geisteswissenschaften bildeten.

2.3 Forschungsarbeit in den Geisteswissenschaften

Es ist wichtig zu betonen, dass Forschung in den Geisteswissenschaften eine andere Grundlage besitzt als in den Naturwissenschaften. In dem Wortlaut von *The Human Experience inside the Humanities at Stanford University* [2] klingt es folgendermaßen:

> Research in humanities "is approached differently than in natural and social sciences, where data and hard evidence are required to draw conclusions. Human experience cannot be adequately captured by facts and figures alone; humanities research employs methods that are historical, interpretative and analytical in nature".

---

[1] Hierzu äußert sich Langacker (1993, 353)[3] folgendermaßen: "Numerous other 'invisible' semantic constructs can be posited and justified. They represent facets of conceptual structure that are crucial to both meaning and grammar even though they are not *per se* either noticed or signalled explicitly. They do, however, leave grammatical tracks that linguists can learn to recognize and interpret. Such constructs are strongly motivated on grounds of descriptive utility: they enable one to account for subtle semantic contrasts and differences in grammatical behavior, and to properly characterize grammatical constructions".

An diesem Punkt ist es wichtig zu überlegen, was Methode bedeutet. Forschung und Methode sind miteinander eng verknüpft, da Forschung ohne Plan und Methode nicht realisierbar ist. In den Geisteswissenschaften sind historische Methoden etwas Besonderes, das in den Naturwissenschaften nicht vorkommt. Aber sowohl den Geistes- als auch den Naturwissenschaften sind analytische und interpretierende Methoden gemeinsam. Es ist daher darauf hingewiesen worden, dass zwischen den beiden Wissenschaftszweigen es häufig nur graduelle Unterschiede gibt und keine Unterschiede in der Wesensart.

2.4 Der individuelle Einsatz

In den Geisteswissenschaften war Forschungsarbeit bisher meistens eine individuelle Leistung. Der Forscher arbeitete alleine, häufig von der Gesellschaft unbemerkt, und leistete unter großem persönlichem Einsatz eine individuelle Denkarbeit, die erst viel später von der Öffentlichkeit bemerkt wurde. Gute Beispiele hierfür sind Ferdinand de Saussures (1857-1913) Arbeit über die Struktur der menschlichen Sprache und über das sprachliche Zeichen, die Arbeit von Sigmund Freud (1856-1939) über die menschliche Psyche und die von Immanuel Kant (1724-1804) über die menschliche Vernunft, die als der Beginn der modernen Philosophie angesehen wird. Diese bahnbrechenden Leistungen, die das Ergebnis vieler Jahre intensiver Arbeit waren, hatten erst viel später einen nachhaltigen Einfluss auf die Gesellschaft.

Heutzutage macht moderne Kommunikationstechnik es möglich, Netzwerke aufzubauen, an denen Forscher mehrerer Richtungen Gedanken austauschen können. Forschergruppen können entstehen und Teamarbeit über Grenzen hinweg ist keine Unmöglichkeit mehr. Als Ergebnis entsteht ein neues Verständnis von Zusammenhängen und dies kann zu einem praktischen Ziel führen, das die Grenzen zwischen Grundlagenforschung und angewandter Forschung teilweise aufhebt. Diesen Zusammenhang hat [5] Unsworth (2005, p. 4) folgendermaßen sehr zutreffend charakterisiert:

> Forschung in den Geisteswissenschaften: "refers to the work of an individual, work that is preparatory to writing, work that results in the publication of a book. Researchers may gather to share insights and critique, but research itself is a solitary enterprise ..... Research in humanities is and has been an activity characterized by the four Rs: reading, writing, reflection, and rustication.
>
> In sciences generally, research is basic or applied. Basic research is motivated by curiosity rather than by a particular goal, and its outcomes tend to be theoretical rather than practical. Applied research usually grows out of basic research, and it usually has practical goals in view from the beginning. But the division is not so neat and much research can be described as one or the other depending on what is being funded.
>
> If we consider humanities research in terms of the basic and the applied, some would say that all humanities research is basic, because it never aims at having a practical application".

Hierzu äußert sich Yamaguchi (2012, p. 9) [7] in ihrem Kommentar zu dem Autonomie-Plan der Universität Malaya. Sie betont in ihrem Kommentar, dass die Geisteswissenschaften grundsätzlich vom Gewinndenken unabhängig sind:

> "Unless the plan concurs with its careful planning and application, it may well nurture the ethic that research is synonymous with saleability. This may be a fatal disadvantage to certain disciplines, particularly those integral to human thinking, whose research output is not directly translatable to commerce and profit".

3 Methodische Unterschiede zwischen Geisteswissenschaften und Naturwissenschaften

Unsworth betont, dass in den Geisteswissenschaften vor allem Grundlagenforschung betrieben wird, obwohl zahlreiche Fälle auftreten, in denen auch eine anwendungsorientierte Forschung möglich ist. In den Naturwissenschaften wird häufig mit Hypothesen oder Modellen gearbeitet, wobei zu betonen ist, dass Modelle im Grunde genommen eine Hypothese darstellen. In den Geisteswissenschaften ist dies auch teilweise möglich. Es ist jedoch sehr wichtig zu betonen, dass Hypothesen und Modelle für sich alleine keine Wirklichkeit darstellen und keine Wirklichkeit ersetzen können. Sie sind daher weder richtig noch falsch. Sie haben nur einen Wert, bis nachgewiesen worden ist, dass diese nicht adäquat sind. Wird nachgewiesen, dass sie nicht adäquat sind, muss eine neue Hypothese entwickelt werden.

Daher sind in den Naturwissenschaften Korrekturmechanismen sehr stark, da die Resultate an direkt messbaren Objekten gezeigt werden können. Diese sind in den Geisteswissenschaften viel schwächer, da die Geisteswissenschaften nicht materiell sind und daher mit messbaren Korrekturmaßstäben schwerer zu behandeln sind. Dies ist z. B. offensichtlich in verschiedenen Grammatikmodellen, die nicht über die Stufen einer Hypothese gediehen sind und daher keine Wirklichkeit darstellen, obwohl daran jahr- und jahrzehntelang gearbeitet worden ist.

Die Ausbildung in den Geisteswissenschaften ist anspruchsvoll und zeitaufwendig. Unserer Ansicht nach muss mit einer durchschnittlichen Ausbildungsdauer von etwa zehn Jahren gerechnet werden, wenn eine Promotion angestrebt werden soll und die Ausbildung als solide zu bezeichnen ist. Auf jeden Fall erfordert eine Promotion in den geisteswissenschaftlichen Fächern durchschnittlich fünf Jahre, selbst wenn daran ununterbrochen und hart gearbeitet wird.

4 Gesellschaftliche Bedeutung der Geisteswissenschaften

Geisteswissenschaftliche Arbeitsplätze haben vielen naturwissenschaftlichen Arbeitsplätzen gegenüber den Vorteil, dass sie sehr viel geringere materielle Ressourcen benötigen. Dies ist von unschätzbarem Wert in einer Welt, in der viele Rohstoffe stets teurer werden und zur Neige gehen. Geisteswissenschaftliche Arbeitsplätze erfordern auch im Allgemeinen keine teuren Laboreinrichtungen, die viele teure Geräte benötigen. Meistens können geisteswissenschaftliche Arbeitsplätze mit Computern auskommen, die ohnehin fast überall vorhanden sind. Sie verlangen aber einen unermüdlichen und kontinuierlichen Einsatz und beschäftigen Arbeitskräfte, die sinnvolle und anspruchsvolle Forschungsarbeit leisten und mit Begeisterung und Zufriedenheit in sinnvoller und origineller Forschungsaktivität engagiert sind.

Wichtig ist es zu betonen, dass die Computer nur Helfer sind und für sich alleine keine Lösungen erbringen. Nach wie vor wird unabhängige Denkarbeit verlangt und zielgerichtetes Handeln benötigt, um unerwartete Ergebnisse in Zusammenhänge einzuordnen. Die Zufriedenheit und das Gefühl, eine sinnvolle Arbeit leisten zu können, sind auch ökonomische, aber leider in der modernen Gesellschaft häufig unterschätzte Faktoren, die eine große Bedeutung haben und besser honoriert werden sollten. Gute Bibliotheken sind in der geisteswissenschaftlichen Forschung unerlässlich. Es gibt berechtigte Zweifel an der Behauptung, dass die elektronischen Medien Bibliotheken überflüssig machen. Bücher speichern Wissen über Jahrhunderte hinweg, sind geduldig und warten darauf, dass in ihnen nachgeschlagen wird. Sie können stets zu Rate gezogen werden, ermöglichen ebenfalls Vergleiche und ruhige Überlegung.

Literatur

[1] The European Science Foundation (www.esf.org/research-areas/humanities) Heruntergeladen am 11. 6. 2011

[2] The Human Experience inside the Humanities at Stanford University (http://humanexperience.stanford.edu/how) Heruntergeladen am 13.6.2011

[3] Langacker, Ronald W.: Grammatical Traces of some 'Invisible' Semantic Constructs. *Language Sciences* 15, 323-355 (1993)

[4] Pétursson, Magnús: Phonetik als Grenzwissenschaft. *Miszellen VI. Hamburger Phonetische Beiträge* 30, 87-104. Hamburg : Helmut Buske Verlag 1979

[5] Unsworth, John: New Methods for Humanities Research. The 2005 Lyman Award Lecture Nov. 11, 2005 (http://www3.isrl.illiois.edu/~unsworth/lyman.htm) Heruntergeladen am 10. 6. 2011

[6] Yamaguchi, Toshiko: The Causative/Inchoative Alternation in Icelandic. In, Saxena, Anju & Viberg, Åke (Eds.): *Multilingualism. Proceedings of the 23rd Scandinavian Conference of Linguistics*, Uppsala 1-3 October 2008. Uppsala: Uppsala University, Acta Universitatis Upsaliensis 2009, pp. 127-140

[7] Yamaguchi, Toshiko: Editorial: UM's (=University of Malaya) Autonomy Plan. *Ergon, Bulletin for the UM Academic Community*, 4 No. 2, October 2012, Issue 7, pp. 8-9

EINIGE GEDANKEN ZUM THEMA „KOGNITION“

Klaus Fellbaum

(ehem. BTU Cottbus)

fellbaum@tu-cottbus.de

Kurzfassung

Der Begriff „Kognition“ ist außerordentlich vielschichtig und wird je nach Anwendung unterschiedlich definiert. Von der Grundbedeutung her meint der Begriff ganz allgemein das *Erkennen* und *Kennenlernen*. Kognition ist (nach Brockhaus) der Sammelbegriff für alle Prozesse und Strukturen, die mit dem Wahrnehmen und Erkennen zusammenhängen; dazu gehören: Denken, Erinnern, Vorstellen, Gedächtnis, Lernen, Planen sowie Sinnesfunktionen wie Hören, Sehen, usw. Ganz sicher spielen aber auch Emotionen eine wichtige Rolle.

Auf welche Weise das Bewusstsein und Emotionen im Gehirn gespeichert sind und funktionieren, ist noch weitgehend unbekannt. Jedoch bieten künstliche, hierarchische, kognitive dynamische Systeme in Form von rückgekoppelten Strukturen hoffnungsvolle Ansätze [1], [2].

Das Thema ist zweifellos zu komplex, um im Rahmen der vorliegenden Ausführungen Lösungen anbieten zu können, aber es ist sicherlich auch schon nützlich, die Problematik zu verdeutlichen und zu hinterfragen.

Die Ausführungen basieren auf einem Vortrag, den der Autor auf der ESSV in Cottbus 2012 gehalten hatte.

1. Einleitung: Was ist Kognition?

Kognition ist ein sehr vielschichtiger Begriff. Geht man von der klassischen Definition aus, so meint der Begriff ganz allgemein das *Erkennen* und *Kennenlernen*. Kognition ist ein Sammelbegriff für alle Prozesse und Strukturen, die mit dem Wahrnehmen und Erkennen zusammenhängen; dazu gehören: Denken, Erinnern, Vorstellen, Gedächtnis, Lernen, Planen sowie Sinnesfunktionen wie Hören, Sehen, usw.

Nachfolgend sollen einige Definitionen von Kognition angegeben werden.

- *Kognition* betrifft alle neuronalen Operationen, bei denen Umweltinformationen über die Sinne aufgenommen, verarbeitet, behalten und für die Entscheidungsfindung verwendet werden (frei nach http://lexikon.stangl.eu/240/kognition/).

- *Kognition* ist der allgemeine Begriff für alle Formen des Erkennens und Wissens. Dazu gehören etwa: Aufmerksam sein, Erinnern, Urteilen, Vorstellen, Antizipieren, Planen, Entscheiden, Problemlösen und das Mitteilen von Ideen. Er umfasst auch die Prozesse der mentalen Repräsentation [3].

- Unter *Kognition* versteht man jene Vorgänge, durch die ein Organismus Kenntnis von seiner Umwelt erlangt. Im menschlichen Bereich sind dies besonders: *Wahrnehmung, Vorstellung, Denken, Urteilen, Sprache…* [4].

Zumeist steht bei der Kognition der *sachliche* Gehalt im Vordergrund; emotionale Komponenten wie das Fühlen und Wollen sind oftmals ausgenommen – obwohl kein Zweifel daran besteht, dass die Kognition Emotionen beeinflusst oder durch sie beeinflusst wird [4], [5], [14].

Übereinstimmung besteht darin, dass die Kognition auf *neuronalen* Prozessen beruht, die im menschlichen Gehirn ablaufen [5]. Wenn wir also über Kognition sprechen, müssen wir uns mit der Anatomie und der Funktion des Gehirns beschäftigen. Das soll im folgenden Abschnitt geschehen.

Die Kognitionswissenschaft basiert auf zahlreichen Disziplinen; Abb. 1 gibt hierzu einen Überblick. Besonders bemerkenswert ist dabei der breite interdisziplinäre Rahmen, der sich von physiologischen über psychologische, naturwissenschaftliche bis zu ingenieurwissenschaftliche Bereiche erstreckt.

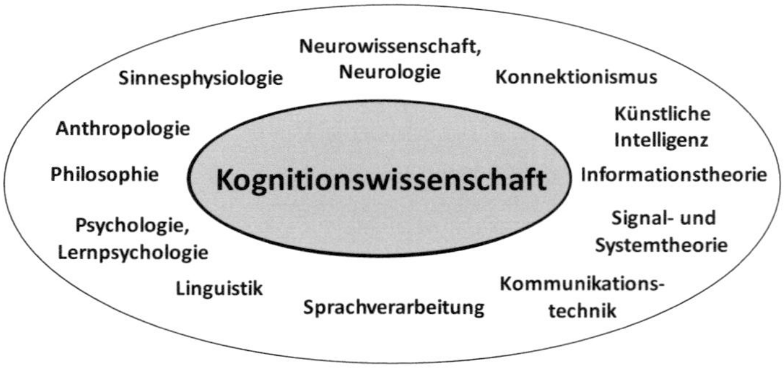

Abb. 1: Kognitionswissenschaft und ihre Teildisziplinen. Angegeben ist lediglich eine Auswahl

Wie verarbeitet und speichert das Gehirn Informationen? Ganz offensichtlich nicht wie ein Computer, also weder digital noch in Form einer „klassischen" Codierung. Die kleinen grauen Zellen (genauer: die Neuronen) sind überall nahezu gleich in Struktur und Funktion; ihre speziellen Fähigkeiten (den „Geist") gewinnen sie in erster Linie durch Vernetzung [6]-[9]. Wir wollen daher auch kurz auf die neuronalen Netze eingehen.

Im nachfolgenden Abschnitt wird versucht, auf der Basis der neuronalen Netze Vermutungen über die Informationsverarbeitung beim Menschen anzustellen. Die Überlegungen führen dann zu den rückgekoppelten kognitiven Systemen, die derzeit intensiv untersucht werden.

Zum Schluss geht es um eine Auswahl von wichtigen, noch ungeklärten Fragen.

2. Zur Anatomie des Gehirns

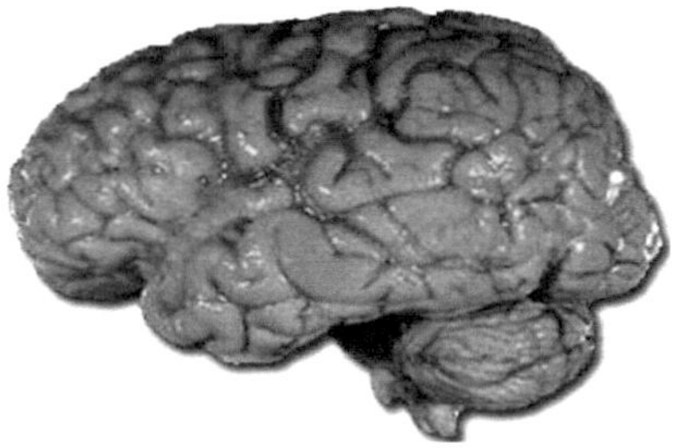

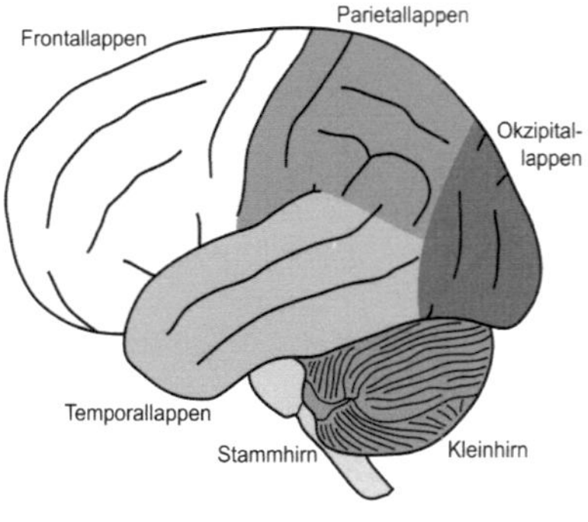

Abb. 2: Anatomie des Gehirns. Links die natürliche Struktur des Gehirns, rechts schematisch die wichtigsten Regionen (Quelle: Wikipedia, verändert)

Die einzelnen Regionen seien nachfolgend kurz beschrieben:

- *Stammhirn*: entwicklungsgeschichtlich ältester Teil des Gehirns. Zuständig für die wichtigsten Lebensfunktionen (Herzfrequenz, Blutdruck, Atmung, Lidschluss, Schluck- und Hustenreflex).
- *Zwischenhirn* (hier verdeckt): Ort des Thalamus ("Tor zum Bewusstsein"). Filter und Verteiler für die Sinneseindrücke, die ins Bewusstsein dringen sollen. Weiterhin: Hypothalamus: Vermittler zwischen Hormon- und Nervensystem.
- *Kleinhirn*: koordiniert Bewegungen und Gleichgewicht.
- *Großhirn*: Cortex; wichtigster Teil: Hirnrinde (Neocortex). Ort des Bewusstseins, der Auswertung und Steuerung von Sinnesfunktionen, des Gedächtnisses, der Denk- und Sprechfähigkeit und vieler weiterer "höherer" Funktionen.

Abb. 3 stellt die wichtigsten "Denkzentren" dar. Generell gilt, dass die linke Seite für die rationalen, sachlichen und logischen Denkprozesse und die rechte Seite für emotionale, musikalische und gestalterische Inhalte zuständig ist.

Von großer Bedeutung ist aber, dass zwischen der linken und der rechten Seite mannigfaltige neuronale Querverbindungen bestehen. Hieraus folgt, dass auch alle Denkprozesse aus einer Mischung von rationalen und emotionalen Komponenten bestehen, wobei die jeweiligen Anteile natürlich sehr unterschiedlich sein können.

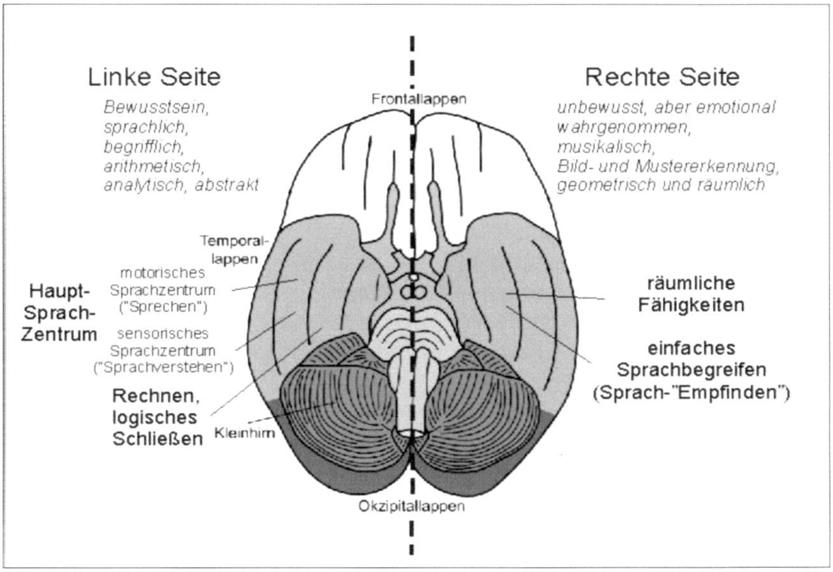

Abb. 3: Die wichtigsten Zentren des Großhirns (Quelle: Wikipedia, verändert)

Sehr ausführliche Darstellungen über die Gehirn-Anatomie und die Funktionen der Gehirnregionen findet man in [7] und [8]. Dabei sind besonders die zahlreichen und sehr eindrucksvollen Bilddarstellungen in [8] hervorzuheben.

Abb. 4 zeigt in stark vereinfachter Form ein einzelnes Neuron. Die Anzahl der Neuronen im Gehirn liegt zwischen 10^{11} und 10^{12}, die Anzahl der Synapsen je Neuron zwischen 10^3 und 10^5; damit ergibt sich als Anzahl der Synapsen eines einzigen Gehirns eine Größenordnung von 10^{14} bis 10^{17}. Daraus folgt, dass die Komplexität eines einzigen menschlichen Gehirns größer ist als diejenige aller jemals gebauten Personal Computer zusammengenommen [7], [9]!

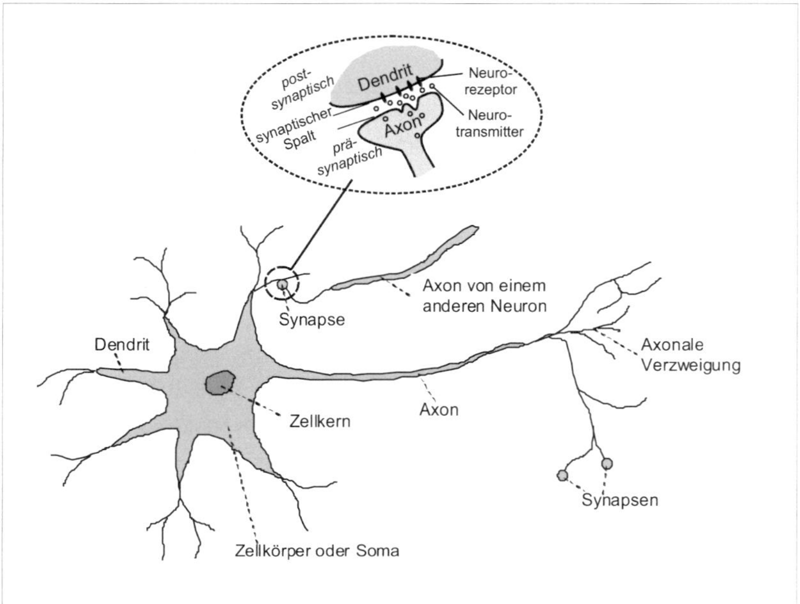

Abb. 4: Neuron (Quelle: [9], verändert)

3. Informationsverarbeitung beim Menschen

Die nachfolgende Abbildung 5 ist als Versuch anzusehen, die menschliche Informationsverarbeitung quantitativ zu erfassen. Es ist schon deshalb lediglich ein Versuch, weil bereits die Quantifizierung eines visuellen oder akustischen Eindrucks mit einer gewissen Willkürlichkeit verbunden ist. Weitgehend ungeklärt ist auch, wie die Informationsreduktion in den menschlichen Sinnesorganen funktioniert, d.h. wie die begrenzte Anzahl von visuellen und auditiven Sinneszellen und die daraus resultierende Informationsreduktion um mehr als 5 Zehnerpotenzen erfolgt, ohne dass die relevanten visuellen und auditiven Informationsinhalte verloren gehen.

Eine weitere drastische Informationsreduktion kommt dadurch zustande, dass fast immer ein "Vorwissen" über die zu erkennende visuelle oder auditive Information vorliegt (man hat fast alles schon einmal gesehen oder gehört). Dieses Vorbewusstsein kann in Form einer Rückkopplungsschleife von der aktuell eintreffenden Information "abgezogen" werden. Es bleibt dann nur noch ein sehr geringer Bitstrom von etwa 10 bis 40 bit/s übrig, der vom Kurzzeitspeicher des Gehirns verarbeitet werden muss. Aber die Reduktion geht noch weiter! Wie im Bild angegeben, ist bereits nach maximal 10 s der Kurzzeitspeicher gefüllt. Der "Abfluss" der Information in das Dauergedächtnis erfolgt dann nur noch mit weniger als einem bit/s. Wenn man sich nun die gewaltige Speicherkapazität des Dauergedächtnisses vor Augen hält, so wird erklärlich, dass sogar bei einem ständigen Informationsfluss aus der Außenwelt nicht einmal ein ganzes Menschenleben ausreicht, um das Gehirn zu "füllen". Tatsächlich gehen Schätzungen davon aus, dass am Lebensende das Gehirn gerade einmal zu einem Drittel gefüllt ist.

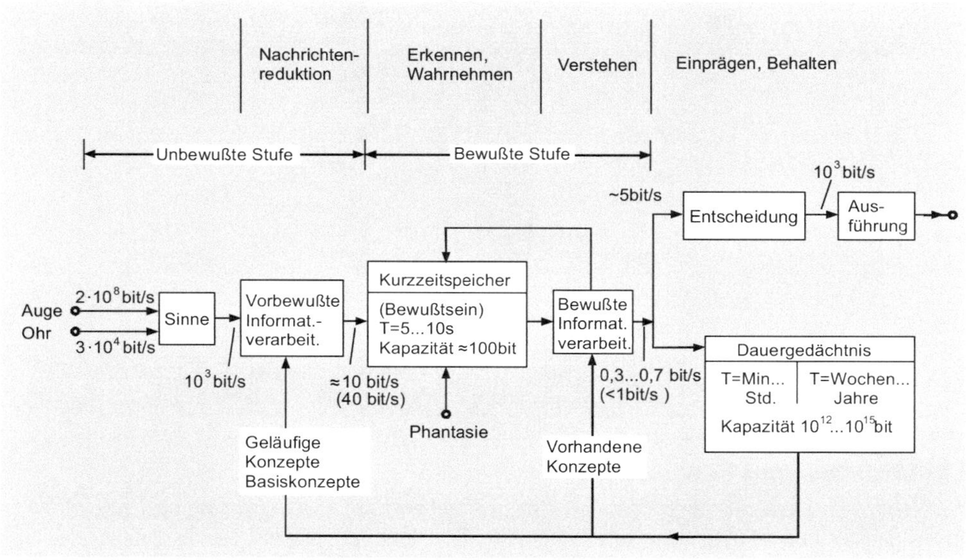

Abb. 5: Informationsverarbeitung beim Menschen (Quelle: [10])

4. Speicherung von Wissen

Wir hatten bereits (Abschnitt 2) Bereiche beschrieben, in denen bestimmte Informationen gespeichert werden. Das bedeutet aber nicht, dass in diesen Bereichen "aufgabenspezifische" Neuronen vorhanden sind. Anders ausgedrückt: es gibt keine derartigen Neuronen; man kann vereinfacht sagen, dass nahezu alle Neuronen von gleicher Struktur sind. Ausnahmen bilden lediglich diejenigen Neuronen, die unmittelbar mit den auditiven und visuellen Sinneszellen verbunden sind. Diese Neuronen führen vermutlich spezielle Transformationsaufgaben durch, wodurch ein von allen übrigen Neuronen verarbeitbarer Datenstrom ermöglicht wird.

Wohin dann der Datenstrom geleitet wird, ist letztlich eine Frage der für eine gerade benötigte Funktion erforderlichen Neuronen-Vernetzung, und diese Vernetzung ist in den zugehörigen Gehirnzentren (Abb. 3) lokalisiert.

Nehmen wir als Beispiel die Erkennung von Wörtern.

„Jedes Wort als Sprachelement muss im Inneren des Gehirns einen Repräsentanten haben (an einfachsten ein Neuron). Sonst könnten wir uns gar nicht an all die Worte erinnern, die wir einmal gelernt haben... Weil Neuronen einen festen Platz im neuronalen Netzwerk haben, können sie dort Worte auf Dauer repräsentieren.“ [6].

Wie der Prozess der Worterkennung abzulaufen scheint, soll Abb. 6 zeigen. Jedes Wort wird durch das Sinnesorgan "Ohr" erfasst und über spezielle Interface-Neuronen in die Neuronenstruktur des Gehirns geleitet. Von dort führt der Weg weiter über verschaltete Neuronenwege zum Hörzentrum, wo die Information ausgewertet wird.

Es gab (und gibt) eine Fülle von Bemühungen, künstliche neuronale Netze zu schaffen, die möglichst genau dem menschlichen Vorbild entsprechen [11], [12]. Die bis heute erzielten Ergebnisse sind jedoch wenig überzeugend. Es ist zwar weitgehend bekannt, wie einzelne Neuronen funktionieren, aber auch die leistungsfähigsten Rechner sind derzeit weit entfernt von dem Ziel, die enorme Komplexität des menschlichen Gehirns nachbilden zu können.

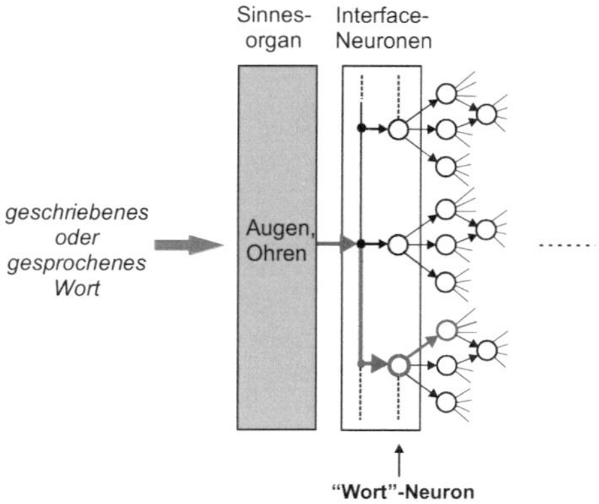

Abb. 6: Vorstellung, wie die Erkennung von Wörtern erfolgen könnte (in Anlehnung an Hilberg [6])

5. Gedächtnis und Bewusstsein

Die bisherigen Betrachtungen bezogen sich weitgehend auf die Erfassung und Speicherung von visuellen und akustischen Informationen. Die letztlich entscheidende Frage, wie aus gespeicherter Information Bewusstsein entsteht, ist damit jedoch weiterhin ungeklärt.

Um zumindest gewisse Teilantworten zu gewinnen, wollen wir uns zunächst etwas genauer mit den Begriffen "Gedächtnis" und "Bewusstsein" befassen.

Abb. 7 zeigt die beiden wichtigsten Arten des Gedächtnisses: das *deklarative* und das *nicht-deklarative* Gedächtnis.

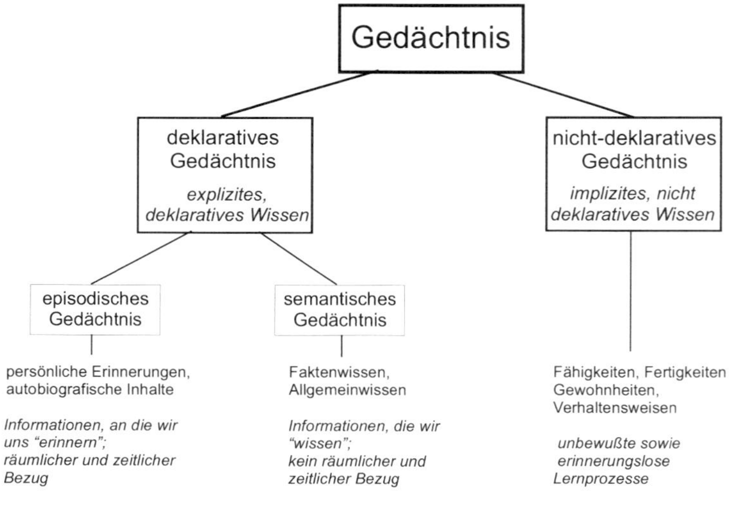

Abb. 7: Formen des Gedächtnisses (Quelle [4])

Vereinfacht gesprochen können wir unterscheiden zwischen einem Gedächtnis, das uns Fakten und Erlebnisse bewusst erscheinen lässt und einem eher unbewussten Gedächtnis, das uns befähigt, Dinge, Situationen, Verhalten usw. quasi automatisch zu bewältigen. Weitere Einzelheiten sind in der Abbildung angegeben.

Offensichtlich spielt der Begriff "Bewusstsein" eine zentrale Rolle. Hierbei unterscheiden wir nach Edelmann [4] zwischen Bewusstseins*inhalten* und Bewusstseins*zuständen:*

- *Bewusstseins**inhalte**:*
  „Von Bewusstsein sprechen wir nur, wenn klare und unterscheidbare Wahrnehmungen bzw. Vorstellungen vorliegen...
  Menschliches Bewusstsein ist untrennbar mit Sprache verbunden. Ein wesentliches Kriterium von Bewusstsein ist die Mitteilbarkeit seiner Inhalte durch verbale Äußerungen".
- *Bewusstseins**zustände**:*
  „Je nach Deutlichkeit der Bewusstseinsinhalte unterscheidet man von der Ohnmacht (*Bewusst*losigkeit) über den Tiefschlaf bis zu einem Zustand höchster Klarheit (volles Bewusstsein) verschiedene Bewusstseinszustände..." [4].

Mit der Definition des Begriffes "Bewusstsein" sind wir allerdings diesem Phänomen selbst leider noch nicht viel näher gekommen. Zwischen den notwendigen Voraussetzungen der Speicherung und der Erkennung (vor allem von Wörtern) einerseits und dem Bewusstsein andererseits liegt offenbar noch ein "Qualitätssprung", der noch nicht geklärt ist. Ein Versuch, zumindest gewisse Komponenten des Bewusstseins plausibel zu machen, wird durch die sogenannten *kognitiven Systeme* vorgenommen, die nachfolgend kurz beschrieben werden.

6. Kognitive Systeme

Derartige Systeme sind dadurch charakterisiert, dass sie einerseits die Umwelt erfassen und zum anderen Einfluss auf die Umwelt nehmen können (Abb. 8).

„Kognitive Systeme müssen ihre Umgebung wahrnehmen können (Analyse), Entscheidungen unter Unsicherheiten treffen (Steuerung) und zielgerichtet auf ihre Umgebung einwirken können (Synthese). Darüber hinaus ist es notwendig, statistische Modelle für Vorhersagen und Regeln für das Verhalten zu entwickeln." (Wolff et.al. [1]).

Ein weiteres, sehr wichtiges Kennzeichen von kognitiven Systemen liegt in ihrer *Dynamik,* d.h. sie müssen auf Veränderungen der Umgebung dynamisch reagieren können.

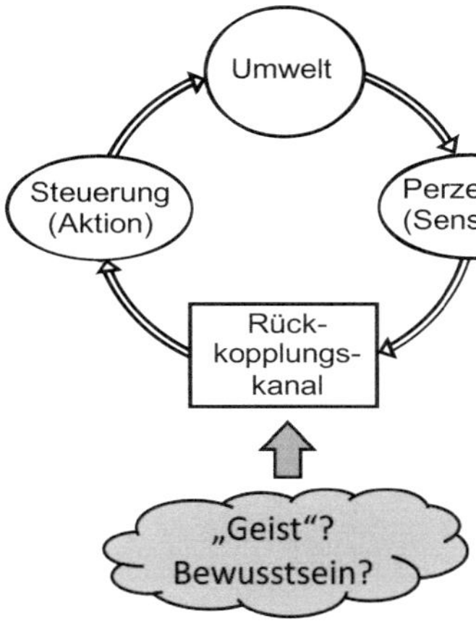

Abb. 8: Rückkopplungskreis (in Anlehnung an Haykin [2])

Systeme mit den genannten Fähigkeiten (vor allem bezüglich der Analyse und Synthese) sind eigentlich nicht neu. Im Prinzip handelt es sich um rückgekoppelte Systeme, die seit vielen Jahrzehnten theoretische und praktisch untersucht worden sind. Siehe hierzu z.B. die

Vorlesungen sowie die zahlreichen Beiträge in den *Studientexten zur Sprachkommunikation* von *R. Hoffmann* [13]. Aber wieder bleibt die Frage weitgehend unbeantwortet, was derartige Strukturen „erkenntnisfähig" oder sogar „kognitiv" macht. Generalisierend formuliert: Wie bringe ich "Geist" oder eben "Bewusstsein" in einen solchen Regelkreis?

7. Schlussbemerkungen

Die bisherigen Ausführungen haben deutlich gemacht, dass noch wichtige Fragen ungeklärt sind. Wir wollen daher abschließend einige dieser Fragen formulieren, ohne dass wir (wie schon mehrfach betont!) plausible oder sogar erschöpfende Antworten hierzu haben:

- Wie ist *Bewusstsein* im Gehirn codiert?
- Wie ist es möglich, dass wir uns eine virtuelle Welt erschaffen konnten (und können)?
- In welcher Weise wird rationales Denken durch *Emotionen* sowie durch *Körpersignale* beeinflusst? Gibt es einen „Bauplan für die Seele"? [14]

Und wenn wir das wissen…

- Wie könnten wir dieses Wissen in einem technischen System realisieren?
- Und schließlich: Wäre das denn überhaupt ein sinnvolles, wünschenswertes Unterfangen?

Literatur

[1] Wolff, M. u.a.: Hierarchische kognitive dynamische Systeme in der Sprach- und Signalverarbeitung. Konferenz "Elektronische Sprachsignalverarbeitung". Cottbus (2012)

[2] Haykin, S.: Cognitive Dynamic Systems. Cambridge University Press. Cambridge UK (2012)

[3] Zimbardo, P.G.: Psychologie. Springer Verlag Berlin, Heidelberg (1995)

[4] Edelmann, W.: Lernpsychologie. 6. Aufl., Verlagsgruppe Beltz, Weinheim (2000)

[5] Rösler, F.: Psychophysiologie der Kognition. Spektrum Akad. Verlag Heidelberg (2011)

[6] Hilberg, W.: Die rätselhafte Fähigkeit des Gehirns, Sprache ohne Hilfe von neuronalen Codes zu verarbeiten. Konferenz "Elektronische Sprachsignalverarbeitung". Cottbus (2012)

[7] Thompson, R.F.: Das Gehirn. 3. Aufl. Spektrum Akad. Verlag Heidelberg (2001)

[8] Carter, R.: Das Gehirn, Anatomie, Sinneswahrnehmung usw. Dorling Kindersley Verlag München (2010)

[9] Stanley, J.; Bak, E.: Neuronale Netze. Computersimulation biologischer Intelligenz. Systhema Verlag GmbH München (1991)

[10] Ohmann, F.: Kommunikations-Endgeräte. Springer Verlag Heidelberg (1983)

[11] Kiebel, S.; Yildiz, B.I.: How does the brain recognize speech-modelling using hierarchical recurrent neural networks? Konferenz "Elektronische Sprachsignalverarbeitung". Cottbus (2012)

[12] Rojas, R.: Theorie der neuronalen Netze. Springer Lehrbuch. Springer Verlag Berlin, Heidelberg usw. (1993)

[13] Hoffmann, R (Hrsg.): Studientexte zur Sprachkommunikation Dresden sowie Systemtheoretische Vorlesungen TU Dresden.
http://www.ias.et.tu-dresden.de/ias/systemtheorie-und-sprachtechnologie/lehre/

[14] Dörner, D.: Bauplan für eine Seele. rororo science sachbuch. Reinbek bei Hamburg, 2. Auflage (2008)

AKUSTIK, UNDE VENIS?

Gunter Ziegenhals

IfM – Institut für Musikinstrumentenbau e.V. an der Technischen Universität Dresden
post@ifm-zwota.de

Abstract: Vor etwa 2600 Jahren beschäftigten sich Gelehrte systematisch mit der Konsonanz von Tönen und den sich daraus ergebenden Tonsystemen. Diese Arbeiten zur Musik stellen aus meiner Sicht die Wurzeln der Akustik dar. Die in der Konsonanz mit ihren Verhältnissen kleiner ganzer Zahlen liegende Harmonie inspirierte durchaus auch andere Wissenschaften. So nannte Keppler sein Hauptwerk Harmonices mundi (Harmonik der Welt), weil er in seinem dritten Gesetz die Verewigung der musikalischen Harmonie im Sonnensystem sah. Auch die Akustik an sich greift den Begriff Harmonie auf. So nennt man die Teiltonreihe eines Signals harmonisch, wenn die Frequenzverhältnisse eine ganzzahlige Reihe (ggf. mit Unterbrechungen) bildet. Es stellt sich nun die interessante Frage: Wie harmonisch sind diese Harmonischen wirklich?

1 Es begann vor 2600 Jahren

Aufgrund ihrer einfachen, weil näherungsweise eindimensionalen Eigenschaften, ist die Saite ein beliebtes Forschungsobjekt der Physik. Die Griechen hatten bereits entdeckt, dass sich harmonische Intervalle aus wunderbar einfachen Zahlenverhältnissen zwischen den Saitenlängen ergeben. Systematische Untersuchungen hierzu werden PYTHAGORAS (6. Jh. v.u.Z.) zugeschrieben. Er verglich Saiten gleicher Beschaffenheit und gleicher Spannung aber unterschiedlicher Länge, oder teilte eine Saite auf einem einfachen Monochord. Man beschäftigte sich seinerzeit mit der Konsonanz und baute darauf Tonleitern auf. Als „Messgerät" diente ein Monochord wie in Abbildung 1 schematisch dargestellt. Ein beweglicher Steg teilt die auf das Gerät gespannte Saite in zwei exakt bestimmte Teile der Längen l_1 und l_2. Ein Normgewicht (definiert gefüllter Wasserbehälter, vielleicht auch ein verwitterungsarmer Stein) hielt die Saitenspannung konstant. Die bei Anzupfen der beiden Saitenstücke erklingenden Töne wiesen entsprechend ein Frequenzverhältnis der Grundtöne von l_2/l_1 auf.

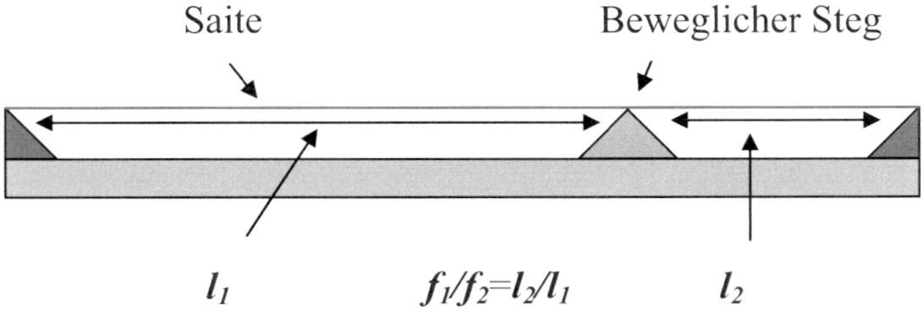

Abbildung 1: Monochord für Untersuchungen zu Tonsystemen

Derartige oder zumindest sehr ähnliche Arbeitsgeräte werden übrigens auch heute noch für Arbeiten in der Musikwissenschaft gebaut. Ein sehr langlebiges Produkt. Dies ist allerdings auch kein Wunder, da es ganz offensichtlich keinerlei update bzw. Versionsaktualisierung benötigt.

Die beschriebenen Arbeiten können zweifellos als die ersten systematischen Untersuchungen auf dem Gebiet der musikalischen Akustik angesehen werden, auch wenn der Begriff der musikalischen Akustik damals sicherlich noch nicht geprägt war. Man beschäftigte sich mit Schall. Andererseits glaube ich mit Recht die musikalische Akustik als Keimzelle der Akustik aufzufassen!

2 Von der Harmonie der Harmonischen

In der Akustik bezeichnet man Teiltonreihen eines Klanges mit ganzzahligen Frequenzverhältnissen als harmonisch bzw. die Teiltöne als Harmonische. Betrachtet wird dabei ein Schallsignal, dessen Ausgangspunkt nicht zwingend nur ein Quelle, spricht ein Instrument sein muss. Die meisten Musikinstrumente arbeiten monofon, sie können jeweils nur einen Ton erzeugen. Spezielle Spieltechniken, wie das Blasen von Multiphonics, bei denen mehrere Grundtöne gleichzeitig angeregt werden, wollen wir hier außer Acht lassen. Man bezeichnet die ganzzahlige Folge von Frequenzen in der Musik auch als Naturtonreihe. Eine besondere Bedeutung hat diese im Falle der Metallblasinstrumente. Deren Eigenfrequenzen und auf diesen werden die einzelnen Töne gebildet, bilden (nahezu) eine solche harmonische Reihe. Von dieser Harmonie ließen sich auch andere Wissenschaften anstecken. Nach der Entdeckung des dritten der nach ihm benannten Gesetze 1618 schrieb Keppler, insbesondere von diesem motiviert, sein im Jahr 1619 veröffentlichtes Werk Harmonices mundi libri V („Fünf Bücher zur Harmonik der Welt“).

Nun liegen die Konsonanz der Töne und die Kepplersche Himmelsharmonie im Verhältnis von Zahlen, im Falle der Konsonanz speziell im Verhältnis kleiner ganzer Zahlen. Betrachtet man die Frequenzverhältnisse der klassischen Stimmungen, so sind die Zahlen in den Verhältnissen aber gar nicht mehr so klein. Betrachten wir die pythagoreische Skala (ohne Versetzungen) so bildet die Septime ein Verhältnis mit dem Grundton von 243/128 und die beiden Partner des Halbtonschritts von 256/243. In der reinen Tonleiter sieht es besser aus. Ohne Versetzungen enthalten 15/8 für die Septime und 16/15 für den großen Halbtonschritt die größten Zahlen. Uns treibt nun die Frage, wie harmonisch passt die harmonische Reihe, also die Reihe der sogenannten Naturtöne in die gängigen musikalischen Skalen. In Anbetracht der in den Skalen vorhandenen Verhältnisse nicht wirklich nur kleiner Zahlen, sollte man dabei die Reihe ruhig etwas weiter abschreiten. Beginnen wir mit dem Grundton der Reihe auf dem Verhältnis 1, so liegt die erste Harmonische bereits in der zweiten Oktave, die vierte in der dritten usw. die 63. Harmonische (also Teilton 64) schließlich in der siebenten Oktave. Wir überstreichen mit 64 Teiltönen somit sechs Oktaven. Das Klavier verfügt über ein klein wenig mehr als sieben Oktaven, eine Orgel über acht. Mit der Betrachtung von sechs Oktaven liegt man also recht gut in Bezug auf Vollständigkeit. Ziel ist die Abweichung der Frequenzen einer harmonischen Reihe von einer auf den Grundton aufgebauten Tonskala (nicht Tonleiter!).

Die Zielstellung wollen wir erreichen, indem wir für die einzelnen Harmonischen die Abweichung vom nächst gelegenen musikalischen Ton einer auf dem Grundton stehenden Skala in cent angeben. Hierzu berechnen wir den cent-Wert für jede Harmonische und bilden die Differenz zum entsprechenden cent-Wert der Skalen. Wir verwenden die bekannte Berechnungsvorschrift und setzen dabei anstelle des Frequenzverhältnisses einfach die Nummer der Harmonischen ein.

$$x[cent] = \frac{1200}{\lg(2)} \lg \frac{f_1}{f_2}$$

Anhand des berechneten cent-Wertes sucht man nun den nächstgelegenen Wert der Skala, bildet die Differenz und hat sein Ergebnis. Für die dritte Harmonische erhalten wir z.B. 1902 cent. Der nächst gelegene musikalische Ton ist die Duodezime (die Quinte über der Oktave). Sie weist in der gleichschwebend temperierten Skala gegenüber dem Grundton einen cent-

Wert von 1900 auf. Unsere Abweichung beträgt also zwei cent. Abbildung 1 zeigt nun die cent-Abweichungen einer harmonischen Reihe in Bezug auf eine reine bzw. gleichschwebend temperierte Skala, basierend auf dem Grundton der Reihe. Ehrlich gesagt, etwas harmonischer hätte ich mir die Sache schon vorgestellt, insbesondere da es sich zugleich um die Naturtonreihe handelt.

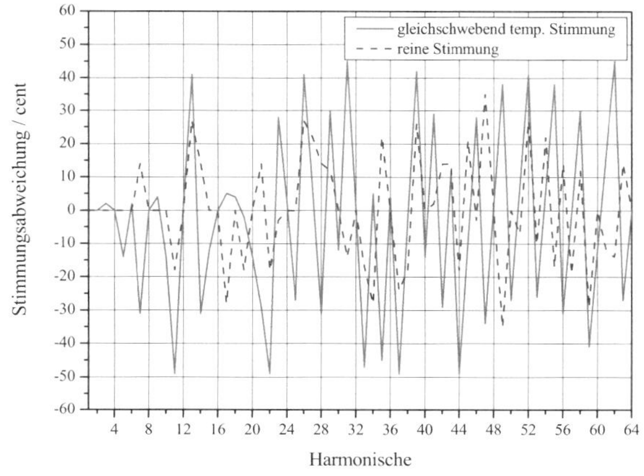

Abbildung 2: Abweichung der harmonischen Reihe von reiner und temperierter Stimmung

Bei der zu Grunde gelegten reinen Skala wird der Faktor 81/80 (21 cent), das syntonische oder didymische Komma vernachlässigt. Dies ist die übliche Anwendung der reinen Stimmung. Sie erfordert 21 Töne pro Oktave. Berücksichtigt man den Faktor 81/80 in der Skala, sieht das Ergebnis ein klein wenig besser aus (Abbildung 3).

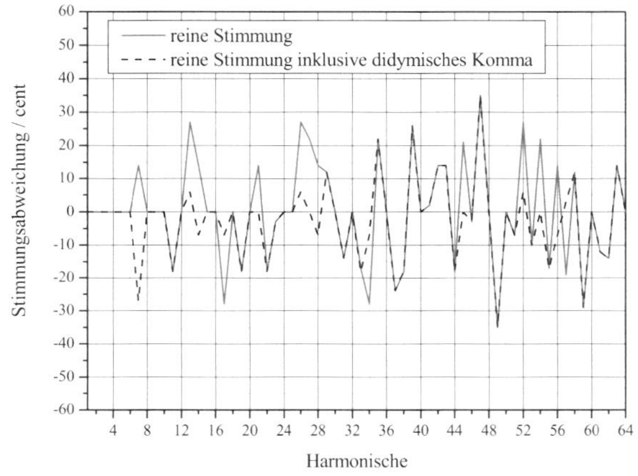

Abbildung 3: Abweichung der harmonischen Reihe von reiner Stimmung, mit und ohne didymische Komma

Tabelle 1 fasst die Werte (ohne Faktor 81/80) zusammen. Zusätzlich sind die den einzelnen Harmonischen nächst gelegenen musikalischen Töne aufgeführt. Die Tonbezeichnungen tragen keine Kennung der jeweiligen Oktave. Man sieht, dass unabhängig von den verbleibenden Abweichungen erst die sechste Oktave der Harmonischen respektive der Naturtonreihe (ab Harmonische Nr. 32) eine vollständige reine Tonskala enthält. Temperiert könnte man sich bereits in der fünften Oktave mit einigen Abstrichen behelfen.

Harmon.		temperiert		rein			Harmon.		temperiert		rein		
Nr.	cent	cent	Diff.	cent	Diff.	Ton	Nr.	cent	cent	Diff.	cent	Diff.	Ton
1	0	0	0	0	0	c	32	0	0	0	0	0	c
2	0	0	0	0	0	c	33	53	100	-47	70	-17	$c^\#$
3	702	700	2	702	0	g	34	105	100	5	133	-28	d^b
4	0	0	0	0	0	c	35	155	200	-45	133	22	d^b
5	386	400	-14	386	0	e	36	204	200	4	204	0	d
6	702	700	2	702	0	g	37	251	300	-49	275	-24	$d^\#$
7	969	1000	-31	955	14	$a^\#$	38	298	300	-2	316	-18	e^b
8	0	0	0	0	0	c	39	342	300	42	316	26	e^b
9	204	200	4	204	0	d	40	386	400	-14	386	0	e
10	386	400	-14	386	0	e	41	429	400	29	427	2	f^b
11	551	600	-49	569	-18	$f^\#$	42	471	500	-29	457	14	$e^\#$
12	702	700	2	702	0	g	43	512	500	12	498	14	f
13	841	800	41	814	27	a^b	44	551	600	-49	569	-18	$f^\#$
14	969	1000	-31	955	14	$a^\#$	45	590	600	-10	569	21	$f^\#$
15	1088	1100	-12	1088	0	h	46	628	600	28	631	-3	g^b
16	0	0	0	0	0	c	47	666	700	-34	631	35	g
17	105	100	5	133	-28	d^b	48	702	700	2	702	0	g
18	204	200	4	204	0	d	49	738	700	38	773	-35	$g^\#$
19	298	300	-2	316	-18	e^b	50	773	800	-27	773	0	$g^\#$
20	386	400	-14	386	0	e	51	807	800	7	814	-7	a^b
21	471	500	-29	457	14	$e^\#$	52	841	800	41	814	27	a^b
22	551	600	-49	569	-18	$f^\#$	53	874	900	-26	884	-10	a
23	628	600	28	631	-3	g^b	54	906	900	6	884	22	a
24	702	700	2	702	0	g	55	938	900	38	955	-17	$a^\#$
25	773	800	-27	773	0	$g^\#$	56	969	1000	-31	955	14	$a^\#$
26	841	800	41	814	27	a^b	57	999	1000	-1	1018	-19	b
27	906	900	6	884	22	a	58	1030	1000	30	1018	12	b
28	969	1000	-31	955	14	$a^\#$	59	1059	1100	-41	1088	-29	h
29	1030	1000	30	1018	12	b	60	1088	1100	-12	1088	0	h
30	1088	1100	-12	1088	0	h	61	1117	1100	17	1129	-12	c^b
31	1145	1100	45	1159	-14	$h^\#$	62	1145	1100	45	1159	-14	$h^\#$
							63	1173	1200	-27	1159	14	$h^\#$
							64	0	0	0	0	0	c

Tabelle 1: cent-Abweichungen der harmonischen Reihe von der gleichschwebend temperierten und der reinen Skala; Die angegebenen cent-Werte gelten jeweils für die aktuelle Oktave.

Betrachten wir ein Instrument, dass als Instrumenteneigenschaft eine harmonische Reihe von Resonanzen aufweist, eine Naturtonreihe. Für die meisten Metallblasinstrumente trifft dies nährungsweise zu. Allerdings sind sie ganz bestimmt nicht bis zur 63. Resonanz musikalisch nutzbar. Lassen wir letzeres außer Acht. Versucht man auf den Resonanzen zu spielen, wird einem das recht sicher gelingen. Die meisten musikalischen Töne sind mehrfach vertreten. Sucht man sich jeweils die günstigsten aus, so liegen die Abweichungen bis auf wenige Ausnahmen im allgemein dem Spieler zur Verfügung stehenden Ziehbereich. Hat man aber einen obertonreichen Klang mit harmonischen Teiltonspektrum vorliegen, wie ihn beispielsweise eine Tonzunge erzeugt, so kann man die nicht zu den musikalischen Skalen passenden, oder auch weniger gut stimmenden Teiltöne nicht einfach „nicht benutzen“ oder ausblenden. Klingen dann mehrere derartige Klänge zusammen, kommt es stets zu mehr oder weniger störenden Dissonanzen.

Da die cent-Skala auf der gleichschwebend temperierten Skala aufbaut, ist es möglich, die lästige, vergleichende Sucherei in einer Tabelle durch einen Algorithmus zu ersetzen: Man runde den berechneten cent-Wert der Nummer der Harmonischen mathematisch auf ganze cent. Diesen Wert teile man durch 100. Nunmehr steht der cent-Abstand bezogen auf den nächsten Ton in Richtung des Grundtones in den zwei Dezimalstellen nach dem Komma (0,01 ... 0,99). Zieht man von dieser gebrochenen Zahl ihren mathematisch gerundeten Wert ab und multipliziert mit Hundert, so erhält man die cent-Abweichung von nächstgelegenen Ton (±(1...49)). Mit dem gleichen Algorithmus kann man übrigens die cent-Abweichung einer beliebigen Grundtonfrequenz f_1 von nächstgelegenen Ton der gleichschwebend temperierten Skala berechnen. Man setzt dazu in der cent-Rechnung als f_2 die zu Grunde gelegte Frequenz des Kammertones a^1, z.B. 440 Hz oder auch 442 Hz ein und verfährt mit dem Ergebnis wie beschrieben. Lediglich nach dem ersten Runden ist noch der Absolutbetrag zu bilden. Für die reine Tonskala ist mir ein solcher Algorithmus nicht bekannt. Es war also der Vergleich mit Tabellenwerten unumgänglich.

3 Die Sache mit dem Klang

Der französische Philosoph, Mathematiker und Naturwissenschaftler Rene Descartes schrieb in seinem 1656 (fünf Jahre nach seinem Tod) erschienen Buch Musicae compendium = Leitfaden der Musik [1]: „Der Zweck des Tones ist letzten Endes, zu erfreuen und in uns verschiedene Gemütsbewegungen hervorzurufen. ... An Mittel zu diesem Zweck oder der Eigenschaften des Tones gibt es vornehmlich zwei: nämlich die Verschiedenheit hinsichtlich seiner Dauer oder Zeit und seiner Stärke in bezug auf Höhe und Tiefe. Von der Beschaffenheit des Tones selbst, womit und wodurch er am geeignetsten erzeugt wird, handeln die Physiker.“ Descartes weist also drei der bekannten akustischen Empfindungsgrößen dem Werkzeugsatz des Künstlers, sei es Komponist oder Musiker zu: Klangdauer, Lautstärke und Tonhöhe. Alle drei Größen sind, sagen wir im Sinne der Musik, hinreichend definiert

- Die Klangdauer über den Notenwert und über das für das Stück geltende Tempo, letzteres angegeben als Anzahl der Viertelnoten pro Minute. Für Parademärsche gelten bzw. galten z.B. folgenden Schrittzahlen = Viertel pro Minute: Preußen 75, Sachsen 96, geschwinde Märsche Preußen 108, Sachsen 115 [2]
- Die Lautstärke wird vom Komponisten den Musikern über die dynamischen Stufen ***piano***, ***mezzo forte*** usw. vorgegeben. Die Skala ist eine relative ohne Bezugspunkt. Es gibt insgesamt 10 Stufen von ***pppp*** (so leise als möglich) bis ***ffff*** (so laut als möglich). Damit realisiert ein gutes Orchester 60 dB Dynamik. Obwohl einem einzelnen Instrument in der Regel diese Dynamik nicht zur Verfügung steht, realisieren Berufsmusiker stets die Differenz zwischen zwei Stufen recht exakt mit einer Schalldruckpegeldifferenz von 6 dB.
- Die Tonhöhe ist durch die geschriebene Note sowie die vorgegebene Stimmtonhöhe (z.B. $a^1 = 440$ Hz) exakt bestimmt.

Descartes grenzt also den Klang aus den „vornehmlichen“ Eigenschaften eines Tones heraus. Ihm war wohl offensichtlich bereits sehr bewusst, dass der Klang, im Gegensatz zu den anderen Empfindungen nicht wirklich (messtechnisch) fassbar ist, zumindest nicht als eine eindimensionale Größe, wie in den anderen Fällen. Klangdauer, Lautstärke und Tonhöhe konnte man schon zu Descartes Zeiten hinreichend genau in Zusammenhang mit der Musik definieren, auch wenn ihm der Schalldruckpegel als Maß noch nicht zur Verfügung stand. Die schwer fassbare Größe Klang schob er, möglicherweise als Notlösung den Physikern zu. Die mussten halt nun zusehen. Und aus der Nummer sind wir streng genommen immer noch nicht heraus. Betrachten wir dazu einmal zwei Definitionen zum Begriff Klang. MILLER 1926 (New York): Zitiert in Risset, Jean-Claude; Mathews, M. V.: Analysis of musical-instrument tones, Physics Today 22(1969)2 beschreibt Klangfarbe wie folgt:

- **Klangfarbe** ist die Eigenschaft die es dem Hörer ermöglicht, Instrumente zu identifizieren.

PRATT und DOAK [3] definierten 1976 Klangfarbe wie folgt:

- **Klangfarbe** ist das Attribut des Höreindruckes, wodurch ein Hörer beurteilen kann, dass zwei Klänge verschieden sind, unter Verwendung anderer Kriterien als Tonhöhe, Lautstärke und Klangdauer".

Durchforstet man die Literatur, so findet man noch weitere von diesen eher ausweichend formulierten Definitionen, präzise jedoch nicht. Das music processing, dem wir uns heute für die Verwaltung von Musikbibliotheken oder für die Transkription von Musik bedienen, kann sehr wohl mittels einfachen Vorstellungen nicht zugänglichen Algorithmen Musikstile, Musikstücke, Instrumente und auch Stimmen innerhalb eines Stückes sicher trennen. Mehr dem Klang im engen Sinne widmet sich die Psychoakustik. Klang ist hier zu Recht keine einzelne, fundamentale Hörempfindung, sondern eher ein zusammengesetztes Phänomen. Mittels der zunächst formulierten Hörempfindungen Rauigkeit, Schärfe und Klanghaftigkeit und den ergänzenden Größen Volumen, Offenheit und Schwankungsstärke lässt sich Klang schon recht gut beschreiben. Obwohl es sich eigentlich um eine eigenständige Hörempfindung handelt, wird die Lautheit hier oft zur Beschreibung von Klängen einbezogen.

Die Größen Volumen, Offenheit und Schärfe repräsentieren in gewisser Weise die bei HiFi-Anlagen der 1970er Jahre und bei Geräten der Musikelektronik heute noch üblichen Klangregelnetzwerke (manchmal auch schon als einfache Equalizer bezeichnet) Tiefen-Präsenz-Höhen. Die Psychoakustikmerkmale Lautheit, Schärfe, Rauigkeit sowie Tonhöhe werden hin und wieder, jedoch nicht einheitlich und auch nicht immer vollständig als fundamentale Empfindungen bezeichnet. Eine fundamentale Empfindung zeichnet sich dadurch aus, dass man sie ändern kann, ohne die anderen fundamentalen Empfindungen zu verändern, sie also in gewisser Weise linear unabhängig sind. Wirklich systematische Untersuchungen dazu sind jedoch nicht bekannt. Inwieweit und ob überhaupt diese Aussage auch auf die Merkmale bzw. Empfindungen Schwankungsstärke, Volumen und Offenheit übertragen oder auch ausgedehnt werden kann, ist zur Zeit nicht bekannt.

Die Eigenschaften der von den Instrumenten abgestrahlten Schallsignale sollten sich je nach Typ deutlich voneinander unterscheiden. Um diesen Gedanken nachzugehen, untersuchte ZIEGENHALS kurze, auf unterschiedlichen Instrumenten, von jeweils mehreren Musikern in unterschiedlichen Räumen gespielte Musikstücke hinsichtlich der von ihnen jeweils im Mittel über die Stücke erzeugten psychoakustischen Merkmale [4]. In die Untersuchungen wurden zehn Gitarren, zehn Geigen, zehn Trompeten und fünf Klarinetten einbezogen. Pro Instrumententyp agierten fünf Musiker und spielten jeweils drei für das jeweilige Instrument typische Musikstücke. Als eines der Stücke wurde stets eine chromatische Tonleiter (auf und ab) gewählt. Die Stücke lagen den Musikern als Notenbild vor, ein optisches Metronom gab den Takt vor. Spielvorgaben gab es bis auf die Bitte ***mf*** zu spielen keine. Die Anspiele zeichneten die Beteiligten zunächst auf, um sie danach off-line zu analysieren. Die für die Experimente ausgewählten bzw. verfügbaren Stichproben repräsentierten ein breites Qualitätsspektrum, ohne jedoch ausgesprochene Superinstrumente, wie altitalienische Geigen aber auch andererseits keinen ausgesprochenen „Schrott“ zu enthalten. Abbildung 4 stellt die Verteilung der Merkmale Lautheit und Offenheit über alle aufgezeichneten Anspiele exemplarisch dar.

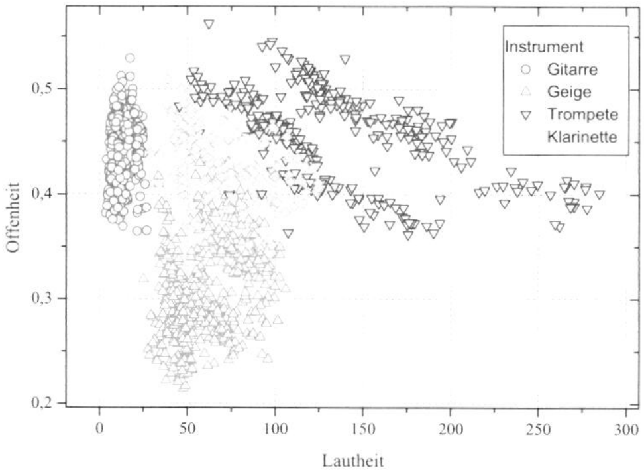

Abbildung 4: Verteilung der Merkmale Lautheit und Offenheit für Anspiele verschiedener Instrumente nach ZIEGENHALS [4]

Wie man sieht, kann man offensichtlich Instrumente, gespielt unter verschiedenen Bedingungen anhand von Klangmerkmalen sehr gut unterscheiden. Damit wäre die MILLERsche Klangdefinition schon einmal bewiesen.

Allerdings trifft dass noch nicht den wirklichen Kern der Sache. Man kann fundamentale Hörempfindungen wie z.B. die Tonhöhe eindeutig einer Skala wie tief … hoch zuordnen. Je nach Fähigkeiten und Übung kann ein Mensch eine mehr oder weniger präzise Zuordnung eines Tones auf dieser Skala treffen. Im Falle der Klangempfindung ist dies jedoch nicht möglich. Es existiert zwar die Formulierung einer Größe „Sensorischer Wohlklang“ (AURES 1985 [5]), jedoch hat diese sich für die Klangskalierung von Musikinstrumenten nicht bewährt. Die von Musikern, öfters noch von Instrumentenbauern an Akustiker gerichtete Frage lautet aber nun: Klingt mein Instrument besser als ein Vergleichsinstrument, welcher Art auch immer? Hier kann unsere Antwort anhand des aktuellen Kenntnisstandes in der Regel nur lauten: „Nun es klingt anders!“ Man kann das „anders“ durchaus auch recht gut beschreiben. Beispielsweise stellten wir fest, dass der Klang lauter, weniger offen und etwas rauer ist. Vor der eigentlich erwarteten Antwort werden wir uns aber wohl noch eine nicht genau definierte Zeit drücken müssen.

Literatur

[1] Descartes, R.: Leitfaden der Musik – Herausgegeben, ins Deutsche übertragen und mit Anmerkungen versehen von Johannes Brockt. Wissenschaftliche Buchgesellschaft, Darmstadt 1978

[2] Allgemeine deutsche Real-Encyklopädie für die gebildeten Stände ..., Band 7. Brockhaus, Leipzig 1935

[3] Pratt, R. L.; Doak, P. E.: A subjective rating scale for timbre
Journal of Sound and Vibration, Volume 45, Issue 3, p. 317-328.

[4] Ziegenhals, G.: Subjektive und objektive Beurteilung von Musikinstrumenten. Eine Untersuchung anhand von Fallstudien. Dissertation TU Dresden 2010, Studientexte zur Sprachkommunikation Band 51 TUDpress 2010 (ISBN 978-3-941298-71-2)

[5] Aures, W.: Berechnungsverfahren für den sensorischen Wohlklang beliebiger Signale. Acustica 59(1985) S. 130

Quo vadis, UASR?

Matthias Wolff[1], *Constanze Tschöpe*[2] *und Ronald Römer*[1]

[1]*BTU Cottbus,* [2]*Fraunhofer IZFP Dresden*
matthias.wolff@tu-cottbus.de

Kurzfassung: Etwa seit der Jahrtausendwende forscht eine mit der Zeit immer größer werdende Arbeitsgruppe am Einheitlichen System zur Sprachsynthese und -erkennung (*Unified Approach to speech Synthesis and Recognition*, UASR). In diesem Artikel blicken wir kurz auf die Anfänge von UASR zurück und zeigen zukünftige Forschungsschwerpunkte auf. Auf drei ausgewählte Themen – die bidirektionale Informationsverarbeitung, die semiotische Informationsverarbeitung und die kognitive zerstörungsfreie Prüfung – wird etwas näher eingegangen. Wir schließen mit einigen Gedanken zu kognitiven Systemen und einem Ausblick.

1 Das einheitliche System zur Sprachsynthese und -erkennung

Basierend auf Vorarbeiten aus den 1990er Jahren wurde etwa um die Jahrtausendwende an der Professur für Sprachkommunikation (heute Professur für Systemtheorie und Sprachtechnologie) der TU Dresden das Konzept eines einheitlichen Systems zur Sprachsynthese und -erkennung (*Unified Approach to speech Synthesis and Recognition*, UASR) entwickelt und erstmals veröffentlicht [1]. Bild 1 zeigt das Original-Blockschaltbild des Systems.

Das Konzept basierte auf der Beobachtung, dass Sprachsynthese und -erkennung im Wesentlichen die gleichen Datenbasen und ähnliche Algorithmen verwenden und dass man einen Sprachsynthetisator als inverses System eines Spracherkenners auffassen kann und umgekehrt. Damals wurden folgende Forschungsziele definiert:

- Verbesserung des Verständnisses der Vorgänge bei der Spracherkennung und Sprachsynthese durch Ausbau einer Plattform, die eine Anwendung des Prinzips der Analyse durch Synthese auf verschiedenen Hierarchieebenen ermöglicht,
- Verbesserung des bisher nur gering ausgebauten Verständnisses der Gründe, warum Spracherkenner Fehler machen, durch Aufbau eines Erkennerzweiges mit transparenter Struktur und der begleitenden Möglichkeit, (auch akustisch) zu bewerten, was ein Erkenner eigentlich „hört",
- Schaffung einer Plattform für die Sprachsynthese auf der Basis statistisch trainierter akustischer Modelle (meist als HMM-Synthese bezeichnet), der ein hohes Qualitätspotenzial zugeordnet wird,
- Schaffung von verbesserten Demonstratoren für die Lehre im Bereich der Signalerkennung und Sprachtechnologie,
- Bereitstellung einer Toolbox für die Gewinnung von Ableitversionen für praktische Anwendungen in der Spracherkennung und –synthese.

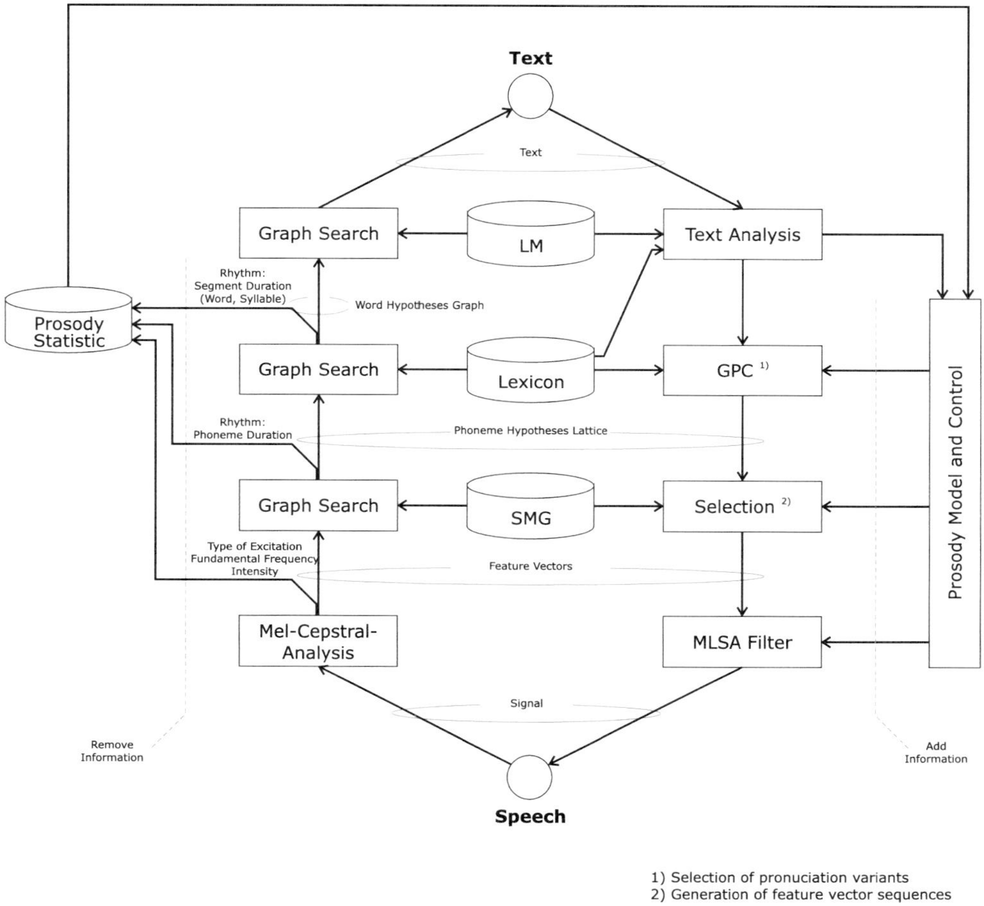

Bild 1: Orginial-Blockschaltbild von UASR aus [1].

Inzwischen wurden die meisten dieser Ziele erreicht (siehe Überblicksarbeiten [2, 3] sowie [4] Abschnitt 7.1). Zwölf Jahre nach der Originalveröffentlichung sieht das Systemschaltbild nun wie in Bild 2 dargestellt aus. Wesentliche Neuerungen und zukünftige Forschungsgegenstände sind die bidirektionale und die semiotische Informationsverarbeitung, auf die in den Abschnitten 2 und 3 näher eingegangen wird.

Von Anfang an wurde das UASR-System – entgegen seinem Namen – nicht *nur* für die Sprachverarbeitung, sondern auch für technische Musterkennung, Musik- und Biosignalverarbeitung verwendet. Dies machte eine Verallgemeinerung zu einem System zur intelligenten Signalverarbeitung notwendig (Details siehe [5]), dessen Blockschaltbild in Bild 3 dargestellt ist. Abschnitt 4 beleuchtet eine zukunftsträchtige technische Anwendung etwas näher.

Sowohl UASR (Bild 2) als auch das System zur intelligenten Signalverarbeitung (Bild 3) sind Spezialfälle eines hierarchischen kognitiven dynamischen Systems nach Bild 4. Dieses ist durch inverse Analyse- und Synthesehierarchien mit gemeinsamen Daten, bidirektionale Informationsverarbeitung sowie eine semiotische Verarbeitung gekennzeichnet. Es sei ausdrücklich erwähnt, dass das System Signal-, symbolische und semantische Ebenen umfasst und damit konzeptionell über die meisten state-of-the-art-Ansätze hinausgeht. Das gilt auch für das Sema-

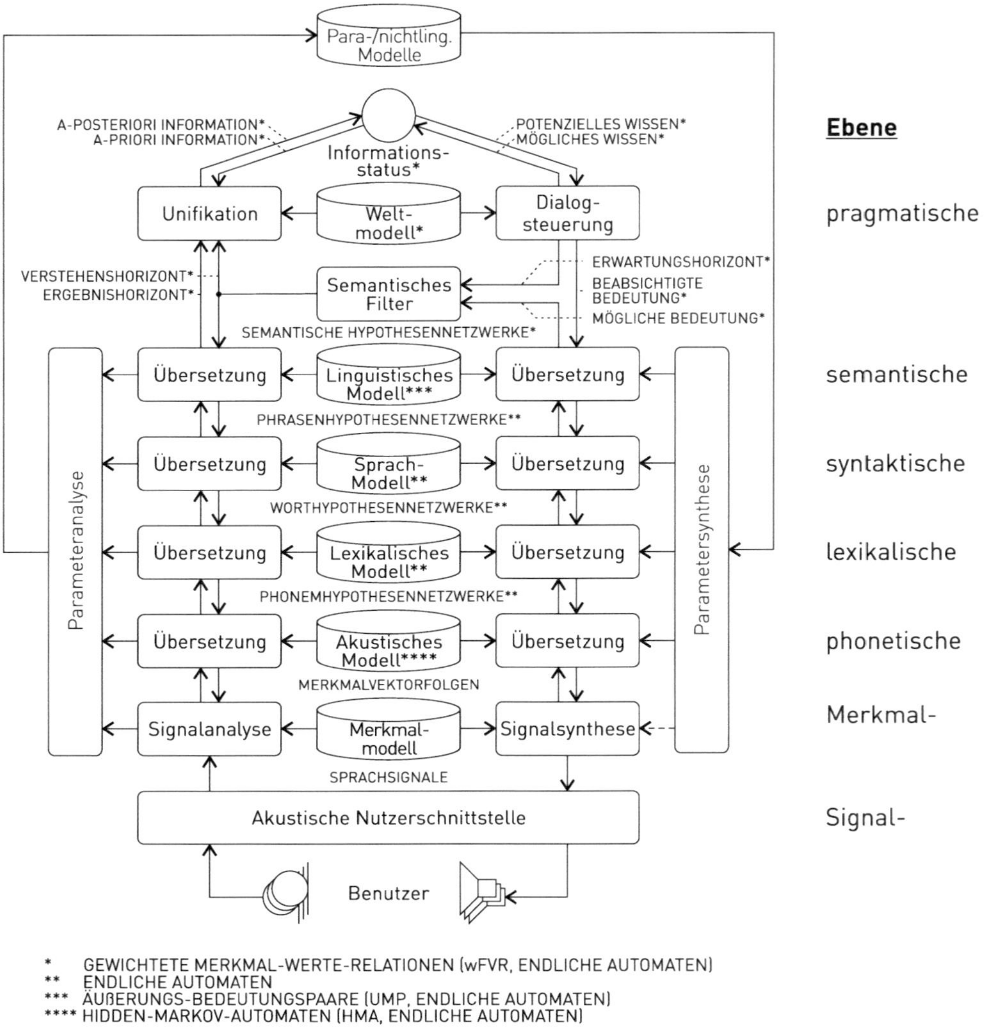

Bild 2: Aktuelles Blockschaltbild von UASR aus [2].

tikmodell in Form von gewichteten partiellen Ordnungen [6, 7, 8].

2 Bidirektionale Informationsverarbeitung

Eine Triebkraft für die Weiterentwicklung der UASR-Technologie im Sinne eines Analyse-Synthese-Systems stellen technische kognitive Systeme dar. Diese Systemklasse hat ihre Wurzeln in der regelungstechnischen Systemtheorie, in der die auftretenden Interaktionen zwischen einem System und seiner Umgebung im Mittelpunkt der Betrachtungen stehen, sie werden als Rückkopplungen verstanden. Diese werden sowohl in der Technik als auch in der Biologie als ein fundamentales Prinzip angesehen; ohne sie wäre kein zielgerichtetes Systemverhalten möglich. Nur wenn die Kommunikationsteilnehmer über Zielvorstellungen verfügen, welche zueinander kompatibel sind, können diese unter Verwendung von Rückkopplungen abgegli-

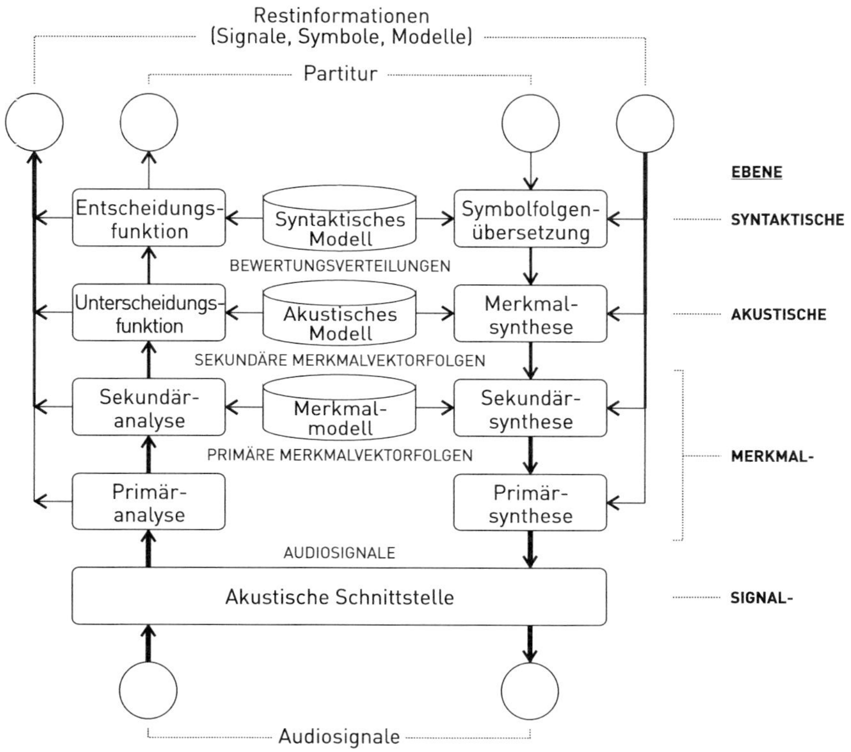

Bild 3: Blockschaltbild eines Systems zur intelligenten Signalverarbeitung aus [5].

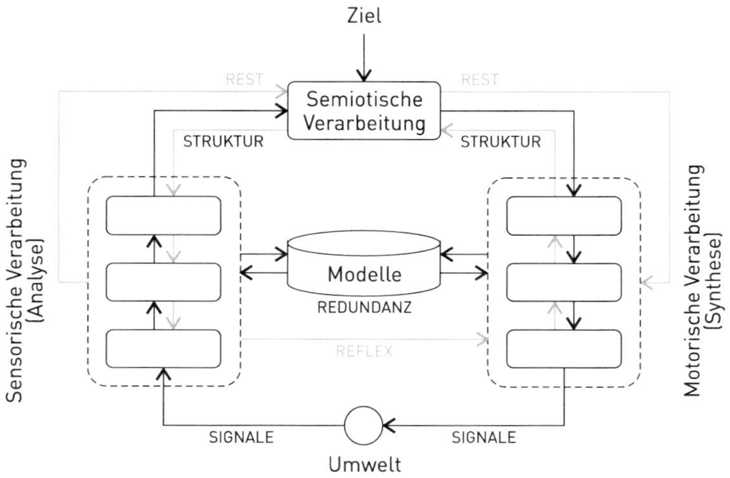

Bild 4: Blockschaltbild eines allgemeinen hierarchischen kognitiven dynamischen Systems.

chen werden. Kognitive Systeme müssen daher ihre Umgebung wahrnehmen können (Analyse), Entscheidungen unter Unsicherheiten treffen (Steuerung) und zielgerichtet auf ihre Umgebung einwirken können (Synthese). Bei der Entwicklung kognitiver Systeme sind naturgemäß biologische Strukturen höherer Organismen von besonderem Interesse. Im biologischen Strukturmodell nach [9], in dem das Zusammenwirken des sensorischen Cortex mit dem motorischen Cortex im Rahmen des Perzeptions-Aktions-Zyklus erfasst wird, kann eine formale Ähnlichkeit zur UASR-Struktur beobachtet werden. Hier findet man ebenfalls hierarchische Analyse-Synthese-Strukturen, die in den einzelnen Hierarchieebenen jeweils durch einen Arbeitsspeicher verbunden sind. Die Existenz der angegebenen Blöcke ist beim Rhesusaffen nachgewiesen worden. Im Gegensatz zum UASR-System liegt im biologischen Vorbild jedoch ein bidirektionaler Informationsfluss zwischen den Hierarchieebenen vor. Die Einführung der bidirektionalen Signalpfade kann mit gespiegelten Kommunikationsprozessen erklärt werden. Die Motivation zur Spiegelung von Kommunikationsprozessen geht auf die Einordnung kognitiver Systeme in die Klasse der finalen Systeme zurück, auf die weiter unten eingegangen wird. Solche Systeme adaptieren sich an die Umgebungsbedingungen, indem sie die Kosten für Fehlleistungen und Täuschungen optimieren. Dies gelingt, wenn die Effekte der eigenen Handlungen in der Umgebung vorhergesagt werden können. Hierfür ist die Ausbildung eines „inneren" Modells der Umgebung notwendig, auf das sowohl die Analyse als auch die Synthese zugreifen können. Die Gewährleistung einer optimalen Kommunikation ist jedoch erst dann gegeben, wenn die bidirektionalen Signalpfade auch eine entsprechende Kopplung aufweisen. Des kann nach dem Bayesschen Prinzip erfolgen. Danach müssen Vorhersage oder eine Erwartung (a-priori) und eine mutmaßliche Beobachtung miteinander verknüpft werden, um eine a-posteriori-Bewertung des eingehenden sensorischen Signals zu erhalten. Eine zweite wichtige Beobachtung stellt fest, dass sich die Struktur einer elementaren neuronalen Verarbeitungseinheit (neuronale Säule) für sensorische oder motorische Cortexareale nicht unterscheiden lässt. Dies lässt auch den Rückschluss zu, dass die Informationsverarbeitung im Cortex ebenfalls auf nur einem einzigen gemeinsam genutzten cortikalen Algorithmus beruht [10]. Erste Grundgedanken zur bidirektionalen Kommunikation zwischen Sender und Empfänger konnten erstmalig von Marko in eine mathematische Form gebracht werden [11]. Konzeptuelle Modellierungsvorschläge zur bidirektionalen Informationsverarbeitung, die sich auf hierarchische Systeme beziehen, sind in [12] publiziert worden. Ein eigenständiges Konzept zur Realisierung des cortikalen Algorithmus unter Verwendung von kaskadierten bidirektionalen Hidden-Markov-Modellen (CBHMM) wurde zunächst in [13] vorgestellt. Nach einer ersten Überprüfung des Konzepts [14] wird derzeit an einer automatenverträglichen Notation des cortikalen Algorithmus gearbeitet. Damit verfolgen wir den bedeutsamen Leitgedanken, dass komplexe Analyse-Synthese-Systeme auf einer soliden systemtheoretischen Grundlage aufsetzen müssen. In der Sprachverarbeitung hat sich die Technologie der gewichteten Finite-State-Transduktoren durchgesetzt, deren universelle Einsatzmöglichkeiten u. a. in der technischen Mustererkennung unter Beweis gestellt werden konnten. Dieser Ansatz erleichtert Verständlichkeit, Modellierung, Wartbarkeit und Erweiterbarkeit, vermeidet die Notwendigkeit der Integration verschiedener Modelle und sorgt für eine leichtere Verständigung von Wissenschaftlern unterschiedlicher Fachrichtungen in einem hoch interdisziplinären Forschungsfeld. Besonders hervorzuheben ist jedoch die vereinfachte Einbindung in technische kognitive Systeme für unterschiedliche Anwendungen. Dabei sind zwei wesentliche Grenzübergänge zu berücksichtigen: der Übergang vom Signal zum Symbol und schließlich der Übergang vom Symbol zur Semantik.

3 Semiotische Informationsverarbeitung

Im vorangegangen Abschnitt wurde bereits darauf verwiesen, dass kognitive Systeme in die Klasse der finalen Systeme eingeordnet werden können [15]. Diese Bezeichnung wurde von N. Bischof – einem international ausgewiesenen und anerkannten Psychologen – geprägt. Solche Systeme zeigen „nach außen" ein scheinbar vernünftiges Verhalten, welches sich jedoch unter Einnahme einer biologischen Perspektive auch als Adaption an die Umgebung erklären lässt. Hierzu ist weder Bewusstsein noch Reflexion notwendig. Finale Systeme adaptieren sich an die Umgebung, indem sie die Kosten für Fehlleistungen und Täuschungen optimieren. Auf diese Art und Weise können finale Systeme Strategien erlernen, die es ihnen ermöglichen, zielgerichtet zu handeln. In diesem Zusammenhang ist es notwendig, sich zu vergegenwärtigen, dass Fehlleistungen und Täuschungen semantische Begriffe sind. Diese Feststellung hat weitreichende Konsequenzen und erlaubt eine Abgrenzung zur Kybernetik, die seinerzeit ähnliche Ansprüche verfolgt hat. Das Vorhandensein einer semantischen Informationsverarbeitung ist das hervorstechende Merkmal von finalen Systemen. Deren Verhalten wird aus biologischer (evolutionärer) Sicht sowohl von mechanistischen Verursachungen (führt zu Reflexen) als auch von semantischen Verursachungen (führt zu zielgerichtetem Handeln und Adaption) bestimmt. Mit dieser Eingrenzung kann schließlich der Geltungsbereich für kognitive Systeme definiert werden. Daraus folgt für das UASR-System, dass dessen hierarchische Struktur durch mindestens eine semantische Ebene fortgesetzt werden muss. Aus der Sicht eines Analyse-Synthese-Systems scheint daher die Einbeziehung einer Dialogmodellierung, welche den Fluss (unsicherer) semantischer Information nachbildet, ein vielversprechender Ansatz zu sein. Ein naheliegendes Vorgehen besteht darin, die Konfiguration der Sprachverarbeitung auf der Analyse- und Syntheseseite semantik- bzw. dialoggetrieben zu gestalten. Ein etablierter Ansatz besteht darin, alle relevanten Information in einem „Informationszustand" zu speichern und darin neu ankommende Information zu integrieren, also ein „Information-State-Update" zu realisieren. Zur Darstellung von Unsicherheit semantischer Information werden geeignete ins Modell integrierte Gewichte (z. B. zur Darstellung von Konfidenzen oder Wahrscheinlichkeiten) verwendet. Diese Gewichte werden dann durch das Update angepasst und dienen als Grundlage für die Ableitung der Dialogschritte. Zur Repräsentation der mit Unsicherheit behafteten semantischen Inhalte (bezüglich der zu identifizierenden Daten und Aktionen) wurde eine neuartige Datenstruktur entwickelt, sogenannte gewichtete „Merkmal-Werte-Relationen" [16]. Solche gMWRen erlauben die Strukturierung von Informationsbestandteilen und stellen eine Erweiterung der in der Sprachverarbeitung bekannten Attribut-Wert-Matrizen um strukturelle Details, Gewichte und damit verbundene Algorithmen dar. Unsicherheit wird durch Gewichte ausgedrückt, welche in Form eines Gewichtshalbrings zur Verfügung stehen [6]. Gewichtete MWRen werden einheitlich sowohl zur semantischen Modellierung der Spracherkennerausgabe (des Erkennergebnisses), des für die Anwendung relevanten Weltausschnitts, des internen Zustands (Informationszustand), des Benutzermodells und der Konfiguration des Spracherkenners (Erwartungs- und Verstehenshorizont) verwendet. Erwartungs- und Verstehenshorizont sorgen für die angesprochene semantikgetriebene Konfiguration des Spracherkenners. Der Verstehenshorizont schränkt dazu das Sprachmodell auf sinnvolle Inhalte ein, um die Erkenngenauigkeit des Spracherkenners zu unterstützen. Der Erwartungshorizont ist der Teil des Verstehenshorizonts, welcher der im normalen Mensch-Mensch-Dialog üblichen Antizipation möglicher Antworten entspricht, während die restlichen Teile auch nicht direkt angesprochene Inhalte bis zu einem gewissen Grad verstehbar machen. Auf der Grundlage von gMWRen wurde ebenfalls ein auf einem Bayes-Update der Gewichte basierendes Verfahren zur Aktualisierung des Informationszustands bezüglich eines Erkennergebnisses entwickelt [17]. Angesichts der Grundstruktur von gMWRen lässt sich eine Menge von gMWRen in natürlicher Weise als nichtsequentielle Sprache eines Petrinetzes auffassen [8]. Setzt man ein Petrinetz als Transduktor ein, so dient es der direkten Übersetzung nichtsequentieller Sprachen. Damit können alle während eines Dialogs generierten MWRen Eingaben bzw. Ausgaben eines Petrinetz-Transduktors (PNT) sein. Die gesamte Funktionalität des semantischen Dialogmodells ist also grundsätzlich durch PNTen implementierbar. Dieser Ansatz verallgemeinert in natürlicher Weise den FST-basierten Ansatz – welcher auf die Verarbeitung von sequentiellen Sprachen beschränkt ist – derart, dass nichtsequentielle Sprachen von PNTen direkt verarbeitet werden können. Das erscheint zumindest auf Semantikebene aus folgenden Gründen sehr vielversprechend:

- Petrinetze sind abwärtskompatibel zu Automaten, d. h. einzelne FST-Komponenten können ohne Nebeneffekte durch PNT-Komponenten ersetzt werden.
- Petrinetzmodelle sind oft intuitiver und kompakter als Automaten-Modelle.
- Petrinetze bieten im Prinzip eine höhere sprachliche Ausdrucksmächtigkeit als Automaten.

Die semantische Ebene dient der Interpretation der auf syntaktischer Ebene erkannten oder zu erzeugenden Äußerungen. Dazu werden diesen Äußerungen sogenannte Bedeutungen zugeordnet. Diese Zuordnung wird durch UMPs (utterance-meaning-pairs) beschrieben [18]. Die Komponente, welche die Übersetzung realisiert, wird als UMP-Transduktor bezeichnet. Da zur Darstellung von Bedeutungen partielle Wörter einer nichtsequentiellen Sprache verwendet werden, ist die Anwendung der allgemeineren Theorie der Petrinetz-Transduktoren sinnvoll. PNTs ermöglichen in natürlicher Weise die Übersetzung zwischen partiellen Sprachen, welche aus partiellen Wörtern bestehen. Ein partielles Wort besteht dabei nicht – wie bei einem FST – aus einer totalen, sondern aus einer partiellen Ordnung auf seinen Symbolen. Da jeder FST ein spezieller PNT ist, ist es möglich, die gesamte Hierarchie eines Analyse-Synthese-Systems durch Kombination von FSTs und PNTs zu realisieren.

4 Kognitive zerstörungsfreie Prüfung

Die UASR-Technologie findet aber nicht „nur“ in der Sprache ihre Anwendung. Auch für die akustische Mustererkennung [4] konnte sie erfolgreich eingesetzt werden. Das zeigen die vielfältigen Anwendungen aus der zerstörungsfreien Prüfung von Bauteilen, Baugruppen, Materialien und Maschinen [19]. Die Palette reicht von Gut-/Schlechtanalysen für sintermetallurgische Bauelementen [20], Lebensdaueranalysen von Magnetventilen [21] bis zur Zustandsüberwachung von Flugzeugmaterialien [22]. Auch „exotische“ Themen wie die Weichheitsprüfung von Tissueprodukten, zu denen u. a. Kosmetiktücher und Papiertaschentücher gehören, konnten dank UASR bearbeitet werden. Bei dieser Anwendung werden Papiersorten zerrissen und die dabei entstehenden Reißgeräusche klassifiziert und Weichheitsklassen zugeordnet. In diesem Fall wurde also ein zerstörendes Prüfverfahren gewählt, was die beinahe unbegrenzten Einsatzmöglichkeiten von UASR unterstreicht.

Es lässt sich vermuten, dass nicht nur die akustische Mustererkennung, sondern der komplette kognitive Kreis aus Abbildung 4 Anwendung findet. Hierin besteht enormes Potenzial für die Zukunft, denn dies ist die Richtung, in die sich die Technik entwickeln wird. Auf Signalebene werden bereits *cognitive radio* und *cognitive radar* verwendet. Diese Anwendungen wurden u. a. von Haykin ausgearbeitet und in [23] und [24] beschrieben.

5 Zusammenfassung und Ausblick

Wir haben kurz die Entwicklung des UASR-Systems und daraus abgeleitete Verallgemeinerungen dargestellt. Wesentliche Meilensteine der Weiterentwicklung von UASR sind die bidirektionale und die semiotische Informationsverarbeitung. Technologisch hat UASR in der Vergangenheit stark von einer strikten Beschränkung auf wenige Basisverfahren profitiert. Hier seien besonders die gewichteten endlichen Automaten (wFST) genannt. Die praktische Realisierung der genannten Weiterentwicklungen wird diese Beschränkung beibehalten. So arbeiten wir zurzeit an Finite-State-Darstellungen der Subsymbol-Symbol-Übersetzung [25, 26], des cortikalen Algorithmus [27] sowie der Semantikverarbeitung [7]. Bei letzterer zeichnet sich wegen der „natürlichen" Nichtsequentialität von Semantik die Notwendigkeit einer Verallgemeinerung auf Petrinetz-Transduktoren [8] ab, von denen endlichen Automaten jedoch ein Spezialfall sind.

Hervorzuheben ist aus unserer Sicht der systemtheoretische Leitgedanke, von den sprachspezifischen Verfahren zu abstrahieren und stattdessen die universell einsetzbare wFST-Technologie zu verwenden. Mit der Verallgemeinerung auf Petrinetze setzen wir diesen Leitgedanken auf der semiotischen Ebene konsequent fort. Ebenso, wie wir mit UASR unterschiedliche nichtsprachliche Anwendungen untersuchen konnten, erwarten wir bei der Einbindung von UASR in ein kognitives System ähnliche Effekte für neuartige technische Anwendungen.

Daher wird auch in Zukunft an nichtsprachlichen Anwendungen von UASR geforscht werden. Hier stehen die oben genannten hierarchischen kognitiven dynamischen Systeme im Mittelpunkt. Wir sind der Ansicht, dass ein „kognitives" System, welches nicht mit natürlicher Sprache umzugehen vermag, diesen Namen nicht verdient. Genau hier liegt die Bedeutung der Ableitung technischer kognitiver Systeme aus UASR: Ihre aus UASR stammenden Algorithmen *sind* in der Lage, auch natürliche Sprache zu verarbeiten und haben somit tatsächlich „kognitives" Potenzial.

Wir sind in diesem Artikel nicht auf die Weiterentwicklung der HMM-Synthese innerhalb von UASR eingegangen, an der jedoch selbstverständlich ebenfalls gearbeitet und geforscht wird.

Literatur

[1] EICHNER, M.; WOLFF, M.; HOFFMANN, R.: *A unified approach for speech synthesis and speech recognition using stochastic Markov graphs.* Proc. ICSLP, Beijing 2000, vol. 1, 701–704.

[2] WOLFF, M.; RÖMER, R.; HOFFMANN, R.: *Hierarchische kognitive dynamische Systeme zur Sprach- und Signalverarbeitung.* In WOLFF, M., editor, Elektronische Sprachsignalverarbeitung 2012. ESSV 2012, volume 64 of Studientexte zur Sprachkommunikation, pages 96–103, Cottbus, Germany, Aug. 2012. TUDpress, Dresden. ISBN: 0940-6832.

[3] HOFFMANN, R.; EICHNER, M.; WOLFF, M.: *Analysis of verbal and nonverbal acoustic signals with the Dresden UASR system.* In: ESPOSITO, A., et al. (Eds.): Verbal and Nonverbal Communication Behaviours. Berlin etc.: Springer 2007 = Lecture Notes in Artifical Intelligence 4775, pp. 200–218

[4] WOLFF, M.: *Akustische Mustererkennung.* Habilitationsschrift, Studientexte zur Sprachkommunikation, Band 57, TUDpress, Dresden, 2011.

[5] WOLFF, M.; HOFFMANN, R.: *An Approach to Intelligent Signal Processing.* In ESPOSITO, A. et al. (Eds.): Behavioral Cognitive Systems, LNCS 7403, pp. 1–18, 2012. Springer-Verlag Berlin Heidelberg 2012.

[6] WIRSCHING, G.: *Calculating semantic uncertainty.* In proc: 2012 IEEE 3rd International Conference on Cognitive Infocommunications (CogInfoCom), pp. 71–76, 2012

[7] WIRSCHING, G.: *Nichtsequentialität in der Sprachverarbeitung mit FST.* In: WOLFF, M. (Hrsg.): *Elektronische Sprachsignalverarbeitung 2012 (ESSV 2012)*, Studientexte zur Sprachkommunikation, Band 64, S. 26–33. TUDpress, Dresden, 2012.

[8] HUBER, M.; LORENZ, R.: *Petri Net Transducers in Semantic Dialogue Modeling.* In: WOLFF, M. (Hrsg.): *Elektronische Sprachsignalverarbeitung 2012 (ESSV 2012)*, Studientexte zur Sprachkommunikation, Band 64, S. 286–297. TUDpress, Dresden, 2012.

[9] FUSTER, J.M.: *Cortex and Mind: Unifying Cognition.* Oxford Press University, 2005.

[10] MOUNTCASTLE, V.: *An Organizing Principle for Cerebral Function: The Unit Model and the Distributed System.* The Mindful Brain (Gerald M. Edelman and Vernon B. Mountcastle, eds.) Cambridge, MA: MIT Press, 1978.

[11] MARKO, H.: *Die Theorie der bidirektionalen Kommunikation und ihre Anwendung auf die Informationsübermittlung zwischen Menschen.* Kybernetik 3 1966, pp. 128-136.

[12] LEE, T.S.; MUMFORD, D.: *Hierarchical Bayesian Inference in the Visual Cortex.* JOSA Vol.20, No.7 July 2003.

[13] RÖMER, R.; HERBIG,T.: *Konzeptionelle Beschreibung des Cortikalen Algorithmus und seine Anwendung in der automatischen Spracherkennung.* In: Hoffmann, R. (Hrsg.): *Elektronische Sprachsignalverarbeitung 2009 (ESSV 2009)*, Studientexte zur Sprachkommunikation, Band 53, S. 33–40. TUDpress, Dresden, 2009.

[14] RÖMER, R.: *Untersuchungen zum Cortikalen Algorithmus unter Verwendung von bidirektionalen HMMs.* In M. Wolff, editor, *Elektronische Sprachsignalverarbeitung 2012 (ESSV 2012)*, Studientexte zur Sprachkommunikation, Band 64, S. 252–261. TUDpress, Dresden, 2012.

[15] RÖMER, R.; WIRSCHING, G.; WOLFF, M.: *Ein Beitrag zu den natur- und geisteswissenschaftlichen Grundlagen kognitiver Systeme.* In: Wagner, P. (Hrsg.): *Elektronische Sprachsignalverarbeitung 2013 (ESSV 2013)*, Studientexte zur Sprachkommunikation, Band 56, S. 93–102. TUDpress, Dresden, 2013.

[16] HUBER, M.; KÖLBL, C.; LORENZ, R.; RÖMER, R.; WIRSCHING, G.: *Semantische Modellierung mit gewichteten Merkmal-Werte-Relationen.* In: Hoffmann, R. (Hrsg.): *Elektronische Sprachsignalverarbeitung 2009 (ESSV 2009)*, Studientexte zur Sprachkommunikation, Band 53, S. 25–32. TUDpress, Dresden, 2009.

[17] WIRSCHING, G.; HUBER, M.; KÖLBL, CH.; LORENZ, R.; AND RÖMER, R.: *Semantic Dialogue Modeling.* Volume 7403 of Lecture Notes in Computer Science, pages 104-113. Springer, 2012.

[18] WIRSCHING, GÜNTHER; KÖLBL, CHRISTIAN: *Language Modeling with Utterance-Meaning-Pairs.* Technical Report, Institute of Computer Science, University of Augsburg, April 2011.

[19] TSCHÖPE, C.: *Akustische zerstörungsfreie Prüfung von Hidden-Markov-Modellen.* Dissertationsschrift, Studientexte zur Sprachkommunikation, Band 60, TUDpress, Dresden, 2012.

[20] TSCHÖPE, C., WOLFF, M.: *Zahnradprüfung mit statistischen Klassifikatoren.* DGZFP-Jahrestagung 2013, Dresden, Mai 2013.

[21] TSCHÖPE, C., WOLFF, M.: *Anwendungen der akustischen Mustererkennung.* In: Wagner, P. (Hrsg.): *Elektronische Sprachsignalverarbeitung 2013 (ESSV 2013)*, Studientexte zur Sprachkommunikation, Band 65, S. 205–210. TUDpress, Dresden, 2013.

[22] TSCHÖPE, C., WOLFF, M.: *Statistical Classifiers for Structural Health Monitoring.* IEEE Sensors Journal, Vol. 9, No. 11, Nov. 2009, pp. 1567–1576.

[23] HAYKIN, S.: *Cognitive Radar.* IEEE Signal Processing Magazine 23 (2006) 1, pp. 30-40.

[24] HAYKIN, S.: *Cognitive Radio: Brain-Empowered Wireless Communications.* IEEE Journal on Selected Areas in Communications 23 (2005) 2, pp. 201–220.

[25] WOLFF, M.; TSCHÖPE, C.; RÖMER, R.; WIRSCHING G.: *Subsymbol-Symbol-Transduktoren.* In WAGNER, P. (Hrsg.): *Elektronische Sprachsignalverarbeitung 2013 (ESSV 2013)*, Studientexte zur Sprachkommunikation, Band 65, S. 197–204. TUDpress, Dresden, 2013.

[26] TSCHÖPE, C., WOLFF, M.: *Zur Formulierung von Hidden-Markov-Modellen als endliche Transduktoren.* In: WOLFF, M. (Hrsg.): *Elektronische Sprachsignalverarbeitung 2012 (ESSV 2012)*, Studientexte zur Sprachkommunikation, Band 64, S. 120–128. TUDpress, Dresden, 2012.

[27] RÖMER, R.; HERBIG,T.: *Cortical Algorithm for Symbolic and Subsymbolic Applications.* In: Mixdorff, H. (Hrsg.): *Elektronische Sprachsignalverarbeitung 2010 (ESSV 2010)*, Studientexte zur Sprachkommunikation, Band 58, S. 150–157. TUDpress, Dresden, 2010.

Die Universitätssammlungen auf dem Weg zu neuen Netzwerken der Wissenskommunikation

Klaus Mauersberger

Einführung

Die Sammlungen der Technischen Universität Dresden sind hinsichtlich ihrer Herkunft, historischen Entwicklung, Einbindung in Lehre und Forschung sowie Grad der Musealisierung höchst disparat. Als Lehrsammlungen an einer technischen Bildungseinrichtung entstanden, erlebten sie über Jahrzehnte, teils über mehr als ein Jahrhundert ihres Bestehens, einen gravierenden Funktionswandel. Allein die den Lehrgegenständen folgende Diversität der Objekte reicht vom Herbarblatt über die Farbstoffprobe bis hin zum Kymographen. Allein die letzterem zugeordnete "Historische Akustisch-Phonetische Sammlung" besitzt eine Spannbreite von Instrumenten und Geräten, die von der frühen Sprachwiedergabe und Elektroakustik über die klassische Experimentalphonetik bis hin zur modernen Spracherkennung und Sprachsynthese reicht. Demgemäß sind auch die Probleme der Unterbringung, Erfassung, Konservierung und Präsentation in den einzelnen Sammlungen sehr unterschiedlich. Auch hinsichtlich des Umfangs unterscheiden sich die Kollektionen beträchtlich. Die hohe Zeit der Sammlungen an unserer Universität war bis in die 1920er Jahre geprägt von einer engen Verquickung des Sammlungsgeschehens mit den Kernaufgaben in Lehre und Forschung. Besonders in den natur- und ingenieurwissenschaftlichen Disziplinen wurde die visuelle Anschaulichkeit zu einem wichtigen didaktischen Prinzip erhoben.

Neben der einer beschleunigten technischen Entwicklung geschuldeten Musealisierung vieler Sammlungen trug nach dem Zweiten Weltkrieg, in der DDR besonders im Zuge der 3. Hochschulreform, der Paradigmenwechsel in den Lehr- und Lernmethoden dazu bei, dass vor allem ingenieurwissenschaftliche Sammlungen an den technischen Hochschulen bald ein Schattendasein fristeten, das sie zu den so genannten "Cindarella Collections" stempelte. Erst mit der Hochschulerneuerung im Gefolge der deutschen Wiedervereinigung hat man sich, auch deutschlandweit, der verborgenen Schätze erinnert. Die 1995 an der TU Dresden erlassene Ordnung über den Umgang mit musealem Gut, die Festschreibung des institutionellen Bewahrerprinzips und der Beratungsfunktion der Kustodie, ist ein deutliches Zeichen dafür und gilt unter den universitärer Sammlungen als vorbildlich. Mit den seit 2010 ausgerichteten jährlichen Sammlungstagungen sowie mit der Gründung einer Gesellschaft für Universitätssammlungen ist die Selbstorganisation der Sammlungsakteure in den letzten Jahren ein gutes Stück vorangekommen. Neuerdings werden die Sammlungen trotz mangelnder Personal- und Finanzausstattung als wertvolle Ressourcen für eine sammlungsbezogene Forschung sowie für die Wissenschaftskommunikation ganz allgemein wiederentdeckt. Im Rahmen einer erweiterten Einbeziehung von Sammlungen in Ausstellungsprojekte wird an der TU Dresden gegenwärtig die Vernetzung der Sammlungen innerhalb der Hochschule sowie über Hochschulgrenzen hinaus betrieben. Der Jubilar Prof. Hoffmann hat an diesem Geschehen stets regen Anteil genommen, Grund genug, die jüngsten Entwicklungen in dieser Festschrift einmal Revue passieren zu lassen.

Der Weg zu einem geordneten Sammlungsgeschehen an der TU Dresden

Blicken wir auf die Sammlungsgeschichte unserer Universität, so wird erkennbar, dass dem Sammlungsgeschehen sehr unterschiedliche Bedeutung und entsprechende Aufmerksamkeit beigemessen wurde. Waren Nutzung von Sammlungen ausgangs des 19. Jahrhunderts noch integraler Bestandteil des Lehrbetriebs, so sind später in den Sammlungsbeständen infolge sich permanent vollziehender Änderungen im Fächerkanon und im Forschungsprofil der Bildungsanstalt große Bewegungen zu verzeichnen. Ein denkwürdiges Jahr in der Geschichte der naturwissenschaftlichen und technischen Sammlungen am Polytechnikum Dresden war 1878. In Ausführung einer Ministerialverordnung erließ die Direktion unter der Ägide Gustav Anton Zeuners erstmals "Allgemeine Normen für die Aufstellung und Fortführung der Inventarverzeichnisse und Sammlungskataloge"[1]. Im Zuge der Campusbebauung in der Südvorstadt kam es zum bislang größten Aufschwung im Sammlungsgeschehen der damaligen TH Dresden. Im Wintersemester 1905/06 verzeichnet das Taschenbuch der Technischen Hochschule zu Dresden die stattliche Zahl von 41 Sammlungen. Damit war ein gewaltiger Schritt von den bescheidenen Lehrutensilien der Anfangsjahre zu einem leistungsfähigen Fundus an eigenständigen, den Lehrfächern zugeordneten Sammlungen vollzogen. Bereits 1901 war für die Vorstände der Sammlungen, die sich in der Regel aus der Professorenschaft rekrutierten, die Amtsbezeichnung "Direktor" eingeführt worden. Als der Bombardierung Dresdens im Februar 1945 große Teile der Hochschule zum Opfer fielen, wurden auch die Sammlungen in Mitleidenschaft gezogen. Wertvolle Sachzeugen gingen unwiederbringlich verloren. Wichtige Bestandteile der nach dem Zweiten Weltkrieg neu formierten Sammlungen mussten förmlich aus dem Schutt geborgen werden. Eine weitere Dezimierung erfuhren die Sammlungsbestände durch Reparationsleistungen an die Sowjetunion. Der Neuanfang nach dem Krieg stand ganz im Zeichen der Reparatur und des behelfsmäßigen Wiederaufbaus der noch vorhandenen Lehr- und Anschauungsmittel. Mühevoll wurden nicht nur die Gebäude wie auch das Inventar instand gesetzt, um den Lehrbetrieb zu gewährleisten. Mehr noch als in den zwanziger und dreißiger Jahren verbreitete sich auch in der Ausbildung von Studenten eine stärkere theoretische Orientierung. Dies leitete einen Wandel im Begriff der Anschaulichkeit ein. Die auf geometrischen Darstellungsformen und durch Visualisierung fundierte Stoffvermittlung wich in einigen Fächern zunehmend abstrakteren Darlegungen. Die so genannte Dritte Hochschulreform hatte ein Übriges getan, so dass mit der Einführung neuer Lehr- und Lernmethoden in den Jahren nach 1968 die herkömmlichen Anschauungsmittel auffallend vernachlässigt und zurückgedrängt worden sind.

Erst in den 1980er Jahren besann man sich erneut auf die reichen Sammlungsbestände, die man vorrangig zur Illustrierung der seit der 150-Jahrfeier der Universität (1978) forciert betriebenen Hochschulgeschichte nutzte. Nach der Einrichtung einer zentralen Kustodie im Jahr 1979 wurde 1987 endlich eine "Ordnung über den Museumsfonds der TU Dresden" erlassen, die den Umgang und Schutz von Kulturgut regelte. Im Zuge der Hochschulerneuerung nach der Wiedervereinigung Deutschlands erhielt die Kustodie den Status einer Betriebseinheit der Philosophischen Fakultät, später den einer dem Rektoratskollegium unterstellten zentralen Einrichtung. Indessen erforderte die sich rasch vollziehende Erneuerung der Lehr- und Forschungsmittel in einem Spannungsfeld von Bewahrung und Selektion in beinahe allen Fächern die ständige Neubewertung technischer Sachzeugen, vornehmlich unter technikhistorischen und musealen Gesichtspunkten. Die Entdeckung längst vergessener Artefakte mit historischem Wert hielt dabei durchaus Überraschungen bereit. Hier schließt sich der Kreis vom einstigen Lehrmittel zum musealen Kulturgut. Ein Reflex darauf war die im Jahr 1998 erlassene und 2004 auf den Kunstbesitz erweiterte "Ordnung zur Bewahrung der naturwissenschaftlichen und technischen Sammlungen, des Kunstbesitzes und der Kulturdenkmale der TU Dresden", die der Nutzung der Kulturdenkmale zu wissenschaftlichen, bildungspolitischen oder kulturellen Zwecken sowie ihre geeignete Präsentation in der Hochschule und auf

[1] Vgl. Sammlungen und Kunstbesitz der Technischen Universität Dresden. Hg. vom Rektor der Technischen Universität Dresden. Leipzig und Dresden 1996, S. 175-177.

Ausstellungen als öffentliches Interesse deklarierte, das einen hohen ideellen und materiellen Wert repräsentiert und als Vermögen der Universität eines besonderen Schutzes bedarf. Grundsätzlich gilt ein institutionelles Bewahrerprinzip, das heißt, die Sammlungen stehen dezentral in der Verantwortung der bewahrenden Einrichtungen (Fachbereiche, Institute, Lehrstühle, Werkstätten), wobei der „zentralen" Kustodie die Anleitungs-, Beratungs-, Koordinierungs- und Kontrollfunktion zukommt. Alle Sammlungen sowie einzelne herausgehobene Sachzeugen ohne Sammlungscharakter sind als Vermögen der TU Dresden im musealen Fonds der Universität zusammengefasst. Entsprechend sind seither die Zuständigkeiten der Kustodie und der bewahrenden Struktureinheiten zum Schutz, zur Erhaltung, Pflege und Nutzung der Sammlungen geregelt.[2] Mit der Einsetzung von Sammlungsbeauftragten in den Wissenschaftsbereichen wurde die Sichtung, Inventarisierung und Dokumentation des musealen Fonds in der Folgezeit wesentlich vorangebracht. Der Kustodie obliegt ferner die Entscheidung bei Aussonderungen, der geregelte Leihverkehr mit Museen und Ausstellungen und die Entgegennahme von Schenkungen und Neuaufnahmen. Gegenwärtig sind in ca. 40 eigenständigen Sammlungen etwa 11 000 Exponate erfasst. Hinzu kommen ca. 30 000 Einzelobjekte der Gesteinsammlungen, 8 000 Farbstoffproben und 350 000 Belege des Herbariums. Mit der Eröffnung der ständigen Ausstellung der Kustodie „Sammlungen und Geschichte der TU Dresden" ist im Jahr 2003 ein Platz musealer Schaustellung eines repräsentativen Querschnitts von Exponaten aus den einzelnen Sammlungen geschaffen worden. Darüber hinaus verkörpert das Projekt „Universitätssammlungen_Kunst+Technik" mit seinen wechselnden Ausstellungen, indessen blicken wir auf eine Anzahl von 20 zurück, auf ganz eigenständige Weise einen Brückenschlag zwischen Kunst und Technik. Eine kritisch-diskursive Ausstellungskultur dürfte dabei auch neue Erkenntnisperspektiven eröffnen. Augenfällig an diesem Projekt ist bereits die inspirierende Wirkung der Kunst im ungewohnten Umfeld. Dieser interdisziplinäre Weg öffnet auch den universitären Sammlungen neue Präsentationsmöglichkeiten. Ein gegenseitiges Lernen und besseres Wahrnehmen von Ingenieurwissenschaft und Kunstproduktion ist dabei mehr als ein gewünschter Nebeneffekt. Durch die Interaktion von Kunst und Wissenschaft dürften auch die scheinbar leblosen Technikobjekte erneut in lebendige Wechselwirkungen sowie in den Austausch der Wissensformen einfließen.

Sammlungsbezogene Forschung, Vernetzung nach innen und außen

Die Sammlungsbezogene Forschung an der TU Dresden nimmt sich gegenüber den bedeutenden naturkundlichen Sammlungen an den großen Universitäten eher bescheiden aus. Immerhin konnte im Zusammenhang mit der Vorbereitung von Ausstellungen ein gewisser Schub an sammlungsbezogener Forschung erreicht werden. Dies betrifft vor allem die Hermann-Krone-Sammlung historischer Fotografien. Die nach einer Werkausstellung im Dresdner Albertinum[3] angebahnte Zusammenarbeit mit dem Getty Conservation Institute war der Höhepunkt einer fruchtbaren Wissenschaftskooperation über Landesgrenzen hinaus. In jüngerer Zeit sind es vor allem Ausstellungen innerhalb der Universitätssammlungen_Kunst+Technik in der „Altana-Galerie" im Görges-Bau, deren Vorbereitung vor allem interdisziplinäre Forschung voraussetzte: Wahr-Zeichen. Fotografie und Wissenschaft (2006), Good Vibrations. Geometrie und Kunst (2008), color continuo. System und Kunst der Farbe (2009/2010), Bilder machen. Fotografie als Praxis (2010), Scheinbar Sein. Faktisches und Virtuelles (2011), terra incognita. Weltbilder-Welterfahrungen (2011). Insbesondere die Sammlung Farbenlehre hat neben der verzweigten Ausstellung "color continuo" bereits durch die Veranstaltungen des „Farbenforums", durch ein e-lerning-Projekt sowie durch Beteiligung an den Jahrestagungen des Deutschen Farbenzentrums einen beträchtlichen Forschungsvorlauf gewonnen. Ein weite-

---

[2] http://www.verw.tu-dresden.de/VerwRicht/Sachwort/download.asp?file=rskustodie0104.pdf

[3] Hesse, W.; Starl, T. (Hg.): Der Photopionier Hermann Krone. Photographie und Apparatur. Bildkultur und Phototechnik im 19. Jahrhundert. Marburg 1998.

res Vorhaben, das historische Forschung erforderte, war die Einbeziehung der Getriebemodellsammlung in das DFG-Projekt „Digitale Mechanismen- und Getriebebibliothek“[4] (DMG-Lib). Selbstverständlich werden die Sammlungen in die hochschulgeschichtlichen Forschungs- und Publikationsvorhaben der Kustodie einbezogen[5]. In der von Prof. Hoffmann betreuten Akustisch-Phonetischen Sammlung wurde erstmals daran gegangen, einen vollständigen Sammlungskatalog herauszugeben[6]. Hinsichtlich der Platzierung der TU-Sammlungen auf internationalen Portalen setzte das Pilotprojekt „Timeline of Photography“ ein erstes Zeichen. Darin wurde Hermann Krones Lehrmuseum im Rahmen der Internet-Präsentation „Constructing Europe“ des internationalen SEPIA II Program (2003) der ECPA (European Commission for Preservation and Access)[7] im Internet präsentiert.

Insgesamt bilden die Kustodie und die Sammlungsbeauftragten eine gemeinsame Plattform der Wissenskommunikation und des Erfahrungsaustausches zum Sammlungsgeschehen an der TU Dresden und sind damit ein Garant für eine geordnete Sammlungstätigkeit, für die Weitergabe von inhaltlichen Anregungen sowie ein Ausgangspunkt für interne und externe Vernetzungen sowie für die Nutzung von Synergieeffekten. Seit einigen Jahren sind auch Bestrebungen in Gange, die universitären Sammlungen deutschlandweit untereinander besser zu vernetzen. 2006 startete am Hermann-Helmholtz-Zentrum für Kulturtechnik der Humboldt-Universität zu Berlin ein von der DFG gefördertes Projekt "Universitätssammlungen in Deutschland: Untersuchungen zu Bestand und Geschichte"[8]. Unter der Ägide von Cornelia Weber wurde am Helmholtz-Zentrum in der Folge ein digitaler Katalog der Universitätssammlungen in Deutschland erstellt, in dem auch die Sammlungen der TU Dresden ausführlich vorgestellt werden[9]. Aus den Projekten der Abteilung Wissenschaftliche Sammlungen und Wissenschaftskommunikation der HUB gingen auch die maßgeblichen Impulse für die Ausrichtung von Veranstaltungen zur weiteren Vernetzung der Universitätssammlungen aus. Als Auftakt widmete sich im Frühjahr 2010 eine erste Sammlungstagung dem Thema „Universitätsmuseen und -sammlungen im Hochschulalltag“ in Berlin, deren wissenschaftliche Leitung vom Hermann-Helmholtz-Zentrum für Kulturtechnik und der Kustodie der TU Dresden getragen wurde[10]. Das Symposium hatte sich zum Ziel gesetzt, gemeinsam nach neuen Aufgaben für Universitätsmuseen und -sammlungen zu suchen sowie Strategien zu entwickeln, um den Fortbestand akademischer Sammlungen sicherzustellen und Zukunftskonzepte zu erörtern, um die traditionellen Universitätssammlungen besser in den Hochschulalltag zu integrieren und den heutigen Ansprüchen von Forschung, Lehre und Wissenschaftskommunikation gerecht zu werden. Darüber hinaus sollte ein Netzwerk für Universitätsmuseen und -sammlungen im deutschsprachigen Raum etabliert werden, um den dringend erforderlichen Austausch von Erfahrungen und Kenntnissen in Gang zu setzen, damit über gemeinsame Strategien nachgedacht, Möglichkeiten der Zusammenarbeit ausgelotet und kollektive Aktivitäten befördert werden können. Auf dem Symposium trat auch der Kanzler der TU Dresden mit einem Beitrag über die Gratwanderung der Universitätssammlungen zwischen Verwaltung und Gestaltung auf. Er hob darin hervor, dass noch immer die Kluft zwischen Bewahrungs-

---

[4] http://www.dmg-lib.org/dmglib/main/portal.jsp

[5] Vgl. Mauersberger, K.: Maschinenbau an der TU Dresden. Ein Beitrag zur Geschichte der Fakultät Maschinenwesen. Illustrierter historischer Abriss mit Auswahlbibliografie, TU Dresden, 2007[1], 2009[2].
Mauersberger, K.: Von der Photographie zur Photophysik. 100 Jahre Wissenschaftlich-Photographisches Institut. Hg. vom Institut für Angewandte Photophysik der TU Dresden, Dresden 2008.

[6] Mehnert, D.: Historische phonetische Geräte. Katalog der historischen akustisch-phonetischen Sammlung (HAPS) der Technischen Universität Dresden, Erster Teil (=Studientexte zur Sprachkommunikation, Bd. 62, hg. von Rüdiger Hoffmann), Dresden 2012.

[7] http://www.iapp.de/krone/timeline/Deutsch/Index2.htm

[8] Weber, C.: Universitätssammlungen in Deutschland - Untersuchungen zu Bestand und Geschichte. In: .hist2006. Geschichte im Netz: Praxis, Chancen, Visionen: http://edoc.hu-berlin/histfor/10_II/(pdf)

[9] http://publicus.culture.hu-berlin.de/sammlungen/

[10] http://edoc.hu-berlin.de/conferences/ums2010

pflicht und mangelnden personellen und materiellen Ressourcen bei vielen Universitätssammlungen Alltag sei. Greife aber solides Verwalten und kreatives Gestalten in der Sammlungstätigkeit vernünftig ineinander, werde auch die Integration der historischen Sachzeugen in die Kernaufgaben von Lehre und Forschung gelingen. Wenn Sammlungen in innovative Lehr- und Forschungsaufgaben eingebunden würden, wenn Publikationen und Ausstellungen über die Universitäten hinaus wirkten, dann würden sie eine gesamtuniversitäre Identitätsstiftung entfalten können und zu einem wichtigen Faktor der Konkurrenzfähigkeit und Exzellenz von Universitäten werden. Daher sollten Strategien entwickelt werden, die Synergieeffekte bewirkten. Gemäß dem Leitbild: Universitäten brauchen Sammlungen - Sammlungen brauchen Universitäten, sollte die Universität ein Ort der Sammlungen bleiben[11]. Das Symposium, das sich einer lebhaften Resonanz erfreute, kann als eine erste größere Bestandsaufnahme der Probleme und Tendenzen des universitären Sammlungswesens in der Bundesrepublik Deutschland gewertet werden. Zugleich war in Berlin eine Aufbruchstimmung zu bemerken, deren Schwung zu weiteren Vorstößen führte.

Fortgesetzt werden sollte der Diskurs nun auf einer zweiten Sammlungstagung an der Universität Jena. Vom 1. bis zum 3. April 2011 wurde diese am dortigen Phyletischen Museum unter dem Thema „Selbstorganisation und Förderung von wissenschaftlichen Sammlungen. Die Empfehlung des Wissenschaftsrates“ ausgerichtet. Dem voraus gegangen waren Anhörungen und Befragungen des Wissenschaftsrates über wissenschaftliche Sammlungen als Forschungsinfrastrukturen, in die auch die Kustodie der TU Dresden involviert war. Der Leiter der Arbeitsgruppe „Sammlungsbezogene Forschung“ beim Wissenschaftsrat, Prof. Bernhard Schink von der Universität Konstanz, trug selbst die Ergebnisse der Befragungen und die daraus abgeleiteten Empfehlungen vor[12]. Darin sind wichtige Punkte angesprochen, die zu einer intensiven Entwicklung der wissenschaftlichen Sammlungen Deutschlands führen sollen. Die Umsetzung der Empfehlung dürfte nur dann gelingen, wenn die für die Sammlungen Verantwortlichen den Prozess selbst in die Hand nehmen und kritisch gestalten. Innerhalb von zwei Tagen sollte daher an der Empfehlung des Wissenschaftsrates gearbeitet und die Grundlage für zukünftige Selbstorganisationsstrukturen, Bewertungskriterien und Zusammenarbeiten geschaffen werden. Die Sammlungsverantwortlichen bekamen auf dieser Tagung die Möglichkeit, eine wegweisende Diskussion zu führen, gleichzeitig zukünftige Organisationsstrukturen zu gestalten und sich über Fördermöglichkeiten zu informieren. Gemäß diesen Richtlinien gliederte sich auch die Tagung in vier Arbeitsgruppen: Selbstorganisation - Standards für wissenschaftliche Sammlungen - Plattformen digitaler Erschließung - Präsentation und Vermittlung.

Wichtig für die künftige Selbstorganisation und Vernetzung der Sammlungen war die Empfehlung, an Universitäten mit relevanten Sammlungsbeständen Sammlungsbeauftragte zu benennen, die unabhängig und übergreifend als Schnittstelle zu den entsprechenden Leitungsgremien agieren. Hier verfügen einige ostdeutsche Hochschulen mit ihren fortbestehenden zentralen Kustodien über einen gewissen organisatorischen Vorlauf. Neben der kustodialen und universitären Ebene ist als ein wichtiges Ergebnis der Tagung auch die Einrichtung einer zentralen, vom Bundesministerium für Bildung und Forschung (BMBF) geförderten Koordinierungsstelle für wissenschaftliche Universitätssammlungen in Deutschland [13], die an das

---

[11] Wormser, W.-E.: Universitätssammlungen zwischen Verwaltung und Gestaltung - das Beispiel der TU Dresden. In: Weber, C.; Mauersberger, K.: Universitätsmuseen und -sammlungen im Hochschulalltag. Aufgaben - Konzepte - Perspektiven. Beiträge zum Symposium vom 18.-20. Februar 2010 an der Humboldt-Universität zu Berlin, ebenda, S. 11-16.

[12] Empfehlungen des Wissenschaftsrates zu Forschungsinfrastrukturen (2011), http://www.wissenschaftsrat.de/download/archiv/10464-11.pdf

[13] www.wissenschaftliche-sammlungen.de
http://www.kulturtechnik.hu-berlin.de/content/wiki/aktuelles

Helmholtz-Zentrum angegliedert worden ist, zu verzeichnen. Diese organisiert die bundesweite Vernetzung der wissenschaftlichen Sammlungen und gilt zugleich als „Appellationsinstanz“, als Anlaufadresse für die Sorgen und Interessen der einzelnen Sammlungen. Die Legitimation eines entsprechenden Gremiums der Selbstorganisation erfolgte zunächst durch das Plenum der Sammlungstagung, sollte aber durch eine nachgeschobene Gremienwahl bestätigt werden. Auch die weiteren Themen wie die Festlegung von Sammlungsstandards, Selbstevaluation der Sammlungen, Vermittlung in Lehre und Öffentlichkeitsarbeit sowie das ganz aktuelle Thema der Digitalisierung und Internetpräsentation der reichen Sammlungsbestände wurde lebhaft diskutiert. Auf einer Abendveranstaltung sprach der ehemalige Vorsitzende des Wissenschaftsrates, Prof. Peter Strohschneider, der ja einige Zeit an der TU Dresden wirkte, über die grundsätzliche Bedeutung von Sammlungen für die Wissenschaft[14]. Er hob dabei die latente Funktion der Sammlungen für völlig neue Forschungsinteressen und -inhalte hervor, die viele Kollektionen heute in einem ganz aktuellen Licht erscheinen lässt. Schließlich waren in Jena auch Vertreter jener öffentlich rechtlichen Förderinstrumente und Stiftungen zugegen, die sich bislang bereits der Sammlungsförderung verschrieben hatten. In diesen Einrichtungen hat offenbar eine Diskussion über die Ausweitung des Inhaltes sammlungsbezogener Forschung begonnen, die hoffen lässt. Insgesamt stimmte die Tagung alle Sammlungsverantwortlichen zuversichtlich und ermutigte dazu, die gegenseitige Kommunikation, Vernetzung und Kooperation zum Nutzen aller voranzubringen.

Blick in die Ausstellung "Dinge des Wissens" anlässlich der 275-Jahrfeier der Georg-August-Universität in der Göttinger Paulinerkirche (2012)

[14] Strohschneider, P.: Faszinationskraft der Dinge. Über Sammlung, Forschung und Universität. In: Denkströme. Journal der Sächsischen Akademie der Wissenschaften, Heft 8(2012), S. 9-26.

Im Jahr 2012 verdichteten sich die Aktivitäten der Universitätssammlungen auf zwei Tagungen. Die dritte Sammlungstagung im Frühjahr fand an der Friedrich-Alexander-Universität in Erlangen[15] statt und trug deutlichen Werkstattcharakter. In Nachfolge der Berliner und Jenaer Veranstaltung wurde der Dialog über die Sammlungen fortgesetzt und weitere Anregungen für eine vielfältige Sammlungspraxis eingebracht. Um Sammlungen in Forschung, Lehre und Ausstellungen zu nutzen bedarf es Kreativität und Sachverstandes. Entsprechend stand der sachgemäße Umgang mit den Sammlungen in seiner wissenschaftlichen und kustodialen Perspektive im Mittelpunkt. Darüber hinaus knüpfte die Veranstaltung an die Bemühungen um künftige Formen der Koordinierung und Selbstorgansisation universitärer Sammlungen an. Im Herbst stand dann das 275-jährige Bestehen der Georg-August-Universität Göttingen an. Aus diesem Anlass gestalteten die historischen Sammlungen der Universität eine beeindruckende Ausstellung „Dinge des Wissens“ in der zur Bibliothek umgebauten Paulinerkirche[16]. Den Impetus des Jubiläums nutzend, richtete die Göttinger Uni zugleich eine zentrale Kustodie ein. So kam es nicht von ungefähr, dass die nunmehr vierte Sammlungstagung ihr Domizil in Göttingen suchte. Vom 4. bis zum 6. Oktober trafen sich im historischen Bibliotheksgebäude die Vertreter universitärer Sammlungen, Kustodien, Universitätsmuseen und ähnlicher Einrichtungen zum Thema „Die Universität der Dinge. Akademisches Sammeln in der Diskussion“ zum Erfahrungsaustausch über aktuelle Themen der Sammlungstätigkeit wie sammlungsbezogene Forschung, Sammlungen in der Lehre, Digitalisierung und Bewertung sowie juristische Aspekte. Den Höhepunkt gemeinsamer Bestrebungen und Interessenvertretung aber bildete die Gründung einer eigenen „Gesellschaft für Universitätssammlungen“, die in der Göttinger Gründungsversammlung nach dem Willen aller Beteiligten umgehend nach dem Vereinsrecht in Angriff genommen wurde. Auf dem Fundament einer eigenen Fachgesellschaft soll auf den kommenden Sammlungstagungen noch stärker auf die fachlichen Aspekte universitärer Sammlungstätigkeit orientiert werden.

Die fünfte Sammlungstagung deutschsprachiger Universitätssammlungen findet dieses Jahr an der Martin-Luther-Universität Halle-Wittenberg statt. Ziel der kommenden Arbeitstagung ist es, in vier sammlungsrelevanten Bereichen konkrete Vorgaben auszuarbeiten: Urheberrecht und rechtliche Belange, Grundfinanzierung, Zentralisierung, sowie die Forschungsaufgabe Restaurierung und Präparation von Sammlungen[17]. Es ist darüber hinaus ein Anliegen der Tagung, möglichst auch mit außeruniversitären wissenschaftlichen Sammlungen und Museen sowie mit Fördermittelgebern verstärkt ins Gespräch zu kommen.

Ausblick: Zeichen eines stabilen Sammlungsalltages

Gegenwärtig zeichnet es sich ab, dass mit den verzweigten Aktivitäten der Koordinierungsstelle, der neu gegründeten Gesellschaft sowie der abgeleiteten Gremien Schwung in das Sammlungsgeschehen gekommen ist, das zumindest Ansätze einer Verstetigung zeitigt. Es gilt nunmehr, die universitären Sammlungen unter Beachtung ihrer Vielfalt und ihrer lokalen Besonderheiten fächer- und standortübergreifend als dezentrale Forschungsinfrastrukturen weiterzuentwickeln und eine dauerhafte bundesweite Vernetzung für ein abgestimmtes Handeln der Akteure zu etablieren. Eine wichtige Aufgabe im breiten Arbeitsspektrum der Koordinierungsstelle wird der Aufbau effektiver Kommunikationswege und Koordinationsstrukturen sein. In Zusammenarbeit mit Experten werden Mindeststandards und Empfehlungen für

[15] Siehe auch: Andraschke, U.; Ruisinger, M. (Hg.): Die Sammlungen der Universität Erlangen-Nürnberg. Begleitband zur Ausstellung, Nürnberg 2007.
[16] Dinge des Wissens. Die Sammlungen, Museen und Gärten der Universität Göttingen. Hg. von der Georg-August-Universität Göttingen, 2012.
[17] http://www.naturkundemuseum.uni-halle.de/sammlungstagung_2013/

den Umgang mit universitären Sammlungen erarbeitet, außerdem werden Beratungen für Sammlungsbeauftragte, Koordinatoren, Kustoden sowie für Universitäten allgemein in sammlungsbezogenen Bereichen angeboten. Ein weiteres Ziel der Koordinierungsstelle ist es, die Sichtbarkeit und damit Nutzbarkeit wissenschaftlicher Sammlungen durch digitale Erschließung und Digitalisierung zu erhöhen. In diesem Zusammenhang wird ein zentrales Portal für Sammlungen und Objekte aufgebaut, das dezentrale Datenbestände verknüpft.

Zu den vom BMBF geförderten Arbeitsgruppen zählt die Fachgruppe "Mindeststandards für wissenschaftliche Sammlungen", in der die entsprechenden Empfehlungen des Wissenschaftsrates in allgemeine Grundsätze gekleidet und schließlich in ein praktikables Arbeitspapier transformiert werden. Dabei geht es namentlich um die Kategorien Objekte, Sammlungen, Interaktion in Lehre, Forschung und Öffentlichkeitsarbeit. Ein wichtiges Thema dabei sind die Standards bei der räumlichen Unterbringung von Sammlungen. Auf den regelmäßig von der Koordinierungsstelle durchgeführten Workshops werden Themen wie "Qualitätskriterien von Sammlungen" sowie "Sammlungskonzepte und Leitbilder" praxisnah erörtert.

Auch die Fördereinrichtungen wie Volkswagen-Stiftung, BMBF oder Deutsche Forschungsgemeinschaft widmen sich immer stärker der sammlungsbezogenen Forschung und stimmen ihre Förderrichtlinien auf die vordringlichen Belange der Sammlungen ab. Auf die DFG-Ausschreibung zur Erschließung und Digitalisierung von objektbezogenen wissenschaftlichen Sammlungen[18] bewarb sich die Sammlung Mathematische Modelle der TU Dresden mit Erfolg. Das Thema des 2012 bewilligten Projekts "Digitales Archiv mathematischer Modelle"[19] widmet sich der "Digitalisierung und Archivierung mathematischer Modelle für frei zugängliche multimediale Präsentation und flexible Recherche via Internet". Große Resonanz in den Sammlungen fand auch die BMBF-Förderrichtlinie „Die Sprache der Objekte – Materielle Kultur im Kontext gesellschaftlicher Entwicklungen“ vom März 2012[20]. Das von Partnern im Umfeld der Farbstoffsammlung sowie der Sammlung Farbenlehre eingereichte Projekt "Farbe als Akteur und Speicher. Historisch-kritische Analyse der Materialität und kulturellen Codierung von Farbe" erfreut sich guter Aussichten, in die engere Wahl zu gelangen. Die jüngste Förderinitiative des BMBF geht von Überlegungen aus, eine Allianz für universitäre Sammlungen unter Einbeziehung von Forschungsmuseen der Leibniz-Gemeinschaft zu bilden. Die DFG hat im Frühjahr 2013 erneut eine Ausschreibung zum Thema "Bildung und Weiterentwicklung von Standards zur Erschließung und/oder Digitalisierung von Objektgattungen in wissenschaftlichen Sammlungen" veröffentlicht[21]. Sie richtet sich an Wissenschaftler sowie wissenschaftliche Service- und Informationseinrichtungen in Deutschland, die objektbezogene wissenschaftliche Sammlungen betreuen und sich in möglichst enger Abstimmung mit weiteren bestandshaltenden Einrichtungen und der nutzenden Wissenschaft für die Bildung bzw. Weiterentwicklung von Erschließungs- und Digitalisierungsstandards für eine spezifische Objektgattung engagieren möchten.

Erwähnt werden soll ferner die erfolgreiche Einbeziehung von TU-Sammlungen in die vom Sonderforschungsbereich "Transzendenz und Gemeinsinn" in Kooperation mit Dresdner Kunst- und Kultureinrichtungen ausgerichtete Summer School "Von der Vitrine zum Web 2.0 - Museen, Bibliotheken und Archive im digitalen Zeitalter"[22] im Herbst 2012. Auch wurde die im Rahmen einer Kooperation mit der Kulturstiftung des Freistaats Sachsen geschaffene Stipendium genutzt, einen Wissenschaftler aus einer osteuropäischen Einrichtung für vier Wo-

[18] http://www.dfg.de/foerderung/info_wissenschaft/archiv/2010/info_wissenschaft_10_26/index.html
[19] http://mg.inf.tu-dresden.de/artikel/dfg-bewilligt-projekt-damm-digitales-archiv-mathematischer-modelle
[20] http://www.bmbf.de/foerderungen/18562.php
[21] http://www.dfg.de/foerderung/info_wissenschaft/info_wissenschaft_13_08/index.html
[22] http://www.sfb804.de/veranstaltungen/sommerschulen/summerschool.html

chen in die Sammlung eines Instituts einzuladen[23]. Ziel dieses Hospitationsprogramms ist es, den internationalen Austausch auf Arbeitsebene mit Osteuropa zu fördern und gleichzeitig die Sammlungen zu unterstützen. Im Oktober 2012 nutzte Prof. Boris M. Lobanov aus Minsk die Möglichkeit, als Gast am Institut für Akustik und Sprachkommunikation der TU Dresden zu weilen. Am Institut wird unter der Ägide von Prof. Hoffmann seit mehr als fünf Jahrzehnten auf dem Gebiet der automatischen Sprachverarbeitung geforscht und gelehrt und die materiellen Zeugen dieser Tradition in der Akustisch-Phonetischen Sammlung aufbewahrt. Infolge der regen Publikationstätigkeit über die Sammlung, durch die an anderer Stelle beschriebenen Zugänge aus Hamburg sowie durch die Beteiligung an Ausstellungen genießt diese Sammlung über ihre Binnenwirkung hinaus ein besonderes Ansehen im universitären Sammlungsgeschehen[24].

Es zeichnet sich in der deutschen Universitätslandschaft deutlich ab, dass die Sammlungen mit der Einrichtung fester Sammlungsbeauftragter, Kustodien bzw. Museen einen deutlichen Aufschwung genommen haben. Trotz unterschiedlicher Modelle der Betreuung von Sammlungen hat sich doch das dezentrale Prinzip der wissenschaftlich-institutionellen Anbindung bei gleichzeitiger musealer Beratungstätigkeit durch Kustodien etc. als vorteilhaft erwiesen. Wichtig wird es sein, die kustodiale Kerntätigkeit, das Erfassen und Erschließen und schließlich die Präsentation der Sammlungen, voran zu bringen. Noch immer ist das an das leidige Problem geringer personellen Ressourcen geknüpft. Voraussetzung dafür ist freilich die Grunderfassung der Objekte, vor allem auf der Basis moderner Datenbanken und Digitalisierungen, wobei letztere nicht Selbstzweck, sondern Mittel zur Erschließung und Sichtbarmachung der wissenschaftlichen Sachzeugen sein sollten.

---

[23] http://www.kdfs.de/initiativen/europa/hospitationen/

[24] Vgl. Hoffmann, R. (Hg.): Elektronische Sprachsignalverarbeitung 2009, Bd. 2 (=Tagungsband des Traditionstages Dresden, 23./24. September 2009 und Katalog der Ausstellung SprachSignale, Dresden, 23. September 2009 bis 21. März 2010), Dresden 2009. Hoffmann, R. (Hg.): Sammeln und Forschen. Gesammelte Beiträge über historische phonetische Geräte. Dieter Mehnert zum 75. Geburtstag (=Studientexte zur Sprachkommunikation, Bd. 55), Dresden 2010.

August Seebeck – der erste Akustiker der Dresdner „Universität"

Peter Költzsch, Technische Universität Dresden
peter@koeltzsch.com

Abstract: Die Akustik als Fachdisziplin einer Hochschule ist in Dresden über große Zeiträume des 20. Jahrhunderts mit den Namen der Wissenschaftler Heinrich Barkhausen (Wirkungszeit an der TH Dresden: 1911 – 1953), Richard Heger (TH: 1910 – 1917), Walter Wolman (TH: 1938 – 1945), Walter Reichardt (TH/TU 1950 – 1968), Wolfgang Kraak (TU: 1966 – 1988), Arno Lenk (TU: 1967 – 1996) und Walter Wöhle (TU: 1970 – 1993) verbunden. Gründliche Recherchen zum Zeitraum des 19. Jahrhunderts haben gezeigt, dass es in der Frühzeit der Dresdner Hochschule auch bereits diese Fachdisziplin gab und mit einem herausragenden Gelehrten besetzt war: mit Ludwig Friedrich Wilhelm August Seebeck (1805 – 1849), einem der großen deutschen Akustiker des 19. Jahrhunderts. Neben seinen Sirenenuntersuchungen („Seebeck-Sirene") und der „Ohm-Seebeck-Kontroverse" ist er auf akustischem Gebiet durch Arbeiten zur Schallreflexion und Schallbeugung sowie zu den Schwingungen von Saiten und Stäben bekannt. Er war vor allem auch ein glänzender Experimentator. August Seebeck war Direktor der technischen Bildungsanstalt Dresden von 1842 – 1849, der Vorgängereinrichtung der heutigen TU Dresden. Er beteiligte sich aktiv an den Schulreformen in Sachsen, insbesondere an der Neugestaltung der naturwissenschaftlichen und technischen Ausbildung. Durch seinen frühen Tod (mit 43 Jahren) im März 1849 konnte er die gerade ausgesprochene Berufung zum ordentlichen Professor der Physik in Leipzig nicht mehr antreten.

1 Biografische Angaben

„L u d w i g F r i e d r i c h W i l h e l m A u g u s t S e e b e c k, der würdige Sohn des Mannes, der einst zu den Koryphäen der Berliner Akademie zählte, ist mitten im kräftigsten Mannesalter ein Raub des unerbittlichen Todes geworden. Geboren zu Jena am 27. Dez. 1805, in Berlin gebildet und hier mehrere Jahre als Lehrer am Cöllnischen Gymnasium mit Auszeichnung tätig, starb er zu Dresden, als Direktor der technischen Bildungsanstalt daselbst, in der Nacht vom 18. auf den 19. März d. J. an den leider immer noch nicht ausgerotteten Menschenblattern. Was der Verewigte für die Wissenschaft war, das bezeugen seine gediegenen Arbeiten im Gebiete der Optik und Akustik, die ihn längst den gründlichsten und einsichtsvollsten Physikern Deutschlands an die Seite stellten; wie viel von seiner Tätigkeit noch zu erwarten stand, das vermögen nur Die ganz zu beurteilen, welche wissen, dass seine bisherigen Arbeiten nur die Früchte kärglich zugemessener Mußestunden waren, und dass sich erst wenige Tage vor seinem Ende in der Berufung zum ordentlichen Professor der Physik in Leipzig ein freierer und mit den Hilfsmitteln der Wissenschaft reichlich ausgestatteter Wirkungskreis eröffnet hatte. Sein Tod ist daher in Wahrheit ein Verlust für die Wissenschaft!" Aus dem Nekrolog für August Seebeck (Annalen der Physik und Chemie 1849)

August war der Sohn des Physikers Thomas Seebeck (1770 – 1831), der 1821 den thermoelektrischen Effekt, den „Seebeck-Effekt", entdeckte, der mit Goethe auf dem Gebiet der Farbenlehre zusammen arbeitete und mit ihm in einem regen Briefverkehr stand. Durch die Reputation des Vaters als Physiker und als ordentliches Mitglied der Preußischen Akademie der Wissenschaften zu Berlin verkehrten auch die Familienmitglieder (also auch der Sohn August Seebeck als eines der zehn Kinder) in dieser oder jener Weise mit den „großen Geistern" der damaligen Zeit. Sie wurden von diesen beeinflusst: in Jena, Bayreuth, Nürnberg, Berlin, durch Johann Wolfgang von Goethe, Wilhelm und Alexander von

Humboldt, durch die Gebrüder Schlegel, durch Hegel, Wieland, Herder, Lorenz Oken, von Knebel, Bettina von Arnim, Schleiermacher, Ludwig Richter, Jean Paul, Johann Heinrich Voß, Novalis, Johann Ludwig Tieck, u. a. m.

Abbildung 1 – Augusts Seebeck (1805 – 1849).

Stahlstich aus „Illustrirter Kalender" 1851. Quelle: BBF/DIPF Bibliothek für Bildungsgeschichtliche Forschung/Deutsches Institut für Internationale Pädagogische Forschung /Archiv

August Seebeck, 1805 in Jena geboren, besuchte Gymnasien in Nürnberg und Berlin, studierte von 1824 – 1828 Mathematik, Naturwissenschaften und Philosophie an der Friedrich-Wilhelms-Universität in Berlin. Seine akademischen Lehrer waren u. a. der Philosoph Hegel, der Naturforscher Alexander v. Humboldt, der Astronom und Direktor der Berliner Sternwarte Encke. August Seebeck promovierte 1830 in Berlin mit der Dissertation „Über den Zusammenhang zwischen Brechungsvermögen und Polarisationswinkel an Körpern von einfacher Strahlenbrechung"; er habilitierte sich dort auch 1831 im Fachgebiet Physik und war dann ab 1831 Privatdozent an der Universität in Berlin. Seine Vorlesungen bezogen sich auf die Fachgebiete Optik und Akustik. Ab 1832 wirkte Seebeck als Lehrer am Cöllnischen-Realgymnasium und zugleich auch an der „Allgemeinen Kriegsschule" in Berlin. Nachdem 1839 das *„Hohe Ministerium der Geistlichen und Medicinal-Angelegenheiten dem Oberlehrer Herrn Dr. Seebeck das Prädicat Professor beigelegt"* [zit. aus dem Programm des Realgymnasiums 1839] hat, wurde August Seebeck 1842 als Direktor der technischen Bildungsanstalt und der Baugewerkenschule Dresden berufen, die er bis zu seinem Tod 1849 leitete. Seebeck erhielt 1849, kurz vor seinem Tod, einen Ruf zum Ordentlichen Professor für Physik an der Universität in Leipzig. Er starb im März 1849 in Dresden; sein Grab befindet sich auf dem Alten Annenfriedhof in der Dresdner Südvorstadt.
August Seebeck wurde 1845 als Korrespondierendes Mitglied in die Königlich Preußische Akademie der Wissenschaften zu Berlin aufgenommen, 1846 erfolgte seine Wahl zum Ordentlichen Mitglied der Königlich Sächsischen Gesellschaft der Wissenschaften zu Leipzig (das ist die heutige Sächsische Akademie der Wissenschaften).

2 Zur Bibliographie von August Seebeck

August Seebeck hat insgesamt 33 Abhandlungen publiziert, davon: 20 in Poggendorff's Annalen der Physik und Chemie, 6 in den Abhandlungen der Königlich Sächsischen Gesellschaft der Wissenschaften zu Leipzig, 3 in Programmen des Realgymnasiums in Berlin und der technischen Bildungsanstalt in Dresden, 3 Buchbeiträge. Von diesen Abhandlungen waren 23 akustischen Problemen gewidmet und 10 optischen bzw. material-wissenschaftlichen Themen. Die wissenschaftlichen Abhandlungen von August Seebeck auf dem Gebiet der Akustik betreffen die folgenden Probleme:

- Experimente mit der akustischen Sirene
- Ton- und Klangerzeugung, Definition des Tones, die Ohm-Seebeck-Kontroverse
- Reflexion, Beugung, Interferenz und Kohärenz von Schallwellen
- Thermoakustische Schallerzeugung: Untersuchungen zum Trevelyan-Instrument
- Schwingungen von Saiten und Stäben, das „Mittönen“ von Platten
- Wahrnehmung von Tonhöhen: Hörbereichsgrenzen, Tonhöhenunterschiede

Von August Seebeck sind zwei Buchbeiträge im „Repertorium der Physik“ von 1842 (107 Seiten) bzw. 1849 (109 Seiten) erschienen. In diesen umfassenden Beiträgen zur Akustik wertet Seebeck aktuelle wissenschaftliche Abhandlungen der damaligen Zeit aus, darunter auch seine eigenen. Schließlich sind zahlreiche Einträge zur Akustik von Seebeck für das Handwörterbuch der Chemie und Physik, herausgegeben zwischen 1842 – 1850, verfasst worden: 78 Stichwörter, z. T. auch mehrseitig, zu allen Grundbegriffen der Akustik.

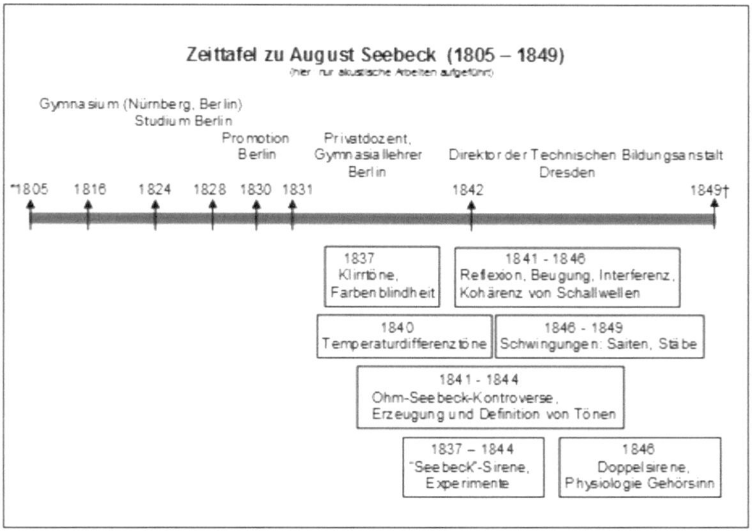

Abbildung 2 – Zeittafel zu August Seebeck

3 Die „Seebeck-Sirene“ – Historie, technische Details, akustische Untersuchungen

Unter einer Sirene wurde ursprünglich ein Gerät zur Schallerzeugung verstanden, bei der in die Zähne eines rotierenden Zahnrades eine dünne Platte oder Pappkarte gehalten und damit bei regelmäßiger Anordnung der Zähne ein tonhaltiger Schall erzeugt wurde. Später bestanden solche Sirenen vorrangig aus Lochscheiben mit Druckluftzufuhr, d. h. ein Druckluftstrom wurde durch eine rotierende Lochscheibe periodisch unterbrochen.

- **1681:** Der englische Physiker **Robert Hooke (1635 – 1703)** demonstriert die Zahnrad-Sirene in der Royal Society zur Erzeugung tonhaltiger Schallsignale.
- **1706:** Der italienische Physiker und Astronom **Vittorio Francesco Stancari (Stancarius) (1678 – 1709)** stellt eine Kammrad-Sirene (mit eingesetzten Nägeln am Radumfang) vor.
- **1799:** Der schottische Physiker **John Robison (1739 – 1805)** ist der Erfinder der Luftsirene. Bei seinem Apparat öffnet ein rotierender Absperrhahn die Druckluftzufuhr aus einem Rohr. Er setzte dieses Gerät faktisch als Musikinstrument ein.

- **1819:** Der französische Physiker **Charles Cagniard de la Tour (1777 – 1859)** baute eine Lochsirene; er gilt allgemein als der Erfinder der Sirene. Seine Konstruktionen: Mehrlochanströmung der Scheibe, Druckluft als Antrieb, mit Zählwerk, Doppelsirene u. a.
- **1826:** Der deutsche Physiker **Ernst Florens Friedrich Chladni (1756 – 1827)** hat 1826 erstmals die Schallerzeugung durch Strömungen als eine besondere Erregungsart von Luftschwingungen bezeichnet, ein „Tönen ohne einen klingenden Körper" [1].
- **1830:** Der französische Physiker **Félix Savart (1791 – 1841)** führte Experimente mit Zahnrad-Sirenen durch.
- **1830: Friedrich Wilhelm Opelt (1794 – 1863),** Geheimer Finanzrat im Königlichen Finanzministerium zu Dresden und Autodidakt auf dem Gebiete der Physik und Musik, muss als „selbständiger Erfinder der mehrstimmigen Lochsirene" angesehen werden.
- **1837: August Seebeck (1805 – 1849)** hat 1837 in seiner ersten akustischen Publikation „Über Klirrtöne" von experimentellen Untersuchungen mit einer Sirene berichtet.
- **1849/1851 Christian Doppler (1803 – 1853)** beschrieb eine Flugrädchen-Sirene als Alarm- und Sicherheitseinrichtung.
- **1850: Carl Sondhauß (1815 – 1886)** verwendete einen akustischen Kreisel (Sirene).
- **1851: Heinrich Wilhelm Dove (1803 – 1879)** entwickelte eine Sirene mit einer Lochscheibe und vier Lochreihen, dazu vier unabhängige Luftdüsen.
- **1862: Hermann von Helmholtz (1821 – 1894)** experimentierte mit einer Doppelsirene, bestehend aus zwei Dove'schen Sirenen, Untersuchung zur Interferenz der Schallwellen.

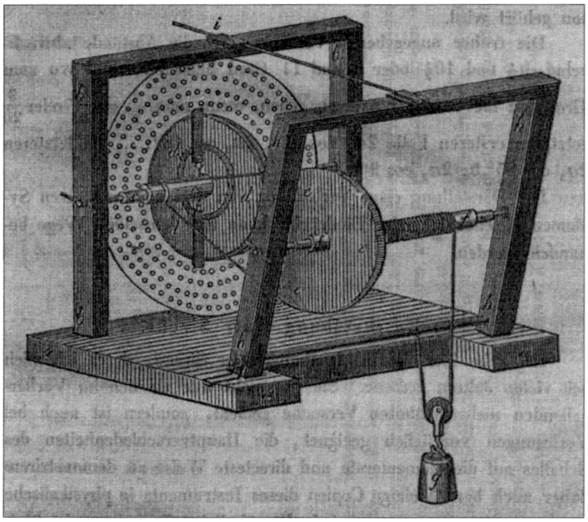

Abbildung 3 – Seebeck – Sirene
Quelle: [2] SLUB Dresden / Deutsche Fotothek

Seebeck begründet die Verwendung der Sirene als zweckmäßigen Schallerzeuger für akustische Experimente: *„Diese Apparate geben gewisse Umstände bei der Erzeugung eines Tones auf eine einfache Weise in die Hand des Beobachters, und können daher zur Beantwortung mancher Fragen in der Akustik benutzt werden, über welche die gewöhnlichen Arten der Tonerzeugung nicht geeignet sind Aufschluss zu geben"* [3].
1849 gibt Seebeck im „Repertorium der Physik. Teil Akustik" [2] eine bildliche Darstellung seiner Sirene: Die Lochscheibe besteht aus *„dünner glatter Pappe (Pressspan)"*, die an eine dickere Holzscheibe angeschraubt ist. Zur Erhöhung des Trägheitsmomentes ist an der Holzscheibe ein Bleiring angebracht. Der geräuschlose Antrieb erfolgt über einen Schnurlauf, der durch ein Gewicht in Betrieb gesetzt wird. Seebeck beschreibt dann den Einsatz der

Sirene bei Lehrvorträgen: *„Mit einer Löcherreihe erhält man einen Ton, der bei zunehmender Geschwindigkeit immer höher wird. Um die Zahlenverhältnisse der Töne auf die einfachste Weise herzuleiten, wendet man am besten eine Scheibe mit vier Löcherreihen, von 40, 50, 60, 80 Löchern, an. Man erhält dadurch die Töne des Dur-Dreiklangs"* [2].

Was ist das Neue an der Seebeck-Sirene?

- Seebeck verwendete eine einfache Sirenenscheibe ("Pappscheibensirene") mit mehreren Lochanordnungen auf konzentrischen Kreisen.
- Seebeck untersuchte mit dem gleichzeitigen Anblasen von Lochreihen mit jeweils einem Luftröhrchen (und von entgegengesetzten Seiten) das akustische Interferenzphänomen.
- Seebeck hat als erster mit ungleichabständigen Löchern gearbeitet, d. h. er führte psychoakustische Experimente bei „gestörtem Isochronismus" der Impulsfolgen durch.
- Seebeck verwendete erstmals die Sirenen-Doppelscheibe, so dass der menschliche Kopf dazwischen angeordnet und damit die kombinierte Wahrnehmung der unterschiedlichen Schallbeaufschlagung des rechten und des linken Ohres untersucht werden konnte.

4 Die Ohm-Seebeck-Kontroverse

In dem Disput zwischen Ohm und Seebeck geht es um den Problemkreis der Tonerzeugung, die Wahrnehmung von Tönen und Klängen, um die Hörbarkeit der Oberwellen, die Verstärkung des Grundtones und um die Definition des Tones überhaupt. Als Beispiele zu ihrer Streitkultur werden einige Ausdrücke aus dem Vokabular genannt, das die Disputanten verwendeten. Da spricht Seebeck von Ohm als „Hochgeehrtester Herr Professor", von seinem „gelehrten Gegner", von den „Ansichten des gelehrten Verfassers, von dem ‚Scharfsinne, welchen man an seinen Arbeiten kennt' ". Und Ohm bezeichnet Seebeck als einen „sorgsamen Beobachter" und seinen „freundlichen Gegner", aber er bekennt auch, dass er es unternehme, „in das Dunkel der S e e b e c k'schen Versuche einzudringen."

Die Ohm-Seebeck-Kontroverse erstreckt sich auf vier Publikationen von Seebeck und auf zwei Publikationen von Ohm aus dem Zeitraum zwischen 1841 bis 1844 (diese enthalten auch das berühmte Ohm'sche Gesetz der Akustik!).

Die Details der Kontroverse können hier nicht dargestellt werden, siehe dazu [4]. Das Fazit formulierte Helmholtz so: *„Lässt man Alles, was S e e b e c k in dem Streite mit O h m behauptet hat, vom Klange gelten, und was O h m behauptet hat, vom Tone, so sind beide ausgezeichnete Akustiker mit ihren Behauptungen im Rechte, und beide Behauptungen können ungestört neben einander bestehen."* [5].

E. Robel schreibt in einer ausführlichen Darstellung der Ohm-Seebeck-Kontroverse die auch in wissenschaftshistorischer Sicht aufschlussreiche Einleitung: *„Interessant ist dieser Streit aber auch in Rücksicht auf die Persönlichkeiten der beiden Männer; welche sich als Gegner gegenüberstanden. Seebeck, der jüngere von beiden, hatte sich bereits durch Arbeiten auf dem Gebiete der theoretischen und Experimentalphysik hinreichend bekannt gemacht, und, von Natur mit einem feinen musikalischen Gehör begabt, war er als geschickter Experimentator berechtigt, die Resultate seiner akustischen Versuche für zuverlässig anzusehen. Ohm, der um einundeinhalb Dezennien ältere Forscher, hatte als Entdecker und Begründer des nach ihm benannten elektrischen Fundamentalgesetzes wenigstens schon im Auslande die ihm gebührende Anerkennung gefunden (...). Im diametralen Gegensatz zu Seebeck war aber Ohm von Haus aus so unmusikalisch, dass er zur Beurteilung der Ergebnisse einfacher akustischer Versuche fremder Hilfe* [d. h. Hörer] *bedurfte (...). Interessant ist aber auch endlich dieser Streit mit Rücksicht auf seinen Ausgang: beide Gegner sanken vor der endgültigen Entscheidung ins Grab und mussten frischen in ihre Stellen einrückenden Kräften die Fortsetzung des unentschiedenen Kampfes überlassen"* [6].

Zum persönlichen Verhältnis zwischen Ohm und Seebeck soll noch ein Auszug aus einem Brief wiedergegeben werden, den Seebeck 1844 an Ohm schrieb:

„Hochgeehrtester Herr Professor! Dresden, den 21. Januar 1844
... Es ist mir sehr erfreulich gewesen, dass meine Beobachtungen an der Sirene Ihre Aufmerksamkeit auf sich gezogen und Ihnen zu einer so interessanten Theorie dieser Klasse von Tönen Veranlassung gegeben haben; und ich kann nur wünschen, dass auch die gegenwärtigen Bemerkungen Ihnen einigen Anlass gewähren mögen, sich weiter mit dem Gegenstand zu beschäftigen, welcher eine wichtige Grundfrage der Akustik betrifft, einer Wissenschaft, an welcher leider gegenwärtig nur wenige Physiker tätigen Anteil nehmen. Sollte Ihr Weg Sie einmal wieder nördlich und an unsere freundlichen Elbufer führen, so hoffe ich, dass Sie sich nicht die Ohren vor den Gesängen meiner Sirene verstopfen werden, wie ich meinerseits nicht verfehlen werden, Ihre persönlich Bekanntschaft zu suchen, wenn es mir einmal wieder beschieden sein wird, die Türme der alten Reichsstadt [Nürnberg] *wieder zu sehen, an welche sich für mich die Erinnerung einer Reihe glücklicher Knabenjahre knüpft. –*
Mit der wiederholten Versicherung vorzüglicher Hochachtung
Euer Wohlgeboren ergebenster A. Seebeck“ [7, S. 188 – 190].

5 Seebeck als Lehrer (Berlin und Dresden) sowie als Direktor der technischen Bildungsanstalt in Dresden

In seiner Berliner Lehrer-Tätigkeit von 1832 – 1842 hatte August Seebeck am Realgymnasium erhebliche Lehrverpflichtungen zu bewältigen (mehr als 20 Wochenstunden) und diese in einem breiten Fächerspektrum: Naturkunde, Physik, Chemie, Technologie, Mineralogie, Mechanik. Zwei Mitteilungen aus den Jahresprogrammen des Realgymnasiums Berlin seien hier angeführt: *„Der Physikalische und Chemische Lehr-Apparat ist in dem abgelaufenen Schuljahr angemessen vermehrt worden. Zu den wichtigeren Erwerbungen desselben gehören: eine* ***akustische Rotationsscheibe****“* (RealGymnBerlin 1838). Und aus dem Programm von 1842 des Realgymnasiums Berlin: *„Jetzt mit dem Schlusse des Semesters scheidet aus: Herr* ***Professor Dr. S e e b e c k****, der seit 10 Jahren den Unterricht der Chemie, Physik und Technologie in den beiden obersten, und zugleich den mathematischen Unterricht in einigen mittleren Classen erfolgreich geleitet, die technologischen Exkursionen beaufsichtigt und als Ordinarius von Obersecunda wesentlich auf die gute Führung der Zöglinge eingewirkt hat. Der ehrenvolle Ruf zu einer Direktorenstelle in Dresden entzieht ihn unserer Anstalt. Die Liebe seiner Amtsgenossen und Schüler, die ihn ungern scheiden sehen, begleitet ihn.“* (RealGymnBerlin 1842).

Seebeck als Lehrer und Direktor der technischen Bildungsanstalt in Dresden :

Seebeck war von 1842 – 1849 Direktor der Anstalt und der Baugewerkenschule in Dresden. Zum 100-jährigen Jubiläum der TH Dresden im Jahre 1928 wird geschrieben:

„Im Jahre 1842 erhielt die Anstalt in dem bisherigen Professor des Realgymnasiums und der allgemeinen Kriegsschule in Berlin Dr. August Seebeck einen neuen Vorsteher, den ersten Direktor, der ihr zugleich als Lehrer angehörte; sein Lehrauftrag erstreckte sich auf die Mechanische Naturlehre und auf die Physik in der Oberen Abteilung. Er war ein reichbegabter, klardenkender Lehrer und ein Physiker von hohen wissenschaftlichen Eigenschaften. Seine Arbeiten über Saitenschwingungen und Schwingungen von Stäben gehören zu den klassischen Untersuchungen der Akustik, die sein Hauptarbeitsgebiet war. Die von ihm konstruierte Scheiben- oder Lochsirene ist auch heute noch in jedem physikalischen Laboratorium in Gebrauch. Ferner ist er der erste gewesen, der die Farbenblindheit wissenschaftlich untersuchte (...)“ [8, S. 138].

Im Programm 1844 der technischen Bildungsanstalt Dresden ist (auf 55 Seiten!) der neue „Lehrplan der technischen Bildungsanstalt“ enthalten, der sichtbar stark vom Realschulgedanken des Direktors Seebeck beeinflusst worden ist. Er enthält innerhalb der Physik das Programm der Akustik (mit einem bemerkenswerten Anteil zur Schallerzeugung):

- Einleitung: Grundbegriffe, Zahlenverhältnisse der Töne, stehende und fortschreitende Schwingungen, theoretische Bestimmung der Fortpflanzungsgeschwindigkeiten.

- Erzeugung des Schalles: Töne durch Schläge, Theorie und Empirie der Saiten; Transversalschwingungen der Membranen, Stäbe, Platten, Glocken; Longitudinalschwingungen der Stäbe, Luftschwingungen, Labial- und Zungenpfeifen, Blasinstrumente.
- Mitteilung und Fortpflanzung des Schalles: Schallgeschwindigkeit in Luft, Wasser und festen Körpern; Stärke, Ausbreitung;
  Kommunikations-, Sprach- und Hörrohr; Interferenz, Kombinationstöne; Zurückwerfung, Echo, Hörsäle; Mittönen und Resonanz; Gehörorgan.

Das Domizil der technischen Bildungsanstalt Dresden war 1842, in dem Jahr, als August Seebeck seinen Dienst als Direktor antrat, in den Gebäuden „Am Jüdenhof" (beim späteren Johanneum). Seebeck bereitete den Neubau der Anstalt am Antonsplatz vor, eine erstaunlich exklusive Lage des Gebäudes in unmittelbarer Nachbarschaft zum Zwinger, zur Sophienkirche, zur Katholischen Hofkirche, zum Schloss! Die Einweihung des neuen Anstaltsgebäudes erfolgte 1846. Das Gebäude wurde 1945 beim Luftangriff auf Dresden zerstört.
Einige Passagen aus der Rede des Direktors Prof. August Seebeck in der Feier zur Eröffnung des neuen Anstaltsgebäudes: *„Wer kann heute voraussehen, welche Aufgaben nach 5, nach 10, nach 20, nach 50 Jahren dem Techniker sich bieten werden? Soll er auf solche gefasst sein, so bedarf er einer festbegründeten, klaren Einsicht in die Grundwissenschaften, auf denen zuletzt alle Anwendung ruht, und in die Methode dieser Anwendung auf die Fachwissenschaften (...)"* Und Seebeck schließt mit den Worten: *„So möge denn dies Haus gesegnet sein in reichem Maße, den Zöglingen eine Schule gediegenen Wissens und sicheren Könnens, eine Schule der Zucht und der Ordnung, der Ehrfurcht vor dem Höheren, der Pflicht und der selbstverleugnenden Hingebung an den Beruf, den Lehrern eine Stätte freudiger Wirksamkeit, gelohnt durch den gedeihlichen Erfolg ihrer Arbeit, gelohnt und gestützt durch das Vertrauen und die Anerkennung der Behörden, der Eltern und Aller, welche an der öffentlichen Wohlfahrt und Bildung in unserem Vaterlande regen Anteil nehmen."* (TechnBildAnstDresden 1847).

6 Seebecks Beitrag zur Entwicklung des sächsischen Schulwesens

Seebeck war nicht nur Wissenschaftler, Physiker und Akustiker, er war auch ein den Gedanken der Realschule und der polytechnischen Ausbildung verpflichteter Pädagoge, der sich mit seiner Tätigkeit als Direktor einer erstrangigen sächsischen Bildungsanstalt aktiv in das Zeitgeschehen einmischte. So war er Mitglied der „Commission zu der vom Königl. Sächs. Ministerium des Cultus und öffentlichen Unterrichtes eingeforderten Begutachtung, den naturwissenschaftlichen Unterricht auf Gelehrtenschulen betreffend", zuständig für das Referat der Realschulen und Realgymnasien [9]. Die Kommission legte im April 1849 einen *„Ersten Entwurf zu dem Schulgesetz für das Königreich Sachsen"* vor. Er führte jedoch nicht zu einer Gesetzesvorlage, wegen der Auflösung des Landtages am 30. 4. 1849 sowie wegen des Dresdner Maiaufstandes und dessen Niederschlagung Anfang Mai 1849. Einige Vorschläge tragen deutlich die Handschrift von August Seebeck, aber auch ansonsten sind die damals erarbeiteten Vorschläge noch heute von Interesse:

- Der Staat ist auch für die Gewährung einer Berufsbildung verantwortlich.
- Die ‚sächsische Schule' soll einen ‚einigen, von dem Kindergarten bis zur Hochschule aufwärts zusammenhängend gegliederten Organismus' bilden.
- Die Schule wird zu einem unabhängigen Organismus im Staate erklärt, das bedeutet die institutionelle Emanzipation von der Kirche.
- Für die Knaben ist die Einrichtung von Realschulen vorgesehen (erstmals in Sachsen!). Sie waren durch den Unterricht in Zeichnen, Mathematik, Naturwissenschaften, Englisch und Französisch gekennzeichnet. Die Stadtschulen für die Mädchen legten den Schwerpunkt des Unterrichts auf die neueren Sprachen, die Muttersprache, Dichtkunst und die vaterländische Geschichte.

- Die ‚Gelehrtenschulen oder Gymnasien“ sollten in einen humanistischen und einen realistischen Zweig (‚Alt-Gymnasien‘ und ‚Real-Gymnasien‘) geteilt werden. Beide sollten auf die Universität vorbereiten. Die geplante Ausgestaltung des Realgymnasiums legte auf Mathematik und Naturwissenschaften sowie eine tiefere Erfassung der neueren Sprachen Wert. Latein sollte obligatorisch sein.
- An den Fachschulen sollte die Vorbildung für einzelne bürgerliche Berufe angeboten werden. Die höheren Fachschulen setzten die Realschule voraus. Als höhere Fachschulen waren vorgesehen die Polytechnische Schule in Dresden, die Gewerbeschule in Chemnitz, die Handelslehranstalt in Leipzig, eine neue Musterzeichen- und Modellierschule in Dresden, die Forst- und Landwirtschaftsakademie Tharandt, die Bergakademie Freiberg sowie die Allgemeine Kriegsschule (für Offiziere) und die Artillerie- und Ingenieurschule.

7 Schlussbemerkungen

August Seebeck war ein außergewöhnlich produktiver Wissenschaftler, der in den knapp 20 Jahren zwischen seiner Promotion und seinem frühen Tod 1849 insgesamt 32 wissenschaftliche Publikationen und drei Buchbeiträge verfasste. Er hat Originäres zur Wissenschaftsdisziplin der Akustik beigetragen. Von ihm stammen die „Seebeck-Sirene“ und das „Seebeck’sche Verfahren“ zur Prüfung auf Farbenblindheit, er war ein glänzender wissenschaftlicher Disputant („Ohm-Seebeck-Kontroverse“). Seine Experimente erstaunen noch heute, z. B. die Doppelscheibensirene zur phasengleichen oder phasenversetzten Beschallung beider Ohren, die schallempfindliche Membran mit angehängten Pendelchen zum Nachweis der stehenden Wellen vor einer Wand, die Realisierung des „gestörten Isochronismus“ von Pulsfolgen durch Sirenenlochscheiben mit ungleichabständigen Löchern u. a. m.. Seebeck hat seine wissenschaftlichen Ergebnisse während der Tätigkeit an Schulanstalten erarbeitet, als Gymnasiallehrer in Berlin (etwa 20 Stunden Unterricht je Woche) und als Direktor der technischen Bildungsanstalt und der Baugewerkenschule Dresden (mit etwa 10 Wochenstunden). Er war ein aktiver Schulreformer in Sachsen, insbesondere zur Realisierung der Realschulidee und der Neugestaltung der naturwissenschaftlichen und technischen Ausbildung. Es wäre nicht unangemessen, dass sich Dresden in der heutigen Zeit des Strebens nach Exzellenz und Elite in der Wissenschaft eines der großen Wegbereiter der Wissenschaft und der Realschulbildung in der Stadt dankbar erinnert. Dazu sollte auch hier in dieser Festschrift ein Beitrag geleistet werden (siehe auch [4]).

Literatur

[1] Chladni, E. F. F.: Über Töne bloß durch schnell auf einander folgende Stösse, ohne einen klingenden Körper. Annalen der Physik und Chemie, Leipzig, Band 8 (1826), S. 453 – 460

[2] Seebeck, A.: Akustik. In: Repertorium der Physik. Eine Zusammenstellung der neueren Fortschritte dieser Wissenschaft. Band VIII. Verlag von Veit & Comp., Berlin 1849. S. 1 – 109

[3] Seebeck, A.: Beobachtungen über einige Bedingungen der Entstehung von Tönen. Annalen der Physik und Chemie, Leipzig, Band 53 (1841), S. 417- 436

[4] Költzsch, P.: Sondhauß-Röhre, Seebeck-Sirene – Wer waren ihre Namensgeber? Schriftenreihe zur Geschichte der Akustik, Deutsche Gesellschaft für Akustik 2012. ISBN 978-3-939296-03-4.

[5] Helmholtz, H. v.: Über die Klangfarbe der Vocale. Annalen der Physik und Chemie, Leipzig, Band 108 (1859), S. 280 – 290

[6] Robel, E.: Die Sirenen – Ein Beitrag zur Entwicklungsgeschichte der Akustik. Wissenschaftliche Beilage zum Jahresbericht des Luisenstädtischen Realgymnasiums zu Berlin. Teil I-IV (1891 - 1900). R. Gaertners Verlagsbuchhandlung Hermann Heyfelder, Berlin

[7] Hartmann, L.: Aus Georg Simon Ohms handschriftlichem Nachlass. Briefe, Urkunden und Dokumente. Gesammelt und mit Unterstützung der Notgemeinschaft der Deutschen Wissenschaft herausgegeben von Ludwig Hartmann, Oberstudienrat in München. Bayerland-Verlag, München 1927

[8] Ein Jahrhundert Sächsische Technische Hochschule 1828 – 1928. Festschrift zur Jahrhundertfeier 1928. Herausgeber: Rektor und Senat. Herstellung: Buchgewerbl. Großbetrieb W. Limpert, Dresden 1928

[9] Moderow, H.-M.: Volksschule zwischen Staat und Kirche. Das Beispiel Sachsen im 18. u. 19. Jahrhundert. Dissertation Universität Leipzig 2006. Böhlau Verlag Köln/Weimar/Wien 2007

Wolfgang von Kempelens Aufenthalt in London:

heißersehnt, jedoch nicht von dem erhofften Erfolg gekrönt.

Alice Reininger

Universität für angewandte Kunst Wien
alice.reininger@chello.at

Abstract: Am 16. Juli 1788 richtete Wolfgang von Kempelen eine Bittschrift an Kaiser Joseph II um ein Privileg für eine Feuer- bzw. Dampfmaschine und für eine zweite Maschine, die nach dem Reaktionsprinzip arbeitete, für die österreichische Monarchie und seiner Kronländer zu erreichen. Kempelen hatte während seiner zweijährigen Reise, die er im Jänner 1783 begann und die ihn durch mehrere europäische Länder führte, auch in England Station gemacht. Auf dieser Reise durch halb Europa wurden in vielen Städten der sogenannte „Schachtürken" und die Sprechmaschine vorgeführt. Diese Reise hatte jedoch noch einen anderen Zweck. Kempelen wollte in England Erfahrungen im Bau von Dampfmaschinen sammeln, um seine Entwicklungen zu verbessern. In London reichte Wolfgang von Kempelen seine Erfindungen beim Patentamt ein und erlangte sogar ein Patent dafür. Er trat in Kontakt mit Dr. Joseph Priestley und Matthew Boulton. Beide besuchten Kempelen in seinem Londoner Quartier und begutachteten die Modelle der Dampf- und Reaktionsmaschine. Ende August 1788 erlangte Wolfgang von Kempelen das heiß ersehnte Privileg für seine beiden Dampfmaschinen. Der Kontakt zu England blieb bestehen. Als ein Verbindungskanal zwischen der Donau und dem Fluss Theiß im Königreich Ungarn von den Gebrüder Kiss errichtet wurde, kam die Kempelensche Dampfmaschine zum Wasserheben zum Einsatz. Bestandteile dazu wurden vermutlich aus England geliefert.

Wolfgang von Kempelen ließ sich nicht davon abbringen, nachdem am 1. Juni 1779 die Vorführung seiner entwickelten Dampfmaschine vor der von der Hofkammer für Münz- und Bergwesen eingesetzten behördlichen Kommission auf Grund eines Berechnungsfehlers abgebrochen werden musste, an seiner Entwicklung weiter zu arbeiten. Zuviel Aufwand und Geld waren bereits in dieses Projekt bis zu diesem Zeitpunkt geflossen.

Hier ist einzufügen, dass zu Beginn des 18. Jahrhunderts in England mit Dampf betriebene Maschinen zum Wasserheben in Bergwerksstollen, sogenannten Newcomen-Maschinen, eingesetzt wurden. Auch im Bergbau von Schemnitz wurde um 1730 eine nach dem Prinzip von Newcomen konstruierte Dampfmaschine eingesetzt. Es war der Sohn des Barockarchitekten Johann Bernhard Fischer von Erlach, Joseph Emanuel Fischer von Erlach, der seine Kontakte nach England spielen ließ und den englischen Ingenieur und Konstrukteur Isaac Potter in das Oberungarische Bergbaugebiet holte, um Neuerungen im Bergbau einzuführen.[1]

In Wien, im Garten des Palais des Fürsten Schwarzenberg, errichtete Joseph Emanuel Fischer von Erlach ebenfalls eine mit Dampf betriebene Maschine, eine „Feuermaschine", die zur Ergötzung des Besitzers und der Wiener Wasserfontainen bis zu 75 Fuß hoch in die Luft schießen ließ und ein Wasserreservoir, welches rund 12.000 Eimer fasste, innerhalb 24

[1] Vozár, J.: English mechanic Isaac Potter constructor of the first fire-engine in Slovakia. In: Studia Historica Slovaca VII, Bratislava 1974, S. 102-139

Stunden füllte. Bis in die zweite Hälfte des 18. Jahrhunderts war diese Dampfmaschine in Betrieb.[2]

Der Abbruch der Vorführung seiner Dampfmaschine hatte für Wolfgang von Kempelen empfindliche finanzielle Einbußen zur Folge. Die in Aussicht gestellte Remuneration von 50 000 Gulden kam nicht zur Auszahlung, das von ihm beantragte Privileg wurde nicht ausgesprochen und jene 3000 Gulden, die ihm jährlich als eine Art Pension in Aussicht gestellt wurden, entfielen. Als zusätzlich die Hofkammer für Münz- und Bergwesen noch ausständige Rechnungen für Arbeiten an der Maschine und für Gold- und Silbermaterial vehement einforderte, drohte man Kempelen sogar seinen Gehalt einzuziehen. Mit einem Bittschreiben an Joseph II. konnte jedoch das Schlimmste verhindert werden und Kempelen weiter Verbesserungen an seiner Dampfmaschine durchführen. Erfolge stellten sich ein und Kempelen ging daran, zwei seiner Maschinen – eine Dunstmaschine und eine Maschine, die nach dem Reaktionsprinzip arbeitete, im Schlosspark von Schönbrunn zu erbauen, um die Wasserkaskaden des neu errichteten Neptunbrunnens in all ihrer Pracht zeigen zu können. Leider wiesen diese beiden Maschinen zum Wasserheben noch immer Entwicklungsfehler auf. Ein reibungsloser Betrieb konnte nicht gewährleistet werden.

Es ist durchaus realistisch, dass die Präsentation des Schachtürken vor einem erlauchten Publikum in der Wiener Hofburg – das russische Großfürstenpaar Thronfolger Paul und seine Gemahlin Feodorowna weilten im November 1781 in Wien – und verschiedene Gespräche über neue technische Errungenschaften in Kempelen den Entschluss reifen ließen, eine längere Auszeit von seiner Arbeitsstelle zu nehmen. In einem Handbillett an Graf Kollowrat, Präsident der Hofkammer für Münz- und Bergwesen, vom 11. Jänner 1782, erlaubte Joseph II. eine zweijährige Karenz Kempelens von seinem Arbeitsplatz. Es hat den Anschein, dass der Monarch nicht ganz vom Nutzen dieser Reise überzeugt gewesen zu sein schien, denn er fand in diesem Handbillett, dass Kempelen diese Reise, *„zu seinem privat Nutzen lediglich unternimmt*“.[3] Trotz dieser eher abwertenden Haltung des Souveräns gewährte dieser Kempelen während der Zeit seiner Abwesenheit die Hälfte seines Salärs als finanzielle Unterstützung. Kempelen wurde zugleich versichert, bei seiner Rückkehr sofort wieder in seine innegehabte Position in der Hofkammer einzusteigen.

Nach einer einjährigen Vorbereitungszeit brach Wolfgang von Kempelen im Jänner 1783 mit dem Schachtürken, der Sprechmaschine und zwei Modellen einer Dampfmaschine – eine Dampfmaschine „Feuermaschine“ und einer sogenannten „Injektionsmaschine“ – zu seiner Reise auf, die ihn durch Deutschland, Frankreich auch nach England führte.

Im Herbst 1783 hielt sich Wolfgang von Kempelen mit seinem Gefolge schon in London auf. Das „Wienerblättchen“ berichtete in seiner Ausgabe vom Mittwoch, 12. November 1783: *„London. Der berühmte Schachspieler des Herrn Kempelen befindet sich nun hier, wo Herr Anton mit diesem Automat ein gutes Spiel machen wird. Das Eintrittsbillett kostet eine halbe Guinee.*“[4]

Die Lancierung von Thickness' „The Speaking Figure and the Automaton Chess-Player, exposed and detected.“ brachte Wolfgang von Kempelen die benötigte Aufmerksamkeit in der englischen Öffentlichkeit. Es ist anzunehmen, dass Wolfgang von Kempelen als Erfinder dieser Attraktion die ersten Vorführungen selbst leitete, um sich einem staunenden als auch einem skeptischen Publikum zu zeigen und diese Illusion zu präsentieren. Danach übernahm Herr Anton, längst mit den Geheimnissen des Schachautomaten vertraut, die Vorführungen. Wolfgang von Kempelen brauchte sich daher nicht um die Organisation der Aufführungen kümmern. Er konnte nun die Zeit für sich und seine Belange nützen.

---

[2] Czeike, F.: Historisches Lexikon Wien, Bd. 5, Wien 1997, S. 174f.
[3] Österreichisches Staatsarchiv Wien: Hofkammerarchiv, Hofresolution vom 11. Jänner 1782, Fasz. 39 H
[4] Das Wienerblättchen, 12. November 1783, S. 39

Gleich nach seiner Ankunft in London musste Wolfgang von Kempelen ein Patent für seine entwickelte Injektionsmaschine, dem Vorläufer einer Dampfturbine, beantragt haben und mit Matthew Boulton bzw. James Watt in Kontakt getreten sein. Dem Patentansuchen wurde stattgegeben und nach einer Bezahlung von 100 Pfund erhielt Kempelen mit 10. April 1784 das Patent Nr. 1428: „*Reaction-machine, set in motion by fire, air, water or any fluid, applicable to other machines requiring a moving power.*"[5] Nach Erhalt des Patentes richtete er am 19. April 1784 ein Schreiben an Matthew Boulton in Birmingham und lud ihn zu einer Vorführung der Dampfmaschinen zu sich in sein Londoner Domizil in der St. James Street Nr. 14, „*next Brooks*", ein.

> *Sir!*
>
> *Since we have agreed, as soon I schal have got the Royal Patent for my Machine, to give You the notice of, I presently do myself the honour to acquaint You, that the Sade [Anm.: said] Patent is allrady in my hands, and now I request the favour of an answer, wether or when You may be pleased, and Your Businesses will allow it, to come to Town, and take a View of my Machine. I now can flatter myself with the advantage to deal with more leisure and more freely with you. Those days I was favoured with Dr. Pristley's Visit, when I took the oportunity to Show him this my machine in action and applyed to several motions. He was vastly satisfied with it, which was no little satisfaction to me. In hope to have the honour to see you as soon as possible I am with greatest Regards*
>
> *Sir*
>
> *your most humble servant Kempelen m[anu] p[ropria]* [6]

Wolfgang von Kempelen erhoffte sich sehr viel von diesem Treffen, vor allem Anstöße zu Verbesserungen bei seinen Entwicklungen, Diskussionen zwischen Fachmännern und vielleicht auch eine Zusammenkunft mit James Watt. Kempelen war begierig zu lernen.

Tage zuvor schon war Dr. John Priestley nach London gekommen, um im Auftrag von James Watt bei Kempelen einer Vorführung der beiden Dampfmaschinen beizuwohnen. Kempelen führte ihm seine Modelle vor. John Priestley dürfte von dieser Vorführung beeindruckt gewesen sein und äußerte sich in einen positiven Bericht darüber bei James Watt. Durch diese Nachricht neugierig gemacht, vielleicht auch etwas beunruhigt und, vermutlich um alle Zweifel auszuräumen, dass Watt der bessere Mann war, folgte Matthew Boulton doch der Kempelenschen Einladung.

Am 13. Mai 1784 wurden Matthew Boulton die Kempelenschen Modelle vorgeführt. Noch am selben Abend schrieb er an James Watt nach Birmingham und beruhigte ihn: James Watt war der bessere Mann und die Watt'schen Erfindungen unschlagbar! Boulton erkannte Fehler in der kempelenschen Dampfmaschine, wich geschickt einer fachlichen Diskussion aus, denn in dieser hätte er Watt'sche Erkenntnisse preisgeben müssen. Einen Konkurrenten konnte man nicht brauchen.

Im ersten und letzten Teil dieses Briefes besprach Boulton allfällige Angelegenheiten, die ihn und Watt betrafen, und angebahnte Geschäfte in Frankreich. Im mittleren Teil nahm er zu seinem Besuch bei Kempelen Stellung und fügte auch eine Skizze zu Kempelen's Injektionsmaschine bei (s. Abb. 1):

> *... I saw Mr. Kemplins Machine at work to day which I suppose I need not discribe to you as I presume Dr. Priestly had already done it. Kemplin seems a very ingenious automaton maker but he wants both knowledge & practise in Steam Engines. As I could*

---

[5] Woodcroft, B.: Alphabetical index of patentees of invention, London 1854, reprinted 1969

[6] Birmingham Archives and Heritage, UK: Manuscript Collection, MS-3782/12/29/24, 29 April, 1784

nor reason with him about his machine without giving him new knowledge I did not enter much into its merits but told him I feard he w.[ould] find himself disapointed in large ones. He reasons much upon an experim[en]t. he made with a Boiler of Perriers 5f[ee]t. Diam.[eter], into which he screwd a pipe 1/2 inch Diam.[eter] & he says it kept up a regular & constant stream of Steam, but he seems to have no Idea if its elastick force & therefore all his calculations are falacious. He is making another Model which hath something like a Cock at each end which are connected with a pin in the Center in such way that by having that pin up the 2 Cocks turn half round & the 2 appertures thereby change sides & thus the Machine will turn in the other way & become convent for drawing Coals (in Modell only) I dont think the friction in the neck so very great because the elastick force of the Steam presses up the socket against a flat bearing & ... [Anm.: Wortkürzel unlesbar] Contra the 2 Arms with weights at the end being just enough to counterballance that power reduces the friction to a very little

A the apperture

B the Lead weights

C the turning flanch which is pressed up by Steam of down by its weights & ought to be made of Steel & then may wear as long as the Coller of a Lathe

I think it upon it whole a pretty innocent thing & I am sorry that Kemplen hath given 100 L (Pounds) to the patent office as he seems to me a good sort of a Man & perhaps may be usefull to us in the Emperors Dominions [7]

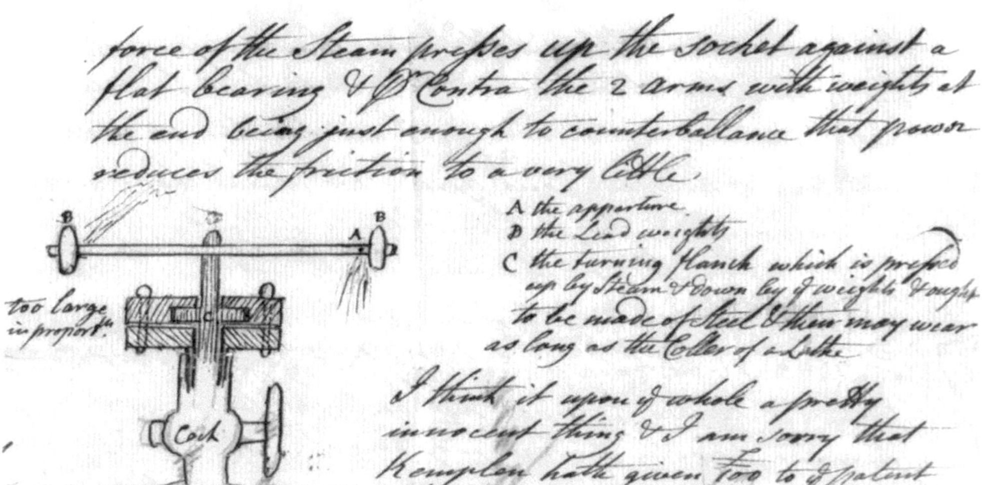
force of the Steam presses up the socket against a flat bearing &c Contra the 2 arms with weights at the end being just enough to counterballance that power reduces the friction to a very little.

A the apperture
B the Lead weights
C the turning flanch which is pressed up by Steam & down by ye weights & ought to be made of Steel & then may wear as long as the Coller of a Lathe

I think it upon ye whole a pretty innocent thing & I am sorry that Kemplen hath given 100 to ye patent office as he seems to me a good sort of a Man & perhaps may be usefull to us in the Emperors Dominions

Abbildung 1 - Detail des Briefes von Matthew Boulton an James Watt vom 13. Mai 1784.
Quelle: Birmingham Archives and Heritage, UK: Manuscript Collection, MS-3147/3/8/3, 13 May, 1784

[7] Birmingham Archives and Heritage, UK: Manuscript Collection, MS-3147/3/8/3, 13 May, 1784

In den Augen Boultons schien Kempelen zwar ein genialer Automatenerfinder bzw. Automatenbauer zu sein, den Wunsch hingegen, Kempelen mit neuesten Erkenntnissen und Erfahrungsberichten in Bezug auf Dampfmaschinen zu versorgen, wollte Boulton unter keinen Umständen erfüllen.

Für Kempelen mussten die beiden Besuche sowohl von Priestley als auch von Boulton unbefriedigend und enttäuschend gewesen sein, die Distanziertheit der Engländer irritierend. Der Wunsch, an neue Informationen und Entwicklungen über die Dampfmaschine von James Watt heranzukommen, erfüllte sich nicht. Man ließ Kempelen mit seinen Problemen allein.

In dem Buch "The Steam Turbine" von Robert M. Neilson, welches 1902 erschienen ist, geht der Verfasser auch auf die Entwicklung einer Dampfturbine von Kempelen ein. Er beschreibt das Patent, welches Kempelen 1784 für „*Obtaining and transmitting motive power*" in London erhalten hatte. Er fügt hinzu, dass im gleichen Jahr James Watt ebenfalls Patentbriefe für „*certain improvements relating to steam-engines*" gewährt wurden.[8] Ob James Watt in diesem Fall von Kempelens offenherziger Preisgabe seiner Entwicklung profitieren konnte, anhand der eigenen Entwicklungsschwierigkeiten jene verbessern konnte oder ob hier zwei Entwicklungen parallel liefen, lässt sich nicht mehr nachprüfen.

1790 knüpfte Wolfgang von Kempelen wieder Kontakte mit England. Er war bereits Inhaber eines Patentes zur Errichtung von Dampfmaschinen für die Länder der Habsburger Monarchie. Darauf wurde auch in dem Antwortschreiben aus London von B. Nicolas Vay, 3. August 1790, Rücksicht genommen. Aus diesem Brief entnehmen wir, dass Kempelen vor hatte, einzelne Bestandteile einer Dampfmaschine in England fertigen zu lassen. Es ist anzunehmen, dass Kempelen für eine Dampfmaschine Bestandteile aus England anforderte, welche beim Bau des Kanals durch die Gebrüder Kiss eingesetzt werden sollte. Die Bestandteile – es handelte sich um den Dampfkessel und andere spezielle Maschinenteile, – sollten nach seiner Beschreibung in England gefertigt und danach über den Hafen Liverpool bzw. Hull nach Hamburg verschifft werden. Leider sind keine weiteren Dokumente oder Spezifikationen darüber erhalten geblieben als diese wenigen Zeilen eines Vorvertrages, ebenso nicht, welche Firma diese Teile fertigte, wann und auf welchem Weg sie ins Königreich Ungarn geliefert wurden.

> *to Kempelen Councilor aulic De son M:[ajesté] M:[ajesté] Imp[ereur] a Vienne*
>
> *Mons[ieur] Le Baron Vay & Wayer having done done us the honour to intimate that you Sir were the proprietor of a Patent for all the dominions of His Imperial Majesty for the sole erection of Steam Engines, & that you were willing to treat with us for the disposal either of the whole or some part of the privileges conveyed to you by that patent. We found ourselves flattered by the offer which we wish to avail ourselves but having no disposition to leave our country, at our time of life & with the engagements of business we are under turn, we now make you the following proposal which we submit to your consideration & hope will prove agreable*
>
> *1st that the patent shall remain your sole right as it now is*
>
> *2d That we shall supply you with the engines of our invention in their most improved state at certain prices to be fix't in a Tarif accepted & signed by you & us. This Tarrif to include only the Mettallicty materials of the Engine & boilers, but no part of the woodwork pumps of mill [Anm: dieses Wort ist unleserlich] work or other machinery which may be required to be wrought by the Engines. The materials to be delivered at those prices at the port of Liverpool or Hull*

[8] Neilson, R. M: The Steam Turbine, London/N.Y./Bombay, 1902, S. 8-10

3rd That we willl furnish you with drawings & directions for erecting the Engine in an proper manner & so as to produce the desired effects, without any charge for the same

4th That we shall provide on your account any pumps or other machinery you may want at the customary prices you also paying all charges on the same from the places they are made to the place of their destination

5th A guarantee to our satisfaction to be appointed in London, as security for performance of this contract & who shall accept our drafts on him for the value of each journal of goods & payable in 6 months from this date of their delivery at Liverpool or Hull

6th That we shall not supply any other person in the dominions of his Imperial Majesty with any other Engines whatsoever

7th That we shall not be obliged to furnish at any time any Materials or Machines which may be prohibited by the laws of this country, nor any drawings or directions for constructing such machinery [Anmerkung: Dieser siebente Punkt ist im Original durchgestrichen, er wurde nochmals überarbeitet wie folgt]:

7th That you shall engage not to make nor purchase from others, any Steam Engines whatsoever other than those of the ancient or NewComens Engines, or such as have been in use previous to our Mounture in the dominions of his Imperial Majesty, & also that by virtue of your patent you shall prevent any other person or persons from importing into these dominions or mentioning any Steam Engines other than what we have described

8th That we shall communicate any improvements we shall make on our Engines from time to time on being allowed for any additional parts which may be required in concequence of such improvement.

Rückseite des Schreibens:

Sir!

I have forget to days, to beg the Favor of You to give me specimen of your Copper money Therefore I take the liberty to beg, to send me one or two of them.

I am your most obedient and humble servent

B. Nic.[olas] Vay[9]

Dass eine mit Dampf betriebene Maschine zum Wasserheben nach den Entwürfen von Kempelen beim Bau des Franzenskanals [auch: Bácser Kanal] eingesetzt wurde, ist in den sogenannten „Wirtschaftsakten" des gräflichen Harrach'schen Familienarchivs nachzulesen. Die von Kempelen entwickelte Wasserschöpfmaschine schien sich auch zu bewähren. Sie schaffte es laut einer Konstruktionszeichnung, in der Minute 12 Eimer Wasser – das sind rund 680 Liter –- 4 Klafter hochzuheben. Der Standort der Maschine war bei Neu-Werbaß [heute: Vrbas, Serbien], wo eine der Hauptschleusen des Kanals errichtet wurde. Dort hatte auch der Maschinist sein Quartier genommen. In den Akten und Berichten über den Kanalbau der nächsten Jahre scheinen keine näheren Beschreibungen auf, ob und wie die Maschine gearbeitet hatte, über Zuverlässigkeit und Reparaturanfälligkeit, Abänderungen in der Konstruktion von Kempelen selbst, Verbrauch an Brennmaterial, ob ein weiteres Modell gebaut und eingesetzt wurde. In einer Bilanz, erstellt am 25. Februar 1795, scheint Kempelens Maschine unter Punkt c) bei jenen Posten auf, die in den schon bestrittenen Ausgaben bis

9 Birmingham Archives and Heritage, UK: Manuscript Collection, MS-3782/12/8/116-117, 18 Jan, 1791

1795 noch nicht aufgelistet wurden: Die Anschaffungskosten der Kempelenschen Dunstmaschine betrugen 7466 Gulden.[10]

Aus dem Archiv in Birmingham ist auch noch eine Spezifikation Kempelens zu einer Dampfmaschine in französischer Sprache erhalten, jedoch ohne die Angabe an wen Kempelen diesen Brief richtete, der an Matthew Boulton weitergeleitet wurde. Nachfolgend die Übersetzung des Schreibens.

Sehr geehrter Herr!

Verzeihen Sie mir, dass ich Ihren Brief so spät beantworte, mit dem Sie mich vor so langer Zeit beehrt haben. Der Grund dafür ist, dass ich bis zu diesem Augenblick nichts Positives über eine Wasserdampfpumpe sagen konnte, die man in diesem Land hier begehren würde. Erst jetzt hat man sich entschlossen, sich eine solche Maschine zu besorgen, um das Wasser hinaufzupumpen. Es handelt sich darum, einen beträchtlichen Sumpf tro-cken zu legen und infolgedessen zu erfahren, welche Größe die Dampfpumpe haben sollte, damit sie dieser Absicht gerecht wird und wie hoch sich die Kosten belaufen würden, falls man sich mit einer Ihrer Erfindungen ausstatten würde.

Was Ihr Angebot angeht, sehr geehrter Herr, wenn Sie uns mit diesen Maschinen beliefern würden, nehme ich mir die Freiheit, mich mit der Absicht an Sie zu wenden und Sie zu ersuchen, mir als Vorbereitung, die folgenden Fragen zu beantworten. Ich schreibe auf französisch, da ich im Englischen nicht ausreichend sattelfest bin, um mich deutlich auszudrücken. Aber Sie können auf Englisch antworten, wenn das für sie angenehmer ist, denn ich habe überhaupt keine Schwierigkeit, Sie zu verstehen. Um Ihnen die Angelegenheit noch angenehmer zu gestalten, schicke ich Ihnen auch die Kopie meiner Fragen, damit Sie das Original behalten können und mir die Kopie zurückschicken, bei der die Antwort daneben steht. Würden Sie die Güte haben, mir Ihre Antwort auf dem selben Weg zukommen zu lassen, wie Sie den gegenwärtigen Brief erhalten haben.

Verehrter Herr, ich habe die Ehre und verbleibe mit der größten Hochachtung, Ihr sehr bescheidener und sehr gehorsamer Diener von Kempelen m.[anu] p.[ropria]

Wien, 20. Januar 1792

Fragen über eine Wasserdampfpumpe, um das Wasser eines Sumpfes abzupumpen

1° Die Hubhöhe würde nur 16 Fuß betragen; oder angenommen, man würde den Dampf in einen Zylinder, der 2 Fuß im Durchmesser ist, füllen und der Weg des Kolbens 8 Fuß betragen, welche Maße sollte der Zylinder der Pumpe haben, die dazu bestimmt ist, Wasser nach oben zu fördern

und folglich wie viele Kubik könnte man in der Minute auf die Höhe von 16 Fuß hinaufbefördern?

Wenn ich diese grundlegenden Daten kennen würde, sollte ich mich dem Fall zuwenden, dass die zu fördernde Wassermenge, einer viel größeren oder kleineren Maschine bedürfte und ich imstande wäre Ihnen die Maße genau anzugeben.

2° Der Kessel für den besagten Zylinder soll /: jenem, den ich schon während meines Aufenthaltes in London anschauen konnte:/ einen Durchmesser von 7 Fuß haben. Es nicht nötig, diesen Kessel aus England kommen zu lassen, denn man kann hier Kupfer zu einem besseren Preis kriegen und unsere Kesselmacher können das auch so gut wie überall sonst anfertigen.

---

[10] Österreichisches Staatsarchiv Wien: Familienarchiv Harrach, Wirtschaftsakte II, Zentrale Verwaltung, Wirtschaftskorrespondenz, Schiffahrtsgesellschaft-Kanal bei Vukovar, Fasz. 8, Lfnr. 146, o. F.

3° Der Regulator, oder Apparat, um die Ventile zu steuern, könnte ebenfalls hier hergestellt werden, um so mehr als ich das Mittel gefunden habe, ihn erstaunlich zu vereinfachen und ihn auf nur einen Hammer (Schlagwerk) zu reduzieren, der einmal auf die eine und dann auf die andere Seite fällt (schlägt), was die Maschine mit der größtmöglichen Genauigkeit arbeiten lässt, dessen ich mich an einem Modell versichert habe, das sehr effektiv mit dem Dampf arbeitet.

4° Das Pendel und das restliche Holzgerüst lässt sich auch hier anfertigen. Es geht nur darum, den großen eisernen Zylinder mit seinem Deckel, seinem Kolben und seiner Hülle aus England kommen zu lassen, danach die kleine Pumpe, die dazu bestimmt ist, Wasser und Luft aus der großen Pumpe zu saugen.

5° Ich ersuche Herrn Bolton, mich wissen zu lassen, zu welchem Preis er mir die obengenannten Teile einer solchen Maschine beschaffen und bis Hamburg zustellen könnte, von wo ich sie dann auf eigene Kosten auf dem Landweg bis hierher weiterbefördern lasse.

6° Ab wann könnten die genannten Teile bereit sein und nach Hamburg transportiert werden?

Übrigens könnte es sein, dass wir auch eine Maschine haben möchten, um Münzen zu prägen. In diesem Fall würde ich mich Herrn Bolton sehr verpflichtet fühlen, wenn er mich in Kenntnis setzen würde über einige Details für die Regierung hier. Das heißt mir anzugeben, in welcher Zeitspanne eine bestimmte Summe zum Beispiel der Krone von England mittels dieser Maschine geprägt werden kann, wie die Maße sind, wievieler Leute es bedarf, diese Maschine zu betreuen, wieviel kostet es die Maschine bis Hamburg zu liefern und wie lange braucht die Lieferung, was kostet der Mann, der sie bis hierher begleiten müsste, um sie zusammenzustellen und uns den Betrieb zu erklären?[11]

[11] Birmingham Archives and Heritage, UK: Manuscript Collection, MS-3782/12/37/15, 20 Jan 1792,

Wolfgang von Kempelen – ein Wegbereiter modernen phonetischen Denkens

Ursula Hirschfeld, Eberhard Stock

Martin-Luther-Universität Halle-Wittenberg
ursula.hirschfeld@sprechwis.uni-halle.de

Abstract: Wolfgang von Kempelen (1734–1804) war der erste „Experimentalphonetiker“, der akzeptable synthetische Sprache erzeugen konnte. Er wollte damit nachweisen, dass Sprache nicht gottgegeben ist, sondern im Sinne Herders als Kommunikationsmittel entstanden ist und auch künstlich erzeugt werden kann. Dabei ging es ihm nicht nur um die Entwicklung einer sprechenden Maschine, sondern auch um deren Verwendung als Hilfsmittel für Taubstumme. Ausgehend von der Sprechmaschine aus dem 18. Jahrhundert wird der Bogen zu einem „sprechenden“ Aussprachewörterbuch gespannt.

1 Einleitung

Seit mehreren Jahren arbeiten wir Hallenser Sprechwissenschaftler mit Rüdiger Hoffmann und seinen Mitarbeitern zusammen, um in Ergänzung des traditionell mit IPA-Transkription ausgestatteten „Deutschen Aussprachewörterbuchs“ (Krech et al 2009) ein „sprechendes“ Wörterbuch zu entwickeln, dessen Stichwörter durch Sprachsynthese hörbar gemacht werden sollen. Wir sehen dabei Parallelen zur Sprechmaschine des Wolfgang von Kempelen: Anspruch, Innovation und Ausdauer (von Kempelen hat fast 20 Jahre gebraucht, bis er eine akzeptabel Laute und Wörter hervorbringende Apparatur vorführen konnte). Es bietet sich also an, in dieser Festschrift als kleine Aufmerksamkeit zum Geburtstag unseres geschätzten Kollegen, ausgehend von der Sprechmaschine aus dem 18. Jahrhundert auf das Projekt „sprechendes“ Aussprachewörterbuch einzugehen.

2 Von Kempelen und seine „sprechende Maschine“

Als Beamter am Hofe Maria Theresias, vielseitig begabt und als Verwalter, Architekt, Physiker, Sprachwissenschaftler, Dichter und in anderen Professionen Tätiger, unternahm von Kempelen verschiedenste wissenschaftliche Experimente. Am bekanntesten sind noch heute der schachspielende Türke (ein „Automat“, in dem sich ein Mensch verbarg) und die *sprechende Maschine* (je nach Quelle auch: *Sprachmaschine* oder *Sprechmaschine*), die er auf Tourneen während der 1780er Jahre in Deutschland, aber auch in London und Paris präsentierte. Auf Leben und Werk dieses Universalgelehrten und Erfinders kann in diesem Beitrag nicht eingegangen werden, es gibt dazu zahlreiche Veröffentlichungen, die insbesondere die Entwicklung der Sprechmaschine beschreiben (vgl. u.a. Reininger 2007, Felderer 2008, Trouvain/Brackhane 2010, Brackhane 2011, Brackhane/Trouvain 2011).

2.1 Von Kempelen als Phonetiker

In seiner Publikation, die 1791 in Wien erschienen ist, bezeichnet er die sprechende Maschine als „Frucht seiner Nebenstunden“ (von Kempelen 1791, Vorerinnerungen S. 4). Zwanzig Jahre lang hatte er versucht, einen Apparat zu bauen, der „die menschliche Sprache“ zufriedenstellend erzeugen konnte. In der 3. Abteilung seines Buches, überschrieben mit „Von den Werkzeugen der Sprache und ihren Verrichtungen“ (a.a.O., 59), zeigt von Kempelen detaillierte Kenntnisse in der physiologischen Phonetik, er beschreibt auf über 100 Seiten – in dieser Reihenfolge – die Stimme, die Lunge, die Luftröhre, den Luftröhrenkopf (Larynx), die Stimmritze oder Luftröhrenspalte (Glottis), die Nase, den Mund, die Zunge, die Zähne, die Lippen (a.a.O., 59 ff.). Die einzelnen Teile der Sprechmaschine ähnelten den menschlichen Sprechwerkzeugen: die Lunge ersetzte von Kempelen durch eine Blasebalg, die Stimmbänder durch eine Dudelsackpfeife und den Mund durch den Trichter einer Oboe, den man öffnen und schließen konnte. Mit dieser Apparatur konnten Wörter und kürzere Sätze in sieben Sprachen hervorgebracht werden. Felderer (2008, 1) bemerkt dazu: „Kempelens wissenschaftshistorisches Verdienst ist es, dass er den ersten ernsthaften Versuch unternahm, die einzelnen Laute nicht mit jeweils verschiedenen Pfeifen zu erzeugen, sondern den Ton einer einzigen Pfeife mit Hebeln, Ventilen und einem weichen Gummitrichter zu formen und zu artikulieren. Zum ersten Mal wurde die Entstehung der Töne auch nicht mehr allein in einer Nachbildung der Anatomie menschlicher Artikulationsorgane gesucht, sondern der entscheidende Schritt zu einer mechanischen und abstrahierenden Synthese gemacht."

2.2 Von Kempelen als Sprachgelehrter und -philosoph

Von Kempelen beherrschte mehrere Sprachen, neben Deutsch sprach er Ungarisch, Französisch, Italienisch, Latein, Englisch sowie „Slavisch" und „Walachisch". Er befasste sich auch mit Übersetzungen und den Beschreibungen dieser Sprachen.

In seinen Ausführungen zur Sprechmaschine beschäftigte er sich in den einführenden Kapiteln mit dem Wesen der menschlichen Sprache. Das 1. Kapitel, die „1. Abtheilung", hat den Titel „Von der Sprache überhaupt" (a.a.O., 1), es beginnt mit dem Satz „Die Sprache im weitesten Verstand ist das Vermögen seine Empfindungen oder Gedanken anderen durch Zeichen bekannt zu machen"; in diesem Kapitel setzt er sich mit den Unterschieden der menschlichen Sprache im Vergleich zur Sprache von Tieren auseinander, er beschreibt die Verständigung zwischen Menschen verschiedener Sprachen durch Zeichen und Gebärden (am Beispiel der Seefahrer), die Gebärdensprache Taubstummer, ehe er sich mit den Zeichen der Sprache beschäftigt und die Sprache unter Verweis auf Herders „Ideen zur Philosophie der Geschichte der Menschheit" (1784) als „Grundfeste der Gesellschaft" (a.a.O., 26) bezeichnet. Auf S. 24 konkretisiert er den oben zitierten einleitenden Satz „Die Sprache ist das Vermögen unsere Empfindungen und Gedanken durch verschieden zusammengesetzte oder aufeinander folgende Laute der Kehle andern bekannt zu machen. Diese Laute nennen wir Buchstaben, Sylben, und Wörter."

Die 2. Abteilung ist überschrieben mit „Gedanken über die Frage: Ob die Sprache von dem Menschen erfunden, oder ob sie ihm anerschaffen worden ist? Ob alle Sprachen aus *einer* Grundsprache entstanden sind?" (a.a.O., 28). Von Kempelen geht gegen die Auffassung Johann Peter Süßmilchs „und anderer" an, dass die Sprache „dem Menschen anerschaffen" wäre (a.a.O., 29). Er bezieht sich auf Schriften von Adelung und Herder; Herders Schrift „Über den Ursprung der Sprache" (1789) war es seiner Meinung nach „vorbehalten in dieser Dunkelheit Licht aufzustecken, und aus Gründen zu beweisen, daß der Mensch sich seine Sprache erfunden hat – nothwendig selbst hat erfinden müssen." (a.a.O., 54). Er wollte damit ausdrücken, dass der Mensch die Sprache – evolutionär – infolge eines immer größeren Benennungs- und Verständigungsbedarfs selbst hervorgebracht hat.

Von Kempelens Berufung auf gleich zwei bedeutungsschwere Publikationen seines unmittelbaren Zeitgenossen Johann Gottfried Herder (1744-1803) sowie auf Veröffentlichungen anderer realistisch denkender Autoren lenkt den Blick auf den historischen Hintergrund seiner Arbeiten, auf das geistige Klima gegen Ende des 18. Jahrhunderts, das wir Heutige als Jahrhundert der Aufklärung und der Französischen Revolution begreifen. Der von ihm offenbar in weniger als einem halben Jahr für die Kaiserin Maria Theresia konstruierte Schach-Türke diente noch der Unterhaltung und ist eher als Kabinettstück einzuordnen: Dagegen war seine über viele Jahre betriebene Forschungsarbeit an einer mechanischen Nachbildung der Sprechproduktion der sehr ernstzunehmende Versuch, zur Lösung von sprachphilosophischen Problemen beizutragen, die in der Wissenschaftskommunität seiner Zeit vielfach heftige Kontroversen ausgelöst hatten.

Ein Beleg für das Letztere ist eben die Tatsache, dass sich auch der heute nahezu unbekannte, damals aber überaus einflussreiche und mit bahnbrechenden Ideen hervorgetretene Aufklärer, Philosoph, Kulturhistoriker und Theologe Herder mehrfach publizistisch mit der Sprachevolution befasste. Als die Preußische Akademie der Wissenschaften zu Berlin 1769 ein Preisausschreiben zum Problem der natürlichen Erklärung der Sprachentstehung (u.a. mit der Fragestellung „Wären die Menschen unter der Voraussetzung, dass sie ihren natürlichen Fähigkeiten preisgegeben sind, imstande, die Sprache zu erfinden?“) veranstaltete, reichte er die bereits genannte Arbeit „Über den Ursprung der Sprache“ ein und erhielt vor sechs weiteren, mit Auszeichnungen bedachten Autoren den ersten Preis. Herder ging in seiner Preisschrift, die 1789 in einer verbesserten Fassung erschien, auch gegen die scholastische Lehre des schon genannten Johann Peter Süßmilch vor, eines Berliner Konsistorialrates, der Wissenschaft und Philosophie allein von den christlichen Dogmen ableiten wollte (1766, 21). Beispielsweise führte er gegen ihn an:

> „Einer der Verteidiger des göttlichen Ursprunges der Sprache findet darin göttliche Ordnung zu bewundern: „dass sich die Laute aller uns bekannten Sprachen auf etliche zwanzig Buchstaben bringen lassen“. Allein das Faktum ist unrichtig und der Schluß noch unrichtiger. Keine einzige lebendigtönende Sprache lässt sich vollständig in Buchstaben bringen, und noch weniger in zwanzig Buchstaben ... Der Artikulationen unserer Sprachwerkzeuge sind so viele, ein jeder Laut wird auf so mannigfaltige Weise ausgesprochen, dass zum Beispiel Herr Lambert im zweiten Teil seines Organon („Neues Organon oder Gedanken über die Erforschung und Beziehung des Wahren“, Leipzig 1764 – Vf.) mit Recht hat zeigen können: „wie weit weniger wir Buchstaben als Laute haben“, und „wie unbestimmt also diese von jenen ausgedrückt werden können“. ... Nun sieht man auch, wie trüglich der Beweis für die Göttlichkeit der Sprache aus ihrer Ordnung und Schönheit werde. Ordnung und Schönheit sind da; aber wann? wie und woher sind sie gekommen? Ist denn diese so bewunderte Sprache die Sprache des Ursprungs? oder nicht schon das Kind ganzer Jahrhunderte und vieler Nationen?“(Herder 1952, 1. Bd., 340 f., 429).

Mit solchen und ähnlichen Gedanken wandte sich Herder, der durch Vermittlung Goethes seit 1776 selbst Generalsuperintendent in Weimar war, dort an der Stadtkirche als erster Prediger wirkte und zeit seines Lebens der Religion anhing, gegen den Dogmatismus der protestantischen Orthodoxie. Sein Denken regte die Religionskritik Lessings und vieler anderer an.

Aus diesem Kontext heraus ist von Kempelens Buch und seine Sprechmaschine zu verstehen. Von Kempelen partizipierte an den aufklärerischen Ideen; publizierend beteiligte er sich am Diskurs, freilich ohne alle Auffassungen der Kritiker zu übernehmen. So behielt er – wie noch gezeigt wird – die problematische Wiedergabe phonetischer Ereignisse mit Buchstaben bei.

Im ersten Kapitel seines Buches widersprach von Kempelen der Annahme einer gemeinsamen Ursprache der Menschheit; am Beispiel von Wörtern und Zahlen aus verschiedenen Sprachen zeigt er, dass diese „nicht aus der Ursprache herausgekünstelt“ sind (a.a.O., 44). Er verweist hier auch auf Unterschiede „in der Syntax und dem Bau der Sprachen“ (ebenda). Dabei wird er gelegentlich auch polemisch, wenn er z.B. schreibt: „Wenn uns doch die Vertheidiger einer Ursprache noch sagen könnten, welche es denn eigentlich gewesen ist, wie sie gelautet, und mit welcher noch lebender Sprache sie die mehreste Aehnlichkeit gehabt hat?“ (a.a.O., 48).

In der 4. Abteilung seines Buches, überschrieben mit „Von den Lauten oder Buchstaben der europäischen Sprachen“ (a.a.O, 178) geht er von einem „Hauptalphabet“ aus, das er bereits im 3. Kapitel kurz beschrieben hat: „Wenn man aus dem gewöhnlichen Alphabethe die überflüßigen Buchstaben c. q. x. y. wegläßt, und die Analoguen B P, D T, G K, u. d. gl: die ohnedieß in den Mundarten beständig mit einander verwechselt werden, für Eines gelten läßt, so werden nicht über 16 Hauptlaute bleiben.“ Hier, im 4. Kapitel, heißt es: „Mein Hauptalphabeth ist also dieses: A. B. D. E. F. G. H. CH. I. K. L. M. N. O. P. R. SCH. J. T. U. W. V. Z.“ (a.a.O., 179, auf den Folgeseiten wird genau erklärt, warum aus dem „gewöhnlichen“ Alphabet – gemeint ist das deutsche – Buchstaben herausgenommen oder hinzugefügt wurden. Es folgt die Beschreibung bzw. ein „Verzeichnis aller in Europa vorkommenden Sprachtöne, jeder Abkömmling bei seinem Hauptbuchstaben angesetzt“. (a.a.O., 183 ff.), über mehr als 200 Seiten, mit Beipielen aus unterschiedlichen Sprachen und phonotaktischen Angaben. Das Kapitel ist eingeteilt in folgende Abschnitte:

- Von dem Alphabethe.
- Von den Selbstlautern.
- Von den Doppellautern.
- Von den Mitlautern überhaupt.
- Von den Mitlautern insbesondere.
- Anhang zu den Mitlautern.

Hier wird bereits deutlich, dass von Kempelen wie im folgenden Kapitel über die Entwicklung, Zusammensetzung und Bedienung der Sprechmaschine stark schriftorientiert ist und die geschriebene Sprache als Basis verwendet, d.h. von den Buchstaben ausgeht, wenn er Lautbildungen beschreibt.

2.3 Von Kempelen als Visionär

Von Kempelen folgte bei der Entwicklung seiner Sprechmaschine aufklärerischen Ideen und wollte Taubstummen eine Stimme geben. In der „Vorerinnerung“, mit der seine Publikation beginnt, schreibt von Kempelen (1791, Vorerinnerungen S. 4): „Aller Nutzen – alles Verdienst, das meine gesammelten Entdeckungen haben dürften, mag wohl nur darin bestehen, daß dadurch bey einigen Taubstummen der Unterricht im Sprechen erleichtern, und ein Theil derjenigen Menschen, die eine fehlerhafte Aussprache haben, durch meine Anleitung davon geheilt werden kann.“

Panconcelli-Calzia schrieb 1948 in „Phonetik als Naturwissenschaft“ im Abschnitt „Phonetik und Kultur“, dass „.. viele Gegenstände des allgemeinen Kulturlebens in Beziehung zur Phonetik stehen. Es ist nur zu bedauern, daß dieser Fragenkomplex bis heute nicht noch ausgiebigere Berücksichtigung gefunden hat. Ein ungeahntes Arbeitsfeld öffnet sich vor uns und verspricht reiche Ernte. Zu seiner Bearbeitung gehört freilich Schwung, Initiative und die Fähigkeit, große Gesichtspunkte überhaupt ins Auge fassen zu können. Wer die Aufgabe der Phonetik ausschließlich darin erblickt, ein Weltalphabet oder ein Lautsystem oder die Existenz der Silbe zu beweisen oder die Ergebnisse einiger spärlicher Untersuchungen in anspruchsvolle mathematische Formeln und Diagramme zu kleiden, der verdient nur den Zuruf: „Il est grand dans son domaine, mais son domaine est très petit.“ (1948:74). Als Wegbereiter modernen phonetischen Denkens hat von Kempelen „große Gesichtspunkte des allgemeinen Kulturlebens“ schon frühzeitig erkannt.

Fabian Brackhane (2011) hat am Institut für Phonetik der Universität Saarbrücken in einer umfangreichen Arbeit die Sprechmaschine von den drei beschriebenen Originalversionen an bis zu den Nachbauten der folgenden Jahrzehnte analysiert und, um von Kempelens Darstellung überprüfen zu können, selbst versucht, nach dessen Angaben einen vergleichbaren Mechanismus zu konstruieren. Von Kempelens Maschine wurde als ein mit Schalltrichter versehenes viereckiges Kästchen vorgestellt, das einige Öffnungen aufwies. In diese musste der Bedienende die Hände einführen, um Federn und Klappen für die Schallmodifikation manipulieren zu können. Die Lösungen, die von Kempelen für die Luftzufuhr sowie die Klang- und Geräuschproduktion gefunden hatte, waren nach Brackhanes Analyse zum Teil erstaunlich naturnah, zum Teil aber auch naturfremd. Es waren Bemühungen und mechanische Ansätze erkennbar, Koartikulation und Prosodie akustisch abzubilden. Trotzdem kann die Synthesequalität angesichts der technischen Möglichkeiten verständlicherweise nur gering gewesen sein. In zeitgenössischen Quellen überwiegen zwar Stimmen, die die Natürlichkeit und Verständlichkeit der synthetisierten Wörter und Phrasen rühmen, dabei ist aber zu bedenken, dass die Hörer bei den Vorführungen, die von Kempelen bei seien Reisen durch Europa veranstaltete und die gewöhnlich nicht die Sprechmaschine, sondern den Schach-Türken in den Vordergrund rückten, keine Referenzmuster hatten, nichts Bestimmtes erwarteten konnten und vermutlich auch entfernte Ähnlichkeiten zwischen Gesprochenem und Synthetisiertem bereits als Sensation erlebten.

Der Wert der Arbeiten von Kempelens ist deshalb wohl in erst er Linie darin zu sehen, dass er, wie schon betont, aus humanistischer Verantwortung für die Versorgung von Sprachbehinderten eine Sprachsynthese für notwendig hielt und dass er, so seine Vision, diese Synthese über ein Modell der Artikulation erreichen wollte. Seine Auflistung der Sprachlaute war zwar, phonologisch betrachtet, unzureichend und auch seine Transkription wurde, greift man auf die oben angeführten Darlegungen Herders zurück, selbst für das zeitgenössische Urteil den phonetischen Gegebenheiten nicht gerecht. Das schmälert aber nicht die Bedeutung seines methodologischen Vorgehens. Nicht durch Spekulation, sondern, wie bereits angedeutet wurde, durch intensive systematische Beobachtung verschaffte er sich die Grundlagen für seine Konstruktion. Seine Beschreibung der Artikulatoren und ihres Zusammenspiels, der Phonemrealisierung und ihrer normgerechten wie dialektalen Varianten sowie der phonotaktischen Besonderheiten im Deutschen zeugt davon. Er ging kontrastiv vor und erfasste die Besonderheiten der einzelsprachlichen Lautbildung, indem er die Lautphysiologien mehrerer europäischer Sprachen miteinander verglich. Mehr als zwei Jahrhunderte später ist sicher manches daran zu korrigieren, von Kempelen erwies sich aber auch darin als Universalgenie, dass er – so die Zeitgenossen – nicht nur Wörter und Aussprüche des Deutschen, sondern auch Gesprochenes in anderen Sprachen synthetisieren konnte.

3 Von der Sprechmaschine zum „Sprechenden Wörterbuch“

3.1 Entwicklung eines „sprechenden“ Aussprachewörterbuchs

Seit den 1950er Jahren ist es für die Halleschen Sprachwissenschaftler ein wichtiges Forschungsgebiet, die deutsche Standardaussprache zu untersuchen und zu beschreiben; bisher sind drei Aussprachewörterbücher erschienen (Krech et.al. 1964, 1982, 2009). Ein „sprechendes“ Aussprachewörterbuch ist seit jeher eine wünschenswerte und notwendige Ergänzung zum herkömmlichen Aussprachewörterbuch, weil es den Zugang zur deutschen Standardaussprache erleichtern und einprägbare Sprechmuster vermitteln kann. Daran arbeiten die halleschen Sprechwissenschaftler und die Dresdner Akustiker seit einiger Zeit gemeinsam, Arbeitsstand, Fragen und Probleme sind verschiedentlich auf Konferenzen vorgetragen und publiziert worden (vgl. Hirschfeld/Hoffmann/Anders/Kruschke 2003, Hoffmann/Hirschfeld/Jokisch/Anders 2004, Hirschfeld/Hoffmann/Jokisch/Lachmann 2005, Hirschfeld/Hoffmann 2006, Hirschfeld/Hoffmann/Lange 2007). In den letzten Jahren sind an der Universität Halle auch mehrere Abschlussarbeiten verfasst worden, in denen es um die Verbesserung der vorhandenen Sprachsyntheseprogramme ging (vgl. Lange 2008, Drechsel 2009, Scheibe-Ahansal 2010, Förster 2011, Kirpeit 2011).

Transkription in gesprochene Sprache umzusetzen, ist für ungeübte Nutzer sehr schwierig. Die in Aussprachewörterbüchern für das Deutsche verwendete internationale Transkription lässt zudem einen gewissen Spielraum. Sie ist, da sie übersichtlich bleiben soll, nicht eng und detailliert genug, um alle Aussprachemerkmale genau zu erfassen. So wird z.B. für die verschiedenen konsonantischen R-Varianten nur ein Zeichen verwendet; für die Akzentuierung wird nur die Akzentstelle angegeben, nicht aber die Mittel, mit denen Akzentvokale bzw. -silben hervorgehoben werden usw.

Durch die Entwicklung der PC-Technik und der Schaltkreisbasis vollzog sich Anfang der 1990er Jahre international der Übergang von parametrischen, ressourcensparenden Verfahren zur sog. konkatenativen Sprachsynthese, bei der kleine, natürliche Sprachsegmente nach bestimmten Regeln zur gewünschten Äußerung verkettet werden. Mit diesem Verfahren, das eine bessere Qualität als die der parametrischen Verfahren liefert, arbeitet auch das am Institut für Akustik und Sprachkommunikation der Technischen Universität Dresden entwickelte Sprachsynthesesystem *Dresden Speech Synthesizer* (DRESS). Speziell für die Einzelwortsynthese in einem Aussprachewörterbuch wurde 2002 auf dieser Basis das Sprachsynthesesystem lexDRESS konzipiert. Seitdem wurden verschiedene Untersuchungen zu dessen Evaluierung und Weiterentwicklung durchgeführt, um die Verständlichkeit, Natürlichkeit und Expressivität der synthetisierten Sprache zu verbessern (vgl. Lange 2008, S.39).

In einem Wörterbuch werden nur Wörter und ggf. Wortgruppen, jedoch keine längeren Phrasen verwendet, deshalb entfällt eine Komponente, die für die linguistische Textanalyse erforderlich und eine Quelle für unerwünschte Artefakte ist: die suprasegmentale Gestaltung zusammenhängender Äußerungen. Dennoch ist die mit der vorhandenen Ausbaustufe des Sprachsynthesesystems DRESS erreichbare Sprachqualität bisher für ein solches Wörterbuch-Projekt unzureichend. Die Hauptursachen sind:

a) aus phonetischer Sicht werden zu wenige Bausteinvarianten (Diphone) verwendet,
b) die suprasegmentale Steuerung (Intonation, Lautlängen, Intensität) ist noch nicht zufriedenstellend.

Daran wird gearbeitet, so dass künftig mit dem auf einer ausreichenden Diphonbasis arbeitenden lex-Editor segmentale und suprasegmentale Merkmale der Sprachausgabe gezielt beeinflusst werden können.

3.2 Entwicklung einer Deutschen Aussprache-Datenbank

In Fortsetzung seiner Diplomarbeit (2011) wird Johannes Förster am Seminar für Sprechwissenschaft und Phonetik der Universität Halle in seinem Promotionsprojekt, wieder in Kooperation mit Rüdiger Hoffmann, eine Plattform für die Erforschung und Beschreibung der deutschen Standardaussprache, die *Deutsche Aussprache-Datenbank* (DAD), entwickeln, die neue und effiziente Wege für die Kodifizierung der deutschen Standardaussprache ermöglichen soll. Ortsungebunden können hier Stichworteinträge bearbeitet oder neu erstellet werden, so dass die Datenbank ein hohes Maß an Aktualität gewährleistet. Vorgesehen ist auch die Einbindung des „sprechenden" Aussprachewörterbuchs auf der Basis des „Deutschen Aussprachewörterbuchs" (Krech et al. 2009).

Literatur

[1] Brackhane, F.: Wolfgang von Kempelen oder: Sprachforschung und Sprachsynthese im 18. Jahrhundert. Sprachreport 1. Mannheim: Institut für deutsche Sprache 2011. pp. 18 – 23. http://pub.ids-mannheim.de/laufend/sprachreport/pdf/sr11-1b.pdf (20.03.2013)

[2] Brackhane, F. / Trouvain, J.: Wolfgangs von Kempelen K. K. wirklichen Hofraths Mechanismus der menschlichen Sprache nebst der Beschreibung seiner sprechenden Maschine. Phonus 16, Univ. Saarbrücken 2011. http://www.coli.uni-saarland.de/groups/WB/Phonetics/contents/phonus-pdf/phonus16/ kommentierte_ausgabe.pdf (20.03.2013)

[3] Drechsel, S.: Zur Optimierung des Diphoninventars für das Sprechende Aussprachewörterbuch – Realisation des Schwa in der Vorsilbe *be-*. Bachelor-Abschlussarbeit. Martin-Luther-Universität Halle-Wittenberg 2009. (unv. Mskr.)

[4] Felderer, B.: Mündigkeit. Institut für Medienarchäologie 2008. http://klangmaschinen.ima.or.at/db/db.php?id=39&table=Object&lang=de&showartikel=1&view=ausstellung (20.03.2013)

[5] Förster, J.: Zur Optimierung eines Diphoninventars für eingedeutschte Namen und Wörter in einem standarddeutschen Sprachsyntheseprogramm – Quantitative Analysen der Standardaussprache des Deutschen im Halle-Korpus. Diplomarbeit. Martin-Luther-Universität Halle-Wittenberg 2011. (unv. Mskr.)

[6] Herder, J. G.: Zur Philosophie der Geschichte. 2 Bde. Berlin: Aufbau 1952

[7] Hirschfeld, U. / Hoffmann, R.: Standardaussprache per Sprachsynthese? In: Hirschfeld, U. / Anders, L. C. (Ed.): Probleme und Perspektiven sprechwissenschaftlicher Arbeit. Frankfurt am Main: P. Lang 2006, pp. 135 – 146. (Hallesche Schriften zur Sprechwissenschaft und Phonetik 18)

[8] Hirschfeld, U. / Hoffmann, R. / Anders, L. C. / Kruschke, H.: Speech Synthesis and Standard Pronunciation of German. In: Proceedings of the 15th ICPhS. Barcelona 2003, pp. 2593 – 2596.

[9] Hirschfeld, U. / Hoffmann, R. / Jokisch, O. / Lachmann, M.: Speech synthesis for a German pronunciation dictionary – phonetic evaluation. In: Vich, R. (Ed.): Electronic Speech Signal Processing. Studientexte zur Sprachkommunikation, 36/2005. Dresden, pp. 446 – 451.

[10] Hirschfeld, U. / Hoffmann, R. / Lange, F.: Prosodic Modeling of Synthesised German Words. In: Proceedings of the 16th ICPhS. Saarbrücken 2007, 2205 – 2208.

[11] Hoffmann, R. / Hirschfeld, U. / Jokisch, O. / Anders, L. C.: LexDRESS – Speechsynthesis for a speaking pronunciation dictionary: First results. In: Fellbaum, K. (Ed.), 15. Konferenz Elektronische Sprachsignalverarbeitung. Cottbus 2004, Tagungsband, pp. 183 – 190. (Studientexte zur Sprachkommunikation Bd. 30)

[12] Kempelen von, W.: Mechanismus der menschlichen Sprache nebst Beschreibung einer sprechenden Maschine, Wien: J. B. Degen 1791. Faksimile-Neudruck 1970, F. Frommann Verlag Stuttgart, Bad Cannstatt, online unter: http://drl.ohsu.edu/cdm/compoundobject/collection/hom/id/3031/rec/1 (20.03.2013)

[13] Kirpeit, K.: Ausgewählte Aspekte der Sprachsynthese für ein *Sprechendes Wörterbuch*. Bachelor-Abschlussarbeit. Martin-Luther-Universität Halle-Wittenberg 2011. (unv. Mskr.)

[14] Krech, E.-M. / Kurka, E. / Stelzig, H. / Stock, E. / Stötzer, U. / Teske, R. (Ed., unter Mitwirkung von Jung-Alsen).: Wörterbuch der deutschen Aussprache. Leipzig: VEB Bibliographisches Institut 1964.

[15] Krech, E.-M. / Kurka, E. / Stelzig, H. / Stock, E. / Stötzer, U. / Teske, R. (Ed., unter Mitwirkung von Jung-Alsen, K.): Großes Wörterbuch der deutschen Aussprache. Leipzig: VEB Bibliographisches Institut 1982.

[16] Krech, E.-M., Stock, E., Hirschfeld, U., Anders, L. C.: Deutsches Aussprachewörterbuch. Berlin/NewYork: de Gruyter 2010.

[17] Lange, F.: Wortprosodie und Sprachsynthese. Diplomarbeit. Martin-Luther-Universität Halle-Wittenberg 2008. (unv. Mskr.)

[18] Panconcelli-Calzia, G.: Phonetik als Naturwissenschaft. Berlin: Wissenschaftliche Editionsgesellschaft 1948.

[19] Reininger, A.: Wolfgang von Kempelen – Eine Biografie. Wien: Praesens 2007.

[20] Scheibe-Ahansal, T.: Zur Optimierung eines Diphoninventars für ein „Sprechendes deutsches Aussprachewörterbuch". Diplomarbeit. Martin-Luther-Universität Halle-Wittenberg 2010. (unv. Mskr.)

[21] Süßmilch, J. P.: Versuch eines Beweises, daß die erste Sprache ihren Ursprung nicht vom Menschen , sondern allein vom Schöpfer erhalten habe. Berlin: Buchladen der Realschule 1766

[22] Trouvain, J. / Brackhane: Zur heutigen Bedeutung der Sprechmaschine von Wolfgang von Kempelen. 2010. http://www.coli.uni-saarland.de/~trouvain/Trouvain_Brackhane_2010.pdf (20.03.2013)

Stationen mechanischer Sprachsynthese vom 18. bis zum 20. Jahrhundert

Fabian Brackhane[1] *& Jürgen Trouvain*[2]

[1]*Institut für Deutsche Sprache, Mannheim*
[2]*Computerlinguistik und Phonetik, Universität des Saarlandes, Saarbrücken*
brackhane@ids-mannheim.de

Abstract: Der vorliegende Aufsatz widmet sich einigen markanten historischen Einzelleistungen auf dem Gebiet der mechanischen Sprachsynthese, die auch heute noch faszinierend, jedoch zumeist nur in groben Zügen bekannt sind. An der hier präsentierten Auswahl erweist sich sowohl die fesselnde Kraft eines einmal als grundsätzlich praktikabel erkannten Konzeptes der stimmlichen Anregung als auch die hieraus resultierende Originalität immer neuer Ansätze, diesem Syntheseprinzip zum technologischen Durchbruch zu verhelfen.

1 Einführung

Die Idee der künstlichen Erzeugung von Sprachschall scheint so alt wie die Menschheit zu sein (vgl. [1]). Bereits aus der Antike sind vom Orakel auf Lesbos ebenso wie auch einige Jahrhunderte später von Albertus Magnus (um 1200-1280) Berichte von „Sprechenden Köpfen" überliefert. Deren „Sprechfähigkeit" bestand allerdings zumeist aus einem von rückwärts in ihre Mundöffnung geleiteten Rohr, an dessen anderem Ende sich ein zutiefst menschlicher Sprecher befand.

Als man sich Mitte des 18. Jahrhunderts in der Lage sah, aufgrund recht verlässlicher anatomischer und physiologischer Erkenntnisse erstmals eine künstliche Nachbildung des menschlichen Sprechapparates zu versuchen, war die interessierte Öffentlichkeit offenbar durch eine Vielzahl mehr oder weniger plumper falscher Sprechmaschinen so enerviert, dass ausgerechnet der zutiefst seriöse Ansatz Wolfgang von Kempelens vielfach auf höhnische Ablehnung stieß (vgl. [2]).

Auch im 19. Jahrhundert behielt das Thema seine Aktualität. Wissenschaftliche Größen wie Hermann von Helmholtz (1821-1894) oder Alexander Graham Bell (1847-1922) befassten sich intensiv mit der Erforschung von Synthese-Möglichkeiten. Aber auch aus den tradierten Ideen der vergangenen Jahrhunderte wurden vielversprechende, wenn auch konventionelle Sprachsynthesekonzepte entwickelt.

Helmholtz war zu Beginn des 20. Jahrhunderts durch die aufkommende Elektrizität in der Lage, gänzlich neue Konzepte insbesondere zur Vokalsynthese zu entwickeln [3], wiewohl auch weiterhin neue, rein mechanische Ansätze erprobt wurden. So von Richard Paget (1869-1955) [4] und Dayton Clarence Miller (1866-1941) [5].

Epochenübergreifend sah man in den Vokalen das Wesentliche einer Sprache und dementsprechend in deren Synthese die zentrale Herausforderung. Den Konsonanten als „Beiwerk" maß man hinsichtlich des Syntheseaufwandes wenig Bedeutung bei [1: 203]. So ist zu erklären, warum es vor und neben „vollwertigen" Sprachsynthesekonzepten auch eine Vielzahl von Versuchen zur Vokalsynthese gab, jedoch keine separaten Konsonantensynthesen. Aus der Menge der historischen Versuche seien an dieser Stelle nur einige Schlaglichter herausgegriffen, um die Entwicklung der mechanischen Sprachsynthese seit dem 18. Jahrhundert nachzuzeichnen.

2 Vokalsynthese

2.1 Die „Vox humana“

Schon früh sahen Forscher in dem ebenso verbreiteten wie hoch komplexen Musikinstrument Orgel eine Art Prototyp der Sprachsynthese. So entwickelt beispielsweise Leonhard Euler (1707-1783) die Idee einer orgelähnlichen Sprechmaschine, auf der Reden gleich einem musikalischen Stück gespielt werden könnten [6].

Die Geschichte der mechanischen Sprachsynthese ist hierbei untrennbar mit der eines speziellen Orgelregisters verknüpft: Bei der „Vox humana“ handelt es sich um eine Bauform der *Lingualpfeifen*, bei denen die strömende Luft durch ein schwingendes Metallblatt (*Zunge* genannt) ähnlich dem Rohrblatt einer Klarinette angeregt wird. Der so entstehende Ton wird durch angefügte Resonatoren gefiltert und verstärkt, wobei Dimensionen und Form des Resonators entscheidenden Einfluss auf die Klangfarbe haben. Über die Namensetymologie des Registers besteht bis heute keine abschließende Einigkeit, es ist jedoch auszuschließen, das beabsichtigt war, die menschliche Stimme authentisch nachzuahmen. Eher scheint es sich um eine funktionelle Stellvertreteraufgabe gehandelt zu haben. Das Wissen hierüber war aber spätestens im 18. Jahrhundert verloren und der Anspruch, dem Register zu einem seinem Namen entsprechenden Klang zu verhelfen, allgegenwärtig [7: 166-167].

Dies wirkte sich auch auf die Konzeption nahezu aller zu dieser Zeit entstandenen Sprachsyntheseversuche aus, von denen hier drei besonders hervorgehoben seien: Die „Vokalorgel“ Christian Gottlieb Kratzensteins (1780), die „Sprechenden Köpfe“ des Abbé Mical (vor 1783) und die „Sprechmaschine“ Wolfgang von Kempelens (1783/91).

2.2 Christian Gottlieb Kratzenstein

Der Naturwissenschaftler Kratzenstein (1723-1795) war über die St. Petersburger Akademie der Wissenschaften mit Euler verbunden. Als diese 1780 in einer Preisfrage nach der Natur und Synthetisierbarkeit von A, E, I, O, U durch eine aus der „Vox humana“ abgeleitete Konstruktion fragte, reichte Kratzenstein bereits im darauffolgenden Jahr ein Traktat und den Prototyp einer „Vokalorgel“ ein. Angesichts der engen Orientierung der Preisfrage an den Ideen Eulers und der überraschend kurzen Bearbeitungszeit, die Kratzenstein scheinbar für die Bearbeitung beider Fragen benötigte, darf eine Konzeption des Wettbewerbes „ad personam“ als wahrscheinlich gelten.

Kratzenstein gelangte in seinen Ausführungen [8] zu der (falschen) Überzeugung, dass die Anregung des die Lunge verlassenden Luftstromes durch den Kehldeckel geschehe, der frei und waagerecht in der Luftröhre schwinge[1]. Basierend auf dieser Annahme entwickelte Kratzenstein je eine Orgelpfeife für jeden der fünf Vokale. Mit Ausnahme derjenigen für [i] waren sie nach dem Prinzip der Lingualpfeifen konstruiert. Kratzenstein hatte indes zutreffend erkannt, dass die Funktionsweise einer herkömmlichen Zungenpfeife, bei der das Metallblatt auf ein hohles Rohrsegment aufschlägt, nicht für eine adäquate „menschliche“ Stimmerzeugung geeignet ist. Als Folgerung aus seiner o.g. These entwickelte Kratzenstein nun Pfeifen, bei denen die Zunge nicht wie üblich auf der Oberseite des Rohrsegments aufschlägt, sondern sich in diesem frei schwingend bewegen kann. Dieses Konzept wurde aufgrund seiner Komplexität in späteren Sprachsynthesekonzepten nicht mehr aufgegriffen (durchschlagende Lingualpfeifen

[1] Der Medizinprofessor Kratzenstein wurde hier wie auch in anderen Aspekten vom physiologischen Autodidakten Kempelen widerlegt!

sind erheblich diffiziler in der Fertigung als aufschlagende), hatte aber im Orgelbau des 19. und frühen 20. Jahrhunderts aufgrund der „zarten" Klangfarbe der hervorgebrachten Töne großen Erfolg.

2.3 Dayton Clarence Miller

Erst durch die Möglichkeit Anfang des 20. Jahrhunderts, einzelne Teiltöne eines komplexen Klanges grafisch darzustellen und zu messen, konnte die Struktur der Vokale näher erforscht werden. Als ein Resultat dieser Forschungen entwickelte Dayton Clarence Miller (1866-1941) eine auf Labialpfeifen basierende Vokalsynthese. Miller erkannte, dass die Klanggestalt eines Vokals und seine Unterscheidbarkeit von anderen Vokalen eng mit der harmonischen Zusammensetzung seines Klanges verknüpft ist. Daher stellte er für mehrere Vokale des amerikanischen Englisch Gruppen aus *Labialpfeifen* zusammen, die – kontrolliert durch den Vergleich mit Oszillogrammen „echter" Vokale – diese nachahmen sollten.

Miller stellte je nach Vokal verschieden große Pfeifengruppen zusammen. Nach Miller waren für [u] sechs Pfeifen (also ein Klang bestehend aus sechs Partialtönen) notwendig, für [a] zehn, für [æ] bereits sechzehn. Die Einstimmung der Grundfrequenz erfolgte über eine Stimmgabel, die übrigen Teiltöne wurden bei ständiger optischer Kontrolle durch das *Phonodeik*, einen Vorläufer des Oszilloskops, beigestimmt [5: 246-250].

2.4 Weitere Konzepte zur Vokalsynthese

Mit den Versuchen Hermann von Helmholtz' geht die Epoche der rein mechanischen Vokalsynthesen ihrem Ende entgegen. Er entdeckte, dass der Mundraum je nach gebildetem Vokal die Resonanz eines anderen musikalischen Tones besitzt. Hierauf aufbauend synthetisierte er Vokale durch elektromagnetisch angeregte Stimmgabeln, deren Teiltöne er jeweils charakteristisch filterte [3].

Als Vorstudien zu einer Sprechmaschine in der Tradition Kratzensteins fertigte Sir Richard Paget in den 1920er Jahren Vokaltraktmodelle aus Plastilin an, die er mithilfe von (aufschlagenden) Zungenpfeifen anregte. Ebenfalls erforschte er die Möglichkeit, Vokale durch elektrische Stromkreise zu erzeugen. Zwar hatten all diese Versuche das Konzept einer neuen, „menschenähnlicheren" Konstruktion der „Vox humana" zur Folge, zu einer umfangreichen Sprachsynthese kam es indes nie [4].

3 Sprachsynthese im 18. Jahrhundert

3.1 Abbé Mical

Die Konstruktion des Abbé Mical (um 1730-1789/90) steht in mancher Hinsicht noch in der Tradition der früheren vorgeblichen Sprachsynthesen. Einmal mehr handelte es sich um „Sprechende Köpfe". Auch ist über die Funktionsweise und das Schicksal der Maschine nur weniges bzw. legendenhaftes überliefert. Es ist ein für unsere Zwecke eher unbefriedigender Bericht über eine Prüfung durch die Pariser Akademie der Wissenschaften erhalten [1]. Allem Anschein nach handelte es sich um eine Maschine, die aus zahlreichen, von labialen wie lingualen Orgelpfeifen abgeleiteten Schallerzeugern bestand und durch eine Stiftwalze – ähnlich der einer Spieluhr – angetrieben wurde.

Die Synthesequalität der Maschine wird als mangelhaft beurteilt [1]. Wohl auch deswegen waren die von ihr erzeugten Sätze auf einem Plakat nachlesbar. Der Legende nach zerstörte Mical sowohl einen früheren Prototyp als auch die 1783 der Akademie vorgestellte Maschine, als sich keinerlei finanzielle Erfolge einstellen wollten [9: 541].

3.2 Erasmus Darwin

Noch weniger bekannt ist über eine Sprechmaschine des Großvaters von Charles Darwin. Erasmus Darwin (1731-1802), einer der berühmtesten englischen Ärzte seiner Zeit, setzte sich mit der menschlichen Sprache intensiv auseinander. Wohl nicht zuletzt zur Überprüfung der eigenen Theorien entwickelte er offenbar auch eine eigene mechanische Sprachsynthese. Diese scheint deutlich vor den anderen hier beschriebenen entstanden zu sein, nämlich um 1766. Das Wenige, das aus zweiter Hand bekannt ist, scheint sie hinsichtlich ihrer Konstruktion und Synthesequalität in die Nähe der Sprechmaschine Wolfgang von Kempelens zu rücken [10].

3.3 Wolfgang von Kempelen

Um ein vielfaches besser dokumentiert als die vorangehenden Episoden ist die „Sprechmaschine“ Kempelens (1737-1807). Zwar kursiert gerade hier eine Vielzahl von Halbwahrheiten und Legenden. Doch wer sich die Mühe macht, Kempelens eigene Veröffentlichung und einige der bemerkenswert zahlreichen zeitgenössischen Berichte kritisch zu lesen, gelangt zu einem vergleichsweise scharfen Bild.

Kempelen hatte, anders als Kratzenstein oder Mical, den Anspruch, eine universelle Sprachsynthese zu konstruieren und somit die Synthese ganzer Sätze unterschiedlicher Sprachen zu ermöglichen. Zudem sollte eine solche Maschine dazu geeignet sein, sog. Taubstummen artikulatorisch anschaulichen Sprechunterricht geben bzw. ihnen eine Art sprachlicher Prothese zur Verfügung zu stellen zu können.

Durch Kempelens Buch „Mechanismus der menschlichen Sprache“ [11] sind wir nicht nur über dessen – für seine Zeit keineswegs allgemein verbreiteten – Erkenntnisse zur Physiologie des Sprechens unterrichtet, sondern haben auch ein so detailliertes Bild von der Konstruktion seiner „Sprechmaschine“, wie es vor- und nachher von keinem mechanischen Synthesekonzept wieder vorliegt. Als Anregungsmodell wählte Kempelen – wiewohl er um die Unzulänglichkeit der „Vox humana“ wusste – eben eine solche Lingualpfeife, deren Zungenblatt er jedoch aus hauchdünnem Elfenbein fertigte und deren Resonator er durch einen flexiblen Gummitrichter als Repräsentation für den Mundraum ersetzte. Analogien für Zunge oder Zähne fehlten indes völlig.

Trotz dieser Einschränkungen wurde die hohe Synthesequalität und die Breite des Repertoires der Maschine von zahlreichen Zeitgenossen explizit betont. Es scheint sich hierbei allerdings zumindest zum Teil auch um quasi autosuggestive Phänomene zu handeln, da die von Kempelens Zeitgenossen beschriebenen komplexen Äußerungen mit keiner der zahlreichen Repliken realisierbar sind, was aufgrund der konstruktionsbedingten Beschränkungen auch nicht anders zu erwarten ist.

Kempelen war sich der Desiderate seiner Konstruktion bewusst. Er räumte sie im „Mechanismus“ seinen Lesern freimütig ein, verbunden mit der Aufforderung, selbst nach Verbesserungen zu forschen. Bereits einige Zeitgenossen Kempelens bauten denn auch mehr oder weniger weiterentwickelte Repliken der „Sprechmaschine“, so dass bereits Goethe 1797 über einen Nachbau berichten konnte [12: 154].

4 Rezeption und Weiterentwicklung im 19. und 20. Jahrhundert

4.1 Kempelens Epigonen

Zu Beginn des 19. Jahrhunderts finden sich in der zeitgenössischen Berichterstattung immer wieder Meldungen über neuerfundene „Sprechmaschinen“. Leider teilen sie allesamt das Schicksal ihrer Vorgänger und müssen heute als verschollen gelten. Auch die zeitgenössische Berichterstattung bricht in allen Fällen nach sehr wenigen – zumeist recht vagen – Artikeln ab.

Beispielhaft herausgegriffen seien hier die Berichte über „Dr. Müllers redende Maschine“ von 1788 [13], die „Sprechmaschine“ des Berliner Bildhauers Leonhard Posch (1750-1831) aus den Jahren 1807/1828, bei der es sich offenbar um eine Weiterentwicklung der Kempelenschen Konstruktion handelte [14: 27-28] und die um 1850 offenbar gleich in mehreren Exemplaren gebaute „Sprechmaschine“ des Musikinstrumentenbauers Carl Salomon Warmholz (1778-1854) [15]. Um den Erwerb der beiden Letzteren bemühte man sich offenbar von offizieller preußischer Seite, nichtsdestotrotz verlieren sich auch ihre Spuren alsbald im Dunkel der Zeit.

4.2 Robert Willis und Charles Wheatstone

In den 1830er Jahren griff Robert Willis (1800-1875) die Arbeiten Kratzensteins wieder auf. Mit einer Vielzahl verschiedener Konstruktionen versuchte er die optimalen Bedingungen für eine möglichst authentische Vokalsynthese herauszufinden. Willis experimentierte hierbei insbesondere mit den Konstruktionsparametern des Resonators sowie dessen Material. Auch die Schallquelle selbst wurde intensiv untersucht [16].

Nahezu zeitgleich mit Willis beschäftigte sich auch der britische Physiker Charles Wheatstone (1802-1875) mit mechanischer Sprachsynthese. Als Ergebnis seiner Auseinandersetzung mit Kratzenstein, Kempelen und auch Willis konzipierte er eine eigene, vorgeblich verbesserte Version der Kempelenschen „Sprechmaschine“ [17], die als einzige aller historischen „Sprechmaschinen“ bis heute erhalten ist[2].

4.3 Joseph Faber und Alexander Graham Bell

Nur wenige Jahre nach den umfassenden (weitgehend) theoretischen Arbeiten von Willis und Wheatstone machte in Deutschland eine weitere Sprechmaschine von sich reden. Die „Euphonia“ des Wieners Joseph Faber[3] nahm für sich (ebenfalls) in Anspruch, eine Weiterentwicklung der „Sprechmaschine“ Wolfgang von Kempelens zu sein. Und tatsächlich lassen einige zeitgenössische Berichte den Schluss zu, dass es sich hierbei um eine durchaus gelungene Sprachsynthese gehandelt haben muss, wenngleich andere Berichte von einer höchst mäßigen Synthesequalität sprechen [1: 18]. Faber stattete – wie bereits von Kempelen vorgeschlagen, seine Maschine zur Steuerung mit einer kleinen Klaviatur aus und versah sie mit einer puppenartigen Verkleidung [18: 67-69].

Der amerikanische Physiker Joseph Henry (1797-1887) entwickelte angesichts der „Euphonia“ die Vision, dass durch die Kombination einer solchen Sprechmaschine mit

---

[2] Nachdem über ihren Verbleib seit den 1920er Jahren Unklarheit bestand, konnte sie unlängst durch den Erstautor wieder ausfindig gemacht werden. Sie befindet sich heute in unvollständigem Zustand in einem Magazin des „Science Museum London“.

[3] Sowohl die Lebensdaten als auch nähere Angaben zur Person sind unbekannt. Dudley & Tarnoczy [19: 164] bezeichnen ihn als „certain Professor Joseph Faber of Vienna“.

der Telegrafie-Technologie die Übertragung beispielsweise von Predigten parallel in zahlreiche Kirchen möglich sei [1].

Alexander Graham Bell (1847-1922) lernte durch seinen Vater, den Phonetiker Alexander Melville Bell (1819-1905), als junger Mann sowohl die Kempelen-Replik Charles Wheatstones als auch die „Euphonia“ kennen und entwickelte unter Anleitung seines Vaters eine eigene Variante der „Sprechmaschine“, die offenbar einige Ähnlichkeit mit derjenigen Fabers hatte. Mithilfe einer solchen Vorrichtung sollten Reden auch großen Menschenmassen verständlich gemacht werden, woraus später indirekt das Konzept des Telefons entstand [1: 19].

Zeitgenössischen Berichten über die Vorführung der „Euphonia“ zufolge beschloss diese zumindest auf ihrer England-Tournée 1846 jede Vorführung mit der Hymne „God save the Queen“ [18: 69]. Auffällig hierbei ist allerdings, dass der Maschine in anderen zeitgenössischen Quellen eine äußerst monotone Sprechweise attestiert wird [1].

4.4 Kempelen-Repliken

Eine Weiterentwicklung der Arbeiten sowohl Kempelens als auch Kratzensteins mit konkretem Nutzungsziel stellen die sog. „Stimm-Mechaniken“ dar, die 1899 durch den Mediziner Johannes Kessel (1839-1907) der Öffentlichkeit vorgestellt wurden [20]. Es handelt sich hierbei um einzelne hölzerne Zungenpfeifen, die liegend auf einem passenden kleinen Blasebalg montiert sind und jeweils einen Einzelvokal oder einen unkomplexen Zweisilbler wie „Mama, Papa, Emma, hurra“ zu produzieren imstande sind [21]. Ursprünglich als Instrument der Rehabilitation hochgradig Schwerhöriger gedacht, unterblieb letztlich eine Weiterentwicklung, die zu einer vollends befriedigenden Synthesequalität und damit auch zu einer konkreten Nutzbarkeit hätte führen sollen.

Die Herstellung dieser Stimm-Mechaniken oblag bemerkenswerterweise mit Hugo Hölbe (1844-1931) einem Vertreter der seinerzeit florierenden Thüringer Spielzeugindustrie, die zu jener Zeit unter anderem auch mit dem Berufsstand des „Stimmenmachers“ für die Ausstattung der in Mode kommenden sprechenden Puppen sorgte.

Auch im Verlauf des 20. Jahrhunderts riss das Interesse insbesondere an der inzwischen legendär gewordenen Sprachsynthese Kempelens nicht ab. Der amerikanische Physiker Robert R. Riesz (1903-1974) präsentierte 1937 einen „Mechanical Talker“ mit aus Gummi und Metall konstruiertem, in einzelnen Segmenten variierbarem Vokaltrakt, der auf Kempelens Entwicklung basierte. Die Steuerung geschah über zehn Pumpventile ähnlich denen einer Trompete. Die verständlichste Äußerung soll „Cigarette“ gewesen sein [22: 207-208].

Ab den 1960er Jahren entstanden etwa ein Dutzend Kempelen-Repliken, die bei aller Treue zur Beschreibung im „Mechanismus“ doch eine verblüffende Variationsbreite im Detail aufweisen. Möglichst eng am Original orientieren sich beispielsweise die Rekonstruktionen durch Nikléczy & Oklaszy in Budapest (2001) [23] und die des Erstautors (Saarbrücken 2007/09, Dresden/Paderborn 2009) [24].

Auch aus pädagogischer Sicht scheint Kempelen einigen Reiz zu besitzen: Für das „Musée des musiques populaires de Montluçon“ fertigte Serge Durin 2001 gleich drei Repliken an, die von den Besuchern ausprobiert werden können. Auch die Autoren erreichten mittlerweile mehrere Anfragen von Universitäten und Schulen bezüglich einer „Bauanleitung“ für eine Kempelen-Replik.

Eine technologisch stark weiterentwickelte mechanische Synthese stellen die anthropomorphen Roboter der japanischen Forschergruppe um Fukui & Ishikawa [25] dar, deren produktive Qualität allerdings in den bereits durch Kempelen beschrittenen engen Grenzen bleibt.

5 Zusammenfassung

Die Idee, Sprache auf rein mechanischem Wege zu erzeugen, hat bis heute ihre Faszination bewahrt, ungeachtet allen Wissens über die hochkomplexen Mechanismen der menschlichen Sprachproduktion. Gerade angesichts der über mehrere Jahrhunderte hinweg immer wieder aufflackernden Begeisterung für die mechanische Realisierung von synthetischer Sprache, wie sie der unten stehende Zeitstrahl verdeutlicht, und vor dem Hintergrund der ebenso jahrhundertelangen Folge mehr oder weniger gescheiterter oder zumindest nicht vollends befriedigender Konstruktionen und Konzepte muss diese Tatsache als zumindest bemerkenswert bezeichnet werden.

Zugleich stellt eben diese Chronologie ehrgeiziger Versuche zwischen anatomischen Studien und genialischer Ingenieurskunst ein spannendes Stück lebendiger Wissenschaftsgeschichte dar, bei dem es nicht immer gelang, die Balance zwischen spektakulären Kabinettstückchen und seriöser Grundlagenforschung zu halten. Zweifelsohne kann jedoch für alle hier vorgestellten Konzepte festgestellt werden, dass es stets die kreative Kraft des dauerhaften Verstehen-Wollens war, die zu immer neuen Ansätzen führte und weniger die Suche nach kurzlebigen populärwissenschaftlichen Attraktionen.

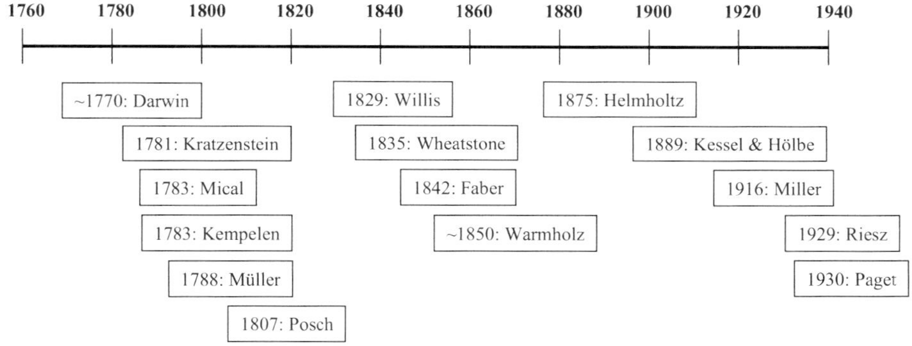

Abbildung 1 - Zeitstrahl der wichtigsten Stationen der mechanischen Sprachsynthese zwischen 1770 und 1930.

Literatur

[1] Hanskins, Th. L. & R. J. Silverman. 1995. Instruments and the Imagination. Princeton: University Press.
[2] Rm.[4] 1784. Windisch, K. G. v.: Briefe über den Schachspieler des Hrn. von Kempelen: Rezension. Allgemeine deutsche Bibliothek, Bd. 58 (1), 275-280.
[3] H. v. Helmholtz. 1896. Die Lehre von den Tonempfindungen als physiologische Grundlage für die Theorie der Musik. Braunschweig: Vieweg.
[4] R. Paget. 1930. Human Speech. London: Toutledge & Kegal.
[5] D. C. Miller. 1922. The Science of Musical Sounds. London: McMillan.
[6] L. Euler. 1761. Lettres à une princesse d'Allemagne sur divers sujets de physique & de philosophie. 137. Brief vom 16. Juni 1761.
[7] Chr. Mahrenholz. 1968. Die Orgelregister: ihre Geschichte und ihr Bau. Kassel: Bärenreiter Verlag.

[4] Der hinter dem Autorenkürzel „Rm" stehende Verfasser ist nicht namentlich bekannt.

[8] Chr. G. Kratzenstein 1781. Tentamen Resolvendi Problema ab Akademia Scientiarum Imperiali Petropolitana ad Annum 1780 Publicae Propositum. St. Petersburg.
[9] J. Gessinger. 1994. Auge und Ohr – Studien zur Erforschung der Sprache am Menschen. Berlin: de Gruyter.
[10] Ph. J. B. Jackson. 2005. Mama and Papa: The Ancestors of Modern-day Speech. Burlington: Ashgate.
[11] W. von Kempelen. 1791. Wolfgangs von Kempelen Mechanismus der menschlichen Sprache nebst Beschreibung seiner sprechenden Maschine. Wien: J.V. Degen. Faksimile-Nachdruck von 1970, Stuttgart: Frommann-Holzboog.
[12] J. W. von Goethe 1893. Goethes Werke, herausgegeben im Auftrage der Großherzogin Sophie von Sachsen. IV. Abtheilung, 12. Band.
[13] Anonymus. 1788. Ueber Dr. Muellers redende Maschine und über redende Maschinen überhaupt. Nürnberg: Grattenhauer.
[14] W. Niemann. 1920. Sprechende Figuren – Ein Beitrag zur Vorgeschichte des Phonographen. Geschichtsblätter für Technik und Industrie. Bd. VII.
[15] Anonymus. 1900. Carl S. Warmholz, ein vergessener Meister und Erfinder. Zeitschrift für Instrumentenbau, Bd. 20, 457-459.
[16] R. Willis. 1832. Ueber Vocaltöne und Zungenpfeifen. Annalen der Physik und Chemie, 397-437.
[17] Ch. Wheatstone. 1879. Reed Organ-pipes, Speaking-machines etc. The scientific Papers of Sir Charles Wheatstone D.C.L, F.R.S. London: Taylor & Francis.
[18] J. Hollingshead. 1895. My Lifetime. London: S. Low.
[19] H. Dudley, T. H. Tarnoczy. 1950. The Speaking Machine of Wolfgang von Kempelen. Journal of the Acoustical Society of America 22 (2), 151-166.
[20] J. Kessel. 1900. Demonstration von Apparaten zur Erzeugung künstlicher Laute. Verhandlungen der Versammlung Deutscher Ohrenärzte und Taubstummenlehrer in München am 16. September 1899, 28-29.
[21] R. Hoffmann, D. Mehnert. 2007. Die Kesselschen Stimm-Mechaniken in der historischen akustisch-phonetischen Sammlung der TU Dresden. Tagungsband DAGA, 401-402.
[22] J. L. Flanagan. 1972. Speech Analysis, Synthesis and Perception. New York: Springer.
[23] P. Nikléczy, G. Olaszy. 2003. A reconstruction of Farkas Kempelen's speaking machine. Proc. Eurospeech 2003 – Geneva, 2453-2456.
[24] F. Brackhane 2011. Die Sprechmaschine Wolfgang von Kempelens – Von den Originalen bis zu den Nachbauten. Phonus 16 – Berichte zur Phonetik, Universität des Saarlandes, 49-148.
[25] K. Fukui, Y. Ishikawa, E. Shintaku, K. Ohno, N. Sakakibara, A. Takanishi, M. Honda. 2008. Vocal cord model to control various voices for anthropomorphic talking robot. Proceedings of the 8th International Speech Production Seminar (ISSP), Straßburg, 341-344.

History and Development of Speech Science and Technology in USSR

Boris Lobanov

United Institut of Informatics Problems NAS Belarus
lobanov@newman.bas-net.by

Abstract: In this article, the history and development of speech science and technology in USSR are described. The prehistory of speech research is summarized, and the organization and the main directions of research in the USSR since the 60's are described. The review of the speech research activity in Soviet Belarus is given and the main achievements in the field of speech synthesis are described.

1 Introduction

In 1991, as the world watched in amazement, the Soviet Union disintegrated into fifteen separate countries. On August 19 of 1991 a group of "hard-line" Communists organized a coup d'état. After three days of massive protest, the coup organizers surrendered, realizing that without cooperation with the military, they did not have enough forces to overcome the power of the entire population of the country. These events were anxiously watched by hundreds of participants of the Congress of phonetic sciences (including the author of this article) which was held at this time in Aix-en-Provence, France.

In the Soviet Union, science and technology was an important part of national policy, practice and identity. Moreover, both science and technology were closely associated with the ideology and practical work of the Soviet state. This was one of the main reasons for the lack of links with the world of science. Soviet scientists had very limited access to foreign literature. They had no practice in foreign languages and rarely participated in international conferences. Their scientific works were usually published in Russian, and therefore were almost inaccessible to foreign scholars. However, there were a large number of scientific areas in which Soviet scientists succeeded. This also applies to speech science and technologies. The purpose of this article is to open slightly the "Iron Curtain" over the history and development of speech science and technologies in the USSR.

2 Prehistory

The world's earliest attempts to produce synthetic speech were made over two hundred years ago [1]. During the reign of Catherine II, The Saint Petersburg Academy of Sciences announced a competition to create a talking machine. In 1779, a German-born Professor Christian Kratzenstein explained physiological differences between five Russian vowels (/a/, /e/, /i/, /o/, and /u/) and made an apparatus to produce them artificially. He constructed acoustic resonators similar to the human vocal tract and activated the resonators by vibrating reeds like in music instruments. The basic structure of resonators is shown in Figure 1. The sound /i/ is produced by blowing into the lower pipe without a reed causing a flute-like sound.

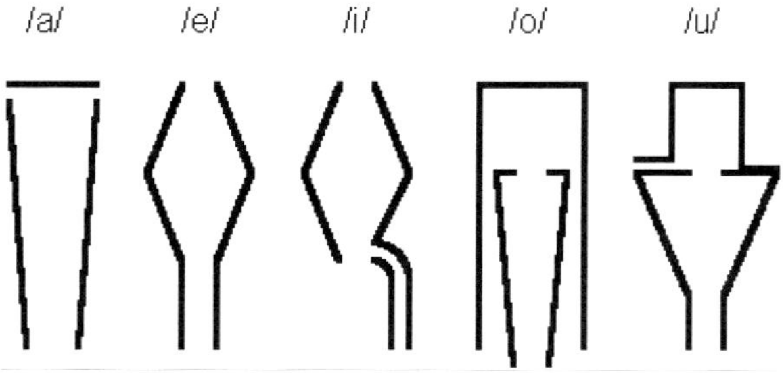

Figure 1 – Kratzenstein's resonators [2].

It is also worth to note the distinguished contribution of Russian mathematician Andrey Markov (1856 – 1922). He developed the theory of stochastic processes [2] which is now called a Markov chain. Nowadays, a hidden Markov model, that is a Markov chain for which the state is only partially observable, is the most effective instrument for speech recognition and synthesis.

The next notable attempt to synthesize speech in Russia already belongs to the 30s of XX century, and is associated with the development of the sound film and electronic music. In Moscow, the electronic music studio engineer Evgeny Sholpo developed a device called variafon. He decided that soundtracks could be created artificially. He "painted" sound waves on a specially designed large scale, photographing them frame by frame, and played them through a finished film projector. Although the work was very time-consuming and inefficient, Sholpo voiced a few cartoons in this way.

Evgeny Murzin who was familiar with Sholpo's work, developed a photo-electronic musical instrument called the ANS Synthesizer. Its name was derived from initials of the influential composer Alexander Nikolayevich Scriabin. He chose a method of speech synthesis using a Fourier series - which is a sum of elementary spectral components in musical acoustics known as a "pure tone." Bank "pure tones" Murzin designed as a glass disc that is very similar to a modern CD. It was covered with a photographic emulsion, and using a special machine, it was recorded in concentric rings 144 photo-optical sound tracks "pure tone". The process of sound synthesis is shown in Fig. 2.

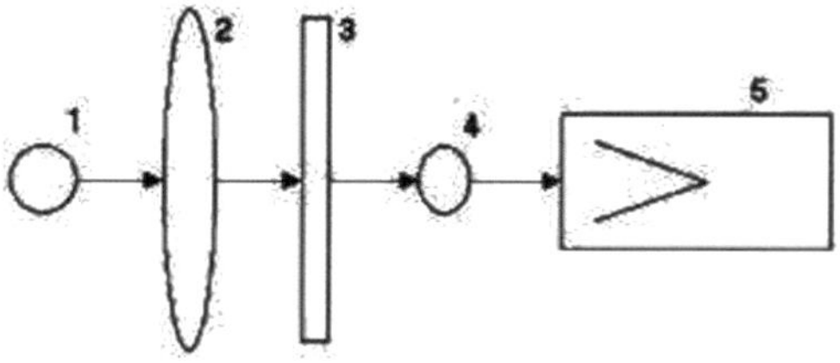

Figure 2 – Functionally-optical circuit synthesizer ANS

The light from the source (1) passes through a rotating disk photo-optical oscillator (2) and intensity-modulated audio tracks. Between the disk and photocell (4) there is a mask (3) with holes for the selection of rays with desired tracks only. The photocell is followed by normal path amplification for projectors (5)

In the early 40's in the Soviet Union the first papers on speech coding and recognition emerged. In 1941-1942 in blockaded Leningrad L. L. Myasnikov completed his doctoral thesis on work related to the system of recognition of isolated spoken sounds - all the vowels and some consonants. In 1943 he published an article in the journal "Successes of Physical Sciences" which described the first device for Russian speech phonemes recognition. The works of Myasnikov outpaced the first foreign works on speech recognition for 10 years.

Immediately after the end of the Second World War, the major investments in this area of science were directed by Joseph Stalin himself. In Moscow, the organization "RI-100" (a "sharashka" or a secret research and development laboratory) was established, where a large group of prisoner mathematicians, physicists and engineers were solving the problems of coding of the speech signal, the voice identification and recognition of keywords in speech. This period of speech research is well described by Aleksandr Solzhenitsyn's in his novel "The First Circle". In the late 1960's the author of this article had the privilege to cooperate with several prototypes of the heroes of this novel.

In the early postwar years, the speech research was conducted mainly in the interests of multiplexing of signals in telecommunication systems. To address these issues at Leningrad Institute of Telecommunications a strong team of scientists led by L.A.Varshavsky and V.S.Fedorovich was created. Either within or in close collaboration with the same team many future leaders of the Soviet speech scientists began their research works. Among them are L.A. Chistovich, L.V. Bondarko, V.I. Galunov, M.F. Derkach et al.

3 The review of the speech research activity in USSR from the 1960's*

A sharp increase of interest in the problem of speech recognition and synthesis both in the USSR and abroad occurred in the early 1960's, with the development of computer technology. Computer companies realized that, in the long run, the computing machine should include a variety of means of computer-human communication, especially, in its most convenient form - a speech dialogue. To solve this problem was a very tempting goal, and it seemed not very difficult to achieve at that time.

The illusion of an easy solution was for all those who were not familiar with the problem. After a report on modest results of the studies, one famous Soviet cyberneticist who was not engaged in a speech signal field of science, said, "The fact that our speech researchers are not able to teach a machine to recognize speech, is a misconception. Mankind has used speech for millions of years, and they cannot understand how it is produced. They need to talk with well-known German Acousticians who certainly can do it".

Under the influence of the public demand and the illusion of triviality of the problem, hundreds of research groups around the world began to work with speech signals. In the 1970s, there were more than 150 teams in the USSR. Until the late 60's, when the main results related to the speech of psychoacoustics and phonetics were obtained, the Soviet scientific school had a leading position in the world.

---

*) The material of this section is partly based on the article [3]

Many Soviet researchers started to learn about the speech synthesis from the book written by M.A. Sapozhkov "The speech signal in cybernetics and communication" (1963). Outstanding contribution to the development of speech researches in the USSR was made by the scientists from Pavlov's Institute of Physiology, Academy of Sciences of the USSR (L. Chistovich, V. Kozhevnikov, V. Lublinskaya, et al.). Their collective monograph "The Speech. Perception and production "(1968) was a handbook for anyone who studied physiology and psychoacoustics of speech.

Phonetic and linguistic problems of speech communication were fruitfully studied by scientific groups of Leningrad, Moscow, and Odessa universities (L.Bondarko, L. Verbitskaya, L. Zlatoustova, R. Potapova, T. Brovchenko, E. Nushikyan, etc.).

The development of various aspects of speech technology was conducted in many organizations. The groups with the most members in this area were:

- Novosibirsk Institute of Mathematics and Novosibirsk State University (N. Zagoruiko, G. Voloshin, V. Velichko, A. Kel'manov, etc.),
- Kiev Institute of Cybernetics (T. Vintsyuk, E. Ludovik, V. Bogino, etc.),
- Minsk Institute of Technical Cybernetics (B. Lobanov, N. Degtyarev, B. Panchenko, etc.),
- Moscow Computing Center of the USSR Ac. of Sc. (V. Trunin-Donskoy, V.Chuchupal, etc.),
- Moscow Institute for Information Transmission Problems (I. Turbovich, G.Tsemmel, V. Sorokin, A. Knipper, etc.),
- Moscow Institute of Radio Communications (A. Pirogov, G. Slucker, etc.).

Coordination of the work carried out through official channels by the Council of speech recognition and synthesis of the USSR Academy of Sciences Presidium (Academician Yury Zhuravlev as chair). However, the most important role was played by an unofficial body, which was, – the all-union seminar on the problem of automatic recognition of auditory images (in Russian abbreviation - ARSO), which was convened annually, and then every two years between 1965 and 1992.

The idea of the ARSO was born during a workshop in 1963 in Novosibirsk, attended by Bondarko, Golubtsov, Zagoruiko, Kozhevnikov and Chistovich, representing the group of mathematicians, engineers, linguists and psychologists. It was decided to organize a school-seminar, where the "school" section included leading specialists in different aspects of the problem who would make summary reports and give educational lectures, while the "seminar" section implied the participants who would report on results of their latest researches.

Various speech research centers (see fig. 3, 4) took part in the ARSO organization in different years, namely:

ARSO-1 (Novosibirsk, Russia, 1965),
ARSO-2 (Trakaj, Lithuania, 1966),
ARSO-3 (Novosibirsk, Russia, 1967),
ARSO-4 (Kiev - Kanev, Ukraine, 1968),
ARSO-5 (Sukhumi, Georgia, 1969),
ARSO-6 (Tallinn, Estonia, 1971),
ARSO-7 (Alma-Ata, Kazakhstan, 1973),
ARSO-8 (Lvov, Ukraine, 1974),
ARSO-9 (Minsk, Belarus, 1976),
ARSO-10 (Tbilisi, Georgia, 1978),

ARSO-11 (Erevan, Armenia, 1980),
ARSO-12 (Odessa, Ukraine, 1982),
ARSO-13 (Novosibirsk, Russia, 1984),
ARSO-14 (Kaunas, Lithuania, 1986),
ARSO-15 (Tallinn, Estonia, 1989),
ARSO-16 (Suzdal, Russia, 1991),
ARSO-17 (Izhevsk, Russia, 1992).

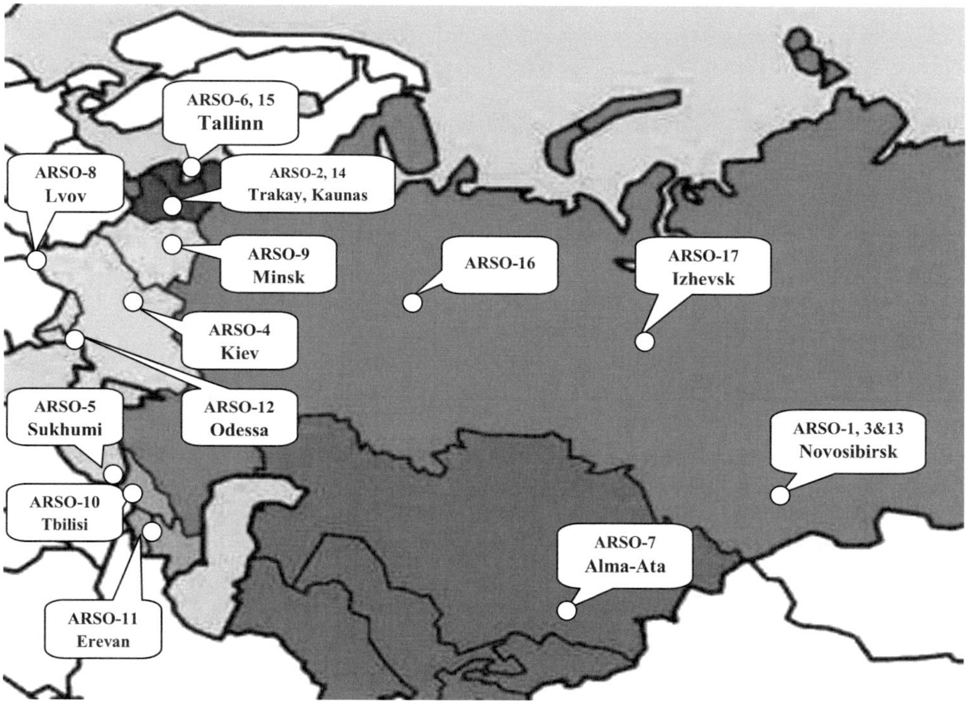

Figure 3 – Map of the ARSO (from 1965 to 1992)

Figure 4 – Members of the ARSO-9 program committee in Minsk
(From left to right: Boris Lobanov, Taras Vintsuk, Valentina Ignatova and Valery Trunin-Donskoy)

Many scholars from different cities participated in the ARSO. For example, on ARSO-9 (Minsk, Belarus, 1976) the total number of registered participants was 239. They represented 73 organizations from 30 cities of the USSR, including:

- Moscow - 74
- Leningrad - 37
- Minsk - 33
- Kiev - 17
- Lvov - 6;
- Penza, Tomsk, Dnepropetrovsk – at 5 persons (15 in total);
- Novosibirsk, Tbilisi, Tallinn, Izhevsk - at 4 person (of 20);
- Kaunas, Odessa, Yerevan, Kuibyshev, Yaroslavl, Poznan (Poland) - at 3 people (18 in total);
- Vilnius, Gorky, Kharkov, Taganrog, Ryazan - at 2 people (10 in total);
- Kazan, Zhitomir, Riga, Frunze, Severomorsk, Aralyk, Warsaw (Poland) - at 1 person (7 in total).

Among the ARSO-9 participants were 15 DrScs (7%) and 75 PhDs (32%). 20% of the ARSO-9 attendants were female participants, and 70% of them had linguistic education.

After disintegration of the USSR the unique ARSO (ARSO-17, Izhevsk, Russia, 1992) was held with only a few dozen participants. For comparison, during the heyday of ARSO-13, in 1984 in Novosibirsk, about 800 participants gathered, which was comparable in size to such an international conference as the 1st Eurospeech 1989 - Paris, France. At this ARSO 291 reports at 14 sections were submitted, namely:

1. Phonetics and prosody - 42
2. Speech production and perception - 21
3. Models of speech dialogue systems - 27
4. Models of speech signals preprocessing - 7
5. Vocoders - 15
6. Phonemic features extraction- 32
7. Segmentation of speech - 16
8. Speech Synthesis - 25
9. Speaker identification and verification - 12
10. Recognition of speech commands - 28
11. Continuous speech and keywords recognition – 21
12. Hardware for speech signals analysis – 8
13. Systems for the speech study - 16
14. Application of speech systems - 21

This section list shows that in spite of the minimal contacts with Western scientists because of the "Iron Curtain", Soviet scientists developed a very wide range of speech communications problems, and they obtained many original scientific results. For example, G. Slutsker [4] and T. Vintsuk [5] in 1968 developed independently the DTW-algorithm of speech recognition, which later became widely used in the world. Based on research results obtained in the 80's industrial samples of speech recognition systems, TTS-synthesizers and voice verification systems were created.

It was a romantic period of search for new scientific results in the study of speech. The ARSO was the central event in the speech community, a regular showcase of the latest achievements. In contrast to large conferences with diverse subjects, which every time gathered new people, the ARSO maintained high stability of key players. "ARSO-members" knew each other well, and it excluded the possibility of false advertising of questionable results. Both developers and customers of speech systems were able to make objective judgments about the team's work level and abilities. After discussions, ARSO-members could adjust the direction of their researches.

Essentially, the APCO played an important role of the informal but effective All-Union Center for the coordination of scientific works in the field of speech researches and technologies.

4 The review of the speech research activity in Soviet Belarus

4.1 The initial stage of speech research

The first group of speech researchers in Belarus was organized by the author of this article in 1965 in Minsk Institute of Radio engineering. At that time, the group included N. Degtyarev , B. Panchenko, M. Fateev and others, many of whom for a long time worked, and some still continue to work in the field.

The group's early studies were aimed at working out of general principles of a speech signals analysis and allocation of informative features that would produce a continuous speech signal as a sequence of phonetic segments. The results of these studies were summarized in the author's PhD-dissertation, "Some questions of the analysis of speech signals", defended in 1968 at Moscow Institute of Radio. The most important results of this work were later published in prestigious international journals [6, 7].

This research became the basis for the development of a rather simple device for speech commands recognition « SESAME – 2*». It was the first device developed in the USSR and, in 1968, it was awarded a silver medal of the All-Union Exhibition in Moscow.

The device consisted of two parts: the analyzer of speech signal features, such as "voice", "noisy", "vowel", etc., and the decision-making unit on relative positioning and a number of features in the speech command. Sufficiently high reliability of recognition of 20 words (including the names of numbers) was achieved, regardless a speaker's voice, volume and tempo of pronunciation.

During the same period, some specialized devices were developed for experimentally-phonetic researches of speech: the Spectrograph and Intonograph. During next years, the devices were used in numerous studies conducted in phonetic laboratories of the Institute of Linguistics of the National Academy of Sciences of Belarus and Minsk Institute of Foreign Languages.

Studies of dynamic spectra of speech gave rise to the development of nonlinear methods for comparing spoken words with their patterns (DTW-method) [5, 6]. In 1969, further development of the DTW method was proposed to solve the problem of detection and recognition of sound combinations in a continuous speech signal. [8].

The beginning of 1970s was marked by the start of work on the creation of speech synthesizers for the Russian language. An important role in the development of Russian speech synthesis was played by the author's visit to the laboratory of Professor Lorenz (Edinburgh University) in 1970. The Lorenz's lab developed one of the first models of formant synthesis of speech signals. It was the formant synthesizer that allowed obtaining by the author high-quality synthesized samples of Russian speech for the first time in history.

---

*) The previous model – «SESAME - 1 – was designed for the purpose of opening the lab door with a voice.

The first, though not a fully advanced model of the Russian text-to-speech synthesizer, "PhonemePhone-1" (see Figure 5) started speaking in the early 70's. Its successful creation is primarily associated with the development of new methods of hardware implementation of formant synthesis of speech signals. As the result of experimental studies, a complete set of phonemes' formant "portraits" was created, which allowed for the first time to create a system of Russian speech synthesis for any text. Later on, an improved version of the synthesizer - "PhonemePhone-2" was constructed. It contained more detailed rules of "phoneme - allophone" transformation.

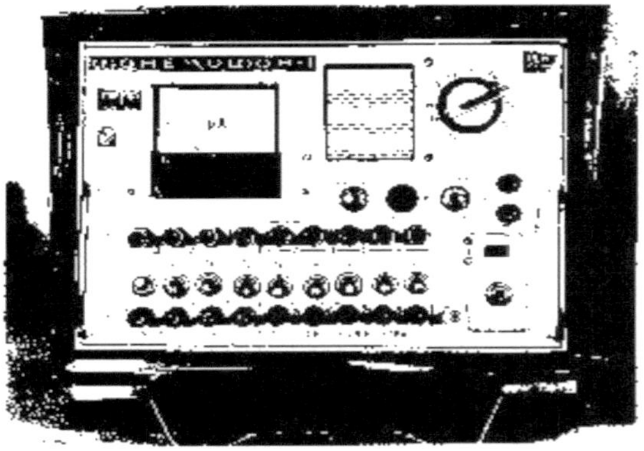

Figure 5 – Synthesizer "PhonemePhone-1"

4.2 Speech Communication Laboratory (1975 - 1987)

The Speech Communication Laboratory was established In December 1974 at the Minsk Branch of the Institute of Communications (MONIIS). The lab played a crucial role in the guidance for developing applications for speech technology in Belarus. At the APCO-9, held in 1976 in Minsk, the first prototype of an automated telephone information service with synthesized voice responses was demonstrated. In the late 70's this service was used for a long time in Minsk as a system of automatic telephone call-around of debtors in long distance calls. By the mid 80's, this system was implemented in many cities of the USSR - from Brest in Belarus to Kamchatka and Sakhalin in Russia.

Figure 6 – Synthesizer "PhonemePhone-3" in Geneva

However, successful implementation of speech synthesizers in real conditions still demanded a lot of work towards further improvements of the technology itself and the quality of the synthesized speech. The main disadvantage of the first synthesis model " PhonemePhone - 1, 2" was a poor quality of the synthesized speech due to the usage of the most simplified models of sounds interaction within speech production (effects of coarticulation and reduction), as well as unsophisticated speech intonation models. In the next version - "PhonemePhone - 3" the additional units of articulation and speech intonation modeling were introduced, which significantly increased the quality of the synthesized speech.

In 1979, the "PhonemePhone-3" was exhibited at the World's Fair "Telecom-79" in Geneva (see Figure 6).

Arthur C. Clarke, the famous science fiction writer, after visiting the USSR pavilion and listening to the speech synthesizer, wrote in a book review, "*You anticipated my fantasies from the "Space Odyssey - 2001" movie.* The Swiss newspaper "Observer" published an article with the following title: "Now Russians study foreign languages with a computer that speaks".

The next landmark in the history of industrial hardware was the creation of a new digital model of a speech synthesizer and recognizer. It became the basis for the speech synthesizer "PhonemePhone - 4" and the voice terminal - "Mars" (Fig. 7), both were constructed for the first time in the USSR in 1983. It became possible due to the efforts of the Design Department, led by V. Afonasev and laboratory staff members N. Degtyarev and V. Shaternik. Voice terminal "Mars" integrated the functions of speech recognition and synthesis for the first time. The algorithm of speech recognition was based on the decision-making DTW method with a set of formant parameters of the speech signal. The "Mars" was designed on the microprocessor. Original technical solutions used in the creation of systems "PhonemePhone" and "Mars" were protected by copyright USSR certificates for inventions.

Figure 7. – Voice terminal - "Mars"

The beginning of 1984 is notable for the final formulation, theoretical and experimental development of a common linguo-acoustic approach to the problem of text-to-speech synthesis, its implementation in the form of technical systems and practical application in automated models of management and communications. The results of these studies were summarized in the author's doctoral dissertation, "A method of automatic text-to-speech synthesis for Russian ", defended in 1984 at the Institute of Electronics and Computer Science, Academy of Sciences of the Latvian SSR. Later, the results were adapted for speech synthesis systems for other European languages. In particular, by 1987, the English version of the synthesizer had been developed in collaboration with E. Karnevskaya, a professor of Minsk Institute of Foreign Languages [9]. The work of the English synthesizer had been

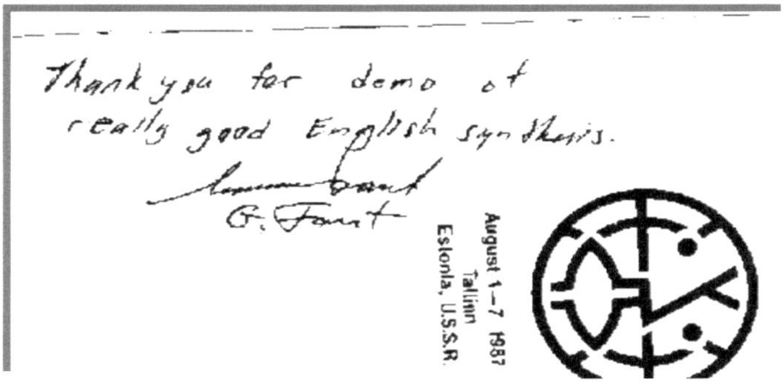

Figure 8 - Facsimile review of G. Fant

demonstrated at the World Congress of Phonetic Sciences and was highly appreciated by the English-speaking experts. The copy of the demonstration review by Professor Gunnar Fant, one of the most prominent researchers in the world of speech, is presented in Figure 8.

4.3 Speech Recognition and Synthesis Laboratory (1988 – 1991)

In 1988, the Speech Communication Laboratory at MONIIS was reorganized into the Speech Recognition and Synthesis Laboratory at the Institute of Technical Cybernetics, Academy of Sciences of Belarus (now - the United Institute of Informatics Problems). The new lab was led by the author of this article who was invited by the Directorate of the Institute for this position. As many still remember well, the end of the 1980s was marked by the appearance of the first personal computers, so naturally, the laboratory paid attention to some questions related to equipping computers with voice systems as new information input and output. The formant method, which had a key role in the development of text-to-speech synthesis systems for a long time, was unsuitable for this purpose because it demanded a huge amount of calculations in real time, which was unrealizable for the PC at that time.

In the late 1980s, a new microwave (MW) method for the synthesis of speech signals was suggested [10]. Instead of formants calculating, this method implied the use of a pre-designed set of microwaves of a natural speech signal. The set consisted of microwave signal segments of the length equal to the period. Their total number, which was required for generating any sound of speech, reached a few hundred. The MW-method was implemented in the synthesizer "PhonemePhone-5" made by Alexander Ivanov. This synthesizer was in a form of a specialized software, oriented towards working with an internal sound card or with an autonomous device that was connected to the RS-232 (see Fig. 9). As a surprise to many, its compactness (only 64K bytes) allowed equipping the first IBM PC-XT and even domestic PC ES1840 with speech synthesis.

Figure 9 – Microwave speech synthesizer

The speech synthesizer was needed and found use in many practical applications. Particularly, it was intended and used for the enhancement of the user interface for the blind computer users[9]. At the beginning of the 1990s, over a hundred of sets of specialized hardware and software products for the blind have been created and distributed by George Losik in Russia, Ukraine and Belarus. The quite legible sound of our Russian synthesizer can still be heard on the Internet or on the widely marketed CD ROM "Talking mouse".

Later on, the synthesizer versions for the Czech and Polish languages were designed on the basis of the MW-method. The author and colleagues spent about 3 months of in those countries on the invitation of the customers. Additionally, an autonomous single-board module of speech synthesis was developed. The Ukrainian-language version of the module was used for the announcements in the Kiev Metro trains for an extended period of time.

5 Conclusion

As described above, in the period from 1960s to 1980s, the USSR supported large groups of successful researchers. During those years, the scientific achievements of the soviet scientists were largely world-class. After the disappearance of the USSR and Republics' withdrawal from it, the scientific community was disintegrated. In addition, the process of liberalization pursued by Russia and other CIS countries virtually instantaneously lifted the 'iron curtain'. This led to an inevitable 'brain drain' where many of the leading scientists and specialists left the country, bringing their experience to the world leading research centers: the U.S., Belgium, Israel, Australia, etc.

Many of the above-mentioned schools of the USSR did not recovered from the brain drain of leading professionals. The situation was also worsened by all the difficulties of economic liberalization of the early 1990's. But despite all this, some of them managed to survive that period thanks to market mechanisms which were running at that time. It can be explained by the fact that in the 1990s it became possible to establish and develop well-functioning private companies, including those in the field of high technology. A brilliant example of such a successful and big company is the Speech Technology Center (STC) in St. Petersburg (see Fig. 9).

Figure 9 – Employees of the CSTs on vacation (http://speechpro.com/company)

In present, a range of research institutes and universities in St. Petersburg, Moscow, Kiev and Minsk continue to work successfully in the field of speech technologies, although the number of their workers is not so quantitatively significant.

Acknowledgements

This work was partially enabled by a grant of the "Kulturstiftung des Freistaates Sachsen". My sincere thanks are to the Kulturstiftung as well as to **Dr. Klaus Mauersberger** and **Kirsten Vincenz** from the Custody of the TU Dresden who initiated my research stay in Dresden.

And last not least, I should like to thank **Prof. Ruediger Hoffmann** for his attention to this work and especially for ***the fruitful cooperation and friendship during the last 20 years***.

Literature

1. Schroeder M. A Brief History of Synthetic Speech. Speech Communication, – 1993, vol. 13, pp. 231-237.
2. Markov A. Distribution of the law of large numbers to values that depend on each other. // Proceedings of the Physical and Mathematical Society of Kazan University. - Series 2. – 1906, Vol. 15 - pp. 135-156. (in Russian)
3. Zagoruiko N. ARSO and speech technologies // Proceedings of the IM SB RAS, "Computer systems", – 1995, Novosibirsk, pp. 3-31. (in Russian)
4. Zagoruiko N. ARSO and speech technologies // Proceedings of the IM SB RAS, "Computer systems", – 1995, Novosibirsk, pp. 3-31. (in Russian)
5. Slucker G. Non-Linear Method of Speech Signals Analysis // Proceedings of the Moscow Research Institute of Radio, N2, Moscow, 1968 – pp. 36-48. (in Russian)
6. Vitsuk T. Spoken words recognition by Dinamic Programming Methods // Cibernetics, N1, Kiev. 1968 – pp. 81-88. (in Russian)
7. Lobanov B. More About Speech Signal and the Main Principles of its Analysis // IEEE Transactions on Audio and Electroacoustics.- 1970, N 3. – pp. 316-318
8. Lobanov B. Classification of Russian Vowels Spoken by Different Speakers // The Journal of the Acoustical Society of America.- 1971, N 2 (2). – pp. 521 – 524
9. Lobanov B., Slucker G., Tizik A. Recognition of Sound Combinations in the Current Speech Signal // Proceedings of the Moscow Research Institute of Radio, N4, Moscow, 1969.- pp. 67 - 75 (in Russian)
10. Lobanov B., The Phonemophon Text-to-Speech System // Proceedings of the XI-th International Congress of Phonetic Sciences, Tallin, 1987.- pp. 100 - 104
11. Lobanov B., Karnevskaya E. MW - Speech Synthesis from Text // Proceedings of the XII International Congress of Phonetic Sciences.- Aix-en-Provense, Franse 1991.- pp. 387 - 391

Auswertung von Sprachsignalen aus Kymogrammen, Sonagrammen und digitalen Aufzeichnungen – ein historischer Rückblick

D. Mehnert, R. Dietzel, S. Kürbis

Technische Universität Dresden, Institut für Akustik und Sprachkommunikation
Email: di.mehnert@freenet.de

Abstract: Die quantitative Untersuchung von Sprachsignalen hinsichtlich ihrer zeitlich veränderlichen Grundfrequenz-Verläufe war eine der Aufgaben für die Experimental-Phonetik, mit der sich zahlreiche Wissenschaftler seit etwa 1890 intensiv beschäftigt haben. Die Sprachsignal-Beispiele wurden dazu so aufgezeichnet, dass sich daraus die Periodendauer der Stimmton-Grundfrequenz und ihre zeitlichen Änderungen ermitteln ließen. Zunächst nutzte man dafür angepasste mechanisch-geometrische Messmethoden. Es folgten Magnetband-Aufzeichnungen mit elektronischen Auswerteverfahren. Moderne Speicher- und Verarbeitungsmethoden gestatten eine umfassende Signalanalyse. An Hand ausgewählter Beispiele werden die frühen Verfahren beschrieben, mit den zeitgenössischen Geräten erprobt und kritisch miteinander verglichen.

1 Vorbemerkung

Innerhalb der Systemtheorie und Sprachtechnologie – dem Berufungsgebiet von Professor Rüdiger Hoffmann – ist die Signalanalyse und -verarbeitung jenes Teilgebiet, dessen historische Anfänge gut dokumentiert sind.

Ein Bestandteil dieser Geschichte ist die Sammlung historischer akustischer und phonetischer Geräte an der Technischen Universität Dresden im Institut für Akustik und Sprachkommunikation. Sie widerspiegelt die Entwicklung der Experimentalphonetik in der Zeit zwischen etwa 1890 und 1960 nahezu lückenlos. Rüdiger Hoffmann hat für den Aufbau dieser Sammlung seit den Anfängen im Jahr 2000 außerordentliches Interesse gezeigt, deren wissenschaftlich-historische Aufbereitung intensiv gefördert und nach Kräften unterstützt. Dank seiner Initiativen konnte diese Sammlung eingegliedert werden in den Bestand der zahlreichen wissenschaftlich-technischen Sammlungen, die von der Kustodie der Technischen Universität Dresden betreut werden.

Der vorliegende Beitrag soll die Verdienste von Rüdiger Hoffmann für den Erhalt historischer technischer Zeugnisse würdigen.

2 Einleitung

Die Ermittlung der Tonhöhen und der Wort- und Satzmelodie lag von jeher im Blickfeld der linguistischen Forschung und war so für die Phonetik von besonderem Interesse. Zunächst waren aus dem Höreindruck des Beobachters nur qualitative Aussagen möglich, um aus den Sprachbeispielen Zeitabläufe (Signal - Pause), Amplitudenverläufe (laut - leise) und Frequenzverläufe (hoch - tief) zu erkennen und zu beschreiben.

In der Anfangszeit der experimentellen Phonetik waren nur diese ohrenphonetisch orientierten Methoden möglich. Diesbezügliche Arbeiten richteten sich auf die von den Linguisten gewünschten detaillierten Beschreibungen von europäischen sowie außereuropäischen Sprachen, dort speziell den Tonsprachen Asiens und Afrikas, wo die Tonhöhenbewegung bekanntlich semantische Information enthält. Außerdem interessierten die Fragen, mit welchen Mitteln in den verschiedenen Sprachen akzentuiert wird. Die wesentlichen Parameter zur Beschreibung des Akzents sind Intensität, Frequenz und Zeitdauer. Mit diesen Begriffen gelang es den Sprachforschern, fortlaufende Sprachsignale und Teile davon inhaltlich zu kennzeichnen und unterscheidbar zu machen.

Der Schritt von der beobachtenden auditiven Phonetik zu quantitativen Methoden erfolgte seinerzeit durch den französischen Phonetiker PIERRE-JEAN ROUSSELOT in Paris. Er gründete 1889 das erste phonetische Laboratorium, bildete auch zahlreiche Wissenschaftler aus anderen Ländern aus, die dann das neue Wissenschaftsgebiet europaweit verbreiteten und in ihren Herkunftsländern neue phonetische Forschungszentren schufen. Einer von ihnen war der Italiener GUILIO PANCONCELLI-CALZIA, der 1911 in Hamburg am Kolonialinstitut ein Phonetisches Laboratorium – das spätere weltbekannte Institut für Phonetik der Hamburger Universität – gründete. Er war ein einfallsreicher unermüdlicher Experimentator, Schöpfer neuartiger Messgeräte, -apparaturen und -verfahren, die er den Fachkollegen vermittelt und empfohlen hat. Vieles ist davon erhalten geblieben und befindet sich jetzt im Institut für Akustik und Sprachkommunikation der TU Dresden [1].

Aus der Vielzahl der Messmethoden und ihrer Geräte wird hier die Tonhöhenmessung näher betrachtet. Diese Auswahl lag nahe, weil fast alle historischen Geräte zur Aufnahme und Auswertung von Sprachproben in der genannten Sammlung vorhanden sind. An Hand einiger Beispiele soll gezeigt werden, mit welcher experimentellen Technik seinerzeit Sprachbeispiele aufgenommen, gespeichert, analysiert und ausgewertet worden sind. Von besonderem Interesse war dabei, wie im Laufe der Entwicklung die Messunsicherheit systematisch verringert werden konnte und sich der experimentelle Zeitaufwand verkleinerte. Besonders reizvoll war es hierbei, frühe Arbeiten und Ergebnisse mit jenen zu vergleichen, die heutzutage in phonetischen Laboratorien erreicht werden.

3 Messmethoden

Die zeitliche Abfolge der praktizierten Messmethoden umfasst vier Abschnitte.

- Kymographische Aufzeichnung auf berußtem Papier und Auswertung mit einfachsten Verfahren zur Messung von Periodenlängen und damit von momentanen Frequenzen,
- Sonagraphische Methoden mit Magnetband-Aufzeichnung und anschließender Grundfrequenzanalyse.
- Analoge Aufzeichnung und elektronische Messung jeder einzelnen Periodenlänge sowie Aufzeichnung ihres Kehrwertes, d.h. der momentanen Frequenz.
- Analoge Aufzeichnung des Sprachsignals, anschließende Digitalisierung und rechentechnische Verarbeitung mit dem Computer.

3.1 Kymographische Aufzeichnung und Auswertung

3.1.1 Historische kymographische Aufzeichnungen

Die Umwandlung von Sprachsignalen in mechanisch aufzeichenbare Schwingungen geht zurück auf ETIENNE-JULES MAREY [3]. Er benutzte einen Einsprech-Trichter mit Schlauchverbindung zu einer Kapsel, die mit einer dünnen Membran bespannt war. Die Membranauslenkungen wurden über einen extrem leichten Hebelmechanismus zu einem Zeiger übertragen, der auf dem berußten Papier einer rotierenden Trommel die Schwingungsvorgänge aufzeichnete [1, S. 22].

Nach Behandlung des Papiersteifens mit einem Fixativ konnte er mit entsprechend angepassten mechanischen Längenmessmitteln ausgewertet werden. Dazu hat LIORET einen Messtisch eingeführt, mit dem Periodenlängen auf ± 0,01 mm ermittelt werden können [1, S. 84].

Um dieses und die folgenden historischen Messverfahren erneut zu praktizieren und nachvollziehen zu können, wurden aus neuen Sprachbeispielen Quasi-Kymogramme erzeugt, indem mit der Technik von heute deren Zeitfunktion als ausgedrucktes Oszillogramm verfügbar ist.

Dabei wurde die Übertragungsfunktion (Bild 2) der historischen Elemente – Schlauch – Kapsel – Zeiger – elektronisch nachgebildet und damit das Signal bearbeitet.

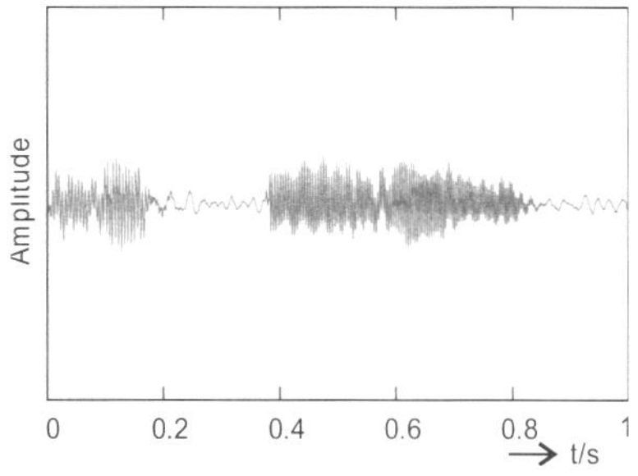

Bild 1: Quasi-Kymogramm vom Beispielwort *Befehl*

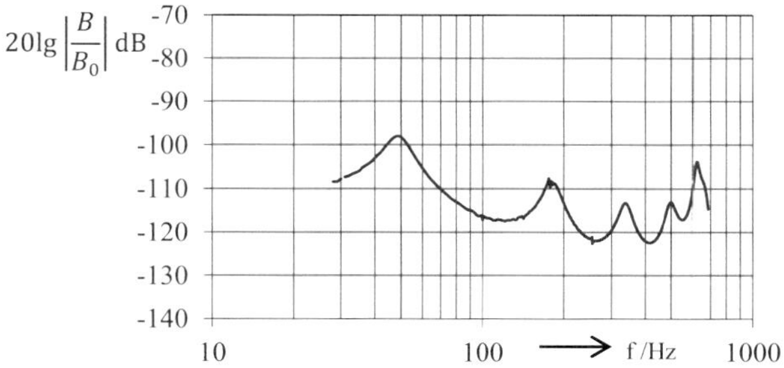

Bild 2: Übertragungsfunktion *B*(*f*) der Anordnung aus Kapsel - Schlauch – Zeiger

Bild 3: Messtisch nach LIORET (1913)

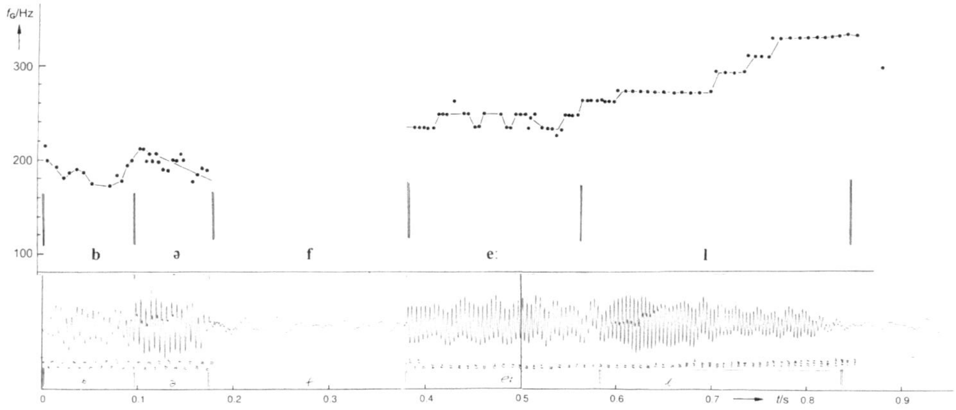

Bild 4: Tonhöhen-Kurve vom Beispielwort *Befehl*. Die einzelnen Periodenlängen wurden mit dem Messtisch von LIORET gemessen und in Momentan-Frequenzen f_G umgerechnet.

Bei derartigen kymographischen Aufzeichnungen musste besonders darauf geachtet werden, dass die Umdrehungsgeschwindigkeit der rotierenden Trommel mit dem berußten Papier so groß war, dass die zu erwartenden Periodenlängen mit den verfügbaren Messmitteln auswertbar waren. Bei männlichen Sprechern liegt der Frequenzhub der Grundfrequenz bei fortlaufendem Sprechen zwischen etwa 100 Hz und 300 Hz, bei weiblichen Sprechern zwischen 200 Hz und 500 Hz. Die Periodenlängen liegen also zwischen 0,1 s und 0,025 s. Sie erfordern deshalb eine Papiervorschub-Geschwindigkeit von mindestens $v_P = 125$ mm/s.

Die technischen Möglichkeiten von Universal-Kymographen erlaubten Werte $v_P = 250$ und sogar bis 500 mm/s [1, S. 22].

Derartige anspruchsvolle Kymographen besaßen einen Supportantrieb. Mit ihm wird die Aufzeichnungstrommel mit dem Papier in axialer Richtung stetig verschoben. Damit ist eine spiralförmige Aufzeichnung der Zeitfunktion in weiten Grenzen möglich. Auf diese Weise konnten sogar gesprochene Sätze von mehreren Sekunden Dauer aufgezeichnet werden.

Bild 5: Ausschnitt aus einem zeitgenössischen Kymogramm, 1959. O. v. ESSEN, Hamburg. Spiralförmige Registrierung. Oben im Bild Stimmgabelschwingung 100 Hz als Zeitmaßstab.

Für die vorliegende Untersuchung eines gesprochnen Satzes (- *Er möchte sich eine neue Wohnung ansehen* - $t_B = 2{,}6$ s Sprechdauer) ist ein Quasi-Kymogramm elektronisch in seiner Länge auf 1500 mm ausgedehnt worden, das entspricht einer kymographischen Aufzeichnungsgeschwindigkeit von 500 mm/s.

Bild 6: Tonhöhen-Messapparat von E. A. MEYER (1911)

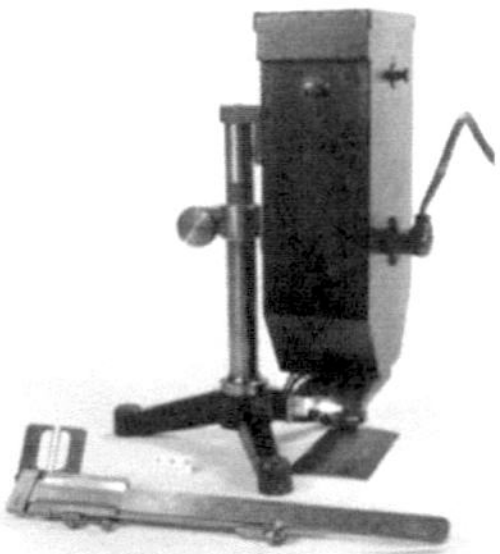

Bild 7: Messprojektor und Messschieber nach F. WETHLO

Weil die beschriebene Periodenlängenmessung mit Mikrometer-Messschrauben zwar ziemlich genau, aber höchst zeitaufwendig war, suchte man nach Verfahren mit geringerem Zeitaufwand, aber mit vergleichbar kleiner Messunsicherheit. E. A. MEYER hat 1911 ein Gerät entwickelt, bei dem jede einzelne Periodenlänge im Kymogramm geometrisch abgemessen und mit Hilfe einer logarithmisch geformten Schablone als Frequenz mit Tonhöhenstufung abgebildet wird. Die Ausmessung der Kymogramme von den hier benutzten Beispielwörtern verkürzte sich erheblich, vgl. Tabelle 1. MEYER gibt beim geübten Umgang mit seinem Verfahren in [7] eine Zeitersparnis bis zu 80 % an. Sein Präzisionsgerät wurde einzeln angefertigt, hatte einen entsprechend hohen Preis, und nur wenige phonetische Laboratorien konnten es anschaffen.

Daraufhin hat F. WETHLO nach einfacheren Methoden und preiswerteren Geräten gesucht. Das Kymogramm liegt in der Brennebene eines Messprojektors mit 10-facher Vergrößerung (Bild 7). Mit einem entsprechend umgebauten Messschieber (Bild 7, unten) lassen sich auf der Mattscheibe des Messprojektors die einzelnen Periodenlängen ausmessen und bei bekanntem Zeitmaßstab in Momentanfrequenzen umrechnen. Die Zuordnung der abgelesenen Periodenlängen zur jeweiligen Lage im Kymogramm ist für die Darstellung der Tonhöhenkurve zwingend notwendig und bedarf einer sorgfältigen Messstrategie, z. B. durch Nummerierung aller Perioden. Dadurch ist der Arbeitsaufwand dieser Methode hoch; er liegt in der gleichen Größenordnung wie beim Verfahren mit dem Messtisch von LIORET.

Deshalb hat WETHLO sein sog. Schnellverfahren vorgeschlagen und praktiziert [5] [6]. Hierbei verschiebt er zwei Gitterlinien mit 5 mm Abstand kontinuierlich parallel zur Zeitachse über das Kymogramm und zählt jeweils die Anzahl der Perioden zwischen den Gitterlinien. Durch Interpolation können auch unvollständig erkennbare Schwingungen einbezogen werden. Durch geeignete Schablonen lassen sich unmittelbar die Periodenlängen in Momentanfrequenzen umrechnen und in einem Diagramm mit der logarithmischen Tonhöhenskala eintragen. Obwohl es ein rein manuelles Verfahren ist, wurde es – auch in Ermangelung anderer Möglichkeiten – noch in einem längeren Zeitraum praktiziert.

3.1.2 Elektronische Nachbildung von kymographischen Aufzeichnungen

Zur praktischen Durchführung der beschriebenen historischen Mess- und Auswerteverfahren mussten aus vorhandenen Sprachbeispielen geeignete Quasi-Kymogramme erzeugt werden.

Dazu wurde die frequenzabhängige Übertragungsfunktion $B(f)$ der Anordnung aus Kapsel – Schlauch – Zeiger (aus Bild 2) elektronisch nachgebildet und als Bewertungsfilter für die einzelnen Beispielwörter benutzt. Damit standen ausgedruckte *„Kymogramme"* zur Verfügung, die vergleichbar mit den aus der zeitgenössischen Literatur bekannten Ruß-Kymogrammen sind (Bild 1).

3.2 Ermittlung der Stimmton-Grundfrequenz mit sonagraphischer Aufzeichnung und Auswertung

Bei einer sonagraphischen Aufzeichnung wird eine Sprachsignalprobe auf einer rotierenden Trommel mit Magnetfolie aufgezeichnet und zur Auswertung permanent wiederholt. Mit einem durchstimmbaren Bandfilter konstanter Bandbreite (Δf = 45 Hz) wird das aufgezeichnete Signal nach der Suchtonmethode spektral analysiert [1, S. 212-213]. Auf der Trommel befindet sich ein so genanntes Faksimilepapier. Darauf werden mit einem elektrischen Registrierverfahren Schwärzungen erzeugt, deren Dichte proportional zur spektralen Amplitude des abgetasteten Zeitfensters ist. Damit war eine quasi dreidimensionale Aufzeichnung der vom Sprachsignal gemessenen Größen möglich. Die Zeit wird auf der Abszisse, die Frequenz auf der Ordinate und die Amplitude durch den Schwärzungsgrad abgebildet. Um die Bewegung der Stimmton-Grundfrequenz f_G deutlicher zu erkennen, wird z.B. deren 10. Oberwelle herausgenommen und in einer entsprechend vergrößerten Skalierung abgebildet.

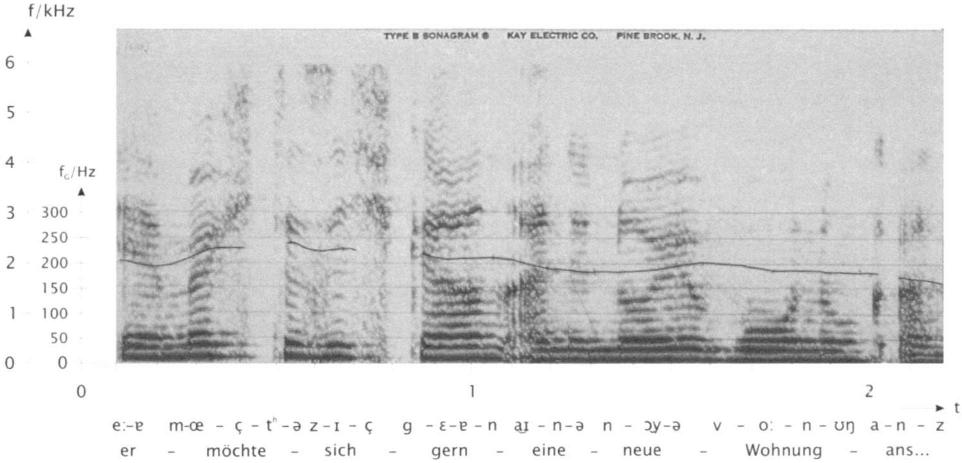

Bild 8: Sonagramm vom Beispielsatz: - *er möchte sich gern eine neue Wohnung ansehen.*

Die Analyse von einer Sprachprobe mit der Länge von 2,4 s dauerte etwa 10 min. Der Zeitmaßstab auf der Abszisse und die Transformation des Ordinaten-Maßstabes müssen nachträglich in das Sonagramm eingetragen werden.

3.3 Elektronischer Grundfrequenz-Analysator

Die Messung jeder einzelnen Periodenlänge eines Sprachsignals beruht auf der Ermittlung des zeitlichen Abstandes von Impulsen, die durch die Nulldurchgänge der aufgezeichneten Glottisschwingung erzeugt werden [1, S. 243-245]. Die so gewonnenen Analyseergebnisse werden mit einem Lichtstrahl-Oszillographen auf kontinuierlich fortbewegten Fotopapierstreifen belichtet und können erst nach fotografischer Entwicklung, Fixierung und Trocknung ausgewertet werden. Der Zeitaufwand für eine Sprachprobe hängt in wesentlichen von der benutzten fotografischen Verarbeitungstechnologie (Handentwicklung oder Automat) ab.

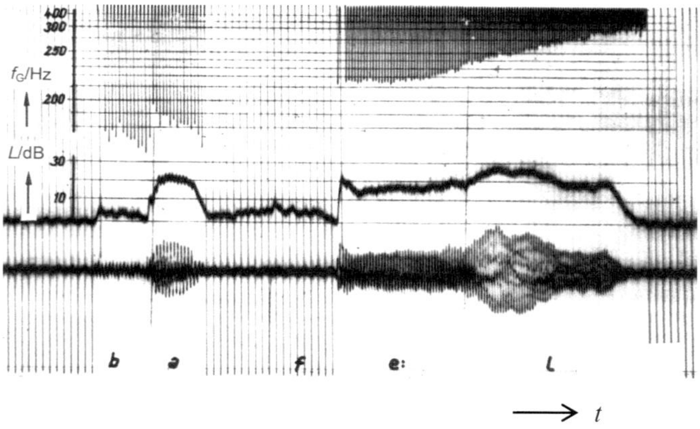

Bild 9: Mehrkanal-Aufzeichnung vom Beispielwort *Befehl*

Im gleichen Registriergerät wurde in späterer Zeit direkt-schwärzendes Fotopapier eingesetzt. Der zeitliche Aufwand für eine Sprachanalyse verringerte sich damit erheblich. Ein weiterer

Vorteil war, dass das Ergebnis der Analyse sofort erkennbar und auswertbar war. Gegebenenfalls konnten während des Versuchs am Gerät Einstellparameter verändert werden.

Bereits 1937 haben GRÜTZMACHER und LOTTERMOSER ein ausschließlich elektronisches Verfahren zur trägheitsfreien Aufzeichnung von Melodiekurven beschrieben [8]. Sie erwähnen darin ausdrücklich als Ansprechpartner F. WETHLO, weil sie überzeugt waren, dass auch die phonetische Forschung daraus Nutzen ziehen könne.

3.4 Rechentechnische Tonhöhen-Ermittlung

Seit etwa 1970 wurde es möglich, die Sprache digitalisiert zu speichern und für die rechentechnische Analyse aufzubereiten. Mit der raschen Fortentwicklung der Datenverarbeitung wurde es möglich, zahlreiche neue Problemstellungen der Experimentalphonetik schneller lösen zu können bzw. überhaupt erst in Angriff zu nehmen.

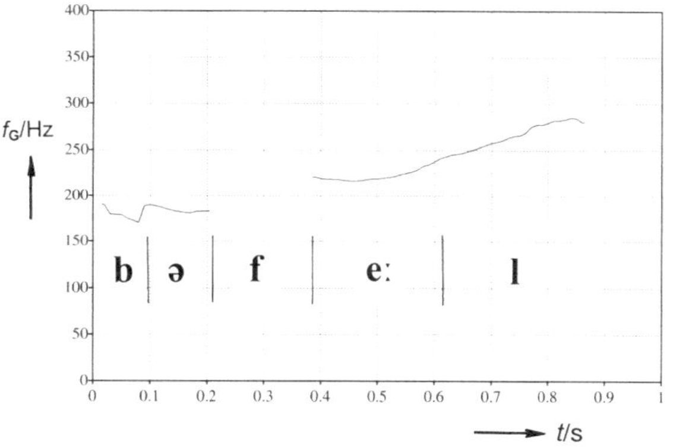

Bild 10: Rechentechnische Ermittlung des zeitabhängigen Grundfrequenz-Verlaufs vom Beispielwort *Befehl* unter Verwendung des phonetischen Analyseprogramms Praat (Version 5.3.32)

4 Kritischer Vergleich der Auswertemethoden

Tonhöhenmessung		Bearbeitungszeit des Sprachbeispiels (Analyse - Grafik - Ausdruck)		
Auswerteverfahren/ Gerätetechnik	Jahr (ca.)	Wort „Befehl" t_{B1}=0.9 s	Wort „Kamel" t_{B2}=0.8 s	Satz „Er möchte sich ..." t_{B3}=2.6 s
H. LIORET – Messtisch	1913	2 h 25 min	2 h 20 min	4 h 40 min
E.A. MEYER – Tonhöhen-Messapp.	1915	45 min	40 min	-
F. WETHLO – Zählverfahren	1950	15 min	15 min	-
F. WETHLO – Längenmessverfahren	1954	2 h 25 min	2 h	-
Sonagraph – Spektralanalyse	1955	10 min	10 min	10 min
Mehrkanal-Analyse – Elektron. Messung	1970	3 min	3 min	3 min
Computer – Programm	1975	30 s	30 s	90 s

Tabelle1:

Verfahren zur Messung von Tonhöhen. Bearbeitungszeiten der nachvollzogenen Messungen mit zeitgenössischen Originalgeräten.

Alle hier beschriebenen Verfahren sind von den Autoren mit den historischen Geräten praktisch erprobt worden. Insgesamt wurden 25 Sprachbeispiele untersucht. Es gelang damit, ein Gespür für die damalige Arbeitssituation zu bekommen und den experimentellen Aufwand nachzuvollziehen. Tabelle 1 gibt einen Überblick über die erforderlichen Bearbeitungszeiten für die hier behandelten Verfahren. Damit können die beachtlichen Leistungen und die Ausdauer früherer Experimental-Phonetiker realistisch eingeschätzt werden.

5 Zusammenfassung

Aus den Beständen der Sammlung historischer phonetischer Geräte der Technischen Universität Dresden sind jene Apparate ausgewählt worden, die zu Beginn der experimentellen phonetischen Forschung zur Messung der Tonhöhen-Verläufe gedient haben. Deren Handhabung wurde an mehreren Beispielen nachvollzogen. Dazu dienten so genannte Quasi-Kymogramme, die aus Teilen vorhandener Sprachinventare mit Hilfe einer nachgebildeten Tiefpass-Filterung erzeugt wurden. Die Ergebnisse werden kritisch miteinander verglichen.

Literatur

[1] Mehnert, D.: Historische phonetische Geräte, Katalog der historischen phonetischen Sammlung (HAPS) der TU Dresden. Studientexte zur Sprachkommunikation. Bd. 62, TUDpress 2012.

[2] Mehnert, D.: Prosodieforschung zu Beginn des 20. Jahrhunderts – Tonhöhenmess- und Analysierverfahren mit historischen phonetischen Apparaten. In: Sammeln und Forschen, Gesammelte Beiträge über historische phonetische Geräte, Studientexte zur Sprachkommunikation, Bd. 55, TUDpress 2010, S. 44-60.

[3] Mehnert, D.; Dietzel, R.; Richter, D.; Landgraf, J.: Experimente zum Übertragungsverhalten Mareyscher Kapseln. In: Elektronische Sprachsignalverarbeitung, Studientexte zur Sprachkommunikation, Bd. 50, TUDpress 2008, S.13-28.

[4] Mehnert, D.; Hoffmann, R.; Dietzel, R.; Kordon, U.: Über den Ursprung der Mareyschen Kapseln. In: Sammeln und Forschen, Gesammelte Beiträge über historische Phonetische Geräte, Studientexte zur Sprachkommunikation, Bd. 55, TUDpress 2010, S. 72-80.

[5] Wethlo, F.: Vereinfachte phonetische Tonhöhenmessung. In: Zeitschrift für Phonetik, 4 (1950), H. 1+2, S. 123-126.

[6] Wethlo, F.: Phonetische Tonhöhenmessung mittels Schablonen. In: Archiv der Ohr- usw. Heilkunde u. Zahn-, Hals- usw. Heilkunde, Bd. 165, (1954) S. 163-167.

[7] Meyer, E. A.: Ein neues Verfahren zur graphischen Bestimmung des musikalischen Akzents. In: Monatsz. f. d. gesamte Sprachheilpädagogik 1911, S. 227-234.

[8] Grützmacher, M.; Lottermoser, W.: Über ein Verfahren zur trägheitsfreien Aufzeichnung von Melodiekurven. In: Akustische Zeitschrift, 2(1937), Bd. 2, S. 242-248.

Sprachkommunikation zwischen Wissenschaft und praktischem Einsatz - Ein Rückblick auf 12 Jahre industrieller Sprachtechnologie-Nutzung

Christian Gruber, Uwe Koloska*, Thomas Falk*, Martin Wenzel*, Robert Schubert**, Diane Hirschfeld*, Franziska Kurnot**

** voice INTER connect GmbH, Dresden*
***Gesellschaft für Mathematische Intelligenz, Radebeul*
Email-Adresse diane.hirschfeld@voiceinterconnect.de

Abstract: Der Lehrstuhl Sprachkommunikation hatte trotz seiner Exotik stets eine ausgeprägte Nähe zu Anwendungen und den Wunsch nach Bereitstellung praktisch einsatzfähiger Systeme (ROSY, TUSY, Dress, UASR) sowie einen guten Bestand an Industrieprojekten, so dass die Ausgründung einiger Unternehmen naheliegende Konsequenz war. Man muss den Weitblick des Lehrstuhls bis heute bewundern, denn obwohl man sich Jahre ja Jahrzehnte schwerpunktmäßig mit Sprachsynthese, Sprach- und Mustererkennung sowie Psychoakustik beschäftigte und die Kommunikation kaum wissenschaftlich präsent war, so ist das Wort Kommunikation bereits im ursprünglichen Namen enthalten und dies auch das Umfeld, welches die Existenz und das Wachstum unseres Unternehmens gesichert hat. Der nachfolgende Artikel skizziert unsere Beiträge zu alltagstauglichen Sprachbedienprodukten und gibt einen Ausblick auf offene und praxisrelevante Forschungsthemen.

1 Vision des sprachbedienten Hauses – die Lücke zwischen Technologie und Alltag

Als 2001 die voice INTER connect GmbH (VIC) aus dem Institut für Akustik und Sprachkommunikation ausgegründet wurde, starteten wir mit der Vision, eine neue Qualität der Gerätebedienung zu realisieren. Sprache als intelligentes, intuitives und berührungsfreies Steuerungsmedium sollte als Komfortmerkmal und ambienter Zugang zu Technik in alle technischen Geräte mit Erklärungsbedarf integriert werden. Der verfügbare Sprachdialog und damit die jederzeit nutzbare akustische Hilfefunktion sollten Bedienungsanleitungen überflüssig machen.

Tatsächlich ist die Faszination und das Innovationspotential von Sprachtechnologie hoch und funktioniert bereits seit 12 Jahren kontinuierlich als Türenöffner bei Kunden. Im Markt sind alle 5-10 Jahre Technologiewellen – wie aktuell wegen Apples Siri - zu beobachten, wo ein erhöhtes Interesse an Sprachbedienungslösungen in allen Branchen aufflammt, das jedoch – aufgrund z.T. mangelhafter Implementierung - bald der Ernüchterung weicht.

Aus Gründen der Akzeptanz und nicht zuletzt der Kosten wegen ist die Auswahl einer Zielanwendung mit hohem Rationalisierungspotential bzw. hohem Kundennutzen unbedingt angeraten, denn Sprachbedienungsanwendungen erfordern eine hohe Sorgfalt bei der technischen Umsetzung und ein interdisziplinäres Team von Experten – neben Software-spezialisten, Experten für Signalverarbeitung und Spracherkennung sind Hardware-spezialisten für das Plattformdesign, Akustiker für die optimale Integration von Lautsprecher und Mikrofon sowie Psychologen bzw. Ergonomen für die Dialog- und Userinterfacegestaltung notwendig.

In 12 Jahren Firmenbestehens können wir auf einige erfolgreiche Beispiele für Sprachbedienprodukte verweisen - mit diversen Freisprecheinrichtungen (Automotive), einer sprachgesteuerten Kaffeemaschine und einem elektronischem Portier (Consumer) sowie

Lösungen zur akustischen Protokollierung von Arbeitsgängen und zur Maschinensteuerung (Industrial) und einem sprachgesteuerten Notrufsystem (Medizinische Rufsysteme).

Als kritische Faktoren für eine breite Vermarktung erwiesen sich folgende Aspekte, die in den nachfolgenden Abschnitten im Detail beleuchtet werden:

- Aufgrund der hohen Ressourcenanforderungen (Speicher und Prozessor) der Algorithmen ist Sprachbedienung mit Mindestkosten um ca. 50 – 15 EUR bei Stückzahlen von 1k bis 10k Stück verbunden, was einen Einsatz in Massenprodukten behindert (Abschnitt 2).
- Störgeräusche, Sprachausgabe und Raumhall als überlagerte Störeinflüsse beeinträchtigen bis heute eine saubere Erfassung von Sprache (Abschnitt 3).
- In praktischen Anwendungen ist die Verarbeitung unbegrenzter Wortschätze aus verschiedenen Gründen nicht angeraten (vgl. Abschnitt 4).
- Sprechervariation, Dialekte, Prosodie und Sprachenvielfalt sind die Ursache von Varianz im Sprachsignal und erfordern große Datenbanken für ausreichend robuste Wissensbasen (Abschnitt 5)
- Beim Design der Anwendung stehen oft technologische Aspekte statt des Nutzers im Mittelpunkt des Designs des Bedienkonzeptes (vgl. Abschnitt 6).
- Die vor Siri zu verzeichnende, fehlende Systemintelligenz enttäuschte die hohe Erwartungen der Nutzer, die eine „Raumschiff-Enterprise“-Funktionalität erwarten (Abschnitt 8).

2 Embedded Plattformen – Basis für ambiente Servicestrukturen

Mit der ersten Produktentwicklung – verbKEY [1] – fokussierte unser Unternehmen bereits auf eine Umsetzung der Sprachbedienung auf einer preisgünstigen, miniaturisierten und stromsparenden Embedded Plattform. Die Entscheidung fiel 2001 für einen flexiblen 16-bit-Festkomma Blackfin-DSP, dessen Familie noch heute die Grundlage unserer Hardware-Plattformen darstellt, und gegen einen ASIC aus, da die abzusehenden Stückzahlen sowie die Anforderungen an Flexibilität eine ASIC-Lösung als nicht wirtschaftlich erscheinen ließen.

Im Zeitraum von 2004 bis 2006 entwickelte VIC eine erste Prototyp-Plattform vicCORE (Abbildung 1), welche sich durch ein modulares Hardware-Konzept auszeichnet: die kostenintensiven und universellen Bauteile wie Prozessor, Flash und Speicher befinden sich auf einer universellen Core-Platine, um Stückzahleffekte nutzen zu können. Die applikationsspezifische Anpassung erfolgt über Trägerboards, die Stromversorgung und diverse Schnittstellen zur Applikation zur Verfügung stellen.

Getrieben durch Kostendruck und VICs Aktivitäten im Bereich der digitalen Sprachkommunikation und beim Freisprechen wurde 2010 unser vicCOM-Modul als Miniaturisierung von vicCORE umgesetzt. Mit 3x6 cm und einseitiger Bestückung sowie den Verzicht auf teure Steckverbinder kann das Modul wie ein Bauteil auf die Trägerplatine des Zielgerätes aufgelötet werden. Aufgrund der geringen Größe und der Stückkosten erfüllt vicCOM2 die ursprünglich formulierten Anforderungen an einen sprachgesteuerten Lichtschalter (Abbildung 1). Auf beiden Hardware-Modulen ist VICs Command&Control-Lösung vicCONTROL verfügbar und in zahlreichen Anwendungen erprobt (vgl. Abschnitt 4).

Neben geeigneten Embedded Plattformen sind in den letzten 5 Jahren im Consumer Markt mit Smartphones und Tablets ernst zu nehmende mobile Plattformen entstanden, die aufgrund der Leistungsfähigkeit ihrer Prozessoren Sprachbedienfunktionen nebenbei übernehmen können. Aufgrund Ihrer Grafikfähigkeit und dem allgegenwärtigen Zugang zum Internet über Wifi können Mobiltelefone als ideales Terminal für intelligenten Wissenszugang und „elektronischer Kokon" betrachtet werden, der den Besitzer mit Komfort und Wissen ausstattet, wo auch immer er sich hin bewegt.

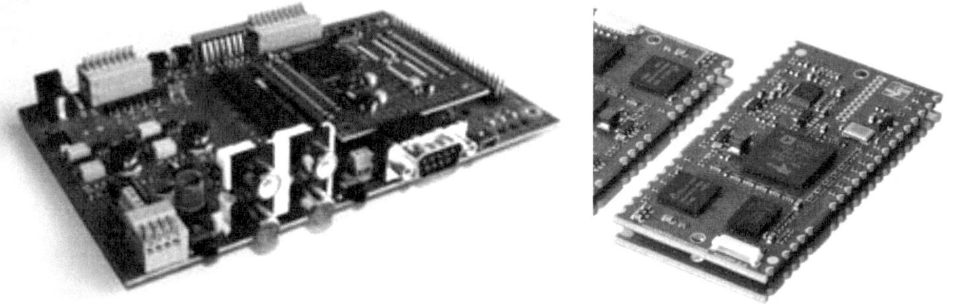

Abbildung 1 – Hardware-Plattformen für Sprachbedienung (links: vicCORE, rechts: vicCOM2),

Interoperabilität und die Paradigmen der verteilten Verarbeitung sowie der zunehmende Ausbau der Städte mit Übertragungsmedien – schnelles Internet, mobiles Internet und wachsende mobile Abdeckung – schaffen die Voraussetzung für ambiente Servicestrukturen. Hausbusse im Wohnumfeld und das Internet der Dinge sowie die zunehmende Durchdringung aller Bereiche zivilisierten Lebens durch IT und Internet sind die Basis für produktübergreifende und systembasierte Funktionen, die über jene eines einzelnen Gerätes weit hinausgehen und die Intelligenz ins Umfeld bringen. Interoperabilität zwischen den Systemen und Standards kann als technische Herausforderung an die Entwickler und deren Fähigkeit betrachtet werden, mit dem Stand der Wissenschaft und Technik Schritt zu halten. Serviceorientierte und semantische Systemarchitekturen und Interface-Standards erlauben automatische Dienstdetektion und Selbstkonfiguration im Netzwerk und beschränken trotz erhöhter technischer Komplexität den manuellen Integrations- und Konfigurationsbedarf.

Mit Energieeffizienz und Energy-Harvesting (der „Ernte" von Energie aus der Umwelt), einem Rückgriff auf organische Materialien (biochemische statt elektrische Prozesse mit wenig Verlustenergie) sowie Integration und Miniaturisierung zur Kosten- und Größenreduktion werden international die Ziele verfolgt, Geräte noch kleiner und kostengünstiger zu gestalten und energieeffizient zu betreiben. Eine Integration in Textilien legt die Technik und Sensorik dem Menschen buchstäblich „auf die Haut".

Unser Unternehmen verfolgt die Vision, das intelligente Haus als Wohnzelle, Auto und Handy als Mobilzelle, sowie das ambiente Büro als Arbeitszelle so mit intelligenter Technik als Verschmelzung einzelner Geräte der IT und Gebäudeinstallation auszustatten, dass diese den Menschen umgibt, umsorgt und ihm alle Bedürfnisse zu Wissenszugang, Kommunikation und Komfort erfüllt, ohne ihn zu bevormunden.

3 Extraktion von Sprache aus Störgeräuschen und Raumhall

Die Sprachübertragung zwischen Sprecher und Hörer bzw. Mensch und Maschine ist durch eine Vielzahl von störenden akustischen Einflüssen beeinträchtigt. Einerseits verändert sich das Sprachsignal selbst, andererseits wird es durch Störeinflüsse additiv überlagert. Je nach Einsatzgebiet wirken sich diese Einflüsse unterschiedlich stark aus.

In geschlossenen Räumen wirkt sich z.B. ganz entscheidend die akustische Umgebung auf das Sprachsignal aus und ändert dessen Klangcharakteristik. Durch Raumresonanzen werden einige Frequenzbereiche gedämpft andere verstärkt. Dies kann im Extremfall dazu führen, dass für die Sprachverständlichkeit wichtige Signalbestandteile verloren gehen. Durch Überlagerung des ursprünglichen Sprachsignals mit störendem Raumhall verringert sich die Sprachverständlichkeit und damit die Zuverlässigkeit der Spracherkennung, weil Raumhall zeitverzögert auftritt und damit das Gesprochene „verschmiert". Nicht zuletzt können all diese störenden Raumeinflüsse auch noch zeitlich veränderlich sein, wenn der Sprecher z.B. seinen Kopf dreht oder sich im Raum bewegt.

Abbildung 2 – links: Konferenzraumsituation – mehrere Sprecher aus verschiedenen Richtungen; rechts: Design-Studie für ein Konferenztelefon

Akustische Störereignisse sind sehr vielfältig und stellen für die Störgeräuschunterdrückung zunehmende Schwierigkeit dar: von stationären Umgebungsgeräuschen wie z.B. Fahrgeräuschen im Auto oder Straßenlärm in mobilen Anwendungen, über instationäre Umgebungsgeräusche wie z.B. Musik im Heimumfeld bis hin zu weiteren Sprachsignalen durch andere Sprecher z.B. in einer Konferenzsituation (Cocktail-Party-Effekt). Ganz entscheidend für die Stärke all dieser Einflüsse sind die räumlichen Distanzen einerseits zwischen Sprecher und Hörer (Mikrofon), andererseits zwischen Störquelle und Mikrofon.

Im Automobilbereich z.B. ist die Entfernung zwischen Sprecher und Mikrofon mit 0,5 m bis 1 m moderat und die Halligkeit gering, sodass Raumhall eine untergeordnete Rolle spielt. Dafür verändert sich die Klangcharakteristik des Sprachsignals erheblich. Zusätzlich besteht ein hoher Lärmpegel durch Fahrgeräusche.

Im Telefoniebereich (Sprachdialoge in der Kundenbetreuung) wirkt sich die Verwendung von Headsets sehr vorteilhaft aus. Der Abstand zwischen Sprecher und Mikrofon ist optimal, so dass sich die Klangcharakteristik nicht verändert und auch Raumhall nicht nennenswert auswirkt. Das im Hörer wiedergegebene Signal überlagert sich als leises Störsignal (Echosignal) im Mikrofon. Aufgrund des hohen Nutzsignalpegels fallen auch Nebengeräusche kaum ins Gewicht. Die einzigen relevanten Störeinflüsse sind Atemgeräusche und Körperschall, der aufgrund der Berührung des Handsets/Headsets entsteht.

Schwieriger wird es bei Verwendung von Smartphones, da diese für die Sprachbedienung nicht direkt an Mund und Ohr gehalten werden, sondern in einem gewissen Abstand zum Mund, um als Nutzer auch das Display sehen zu können. Durch den etwas größeren Abstand zum Mikrofon kann sich Raumhall in größerem Räumen bereits negativ auswirken. Auch das Verhältnis zwischen Sprach- und Störsignal verschlechtert sich. Da mobile Geräte in jeder denkbaren Umgebung verwendet werden, ist hier mit der ganzen Bandbreite an Umgebungsgeräuschen zu rechnen.

Die wissenschaftliche Forschung hat in den vergangenen Jahren bereits eine ganze Reihe an Lösungen hervorgebracht. Stationäre Störgeräusche wie z.B. Fahrlärm im Auto und selbst geringfügig instationäre Geräusche wie z.B. Messelärm können heutzutage bereits recht gut mit Hilfe von Störgeräuschreduktionsalgorithmen bereinigt werden ([12]). In einigen

Anwendungsfeldern kann man sich zunutze machen, dass das störende Signal (Sprachausgabe) für das Spracherkennungssystem bekannt ist. Hier kommen Echokompensationsalgorithmen zum Einsatz. Im Automobilbereich kann man mit Hilfe dieser Algorithmen z.B. das Radiosignal aus dem Mikrofonsignal filtern. Im Bereich der Spracherkennung ist diese Funktion als Barge-In bekannt.

Die größte Herausforderung an die Spracherkennung stellt die für den Nutzer komplett unsichtbare Integration von Spracherkennungssystemen in das Umfeld des Nutzers, das heißt den umgebenden Raum, dar („Raumschiff-Enterprise-Szenario"). Da in einem solchen Szenario das Mikrofon bzw. auch mehrere Mikrofone unter Umständen weit entfernt vom Sprecher in Wänden oder technischen Geräten versteckt werden, wirken sich alle genannten Störeinflüsse stark aus. Das Sprachsignal ist durch Raumhall, der sich auch negativ auf die Echokompensation auswirkt, stark beeinträchtigt, der Sprachsignalpegel ist gegenüber störenden Nebengeräuschen sehr gering.

VIC hat für eine robuste Spracherfassung in diesem Szenario im Projekt AUTAGEF ([2]) eine Lösung mit verteilten Mikrofonarrays, den patentierten Sensorbus, entwickelt ([14]). Dieser zeichnet sich durch zentrale Steuerung sowie mehrkanalige, parallele und hochsynchrone Audioübertragung von bis zu 12 Sensorknoten an eine Sensorzentrale aus. Damit lässt sich u.a. stets das zum Sprecher am nächsten gelegene Mikrofon für die Spracherkennung auswählen. Dies erhöht die Raumabdeckung, so dass eine Sprachbedienung von verschiedenen Positionen bzw. auch bei Bewegung im Raum möglich wird. Weiterhin können durch ein geeignetes Beamforming Störsignale, die aus einer anderen Richtung als das Sprachsignal eintreffen, gegenüber dem Sprachsignal gedämpft werden. Auch lässt sich die Halligkeit des Sprachsignals in Räumen mit Hilfe von Mikrofonarrays durch den Einsatz mehrkanaliger Enthallungsalgorithmen reduzieren. Durch Verfahren zur blinden Quellentrennung können mehrere Sprecher im Raum oder Sprecher von Störquellen getrennt werden. Diese Ansätze werden zukünftig durch VIC weiter erforscht.

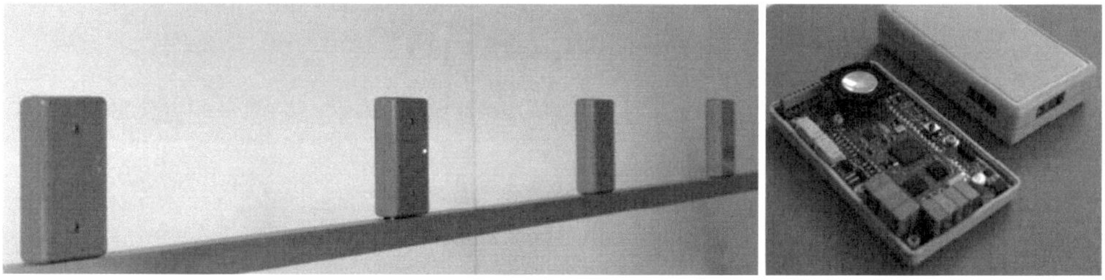

Abbildung 3 – links: Sensorbus mit Mikrofonknoten; rechts: Mikrofonknoten (geöffnet) zur Beschallung und optimalen Erfassung von Sprachsignalen im Raum

Zusätzlich zu all diesen Vorverarbeitungsalgorithmen lässt sich der Einfluss von akustischen Störungen auch mit Hilfe geeigneter Sprachmodelle verringern. So können z.B. Störgeräusche oder auch Raumhall teilweise modelliert werden. Dies hilft dem Spracherkenner, besser zwischen relevanten und nicht relevanten Signalbestandteilen zu unterscheiden. Aktuelle Entwicklungen auf dem Gebiet der akustischen Szenenanalyse helfen, sowohl Sprachmodelle als auch Modelle für Umgebungsgeräusche weiter zu verbessern. Dies wird zukünftig dazu beitragen, die Genauigkeit von Spracherkennungssystemen weiter zu verbessern.

4 Anpassung an die Zielanwendung über Wortschatz und Sprachmodell

Während der erste Embedded Erkenner, verbKEY, noch ein DTW mit variablem Suchraum war, der mit hohem Trainingsaufwand und evolutionären Verfahren zur Multiparameter-Optimierung an die Zielanwendung angepasst werden musste ([1]), und der sich durch eine geringe Sprecherunabhängigkeit und starke Situationsabhängigkeit auszeichnete, war der ab 2005 genutzte phonKEY [9] ein Phonemerkenner in HMM-Technologie. Dieser zeichnete sich durch sprecherunabhängige Erkennung, sowie Komfort bei der Definition neuer Vokabeln als Textliste aus. Die manuelle Erstellung von BNF-Grammatiken, die Vokabeldefinition und die Verwendung von Aussprachevarianten für jedes Wort im Lexikon erforderten große Sorgfalt bei der Entwicklung. Eine Optimierung der Sprachbedien-Applikation war stets mit umfangreichen Feldtests verbunden, bei denen die Erkennungsrate manuell erfasst und optimiert wurde.

Für einen großen Kunden im Automotive-Bereich entwickelte unser Unternehmen 2008 modellbasierte Entwurfstools für ein einheitliches GUI- und Sprachdialog-Design in Multimedia-Anwendungen. Diese erlaubten zum einen den grafischen Entwurf von Vokabularen und Grammatiken, zum anderen die Validierung der Statemachines im Ergebnis des Entwurfsprozesses und die vollautomatische Codegenerierung für die Sprachdialog-Applikation für die Fahrzeugplattform. Teile des damals gewonnenen Knowhows finden sich heute im vicDesigner, unserem grafischen Entwurfstool für unsere vicCONTROL-Sprachbedienung wieder.

Neben diesen Command&Control-Anwendungen ist bei automatischer Verschriftung (z.B. beim akustischen Beratungsprotokoll in Finanzanwendungen) ein Streben nach unbegrenzten Wortschätzen zu verzeichnen. Hier ist ein vollständiges Training der Wissensbasen des Spracherkenners ungleich schwieriger, da entsprechende Abdeckungen an Sprechern und Sprache bzw. Texten erforderlich sind (vgl. nächster Abschnitt). Unter sorgfältiger Vorverarbeitung gesammelter Texte aus dem Internet läßt sich ein Trainingskorpus für ein Sprachmodell mit überschaubarem Aufwand generieren, es besteht jedoch das Problem, dass die Abdeckung der Zieldomäne aufgrund der Art der verwendeten Texte nicht ausreichend ist. Voice INTER connect arbeitet daher aktuell an Verfahren zur automatischen domänenspezifischen Suche und Aufbereitung bzw. Normalisierung von Texten.

5 Sprechervariation, Dialekte und Sprachenvielfalt

Sprachliche Unterschiede zwischen Menschen unterschiedlicher Herkunft sind für jeden "Spracherkenner" egal ob Mensch oder Maschine ein Riesenproblem. Davon können gerade die Sachsen ein Liedchen singen, werden sie doch vom Rest der Welt ob ihres putzigen Dialekts belächelt und oft nicht für voll genommen. Auch ein Spracherkenner (sei es als App auf dem Smartphone oder eingebettet in einen Kaffeevollautomaten) wird oft nicht angenommen, weil schon kleine Aussprachevariationen des Sprachbefehls völlig falsche Ergebnisse hervorbringen können. Dazu kommt noch eine Vielfalt an Sprachen, Dialekten, Akzenten, Wortwahl und - weil wirklich jeder Mensch anders spricht - von Sprecherinnen und Sprechern jeden Alters. Insbesondere Alltagsanwendungen im Automobil bzw. auf dem Mobiltelefon erfordern aufwändige Aufnahme-Setups (auf der Straße, im Auto, auf öffentlichen Plätzen).

An der Schließung dieser Daten- und damit Akzeptanzlücke arbeitet die wissenschaftliche Gemeinschaft schon viele Jahre. Aktuell sind Spracherkennungsanwendungen zwar durch eine recht gute Erkenner-Performanz gekennzeichnet, überzeugen jedoch nicht sofort Jeden, für bestimmte Aufgaben nur noch Sprache als Eingabemedium zu verwenden. Da aktuelle Spracherkenner zum größten Teil auf statistischen Verfahren beruhen, sind für deren Training eine große Menge an realen Sprachdaten mit Metadaten und Annotationen nötig.

Diese Datenmengen und insbesondere der Annotationsbedarf stellen eine große Hürde für jeden Hersteller von Spracherkennungssoftware dar. Um diese Situation zu verbessern, sind zur Jahrtausendwende einige mit erheblichen öffentlich Mitteln geförderte Projekte zur Datenakquise gestartet worden oder waren Bestandteil von großen Verbundforschungsvorhaben (SpeechDat,[10]; PhonDat, Verbmobil, [11]). Die Datenbanken werden trotz öffentlicher Förderung über Organisationen wie das BAS, LDC oder ELRA kommerziell vermarktet. Die an den Projekten beteiligten Großunternehmen verfügen meist über Nutzungsrechte, aber für ein mittelständisches Unternehmen kann die Unterstützung eines Spracherkenners in allen europäischen Sprachen schnell zur Investitionsfalle werden.

Abbildung 4 – links: Korpusaufzeichnung für Haushaltgerätebedienung im Homelab, rechts: Mobilab-Aufnahmesystem

Als Antwort auf dieses Datendilemma entwickelte unser Unternehmen das Mobilab-System zur stationären oder mobilen automatisierten Aufnahme mit bis zu 8 Kanälen parallel in hoher Qualität ([5] und Abbildung 4) sowie Tools zur effektiven Bearbeitung und teilautomatischen Sprachdatenverwaltung WiGE [3] und setzte diese in zahlreichen Projekten erfolgreich ein: unter anderem in einem Projekt zur Aufnahme eines Referenzkorpus für die Bewertung von Spracherkennung für Haushaltsgeräte (Apollo-Korpus, [4]), im Automobilbereich, für die Optimierung von Spezialerkennern [6] und für zahlreiche kundenspezifische Datenbanken, u.a. für Russisch, Englisch und Arabisch.

Das WiGE-System wird zur Steuerung des Aufnahmeprozesses verwendet, um die Aufnahme zu automatisieren und die Qualität der Aufnahmen kontinuierlich zu sichern. Durch die nachfolgenden automatisierten Arbeitsgänge wie Extrahieren und Annotieren der gelungenen Aufnahmen kann viel manuelle Arbeit gespart werden. So war es mit einem begrenzten Budget möglich, schnell hochwertig annotierte Sprachdaten für die unterschiedlichsten Aufgaben zur Verfügung zu stellen.

Einer dieser Spezialerkenner ist im AzAR-Projekt [7] entstanden und erlaubt durch sein spezielles Trainings- und Testdatenkorpus die Erkennung von Ausspracheproblemen für russische Muttersprachler, die Deutsch lernen. Dieser Ansatz ist im Projekt Euronounce [8] auf weitere osteuropäischen Sprachen ausgebaut worden, so dass neben Russisch auch Polnisch, Slowenisch und Tschechisch unterstützt werden. Aktuell wird AzAR gerade für eine Anwendung in der Rehabilitation von Schlaganfallpatienten angepasst und für die mobile Nutzung auf eine Client-Server-Architektur umgestellt.

Die serverbasierte Datenverarbeitung sowie mobile Clienten (Smartphone, Tablets) bieten neben flexibler Nutzung und Ortsunabhängigkeit für den Anwender ganz neue Möglichkeiten der Datenerfassung eben auch unter Alltagsbedingungen, womit sich die Datenlücke endlich auch für KMU schließen lässt.

6 User Interface-Gestaltung und Ergonomie

Technologische Forschung ist aufwändig und die Vermarktung neuer Produkte muss in immer kürzeren Zyklen von der Idee bis zur Produktreife erfolgen. Eine Abgrenzung vom Wettbewerb erfolgt zumeist über zusätzliche technische Funktionalitäten.

Dieser technokratische Ansatz (alles, was technologisch möglich statt alles was ergonomisch nötig) muß jedoch zunehmend infrage gestellt werden: Was nützt die neue Kaffeemaschine mit automatischem Abschaltschutz, Erkennung des Wasserstandes zur Anpassung der Brühzeiten und selbständigem Entkalkungsprogramm, wenn der Anwender kaum in der Lage ist, den Einschaltknopf zu finden? Die Konzentration auf technologische Möglichkeiten zu Ungunsten der Ergonomie lässt gerade in einer zunehmend älter werdenden Gesellschaft, die nicht zeitlebens mit Elektronik vertraut ist, Vorbehalte gegen Neuerungen wachsen. Es gibt aber inzwischen - z.B. bei Apple-Produkten – auch Erfolgsstories, bei denen Ergonomie neben den technischen Aspekten eine zentrale Rolle für den Produkterfolg spielt. Insofern lohnt sich in der Zukunft eine Investition in ergonomische Aspekte, da der Verbraucher zunehmend neben Design auch auf Ergonomie wert legt. Auch bei VIC ist das Bewusstsein für eine sorgfältige Gestaltung der Nutzerschnittstelle stark ausgeprägt – insbesondere bei Betrachtung multimodaler Bedienkonzepte.

Abbildung 5 – links: Prototyp eines sprachgesteuerten Kaffeeautomaten; rechts: Waschmaschine mit akustischer Bedienungsanleitung

Doch wie können die Bedürfnisse des Nutzers Eingang in den Entwicklungsprozess eines Produkts finden? Bereits in der Konzeptionsphase müssen Use cases nicht nur theoretisch hergeleitet, sondern konkret beim Nutzer erfragt werden. Dies setzt voraus, dass eine ausführliche Recherche des Marktpotentials und der Zielgruppe stattgefunden hat. Im Idealfall wird ein Prototyp Probanden zur Verfügung gestellt und im Feldtest praktisch erprobt. Die Ergebnisse fließen dann in die Weiterentwicklung ein.

Für die Entwicklung von Produkten im Bereich der Sprachkommunikation ist außerdem eine interdisziplinäre Zusammenarbeit ideal. Ein enger Austausch von Ingenieurs- und Computerwissenschaftlern mit Humanwissenschaftlern und Designern führt zu einer verbesserten Benutzerfreundlichkeit besonders an der Schnittstelle zwischen Maschine und Mensch.

Die Erweiterung herkömmlicher Bedienmodalitäten um das Medium Sprache bedingt sorgfältige Planung. Eine Sprachbedienung kann beispielsweise nur dann von Nutzen sein, wenn sie einfach, klar strukturiert ist und der natürlichen Sprache des Nutzers nahe kommt. Anstatt wie in grafischen Menüs weit verzweigte Strukturen nachzubilden, muss eine Funktion schnell verfügbar sein. Also nicht "Hausautomation – Wähle Wohnzimmer – Wähle Jalousien – Jalousien hochfahren", sondern ein direkter Zugriff "Jalousien hoch" muss zum gewünschten Ergebnis führen. Die Festlegung der Vokabeln setzt eine große Sorgfaltsleistung voraus, da eine Verwendung von Synonymen aufgrund subjektiver Faktoren sehr wahrscheinlich ist, und verschiedene Aussprachevarianten berücksichtigt werden müssen. Zur Gewöhnung des Nutzers können vorteilhaft bekannte Bedienmodalitäten mit neuen kombiniert werden. So kann der Nutzer einer multimodalen Bedienung alle auf einer GUI angezeigten und beschrifteten Bedienelemente auch als Sprachbefehl nutzen und hat so eine implizite Hilfestellung zum verfügbaren Befehlssatz.

Eine wertvolle Ergänzung der Sprachbedienung besteht in der Nutzung zusätzlicher Sensoren als Kontextgeber. So können Bewegungssensoren dem System vermitteln, in welchem Raum der Befehl ausgesprochen wurde, um ein Verstehen im Kontext zu erreichen - gemeint sind die Jalousien im Wohnzimmer. Im Zweifelsfall muss es dem System möglich sein, mit dem Anwender in einen Klärungsdialog zu treten.

All diese Innovationen können nur dann vom Anwender akzeptiert werden, wenn er nicht das Gefühl der Überwachung oder Bevormundung hat. Der Mensch muss immer das Gefühl haben, die Technik kontrollieren– sprich: sie abschalten – zu können, und sie nicht als Eindringling in die Privatsphäre, sondern als Ergänzung in Sachen Komfort und Bedienbarkeit begreifen.

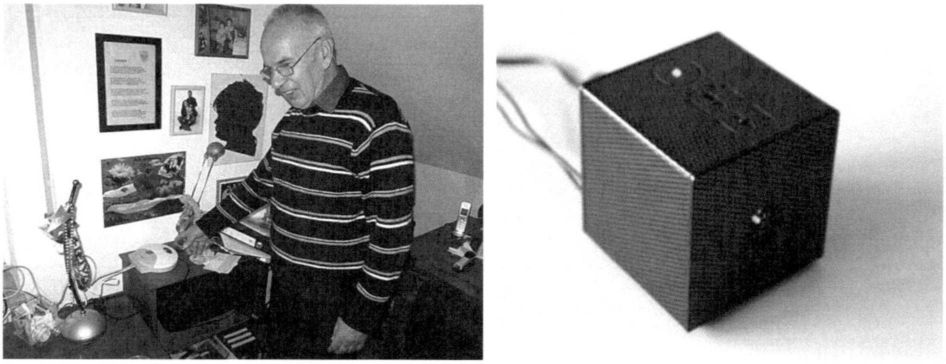

Abbildung 6 – Links: Herkömmliches ([**2**]); Rechts: Sprachbedientes Hausnotruf-System.

7 AUTAGEF als Prototyp für eine ambiente Sprachkommunikations-architektur

Im Projekt AUTAGEF [2] wurden Lösungen entwickelt, die sowohl den technologischen als auch ambienten Anforderungen einer Sprachkommunikation im häuslichen Alltag gerecht werden ([13], vgl. auch Abschnitt 3). Besonderer Schwerpunkt ist hierbei die Gefahrenmeldung und -rufauslösung im Notfall. Ähnlich wie bei der Ambient-Musik, die der Zuhörer als hintergründig erlebt und ihr nur sehr wenig Aufmerksamkeit schenkt, muss ein intelligentes Notrufsystem 24 Stunden lang im Hintergrund unauffällig funktionieren. Nur wenn der Anwender das Gefühl eines stillen, zurückhaltenden Begleiters hat, der lediglich im Fall der Aufmerksamkeitszuwendung unmittelbar einspringt, kann er einen Eingriff in seine Privatsphäre akzeptieren und gewinnbringend einsetzen. Das Bedürfnis nach persönlicher Sicherheit und die schnelle Hilfe im akuten Notfall sind weitere Faktoren, die die Akzeptanz steigern.

8 Sprachstruktur und Sinn gesprochener Sprache

Sprache ist die Äußerungsform des sich reflektierenden menschlichen Bewußtseins, seiner Reflexionsfiguren durch Zeichen und Metazeichen [15]. Als solche kann sie durch technische Verarbeitung wohl niemals vollständig beherrscht, d.h. verstanden und gesprochen werden. Die dafür nötigen Sinnprozesse und Bewußtseinsvollzüge lassen sich ohne Welterfahrung und Denkvermögen nicht reproduzieren. Praktikabel erscheint allerdings, durch die sprachwissenschaftliche Reflexion ihre Logik zu rekonstruieren. Das Ziel kann dann als *sprach-ähnliches Verhalten* neu definiert und umgesetzt werden: durch die datentechnische Abbildung ihrer Sinngehalte und die rechentechnische Simulation ihrer Sinnvollzüge – bis zu einem gewissen Niveau.

Abbildung 7 - Sprachhandlungs-Übersetzung Deutsch-Chinesisch im EUROFON

Dabei stellt sich zuerst und unmittelbar das Problem der Verdeckung der höheren Ebenen der Zeichengestalt (der sigmatischen Dimension) durch die jeweils tieferen: Direkt beobachtbar ist lediglich die Lautgestalt (sigmatische Ebene) – bei vorhandener Kenntnis dieser Gestalt *als Zeichen* überhaupt. Erst das Wissen um die Bedeutungsprägung (semantische Ebene) der einzelnen Ausdruckselemente einer Muttersprache aber (Phoneme, Morpheme, Lexeme, Prosodeme, Äußerungs- und Diskurszeichen) erlaubt ihre schrittweise – teils lineare, teils auf ihre Bedeutung und ihr Ganzes vorgreifende – Identifizierung in einem gegebenen Zeichenkomplex.

Auf dieser Ebene stehenzubleiben, sei es auch mit umfangreicher Information über die (aufgrund ihrer Häufigkeit und Korrelation) *allgemein erwartbaren* Zeichenfügungen, heißt jedoch, gerade das Wesentliche des Sprachsystems zu verfehlen: die Mehrdimensionalität des Zeichengeschehens in seiner logisch-gestuften Reflexion und wechselseitigen Durchdringung (Sigmatik, Semantik, Pragmatik und Syntaktik). Insbesondere würde damit das Charakteristische der Sprache unterschlagen: Bedeutung ausdrücken zu können. Denn interessant ist immer nur, was noch nicht zuvor gesagt, und wie es im jeweiligen Kontext gemeint wurde.

Für die Zeichenhypothesen ist dazu auf der Grundlage der Handlungseinbettung (Kontext, pragmatische Ebene) ihre *konkrete Bedeutung* zu bestimmen – ihr objektiver Bezug (Referenz) auf Reales. Dies kann zwar die Bedeutungseinführung umfassen, doch generell und für den ganzen Zeichenkomplex muss dazu erst die jeweilige *allgemeine Bedeutung* abgerufen werden – ihr subjektiver Gehalt (Vorstellung) unabhängig von einzelnen Sprachvollzügen, aber auch von beteiligtem Subjekt und faktischer Wirklichkeit. Dieser Übergang vom *Das* der Zeichengestalt zum *Was* des Zeichengehaltes aber erschließt erst die semantische Dimension. Diese hat ihrerseits eine sigmatische Ebene der Bezeichnung (durch Namen), eine semantische der Benennung (durch Begriffe), eine pragmatische der Prädikation (durch Relationen) und eine syntaktische der Verbindung von Gehalten.

Jeder Sprechakt ist in seiner pragmatischen Dimension zugleich (soziale) Ausdruckshandlung und damit real und intersubjektiv wirksam: deine und meine Welt verändernd. Hierin äußert sich auch der dialogische Grundcharakter der Sprache (unabhängig vom eigentlichen Gespräch). Es lassen sich wiederum vier Funktions-Ebenen unterscheiden: (lokutiv) Information, (illokutiv) Ausdruck, (perlokutiv) Wirkung, (exekutiv) Rolle.

Die syntaktische Dimension schließlich als Ort der Zeichenverbindung stellt das Ganze dar, das es integriert und so zum Medium werden lässt. Durch ihre spezifischen Meta-Zeichen der syntaktischen Kategorien enthält (und reguliert) ihr Vollzug sich selbst. Hier zeigt sich, welche Zeichenhypothesen sich überhaupt sinnvoll (d.h. mit konkreter Bedeutung) kombinieren lassen.Zu ihr gehört die sigmatische Ebene der Phonotaktik und Morphologie, die semantische der Grammatik, die pragmatische der Dialogik und Rhetorik und die syntaktische der Stilistik.

Erst wenn alle Dimensionen ausreichend entwickelt (d.h. formal reflektiert) vorliegen, läßt sich eine akustisch gegebene Sprachhandlung wirklich technisch nachvollziehen. Damit vereinfacht sich auch die Teilaufgabe der Dekodierung in der sigmatischen Dimension substantiell (d.h. die Suche nach der intendierten Zeichengestalt), denn sie fällt mit der Analyse der höheren Dimensionen zusammen (der Suche nach den Zeichengehalten). Hier ergibt sich sodann zugleich die Möglichkeit, verlorene Teile oder Unverständliches wirklich zu rekonstruieren, also dem Zeichengeschehen robust zu folgen. Ein solcher semiotischer Erkenner-Parser bildet zusammen mit einem analog entworfenen Generator aber auch erst die Grundlage, den menschlichen Sprachhandlungen auf medialer Stufe technisch zu begegnen, d.h. in ihrer logischen Eigendynamik, ohne bloße Nachahmung ihrer Zeichengesten. Diese Technik befähigt nicht nur zum Aufbau einer hochwertigen sprachlichen Mensch-Maschine-Kommunikation, sondern läßt sich auch in der Übersetzung von Sprachhandlungen in eine andere Muttersprache anwenden (elektronischer Dolmetscher).

Mit dem EUROFON-Projekt [16], [17] wird genau dieses Ziel verfolgt. Dort konnte bei der wissensbasierten, verstehenden Übersetzung von Dialogen zwischen dem Deutschen und dem Chinesischen bereits ein gewisser Fortschritt erzielt werden.

9 Zusammenfassung und Ausblick

Es wurde gezeigt, dass die Kerntechnologie heutiger Spracherkenner (Akustisches Frontend und Spracherkenner) robust und leistungsfähig ist, jedoch zur praktischen Anwendung große Lücken klaffen. Am deutlichsten betroffen sind die Robustheit der Spracherkennung gegen Raumeinflüsse und Variation des Spracherfassungskanals einerseits, sowie die höheren linguistischen Verarbeitungsstufen und deren syntaktisches und semantisches Korrekturpotential andererseits. Eine intelligente Nachverarbeitung der Klassifikationsergebnisse eines Spracherkenners erlaubt die Anwendung von Verfahren zur gesprächsbegleitenden, fortgesetzten inhaltlichen Vorhersage und Verifikation des Gesprochenen, welche einerseits die Erkennungsqualität erst handhabbar erscheinen lassen, und andererseits den Aufwand des Dekodierprozesses durch Beschränkung auf Topic und Domäne soweit absenkt, dass er zeitlich und ressourcenmäßig für ein Embedded System praktikabel erscheint.

Schließlich ist die Sorgfalt und Kontinuität der Weiterentwicklung und Bündelung von Sprach-Knowhow sowie die kontinuierliche Investitionsbereitschaft in Köpfe und Verfahren ausschlaggebend für nachhaltigen Erfolg. Aufgrund der Komplexität der algorithmischen Verfahren und des Aufwandes der Datensammlung ist ein einzelner Wissenschaftler mit seiner Lebensarbeitszeit nur in der Lage, einen kleinen Beitrag in einem sprachverarbeitenden System zu leisten. Neben der wissenschaftlichen ist es eine kommerzielle Herausforderung, eine unter allen Umständen funktionierende und durch den Anwender akzeptierte Anwendung zu schaffen. Für eine erfolgreiche Produkteinführung müssen Technik und Ergonomie eine Einheit bilden. Durch vorausschauende, den Nutzer einbeziehende Produktentwicklung sowie interdisziplinäre Zusammenarbeit ist die Überführung wissenschaftlicher Erkenntnisse und technologischer Fortschritte in die Praxis möglich.

10 Literatur

[1] Torsten Rudolph. Evolutionäre Optimierung assoziativ-dynamischer. Worterkenner. Dr.–Ing.–Dissertation, Technische Universität Dresden. Fakultät Elektrotechnik,April 1999

[2] www.autagef.de

[3] D. Hirschfeld, U. Koloska: Integrierte multimodale Sprachdatenverwaltung mit dem WiGE System. In: 15. Konferenz Elektronische Sprachsignalverarbeitung, Tagungsband 30, Studientexte zur Sprachkommunikation 24, 2004, pp. 222 - 228

[4] J. Helbig, D. Hirschfeld, U. Koloska, J. Maase, T. Westfeld: Toward an Evaluation Standard for Speech Control Concepts in Real-World Scenarios. In: EUROSPEECH-2003, pp. 1553 - 1556

[5] M. Albrecht, D. Hirschfeld, U. Koloska: Mobiles Aufnahmesystem für Sprachtechnologie-Anwendungen. In: Tagungsband der 28. Jahrestagung der Deutschen Akustischen Gesellschaft für Akustik e.V. (DAGA), 2002

[6] U. Koloska, R. Römer: Performance Optimisation of Speaker Dependent HMM – Based on Speech Recognition Systems. MMSP 2002, 5th IEEE Workshop on Multimedia Signal Processing, December 9 – 11, St. Thomas, US Virgin Islands

[7] D. Hirschfeld, R. Hoffmann, O. Jokisch, U. Koloska (2005): Pronunciation Learning and Foreign Accent Reduction by an Audiovisual Feedback System. First International Conference on Affective Computing & Intelligent Interaction, ACII October 22 - 24, 2005, Beijing, China

[8] N. Cylwik, R. Hoffmann, R. Jäckel, O. Jokisch, A. Ronzhin, M. Rusko, R. Sabo, A. Wagner: Multilingual Speech Data Collection for the Assessment of Pronunciation and Prosody in a Language Learning System. Proc. 13th Intern. Conf. Speech and Computer (SPECOM), St. Petersburg, June 2009

[9] Estelmann, Jens: Phone and word based confidence scores for command and control applications, In: Electronic Speech Signal Processing ESSP 2005, Prague 2005; Studientexte zur Sprachkommunikation, Volume 36.

[10] www.speechdat.org.

[11] Burger, S., Weilhammer, K., Schiel, F., & Tillmann, H. G. (2000). *Verbmobil data collection and annotation.* In Verbmobil: Foundations of Speech-to-Speech Translation (pp. 537-549). Springer Berlin Heidelberg.

[12] C. Gruber, D. Hirschfeld, G. Kinast, R. Petrick: *Comparison of Signal Enhancement Techniques in Communications and Speech Control Tasks for a Single-DSP in-Car Application.* Biennial on DSP for in-Vehicle and Mobile Systems, Sesimbra (Portugal) 2005, Paper M2-6

[13] D. Hirschfeld, O. Jokisch, K. Kabitzsch, J. Ploennings, U. Ryssel: Generation of Adapted, Speech-based User Interfaces for Home and Building Automation Systems. WFCS 2008. IEEE International Workshop on Factory Communication Systems; Volume, Issue , May 21 - 23, 2008, pp. 445 – 452

[14] Dachselt, F., Gruber, C., Hirschfeld, D.: Ambiente Sensorsysteme für Gefahrenerkennung, Kommunikation und Bedienkomfort - Audiosensorik im Projekt AUTAGEF, 6. AAL-Konferenz, Berlin, 2013

[15] Heinrichs, Johannes. Philosophische Semiotik, Teil II: Sprache. Steno, München. 2. Aufl., 2008.

[16] BMWi-ZIM, Projekt KF2037603 (2012-2014) Eurofon-CE22 – Lernender Europäisch-Chinesischer Kommunikationsapparat

[17] Däßler, Klaus. Eurofon, persönlicher digitaler Spontanübersetzer. Interne Dokumentation. Gesellschaft für Mathematische Intelligenz, Radebeul, 2005-2013.

Technology Transfer for Speech Processing Applications

Oliver Jokisch
Deutsche Telekom AG, Leipzig University of Telecommunication (HfTL)
Institute of Communications Engineering (ICE)
jokisch@hft-leipzig.de

Abstract: The article illustrates speech technology transfer of more than one decade. Some examples in speech synthesis, speech corpora development and pronunciation tutoring reflect experiences of GWT (the transfer partner of TU Dresden) and demonstrate a bidirectional know-how transfer between scientific and industrial partners.

1 Introduction

The contributions from Dresden in acoustics and speech analysis since 1911 – connected to professors like Heinrich Barkhausen, Walter Reichardt (from 1950) or Walter Tscheschner (from 1969) – are well-known and also referenced in this Festschrift. In speech processing, early developments involved prototypes in speech coding such as a vocoder in 1957 and several devices for parametric speech synthesis from 1962 to 1987 in cooperation with industrial partners (e. g. with GDR computer producer Robotron). This alliance of teaching, fundamental research and applied research has been continued by Prof. Rüdiger Hoffmann and his group since 1992. In cooperation with Fraunhofer institutes for applied research and corporate R&D departments, numerous projects in speech recognition, speech synthesis and database development were initiated. Additionally, Hoffmann supported the dissemination of speech technology by co-founding the companies Gesellschaft für Signalverarbeitung und Mustererkennung mbH (GeSIM) and voice INTER connect GmbH.

To ensure professional project management at the interface between university research and commercial application, he established the signal processing department within GWT-TUD GmbH (the technology transfer company of TU Dresden) in 1998. This article addresses technology transfer for speech processing applications and illustrates exemplary project results.

2 Knowledge and technology transfer in Dresden

2.1 Partnering concept

GWT-TUD GmbH – founded as knowledge and technology transfer company of TU Dresden – is acting as 'temporary company' for scientists of Saxonian universities. GWT realizes commercial projects and monitors time schedule, quality and financial budget. The service includes marketing, customer acquisition, contract negotiations, human and material resource management – while scientists can focus on research and development. GWT belongs to the leading enterprises of this kind in Germany. The service charge depends on project type (private, public or mixed funding), project complexity etc. and starts at ca. 12 % of project's gross total.

2.2 Exemplary research and development in speech processing

The following sections introduce three typical application areas in speech processing – speech synthesis, speech corpora development and pronunciation tutoring.

The described technology transfer initially based on fundamental and applied research in previous cooperation projects – such as the national Verbmobil project in the early 1990ies. The project results involved submodules e. g. text-to-speech (TTS) synthesis within a dialog system to demonstrate basic functions. Industrial project partners as e. g. the corporate research department of Daimler AG in Ulm (Germany) commanded a baseline TTS system in 1998 but specified additional requirements for real world applications such as a female corporate voice (for navigation system) with high intelligibility and naturalness or different interfaces and operation systems.

The specified tasks requested complex knowledge in research and development, an own experimental platform but also a lot of routine and optimization work which is not fully covered by academic research. Consequently, this knowledge and technology transfer was separately contracted by the industrial partners. In later projects with development departments of Infineon Technologies AG and Siemens AG (both located in Munich), we developed derivative TTS systems and submodules for the use in embedded environment under low-resource restrictions (memory on chip, calculation time etc.). The qualified feedback from the partners regarding the developed prototypes and applications was leading to new research questions at TU Dresden – in some cases concerning fundamental research as well. Additionally, prototypes were made available for teaching purpose so that the technology transfer as a whole can be considered as win-win situation for university research, commercial partners and students.

The quality of speech processing applications – in particular in speech synthesis – depends a lot of available speech corpora for training and localization/personalization. In a further section, the article shortly describes an according database project with Siemens CT in the multilingual environment. To demonstrate the cooperation with smaller companies in education and development, the next section illustrates some efforts in pronunciation tutoring technology which was developed in cooperation with the enterprises voice INTER connect GmbH and REZO Computerservice GmbH.

3 Speech synthesis technology

3.1 Dresden Speech Synthesizer (DRESS)

Stimulated by a speech synthesis solution on PCMCIA card (VoiceCard [1]) and the mentioned Verbmobil project (targeting on higher acoustic quality), several synthesis modules – including formant synthesis, concatenative (diphone-based) synthesis, text processing and prosody generation – have been developed [2].

The first GWT projects from 1998 till 2000 dealt with the software integration and improvement of these heterogeneous synthesis components for a general purpose text-to-speech (TTS) system. The design involved:

- Experimental setup (alternative modules and processing paths) and real-time capability,
- Multilingual databases and several voices,
- Strict code/data separation and different operating systems,
- Configurable modules for different application domains.

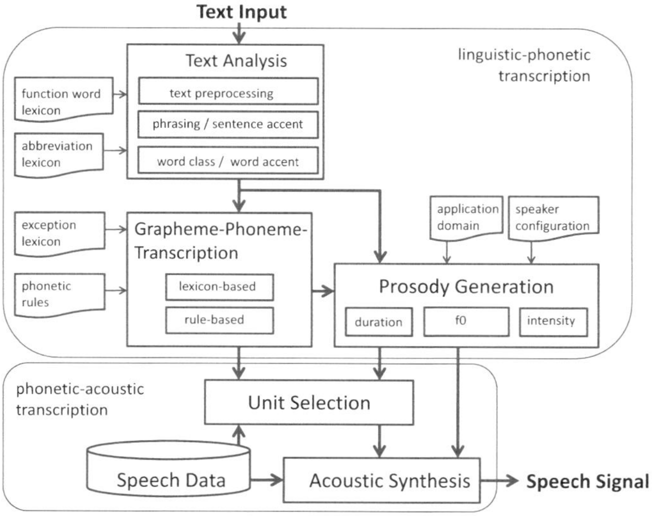

Figure 1: Processing levels and modules of DRESS.

The resulting baseline system was called Dresden Speech Synthesizer (DRESS) [3, 4],based on concatenative PSOLA synthesis in time domain. Figure 1 shows the block diagram of DRESS. Main challenge was the interface adaptation for existing modules from different projects. Consequently, some modules formed bottlenecks with regard to processing quality and software technology – in particular on linguistic and prosodic level. During the multimedia and speech technology hype in the end of 1990s, several development projects in speech synthesis were acquired – including acoustic synthesis and voice optimization for Daimler AG, a TTS solution on Antares DSP board for the former T-Nova (Deutsche Telekom AG) and a TTS module for an interactive voice response (IVR) server of Globana Teleport GmbH. The hybrid multi-level prosody module in [3] has been patented by T-Nova.

3.2 Embedded speech synthesis – microDRESS and ePapageno

Around year 2000, TTS systems were considerably improved which resulted in memory requirements of several (partly a few hundred) megabytes – unacceptable for many applications on embedded systems. Such applications often require small footprint and low processing power (usually connected with restricted battery capacity). These requirements may be met if the text processing is changed from common data-driven algorithms to rule-based processing. Furthermore, the inventory should be as small as possible (diphone inventory) and should be stored in a compressed manner. In the mentioned cooperation with Infineon Technologies AG, a modified synthesis system microDRESS for German and English was developed [5] with a footprint of less than 1 megabyte per language. Simplified block diagram is shown in Figure 2.

The embedded target system of Infineon (see Figure 3) requested optimization steps like reduced computing power and small object code size, small external memory for compressed voice inventory and lexicons but also an optimized data flow and easy portability.

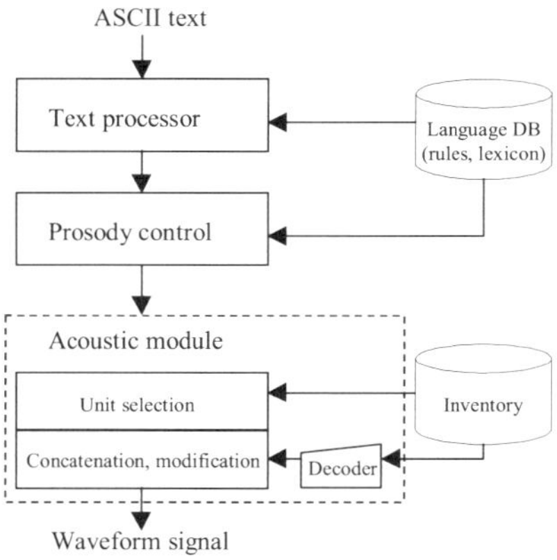

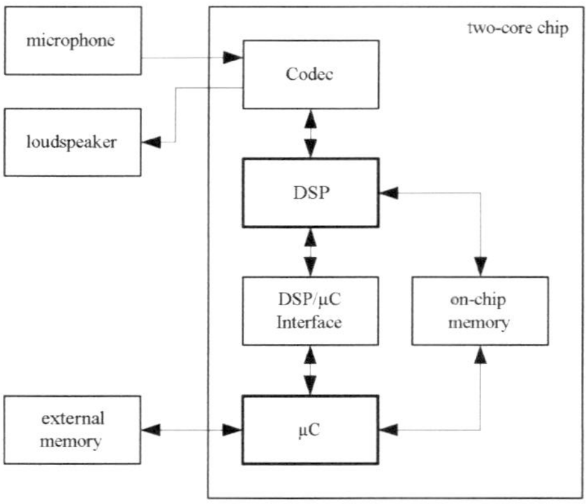

Figure 2: Block diagram of microDRESS [5]. **Figure 3:** Prototypical speech chip [6].

Compared to the baseline DRESS system, microDRESS does not show essential quality losses apart from the influences of telephone bandwidth which is appropriate for many embedded applications. Figure 4 compares the Mean Opinion Scores (MOS "overall quality", scale from 1 "insufficient" to 5 "excellent") for microDRESS stimuli with natural reference, DRESS stimuli and stimuli of two commercial TTS systems (marking typical quality expectation at this time). The test involved 20 listeners and 10 utterances. With uncompressed inventory, the quality of microDRESS (mdress) was not degraded compared to the baseline system DRESS (dress). An inventory coding similar to ADPCM (mdress*) caused an acceptable audible quality loss. The additional limitation to telephone bandwidth resulted in a clear quality loss of almost 1 MOS degree (mdress**). Indeed, experience showed that telephone bandwidth is widely accepted by users if presented via telephone set.

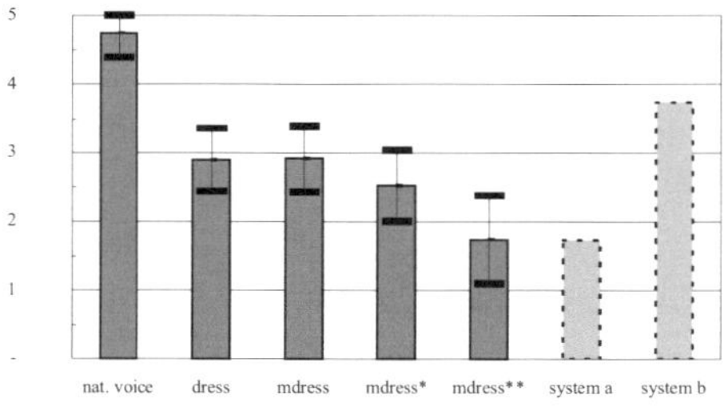

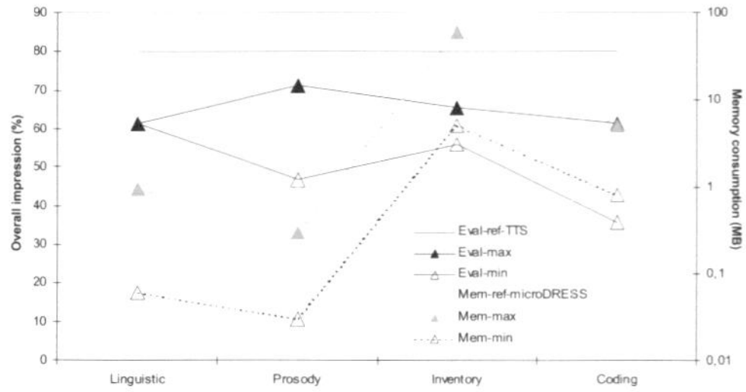

Figure 4: Perceptual test of microDRESS [7]. **Figure 5:** Component effect on overall quality [7].

The modified TTS components (linguistic processing, prosodic model, unit inventory and inventory coding) were separately investigated but basing on a few assumptions [7], a cost-value metrics was predicted in terms of memory use versus auditory quality (Figure 5). It emphasizes that the memory resources for linguistic and prosodic processing are less critical. The unit inventory (including bandwidth and coding scheme) seems to be the cost-value bottleneck in scalable speech synthesis. Further Siemens projects were directed to a derived acoustic module for their corporate embedded synthesizer ePapageno – based on codecs from mobile communication. The involved one-step decoding and synthesis [8] was patented. The practical constraints of corporate R&D also stimulated the further research at TU Dresden. Advanced synthesis approaches of Strecha et al. achieve a memory consumption of less than 100 kB (code and data of complete acoustic synthesis).

4 Speech corpora and annotation

Multilingual localization and personalization in speech processing applications – in particular in speech synthesis – require the generation and evaluation of various speech databases – e. g. the voice inventory and a prosodic database for training. In cooperation with Siemens CT from 2002 till 2005, we prepared databases for several European languages.

First steps involved a casting of 5 to 8 female speakers per language. Figure 6 presents the perceptual ranking among six UK English speakers by preference decisions of 25 listeners. The correlation in decisions of native and non-native listeners (some not familiar with the target language) could be observed across all languages – except for a Mexican speaker in a Spanish casting (dialect effect) – and was surprisingly high. The intermediate evaluation results leaded to further research on objective (instrumentally measured) voice parameters correlating with listener's preference as described in [9].

Figure 7 shows the averaged f0 mean values (pitch of the voice) of speakers with an equal rank 1 to 5 in German, UK and US English, Spanish and French as an example. The diagram suggests a cross-lingual preference for lower female voices.

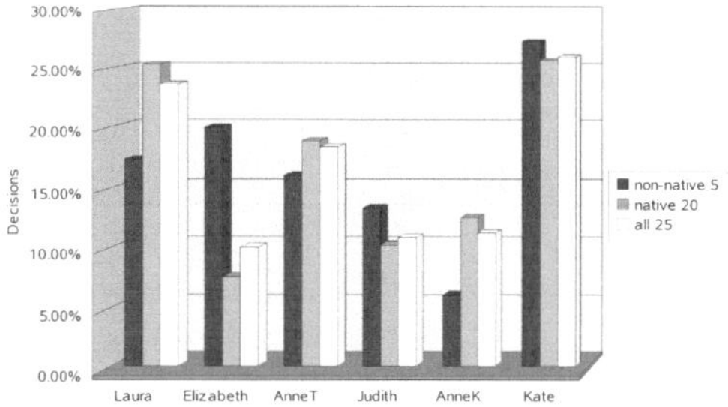

Figure 6: Perceptual ranking of UK voices [9].

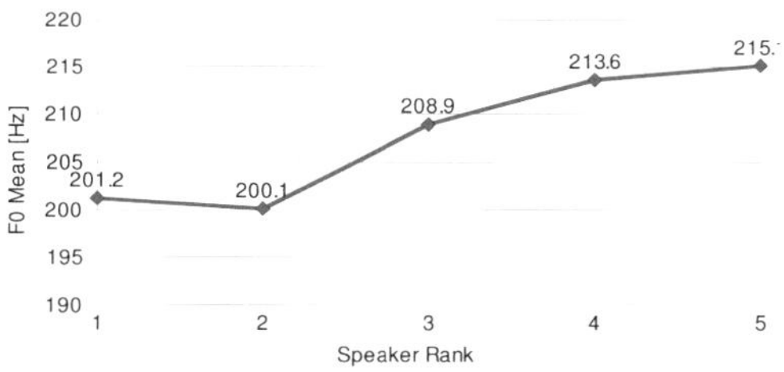

Figure 7: Average pitch – sorted by rank [9].

Ensuring high quality of speech and descriptive data, advanced database projects require automatic procedures for collection, segmentation and annotation to reduce time effort and labor costs. Continuing the Siemens cooperation, we developed a semi-automatic software framework [10] involving manual segmentation and evaluation processes (overview in Figure 8) within the European project "Technology and Corpora for Speech to Speech Translation" (TC-STAR) in 2006, aiming at speech corpora for building advanced TTS systems as well as for intra-lingual/inter-lingual research on voice conversion and expressive speech. The resulting corpora for UK English, Spanish and Mandarin include voice recordings at 96 kHz/24 bit and consist of different read parts: e. g. novels and (expressive) parliamentary speech. In total, 10 hours of net speech per voice correspond to 90,000 running words in 5,558 utterances which needed to be annotated.

Phonetic and linguistic-prosodic annotation processes are denoted in the Figures 9 and 10. The different processing paths and interfaces enabled consistent manual and automatic labels. To support a robust prosodic segmentation, only minor and major phrases/accents were marked.

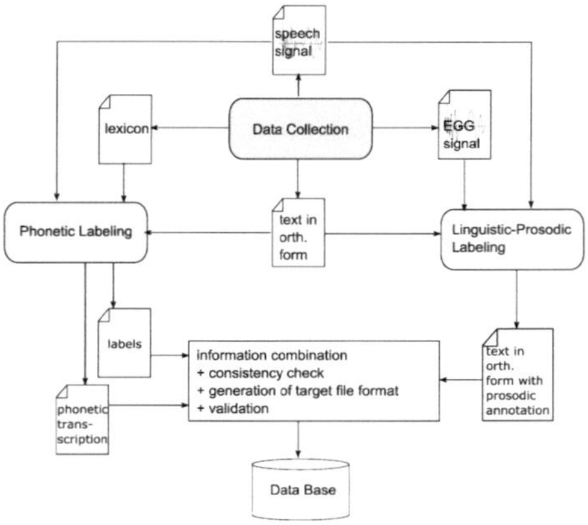

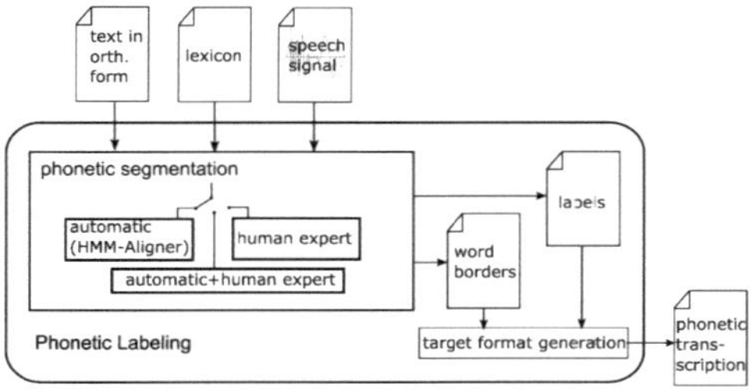

Figure 9: Phonetic segmentation/annotation [10].

Figure 8: TCSTAR process chain [10].

Figure 11 summarizes the success rates (SR) of the phrase marking based on prosodic analysis and pause detection. We created the UK English voices "Laura" and "Ian". The part of manually annotated data for training and evaluation amounted to 28.4 % (voice "Laura").

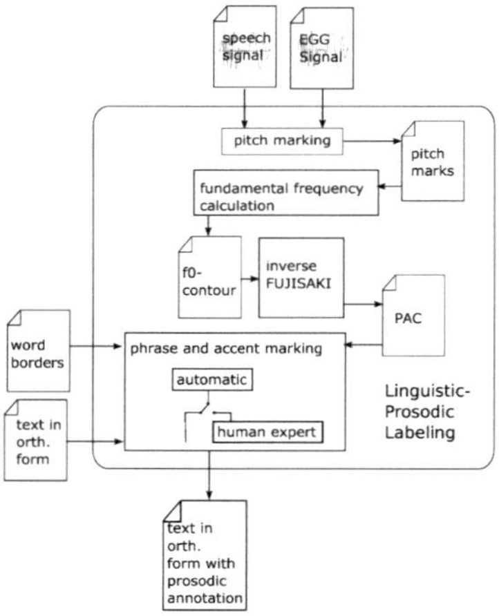

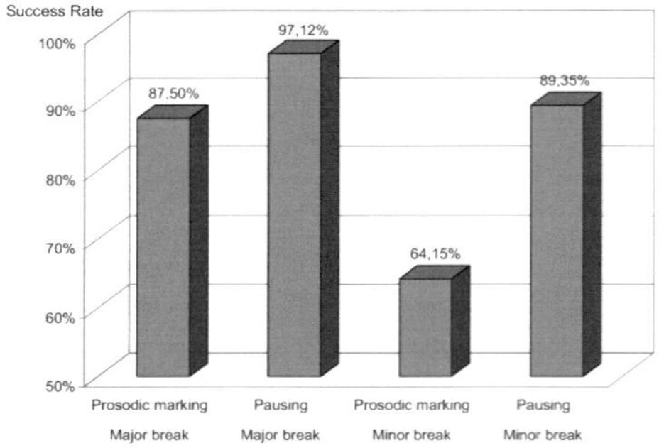

Figure 11: Evaluation of phrase marking [10].

Figure 10: Linguistic-prosodic annotation [10].

5 Pronunciation tutoring technology

In the following, the technology transfer with local enterprises is illustrated. Further education company REZO Computerservice GmbH extended the professional training for Russian migrants with German language courses. The teachers were dissatisfied with existing computer-assisted tools which did not include a distinct user feedback. In cooperation with speech technology company voice INTER connect GmbH, we initiated two research projects 2004 – 2007 (funded by national agencies AiF and SAB) aiming at the "Automat for Accent Reduction" (German acronym: AzAR) [11]. The resulting software enabled the interactive training of second language (L2) pronunciation for native speakers from the Slavonic language group. Beside animated articulatory organs, position and strength of mispronunciation are represented by a color scale. Figure 12 shows the graphical user interface of AzAR. Despite a positive user feedback, the subsequent product marketing was less successful. Nevertheless, AzAR results led to succeeding research projects under guidance of TU Dresden (e. g. Euronounce) and to new scientific partners, extended linguistic research and databases for Polish, Czech and Slovak.

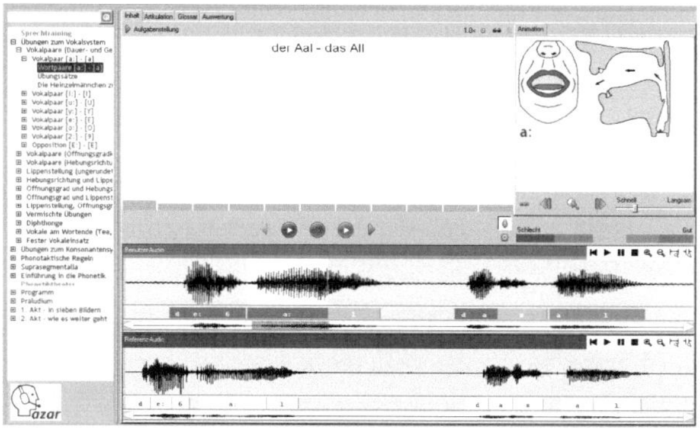

Figure 12: User interface of AZAR 3, version 2010.

In a further step, didactic concept and tutoring technology were adapted to the special requirements of young children aged 3+ years. The prototypical embedded system LISA [12] – extended by microphone and loudspeaker – was integrated in a puppet and can lead simple dialogs. For navigation in educational books, a barcode scanner was connected (Figures 13 and 14).

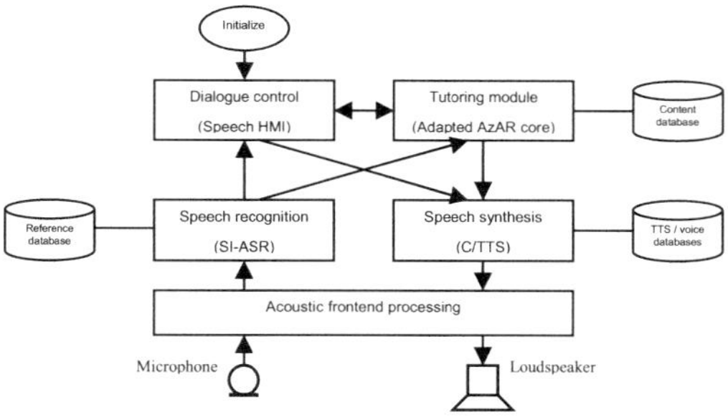

Figure 13: Block diagram of LISA [12].

Figure 14: LISA demonstrator [12].

6 Conclusion

The examples of technology transfer demonstrate a fruitful and 'bidirectional' cooperation with commercial partners – often stimulating new fundamental research but also enhancing teaching horizon at TU Dresden. In the described cases, only pre-stages of products were achieved which requested further developments of the commercial partners.

7 Acknowledgment

I would like to thank my former colleagues at TU Dresden and GWT for their support[1] – in particular Prof. Rüdiger Hoffmann, PD Dr. Ulrich Kordon, Prof. Hongwei Ding, Dr. Diane Hirschfeld, Guntram Strecha, Dr. Sören Wittenberg, Rainer Jäckel and Henry Urban.

[1] I joint the group of Prof. Rüdiger Hoffmann 1995 – 2012, worked as GWT project manager 1998 – 2007 and, at present, hold the Chair of Signal and System Theory at Leipzig University of Telecommunication (HfTL).

References

[1] U. Kordon, W.-J. Fischer, and H.-J. Holland. Pcmcia-card für ein sprachsynthesesystem. *Proc. DAGA 95 - Fortschritte der Akustik, Saarbrücken*, pages 1003–1006, 1995.

[2] D. Hirschfeld. *Das Text-to-Speech System. Algorithmen, Programmbeschreibungen, Dateninventare.* TU Dresden, 1996. Technical report.

[3] O. Jokisch, D. Hirschfeld, M. Eichner, and R. Hoffmann. Multi-level rhythm control for speech synthesis using hybrid data driven and rule-based approaches. *Proc. ICSLP 98, Sydney*, pages 607–610, 1998.

[4] R. Hoffmann, D. Hirschfeld, O. Jokisch, U. Kordon, H. Mixdorff, and D. Mehnert. Evaluation of a multilingual tts system with respect to the prosodic quality. *Proc. ICPhS 99, San Francisco*, pages 2307–2310, 1999.

[5] R. Hoffmann, O. Jokisch, D. Hirschfeld, G. Strecha, H. Kruschke, and U. Kordon. A multilingual tts system with less than 1 megabyte footprint for embedded applications. *Proc. ICASSP, Hongkong*, pages 532–535, 2003.

[6] M. Schnell, O. Jokisch, M. Küstner, and R. Hoffmann. Text-to-speech for low-resource systems. *Proc. IEEE Workshop on Multimedia Signal Processing (MMSP), St. Thomas, US Virgin Islands*, 2002.

[7] O. Jokisch, R. Hoffmann, M. Eichner, S. Werner, H. Kruschke, and U. Kordon. The influence of the tts system configuration on the perceived quality of synthesized speech. *Proc. ISCA Workshop on Auditory Quality of Systems, Mont-Cenis, Germany*, 2003.

[8] G. Strecha, O. Jokisch, M. Eichner, and R. Hoffmann. Codec integrated voice conversion for embedded speech synthesis. In *Proc. Interspeech, Lissabon*, pages 2589–2592, 2005.

[9] U. Hain, O. Jokisch, and L. Coelho. Multilingual voice analysis: Towards prosodic correlates of voice preference. In *Proc. Elektronische Sprachsignalverarbeitung (ESSV) 2009 (Studientexte zur Sprachkommunikation Bd. 53), Dresden*, pages 215–221, 2009.

[10] O. Jokisch, S. Wittenberg, M. Cuevas, H. Hussein, G. Strecha, H. Ding, and R. Hoffmann. Towards an automatic process chain for the speech corpora annotation. In *Proc. SPECOM, Moscow*, pages 869–876, 2007.

[11] O. Jokisch, U. Koloska, D. Hirschfeld, and R. Hoffmann. Pronunciation learning and foreign accent reduction by an audiovisual feedback system. In T. Tan J. Tao and R.W. Picard, editors, *Affective Computing and Intelligent Interaction (ACII Beijing)*, pages 419–425. Springer LNCS-3784, Berlin, 2005.

[12] O. Jokisch and R. Hoffmann. Towards an embedded language tutoring system for children. In *Proc. Workshop on Child, Computer and Interaction (WOCCI), Chania, Greece*, 2008.

EINE KURZE GESCHICHTE ÜBER DIE LEHRE

Mathias Kortke, Sören Wittenberg

Professur Systemtheorie und Sprachtechnologie
Mathias.Kortke@TU-Dresden.de, Soeren.Wittenberg@TU-Dresden.de

Kurzfassung: Die wissenschaftlichen Leistungen von Professor Dr.-Ing. habil. Rüdiger Hoffmann und seiner Professur *Systemtheorie und Sprachtechnologie* sind national und international durch eine Vielzahl von Veröffentlichungen bekannt. Weniger bekannt sind vielleicht die didaktischen Leistungen auf diesen Gebieten. Der vorliegende Beitrag gibt einen Rückblick auf 11 (und noch mehr) Jahre Lehre. Der Fokus ist auf die Lehrveranstaltungen der Systemtheorie und der automatischen Spracherkennung gerichtet. Durch eine statistische Auswertung und die Betrachtung eines roten Fadens durch das Studium wird die hohe Qualität und vorbildliche Strukturierung der angebotenen Ausbildung aufgezeigt. Im Abschluss verdeutlicht ein Überblick über die Verwendung neuer Medien in der Lehre den stetigen Wunsch von Professor Rüdiger Hoffmann, die vermittelten Lehrinhalte einfacher zugänglich zu machen.

1 Lehre?

Jeder Hochschullehrer ist verantwortlich für Lehre und Forschung – so ist es geregelt. Viel, so auch hauptsächlich in diesem Buch, wird über letztere – die Forschung – geschrieben. Wer aber schreibt über das ganz Alltägliche – die Lehre?

In diesem Artikel soll nun auch endlich einmal der tägliche „Kampf" im Hörsaal gewürdigt werden – so z. B. der Wettstreit um den größeren Schallpegel und die Verbesserung des Signal-Rausch-Verhältnisses. Legendär ist in diesem Zusammenhang schon das Zitat von Professor Dr.-Ing. habil. Helmut Schreiber: „Ich bin für das Nutzsignal zuständig und Sie für das Störsignal ..."

2 Systemtheorie

2.1 Wie alles begann

Die Systemtheorie hat eine langjährige Tradition an der Fakultät Elektrotechnik und Informationstechnik der TU Dresden. Ihre Anfänge reichen hier bis in die 60er Jahre des 20. Jahrhunderts zurück. Maßgeblich hierfür war Professor Dr.-Ing. habil. Dr. e. h. Dr. e. h. Gerhard Wunsch, der von 1969 bis zu seiner Emeritierung im Jahr 1990 als ordentlicher Professor für *Systemtheorie* berufen war. Mit seinen drei im Verlag Technik Berlin erschienen Bänden zur Systemanalyse: Band 1: *Lineare Systeme* [1], Band 2: *Statistische Systemanalyse* [2] und Band 3: *Digitale Systeme* [3] stellte er nicht nur den Studierenden ausgezeichnete Lehrbücher zur Vertiefung des Vorlesungsstoffes mittels zahlreicher Beispiele und Übungsaufgaben zur Verfügung, sondern strukturierte damit gleichzeitig das gesamte damalige Wissensgebiet der Systemtheorie. Unter der Mitwirkung von Professor Dr.-Ing. habil. Helmut Schreiber, Inhaber der Professur *Systemtheorie* von Januar 1991 bis September 2002, wurden die drei Bände neu gegliedert und in der Symbolik an eine international gebräuchliche Notation angepasst. Die drei neuen Bände sind unter den Titeln *Digitale Systeme* [4, 5, 6], *Analoge Systeme* [7, 8, 9] und *Stochastische Systeme* [10, 11, 12] über 3 Jahrzehnte in verschiedenen Verlagen erschienen und während dieser Zeit inhaltlich kontinuierlich weiterentwickelt, aber in ihrer Struktur nicht mehr wesentlich verändert worden. Es ist der besondere Verdienst von Professor Helmut Schreiber, das Wissen für die Vorlesungen pädagogisch so aufbereitet zu haben, dass die „... häufig sehr komplizierten und abstrakten Zusammenhänge der Systemtheorie ... für den Durchschnittsstudenten noch einigermaßen genießbar bleiben" und „... dass das Ergebnis 'gerade noch nicht' falsch ist" [13].

Auch andere Hochschullehrer der Fakultät haben das Wissensgebiet Systemtheorie in der Forschung erweitert und besonders in der Lehre präsentiert und mitgestaltet. Erwähnenswert sind hier für die Zeit der 80er Jahre bis 2002 insbesondere Frau apl. Professor Dr.-Ing. habil. Renate Merker (besonders auf dem Gebiet der zellularen Systeme) sowie Professor Dr.-Ing. habil. Albrecht Reibiger und Professor Dr.-Ing. habil. Wolfgang Schwarz mit ihren Lehrveranstaltungen *Grundlagen technischer Systeme*.

Im September 2002 ging der Inhaber der Professur *Systemtheorie*, Professor Helmut Schreiber, mit 65 Jahren in den Ruhestand. Die Professur wurde als solche nicht wieder besetzt. Mit den sich daraus ergebenden Lehraufgaben beauftragte die Fakultät für Elektrotechnik und Informationstechnik ab dem Wintersemester 2002/03 Professor Dr.-Ing. habil. Rüdiger Hoffmann, den Leiter der Arbeitsgruppe *Sprachkommunikation*. Mit den hinzugekommenen Aufgaben in Lehre und Forschung wurde ab Oktober 2002 daraus die Arbeitsgruppe *Systemtheorie und Sprachkommunikation* und seit 2007 die Professur *Systemtheorie und Sprachtechnologie*.

Für Professor Rüdiger Hoffmann ist die Systemtheorie kein unbekanntes Stoffgebiet, hat der „Geheime Zellularrat" doch parallel zur Tätigkeit im VEB Elektromat Dresden an der TU Dresden in Lehre und Forschung mitgearbeitet und im Jahr 1978 seine Dissertation A mit dem Titel „Beitrag zur Zuverlässigkeitstheorie binärer zellularer Systeme" bei Professor Gerhard Wunsch angefertigt und verteidigt. Mit seiner Habilitation (damals: Facultas docendi und Dissertation B zum Dr. sc. techn.) im Jahr 1985 mit dem Titel „Stochastische zellulare Systeme / Grundlagen" knüpfte er an diese wissenschaftliche Arbeit an.

Seit 2002 setzt Professor Rüdiger Hoffmann nun die Kontinuität in der Lehre auf dem Gebiet der Systemtheorie der Professoren Wunsch und Schreiber fort. Manchmal erfordert das auch einen Spagat zwischen den Lehrveranstaltungen. So lesen wir in den (oben zitierten) BAR-News 55 den Vorlesungsspruch: „Professor Hoffmann: 'Ich sag's ja nur, damit Sie nicht denken, ich sei schizophren oder so.' (Benutzung von f_x und p_x als Dichtefunktion in verschiedenen Vorlesungen)".

Weitere Zitate von Vorlesungssprüchen zeigen, dass es auch bei „Hoffmanns Erzählungen" im Hörsaal recht locker zugehen kann: BAR-News 50: „Nun ja, wenn Sie zur Unendlichkeit noch ein bisschen dazuzählen, dann juckt das die Unendlichkeit wenig ...", BAR-News 53: „Studenten: 'Das Mikro ist aus!' Professor Hoffmann: 'Ja, ich hör's. Aber ich weiß auch nicht, was ich machen soll.'", BAR-News 49: „Klein Phi von Omega heißt Phasenfrequenzgang. - Ja ja, klein Phi macht auch Mist." BAR-News 51: „Differenzengleichungen sind ja quasi so 'was wie Ableitungen für arme Leute." oder BAR-News 48: „Ich kann hier ja nicht einen Strom von einer Spannung abziehen. Zumindest macht das keinen guten Eindruck."

2.2 Statistik zu den Lehrveranstaltungen Systemtheorie in den Jahren 2002 – 2013

An dieser Stelle soll in einer kurzen Übersicht aufgelistet werden, wer die vielen Studierenden im Fach Systemtheorie in den letzten 11 Jahren unterrichtet hat, ohne dabei zu sehr in die Details zu gehen. Die Hörerzahlen wurden anhand der geschriebenen Klausuren inklusive der Nach- und exklusive der Wiederholer des gleichen Jahres ermittelt.

2.2.1 Die Lehrveranstaltungen *Systemtheorie I und II*

Im dritten und vierten Semester des Grundstudiums an der Fakultät Elektrotechnik und Informationstechnik besuchen die Studierenden der Studiengänge Elektrotechnik, Informationssystemtechnik und Mechatronik die Lehrveranstaltungen *Systemtheorie I und II*.

In der Modulbeschreibung heißt es: „Das Lehrgebiet Systemtheorie vermittelt die allgemeinen begrifflichen und methodischen Grundlagen zur Beschreibung (Darstellung, Modellierung) dynamischer Vorgänge in Natur und Technik. ... Die stoffliche Gliederung nach den Gesichtspunkten diskrete und kontinuierliche Zeit sowie diskrete und kontinuierliche Signalwerte führt auf eine überschaubare Klassifizierung in digitale Systeme (*Systemtheorie I*), zeitdiskrete Systeme und zeitkontinuierliche Systeme (*Systemtheorie II*), wobei innerhalb jeder dieser Klassen einerseits zwischen linearem und nichtlinearem und andererseits zwischen statischem und dynamischem Verhalten unterschieden wird.“

Vortragender: Prof. Dr.-Ing. habil. Rüdiger Hoffmann (vertretungsweise: PD Dr.-Ing. Ulrich Kordon, apl. Prof. Dr.-Ing. habil. Renate Merker)

Übungsbetreuer: Dr.-Ing. Matthias Eichner, Dr.-Ing. Ute Feldmann, Dipl.-Ing. Stephan Hübler, Dr.-Ing. Oliver Jokisch, PD Dr.-Ing. Ulrich Kordon, Dipl.-Ing. Mathias Kortke, Dr.-Ing. Steffen Werner, Dr.-Ing. Sören Wittenberg und Dr.-Ing. habil. Matthias Wolff

Lehrumfang: Wintersemester (*Systemtheorie I*): 2 Semesterwochenstunden Vorlesung, 1 Semesterwochenstunde Übung (2 × 3 Übungsgruppen zweiwöchentlich im Wechsel)

Sommersemester (*Systemtheorie II*): 2 Semesterwochenstunden Vorlesung, 2 Semesterwochenstunden Übung (6 – 8 Übungsgruppen an 2 Tagen pro Woche)

Lehrbücher: *Digitale Systeme* [6], *Analoge Systeme* [9] und Sammlung von Übungsaufgaben, Prüfungsklausuren und Formelsammlungen [14]

Vorlesungsbegleitendes Online-Skript auf der Lernplattform OPAL:
Systemtheorie I: https://bildungsportal.sachsen.de/opal/auth/repo/go?rid=1110474793,
Systemtheorie II: https://bildungsportal.sachsen.de/opal/auth/repo/go?rid=1110474792

Studienjahr	2002/03	2003/04	2004/05	2005/06	2006/07
Hörer	263	291	340	314	243
Notenmittel	3,44	3,25	3,08	2,88	3,20
durchgefallen	48 (18 %)	58 (20 %)	35 (10 %)	20 (6 %)	20 (8 %)

Studienjahr	2007/08	2008/09	2009/10	2010/11	2011/12
Hörer	189	255	228	239	225
Notenmittel	2,70	2,84	3,05	3,44	3,14
durchgefallen	7 (4 %)	18 (7 %)	20 (9 %)	40 (17 %)	33 (15 %)

Tabelle 1 - Statistik zu *Systemtheorie I und II*

2.2.2 Die Lehrveranstaltungen *Systemtheorie III*

Zur Verdeutlichung der Qualität dieser Lehrveranstaltungen sei hier sinngemäß Professor Rüdiger Hoffmann zitiert: „An der Vorlesung Systemtheorie III möchte ich eigentlich nichts ändern; sie ist über Jahre gewachsen und vortrefflich ausgearbeitet.“

Dazu heißt es in der Modulbeschreibung: „... Den Schwerpunkt des Lehrfaches *Systemtheorie III* bilden Methoden zur Untersuchung statischer und dynamischer Systeme unter der Einwirkung stochastischer Signale. ... Die Übertragung stochastischer Signale durch Systeme wird insbesondere für nichtlineare statische Systeme (Transformation der Dichtefunktion) und für lineare dynamische Systeme (Transformation des Leistungsdichtespektrums) herausgearbeitet.“

Vortragender: Prof. Dr.-Ing. habil. Rüdiger Hoffmann (vertretungsweise: Dipl.-Ing. Mathias Kortke)

Übungsbetreuer: Dipl.-Phys. Till Moritz Eßinger, Dipl.-Ing. Thomas Fehér, Dr.-Ing. Ute Feldmann, Dipl.-Ing. Mathias Kortke und Dr.-Ing. Steffen Werner

Lehrumfang: Wintersemester: 2 Semesterwochenstunden Vorlesung, 2 Semesterwochenstunden (ab 2012/13 1 Semesterwochenstunde) Übung (1 Übungsgruppe)

Lehrbücher: *Stochastische Systeme* [12] und Sammlung von Übungsaufgaben, Prüfungsklausuren und Formelsammlungen [15]

Vorlesungsbegleitendes Online-Skript auf der Lernplattform OPAL:
https://bildungsportal.sachsen.de/opal/auth/repo/go?rid=1107755019

Studienjahr	2002/03	2003/04	2004/05	2005/06	2006/07	2007/08
Hörer	117	107	106	115	119	90
Notenmittel	2,46	3,16	3,12	2,36	2,51	2,27
durchgefallen	8 (7 %)	9 (8 %)	14 (13 %)	1 (1 %)	3 (3 %)	1 (1 %)

Studienjahr	2008/09	2009/10	2010/11	2011/12	2012/13
Hörer	67	96	112	110	82
Notenmittel	2,36	2,65	2,25	2,56	2,48
durchgefallen	0	6 (6 %)	3 (3 %)	3 (3 %)	0

Tabelle 2 - Statistik zu *Systemtheorie III*

2.2.3 Die Lehrveranstaltungen *Stochastic Signals and Systems*

Für die Studierenden des Master-Studienganges “Nanoelectronic Systems” wurde eine englischsprachige Fassung der Lehrveranstaltungen *Systemtheorie III* ausgearbeitet und ab dem Wintersemester 2011 angeboten. Die dazu notwendige Übersetzungen des Vorlesungsskripts, der Übungsaufgaben und der Formelsammlungen ins Englische übernahm Mathias Kortke unter Mitarbeit von Till Moritz Eßinger.

Vortragender und Übungsbetreuer: Dipl.-Ing. Mathias Kortke

Lehrumfang: Wintersemester: 2 Semesterwochenstunden Vorlesung, 2 Semesterwochenstunden Übung (1 Übungsgruppe)

Lehrbücher: *Stochastische Systeme* [12] und Sammlung von Übungsaufgaben, Prüfungsklausuren und Formelsammlungen (auf Englisch) [16]

Vorlesungsbegleitendes Online-Skript auf der Lernplattform OPAL:
https://bildungsportal.sachsen.de/opal/auth/repo/go?rid=2786328577

Studienjahr	2011/12	2012/13
Hörer	8	11
Notenmittel	2,30	1,91
durchgefallen	0	0

Tabelle 3 - Statistik zu *Stochastic Signals and Systems*

2.2.4 Die Lehrveranstaltungen *Einführung in die Systemtheorie*

Die Lehrveranstaltungen *Einführung in die Systemtheorie* basieren auf ausgewählten Kapiteln der Lehrveranstaltungen *Systemtheorie I und II* und wurden ursprünglich für Studierende der Informatik und Wirtschaftsingenieurwissenschaften im Nebenfach konzipiert. Seit dem Sommersemester 2013 besuchen auch die Studierenden des Studienganges *Regenerative Energiesysteme* diese Lehrveranstaltungen.

Vortragender: PD Dr.-Ing. Ulrich Kordon

Übungsbetreuer: Dipl.-Ing. Stephan Hübler, Dr.-Ing. Oliver Jokisch und Dipl.-Ing. Mathias Kortke

Lehrumfang: 2 Semesterwochenstunden Vorlesung, 1 Semesterwochenstunde Übung (Wintersemester: 1 Übungsgruppe, Sommersemester (Studiengang *Regenerative Energiesysteme*): 4 Übungsgruppen)

Lehrbücher: *Digitale Systeme* [6], *Analoge Systeme* [9] und Sammlung von Übungsaufgaben, Prüfungsklausuren und Formelsammlungen [14]

Studienjahr	2007/08	2008/09	2009/10	2010/11	2011/12	2012/13
Hörer	7	7	19	20	15	19
Notenmittel	2,33	3,54	3,77	3,52	3,37	3,68
durchgefallen	0	0	3 (16 %)	5 (25 %)	5 (33 %)	3 (16 %)

Tabelle 4 - Statistik zu *Einführung in die Systemtheorie*

3 Spracherkennung – Ein roter Faden im Studium

Die Professur von Professor Dr.-Ing. habil. Rüdiger Hoffmann bildet umfassend auf dem Gebiet der Systemtheorie und Sprachtechnologie aus. Wird einzig die Ausbildungslinie auf dem Gebiet der automatischen Spracherkennung betrachtet, so ergab sich vor der Umstellung auf das modularisierte Studium im Wintersemester 2010/11 infolge des Bologna-Prozesses [17] folgende Verteilung der Lehrveranstaltungen auf die Semester 3 bis 8 in den Diplomstudiengängen Elektrotechnik (Schwerpunkt Informationstechnik) und Informationssystemtechnik (Schwerpunkt Kommunikationsakustik):

- *Systemtheorie* (3. – 5. Semester)
- *Signalverarbeitung* (5. Semester)
- *Technische Sprachkommunikation* (6. Semester)
- *Signalanalyse und -erkennung* (6. Semester)

- *Akustische Mustererkennung* (7. Semester)
- *Technische Sprachkommunikation* (7. Semester, Praktikum)
- *Spracherkennung* (8. Semester)

Durch diese Aufteilung war bzw. ist in den auslaufenden Studiengängen eine umfassende Ausbildung sichergestellt, die zur notwendigen Handlungskompetenz auf dem Gebiet der automatischen Spracherkennung führt. Davon zeugen zahlreiche Diplomarbeiten (z. B. [18, 19, 20, 21, 22, 23]), die im Umfeld des an der Professur entwickelten Systems UASR entstanden sind und zur Fortentwicklung des Systems beigetragen haben.

3.1 UASR – Das System zur Spracherkennung

UASR ist die Abkürzung von "Unified Approach for Speech Synthesis and Recognition" – einem einheitlichen Ansatz für die automatische Erkennung und Synthese gesprochener Sprache [24]. Das System ist in die beiden gegenläufigen Verarbeitungsstränge *Spracherkennung* und *Sprachsynthese* unterteilt, deren Kopplung über gemeinsame Datenbasen erfolgt. Die Spracherkennung des hierarchisch aufgebauten Systems folgt dem Analysator-Klassifikator-Konzept nach [25], welches die getrennte Betrachtung von Signalanalyse und nachfolgender Erkennung vorsieht. Diese Unterteilung ist auch in der Ausbildung auf dem Gebiet der Spracherkennung sichtbar. So erfolgt die Qualifizierung zur Signalanalyse in den Lehrveranstaltungen der frühen Semester: *Systemtheorie*, *Signalverarbeitung*, *Technische Sprachkommunikation* und *Signalanalyse und -erkennung*. In diesen Veranstaltungen wird von allgemeinen Verfahren zur Signalanalyse (z. B. FOURIER-Analyse) ausgehend auf spezielle Verfahren zur Analyse von Sprachsignalen (z. B. Cepstralanalyse) übergegangen. Die Spezialisierung der betrachteten Verfahren entlang der Ausbildungslinie erlaubt die tiefgründige Herleitung und Behebung verfahrensbedingter Einschränkungen. Für die Lehrveranstaltung *Spracherkennung* sind die Lehrinhalte aller genannten Lehrveranstaltungen notwendig. So ermöglicht beispielsweise die am Anfang der Ausbildung stehende Systemtheorie mit der Einführung allgemeiner Betrachtungen zu Automaten eine geschlossene Beschreibung der automatischen Spracherkennung mittels endlicher Automaten am Ende der Ausbildung. Die allgemeinen Klassifikationsansätze (z. B. BAYES- und Linearklassifikator) werden hingegen in den Lehrveranstaltungen *Signalanalyse und -erkennung* und *Akustische Mustererkennung* vermittelt.

3.2 Modularisierung – Geht der rote Faden verloren?

Die modularisierte Studienform ermöglicht die interessengerechte Belegung von sogenannten *Modulen*, also inhaltlich abgeschlossenen Einheiten, deren individuelle Kombination erst am Ende des Ausbildungsweges alle erworbenen Kompetenzen ergibt [26]. An der Professur *Systemtheorie und Sprachtechnologie* wurden die Module

- *Systemtheorie*,
- *Signaltheorie*,
- *Intelligente Audiosignalverarbeitung* und
- *Sprachtechnologie*

formuliert. Die Gesamtheit dieser Module bildet die inhaltlichen Schwerpunkte aller Lehrveranstaltungen vor der Modularisierung ab. Um die interessengerechte Modulauswahl zu ermöglichen, müssen bisher vorausgesetzte Lehrinhalte in den verschiedenen Modulen wiederholt bzw. mehrfach eingeführt werden. Im Ergebnis bewirkt die Modularisierung eine Straffung und Doppelung bisheriger Lehrinhalte.

4 Neue Medien in der Lehre

Kontinuität ist ein Kerngedanke in der Lehre, ein anderer – die Innovation. Diesen Gedanken folgte im Zeitraum 2000 bis 2004 auch das Bundesministerium für Bildung und Forschung (BMBF) mit der Förderinitative *Neue Medien in der Bildung*, welche als erste ihrer Art auf dem Gebiet des universitären eLearnings förderte [27]. Professor Rüdiger Hoffmann sah das Potential der Initative und bekam im Kooporationsprojekt *eL-IT* – eLearning-Module für die Studiengänge der Informations-, Kommunikations- und Medientechnik – zusammen mit der Brandenburgischen Technischen Universität Cottbus, der Technischen Universität Berlin und der Universität Kassel die Möglichkeit, Module einer multimedialen Lehr- und Lernplattform zu entwickeln [27]. Im Projektzeitraum vom 01. 06. 2001 bis 31. 12. 2003 wurden so die Präsenzvorlesungen *Signalverarbeitung* und *Psychoakustik* didaktisch und multimedial an die sich durch die Neuen Medien ergebenen Möglichkeiten (Animationen, Graphiken, Video, Audio usw.) angepasst und online gestellt. Die Abbildung 1 zeigt ein Bildschirmfoto des Lernmoduls *Signalverarbeitung* das von Professor Rüdiger Hoffmann und seinen Mitarbeitern Margitta Lachmann, Ulrich Kordon und Steffen Kürbis entwickelt wurde und noch heute von den Studierenden dankend angenommen wird. Als wichtiger Innovationsschritt innerhalb der Lehr- und Lernplattform gilt die Integration von Sprachdiensten (Abbildung 1 links unten) durch die Mitarbeiter Matthias Wolff und Matthias Eichner. Sie integrierten eine akustische Sprachsynthese zum Vorlesen der Inhalte, sowie eine akustische Spracherkennung zur Navigation innerhalb der Module oder zur mündlichen Durchführung von Multiple-Choice-Tests.

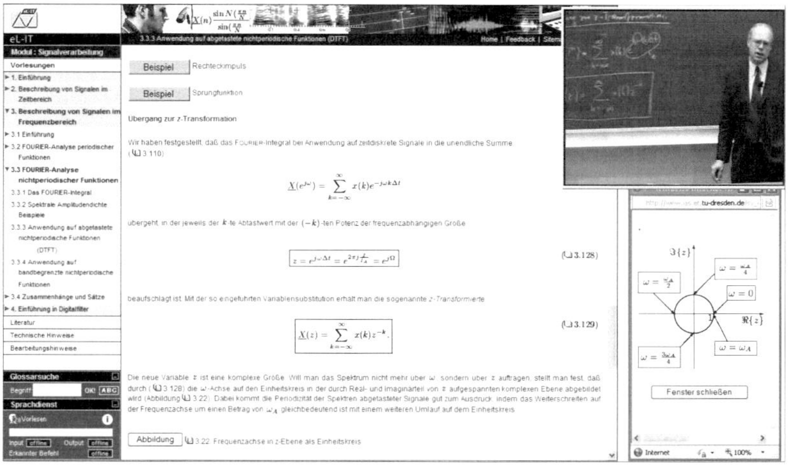

Abbildung 1 - Bildschirmfoto des *eL-IT*-Lernmoduls *Signalverarbeitung*.

Im Jahr 2008 entstand die Idee, die Erkenntnisse des Projekts *eL-IT* erneut für die Lehre einzusetzen und den Studierenden vorlesungsergänzendes Lehrmaterial in Form von HTML-Seiten der Vorlesungsskripte und web-basierten Demonstratoren zur Verfügung zu stellen. Die Erstellung der Vorlesungsskripte [28, 29, 30, 31] und deren Integration auf der Lernplattform OPAL stand im Mittelpunkt eines Multimediaprojektes [32], das in den Jahren 2008 und 2009 durch den Multimediafonds der TU Dresden gefördert und von Matthias Wolff und Mathias Kortke koordiniert wurde.

Die Erstellung der Vorlesungsskripte wurde von der leitenden Idee getragen, für die verschiedenen Präsentationsmöglichkeiten der Vorlesungen nur eine einzige Datenbasis nutzen und pflegen zu müssen.

Bei den Präsentationen der Vorlesung handelt es sich um:

- das vom Vorlesenden genutzte Vorlesungsskript,
- Folien zur Vorlesung sowie
- die HTML-Seiten auf der Lernplattform OPAL.

Das Konzept, für diese einheitliche Datenbasis das Textsatzsystem LaTeX zu nutzen, hat sich sehr bewährt. Problematisch dabei ist lediglich die mehrfache Nutzung von Abbildungen, strukturierten Texten und mathematischen Formeln in den verschiedenen Präsentationen. Hierbei wurde die jeweilige Anpassung mittels Compiler-Direktiven direkt in den LaTeX-Quellen vorgenommen. Im Ergebnis wurde eine automatische Erstellung der HTML-Seiten aus den LaTeX-Quellen implementiert. Hierbei konnte auf Erfahrungen mit den Werkzeugen `make`, `pdflatex` und `latex2html` zurückgegriffen werden.

Interaktive Demonstratoren unterstützen die Sicherung der vermittelten Lehrinhalte. Infolge der sich stetig vereinfachenden Programmierung grafischer Benutzerschnittstellen lassen sich viele Vorlesungs- bzw. Lehrbuchbeispiele aus [33] visuell veranschaulichen und interaktiv unterlegen. Diesen technischen Möglichkeiten hat sich die Professur *Systemtheorie und Sprachtechnologie* nicht verschlossen, sondern sie aktiv unterstützt. Im Rahmen eines Multimediaprojektes [32] wurden die Java-Applets bzw. Java-Webstart-Anwendungen „SignalANalyse und -SYnthese – SANSY" [34] und „Lineares zeitinvariantes System – LTIS" [35] für die Lernplattform OPAL entwickelt und in diese integriert. Beide Demonstratoren sind in [32] beschrieben. Eine genauere Betrachtung sollen zwei Beispiele aus den Lehrveranstaltungen *Signalverarbeitung* und *Akustische Mustererkennung* erfahren.

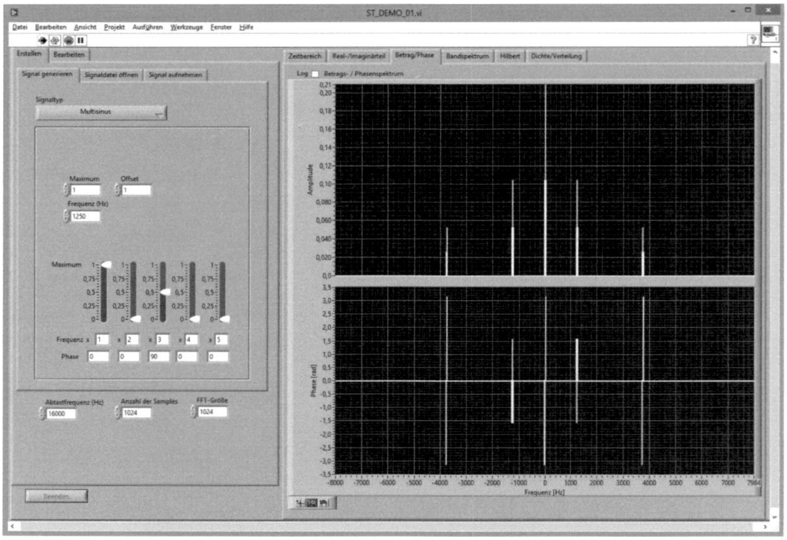

Abbildung 2 - Demonstrator *Analyse*: Darstellung des Betragsamplituden- und Phasenspektrums eines Multisinussignals. Quelle: Steffen Kürbis (IAS)

Die Veranschaulichung von Signalanalyseverfahren (z. B. Diskrete FOURIER Transformation) beschränkt sich in den Lehrveranstaltungen auf einfache Signale, die im zeitlichen Rahmen und mit angemessenem Aufwand dargestellt werden können. Praktisch auftretende Signale sind deutlich komplexer und nur rechentechnisch analysierbar. Da aber gerade die Analyse derartiger Signale zum Verständnis beitragen kann, hat der Professurmitarbeiter Dipl.-Ing. Steffen Kürbis einen einfach zu bedienenden Signalanalysator implementiert. Die Besonderheit dieses

Demonstrators ist die strikte Einhaltung der in den Lehrveranstaltungen präsentierten mathematischen Zusammenhänge. Eventuell auftretende Phänomene können so nachgerechnet und ihre Ursache untersucht werden. Ein typischer Einsatz im Lehrbetrieb ist die Generierung von verschiedensten Signalen und die Visualisierung von deren Betrags- / Phasenspektren oder Amplitudendichten / -verteilungen.

Das zweite Beispiel veranschaulicht den seriellen Perzeptron-Lernalgorithmus, der in der Spracherkennung zur Bestimmung der Trennfunktion eines Linearklassifikators verwendet wird. Der Linearklassifikator kann z. B. zur Unterscheidung der deutschen Langvokale anhand der ersten beiden Vokalformanten eingesetzt werden. Dieser Einsatz ist in [33] Abbildung 8.2 dargestellt und wurde vom Professurmitarbeiter Dr.-Ing. Sören Wittenberg in einem interaktiven Demonstrator für zwei Vokalklassen umgesetzt (Abbildung 3). Der Demonstrator berechnet anhand von eingetragenen Vokalrealisierungen sequenziell eine Trennfunktion, die den sogenannten Merkmalraum in zwei Bereiche unterteilt und damit die für die Klassifikation notwendigen Klassengebiete definiert. Jede Veränderung der Trennfunktion wird direkt im Merkmalraum dargestellt, wodurch die schrittweise Verbesserung der Lösung veranschaulicht werden kann. Interaktives Einfügen weiterer Vokalrealisierungen führt zur erneuten Anpassung der Trennfunktion.

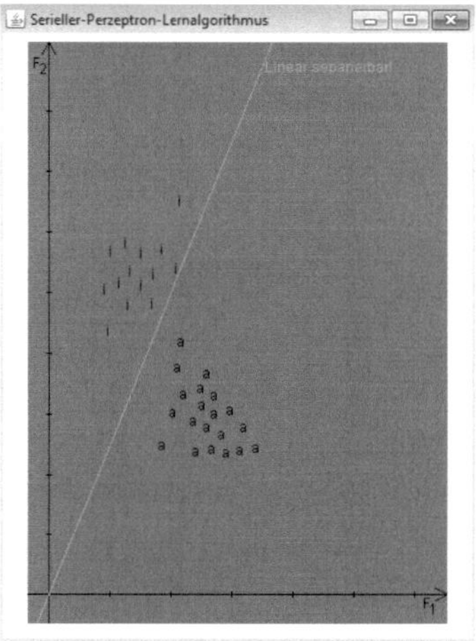

Abbildung 3 - Demonstrator *Erkennung*: Visualisierung des seriellen Perzeptron-Lernalgorithmus. Quelle: Sören Wittenberg (IAS).

Literatur

[1] WUNSCH, G.: *Systemanalyse*. Bd. 1 Lineare Systeme. 3., bearbeutete Auflage. Berlin : Verlag Technik, 1972

[2] WUNSCH, G.: *Systemanalyse*. Bd. 2 Statistische Systemanalyse. 2., durchgesehene Auflage. Berlin : Verlag Technik, 1970

[3] WUNSCH, G.: *Systemanalyse*. Bd. 3 Digitale Systeme. 1. Auflage. Berlin : Verlag Technik, 1971

[4] WUNSCH, G. ; SCHREIBER, H.: *Digitale Systeme*. 3. Auflage. Berlin : Verlag Technik, 1989

[5] WUNSCH, G. ; SCHREIBER, H.: *Digitale Systeme*. 4. Auflage. Berlin Heidelberg : Springer-Verlag, 1993 (Springer-Lehrbuch)

[6] WUNSCH, G. ; SCHREIBER, H.: *Digitale Systeme*. 5. Auflage. Dresden : TUDpress Verlag der Wissenschaften GmbH, 2006 (TUDpress Lehrbuch). – ISBN 10: 3938863846, ISBN 13: 978–3938863848

[7] WUNSCH, G. ; SCHREIBER, H.: *Analoge Systeme*. 2. Auflage. Berlin : Verlag Technik, 1988

[8] WUNSCH, G. ; SCHREIBER, H.: *Analoge Systeme*. 3. Auflage. Berlin Heidelberg : Springer-Verlag, 1993 (Springer-Lehrbuch)

[9] WUNSCH, G. ; SCHREIBER, H.: *Analoge Systeme*. 4. Auflage. Dresden : TUDpress Verlag der Wissenschaften GmbH, 2006 (TUDpress Lehrbuch). – ISBN 10: 3938863676, ISBN 13: 978–3938863671

[10] WUNSCH, G. ; SCHREIBER, H.: *Stochastische Systeme*. 2. Auflage. Berlin : Verlag Technik, 1986

[11] WUNSCH, G. ; SCHREIBER, H.: *Stochastische Systeme*. 3. Auflage. Berlin Heidelberg : Springer-Verlag, 1992 (Springer-Lehrbuch)

[12] WUNSCH, G. ; SCHREIBER, H.: *Stochastische Systeme*. 4. Auflage. Berlin : Springer-Verlag, 2005 (Springer-Lehrbuch). – ISBN 10: 354029225X, ISBN 13: 978–3540292258

[13] SCHREIBER, H.: OffenBARung: Systemtheorie. In: *BAR-News* der Fachschaft Elektrotechnik an der TU Dresden (2001), Juli, Nr. 35, 14–18. http://fsr.et.tu-dresden.de/de/downloads/finish/3-barnews/29-barnews-35

[14] SCHREIBER, H. ; MERKER, R. ; HOFFMANN, R.: *Systemtheorie I/II*. Version: 2011. http://www.ias.et.tu-dresden.de/ias/fileadmin/user_upload/sprache/texte/Lehre/SystemtheorieI_II/st12.pdf. Web version. – Sammlung von Übungsaufgaben, Prüfungsklausuren und Formelsammlungen

[15] SCHREIBER, H. ; MERKER, R. ; HOFFMANN, R.: *Systemtheorie III*. Version: 2011. http://www.ias.et.tu-dresden.de/ias/fileadmin/user_upload/sprache/texte/Lehre/SystemtheorieIII/st3.pdf. Web version. – Sammlung von Übungsaufgaben, Prüfungsklausuren und Formelsammlungen

[16] HOFFMANN, R. ; KORTKE, M.: *Stochastic Signals and Systems*. Version: 2011. http://www.ias.et.tu-dresden.de/ias/fileadmin/user_upload/sprache/texte/Lehre/StochasticSignals/sss.pdf. Web version. – Collection of Exercises, Exams, and Formularies

[17] THE EUROPEAN HIGHER EDUCATION AREA: *The Bologna Declaration of 19 June 1999. Joint declaration of the European Ministers of Education*. http://www.ehea.info/Uploads/Declarations/BOLOGNA_DECLARATION1.pdf, 1999

[18] WERNER, S.: *Angepasste Merkmalextraktion für ein kombiniertes Spracherkennungs-Synthesesystem*, Institut für Akustik und Sprachkommunikation, Technische Universität Dresden, Diplomarbeit, 2000

[19] ESTELMANN, J.: *Sprecheradaption in einem kombinierten Sprachsynthese-/Spracherkennungssystem*, Institut für Akustik und Sprachkommunikation, Technische Universität Dresden, Diplomarbeit, 2003

[20] KÜHNE, M.: *Stimmaktivierung eines Spracherkenners*, Institut für Akustik und Sprachkommunikation, Technische Universität Dresden, Diplomarbeit, 2004

[21] DIENEROWITZ, S.: *Tools zur Grammatikerzeugung für einen phonembasierten Spracherkenner*, Institut für Akustik und Sprachkommunikation, Technische Universität Dresden, Diplomarbeit, 2005

[22] WITTENBERG, S.: *Kanaladaption für ein Internet-Frontend eines Spracherkenners*, Institut für Akustik und Sprachkommunikation, Technische Universität Dresden, Diplomarbeit, 2006

[23] DUCKHORN, F.: *Optimierung von Hidden-Markov-Modellen für die Sprach- und Signalerkennung*, Institut für Akustik und Sprachkommunikation, Technische Universität Dresden, Diplomarbeit, 2007

[24] HOFFMANN, R. ; EICHNER, M. ; WERNER, S. ; WOLFF, M.: The Project UASR (Unified Approach for Speech Synthesis and Recognition) - A Progress Report. In: *DAGM Speech Processing Workshop* (2003), S. 17–24

[25] WOLFF, M.: *Akustische Mustererkennung*. Dresden : TUDpress Verlag der Wissenschaften, 2011 (Studientexte zur Sprachkommunikation, Bd. 57). – ISBN 978–3–942–71014–5

[26] BUTTNER, P. ; VOCKE, Ch.: Modularisierung von Studiengängen: Grundsatzüberlegungen. In: *Beiträge zur Hochschulforschung* 26 (2004), Nr. 02, S. 6–27

[27] FELLBAUM, K. ; GÖCKS, M.: *eLearning an der Hochschule*. Aachen : Shaker Verlag, 2004. – ISBN 978–3–8322–2531–5

[28] HOFFMANN, R. ; KORTKE, M. ; WOLFF, M.: *Vorlesungsbegleitendes Online-Skript Systemtheorie I*. Version: 2009. `https://bildungsportal.sachsen.de/opal/auth/repo/go?rid=1110474793`

[29] HOFFMANN, R. ; KORTKE, M. ; WOLFF, M.: *Vorlesungsbegleitendes Online-Skript Systemtheorie II*. Version: 2009. `https://bildungsportal.sachsen.de/opal/auth/repo/go?rid=1110474792`

[30] HOFFMANN, R. ; KORTKE, M. ; WOLFF, M.: *Vorlesungsbegleitendes Online-Skript Systemtheorie III*. Version: 2009. `https://bildungsportal.sachsen.de/opal/auth/repo/go?rid=1107755019`

[31] KORTKE, M. ; HOFFMANN, R.: *Online Script Stochastic Signals and Systems on the OPAL-E-Learnung-Plattform*. Version: 2011. `https://bildungsportal.sachsen.de/opal/auth/repo/go?rid=2786328577`

[32] HOFFMANN, R. ; KORTKE, M. ; WOLFF, M.: Abschlussbericht zum Projekt „Multimediale Vorlesungsergänzung zur Systemtheorie und Signalverarbeitung" / Professur für Systemtheorie und Sprachtechnologie. TU Dresden, 22. Dezember 2009. – Abschlussbericht. – 11 S.

[33] HOFFMANN, R.: *Signalanalyse und -erkennung: Eine Einführung für Informationstechniker*. Berlin etc. : Springer, 1998. – ISBN 3–540–63443–6

[34] STRECHA, G.: *SignalANalyse und -SYnthese – SANSY*. Version: 2009. `https://bildungsportal.sachsen.de/opal/url/RepositoryEntry/1110474792/CourseNode/80976176336594`

[35] GAMBOA ROSALES, H.: *Lineares zeitinvariantes System*. Version: 2009. `https://bildungsportal.sachsen.de/opal/url/RepositoryEntry/1110474792/CourseNode/81092392370974`

Autorenverzeichnis

Altinsoy, E. 177
Ascoli, A. 45
Bissiri, M. P. 234
Brackhane, F. 319
Braun, A. 226
Campbell, N. 154
Capuano, V. 249
Cordasco, G. 249
Corinto, F. 45
Dietzel, R. 339
Ding, H. 133
Duckhorn, F. 96
Eichner, M. 171
Esposito, A. 249
Falk, T. 347
Faundez-Zanuy, M. 249
Fehér, T. 185
Fellbaum, K. 261
Fuder, G. 201
Fujisaki, H. 69
Gebremedhin, Y. B. 139
Gruber, C. 347
Hess, W. 29
Hinterleitner, F. 117
Hirschfeld, D. 347
Hirschfeld, U. 311
Höge, H. 36
Hübler, S. 171
Hussein, H. 241
Jokisch, O. 359
Kačič, Z. 103
Karpov, A. 82
Klippel, W. 207
Koloska, U. 347
Költzsch, P. 295
Kordon, U. 185
Kortke, M. 367
Kraft, L. 226
Kraljevski, I. 139
Kröger, B. J. 218
Kroschel, K. 193
Kürbis, S. 185, 339
Kurnot, F. 347
Lacroix, A. 23
Lobanov, B. 327
Marschner, U. 59
Mauersberger, K. 286
Mehnert, D. 339
Mekyska, J. 249
Mixdorff, H. 241
Möbius, B. 88
Möller, S. 117
Paulus, E. 146
Pétursson, M. 256
Pfeifer, G. 59
Reininger, A. 303
Rhonzhin, A. 82
Riviello, M. T. 249
Römer, R. 276
Schubert, R. 347
Senger, V. 45
Starke, E. 59
Stock, E. 311
Strecha, G. 96
Tetzlaff, R. 45
Trouvain, J. 319
Tschöpe, C. 276
Unoki, M. 109
Vich, R. 15
Wagner, P. 75
Wenzel, M. 347
Werner, S. 125
Wittenberg, S. 367
Wolff, M. 11, 276
Yamaguchi, T. 256
Ziegenhals, G. 269